P9-CNE-564

DATE DUE

NOV 2 2 1993			
Dec 3 1993			
JAN 0 6 1997			

DEMCO 38-297

The American Family

CROWELL TEXTS BY RUTH SHONLE CAVAN

The American Family, Fourth Edition
American Marriage: A Way of Life
Criminology, Third Edition
Marriage and Family in the Modern World: A Book of Readings,
Third Edition

Ruth Shonle Cavan

PROFESSOR EMERITUS OF SOCIOLOGY AND SOCIAL WORK, ROCKFORD COLLEGE

New York   THOMAS Y. CROWELL COMPANY   Established 1834

The American Family

FOURTH EDITION

Library of Congress
Catalog Card Number:

69-13254

Designed by
Barbara Kohn Isaac

Manufactured in the
United States of America

PREFACE

THE AMERICAN FAMILY, Fourth Edition, presents a sociological analysis of the contemporary American family, touching when necessary on other cultures and our own past to clarify and emphasize present-day conditions and trends. The family is regarded as the basic unit in the social structure, providing the child with his initial socialization into social-class and ethnic subculture, and both aiding and obstructing his later social mobility. Interaction within the family is presented as the result of personality characteristics on the one hand and social roles on the other. Changes within the family are analyzed in terms of both the different stages in the family life cycle and changing external pressures.

Part One, Characteristics of the American Family, first compares features of families in other cultures, goes on to discuss nine issues currently confronting the American family, and examines, finally, the merging cultural aspects of rural and urban-suburban families in order to describe the basic type of American family.

Part Two, Social and Cultural Configurations of the American Family, places the family within the context of current subcultures— social class, ethnic, and racial. Particular emphasis is placed upon the process of horizontal and vertical mobility and the ways in which they affect the family. An analysis of downward mobility, rarely studied, is included. Intermarriage between racial or cultural groups is analyzed.

Part Three, The Cycle of Family Life, follows the individual from adolescence and the dating period through the various stages of family life to old age, widowhood, and dissolution of the nuclear family through the death of the remaining spouse.

In the single chapter of Part Four, Adjustment of Family and Society, trends toward greater integration of the family into the social organization and increased integration within the family are examined.

Although essentially the same in its organization and point of view as the 1953 and 1963 editions, the Fourth Edition of *The American Family* has been extensively rewritten to take account of changes both in external social conditions and in attitudes and values regarding family goals and behavior. In addition, research carried out since 1963 has been incorporated into the discussion, sometimes replacing earlier and outmoded findings.

The Fourth Edition follows the general plan of the Third. Rural and urban families are presented as minor variations of a basic American family type. Social-class, ethnic, and racial differences are also conceived as variations on the basic type, although these differences are often blurred by the prevailing trend of upward mobility. The issues in the American family (Chapter 2) have been made current. Development through the family life cycle provides the structure for Part Three.

For assistance in the preparation of this new edition, my thanks are due to no one person, but rather to all those who aided in the formulation of the basic concepts, as well as the many professional friends and users of the textbook who over the years have communicated to me their criticisms, commendations, and suggestions. Acknowledgment is also due to Northern Illinois University, where I have been on the teaching staff while preparing the Fourth Edition, and to the many students who have discussed in class and willingly written papers on problems and patterns of dating and adjustments of early marriage.

RUTH SHONLE CAVAN

October, 1968
DeKalb, Illinois

CONTENTS

III   The Cycle of Family Life

IV Adjustment of Family and Society

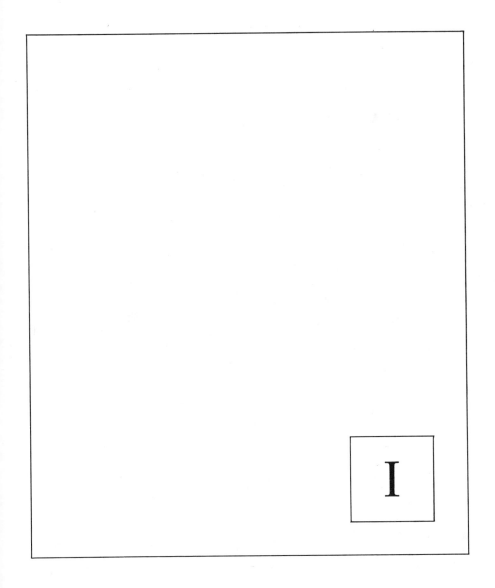

I

The Present Status of the
American Family

$$I$$

Characteristics of the American

Family

THE FAMILY is a deeply rooted institution in the United States it; is by far the most favored group with which adults associate themselves. All but about 10 per cent of people marry at some time during their lives—and the unmarried, in addition to those who have preferred to live as singletons, include certain nonmarriageable groups, such as the chronically ill or incapacitated or prisoners serving long terms. The marriageable group that chooses not to marry is very small. Moreover, youth eagerly seek the status of married people; half of young women are married by the time they are 21 and half of young men by the time they are 23. Most of the other half soon follow the early marrieds into matrimony. It is true that the present eagerness for marriage does not always lead to happiness. The divorce rate is one of the highest among all societies that keep records. Neither the divorced husband nor wife, however, regards divorce as the end of married life; the great majority of divorced people sooner or later marry another mate and continue their status as a husband or wife in a new marital situation.

Not only is marriage eagerly sought as the preferred adult relationship, but children are almost invariably included as part of the marriage plan. Couples who find themselves unable to have children file so many applications to adopt children with child-placing agencies that they cannot all be filled.

Not marriage alone, therefore, but family life is the preferred mode of living for adults of all ages in the United States. One may fairly ask if this situation is not true also for other societies. It is true that all societies known, past or present, have had a definitely formed family as one of their important institutions. Rarely, however, has marriage been as personalized a relationship and as eagerly sought by young people as in the United States at the present time.

Universal Aspects of the Family

An anthropologist, La Barre, has sought the origin of the family in the complementary biological characteristics of man, woman, and child.[1] The human infant is equipped with a large brain, a helpless body, few instincts by which it might preserve its own life, but with the capacity for continued learning over many years. Survival depends upon continuous hourly care. The mother is equipped first to produce the child over a period of nine months and then to provide suitable food for it, not only during its early months, but over several years of time—as shown by some societies in which children secure at least part of their sustenance by nursing until the age of three. The mother, occupied with child-bearing and infant care, is unable to care adequately for all her own needs or for all the needs of her growing brood. She depends, therefore, upon her mate for supplemental care. The man, equipped with larger bones and muscles and unburdened with pregnancy and nursing, is able to be more active than the woman. At the same time, his sexual drive is potentially active at all times and the woman is equipped to be receptive at almost all times. The man is bound, therefore, to the woman for ready gratification of his sexual desires. A mutual relationship of biological dependence and satisfaction develops that gives at least some degree of exclusiveness and permanence to the relationship.

When an attempt is made to find the essential, universal functions of all families everywhere, only a few functions appear. Murdock, working with anthropological material, lists four basic functions: sexual, reproductive, economic, and educational—all regarded as necessary to the survival of society.[2] Families are not limited to the fulfillment of these functions, but all families seem to exercise them.

Over and above these biological bases and minimal functions, a

[1]Weston La Barre, "Appraising Today's Pressures on Family Living," *Social Casework*, 32 (February, 1959), 54–55.
[2]G. P. Murdock, *Social Structure* (New York: Macmillan, 1949), p. 10.

large cultural superstructure has developed. In the long history of the human race with its many divisions into separate societies and cultural groups, great diversity of family forms and functions has evolved.

Definitions of the Family

Many definitions have been composed both for the family as a universal institution and for the American family alone. Such definitions emphasize the common features rather than the diversities of families. Burgess and Locke, research specialists in the field of the family, use an inclusive definition of the family with the following items:[3]

1. The family consists of persons united by the bonds of marriage (husband and wife), or blood or adoption (parents and children).
2. The members of the family typically live together as one household. The size of the household may vary from the extended family to the marital group of husband and wife.
3. The family members enact roles socially prescribed and endorsed by the individuals. Interaction in terms of these roles gives a unity to the family.
4. The family maintains a common culture derived mainly from the general culture as brought to the family by husband and wife.

Other concepts, especially of the American family, give importance to individual characteristics and personality factors. For example, Hess and Handel concentrate upon the interplay among family members as they seek to satisfy personal needs within the family, and hence to maintain the family as a group but at the same time keep their individuality without complete submergence in the family.[4] "Separateness and connectedness are the underlying conditions of a family's life, and its common task is to give form to both." Through interaction among the various members, the family comes to function systematically, usually in harmony with community mores, but without the domination of predetermined roles.

The Bureau of the Census, interested in statistical compilations, defines the family as follows: "a group of 2 persons or more related by

[3]Ernest W. Burgess and Harvey J. Locke, *The Family* (New York: American Book Co., 1950), pp. 7–8.

[4]Robert D. Hess and Gerald Handel, *A Psychosocial Approach to Family Life* (Chicago: University of Chicago Press, 1959), pp. 1–19.

blood, marriage, or adoption and residing together."⁵ This general definition is supplemented by definitions for various combinations of family members living together. Nothing is included about interaction or family culture.

The American Family Compared with Other Types

The family in the United States is a blend of traditional forms brought to this country by the varied migrating peoples that have formed American society. This ever-changing blend has been modified by the impact of, first, settling in a wild country, and second, bringing that country to a high state of industrialized urbanism. The basic biological factors and the minimum functions have been overlaid many times by cultural veneers and the total family form twisted and molded to fit the needs of people and of the changing society.

MONOGAMY

American marriage carries on the long European tradition of one husband paired with one wife. In all societies, monogamy is the most commonly found type of marriage, necessarily so since the number of men and women is approximately the same in any society unless the exigencies of life or migrations, war, and the like seriously disturb the sex ratio. However, unlike the United States, where monogamy is the only legally and morally approved form of marriage, many societies, in addition to the practice of monogamy, permit or encourage polygamy—the pairing of either husband or wife with two or more persons of the other sex.

The most common competitor to monogamy is polygyny, wherein one man is officially united in marriage to two or more women. For example, the traditional Moslem practice was for the man of means to marry more than one woman, the practice being supported by the statement in the Koran, ". . . marry of the women who seem good to you two or three or four, and if ye fear that ye cannot do justice then one . . ." With the westernization of Moslem countries, the practice is dying out. It is forbidden in Turkey and applies to only about 2 per cent of mar-

⁵*Current Population Reports, Population Characteristics: May 1, 1962,* Series P-20, No. 116 (Washington, D.C.: Bureau of the Census, 1962), p. 5.

riages in Egypt. In Iraq the percentage is about 9; in Saudi Arabia the practice is more commonly followed.[6]

Peripheral to polygyny is concubinage, a system whereby in addition to his legal wife or wives, a man may have a permanent and responsible relationship to one or more women known as concubines. He is not legally married to them but has certain responsibilities for their care and the care of their children. The system was in use in China from an early period, the concubines becoming members of the man's household. Their status was low, but their children were accepted without stigma. Concubinage was made illegal in China in 1936, but continued in practice. The Moslem husband, in addition to his several wives, was permitted to have concubines chosen from among his slaves for whom he assumed special responsibilities. In other societies also, polygyny and concubinage were permitted; many primitive societies practiced both. Any form of polygyny or concubinage was limited to men with sufficient means to support more than one wife and the assembled children of all. The practice was also limited by the number of women available. It is important to note that both polygyny and concubinage were legally recognized and supported by moral codes. They were practiced publicly, and no stigma was attached to women who entered into these relationships, although not all levels of wives had equal family or social status.

Two other forms of marriage deserve mention, although both occur so rarely as to be simply cultural oddities. One is polyandry, or a system whereby one woman has two or more husbands; this system has been found in a few small primitive societies in the Far East. Group marriage has been found in a few primitive societies; men joined in small groups have individual wives and in addition have sexual access to the wives of the other group-members.

In the United States, although monogamy is the only form of marriage legally permitted and morally approved, certain variants have appeared in the past with the approval of limited organized groups though never with legal sanction. The most persistent variant was the practice of polygyny, which was officially approved by the Mormon church from 1852 to 1890, and sometimes secretly practiced during limited periods both before and after these dates. The practice was always denounced by non-Mormons and resulted in continued legal prosecutions. Under these pressures it was eventually "outlawed" by the Mormon church.

Another variant, also highly disapproved by the general public, but sanctioned by a small organized group, was a form of group marriage

[6]Dorothy Fahs Beck, "The Changing Moslem Family of the Middle East," *Marriage and Family Living*, 19 (1957), 340–47.

practiced by the Oneida Community, a religious colony that existed from 1848 until about 1880 when it was dispersed. The Community was communistic in the sense that everything was shared; individual achievements and relationships were regarded as selfish and self-seeking. Formal marriages were not recognized or permitted. Sexual relations could take place between any man and any woman, but not on a purely promiscuous basis; some control was exercised by the Central Committee in charge of the Community, with arrangements made by a go-between. These relationships were not expected to result in pregnancy; the man's responsibility was to exercise self-control and to withdraw before ejaculation. In an attempt to breed a superior type of human being, children were to be produced only by couples paired for their fine qualities. These pairings had to receive the approval of the controlling group and were not necessarily based upon the attractiveness of the man and woman to each other. Children were regarded as belonging to the Community and after infancy, which they spent in the care of their mothers, were reared in groups with the best of care. As was true in the case of the Mormons, outside public disapproval was severe. However, also as with the Mormons, the system of sex relations was not licentious or promiscuous but was subject to close control by the ruling body.

Individually and secretly, many variants to monogamy occur in the United States. Some are accepted with leniency, although they are subject to various legal penalties. Occasionally someone—usually a man —marries two (usually no more) wives, going through all the legal forms of securing a license, having the marriage performed by a qualified official, and having the marriage registered. The man accomplishes this only with great secrecy and deception to prevent the wives, police, and public from becoming aware of the situation. Known as bigamy, this practice when discovered subjects the man to a criminal trial. Informal sex relations with someone other than the wife, known as adultery, are also illegal. Laws vary from state to state regarding penalties; however, the laws are rarely strictly enforced. Adultery does not have legal or moral sanction, but is a kind of *sub rosa* practice that one might say exists in the folkways but without approval of the mores.

Divorce

There are a number of ways in which marriage as a functioning relationship may be terminated: by death of one spouse, informal separation or desertion by one spouse, legal separation, annulment, and divorce. Disregarding natural death, divorce is the most frequent method used to terminate the marital relationship; it does not necessarily cancel obligations between the former mates and to the children. Divorce is a way of giving flexibility to marriage; by it a husband or wife may free himself or herself from a relationship that has become onerous, and become available for another marriage if it is desired.

All states in the United States permit legal divorce, but under conditions that vary from state to state. The laws are permissive; that is, one spouse may avail himself of the legal privilege of ending the marriage under the legal conditions in force, but no one is forced to divorce, and each spouse is privileged to contest a suit for divorce brought by the mate. The present attitude in the United States toward divorce is very tolerant, with the result that the divorce rate in the United States is extremely high as compared with European countries.

Other societies vary in their provisions for divorce. Italy, Spain, and some other Catholic countries have no provision for divorce. At the other extreme, in the early days of communism Russia permitted a divorce by the simple method of application for divorce by either husband or wife and the payment of a small fee. Obligations of the father for support of his children, however, continued. By laws of 1936 and later dates, divorce in Russia became much more difficult to secure and required a court hearing. The traditional Moslem method of divorce consists of the husband repeating three times that he has divorced his wife, although he continues to have certain obligations, especially for his children. Unless the right of divorce is stated in the marriage contract, the wife may not divorce her husband. England for a long time did not permit divorce except by Act of Parliament, and divorce is still more difficult to secure there than in the United States or the Scandinavian countries.

Divorce rates are in part a reflection of laws, but perhaps more a reflection of attitudes toward the permanence of marriage and toward its religious and social significance. In the United States, various religious groups, notably the Roman Catholic Church, are opposed to divorce and severely penalize members who secure a divorce. Other religious groups disapprove of divorce but do not erect barriers or penalties, and still others regard divorce as a private matter. Judging by the high divorce rates in the United States, one is forced to conclude that the public attitude generally is tolerant or favorable toward divorce.

CHOICE OF A MATE

In the United States, each person upon reaching a certain age set by law in each state is free to choose his own mate. If the desired person agrees, marriage may follow. Laws set a few prohibitions to marriage besides that of a minimum age, such as feeblemindedness, insanity, certain diseases, and close kinship. In practice, certain informal or institutional restrictions limit personal choice. For example, parents may object to a specific choice; some religious groups strongly disapprove and may penalize marriage outside the religion; public opinion looks askance at certain types of marriage.

The relative freedom of choice of mate in the United States by persons who may still be in their teens or early twenties is in sharp contrast to the methods of many other countries. China, Japan, India, and the Moslem countries traditionally followed a quite different method, whereby the parents selected their children's future spouses on the basis of the social and economic status of the family as well as the personal suitability of the young people. Typically, the young couple did not see each other or converse with each other prior to marriage. Romantic love as a factor in mate selection was unheard-of, although the couple might later come to love and respect each other. In many countries these family-controlled methods of mate selection are beginning to disappear under the influence of more recent custom, whereby girls are no longer secluded within the family confines but are able to meet other young people through friends or at school or work. However, in general, family control of mate selection is still a strong factor in most instances. The United States' method of placing complete freedom in the hands of young people is regarded in these countries as hazardous and conducive both to unstable marriages and to socially unsuitable mates. Parents are regarded as lacking in responsibility toward their children.

ENDOGAMY

Endogamy refers to both the principle and practice of marrying within the subculture to which a person belongs, whether this is defined by race, religion, social class, or ethnicity. The opposite term, exogamy, refers to the principle and practice of marrying outside one's subculture or some smaller subdivision. For example, in many societies, one may not marry within the close kinship or clan (exogamy) but must marry within the larger subculture (endogamy). In traditional Indian society, a person could not marry within the village but was compelled to marry within his caste. In the United States, the principles and practice of endogamy are less rigorously defined and enforced than in some societies, but social expectations and preferences support racial, religious, social class, and ethnic endogamy, although the policy of individual choice of marital partner permits exogamous marriages.

FAMILY STRUCTURE

In the United States, the typical family is the conjugal family, in which the basic relationship is between husband and wife. They and their children who are still living at home form the family. Since this type of family has been found to be the basic unit in all societies, it is also referred to as the nuclear family.[7] Variants of the type are the childless husband and wife, the widow, widower, or divorcee and their children, or brothers and sisters who continue to live together after the death of the parents.

The strongest family tie in the United States is the legal contract of marriage between husband and wife. This is in contrast to some family systems in which the strongest tie is established by blood relationship through descent from a common ancestor.[8] Such a family as the latter is consanguineous. The most common type is patrilineal; that is, it traces the blood line through the males; less common is a matrilineal system with the blood line traced through the females. In either type, marriage is less a tie between husband and wife than between father and daughter-in-law in the patrilineal system or mother and son-in-law in the matrilineal system.

Any family system is held intact by a set of related policies and practices. The conjugal or nuclear family of the United States is supported by a bilateral concept of descent; that is, a person is regarded as descending from the lines of both parents rather than exclusively from either the father or the mother. The nuclear family therefore is not absorbed into either the paternal or the maternal family. In residence the nuclear family is neolocal, that is, it establishes a new place of residence separate from that of the husband's father (patrilocal) if the society is patrilinear or from the wife's mother (matrilocal) if the society is matrilinear. A neolocal residence gives opportunity for autonomy of the couple and frees them from either a patriarchal or a matriarchal system of control.

Roles within the family also support the family system. In a con-

[7]Murdoch, *op. cit.*, pp. 1–2.

[8]William J. Goode, *The Family* (Englewood Cliffs, N.J.: Prentice-Hall, 1964), chs. 5 and 6.

jugal neolocal family, husband and wife work out their own roles, usually conforming to some generally recognized system. In the United States the husband is usually considered to be head of the family, whose primary role is chief wage-earner. The wife's principal domain is the home, with the secondary role of employed woman largely a matter of choice. Husband and wife are companions and sexual partners; together they produce and rear children.

The patrilineal, patrilocal, patriarchal family system places the headship in the hands of the oldest male. His wife, his sons, his daughters-in-law, and his grandchildren are subordinate to him. They have roles relative to each other and certain areas of freedom but the generational hierarchy with male dominance is basic. In the matrilineal, matrilocal, matriarchal family a similar system prevails, although it is rare that a truly matriarchal pattern of control develops. The economic unit is not limited to the husband or to the parents jointly, as in the American nuclear family, but is composed of the family as a whole.

The above statement is a very sketchy and somewhat idealized statement of the patrilineal or matrilineal family. There are several types depending upon whether land or other property passes from father to one son, or whether property is held jointly by all the males. From time to time, due to the exigencies of deaths or failure to marry, an individual family may resemble the nuclear family. Considered as a family system, however, it is very different from the nuclear family of the United States.

The patrilocal and the matrilocal families, with several generations and collateral relatives living under one roof or in a cluster of houses, is referred to as an extended family. In the United States, it is not anticipated that married children will continue to live with the parents of one of the couple; each marriage marks the start of a new conjugal (nuclear) family, separate in place of residence, self-supporting, and in control of its own affairs. This type of family is not only the most common type in the United States but the ideal type. The nuclear family is not, however, isolated from relatives. A number of related nuclear families often form a social kinship web on a voluntary basis.

Functions of the Family

In the United States, the exclusive functions of the family are primarily of a personal nature. For the husband and wife, the family ideally provides companionship, love, sexual satisfaction, children, and security. The family is regarded as the ideal instrument for the early formation of a child's personality and as the intimate group that guides the adolescent on his way toward maturity. In order to carry out these functions, the family shares a household and thus provides a shelter in which many utilitarian functions are performed both as a way to meet the material needs of the family and as the framework for the inter-action that leads to the achievement of the more personal goals first listed. However, many of the utilitarian functions are shared with other, more highly specialized institutions, such as schools, churches, welfare services, and economic and governmental institutions.

The American family is often called a weak institution in comparison with the more powerful economic and governmental institutions. This view overlooks the relation of the family to other institutions in a demo-cratic society. The adults who operate the various institutions, who are employers, employees, members of a union, on boards of directors, and voting citizens, are also family members. The adult members of families are in a position to safeguard the family from encroachments of specialized institutions and at the same time to institute movements to supplement the services provided by the family.

In societies with strong extended family systems, many of the func-tions performed in the United States by specialized institutions are ex-clusively the responsibility of the family. Care of the old, the handi-capped, and the ill, maintenance of all members, religious observances of a family or ancestral type, performance of household duties, control of all members, and education of children are within the province of family duties. Other functions that in the United States belong to the individual are functions of the extended family; for example, self-support on the part of adults and the mutual selection of mates.

In the pioneering and settlement period of the United States, the family, although primarily conjugal in form, carried many of these same responsibilities. The pioneer and later the rural family had few resources except within its own circle for the production and prepara-tion of food and clothing, education of children, care of the sick and old, recreation, religious observances, and many other functions now per-formed by other institutions. In time these functions became the special vested interests of the families, and when urban development called for a higher level of performance and provided the skills and facilities for its achievement, many families were reluctant to relinquish their re-sponsibilities. By the late 1960's, however, the transition from the multifunctioned family to the personal-needs centered family had vir-tually been accomplished. Supporting this family on an informal basis, and cushioning it against severe crises, is the kinship web.

The Nuclear Family and the Kinship Web

For a number of years sociologists have debated as to whether the nuclear family is an isolated group, cut off from kinship ties. One study after another has disproved complete isolation from as well as complete inclusion in an extended family. A midway position, known variously as the modified extended family, the kinship network, or the kinship web, has been uncovered as characteristic of many nuclear families. Such a kinship web is not a cultural imperative, applicable to all subcultures, but is a matter of circumstance and choice.[9]

The position of the nuclear family within the kinship web is important in understanding roles, types of interaction, and distribution of functions.

PHYSICAL ISOLATION

The nuclear family may or may not live in isolation from other nuclear families related to it by blood or marriage. Certainly when immigrants or migrants leave the home of their childhood and youth and eventually settle with the breadth of an ocean or a continent between them and their parental families, they tend to be isolated physically, whether the migrating unit is an individual or a married couple. During the years when the population of the United States was growing mostly by immigration and cities were growing primarily through either immigration or migration from rural areas, the isolated nuclear family was a very common type. During this same period—an extended one—lack of means of travel and communication made a close tie impossible. The isolation was not only physical but psychological and social. Identification with the parental family was weakened or disappeared entirely, and social contacts were possible only at long intervals if at all. The nuclear family, especially when isolated from kinfolk, was an event of a particular historical stage in the development of the United States.

Isolation is often also a phase of the long-term development of specific families. The couple migrating, whether they come from another country or into cities from the rural area of the United States, remains nuclear only for the period of time during which their children are living

[9]Gerald R. Leslie, *The Family in Social Context* (New York: Oxford University Press, 1967), ch. 2; Marvin B. Sussman, "The Isolated Nuclear Family: Fact or Fiction," *Social Problems*, 6 (Spring, 1959), 333–40.

at home. With marriage of the children, the once nuclear family becomes part of a kinship circle composed of an elderly nuclear family and as many new nuclear families as there are children. When grandchildren are born the structure again changes, with three generation levels. If the new nuclear families migrate, isolation may be resumed.

When a nuclear family becomes rooted in a particular locale, at least some of the children, when they marry, are likely to establish themselves nearby. This is especially true if the locale has varied and ample opportunities for employment. Even when related nuclear units scatter geographically, present means of transportation and direct communication make possible visits and conversation with an ease that was unheard-of a few decades ago.

Kinship Web Defined

These contacts, whether physical or conversational, do not destroy the independent nuclear units. They do not establish an extended family; but they do create a kinship web within which interaction tends to be more intense than between friends or employer and employee.

In contrast to the extended family, the kinship web is a voluntary association of related nuclear units based on affection, sentiment, and memories. The units tend to live separately, perhaps at some distance from each other, by choice. Each unit is financially independent, autonomous in decision-making, and has a semi-closed system of roles. Nevertheless, the units feel a sense of identification with each other and are proud or ashamed according to the achievements or misconduct of related nuclear units. The common surname of many of the units gives a sense of identification and proclaims the relationship.

Structure of the Kinship Web

Various types of relationships exist within the kinship web. Usually the relationship between children and their parents is the strongest and most influential that a child may experience. Unlike the extended family, the nuclear family is based in part on the assumption that each child will become independent of his parents psychologically and often socially during adolescence and soon thereafter financially. As a young adult, the child is expected to marry a mate of his own choice—who also chooses him. At this point the conjugal relationship becomes dominant and the parent-child relationship becomes subordinate. The unit of parent and child is called the family of orientation from the point of view of the child—the family in which the child had his origin. From the parents' point of view, the family is in the stage of procreation. Whether a given family is thought of as a family of orientation or a family of procreation depends upon whether one views it from the child's or the parents' standpoint. In the life experience of one person, the transition from the family of orientation to the family of procreation comes with marriage and the birth of children.

Marriage extends the family ties through the marriage of the son of one family of procreation with the daughter of another family of procreation. The two parental families are at the point of transition from procreation to gerontation—the family of old people.[10] Another term, useful but not widely used, is the affinal family, which refers to the family of the spouse, to which one is related by marriage. Members of the affinal family are in-laws.

Although this relationship may seem complex, the technical terminology refers to familiar relationships. Parents and children have already been mentioned. With a new conjugal unit, through marriage, come in-laws—two fathers-in-law and two mothers-in-law, one son-in-law and one daughter-in-law. With the birth of children comes the grandparent-grandchild relationship.

The above relationships are usually the closest ones in the kinship web, most fraught with emotion, most competitive as between units, and most helpful to each other. Lying somewhat beyond these closely related groups stand the siblings of the grandparents and of the parents of the middle generation. These are the uncles and aunts, and their children, the cousins. As generation is added to generation and one marriage is followed by another, the kinship web extends into more and more remote relationships, until contacts are lost. Occasionally the sense of family extends into these peripheral relationships. Families may organize, keep a written roster, elect a secretary, and at intervals hold extensive family reunions when news is exchanged and the boundaries of the kinship re-established.

The kinship is held together not only by sentiment and a feeling of identification, but by overt behavior, including forms of practical aid on a loosely reciprocal basis, informal social contacts, and pressures for social control. The different types of interaction vary between social groups such as social class and ethnic groups. For example, in the small but exclusive upper class, the kinship interrelations tend to be formal

[10]Marvin B. Sussman, "Relationships of Adult Children with Their Parents in the United States," in Ethel Shanas and Gordon F. Streib, *Social Structure and the Family: Generational Relations* (Englewood Cliffs, N.J.: Prentice-Hall, 1965), p. 74.

and authoritative and may more appropriately be said to form a modified extended family. The balance maintained between nuclear units also varies according to the stage of the family life cycle. Specific characteristics of the kinship web are discussed at appropriate places in this text.

Coordination of Characteristics

The characteristics of the family are not haphazardly put together. The United States family makes sense; so do the family forms of other cultures. In the United States, monogamy is a matter of deep moral values. In the past, polygyny might have been beneficial under some circumstances. In a new country with an agrarian economy, additional wives and children may function to bring land into cultivation more quickly than one man and woman and their children alone can do. It must be assumed, however, that the husband could weather the long period before children are old enough to be productive. It must also be assumed that there are excess women. In the settling of the United States, men came first and penetrated the wilderness alone. Women were at a premium on the frontier; even one wife was eagerly sought as a helpmate. The Mormons, drawing on another line of moral reasoning, established polygyny, which thrived in Utah and undoubtedly hastened its development. The Mormons entered Utah as an organized religious and social group, able to give support and encouragement to each other; no man faced the wilderness alone. Instead of a shortage of women there was soon a surplus, for more women than men became converts to Mormonism. Although polygyny came to an end under outside pressure, one may well question whether it could have survived unmolested to the present, now that Utah is a well-settled state with many industries and a lack of new land to be opened to cultivation.

In general, monogamy now seems better suited than polygyny to the present industrial, urban society, where children are a luxury rather than a utility, and often the employment of both father and mother seems necessary for the rearing of the children of one wife.

Monogamy may be patriarchal in nature, especially when the sons bring their wives to the father's household and rear their children there. Any large group living in a common household and working in a common economic enterprise requires some organization. The over-all division of labor usually recognized the absorption of the wife in childbearing and rearing, whereas the husband was free to occupy himself with the economic production that was basic to the well-being—even the survival—of the entire family. So long as the United States was primarily agrarian, a modified patriarchal family, usually called a paternal family, existed. With urbanization, the authority of the husband declined. The trend toward the equalitarian nuclear family, furthered by the way in which the country was settled, continued. It is doubtful whether the large patriarchal family could survive in an industrialized urban society. Certainly immigrant families with traditional patriarchal organization have lost these qualities during the first generation in American cities. Also, formerly strongly patriarchal countries that are becoming urbanized find the family changing toward the equalitarian nuclear type.

Both the freedom of youth in the choice of a mate and the tolerance of divorce are harmonious with the concept of the equalitarian nuclear family. The nuclear family tends to be the concern chiefly of the married couple; they enter it of their free will and the implication is that they should be free to leave it. It is also possible that with the high degree of freedom allowed, divorce gives support to monogamy. The groups that maintain lifelong monogamy, such as the Catholics, impress on their members from infancy onward the sacred value of the family and the moral impossibility of divorce. Even so, there is not perfect conformity to the Church teachings.

Roles fit the type of marriage and family. When the family is pared down to husband and wife and a small number of children, patriarchy has little meaning. The employment of the wife, which is becoming more and more customary at some stage of married life, further undermines patriarchal inclinations of the husband. Activities tend to be carried out on a personal basis—the father cannot supervise or control all activities of all members, and there is no longer a need for elaborate organization.

By the same token, under other conditions the large patriarchal family was a sensible and workable organization. The family in an agrarian economy is an economic and social unit, an agency of welfare, an educational institution for children, and a system of justice. It is, in fact, an institution that calls for strata of leadership, specific roles, and coordination of activities. It has seemed to thrive primarily in a stable agrarian economy and to decline with migration of small units or of individuals from the home base or with the growth of modern industry and large cities. The Mormons were an exception in that immigrants were quickly absorbed into a polygynous patriarchal system.

Family and Social Organization

It has already been implied that the family type is related to the social organization.[11] Given any type of social organization—isolated farmstead, village, or metropolis; household industries or factories; independent economic enterprise or communism; primitive preliterate tribe or highly sophisticated society—the family type becomes adjusted to the remainder of society. Although a general correspondence can be made between stable agrarian societies and patriarchal families and between mobile, industrial, urbanized societies and equalitarian nuclear families, an absolute and rigid correspondence does not exist. The fact of adjustment between the family and other parts of the social organization seems to be important, rather than the type of adjustment. When such an adjustment has been achieved, a stable type of family evolves into which children are socialized. A certain kind of family life can be anticipated by each member of the family. Likewise, what the family can be expected to do as a unit can be anticipated by the other institutions in the society. The family in turn can anticipate what functions other institutions will perform. The small or nuclear family does not carry the entire burden alone; the extended family, the kinship web, the community as a whole, and other institutions can be counted on for certain functions.

This coordination, once achieved, tends to continue until some drastic change occurs, which may be imposed upon the society from the outside. A situation that has occurred repeatedly is the invasion and overwhelming of a stable culture by an alien cultural group, especially when it has superior weapons, technical skills, and education. Conquering armies and military occupation disturb family forms; when the conquerors set out by decree to change the values and forms of the society, old forms of family life may be quickly disturbed and new ones instituted, almost invariably with an intervening period of opposition and confusion. An example in the past of the United States was the effect of the white invasion and imposition of change on Indian tribes. More recent is the change wrought by the Communists in Russia; and still more recent, the changes that occurred in China under communism, and in Japan under the impact of the United States occupation.

[11]M. F. Nimkoff, editor, *Comparative Family Systems* (Boston: Houghton Mifflin, 1965), chs. 3 and 4.

The changes have affected the entire social organization in each case, the family having been only one of many institutions to be altered.

Other changes affecting family life occur within the society. In country after country, the growth of industrialization has been accompanied by the growth of cities and the decrease of rural life. As a consequence, the rural family was forced to change to fit into the urban patterns. These changes, which were dominant in the United States from the time of the Civil War until World War I, are now occurring in Middle and Far Eastern countries where industrialization is still in process.

Sometimes a revolutionary social or religious leader will set in motion trends that call for drastic changes in family life; for example, Mohammed in the Middle East, and Joseph Smith, who founded the Mormon church.

When these and other changes occur, the family is usually in a state of discord with other parts of the social organization. If the family changes—if it discards or acquires functions—then typically other social institutions must correspondingly assume or discard some of their functions.

When the United States was settled by successive migrations from region to region, from East to West, many community functions were left behind. The family increased its functions and spread them to cover the lacks. When no minister was at hand, families recognized the common-law marriages of their members. The services of a doctor were replaced by home remedies. The work of the skilled craftsman was assumed by family members. At a time when fine homes were being built in the East, members of a family or neighborhood raised log cabins on the frontier, often only a few hundred miles away.

As the country was settled and states organized, new needs developed that the family could not satisfy. For example, the growth of democracy in the United States made it mandatory to have an educated citizenry who could read, listen, come to decisions, and vote intelligently. The family could not supply the type of education needed; public schools were the answer. In the mid-1800's, when public schools were on the increase, many families objected to the demand that their children exchange their useful services to the family for education beyond that experienced by the parents. In modified form, this protest is still evident among poorly educated rural families that migrate into large urban centers. Thus the family is forced to yield some of its autonomy over its individual members.

When the frontier closed and the flow of population turned back to the cities as factories called for workers, the reverse process began and families contracted. The expanded functions of the rural family were unsuited to the demands of city life. Under these new conditions, the family lost functions, sometimes through the simple inability to carry them out in the impersonal city where an individual could lose his identity and family contacts in the space of a few city blocks; sometimes because of the different demands made by the city for skills for which the family could not train children; and sometimes because of the dispersion of the family members into offices, factories, and schools.

In time, however, the family readjusts itself to the new situation, expanding its functions or curtailing them to fit into the total social organization. The changes do not mean that traditional values or functions are necessarily lost altogether. They may simply be transferred to other institutions. On the other hand, new functions may accrue to the family. It cannot be assumed, however, that the only change is in what agency performs the old functions. Changes occur also and often with great pain in the values held dear by families and by society itself.

At the present time, the American family is in a state of contraction, with a residue of few though vital functions. It is also only partially in a state of equilibrium with other social institutions.

Questions

1. Why is the married state more eagerly sought by young people in the United States than in many other countries?
2. Which definition of the family seems most useful in understanding the American family?
3. How do you account for the present form and functions of the American family?
4. If you had to choose some other form of marriage than monogamy, what form would you prefer? Why?
5. What are the advantages of selection of the mate by family elders? For a class project, let each student or a committee of students inquire among their friends as to their reaction to mate selection by their parents. What is their reaction?
6. What advantages for the American family does the kinship web have over both the extended family and the nuclear family?
7. Compare the American family with the traditional Chinese or Moslem family. See the Anshen and Beck references in the Bibliography for additional material.

8. Does the extended patriarchal family adjust well to the modern industrial city? Why?
9. If the United States' physical and social structure were destroyed by war or natural catastrophe, what immediate and permanent changes might be expected in the family?

Bibliography

ANSHEN, RUTH NANDA, ed., *The Family: Its Functions and Destiny*, rev. ed. (New York: Harper & Row, 1959), chs. 1–12.

BECK, DOROTHY FAHS, "The Changing Moslem Family of the Middle East," *Marriage and Family Living*, 19 (1957), 340–47.

CAVAN, RUTH SHONLE, ed., *Marriage and Family in the Modern World, A Book of Readings* (New York: Crowell, 1969), chs. 1 and 4.

GOODE, WILLIAM J., *The Family* (Englewood Cliffs, N. J.: Prentice-Hall, 1964).

LA BARRE, WESTON, "Appraising Today's Pressures on Family Living," *Social Casework*, 32 (February, 1951), 51–57.

LESLIE, GERALD R., *The Family in Social Context* (New York: Oxford University Press, 1967), ch. 2.

MURDOCH, GEORGE P., *Social Structure* (New York: Macmillan, 1949).

NIMKOFF, M. F., ed., *Comparative Family Systems* (Boston: Houghton Mifflin, 1965).

PARSONS, TALCOTT, "The Normal American Family," in Seymour M. Farber, et al., *The Family's Search for Survival* (New York: McGraw-Hill, 1965), 31–50.

———, "The Social Structure of the Family," in Ruth Nanda Anshen, *The Family: Its Function and Destiny*, rev. ed. (New York: Harper & Row, 1959), ch. 13.

QUEEN, STUART A., and ROBERT W. HABENSTEIN, *The Family in Various Cultures* (Philadelphia: Lippincott, 1965).

SUSSMAN, MARVIN B., "The Isolated Nuclear Family: Fact or Fiction," *Social Problems*, 6 (Spring, 1959), 333–40.

WINCH, ROBERT F., and ROBERT MCGINNIS, eds., *Selected Studies in Marriage and the Family* (New York: Holt, Rinehart, and Winston, 1953), chs. 2 and 3; also Winch, McGinnis, and Herbert Barringer, rev. ed., 1962.

2

Issues in the American Family

As THE FAMILY has adjusted from rural agrarian life to urban industrialized life it has seemed at times about to disintegrate. In the period after World War I, writers sounded the alarm under such titles as *The Drifting Home, The Fate of the Family, Must We Scrap the Family?, What Is Happening to Marriage?* and *What Is the Family Still Good For?* The family survived the postwar adjustment and prosperity of the 1920's, the depression of the 1930's, as well as World War II and the greatly increased prosperity of the 1940's and 1950's. Writers no longer fear its disintegration, but they recognize that changes have occurred. Some of the changes seem to have reached a state of at least temporary stabilization; others are still in process of adjustment. There are still many areas of discord within the family, and between the family and other parts of the social organization, which are matters of great public concern. Some of them involve values that seem to be threatened; others involve policies on how to meet recognized individual and family needs. Some of these matters of concern are presented here, though more detailed discussion is reserved for later chapters of the book.

The Basic Meaning of Marriage

Monogamy as the approved form of marriage is unquestioned, although the degree of permanency desirable for any one union is an unsettled issue. Underlying the form of marriage, however, is a deeper concept, the meaning of marriage.

In the United States in the past century a strong belief inhered in marriage as a sacred, divine, and holy institution entered into as a permanent relationship. Marriage was instituted by God and not to be tampered with by man, and its chief purposes were regulation of sex and the production and care of children; this view was upheld by both the Protestant and Catholic religions. Debate over this point of view was strong in the last quarter of the nineteenth century, primarily in connection with the increased rate of divorce, since divorce constituted a definite tampering by man with marriage. The clergy was generally forbidden to perform the marriage service for a divorced person. Although many denominations have altered their stand to the extent that the clergy may now marry divorced persons, the Catholic Church still maintains the view that the family is regulated both by natural and divine laws and opposes divorce as a bold attempt by man to interfere with divine laws.

As the concept of marriage as sacred and inviolable yielded before contrary opinions, it tended to be replaced by the idea that marriage was a social obligation. The social functions attributed to marriage were similar to those supported by the earlier concept—regulation of sex and the production and rearing of children. It was asserted that security of persons, and of family life, demanded restrained sex activities and the strength of the nation depended upon maintenance or increase of the population. The family was also felt to be obligated to produce children in order that the family name might be perpetuated and that property, such as a family farm or business, might be passed on to succeeding generations.

Both the sacred and the social concepts placed emphasis upon the relation of marriage to the larger society and minimized the happiness of the individual members as the chief goal of marriage. Marriage and family life were end-values to society and not means by which individuals gained happiness for themselves. The sacred and social concepts were supported by some degree of necessity, for they were the outgrowth of a social situation in which not only social welfare but personal survival depended upon a strong and continuing family life.

However, the social concept of marriage, unlike the sacred, allowed room for a strong secondary motive of personal happiness. Without happiness, and especially with conflict, the family could not function for social betterment, the argument ran. Husband and wife would refuse to play their roles and achieve the desired functions, and children's lives would be warped or ruined if parental concord was absent.

As the necessity for the family to perform utilitarian functions declined, less was said about marriage as a social obligation. This concept, current from about 1880 to 1920, was challenged by a third concept and one widely held at present: that marriage exists primarily for the personal happiness of husband and wife. If happiness is achieved, the marriage is successful. Sacred values are left to the church; social values to a number of other agencies.

Thus, at the present time three concepts of marriage exist: the sacred, the social, and the personal. The sacred concept is usually limited to strongly organized groups, like a religion, which through control of its members succeeds in bringing marital and family conduct into rather close coordination with the ideal norm. The social concept is supported by many religious groups, which, though they have abandoned the strictly sacred interpretation, uphold the social. As far as individuals are concerned, they now feel free to choose among the sacred, social, and personal interpretations.

At present, therefore, there is lack of uniform opinion as to the basic meaning of marriage. Different institutions support conflicting views, and many unaffiliated people attempt to work out an individual concept, or simply try to solve each marital problem as it arises without having a clear idea of the basic meaning of marriage either to society or to themselves.

The issue is clear: What is the purpose of marriage? Is marriage primarily for the purpose of accomplishing certain religious values? Is it to support the social order? Is its main purpose personal happiness of husband and wife? Or should marriage and family life contribute to all three functions? If so, how may the three functions best be coordinated?

How Can People Best Adjust to Divorce?

Until approximately the end of World War II, the chief reaction to divorce was consternation over the increasing rate and fear that the family as an institution was threatened by this increase. The high rate reached in 1945–46, which was followed by a slight decline and stabilization at a higher level than at any time prior to World War II, shocked laymen and family specialists alike into realizing that lamentations would not reverse the trend. Actually, the high rates were simply a culmination of an upward trend that began prior to the Civil War.

Many people believe that the reason for the increasing rates has been the change from strict to more lax divorce laws. The greater change has been in the increased tolerance toward divorce. During the colonial period, in a number of the colonies divorces were obtainable for a number of reasons, and early national practices were liberal. After the Civil War, divorce laws tended to become more restrictive.[1] However, the attitude toward divorce became more tolerant and the granting of decrees steadily increased. Groups that accept the sacred concept of lifelong marriage continue to be opposed to divorce; those who regard marriage as a personal contract speak of the well-being of husband, wife, and children. If the marriage does not work out well, it cannot fulfill its social functions nor contribute to the happiness of husband and wife and the personality development of the children. It has been argued that it is immoral to continue a nonfunctioning marriage, and that a divorce, far from being immoral, is actually moral.

Remarriage also has come in for criticism. In the period after the Civil War, public opinion held that remarriage was a right only of the innocent party and that a proposal of marriage from a divorced man was an insult to a woman. The clergy generally refused to marry divorced persons, although a justice of the peace or judge would do so. This attitude of disapproval has changed, although in some Protestant denominations and in the Catholic Church the clergy are forbidden to perform the marriage ceremony for a divorced person. Far from being considered unsuitable for remarriage, divorced persons have a higher rate of marriage, age for age, than have the widowed or single persons entering their first marriage. According to one estimate, the proportion of divorced persons who will eventually remarry is more than two-thirds of women and three-fourths of men.[2]

Several issues stem from the divorce situation as it now stands.

Are the rather complacent approval of divorce as a way to "solve" an unhappy marriage and the acceptance of the present high rate justified in terms of present social conditions? Another war and postwar adjustment undoubtedly would send rates up again.

Many divorces involve young children. Is the cliche so often heard justified—"It's better for the child to have divorced parents than to live in the midst of conflict"? Are there other alternatives than conflict or divorce? To what extent do parents who are contemplating divorce really consider the welfare of the children?

In view of the penchant of Americans for marriage, divorced people are out of step with normal social life. How can they adjust to the status

[1]Arthur W. Calhoun, *A Social History of the American Family* (New York: Barnes and Noble, 1960), various references in Vols. I, II, and ch. 12 in Vol. III.
[2]Paul C. Glick, *American Families* (New York: Wiley, 1957), pp. 135, 139.

of being divorced? Many marry another partner. Is this an adequate solution? What of those who do not remarry?

Should Young People Have a Free Hand in Selecting a Mate?

Selection of the marital partner is now regarded as an individual right of the couple involved. With the prevailing youthful age of marriage, this selection often takes place when at least the girls are still adolescent and not regarded as adult in many areas of life; for example, they cannot vote. Complete freedom of mate selection is of fairly recent origin in this country and, as has been pointed out, does not exist at all in many societies where the elders of the family are completely responsible for selecting their children's spouses.

In the period prior to World War I, several features of social life in the United States placed mate selection under the supervision of parents and neighbors: more people lived in rural and small-town communities, where "everyone knew everyone else," thus creating an informal but effective check on unsuitable courtships; young people tended to select mates from among friends whom they had known from childhood and whose personal characteristics and family status were well known to them and their parents; few young people had access to automobiles as a part of the courtship equipment; family activities were customary, with relatively few social activities for the young alone, and these, when they occurred, were under adult chaperonage.

The transfer of the population from rural communities to large cities introduced a new approach to mate selection through long-continued dating under the control of young people themselves. It is difficult to assess the relative effectiveness of mate selection under adult supervision and the current autonomous mate selection by quite young people. Not all the ills, nor all the joys, of marriage can be attributed to the new method. However, four problematic situations can be selected that seem closely related to unsupervised dating and choice of a mate.

One problem concerns the qualities of the chosen mate. When adults kept their hands on the reins of mate selection, the tendency was to define a "good" marriage as one in which the man and woman came from the same social, ethnic, and religious background. A coup might be gained by one set of parents if the mate was of slightly better social status, the other set of parents countering with satisfaction in the beauty of a girl of slightly lower position than their son, or of the fine position or income of a man of slightly lower status than their daughter. In some way the inequality of status was balanced out. On the personal side, parents of the girl approved of a young man who was of good character and had promise of being the proverbial good provider; parents of the man approved of a girl who was attractive, above reproach morally, and had the potentialities of being a good mother and home-maker.

With young people themselves in charge, these qualities are often overlooked. In an urban situation they are less easily discovered and often seem less necessary than in a rural setting. Personal attractiveness and appearance of the girl and attractiveness of the young man as well as his rating as a "good spender" often take precedence in young minds over practical considerations of stability and the ability to shoulder the responsibilities of marriage and children.

Is this change in qualities sought a detriment to marriage?

A second concern is the apparent increase in marriages between members of different cultural or racial groups. Marriages or illicit liaisons between men and women of different backgrounds are not new, as witness the unions between European explorers and Indian women, between white plantation owners and women slaves, or between military men and the women of almost any country where they are stationed, regardless of race, religion, or type of culture. Our concern here is not with the illicit unions but with marriages, which set up a permanent union and open the way for the birth of children. More than formerly, young people meet persons of other racial and cultural backgrounds at work, in school and college, and in the course of recreation. Young people may fear intermarriage and confine their social and dating activities to their own groups. Others are intrigued by the differences and enter into dating but withdraw before falling in love. But intermarriages of various types are now numerous and are in line both with our general democratic attitudes and with the prerogative of young people to choose their own mates. Public opinion is opposed to many of these marriages, especially the interracial ones; many organized religious groups are opposed to interreligious marriages; parents have misgivings about almost any type of marriage in which husband and wife have widely different backgrounds. In general, people are still in the stage of lamenting the trend toward intermarriages and of trying to prevent them. Perhaps a more realistic approach would be to accept them and discover how the necessary adjustments between husband and wife and between the couple and their families and the community might be achieved. The Catholic Church is virtually the only organized group that has devised any means of coping with marriages of its members to nonmembers; the plan, however, is directed toward keeping the Catholic member within the Church and bringing children into the Church. Little concern is shown for the non-Catholic member or for compromising the differences that almost inevitably appear in the marriage.

Are intermarriages as hazardous as they seem? Ought laws to be passed to regulate or forbid intermarriages? If so, to what types of intermarriage ought they apply? Or, ought all religious groups provide some type of compromise? Ought courses of study be made available to young people to provide greater understanding of the effects that intermarriage may have on them as a family and possible ways of mitigating adverse effects?

A third outgrowth of youthful autonomy in mate selection is the trend toward early marriage. When is a marriage "early"? According to English common law, a girl of 12 and a boy of 14 could marry. Some Eastern countries still permit marriage during preadolescence, although the custom is fading. In our own colonial days, Puritans married young —girls at 16 or younger and many men before they were 20; in North Carolina, marriage of girls of 13 was not unusual and the customary age was 16.[3] An unmarried woman of 20 was "reckoned a stale maid."

At present the epithet "teenage" marriage is derogatory. Nevertheless, half of all girls are married while still in their teens, although in the last two years of 18 and 19. Teenage or early marriage now by popular usage refers to marriage of young people who are still of school age, that is, below 18. In 1959, among brides making their first marriage, 18 per cent were under age 18; among grooms, however, only 1.8 per cent were under age 18, and the majority were aged 21 or over.[4] The early or teenage marriage about which so much disapproval clusters actually refers to the marriage of girls under age 18. The group may be further narrowed. Lower-class girls have traditionally married in the mid-teens; the marriage that arouses consternation is of middle-class girls who are usually considered school girls and not candidates for early marriage.

In light of the above explanation, what are the objections to middle-class mid-teen marriages for girls? Lack of maturity to accept the role of the middle-class adult woman? Insufficient education for companionship with the slightly older, better educated man she will marry? The suspicion or actual fact of premarital pregnancy?

If such deficiencies exist, what can be done about the situation? Should the legal age of marriage be raised? Should the school-age part-

[3]Calhoun, op. cit., I, 67–68, 245–46.

[4]Vital Statistics of the United States, 1959, Vol. I, Sec. 9, "Detailed Marriage Statistics for the Marriage-Registration Area" (Washington, D.C.: Government Printing Office, 1961), p. 60.

ner remain in school? Should marriages of those under legal age be annulled? Should abortion for premarital pregnancy of teenage girls be made legal? Should parents try to recapture the control of mate selection? Can teenagers themselves be taught to function more effectively in delaying marriage?

The fourth matter of concern in our present dating and mate-selection system is the practice of premarital sex relations. Since this is one of the most controversial moral issues of the day, it will be considered under a separate heading.

Should Sex Relations Be Reserved for Marriage?

The social norms of the past sternly forbade sexual intimacies outside of marriage. Officially religion, law, and the popular mores allowed for no deviation. Unofficially there was recognition of a double standard whereby the behavior of unmarried young men was condoned if they indulged in casual sex relations with women of uncertain morals. For these men sex had two connotations: especially in their youth, it was regarded as a right of virile young manhood and a source of physical pleasure; with marriage it assumed in addition social values in that children were desired and highly valued. For the girl of two generations ago, sex tended to have primarily the social value; many middle- and upper-class girls were reared with the idea that sex was "dirty," that a girl "submitted" because she owed this duty to her husband and also because it was the only means by which children might be attained. Strict chastity for all women except a limited group of lower-class casuals and prostitutes was almost universal. The girl who deviated from this code was pitied or reviled as a "fallen woman" who brought lasting shame and disgrace to herself and her family.

The trend has been away from these mores for some years. Young women, seeking equality with men, made the measure of that equality identity of privileges in a number of fields, including the same degree of freedom of sex expression accorded to men. As an abstraction, many people agreed; young women themselves have hesitated to turn the abstract privilege into reality. Nevertheless, the trend has been for teenage girls and unmarried young women to permit greater intimacy prior to marriage than they did formerly. The intimacy often stops with petting, as most girls are well aware of some of the more obvious dangers of premarital intercourse—ruined reputation, pregnancy, and venereal disease. Middle-class girls look for a rationalization to justify premarital intimacies; the most frequent is that being in love justifies them. Lower-class girls have a simpler rationalization: intimacies are a natural type of behavior in view of the potency of the sex drive.

Among young men, the double standard continues to function: sex without responsibility with girls who make a practice of casual or promiscuous sex relations; sex on the basis of friendship or love with girls they would regard as of equal social status.

New conceptions of sex experience have developed, applicable both before and after marriage. Now, young women look for personal satisfaction and pleasure in sex, similar to that long experienced by men. In addition, for both men and women, sex has attained additional valuation as an expression of love and as a means of expanding the personality. The social valuation related to children has not been lost, but it is no longer the only one for women, and often its aura has been dimmed by the decreased number of children in the modern family. When the short period of childbearing has ended, values other than reproduction must be found for sex relations.

The separation of sex from childbearing in people's thinking and its partial accomplishment through the effective use of contraceptives implies the possible freeing of sex from marriage. If sex has positive values in itself—if it is good and normal—why confine it to marriage? Or, in marriage, why confine it solely to the spouse? Especially why is it not a justifiable part of courtship between two people in love with each other? Many persons who would regard it as reprehensible for a young unmarried couple to produce a child are willing to condone premarital sexual relations and to regard them as the privilege of the two individuals involved. Many others, concerned with family stability, fear the effect on the personalities of the young couple and the subsequent effect on the stability of their marriage. Others condemn the act because it may result in conception. Still others continue to hold the social code of the past: that sex outside of marriage is sinful and a highly immoral act.

Here, then, is an unresolved issue of social, moral, and personal import with great emotional content: are premarital or extramarital sex relations ever justified and, if so, under what conditions?

The Population Explosion on a Family Level

Family planning (referring both to limitation of the total number and to spacing of children) and population explosion are two sides of the same coin. In the United States, population explosion is an abstraction in the sense that we have food and living space for the present population or for reasonable increases. The situation here differs from that in some parts of the world where population growth threatens slow starvation. In the United States, the population explosion is feared largely by individual families to the extent that with a large number of children they will be unable to maintain a high standard of living. This fear is especially marked on the part of the middle class and of upwardly mobile groups.

The conflict over artificial limitation of families was originally conducted on an ideological and theological basis, and was closely related to different concepts of the meaning of marriage. Marriage as a sacred institution included the concept that the chief basis of marriage and of sexual relations was the production of children. With the gradual shift in attitude among many groups to the concept of marriage as a personal contract, the significance of children also changed. After a long and bitter struggle between adherents of the two concepts, it is now generally conceded by most people that family limitation has some merits. Those who hold to the sacred concept view limitation as primarily a means of promoting responsible parenthood; that is, with consideration for the mother's health, the parents' ability to provide material necessities for their children, the availability of housing, and the general population conditions of the country.[5] Not only the Catholic Church but many Protestant denominations qualify their approval of family limitation by these and similar conditions. According to such statements, family limitation is not a matter of individual wishes, but is designed to promote more responsible parenthood for the maximum number of children the parents are prepared to rear.

Another ideology has grown from the concept of marriage as a personal contract. An official of the Planned Parenthood Federation of America, the leading proponent for planned families, has written that "Planned parenthood is the utilization of medical knowledge for the procreation of the number of children any given couple want to have, born when the family is ready for them."[6]

The ideological conflict has prevented the formulation of a national policy regarding the optimum size of family needed for the growth of a strong nation or for personality development of parents and children.

A secondary conflict has developed and at present is even more of a public issue than the ideological difference. This issue concerns the various means of controlling births, whether to limit the complete num-

[5]The Rev. John A. O'Brien (Research Professor of Theology, University of Notre Dame), "Let's Take Birth Control Out of Politics," *Look*, 25 (October 10, 1961), 67–68ff.

[6]David Loth, "Planned Parenthood," *Annals of the American Academy of Political and Social Science*, 272 (November, 1950), 95–101.

ber of children or for the purposes of spacing births. One point of the debate concerns the type of contraceptive to be used. The Catholic Church officially maintains the stand that it has held for some years: the only approved method of contraception is the use of the rhythm method, that is, abstinence from coitus during the portion of a woman's monthly menstrual cycle when she is fertile and could readily conceive. Many types of contraceptives have been in use for many years, with varying degrees of effectiveness. The controversy over contraception came into sharp debate around 1960 with the introduction to the public of a pill to be taken orally 20 days out of 30.[7] When so taken, month after month, the pill prevents ovulation and hence the possibility of pregnancy. The reliability of the method, and the simplicity of its mechanics compared with most other methods, led to its widespread adoption. Many secondary issues arose. Since the pill can be used to merely regulate the occurrence of the menstrual period, members of groups opposed to the use of contraceptives have urged that its use as a regularizer is not a violation of the stricture against contraceptives, even though an incidental effect is the prevention of ovulation. Another secondary dispute has occurred over the program developed in some cities by nonofficial organizations to teach the use of and perhaps provide the pill to unmarried women who have given birth to one child and who might be expected to produce additional children, often without a reasonable prospect of marriage or self-support. This program has been decried by others as encouraging nonmarital sex relations, which they define as being immoral. A third point of the debate concerns the distribution of pills to unmarried girls in anticipation of coitus. Again questions of morality have come up.

A second subject that has come under heavy discussion during the 1960's concerns induced abortions, that is, abortions deliberately caused at the wish of the pregnant woman, as opposed to spontaneous abortions (miscarriages) that occur from natural causes, or therapeutic abortions performed primarily for medical reasons. Only therapeutic abortions are legal. Until 1967, state laws limited therapeutic abortions to cases in which the life of the mother was at stake or, in a few states, the health of the mother. A slow movement to liberalize these laws has been developing over a long period of time. Various arguments have been cited in support of more liberal laws. Chief among them is the fact that a very large but unknown number of illegal abortions takes place every year, some under unsanitary conditions and by inexperienced persons, leading in a small but unknown percentage of cases to permanent injury or death of the woman. Those favoring more liberal

[7]The pill is a synthetic substitute for the natural hormone progesterone, which prevents ovulation when secreted by a woman's body.

abortion laws also point to the fact that some pregnancies result from an illegal act, such as rape or incest; that the mother may be a young girl who has not reached the age of consent; or that certain diseases the mother may contract, or the use of certain drugs, are known to result in physical or mental abnormality of the baby in some instances, though there are no methods of determining which children will be so affected. Other arguments emphasize economic or social handicaps of the mother which might prevent adequate opportunities for the child; and still others, that if the child is not wanted, it will not be loved.

Those opposed to such laws point to the fact that legal abortion would not put an end to all illegal abortions, since many women wish to keep the fact of the abortion a secret or simply do not want the child. The strongest arguments hinge on the fact that life begins with conception, so that any abortion may therefore be defined as destruction of a human life. Catholics are also concerned with the destruction not only of life but of a human soul.

A break in the public debate—but not an end to it—came in 1967 when two states passed laws to permit legal abortions on certain grounds in addition to preserving the life of the mother. Colorado and North Carolina modified their laws in April and May, 1967, respectively, both of them basing the new law on a model code drafted by the American Law Institute. The main features of the new laws make abortion legal whenever the pregnancy (1) results from incest or rape, (2) threatens grave damage to the woman's physical or mental health, or (3) is likely to result in the birth of a child with a severe mental or physical defect. Although some other states have followed the lead of these two, the movement toward liberalization will probably be slow, as those opposed to and those in favor of changing the laws marshal their forces state by state.

In the debate now in progress, the basic issue concerns the conflicting values that are placed on abundance of children, human life, health of the mother, standard of living, and the individual wishes of husband and wife.

Should Upward Social Mobility of Families Be Controlled?

A marked feature of the present period of material abundance is the upward mobility of many families. Near-full employment and higher incomes have led to a general stream of upwardly mobile individuals and families seeking a place in the sun of a higher social class than the class of their origin. Evidence of such an upward movement has been found among some portion of each social class. Different writers discuss the *nouveau bourgeoisie* (new middle class) moving from upper-lower into lower-middle class, the *parvenu* (upstart) pushing into upper-middle class from lower-middle class, while the lower-upper class exerts pressure as *nouveau riche* aspirants to membership in the upper-upper class.

The movement is not cataclysmic; members of a lower class do not customarily leap-frog over intervening classes into a markedly higher class. But the movement is not the older, slow kind of transition whereby the upwardly mobile learned the culture of the next class above them as they slowly accumulated the money to maintain the life-style of the superior class. The present movement is rapid and carries the family into the next higher class in material culture—the right make of car, the house in the correct suburb—while it still clings to the old familiar values and life-style of the class of origin.

It seems feasible to suggest that there are now two vertical hierarchies—one, the old fortress-like class structure, with the social class at each level resisting invasion of newcomers, the other a fluid, mobile structure, in which each segment pushes persistently and rapidly upward, although not with revolutionary force. The disjuncture between the static and the mobile hierarchies raises questions for the family that perhaps existed earlier as problems of only very few families. These questions now pertain to large segments of each class. Some of these questions are:

To what extent will solidly based classes continue to resist the social encroachments of the upwardly mobile classes? Will the mobile families force their way in and thus undermine the stability of the former higher class with resulting social disorganization?

What effect will the resistance and rejection by the higher class have on the intruding families? Will some favored members be accepted and others rejected, thus creating disruption in the mobile groups and families? Will rejected members or entire families feel frustrated and antagonistic to the point of neurotic or criminal behavior?

Finally, to what extent is the acquirement of the material goods necessary for upward mobility based on credit? Is the financial status of the mobile families sufficiently firm to withstand the effects of a long economic recession or depression; or will families be plunged into downward mobility that will carry them to their original status or even lower?

Since our democratic way of life includes the privilege of attempting to improve one's position, how can upwardly mobile families protect themselves against disruption and personal ill effects?

The Confusing Roles of the American Wife

The family of our immediate past had developed roles for husband and wife that supplemented each other. Children as they arrived also were immediately ascribed roles, not only in relation to their parents but in relation to each other in terms of age, ordinal position, and sex.

The husband was the openly acknowledged head of the family, with well-defined duties: to earn or provide the living for his family, to provide the final but benevolent authority on matters of discipline and in decisions affecting the family as a whole, to maintain community contacts, and to vote in community and national elections. The wife was a junior partner, who contributed her opinions but accepted the decisions of her husband, attended to the details of the household and the daily training of the young children, and found her chief community outlets through the church and its attendant welfare activities. On the farm and in the village her time was well filled with the necessities of family life. In the cities some wives found it necessary to work to aid their husbands, but carried out this work in the same spirit that they did their housework, as a supplement to the husband's functions.

These roles were not only well coordinated but were relatively fixed by custom. Girls and boys learned in advance what their adult roles were to be, and when the time came were prepared to carry them out. The stability of the coordinated pattern of roles gave to the family the attribute of dependability as a part of the social structure.

More recently, the trend has been away from fixed roles for all members of the family, but especially so for women. In fact, during the period preceding World War I women became a storm center. The more aggressive women organized into a militant feminist movement, while a minority not only adapted their roles to changed conditions but demanded new roles for themselves and sought to force those still content with the wife-and-mother role into roles previously the stronghold of men. Under the battle cry of equality, the feminist spearhead sought identity of activities with men educationally, vocationally, and politically, and of personal activities including minor and major vices. During the 1930's the situation tended to stabilize itself, but not around a new array of fixed roles. The stabilization was based on a choice of roles for women, with men more or less reluctantly conceding the right of a woman to make a choice, but not necessarily the obligation of man to accommodate himself if she chose other than the wife-and-mother role.

The demands for workers during World War II carried great numbers of women into paid employment. Although many returned to marriage and family life when the war ended, the percentage that remained employed was high. More important was the fact that women's position in business, industry, and the professions was assured. Women no longer felt a compulsion to work to demonstrate their right to do so; they no longer had to justify their employment by necessity or by the desire for a career. They could simply work if they wished. Moreover, husbands accepted their wives' new role and adjusted their own roles accordingly. It is important to note that the men and women of the postwar period who accepted the new roles were not the ones who had fought the battle over women's rights just before and after World War I, but were of the next generation—the sons and daughters of the men and women who had struggled through the role adjustment in the earlier period.

Although the coordination of roles for men and women on the new basis of employment for women is well on its way to adjustment, women have not yet effectively adjusted their own multiple roles. Two of the remaining problematic areas worthy of discussion are the wife's conception of her status with reference to that of her husband, and her inability to alter her concept of motherhood in relation to her employed role.

Many young women wish to be "little women" in relation to their husbands. This phrase implies inferiority and subordination of the wife's status relative to the status of her husband. Moreover, it implies her acceptance of this status, an attitude that is the direct opposite of that of her feminist mother or grandmother, who insisted on equal status. Surveys of college students made over the past 20 years show a persistent trend of well over half of women students to seek a mate who is older, more intelligent, and better educated than themselves. These attitudes contrast strangely with the trend of women into employment where they must meet men on a basis of equality. It also contrasts with the replies of men college students, who are much more ready than women for equal status with their future spouses. Many of the inequalities women seek are actually carried into practice; for example, men on the average are between two and three years older than their wives.

What are the implications for marriage and family living not only of actual inequalities but, more significantly, of the attitude of many young women that they wish to be less well equipped by nature, education, and years of experience than their husbands? Are these simply college-girl attitudes? What do such inequalities do for companionship?

Is the "little woman" role compatible with the demands of the 1960's, when many young women are being forced into the headship of the family by military separation or by divorce? Does "little womanhood" fit the wife for the triple role many women will play of homemaker, mother, and employed woman?

The second confusion in the roles of women concerns the rearing of children. Americans hold firmly to the idea that the mother should rear her children personally, especially in their preschool years. In favor of this, cases are cited of young children who languish from lack of personal care and love, who feel so insecure that they never gain self-confidence, and who grow up feeling unloved and unwanted. Counter arguments support the right of the mother to delegate their care, if she is bored by childrearing or feels that she is not making full use of her education in confining herself to housekeeping and the care of small children. Others point to children who are not reared by their mothers and who seem to suffer no ill effects—children of the upper class who are reared by nurses and tutors; children in residential schools from an early age (as in England); and children in the kibbutzim (collective settlements) of Israel, where they spend most of the 24 hours in special living units separated from their mothers.

What is the answer for American mothers? Should they remain at home when their children are small, even though they are bored or feel they are wasting education and talents? Should they perhaps be educated solely for the role of homemaker and mother? If the mother is employed, what is best for the children: care by an older brother or sister? By an accommodating neighbor? A housekeeper? Or should American mothers explore the possibilities of full day care in nurseries or weekday residential care for older children, both of which are now little used in the United States? In view of the steadily increasing percentage of mothers of preschool children who are accepting employment, the question of adequate care for children is a vital and growing problem.

Is the Loss of Functions Detrimental to Family Life?

There is much concern about the segmental character of modern family life. As older or even middle-aged persons recall the family life of their youth, it was much more inclusive than at present. Only in very isolated rural areas has the family retained sufficient practical functions to be thought of as physically self-sustaining, and the almost complete self-sufficiency of the pioneering period is now historical rather than even within the past experience of the living. The loss of functions which began with the settled community has accelerated with increasing urbanization. Moreover, the process has reached out from the cities into the villages and rural areas. The tangible crafts that have been lost are the ones most often referred to with a nostalgic tone of voice; the pans of browned bread on the kitchen table, the rows of canned fruit on the shelf, the party dress that the mother of the family sat up half the night to complete, are the things regretted by those who experienced them in their youth. Interestingly enough, most of the lamented art- and crafts are those of women; either the activities of the father were less obvious to the children, or he had left the home and farm crafts behind him a generation earlier and it is now accepted that he should not do them.

More significant but less often mentioned than the abandonment of the tangible crafts and the practical physical activities is the loss of the social activities of the home. The earlier family was not only physically but also socially self-sufficient. The family as a whole more often than at present picnicked, attended the Chautauqua, explored the nearest city on a Sunday railway excursion, and visited or entertained other families. Also the fact that more work was done in the home created a social situation as parents and children of different ages joined in the tasks on a cooperative basis, with each doing work suited to his age and sex. It is, in fact, the social inclusiveness of family life that is regretted, of which the physical crafts stand in memory as symbols.

In contrast to this inclusive family life of the past, the family life of today seems to be composed of segments of experience that are different for each member and often unintegrated within the experience of each one. The parents do not know their children's friends, or meet them only casually without acquaintance with their parents. Children of different ages and sex each have a private circle of friends. Husband and wife plot their days along totally different lines that rarely intersect.

The gradual shortening of the work week and the consequent increase in leisure for employed members also affects the pattern of family life. There is also less compulsion for adolescents to have part-time employment while still attending school. The increased leisure may permit time for a renewal of family life, assuming that all members have off-hours at the same time. However, if individual activities are still pursued, increased leisure may increase the splintering of family life.

What are some of the results for the family of individual activities versus family activities? Undoubtedly, the entrance of adults and children alike into a variety of nonfamily associations changes the character of the family. It loses unity, interdependence, common goals, and participation through which parents pass on to children the family and general culture. On the other hand, through nonfamily agencies each member acquires experience and knowledge beyond the scope of the family and relates himself to the larger community. These questions may well be asked: is inclusive family life too limited, especially in the modern city? Is it simply a relic from the rural past? What contribution can the family make to fit its members to adjust to city life? Is the movement to the suburbs a mass attempt to restore the unity of family life?

Old Age—A New Dimension of Married Life

Several factors have combined to create a new phase of marriage and family life, extending into the period after children have become adults and left the home and later into the period of retirement from paid employment. Smaller numbers of children, born earlier in life to the parents, and hence leaving home when the parents are still middle-aged, account for one aspect of this new dimension: the resumption by parents of the roles of husband and wife as their dominant roles. The generally accepted retirement age of 65 precipitates the couple into another phase of married life, with lowered income and destruction of the husband's principal life role as a productive worker. Although both the shift to postparental status and to retirement status affects both husband and wife, the former seems to call for the more acute adjustment on the part of the wife, the latter on the part of the husband.

In addition to the above social factors, several biological factors are also present. The menopause of the wife terminates any possibility of further parenthood and calls for new self-conceptions of maturity instead of youthfulness. During middle and old age the declining sexual potency of the husband leads to somewhat similar reevaluations of self-conceptions. For both, the added years strip away many of the attributes of youth such as attractive physical appearance, physical strength, and speed of learning new skills or grasping new abstractions. These biological and physical changes are not new, but the length of time that men and women now live has created a long span of time when the marriage must adjust to these changes. Finally, husband or wife dies, and the remaining partner must make another adjustment as widow or widower, or remarry and repeat the process of early marital adjustment.

Each change calls for abandonment or decline of previous self-conceptions and roles and the adoption of new ones. Changing self-conceptions and roles are typical of each transition in the family life cycle, from infancy onward. The transition is simplified when the new roles can be known in advance and when means exist to facilitate the transition. Transitions are welcomed when the new self-concepts and roles promise rewards in the way of a more favored status, expanded pleasures, or increased income. The transition to old age and to some extent to middle age often does not hold out such promises.

In general, valued roles are lost regardless of the person's wishes in the matter, and changes in self-concepts are rather forcibly demanded. The mother becomes an in-law, the retired man is "on the shelf." Income often decreases not as a temporary exigency of economic conditions but as a permanent condition of life. With the present long life span, these situations cannot be regarded as characterizing simply the last few years of the person's life. If discontent and maladjustment are to be avoided for years to come, the situations must be accepted. Since the increased expectancy of long life is relatively new, the culture has not yet developed ways to make the transition simple nor created satisfying new self-conceptions and roles for the old. Nevertheless, some attempts have been made.

The old family has more economic security than it did due to the passage of the Social Security law in 1935 and the subsequent development of industrial pensions. The level of income may be lower than it was when it was earned, but the family has the compensation of security and of independence from support by relatives.

Housing especially planned for the income and needs of older people is under way.

Many social clubs and some community centers designed for older persons are springing up all over the country.

In time, grandparenthood restores some of the aspects of the parental role and adds new satisfactions through pride in the continuity of the family into a new generation.

The chief loss is in the failure of any of the institutions of society to devise for the man an adequate substitute for his previous self-concept as a productive earner and to provide a means of his acting out such a new role. A few men are retained on their jobs into old age; a few, retired from one position, are able to find other employment. Some are glad to be released from work. But, by and large, older men are displaced persons without a satisfying role to play. What is usually available is some form of recreation, such as travel, social clubs, or crafts. Recreation, at one time frowned upon in Puritan culture, has gained a recognized place, but normally as a supplement to work. The steady worker, the creative producer, has much higher status than the wastrel or the playboy. Almost the only role offered by business or organized community groups to the retired man is that of professional playboy. To adopt this role, the man not only has to change his activities but to reverse his self-concept and his role. Many refuse, and seek individual solutions; many others remain frustrated and unhappy. Whatever solution is reached by the individual man, his relationship with his wife is affected. Unless he continues to work, the older schedule of meals, bed-time, rising time, and daily activities changes. The husband is often at home during much of the time. Can the wife change her routines and roles sufficiently to include her husband in homemaking? Will the husband accept such a subordinate role to his wife? Like the playboy role, this is regarded as a low-status role, especially by the generation of men now in or approaching retirement.

The issue of making old age productive and satisfying will remain until some adequate solution is found; the length of life is still increasing, and consequently the number of old people in the population continues to increase. What are some possible solutions? Ought old age be redefined and the age of forced and customary retirement raised? Ought part-time jobs (filled now by many mothers of young children) be arranged for older men? Is there a place for some men as consultants or advisers to younger persons in their field of work? Could they be organized into corps of volunteers for needed but perhaps unpaid community work?

The adjustment problems of older women seem less acute and more readily solved. Undoubtedly the most distressing problem is that attendant upon adjusting to widowhood, an adjustment that the wife is called upon to make more often than the husband inasmuch as the length of life of most women exceeds that of men.

Questions

Questions are contained in the text of this chapter, at the end of each section.

Bibliography

It is the intention of this chapter to arouse interest in current issues and to encourage the student to review his own opinions. As each issue is discussed in the later chapters, appropriate bibliographical references are given.

$$3$$

The Rural, Urban, Suburban
Composite Family

SINCE 1790, when the first population census was made, the rural farm and village or small town population has decreased from 95 to about 30 per cent of the total. At first the decrease was slight from decade to decade, then very rapid with only minor periods of slow decrease, chiefly during economic depressions. The corollary to the decrease in rural population was a corresponding increase in city population. Large cities of 100,000 population and over also increased. Prior to 1820 no city of 100,000 existed in the United States; by 1930, almost a third of the population lived in such cities. The seeming stabilization of large cities since 1930 at about 30 per cent of the population is deceptive, for it has been accompanied by a tremendous increase in suburbs that encircle cities not once but several times and extend outward in star-shaped configurations along the main lines of transportation. Many suburbs become annexed to cities, but the growth into outlying areas continues.

A detailed analysis of where people lived in 1960 is given in Figure 1. More than half the population lived in urbanized areas, with 32 per cent in the central cities and 21 per cent in the fringe or suburban areas. Isolated cities, usually small or moderate in size, accounted for only 16 per cent of the population, rural communities for 22 per cent, and farms for only 9 per cent.

Significant also is the rate of population growth for each type of community. The increase since 1950 in the suburban areas has been phe-

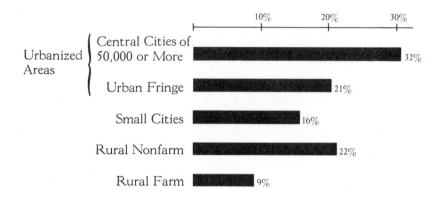

FIGURE 1   *Distribution of Population by Type of Community, 1960.*

Over half the population lives in or is under the influence of cities of 50,000 or more population. Since 1950, fringe areas have had the greatest increase; rural population has declined slightly.

SOURCE: *United States Census of Population, 1960, United States Summary, General Population Characteristics* (Washington, D. C.: Government Printing Office, 1961), pp. VIII–IX, 1–143. Figure for farm population from *Statistical Abstract of the United States, 1961* (Washington, D. C.: Government Printing Office, 1961), p. 613.

nomenal—81.5 per cent. Central cities in the midst of their suburbs have increased by 20 per cent. Cities and villages outside the metropolitan city-suburban complex have had only a modest increase. The farm population, once the stronghold of the nation, declined from 16 per cent to 9 per cent of the total population.

Summarizing the trend, until about 1920–30 the country was still predominantly rural so far as place of residence and family culture were concerned. From 1930 on very large cities tended to become stable in percentage of population. During this same period and especially after 1940, the growth of suburbs brought many additional people within the immediate ring of influence of cities.

The Rural Family

So far as numbers are concerned, the rural family is a disappearing type, although so long as products must be grown in the soil there is no reason to believe that it will disappear entirely. One of the chief interests at present in the rural family is the fact that the basic pattern of the American family was set during the decades when the nation was primarily rural in social organization and culture. Some of the issues discussed in the preceding chapter are an outgrowth of the transfer of rural values and customs to a city environment.

THE PIONEER RURAL PAST

Although in earlier years hunters, trappers, and Indian traders had traversed the land, permanent settlement was made not by these transient and nonfamily men who gathered the natural bounty of the land, but by permanent residents on farms where a living was made by cultivating the same plot of land productively year after year. Migrants were induced to settle by the government policy of buying land from the Indians, surveying it, and selling it to settlers in plots of not less than 80 acres, for $1.25 per acre. By 1850 the westernmost surveyed land covered Michigan, half of Iowa, most of Arkansas, and parts of Wisconsin.[1] Settlers without the necessary cash to buy land moved further and settled on unsurveyed land which, when surveyed, they were allowed to buy. Thus, as one area became settled, the pioneers pushed westward into the next unclaimed area. The Homestead Act of 1862, granting land without cash payments, further stimulated westward migration. Increases in population were fabulous. In 1860, 300,000 people occupied Minnesota, Dakota, Nebraska, and Kansas; by 1870 the number had increased to almost a million and by 1880 to two and one half million. Families that took up homesteads had almost no cash; they built sod or log huts and labored hard to make their farms productive. One historian notes that never in the nineteenth century had so great a proportion of the farm population lived under pioneer or semi-pioneer conditions as in the post-Civil War period.[2]

PIONEER INFLUENCE UPON THE FAMILY

The present popular American concept of the ideal family was established during the pioneer period, and many older people still cling to that ideal or remember it with nostalgia from their childhood. This family was not only the rural family, but a special kind of rural family. Contrary to most earlier practices, each pioneer family lived upon its own wide acres. Before the development of widespread industry and commerce, most people of necessity raised their own food and made

[1]Carl Russell Fish, *The Rise of the Common Man, 1840–50* (New York: Macmillan, 1927), pp. 152–55.

[2]Allan Nevins, *The Emergence of Modern America, 1865–78* (New York: Macmillan, 1927), pp. 154–55.

many of their own implements. They were therefore rural in the sense of being self-sufficient. The American farm ideally was owned by the man who lived upon it and worked it. The belief in the positive value of ownership was in part a reaction to the peasant system of Europe that lay in the background experience or family history of many American families; and it was in part a result of the luxuriant expanse of land waiting for cultivation. The ideal farm was not so large, however, that it could not be worked by the farmer, his wife, and growing children, with perhaps the aid of a hired man. This was the ideal—the family-sized farm owned, occupied, and operated as a family enterprise to provide a good living for the family. The farmer was comparable to the owner-artisan who owned his home and small business in the town or city, doing the work himself with perhaps the aid of an apprentice or two. In both cases business merged with family life, and the objective was not thought of as amassing wealth or building a commercial enterprise so much as finding a satisfying and integrated mode of life that encompassed the entire family.

The family was the economic and social unit that moved into the opening West. Although husbands sometimes preceded their wives and young men sometimes bought land or took a homestead before marriage, soon wives, children, and sweethearts followed. Affection and desire for companionship were not the only motives at work, for each family unit had to be self-sustaining to a high degree; the skills of a woman were needed to supplement the work of a man, and the children soon grew to useful stature. The pioneer situation therefore encouraged early marriage and a high birth rate. Family life was highly valued.

Moreover, the communal unit was the family, for the principal pattern of settlement was farm by farm, each owner living upon his own land and often definitely isolated in a period without good roads, telephones, rural free delivery of mail, or radios. A distance of even a few miles might isolate the family, as this description of a farm in Otsego County, New York, in 1848 emphasizes:

> Our new home was in a comparative wilderness; not a house was in sight. The nearest neighbors on the south and east lived over a mile from us. On the west, the nearest lived three fourths of a mile, and on the north over one fourth of a mile; and a thick dark forest intervened.[3]

The family was therefore an interdependent social unit, with all lines of interaction turning inward.

[3]H. C. Wright, *Human Life: Illustrated in My Individual Experience* (Boston, 1849), quoted in J. H. Kolb and E. de S. Brunner, *A Study of Rural Society* (Boston: Houghton Mifflin, 1946), p. 203.

The pioneer family, moreover, was the nuclear unit of two generations. Never before had so many small family groups been so completely dependent upon their own resources. This pioneer trend differed from the colonial type of settlement in which the family was subordinate to the village. New England was settled primarily by community groups made up of a number of families who established villages, with farms lying beyond them. Churches were quickly established and the community functioned as a unit in cooperative work and the control of deviant conduct.

Because the conditions of pioneering demanded family integration and organization, the family remained semipatriarchal; at the same time, however, the need for labor gave the wife and children unusual importance and status. Women were in great demand on the frontier, and men competed for each unmarried woman who appeared. The seeds of equality were thus planted in the pioneer land as a result of the hard conditions of life, at a time when in the East certain women intellectuals were demanding equality with men as a matter of principle.

The necessity for coping with new conditions called for strength of character, ingenuity, and independence on the part of all. Whereas in the East social classes had begun to develop and individuals had an ascribed status based on family status, in the pioneer areas social classes scarcely existed and prestige accrued to the industrious, the planners, and the rational thinkers. Abundance of productive land, easily acquired, also smoothed out potential class differences. The leveling effect of the frontier was probably the most important factor in the development of the middle-class family, the present dominant type. In the East, where an aristocracy had developed that looked to Europe for standards of taste and culture, the middle class was relatively weak, the lower class strong. In the South, the distinction between upper and lower was even more sharply drawn. By contrast, at the time that the middle class was growing in strength in the Middle and Far West, the upper limit to which it might climb was undetermined. A sufficient number of pioneering families gained comfort and status in their lifetime, and achieved a social position above that of their parents to the East, to make any degree of upward social mobility seem a possibility. The opportunity to try to improve one's position seemed open to any who were willing to move west and undertake the task of clearing the land or developing natural resources. Liberty and equality were key words, born of the times, and had their effect on the family as on other institutions.

The settlement of the West by individual farms, the relative isolation of the families, and the delay in founding organized government and such regulatory institutions as courts, churches, and schools threw tremendous responsibility upon families. Each family supplied its own protection, control of its members' conduct, care of the ill, religious services—even the marriage ceremony in the more remote areas, until such time as the minister's circuit brought him to the neighborhood to validate the marriage.

Such a life of family self-reliance inculcated independence in each member. As a result, when children grew to adulthood they exercised great freedom of choice over selection of a spouse, with only informal guidance by parents, and were also free to decide upon their future occupations and places of residence. Families were large, and children who were not needed to operate the parental farm filtered off to the newer land to the west or trickled into the newly founded cities.

The pioneering period thus made a number of contributions to the American family. It strengthened family unity and organization and broadened the scope of family functions at a time when, in the East, rural family functions had begun to decrease as dependence upon factory-made goods grew. The organization of the family, however, became more flexible, with greater equality between husband and wife. The self-reliance taught by pioneer conditions and the ever-beckoning opportunities of new areas freed younger adults from family ties in a process that was repeated again and again across the country.

In its adjustment to pioneer conditions the family demonstrated its adaptive qualities and changed in various ways from the village-bound family of the East. Nevertheless, the changes were of degree rather than kind; the essential family pattern remained the same, for the East in spite of its villages and small cities was essentially rural in its economic basis and dependent upon farms and the productive capacity of each family.

Present Day Rural Families

The pioneering period saw the development of other types of farm than the one described, though that one was the dominant type. In the southeast the plantation was typical, in mountainous areas small subsistence farms, in the West large ranches, and in Utah among the Mormons a communal type of living. With the exception of the Utah communal farm, the other types continue. They differ from the early period, however, in that all except the small subsistence farms have tended to move away from an inclusive type of life and have become business enterprises. This change has been accomplished through the mechanization of farming.

Mechanization of Farms

With mechanization the pattern of living for the owner's family changes, as does the relationship of the family to the rural community. No longer is the family so closely tied either to the farm or to the rural neighborhood. The owner's wife and children no longer take direct part in the farm work; fresh vegetables, chickens, eggs, and the like are supplied to the family by the tenant. Meat stored in the locker often comes from the neighbor who is still doing family farming. The main crop of the farm tends to be more highly specialized, and the owner buys products that he formerly raised for himself. When the commercial farmer buys his own machinery and employs workers, he breaks his tie with his neighbors who are still operating machinery on a cooperative basis. Often the center of interest shifts from the neighborhood to the more distant town or small city, not only for business purposes and shopping, but for recreation and education. Such a family is further set apart by reason of its prosperity, for the farmer who has achieved success that for some reason is beyond the grasp of some of his neighbors associates with other commercial farmers in the area who form a rural upper class. Being freed from daily tasks and sufficiently prosperous, he may take his family to Florida in the winter. Kimball, in discussing the development of commercial farming in Tuscola County, Michigan, states that a sufficient number of farmers from this one county winter in Florida to have formed a Tuscola County club there.[4]

Large Commercial Farms and the Exodus to the City

Increased use of machines on the farm has been accompanied by a decrease in the number of farmers needed to cultivate a given acreage. According to an Oklahoma study, each tractor added to the farm was associated with the loss of three or four persons. The decreased labor requirement might simply eliminate the necessity for farm laborers or might release sons of the farmer, or, when small farms were sold to create a larger farm for someone, entire farm families might leave the area.

The trend is for large farms to move from cultivation by tenants, sharecroppers, or migrant workers to complete mechanization with hired laborers who are paid cash wages.

[4]Solon T. Kimball, "Rural Social Organization and Co-op Labor," *American Journal of Sociology*, 55 (1949), 38–49.

REDUCTION OF RURAL ISOLATION

The rural changes so far discussed have been of the type that frees many family members and employed farm laborers from their tie to the land. Another type of mechanization brings to those who remain on farms many aspects of culture and the range of knowledge and news formerly limited to people living in cities. In the late 1950's, 53 per cent of farm families had television sets, 65 per cent had telephones, 80 per cent had automobiles, and almost all families had radios.[5] Good roads make nearby villages and cities accessible, and increase attendance of farm families at church, motion pictures, and various cultural events. Farm children increasingly attend community schools. As a consequence, local areas are fast losing their piquant flavor of individuality. The hayseed, the hick, the hillbilly are being replaced by well-dressed and well-informed farm families.

The means of mass communication not only reduce the gap between rural and urban families but also provide anticipatory socialization in urban living for those who plan to move to cities. Preparation for urban life also comes through college attendance by farm youth. Research in Iowa indicates that 61 per cent of the farm boys who plan to farm do not aspire to more than high school education.[6] Farm boys who do not expect to remain on the farm plan to limit their education to high school in only 19 per cent of cases, while 81 per cent plan on college or some other type of training, thus preparing themselves for urban-type occupations.

Although rural migrants into cities have had preparation for city life, they also carry with them into cities many ingrained attitudes and customs developed in the rural setting. Urban culture thus constantly receives an infusion of rural culture as well as of rural migrants. This exchange of culture tends to bring rural and urban family life into closer similarity.

Comparison of Rural and Urban Families

Rural and urban families are basically alike, each having the characteristics common to the American family as given in Chapter 1. They

[5]*Statistical Abstract of the United States, 1961, op. cit.,* pp. 634–35.
[6]Lee G. Burchinal, "Differences in Educational and Occupational Aspirations of Farm, Small-Town, and City Boys," *Rural Sociology,* 26 (June, 1961), 107–21.

differ primarily in the degree to which each type of family has each characteristic.

The material summarized here comes from a number of different studies, using different concepts of urban and rural. The term "farm family" refers to people actually engaged in farming; "rural nonfarm" to small, closely settled communities under 2,500; and "rural" to a combination of the above. "City" or "urban" family refers to the family in all communities of 2,500 or more, unless otherwise stated. Wherever possible, the size of the city used in a given study is specified.

FAMILY MEMBERSHIP

Rural families are more likely than urban families to be complete units with husband, wife, and children present. However, the rural family does not stand in sharp contrast to the large-city family. For example, Table 1 shows the number of disrupted marriages per 1,000 married women in rural and urban centers of different sizes. Women who are separated from their husbands or divorced form a much higher proportion of all married women in large cities than in small cities, with "other rural" (village and farm) having a ratio only about a third that of large cities.

TABLE 1

NUMBER OF DISRUPTED MARRIAGES PER 1,000 MARRIED WOMEN, IN 1960, BY SIZE
OF PLACE

	Urbanized areas		Other urban places		Rural	
Type of disruption	Central cities	Urban fringe	Places of 10,000 or more	Places of 2,500 to 10,000	Places of 1,000 to 2,500	Other rural
Separation	50	20	32	26	21	17
Divorce	65	37	51	40	33	20
Both types	115	57	83	66	54	37

SOURCE: Paul C. Glick, "Marriage Instability: Variations by Size of Place and Region," *Milbank Memorial Fund Quarterly*, XLI, 1 (January, 1963), 43-55. Source of data, U. S. Census, 1960.

The number of children per 1,000 married women gradually increases from large cities to the rural farm, according to Table 2. There is no sharp break at any point. Rural families are slightly more desirous of having children than are city families, according to a study of Detroit wives and Michigan farm wives. The mean (average) number of children preferred by Detroit wives was 3.42; and by farm wives, 3.57.[7]

The sex ratio, which is one factor that affects the chances for marriage, varies widely between urban and rural. In "other rural" areas there are 106 men to 100 women. In cities of various sizes, from populations of 1,000 up to large cities, the number of men falls short of the number of women, ranging from 93 to 96 men per 100 women.[8] The uneven balance of the sexes is especially marked for ages 20 to 24, when marriage rates are high. In cities of various sizes there is a shortage of 10 to 15 men per 100 women in these ages; in small communities, conversely, there are 17 extra men for every 100 women. These unbalanced ratios are one factor that contributes to spinsterhood in some cities and bachelordom in some rural areas.

TABLE 2

AVERAGE NUMBER OF CHILDREN EVER BORN PER WOMAN, AGED 45 AND OVER, WHO HAD EVER BEEN MARRIED, BY SIZE OF COMMUNITY, 1964

Community	Average number of children
Total population	2.7
Standard metropolitan statistical areas	2.4
Central cities	2.3
Outside central cities	2.5
Nonmetropolitan areas	3.2
Farms	3.6

SOURCE: *Statistical Abstract of the United States, 1967* (Washington, D.C.: Government Printing Office, 1967), p. 52.

EDUCATION

Farm families have less interest in education for their children, and the children secure fewer years of schooling than is true for urban families. However, there is no sharp contrast between a near-illiterate rural group and a highly educated urban group, when region of the country and school facilities are taken into consideration. At the kindergarten level less than half as many rural as urban children attend, with the

[7]Robert O. Blood and Donald M. Wolfe, *Husbands and Wives: The Dynamics of Married Living* (Glencoe, Ill., Free Press, 1960), p. 118.

[8]*United States Census of Population, 1960, United States Summary, General Population Characteristics* (Washington, D.C.: Government Printing Office, 1961), p. 1–149.

rural nonfarm falling between these two rates.[9] During elementary and most of high school the farm boys and girls fall only slightly behind the nonfarm and urban children. With college, the difference becomes greater. For example at ages 20 to 21, 19 per cent of rural farm males are in school, 21 per cent of rural nonfarm, and 31 per cent of urban. The "school" typically would be college. The percentages of farm, rural nonfarm, and urban girls who are in school at any given age show only slight variations, not always in favor of the city girls. At ages 16 and 17, the last 2 years of high school, a slightly higher percentage of both farm and rural nonfarm girls are in school than of city girls. At ages 18 and 19, the percentage of city girls slightly exceeds that of rural nonfarm and farm girls, but at ages 20 and 21, 17 per cent of farm girls are in school (college), compared with 12 per cent of rural nonfarm and 13 per cent of urban girls. For both rural nonfarm and urban communities, for each age after high school, males greatly exceed females in school attendance. Farm girls, however, attend in almost the same proportion as farm boys.

These figures seem to indicate that farm boys as a class fall behind town and city boys in education, whereas farm girls at least keep pace with town and city girls and virtually equal farm males in education. In an earlier part of this chapter, a study of high school boys was cited which showed that those who expected to farm did not plan on college whereas those who planned upon some urban occupation more often expected to attend college. We know that farm girls migrate to cities in larger proportions than farm boys: perhaps they are preparing to enter such urban occupations as business, nursing, or teaching.

FAMILY AND KINSHIP INTERACTION

Few if any differences have been found between rural and urban patterns of family interaction or family organization. The earlier fear that the city family was fast moving toward disintegration led to a study of participation of family members in home activities and in joint outside activities.[10] A simple questionnaire was given to a probability sample in a rural area, village, and small, medium-sized, and metropolitan cities. The slight differences that appeared in the scores of family participation did not fall into any logical pattern, and were not statistically

[9]*Current Population Reports, Population Characteristics, July 24, 1961*, Series P-20, No. 110 (Washington, D.C.: Bureau of the Census, 1961), p. 10.

[10]William H. Key, "Rural-Urban Differences and the Family," *Sociological Quarterly*, 2 (1961), 49–56. See discussion of kinship web, Chapter 1.

significant except for women, whose scores for participation were highest in rural areas, lowest in villages, with the three cities falling between. The differences, however, are not marked, even though statistically significant.

The same study included a questionnaire on participation of the men and women with relatives. This part of the study grew out of the common belief that the urban family was not only nuclear in form but was well isolated from other branches of the extended family. Again, for both men and women score differences were slight and did not show any progression with size of community. The village scores again were lowest. City people were in contact with relatives, visiting with them, engaging in joint activities, and borrowing from and lending to them as often as rural people.

The author suggests that the older concept of the isolated urban nuclear family may have had its origin in the early part of this century when many immigrant families and detached individuals crowded the city, many of whom were without relatives. In the period since, relatives have immigrated; also, these families have been augmented by children and grandchildren, many of whom live in the same city. Many of the original immigrants came from rural communities in Europe where kinship ties were very strong, and they have tended to pass on to their descendants some of the older family loyalties.

It is also suggested that the large number of secondary contacts in the city gives added importance to such intimate intrafamily contacts that exist. In rural areas spatial separation of kinship units turns the immediate family in upon itself. The village, with the lowest rates of both family and kinship participation, has neither social nor spatial isolation and hence permits the growth of neighborhood contacts that serve many of the same purposes that the family contacts serve in the city and on the farm.

A comparison of family interaction in metropolitan Detroit with that in a southeast Michigan farming area revealed few major differences.[11] In both areas the making of decisions fell into the same pattern of distribution between husband and wife. The husband predominated in decisions about his work and choice of a car, the wife in decisions about her work and certain household matters. But the shared decision was most characteristic on matters pertaining to insurance, vacations, housing, and medical services. If we think of the rural family as leaning toward a patriarchal pattern and the urban as predominantly equalitarian, the study did not support these views. In both rural and metro-

[11]Blood and Wolfe, *op. cit.*, p. 24.

politan areas in Michigan many decisions were made jointly or were delegated to the person who seemed best able to make them. In the overall situation, the husband had somewhat more influence than the wife, in both city family and on the farm.

The Michigan study also analyzed the assignment of household tasks between husband and wife.[12] Husbands in both rural areas and cities predominated in repairs and care of lawn and walks, wives in household tasks. However, in rural areas wives somewhat more often carried on the customary male jobs as given above, but they did not engage in heavy types of physical work.

The rural Michigan family much more often than the urban family raised vegetables for its own use, and women canned and froze foods and made baked foods.[13] Another traditional woman's task, sewing, is no longer common in either rural or city family. The authors of the study comment that both farm and city wives contribute to the family, the farm wife through producing and canning or freezing food, and the city wife through outside paid employment.

Finally, the Michigan study compared city and farm families on disagreements between husband and wife.[14] In general, the areas of disagreement were the same, with some minor differences related to the type of community. Money was a matter of disagreement among many families. In the city the disagreements concerned extravagance, prices, and housing decisions; on farms, they centered on the purchase of durable goods, what the family could afford to buy, and the priority of purchases. In the city disagreements over recreation concerned differences in interests and the amount of time spent on recreation; in the farming community, the wife simply craved more recreation than she had. The city wife more often than the farm wife was involved in clashes with her husband over such moral issues as drinking or seeking the companionship of other women. Discipline of children was a matter of disagreement in both types of families.

PERSONALITY DEVELOPMENT OF CHILDREN

The question of the relative advantages of rural or urban environment for the rearing of children has engaged the attention of a number of child and family specialists.[15] A study made in Ohio in the 1940's seemed to indicate that farm and rural nonfarm children were superior in per-

[12] *Ibid.*, p. 58.
[13] *Ibid.*, pp. 82–83.
[14] *Ibid.*, p. 241.

sonal and social adjustment to children in a city of 17,000 people in the same area. The children were given the California test which yielded scores on self- or personal adjustment and on social adjustment. The test of personal adjustment included six phases of adjustment: self-reliance, feelings of personal worth, feelings of belonging, sense of personal freedom, social withdrawal tendencies, and nervous symptoms. The test of social adjustment was based on a test of the child's attitudes toward social standards, social skills, freedom from antisocial tendencies, and family, school, and community relationships. However, more recent studies of farm, nonfarm, and urban children made in two Iowa communities with the California test failed to show any significant differences between rural and city school children. A fourth study of a combined aggregate of children from Iowa, Ohio, Kansas, and Wisconsin shows no significant differences, with one exception: in the last study, city children had a greater propensity for daydreaming than had rural children. In the last study the Rogers' test of personality adjustment was used, which covers feelings of personal inferiority, social maladjustment, family relationships, and daydreaming. In all these studies, the rural areas were adjacent to the cities, thus ruling out many regional differences. However, none of the cities was over 20,000 in population, and some were as small as 2,500. Personal and social adjustment of large-city children was not compared with that of rural children.

The conclusion may be drawn that farm, rural nonfarm, and small city social and cultural influences are not sufficiently different to cause personal and social adjustment of children to differ.

COMMUNITY PARTICIPATION

The previous paragraphs have shown that very little difference exists between farm and city families with respect to intrafamily and kinship participation. Is there a difference in participation in community activities and institutions? For Protestant church activities, the answer is yes, according to a study of a small sample of Iowa farm and nonfarm families.[16] The size of nonfarm communities is not given.

As is true of other characteristics in which farm and nonfarm families differ, the degree of difference is not great enough to think of the families as contrasting with each other. Over 50 per cent of both farm

[15]Lee G. Burchinal, Glenn R. Hawkes, and Bruce Gardner, "Adjustment Characteristics of Rural and Urban Children," *American Sociological Review*, 22 (1957), 81–87. Several studies are summarized.

[16]Lee G. Burchinal, "Farm-Nonfarm Differences in Religious Beliefs and Practices," *Rural Sociology*, 26 (1961), 414–18.

and nonfarm husbands and wives attended church "practically every Sunday," with the farm wives having the highest percentage of weekly attendance—72 per cent. Nonattendance accounted for 22 per cent of farm men and 38 per cent of nonfarm men, and 3 per cent of farm wives and 20 per cent of nonfarm wives. Farm men and women participated in church activities only slightly more often than the nonfarm, the differences in mean activities not being statistically significant.

Interestingly, this study demonstrates the way in which farm practices are carried over into nonfarm life by city migrants. The sons and daughters of the farm families who were queried about religion were students at Iowa State University and it seems safe to say headed toward future nonfarm life. Farm girls and to a slight extent farm boys attended church more frequently than the nonfarm students. They also carried over conservative religious beliefs later, as they entered into urban life. At least some remnants of their rural beliefs and practices seemed to go with them.

CONCLUSIONS ON RURAL AND URBAN FAMILIES

The comparisons that have been cited tend to be of families in farm and urban areas that are adjacent to each other and therefore share the same regional culture. It seems certain that greater contrasts could be found by comparing the least sophisticated farm families with the most sophisticated urban families—or vice versa. Social class and ethnic differences have been ruled out to some extent. These comparisons of families with essentially the same subcultural elements show markedly little difference in family forms, education and personality development of children, interaction within families and kinship groups, and community participation in religious life. There are virtually no contrasts where urban families and rural families fall into discrete types. When data are available, the conclusion is that a gradation in differences appears according to size of community.

Some of the differences are rather obvious ones related to occupation. For example, the farm wife has additional household tasks because she prepares food for winter use, whereas the city wife works, earns money, and buys food. They are meeting the same type of family needs. Specific points of disagreements between husband and wife differ because of farm-urban differences, but the areas of disagreement remain the same.

Other differences show a slight tendency for farm families to be more conservative than urban families—to have moved less far from the traditional rural family from which all families have at some time moved. Nevertheless, present day rural families more closely resemble urban families than the traditional farm family; and urban families retain more rural characteristics than is sometimes believed.

Urban-Suburban Families

The clustering of families on a voluntary or enforced basis in segregated communities within cities has been recognized for many centuries in countries all over the world. The rich had their areas, the poor theirs; groups that were ostracized but not exiled had special residential areas. This general knowledge was formalized in the United States by ecological and social class studies of the 1920's and later.

TYPES OF URBAN FAMILIES

One of the first attempts to equate family type with spatial areas in cities was made by Ernest R. Mowrer, who produced a formulation that was further elaborated by Burgess and Locke.[17]

Types of families were viewed as part of the general life pattern that developed in different types of areas, distinguished on the basis of the ecological zones now familiar to most sociology students. Briefly, the urban ecological pattern consisted ideally of successive zones encircling the central part of the city (Zone I), which was devoted to business. Second came a zone of deterioration (the slums, homeless-man areas, and rooming-house areas), with a characteristic type of family, the emancipated. This family usually consisted of a young couple, both employed, detached from parental family ties, and rootless in the social organization; one may surmise that many were migrants from rural areas. Zone III was the lower-class immigrant zone with a semipatriarchal family carried over from the place of origin. Fourth was the lower-middle-class workingman's zone, with a patricentric family, in which the husband and wife were often the descendants of the families of an earlier generation in Zone III. The fifth zone was given over to apartment houses occupied by upper-middle-class equalitarian families in which wives as well as husbands were well educated and of older American heritage. The sixth and final zone was the suburban, visualized as being of native American population, upper-middle and upper class, living in single homes, and matricentric in type, in that the husband,

[17]Ernest R. Mowrer, *The Family* (Chicago: University of Chicago Press, 1932), pp. 187ff.; Ernest W. Burgess and Harvey J. Locke, *The Family from Institution to Companionship* (New York: American Book Co., 1950), ch. 4.

who usually worked in the inner city, had little time to spend with his family. This zonal formulation was based upon research in industrial cities, chiefly in the North, and notably in Chicago.

Since this formulation was made, numerous changes have occurred in American cities. The concentric circles have been cut across by long tongues of people of some particular subculture; in Chicago, for example, Negroes of southern origin have carried some of the practices of the second zone through several successive zones, while other parts of the city are snug neighborhoods of middle- and upper-class Negro families. Slum clearance and urban redevelopment have introduced into zones two and three new housing designed for middle- and upper-class families. Perhaps the most spectacular change has been in the phenomenal growth of suburbs, not only of the old suburbs, but in a short space of time of new rings of suburbs beyond them.

Although suburbs had never been all upper class (there were industrial suburbs at earlier periods), the new suburbs built after World War II represented in individual suburbs all the social classes, from small clusters of squatters' shacks along some creek to upper-class homes surrounded by wide lawns. Negroes had their suburbs; certain religious and other ethnic groups theirs. However, most of the mushroom growth of the newly built suburbs consisted of middle-class families, often coming into the urbanized area from smaller distant communities or escaping from the confines of the inner city with the birth of the first child. Many families were upwardly mobile.

The startling suddenness with which these new suburbs grew focused the attention of many social scientists upon them, including the family sociologists. "Is a New Family Form Emerging in the Urban Fringe?" queried one article in 1953, and in 1955 another sociologist titled her article, "The Challenge of the New Suburbs."[18] The first reaction to the proliferation of suburbs was that there must necessarily be a new family form to correspond to the new suburbs. Just as the earlier conception of rural and urban families had been that they were opposite types, so in the 1940's and 1950's another polar concept developed—the suburban family had characteristics that were the opposite of those of the city family.[19] People who moved to the suburbs were thought to be protesting against the crowded city and its impersonality. Many people

[18]E. Gartly Jaco and Ivan Belknap, "Is a New Family Form Emerging in the Urban Fringe?" *American Sociological Review*, 18 (1953), 551–57; Sidonie Matsner Gruenberg, "The Challenge of the New Suburbs," *Marriage and Family Living*, 17 (1955), 133–37.

[19]For a discussion of changing concepts of suburban living, see Anselm Strauss, "The Changing Imagery of American City and Suburb," *Sociological Quarterly*, 1 (1960), 15–24.

visualized the suburb as the ideal place in which to rear children, to spend long leisurely weekends working on the lawn, to gain the security of homeownership, and at the same time have the advantages of city jobs and services. In this formulation certain practical matters were overlooked, such as the increased demand for workers in the city, the great shortage of housing resulting from below-normal building during the depression and World War II, and the increased number of children, which made individual homes and play space seem more desirable than city apartments, even had there been space within the city to build additional apartments. Growth at the fringe of cities seemed to meet many practical as well as idealistic needs.

CHARACTERISTICS OF SUBURBAN FAMILIES

During the first great push into the suburbs, several studies were made in the attempt to find the motivations for moving. These studies showed that the suburban families were predominantly urban in origin; they came both from the central city and from other cities or in a minority of cases directly from rural areas. A study of Milwaukee families living in the urban fringe showed that 60 per cent of the families had moved out from Milwaukee, 20 per cent from the large suburbs, 12 per cent from other fringe areas in the county, and 8 per cent from outside the county.[20] Most of the latter 2 groups were originally from an urban background. Of the fringe families around Madison, Wisconsin, 74.6 per cent had moved from a city, 17.6 per cent from villages or farms, whereas 7.8 per cent had made no moves since marriage.[21] A few of the families had made two moves, rural→urban→fringe or urban→rural →fringe. These studies do not show movement of families away from fringe areas, although some families undoubtedly leave the fringe area to move into the city or entirely away from the urbanized area.

The reasons for movement to the fringe and also the type of fringe community preferred show a desire to escape from some of the handicaps of the large city but not a desire to live under rural conditions. Less congestion, more building space, and better conditions for rearing children motivated the centrifugal movement in Madison, Milwaukee, and Flint, Michigan.[22] Along with their greater freedom from density

[20]Richard Dewey, "Peripheral Expansion in Milwaukee County," *American Journal of Sociology*, 54 (1948), 118–25.

[21]Myles W. Rodehaver, "Fringe Settlement as a Two-Directional Movement," *Rural Sociology*, 12 (1947), 49–57.

[22]Amos H. Hawley, *Human Ecology: A Theory of Community Structure* (New York: Ronald, 1950), p. 424.

and city restrictions, the fringe residents wanted urban services. The Milwaukee fringe families wanted to have a food market, grade school, and drugstore within walking distance. Within a mile-and-a-half radius they wished to have beauty parlors, gas stations, a high school, churches, parks, and motion-picture theaters. Proximity of taverns was thought undesirable. Among utilities listed as essential were electricity, telephone, public transportation, sewer, garbage collection, ash collection, gas connections, and street lights. Highly desirable were a public water supply, sidewalks, and door-to-door mail service. Nearness to employment was less essential than proximity of services used by children or in the operation of the home. Fringe families desire urban services and are content with separation of home from place of work; they dislike the congestion and density of the city itself.

The fringe area as a whole is not homogeneous. It breaks up into communities, some incorporated and some informal, varying in size from a dozen families clustered together with a few services to completely formed small cities. Each of these communities has a high degree of homogeneity—more so than an independent community that is unrelated to a central city. This greater homogeneity is possible because no one fringe community, large or small, is wholly independent, and therefore it is not forced to supply a full coterie of stores, schools, churches, and other services. Communities may depend upon each other for some specialized services, and all are within easy reach of the central city for other services. Therefore the occupational diversity within the fringe community may be narrow: many such communities have no doctor, dentist, newspaper, high school, motion-picture house, or retail stores that sell durable goods. Or the community may be served by a doctor who is a general practitioner, but have no local specialists, or by a newspaper that emphasizes local events but does not subscribe to a national press service. The occupational homogeneity is related also to the economic level of the community. Many fringe communities are promoted by one or two real estate companies that buy up plots of farm land and determine in advance the size of lots and quality of housing to be built, either building a quantity of houses for sale, or building a demonstration house that tends to set the pattern. Lines of transportation, natural scenery or lack of it, nearness to factories, all help to increase the homogeneity of the fringe community. Ordinarily there is less diversity of occupation, income level, and social class in the suburban-fringe communities than in the independent city. These communities fall into certain types, such as upper-class suburbs whose residents may be almost exclusively drawn from large-scale proprietors and successful professional men; middle-class suburbs whose employed members are clerical workers and in minor managerial positions; industrial suburbs that supply operatives to factories located within the suburb or on the edge of the city.

Fringe areas may differ from central cities in population characteristics that are related to the family. A study of Michigan farming, fringe, and city areas showed that the fringe population more nearly resembled the rural than the strictly urban (Table 3). The fringe population, as compared with that of the city, had a lower proportion of foreign-born, fewer Negroes, a higher sex ratio (excess men), younger adults, and many more children. Whether these relationships would hold also for other areas would depend in part upon the occupational structure.

The discussion so far has tended to emphasize some of the distinctive qualities of the fringe population and fringe family life. Both fringe and central-city families are subjected to many of the same urban influences and face similar adjustments.

TABLE 3

COMPARISON OF CITIES, FRINGE AREAS, AND FARM AREAS, MICHIGAN

	Race and nativity				Age			
	Native-born white	Foreign-born	Negro	Sex ratio	Under 21	21–64	65 and over	Fertility ratio
Urban	77.0%	16.4%	6.6%	102	33.6%	61.8%	4.8%	285
Fringe area	88.4	9.3	2.3	114	39.5	55.8	4.7	451
Adjacent farming area	92.3	7.4	0.3	114	39.8	52.1	8.1	470

SOURCE: J. Allan Beegle, "Characteristics of Michigan's Fringe Population," *Rural Sociology*, 12 (1947), 259. The fertility ratio was computed by dividing the number of children under 5 years of age by the number of females aged 15–44 and multiplying by 1,000.

REACTIONS TO SUBURBAN LIVING

The suburbs are no longer a new phenomenon in urban growth; they are an established part of the metropolitan area. Some of the earlier characteristics of suburban families are changing. The young families that moved into fringe areas in the late 1940's and early 1950's are no longer young; children are of high school or college age and often are moving from the suburb back to the central city or into other, newer suburbs. Their parents, now past the childrearing stage, often return to the central city as offering greater convenience for work, diversity of shopping, or cultural life. Families of all stages of the family life cycle replace them in the suburbs, making of the once child-dominated community a community of diversified families.

Meanwhile, the city itself is tending to clear slums near the central area, replacing the old tenements or dilapidated fine homes with modern apartments, some geared to families with children, others planned for the middle-aged couple. Thus the physical contrast in housing between the inner city and the bright new suburb, no longer bright or new, is lessening.

The earlier expectations of the suburbs for childrearing have not always been met. Suburbs tended to be self-segregated areas, racially, religiously, and in socioeconomic status. In a period of increased desegregation in many areas in the nation as a whole, suburban children were being reared without a realistic rubbing of elbows with any children or adults other than their own cultural, racial, and family type. Many parents expressed concern;[23] others, however, especially when upwardly mobile, found the new suburb a convenient place to start their upward trek. The new suburb at first is a community of strangers among whom past social class placement may be lost. Moreover, the successful upwardly mobile family may repeatedly move from one suburb to another of higher class until it reaches its upward limit.[24] Parents and children alike may associate with some families rooted in the social class level of the suburb and also with other upwardly mobile families seeking the same goals as their own.

Some people express concern over the dullness of life in the suburbs, the uniformity, and the lack of cultural stimulation.[25] They fear the effect of these conditions on their children and themselves.

Mowrer, on the basis of his own research and that of others, sums up the suburban situation in the 1960's by calling attention to the diversification of types of suburbs and their similarity to types of communities within the city proper.[26] Each type of suburb has its own life style. When differences seem to exist between city and suburb, a strong factor is the life style already developed by families, which they seek to express more fully in one or another suburb. An overall view of

[23]Gruenberg, *op. cit.*

[24]The struggles of the suburban family with upward mobility are given in semi-fictional form in John Keats, *The Crack in the Picture Window* (Boston: Houghton Mifflin, 1957).

[25]Strauss, *op. cit.*, with citation of an unpublished paper by Nathan Glazer.

[26]Ernest R. Mowrer, address to the Midwest Sociological Society, 1962; see also his chapter in William M. Dobriner, ed., *The Suburban Community* (New York: Putnam, 1958), pp. 147–64.

suburbs, old and new, industrial and residential, and of different races, ethnic groups, and social classes, does not support the concept of a single suburban life style (or family type) per se.

Adjustment of Rural Families to Cities

Many families that leave farms do not move to large cities, but simply to a nearby small town. This move is especially true of the retired farmer who may still retain management of his farm, or the old couple, widow, or widower who finds farm work too arduous. Farm people who migrate to larger cities are more likely to be young detached people or young adult families in search of work. The places they fit themselves into in city life are closely related to the skills they have and the antici- patory socialization into city life they have experienced. The young person who has prepared himself or herself through education for a vocation typical of the city finds a more satisfactory niche than the one who has a poor education and no urban skills. The displacement of farm laborers by machinery, especially in the South, has sent thousands of whites and Negroes alike into southern and northern cities poorly prepared to find work or to adjust to the demands of city life. Poorly educated and accustomed to a low level of living, they primarily add to the unskilled lower-class stratum that exists in every large city. Rural migrants who are prepared for the transition fit into whatever economic and social level they are prepared to fill.

Studies of rural migrants to cities tend to emphasize the unskilled contingent and their many problems of adjustment, both social and eco- nomic. The tendency is to overlook another aspect of the situation which pertains to both the uneducated and the prepared. They bring with them into the city some of the rural family values that have al- ready been discussed. Thus the city not only imposes urban character- istics of family life on rural migrants, but also receives a constantly re- newed infusion of rural values from these same migrants. This rural infusion is augmented by the influence of migrants from other cultures, whether within the United States (Puerto Rico, for example) or through immigration. Typically, these alien-culture newcomers have been rural in background. Their entrance into urban life is likely to be more abrupt than that of migrants within the mainland of the United States, be- cause of the language difficulty and broader cultural differences. Their period of adjustment, therefore, is often more disruptive and may extend over several generations. As they become adjusted they often cling to some of the old family patterns, notably respect for the elders in the family and a strong feeling of family unity that extends to the kinship group.

The implantation of certain elements of rural family life tends to counterbalance the fragmenting effect of urban life. Young detached people who enter the city without family or kinship contacts there are subjected to considerable buffeting by diverse city patterns of conduct. The city-born children of immigrants also often go through a period of detachment from social and family controls, a condition that also prevails among some of the lower-class migrants to northern cities from the South. These disturbances are often transitional in the lives of those who experience them. Jobs are found, contacts are made, marriage brings some degree of security and stability, and the misplaced rural person becomes assimilated into urban life; but he often retains or revives some rural values and customs.

The Urban Adjustment of the Rural White Family

Undoubtedly the most marked migratory adjustment any rural white family makes occurs when the southern rural family moves to the northern industrial city. This type of migrant has been the subject of numerous studies.

The migrating unit is either the family or the individual. Unmarried men often crowd into new industrial areas. The migrating family tends to have the following characteristics: unfamiliarity with urban living, but with the men maintaining trading contacts in nearby small cities; semipatriarchal organization; the women and children from an early age active in farm work; four or five years of schooling; early marriages; crude home equipment; low income.[27] These migrants would find themselves in a foreign land when they migrate north were it not that a call for workers spreads through a community or among relatives, and often families or individuals who know each other congregate in the same industrial town. In addition, a feeling of camaraderie springs up among southern migrants from specific areas, who easily recognize each other's

[27]F. D. Alexander, "Family Life in a Rural Community," *Social Forces*, 18 (1939–40), 392–402; Margaret Hagood, *Mothers of the South: Portraiture of the White Tenant Farm Family* (Chapel Hill: University of North Carolina Press, 1939); Charles P. Loomis and J. Allan Beegle, *Rural Social Systems* (Englewood Cliffs, N.J.: Prentice–Hall, 1950), section on "Family and Informal Groups as Social Systems"; Nora Miller, *The Girl in the Rural Family* (Chapel Hill: University of North Carolina Press, 1936).

regional origin by mode of dress and speech. There is therefore a certain transfer of southern culture to the urban area that tempers the impact of the city.[28]

The degree of cultural change is much greater than would be true for a northern rural family migrating into a northern city. The standard of education for children is a case in point. The child who in the South is expected to drop out of school after grade school or perhaps after only a few years in school to work on the farm is required in the northern city to attend until the age of 16 or 18, according to the state laws. Parents and children alike may fail to appreciate the necessity for the required education or the restrictions on child labor. Early marriage also runs counter to northern standards. The rural white family maintains a close watch over its daughters until they marry, with marriage occurring soon after a girl begins to attract the attention of young men. In the city, such supervision is difficult to maintain, and of longer duration. Girls may be eager for the excitement of city life and lack the sophistication to control their contacts with strangers. Families, unaccustomed to electrical household equipment and indoor plumbing, often misuse these facilities. Many are the jokes regarding such misuse told by northerners at the expense of southern families.[29]

Southern rural families are not well prepared in advance for the change. The lure of the industrial North is largely economic, and little preliminary interest in cultural change exists. The low educational level, absence of reading habits, and absence of radios in some rural homes prevent adequate anticipatory socialization.

In some northern cities the white migrant finds himself living, working, and sharing neighborhood services with Negroes, whom he had previously regarded as inferior. His conception of his status is badly shaken. Or he may live among an ethnic Catholic group, whereas all his former associations had been with Protestants like himself. Again, he must adjust his ideas of the relative status of religious groups.[30]

Irregular employment leads to further mobility and earns the migrant a reputation for unreliability. A lay-off, depression, or long-drawn-out strike sends a wave of southerners back home for a prolonged visit until employment in the North improves. Thus, longing for the old home competes with the economic lure of the North.

North or South, the rural migrant tends to enter at the lower end

---

[28]Lewis M. Killian, "Adjustment of Southern White Migrants to Northern Urban Norms," *Social Forces*, 32 (October–May, 1953–54), 66–69.

[29]E. D. Beynon, "The Southern White Laborer Migrates to Michigan," *American Sociological Review*, 3 (1938), 333–43.

[30]Killian, *op. cit.*

of the social scale. In his search for housing, he usually finds himself crowding into the low-rent or slum area.[31] In Flint, Michigan, only about half as many migrants as total population owned their homes, or lived in homes with basements (implying central heating) or running water.[32]

Vocationally, too, the rural migrant must change his ways. Accustomed only to farming by hand methods or with the aid of a mule for power, he is not fitted for skilled urban labor. In Flint, Michigan, 68 per cent of southern white migrants who were employed were unskilled laborers, as opposed to 54 per cent of the total employed population who fell into this classification.

Lack of early adjustment is shown by the tendency, already mentioned, of migrants to return South whenever work is slack. In general, close contacts and continued visiting with parents prevent early adjustment to and identification with the city.[33] In time, adjustment to the city is made. In Flint, later adjustment is indicated by their wide distribution throughout the city after they gain a foothold and the high percentage of marriages (48.5) made with Michigan-born persons.

Questions

1. What changes in rural–urban distribution of population have occurred since 1790? What are the main factors that account for the changes?
2. In what ways is the rural family a disappearing type?
3. What qualities did the pioneer period contribute to the American family? Which of these qualities are still evident in the family?
4. How is rural family isolation reduced?
5. In what ways is there a two-way exchange of culture between rural and urban families?
6. What differences exist between rural and urban families? Do rural and urban families represent two distinct types of family?
7. Discuss the concept that the suburban area is developing a new type of family.

[31]Howard Beers and Catherine Heflin, "The Urban Status of Rural Migrants," *Social Forces*, 23 (1944), 33–34.

[32]Beynon, *op. cit.*

[33]Harry K. Schwarzweller, "Parental Family Ties and Social Integration of Rural to Urban Migrants," *Journal of Marriage and the Family*, 26 (1964), 410–16.

8.   How do suburban families and urban families resemble each other? How do they differ?

9.   When does the rural family have difficulty in adjusting to urban life?

10.   How do close contacts with parents and other close relatives help migrants? How do they hinder?

Bibliography

HISTORICAL BACKGROUND

ADAMS, JAMES TRUSLOW, *The Epic of America* (Boston: Little, Brown, 1933).

CAVAN, RUTH SHONLE, ed., *Marriage and Family in the Modern World, A Book of Readings* (New York: Crowell, 1969), ch. 2.

COLE, ARTHUR CHARLES, *The Irrepressible Conflict, 1850–1865* (New York: Macmillan, 1934).

FISH, CARL RUSSELL, *The Rise of the Common Man, 1840–1850* (New York: Macmillan, 1927).

NEVINS, ALLAN, *The Emergence of Modern America, 1865–1878* (New York: Macmillan, 1927).

HISTORY OF THE AMERICAN FAMILY

CALHOUN, ARTHUR W., *A Social History of the American Family from Colonial Times to the Present* (3 vols.; Cleveland: Arthur H. Clark Co., 1919; also Barnes and Noble, 1945; reprinted in paperback, 1960).

RURAL AND URBAN FAMILY LIFE

ALEXANDER, F. D., "Family Life in a Rural Community," *Social Forces*, 18 (1939–40), 392–402.

BEERS, H. W., "A Portrait of the Farm Family in Central New York," *American Sociological Review*, 2 (1937), 591–600.

BLOOD, ROBERT O., and DONALD M. WOLFE, *Husbands and Wives: The Dynamics of Married Living* (New York: Free Press, 1960).

BURCHINAL, LEE G., "Differences in Educational and Occupational Aspirations of Farm, Small-Town, and City Boys," *Rural Sociology*, 26 (June, 1961), 107–21.

_____, "Farm–Nonfarm Differences in Religious Beliefs and Practices, *Rural Sociology*, 26 (1961), 414–18.

_____, GLENN R. HAWKES, and BRUCE GARDNER, "Adjustment Characteristics of Rural and Urban Children," *American Sociological Review*, 22 (1957), 81–87.

DAVIS, ALLISON, B. B. GARDNER, and M. R. GARDNER, *Deep South* (Chicago: University of Chicago Press, 1941), Part II.

FREEDMAN, RONALD, *et al.*, eds., *Principles of Sociology* (New York: Holt, Rinehart and Winston, 1956), pp. 433–39, 462–71.

HAGOOD, MARGARET, *Mothers of the South: Portraiture of the White Tenant Farm Family* (Chapel Hill: University of North Carolina Press, 1939).

KEY, WILLIAM H., "Rural-Urban Differences and the Family," *Sociological Quarterly*, 2 (1961), 49–56.

OGBURN, WILLIAM F., and MEYER F. NIMKOFF, *Technology and the Changing Family* (Boston: Houghton Mifflin, 1955).

SUBURBAN FAMILY

BELL, WENDELL, "Familism and Suburbanization," *Rural Sociology*, 21 (1956), 276–283.

BERGER, BENNETT, *Working-Class Suburb* (Berkeley: University of California Press, 1960).

DOBRINER, WILLIAM M., ed., *The Suburban Community* (New York: Putnam, 1958), chapter by Ernest R. Mowrer, pp. 147–64.

GANS, HERBERT J., "Urbanism and Suburbanism as Ways of Life: A Re-examination of Definitions," in Arnold M. Rose, ed., *Human Behavior and Social Processes: An Interactionist Approach* (Boston: Houghton Mifflin, 1962), ch. 33, pp. 625–48.

JACO, E. GARTLY, and IVAN BELKNAP, "Is a New Family Form Emerging in the Urban Fringe?" *American Sociological Review*, 18 (1953), 551–57.

KTSANES, THOMAS, and LEONARD REISSMAN, "Suburbia—New Homes for Old Values," *Social Problems*, 7 (Winter, 1959–60), 187–95.

MOWRER, ERNEST R., "Sequential and Class Variables of the Family in Suburban Areas," *Social Forces*, 40 (1961), 107–12.

STRAUSS, ANSELM, "The Changing Imagery of American City and Suburb," *Sociological Quarterly*, 1 (1960), 15–24.

VON RHODE, C., "The Suburban Mind," *Harper's Magazine*, 192 (April, 1946), 289–99.

URBAN ADJUSTMENT OF MIGRANT FAMILIES

KILLIAN, LEWIS M., "Adjustment of Southern White Migrants to Northern Urban Norms," *Social Forces*, 32 (October–May, 1953–54), 66–69.

LEYBURN, G., "Urban Adjustments of Migrants from the Southern Appalachian Plateau," *Social Forces*, 16 (1937), 238–46.

OMARI, THOMPSON PETER, "Factors Associated with Urban Adjustment of Rural Southern Migrants," *Social Forces*, 35 (October–May, 1956–57), 47–53.

II

Social and Cultural
Configurations of the
American Family

CHAPTER

4

Social Classes, Ethnic Groups,

and Mobility

FAMILIES DO NOT exist as independent units but form large groups that have many similarities of culture and bonds of friendship and affection. These large groups share in the common characteristics of American families but at the same time are sufficiently different to be thought of as subcultures or variants of the general type of American family. The subcultures that seem most important to the family and that are discussed here are social classes and ethnic and religious groups.

Social Classes

The most fundamental grouping of families is into social classes.

DEFINITION OF SOCIAL CLASS

A comprehensive definition of the term social class is given by W. Lloyd Warner and Paul S. Lunt in one of the first scientific studies of the American social class system:

> By class is meant two or more orders of people who are believed to be, and are accordingly ranked by the members of the com-

munity, in socially superior and inferior positions. Members of a class tend to marry within their own order, but the values of the society permit marriage up and down. A class system also provides that children are born into the same status as their parents. A class society distributes rights and privileges, duties and obligations, unequally among its inferior and superior grades.[1]

According to this definition, the family is the basic unit in the social-class system. The family gives each new-born child his first social-class placement and trains him into the culture of the class; any change in class position while the child is young is made by the family; change in class position that an individual may make later wrenches him away from the family.

The tendency for people to marry within their class makes both for continuity of the social class and for a reduction of possible conflicts of values and roles within the family. When marriages occur, as they do, between members of different social classes, the probability of such conflicts increases.

QUALITY OF SOCIAL CLASSES

Related to but not synonymous with social class is the concept of social stratification, or the ranking of people according to certain characteristics that can be placed in rank order. Characteristics often used in the United States as the basis for studies of stratification are income, years of schooling, and occupations ranked according to the public prestige accorded each occupation. Although the correlation between such rankings as are found in large groups of individuals is far from perfect, in a general way high ranking on one category is associated with high rankings on the other two, middle rankings are found to go together, and persons with low rankings on one also tend to have low rankings on the other two. There are, however, no sharp breaks at different points along the ranks to indicate the boundaries between social classes. The class most distinctly set off is a small elite group at the top of the various scales.[2]

These and similar findings suggest that the division into social classes is artificial. Such a view, however, overlooks several other important characteristics of social classes in addition to the differences in rankings on the three characteristics already mentioned.

---

[1]W. Lloyd Warner and Paul S. Lunt, *The Social Life of a Modern Community* (New Haven: Yale University Press, 1941), p. 82.

[2]Werner S. Landecker, "Class Boundaries," *American Sociological Review*, 25 (1960), 868–77.

Income, education, and occupational prestige are economic in nature and, with the things that money can buy, represent differences in the material culture of social classes, such as the costliness of a dwelling or a car, the number of cars owned, and the number and variety of luxury leisure-time items such as summer or winter homes, yachts, racing horses, sports equipment, and the like. Social classes can be ranked up to a certain point on the possession of these and similar items.

However, the true essence of social class subculture, and the phase of most importance from the point of view of the family, lies in the intangible aspects of the class subculture—the beliefs, values, and goals. These intangibles differ from class to class in a qualitative manner; they are not simply a matter of more or less of some characteristic, and therefore do not fall into rank orders. Their differences mark the boundaries between the social classes. One brief example may be given. Each social class tends to have a certain range of years of schooling. But the essential difference between the classes is in the value attached to education. In the higher classes education in and of itself is a matter of prestige. The college degree has an intrinsic value; it is the mark of a gentleman, a symbol of culture. Also, education opens the door to many lucrative occupations. In the lower social levels, education beyond elementary school is regarded as useless and a waste of time; some practical use of time, early employment, and an income however small are of higher value than an education that seems to lead nowhere and which in fact may alienate the person from his family.

The various elements of each class subculture tend to become coordinated and to support each other. Taken together, they constitute a way of life or life-style, into which each child is socialized by his family. His social class becomes his social world within which he lives. The child becomes a part of and adjusted to his class subculture and therefore not readily adjustable to another subculture.

The cultural cohesiveness of a social class is supported by the fact that families of a given class tend to live together in one, or in a large city in several similar, geographic areas. People living in a given social-class area rarely penetrate the areas of other social classes and have little firsthand knowledge of the family life of other social classes than their own. Members of different social classes may meet as individuals in school, stores, and places of amusement, worship, or work; however, even such contacts are limited since the institutions named often serve only one geographic area that may be inhabited by only one class, or appeal only to the interests of one class, or set up barriers between members of different classes. Contacts that occur often are formal and impersonal.

Family life and especially the lives of women and children are likely to be limited by the geographic boundaries of the social-class area. Within these boundaries, each class develops its own integrated family and community culture, in which its children are reared, and within which courtship and marriage tend to take place. So important are these intimate associations in the maintenance of class subculture that they have been made the central point in one definition of social class.

> Social class . . . as used by American sociologists, refers to roles of intimate association with others. Essentially, social classes in this sense denote strata of society composed of individuals who accept each other as equals and qualified for intimate association.[3]

CLASSIFICATION OF SOCIAL CLASSES

Present studies of social classes in the United States stem from the research and publications of W. Lloyd Warner and his associates.[4] Warner's classification is still widely used: upper-upper class; lower-upper; upper-middle; lower-middle; upper-lower; and lower-lower. Small communities often have few members in the upper class and these few tend to associate with the upper-middle class; in studies of such communities, therefore, upper class and upper-middle are grouped together for purposes of discussion. Likewise, the upper-lower class and the lower-middle class may be combined under the title of the common man or the working class. When the upper-lower class is upwardly mobile, this combination may be defensible.

NUMERICAL DISTRIBUTION OF SOCIAL CLASSES

People are unevenly distributed among the social classes. An estimate for the United States published in 1950 and illustrated in Figure 2 placed slightly more than a third of the population in lower-middle class and another third in upper-lower class. The remaining third was unequally divided among upper class (3 per cent), upper-middle (9 per cent), and lower-lower (17 per cent).

For any given community the percentages might vary, depending in part upon educational and occupational opportunities. The federal or state capital, the university city, or the art colony would have a

[3]Seymour Martin Lipset and Hans L. Zetterberg, "A Theory of Social Mobility," *Transactions of the Third World Congress of Sociology*, 2 (1956), 155–77; also in Reprint Series in the Social Sciences, No. 176 (Indianapolis: Bobbs–Merrill).

[4]The first of a number of books was Warner and Lunt, *op. cit.*

disproportionate number of people in the upper-middle class; the industrial town or suburb, a high percentage of lower class; and the old

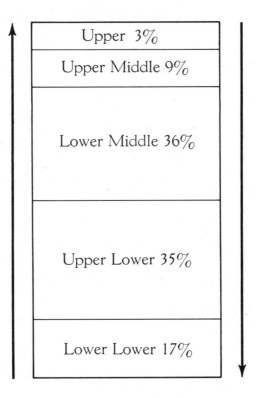

FIGURE 2   *Estimated Distribution of Population in the United States by Social Class.*

In older communities, the upper class may be divided into upper and lower-upper. Locally, the distribution depends upon the type of community: heavy industry increases the proportion of the lower-lower class; a state capital or a university city has few lower- but more middle- and upper-class people. The social class in which a person is born and reared influences his personality and family life. In the American open-class system an individual's social-class placement may change either up or down (arrows). Such a change creates family tensions and schisms.

SOURCE: Carson McGuire, "Social Stratification and Mobility Patterns," *American Sociological Review*, 15 (1950), 200.

expensive resort city more than its proportionate share of upper class. Within a large city or metropolitan area, local areas and individual suburbs would each reflect the subculture of a distinct social class. As social classes vary so also do family life and childrearing.

Ethnic Families

A second important subcultural grouping of families is into a variety of ethnic groups. In each social class there are some people whose mode of living is not thoroughly American but is derived from an alien culture. With only a few exceptions, these people are either foreign-born or the recent descendants of the foreign-born.[5] When such groups think of themselves as more closely affiliated with the nationality of their birth or of their recent ancestors than with American culture, they are called ethnic groups.

The period when the assimilation of foreign-born groups was one of the most serious of social problems and fascinating of social processes has passed. Restrictive legislation of the 1920's, the depression of the 1930's, and the two world wars reduced the once powerful stream of immigration to a mere trickle. The immigrants who crowded northern industrial cities prior to 1914 are now either old or have already died. However, in limited numbers new ethnic groups arrive, chiefly Mexicans and Puerto Ricans, to repeat the adjustment process of the earlier groups.

Although ethnic groups have some characteristics in common, they do not merge into one common interacting social group. Each alien cultural group of the past has its own descendant ethnic group in the present. There is a Norwegian ethnic group, an Italian, a German, and so on. Not all descendants of foreign-born families can be classified as ethnic; only those that cling together with a certain degree of social isolation from other ethnic groups and from Americans should be termed ethnic. Individuals and families that have merged completely into the American pattern of culture and the American social world and who no longer think of themselves as Norwegian or Italian or German, as the case may be, are no longer ethnic.

Groups of non-Caucasian origin also fall into the classifications of ethnic or American. If they maintain a distinctive culture brought with them from their homeland—for example, Chinese who huddle into urban "Chinatowns"—they are ethnic. If they have exchanged their native culture for American culture, as the Negroes have, they are culturally American. The family life of non-Caucasians, therefore, is not discussed separately from the two basic divisions of ethnic and Ameri-

[5]American Indians are the chief example of nonforeign-born people who nevertheless have not accepted the American culture.

can. Nevertheless, racial affiliation may have a relationship to family life, either because the group is set apart through prejudice, or because members of different races have intermarried.

THE PROCESS OF ETHNIC ADJUSTMENT

The adjustment of ethnic families is closely related to the social-class structure. The original stages of adjustment more often than not take place within the framework of the lower class. Once this adjustment has been made the ethnic families or their descendants enter into the social-class hierarchy, often, however, taking some cherished elements of their orginal culture with them and thus introducing diversity into the middle and upper classes.

The most persistent ethnic characteristic is the religious faith of each group. Catholicism and Judaism have flourished in a culture that orig-inally was primarily Protestant. Protestant sects that originated in Europe have handed their faith down from generation to generation. Newer religious faiths that originated in the United States also differ-entiate people and sometimes require special family observances. In the course of a few generations, ethnicity may be said to fade out, and religious affiliation becomes the dominant difference among groups for-merly ethnic in other ways.

Racial Subgroups

The largest nonwhite racial group in the United States is Negro, and it is an old segment in the population since few Negroes entered the United States after the importation of slaves became illegal in 1808. Under the conditions of slavery the Negroes lost their original African culture and became acculturated to America, with the modification of their status as slaves. Since the Civil War they have moved slowly but steadily into the American culture, with certain idiosyncrasies of social class and family life that seem traceable primarily to their exclusion from full participation in American social life.

Negroes are sometimes referred to as forming a caste in American social life. It is true that a barrier exists between the whites and Ne-groes that is supported by mores or merely by folkways. However, within the racial social structure, social classes similar to those in the white segment of the population have existed. A caste implies that members of the caste remain at virtually one level, but even during the slave period Negroes were not all of one social level. A small number of Negroes were free and formed a social class well above the slaves. Within the slave population several grades were observable; for example, house servants, skilled craftsmen, and field hands.

The separation between whites and Negroes has never been complete. Personal servants, although separated from their white masters and mistresses by wide social distance, nevertheless were in close daily contact with them and apparently often served as protectors and comforters in times of stress. Sexual union between white men and Negro slave women was a common occurrence judging from the great proportion of Negroes of moderate or light color. (The tendency of light Negroes to marry each other perpetuates the presence of light Negroes in the race.)

Instead of regarding Negroes as a caste, it is more nearly in line with reality to regard them as forming a distinct social-class system roughly parallel with the white system. As barriers between the two races break down and they are able to communicate and participate in joint activities more freely than in the past or the present, differences between the two social-class systems may decline.

Smaller aggregates of non-Caucasian groups than the Negroes also exist in the United States, each living a somewhat distinctive life: examples are the Chinese, Japanese, Filipinos, and various Indian and Eskimo tribes. Although the total number in each of these groups is not large, their concentration in certain regions or cities and their tendency to live in segregated areas make for small cultural islands. Unlike Negroes, these groups tend to perpetuate their original culture.

Social Mobility

Social mobility refers to the movement of persons, families, or larger groups from one position in the social structure to another. The movement may be limited in nature. A person may move from one occupation to another of equivalent status, for example, from teacher to social worker. A person may leave one religion and affiliate with another or change political parties, but remain in the same class level. Another type of movement takes the person into a higher or lower level of prestige in some one area of life. With additional training, a practical nurse may become a professional nurse, or a workingman may successfully become foreman and superintendent. Other types of mobility are more extensive and involve movement from one subculture to another.

HORIZONTAL MOBILITY

The movement from one group to another of equal standing and prestige constitutes horizontal mobility. The change by one member of a family from one social group to another group of equivalent status is not of too great importance unless the change also entails a change of values for the mobile member that then conflict with the values still held by the other members of his family. Such a situation might occur if one member turned from a religion with one creed and set of values to a religion with a very different or even opposed creed or values.

When the entire family changes, the probability of internal conflict is reduced. The slow transition of an ethnic family from a foreign culture to American culture of equivalent status may take place smoothly. If, however, as often happens, the older family members tend to remain identified with the foreign culture and the younger members to reject the old and identify with the American culture, intrafamily conflict may result.

The avenue of horizontal mobility for one person may be through marriage to a member of a different ethnic, religious, or racial group. This situation is especially poignant, since each family may feel it has lost a member and the married couple are at least partially alienated from both families, and in addition may be faced with working out an adjustment of their conflicting sets of beliefs, values, and customs.

VERTICAL MOBILITY

The passage of an individual or family from affiliation with one social class into affiliation with another class of higher or lower status is known as vertical social mobility. The family is downwardly mobile when it moves from a high stratum to one with less prestige and fewer valued possessions; or the family may be upwardly mobile and succeed in establishing itself in a stratum further up in the hierarchy than the one to which it previously belonged.

In the United States, upward mobility is the more frequent process of the two, chiefly because of the many opportunities afforded in this country for children to surpass their parents in education and occupational opportunities. In other cases, a person may occupy a higher stratum in middle age than he had in youth. The process of mobility is complex and often frustrating, as will appear from the detailed analysis in Chapter 9.

Downward mobility is not unknown in the United States, although it is minor in trend and little discussed. Individuals may be unable to maintain their early position or that of their parents. During a long depression, such as that of the 1930's, many families experience downward mobility and become stabilized at a lower level without any success in later regaining their former class even after prosperity has replaced the depression.

The major trend of upward mobility begins with a combination of educational, occupational, and income factors. This combination opens the way to mobility but does not complete the process. The formal education-occupational status and the material symbols of status that money can buy do not guarantee acceptance into another social class. It is necessary that the family should be accepted into the informal primary groups—the family gatherings, the friendship cliques—of the class; the final act of acceptance is approval of the marriage of the newcomer with an established member of the other class.

In the process of becoming accepted, the upwardly mobile family is likely to commit many gaucheries from the point of view of the established class. Crudities of manners, unfamiliarity with values, customs, even fads, and conspicuous buying all offend the higher class and harden the protective wall of rejection erected to keep out newcomers.

Most studies of mobility do not cover the entire range of mobility nor its effects as they are related to family organization, goals, and roles. Sorokin's study of social mobility, published in 1927, is concerned chiefly with movement based on economic, political, and occupational changes.[6] Warner and his associates assert the ever-present flow of people up and down but are primarily interested in defining social classes and their relationship to each other; nevertheless, illustrations of mobile families are included in their books.[7] Post-World War II studies have been primarily concerned with economic indices of stratification and rates of mobility.

Mobility as a social-class phenomenon and its effect on the family have been neglected. Nevertheless, at least four mobile groups that seem to be the equivalent of new social classes have been suggested or clearly identified. Each is in transition between two relatively stable classes.

1. The *nouveau riche*, the new-rich described by Warner under the title lower-upper class, seeks entrance to the upper-upper class.

[6]Pitirim Sorokin, *Social Mobility* (New York: Harper, 1927); also published under the title *Social and Cultural Mobility* (Glencoe, Ill.: Free Press, 1959).
[7]Warner and Lunt, *op. cit.*

2. The *parvenu* (newcomer, upstart) is the name applied in one study
    to a rapidly upwardly mobile middle-class segment of the popu-
    lation that regards itself as upper-middle class but lacks many of
    the noneconomic qualifications for this class.[8]

3. *Black bourgeoisie* (black or Negro middle class) is the term applied
    to a similar rapidly upwardly mobile segment of the Negro popu-
    lation.[9]

4. *Nouveau bourgeoisie* (new middle class) is the name suggested for
    the very large mobile group that is working its way upward from
    upper-lower to lower-middle class.[10]

The four authors, working independently, have not chosen terms
that fall into a series indicating the position of the mobile classes in
the social-class hierarchy. In each case, however, the name chosen implies a group that is taking the initiative in an aggressive manner in
trying to force an entrance into a previously formed social class. Several
points are emphasized in all the studies. The basis for the upward thrust
is a large increase in income usually acquired over a short period of
time. On the basis of this income, the upwardly mobile families buy
some of the material symbols of the social class into which they are
trying to move. They do not, however, have the intangible qualifications of the higher class, and are therefore rejected by the higher class.
Acquiring these qualifications in a superficial manner becomes a central
goal about which family life and the training of children are organized.

These families are in cultural transit between the class in which they
were originally socialized and the higher class into which they are trying to become acculturated. Their position is marginal to both classes;
they fit into neither. In time, many will succeed in their ambition, at
least as far as their children or grandchildren are concerned; but inevitably some will fail and slip back into the class of origin.

It may be concluded that at present the social class hierarchy actually consists of two parallel series of classes. One is composed of the
stable or core classes whose families have held their positions for more
than a generation or two. A second series of classes falls into an intermediate position between the stable classes; it is composed of mobile

[8]The term was used by Harold M. Hodges of San Jose State College for an upwardly mobile group discovered during a study of social class in a three-county
metropolitan area in California. It is described in "Is the Upper-Middle Class
Really Two—A Proposal," mimeographed.

[9]E. Franklin Frazier, *Black Bourgeoisie: The Rise of a New Middle Class in the
United States* (Glencoe, Ill.: Free Press, 1957).

[10]Robert H. Bohlke, "Social Mobility, Stratification Inconsistency and Middle
Class Delinquency," *Social Problems*, 8 (Spring, 1961), 351–63.

families, which are sometimes so numerous at one level in a community that they function like a social class in their own right.

It is theoretically possible that a third hierarchy might exist, of downwardly mobile families. In the United States, downward mobility is likely to be a family affair and not to affect large segments of the population. However, from time to time, the downward trend is pronounced and may affect all social classes to some extent. The nationwide depression of the 1930's affected all classes but was especially disastrous to the lower-middle and upper-lower classes and forced many families into a downward process from which at least the older members never recovered. Locally, the removal of a large industry from one small city to another may strand workers and radically change their class position.

Integration of the Subcultures

The emphasis on differences should not blind us to the fact that the various subcultures are closely bound together to form one large functioning society. The integration is achieved in various ways. The subcultures all accept certain principles or basic values, already enumerated in Chapter 1, so far as marriage and the family are concerned. The freedom to move from subculture to subculture—or at any rate to attempt to move—also gives a sense of oneness to society. Incoming foreign-culture groups are expected and urged to acquire the dominant American culture.

At the same time that avenues are open for a merging of subcultures and the passage of people from one subculture to another, certain roadblocks are set up that slow the process. Established groups are often not at all eager to accept persons or families of different origin or culture. These roadblocks cause some families to become stabilized in their own subcultures and slow down the process for others. Although the rejection may be frustrating to the upwardly mobile family, it may benefit social stability since it assures that the marginal group will be forced to acquire and internalize the values of the core group before acceptance, rather than to plunge into a new position on a wave of prosperity and high income without the stabilizing and organizing values of the established group.

The chief directions of mobility are horizontal, as seen among ethnic groups, and vertically upward. At all times a minor downward trend is present for families or individuals; at times of widespread unemployment it may affect a large portion of certain class levels.

The importance of subcultures for a study of the American family touches on several phases of family life: the organization of the family in terms of subculture values; the training of children in these values; the process of transition from one subculture to another, either horizontally or vertically; and the intergenerational aspects of these processes. The continued influx of new cultural groups and the constant social mobility give these phases of family life a fluid quality that is counterbalanced by processes of integration.

The chapters that follow present material on families in the stable or core social classes and the mobile marginal groups; horizontal mobility as illustrated by ethnic families; vertical upward and downward mobility of families; and intermarriage as a process of transition.

Questions

1. What is the difference between stratification and social class? Which concept is most useful in a study of the family?
2. Discuss the relation of cohesiveness of a social class to residential areas.
3. In a given community, what are some factors that might affect the distribution of people into different social classes?
4. Why should the concept of social class be brought into a study of the family?
5. What is an ethnic family? What processes of adjustment does an ethnic family typically make? Are there similarities between ethnic adjustment and the adjustment made by rural families that have moved into a city?
6. Are the Negroes a caste? An ethnic group?
7. What are the different types and avenues of social mobility?
8. Relate the concepts *nouveau riche*, *parvenu*, and *nouveau bourgeoisie* to social mobility.
9. What are some of the effects that social mobility has on families?

Bibliography

BOHLKE, ROBERT H., "Social Mobility, Stratification Inconsistency and Middle Class Delinquency," *Social Problems*, 8 (Spring, 1961), 351–63.

CAVAN, RUTH SHONLE, ed., *Marriage and the Family, A Book of Readings* (New York: Crowell, 1969), ch. 3.

———, "Subcultural Variations and Mobility," in Harold T. Christensen, ed., *Handbook of Marriage and the Family* (Chicago: Rand McNally, 1964), ch. 14.

FRAZIER, E. FRANKLIN, *Black Bourgeoisie* (Glencoe, Ill.: Free Press, 1957).

———, "The Negro Middle Class and Desegregation," *Social Problems*, 4 (April, 1957), 291–301.

JANOWITZ, MORRIS, "Some Consequences of Social Mobility in the United States," *Transactions of the Third World Congress of Sociology*, 3 (1956), 191–201; also in Reprint Series in the Social Sciences, No. 135 (Indianapolis: Bobbs-Merrill).

LIPSET, SEYMOUR M., and HANS L. ZETTERBERG, "A Theory of Social Mobility," *Transactions of the Third World Congress of Sociology*, 2 (1956), 155–77; also in Reprint Series in the Social Sciences, No. 176 (Indianapolis: Bobbs-Merrill).

SOROKIN, PITIRIM, *Social and Cultural Mobility* (Glencoe, Ill.: Free Press, 1959).

WARNER, W. LLOYD, and Associates, *Democracy in Jonesville* (New York: Harper, 1949).

———, and PAUL S. LUNT, *The Social Life of a Modern Community* (New Haven: Yale University Press, 1941).

———, MARCHIA MEEKER, and KENNETH EELLS, *Social Class in America* (Chicago: Science Research Associates, 1949).

5

Upper-Class Families

THE UPPER CLASS not only constitutes the smallest of the classes but it is the one most sharply set off from an adjacent class.[1] The upper class tends, even in democratic America, to form a small aristocratic elite that resists invasion from below. However, the general process of upward mobility brings aspiring groups to the portals of the upper class even though they do not have all the attributes for acceptance. Therefore, the upper class can be separated into upper-upper and lower-upper, for which the term *nouveau riche* has already been suggested. A cultural variant occurs in the Negro upper class.

The Upper-Upper-Class Family

Families in the upper class are firmly entrenched, not only in class culture, but in an extended family or kinship system that gives firmness and continuity to the family.

THE HISTORICAL FAMILY

The upper-upper-class family typically regards itself not as an independent unit but as a stage in the development of a historical family. It

[1]Werner S. Landecker, "Class Boundaries," *American Sociological Review*, 25 (1960), 868–77. By a study of stratification based on ranking of educational, occupational, income, and ethnic status, Landecker found that the highest stratum was sharply set off from the next highest stratum and that other breaks in the rankings were less marked.

venerates the past generations whose accomplishments laid the foundation for the present family status. European ancestry of worth is respected, but real pride is felt for the ancestors who established themselves in the American community through individual energy and ability. Their early descendants consolidated the position won by the original American ancestors and passed on to their children an impregnable position of prestige, coupled with adequate stable income based on inherited wealth. The Lowells, Roosevelts, and Lees are examples of long-established upper-upper-class families.

The Lowell family is a recognized upper-upper-class family of Boston, best known at the present time for Abbot Lawrence Lowell, president of Harvard University from 1909 to 1933, and his poet-sister Amy Lowell; and in the past for James Russell Lowell. A family that has provided outstanding leadership in public affairs, education, the courts, the church, and the cotton industry, it had its roots in this country in Percival Lowell, classified as a gentleman in England, who emigrated to America in 1639.[2] The family required several generations to establish its prestige in America. Percival's great-great-grandson John set the family pattern, which still continues, of graduation of the men from Harvard and leadership in the professions and community affairs, supported (later) by wealth from the lucrative cotton manufacturing of New England. By 1800 the "high places of Boston were permeated with Lowell poets, manufacturers, diplomats, judges, historians, ministers, and educators," representing various branches of the family. Franklin Delano Roosevelt, an acknowledged member of the upper-upper class, was a descendant on his mother's side of Philip De la Noye, who landed at Plymouth in 1621.[3] Philip had a grant of land at Fairhaven, Massachusetts, on part of which the family home still stands. Richard Lee, the founder of the Lee family of Virginia that early gained prominence in public affairs, which continued until the Civil War, came to America in 1640.[4]

Although in eastern cities, eight and nine generations have helped to establish the upper-class family, in more recently settled regions a lesser number of generations has similarly established an upper class, and become accepted as such in the local area. In the Middle West, for example, five generations of residence with perhaps four generations of leadership give the necessary prestige; in the Far West, the family his-

[2]S. Foster Damon, *Amy Lowell, a Chronicle with Extracts from Her Correspondence* (Boston: Houghton Mifflin, 1935), p. 20.

[3]Rita Hall Kleeman, *Gracious Lady: The Life of Sara Delano Roosevelt* (New York: D. Appleton–Century, 1935).

[4]Burton J. Hendrick, *The Lees of Virginia: Biography of a Family* (Boston: Little, Brown, 1935), p. 3.

tory may be shorter. Often these families of the Middle and Far West look with pride to connections with older established families of the East. But often also they owe their origins to persons of force and initiative who assumed leadership in a new community that they never could have demonstrated in an eastern city where the social-class lines were firmly established with prestige and power fixed in a limited number of families.

Family continuity is emphasized by both material and nonmaterial symbols. Family names are important, as is a family crest if one exists. The importance of names attaches both to the surname and to given names. In the case of the late President, Franklin and Delano as well as Roosevelt are family names. In the Saltonstall family in Boston, Nathaniel, Richard, and Leverett appear generation after generation, and the Quincy family had four generations of Josiahs.[5] Portraits also are symbols of family continuity, and give substance to the legends that arise of the beauty of the women and the bravery of the men of past generations. Certain professions or businesses are handed down from generation to generation, a son often being trained from earliest childhood for entrance into the family occupation. The medical profession may characterize one family, the ministry another, some specific business another.

THE MODIFIED EXTENDED FAMILY

The upper-upper-class family has not only historical continuity but also functioning lateral relationships. It consists of nuclear units closely interconnected by blood ties, marriage, past history, and present joint ownership of property. The great family thus includes uncles, aunts, and cousins of various degrees of closeness, organized into conventional nuclear units but functioning also as a modified extended family. Moreover, the tendency of members of the small upper-upper class to marry within the class—even within the larger family, as cousin with cousin—has created a complicated system of relationships, so that it often may be truthfully said that the entire upper-upper class in a given community tends to be a related kinship group. The family histories of the Lowells, the Lees, and the Roosevelts all include such marriages.[6] More recently developed upper-class families also show the same tendency,

[5]Cleveland Amory, *The Proper Bostonians* (New York: Dutton, 1947), p. 19.

[6]Amory, *op. cit.*, pp. 20–21; Allison Davis, Burleigh B. Gardner, and Mary R. Gardner, *Deep South* (Chicago: University of Chicago Press, 1941), pp. 87–90; Ferris Greenslet, *The Lowells and Their Seven Worlds* (Boston: Houghton Mifflin, 1946), p. 113; and numerous other references.

according to Lundberg's popular study of America's sixty wealthiest families.[7]

The larger family is often held together, also, by joint property or by ownership of adjacent pieces of property by family members. In the South the extended family group is held together partially by the joint ownership of plantations or by the operation under one management of plantations owned by branches of the same family.[8] Lundberg discusses the great industries and trust funds in which the accumulated assets of America's wealthiest families are concentrated and passed on intact—and, indeed, greatly augmented—from generation to generation, the numerous members of each generation receiving ample income but no one person individually owning the industry or the capital of the trust fund.[9] The concentration of wealth is aided by the intermarriages that occur between close or remote cousins.

Family ties are very strong. One is a member of the larger family first, of the nuclear family second. Family organization therefore tends to be on a kinship rather than a marital basis, with the headship resting in the oldest person or in a group of collateral elders. Since women often survive their husbands, the head of the extended family may be a woman.

The elderly heads hold somewhat the same position in the extended family that the elders hold in primitive societies. In their youth they knew members of at least two preceding generations whose lips repeated the legends of still earlier generations. Family victories are thus preserved—sometimes family defeats. Children are compared to earlier members of the family and expectations are established that these children will equal or surpass the feats of their ancestors. Admired personality traits of the ancestors are held before children in their impressionable years. The old men of the family hold the professional and business secrets that have spelled success in the past. Thus, as with primitives, the elders of the upper-upper class are the repository of legend and wisdom for both the social class and the particular family group.

The elders wield great power over both adult and youthful descendants, often determining such matters as type and place of education, occupation, and selection of the spouse. If, as often happens, they hold the joint family property and wealth, they possess an enormous authority since they may control the amount of income of younger mem-

[7]Ferdinand Lundberg, *America's 60 Families* (New York: Vanguard, 1937), pp. 9–22.
[8]Davis, Gardner, and Gardner, *op. cit.*, p. 277.
[9]Lundberg, *op. cit.*, ch. 2.

bers. Thus middle-aged men who, in other social classes, would be independent heads of their small families and control their own social and economic destinies, in the upper-upper class may still play the role of dependent sons to their old parents.

Cultural Unity

Since, in a given community, all upper-upper-class families tend to have established themselves at approximately the same period of time, they represent the same ethnic stock and cultural traditions. In New England and Virginia, the stock tends to be English. People of other ethnic stocks, more recently arrived, are not readily acceptable in the circles of the upper-upper class, regardless of amount of education, cultural sophistication, or wealth. In Boston, for example, among 2,350,000 people in the 1940's, 8,000 were included in the *Social Register*.[10] Among these 8,000 were listed the names of only one Jewish man and less than a dozen Catholic families, although the population of Boston was 79 per cent Catholic. Ethnic groups that came after 1850—Irish, Italian, Jewish, and Polish as well as other European nationalities—were almost unrepresented. Among the upper classes represented by the 8,000 families in the *Social Register* is a smaller group, an ultra-upper class, called by Amory "the Proper Bostonians." This group has not only a uniform ethnic background but a high degree of similarity in the family histories. The general pattern includes entrance of the original members into the colonies, although they may not have been leaders in colonial life; establishment of a family fortune between the periods of the Revolutionary and the Civil wars through an international merchant prince; wise investment of the fortune to form the basis of inherited wealth; often, continued production of wealth through industry and railroading; education of the male members at Harvard; local community leadership including philanthropic operations, often supplemented by state, national, and international statesmanship; entrance of some members of the family into the professions of education, law, medicine, but with other members of the family continuing as astute businessmen; limited travel abroad primarily to England with development of cultural interests.

In the middle states of the Deep South, the families are of English or French ancestry. Emphasis, however, is not placed on this remote ancestry but on the status of the family prior to the Civil War.[11] The pre-Civil War cultural pattern included ownership of a large plantation

[10]Amory, *op. cit.*, pp. 12–13.

and many slaves, extravagant living, and lavish entertainment of guests. Although wealth was diminished by the Civil War, the upper-upper-class families attempt to maintain the plantation home as well as the city house, and cling to both the material furnishings and the memories of the past. So immersed may the families become in the past that they fail to maintain political or community leadership in the present. Status rests on membership in a family with a glorious past rather than upon present accomplishments.

Cultural unity is also maintained by the withdrawal of the upper-upper class from the common public institutions. The class tends to form an isolated social world, protecting its isolation by a system of exclusive social contacts. Nurses, tutors, governesses, and maids stand as a bulwark, both physically and in the training they give, between the children of the upper-upper class and children who might be met in a freer existence. Later the children attend private day or boarding schools, which admit only children of the upper social classes. Colleges and universities are no longer so exclusive as formerly, although within the institutions small exclusive clubs may exist. In the adult community, clubs, large and small, to which membership may be gained only upon election, also support the social isolation. In his discussion of the First Families of Boston, Amory emphasizes the function of upper-class clubs in maintaining the social status of their members.[12] It is virtually impossible for any except the descendants of earlier members to gain election to membership. The clubs thus are an adjunct of the families.

Upper-upper-class families are thus welded into community solidarity through their common ethnic and cultural background and present exclusive social experiences. This solidarity is at the basis of the almost impenetrable barrier erected in older cities against intrusion of upwardly mobile families.

ECONOMIC BASIS

Three factors characterize the economic basis of upper-upper-class families: the income must be adequate to maintain the standards of the class; the income is based primarily on inherited rather than newly acquired or currently earned wealth; and in each locality certain sources of income give prestige. Each point merits some discussion.

Although the upper-upper class is not usually characterized by ostentatious display, the style of living rests upon a liberal expenditure of

[11]Davis, Gardner, and Gardner, *op. cit.*, pp. 73–75.
[12]Amory, *op. cit.*, pp. 354–59.

money. The education of children through tutors, private schools, travel
or study abroad, and in high-fee universities in the United States is
expensive. The operation of a city and one or more country homes, both
of which are perhaps open at the same time, again requires a large income for maintenance and servants. Support of philanthropies, an
upper-upper-class community duty, calls for excess money. A family
that spends lavishly and exceeds its income may hold its position for a
generation but is disapproved by other families and soon loses its position of prestige, unless the next generation can recoup the losses or
succeeds in marrying into a family of wealth. The marriage may be to
a wealthy member of a slightly lower class, although such a marriage
weakens the personal status of the upper-class member.

The factor of inherited income is linked both to long establishment
of the family and also to stability of the source of wealth. Important
in inherited wealth is the rather common practice on the part of the
first producer of outstanding wealth of establishing trust funds, which
securely safeguard the capital and permit subsequent generations to
use only the income. An example of this procedure is found in the will
of William Rockefeller, brother of John D. Rockefeller. When he died
in 1922, he left a fortune of 50 million dollars, a portion of the income
of which was to be divided among his children and grandchildren; the
principal, however, was to remain intact for division among his great-
grandchildren.[13]

The source of wealth varies from one community to another. In
Boston, the acceptable sources are, first, merchandising in the early
nineteenth century and, second, certain industries, such as the cotton
mills operated by members of the Lowell family. In the Deep South,
the prestige-carrying source of family wealth is the large plantation
established by an ancestral planter; in New York City, it is real estate;
among more recently established families, industrial and railroad development and extraction of metal have ranked high.

RESIDENTIAL STABILITY

Since upper-upper-class prestige rests in part upon the length of time
that the family has held a position of leadership in the community,
residential stability is common to the families of this social class. Frequent moving from one community to another causes a break in the
family continuity. Even though a family that has newly moved into a
community is related to an upper-upper-class family elsewhere, it may

[13]Lundberg, *op. cit.*, p. 49. See also Amory, *op. cit.*, pp. 32–34.

not be fully accepted into the upper-upper class of the new community. Each kinship group has its own favorite central locale: the Lowells in Boston, the Roosevelts in New York City and Hyde Park; and the Du Ponts in Wilmington, where twenty-four Du Pont estates are located.[14]

NUCLEAR FAMILY ORGANIZATION

Within the modified extended family, as based on descent, the nuclear families function on a conjugal basis.

The nuclear units tend to be patrilinear. The given names of the husband's ancestors take precedence in naming the children; the wife is expected to minimize the traditions of her family and to extol those of her husband's; sons are important to carry on the family name. By the time the elderly wife becomes head of the family in her widowhood she usually is an excellent carrier of the culture of the husband's family. The husband, if he owns property individually, manages the finances of the family during his lifetime and sometimes creates a trust for their management after his death along lines laid down by him.

Socially, however, husband and wife tend to be on an equal basis. Friends are entertained at home with husband and wife as host and hostess. The two travel together, belong to some social clubs together, and attend concerts, opera, and the theater in each other's company. The men's clubs to which the husbands alone may belong are matched by women's clubs to which their wives belong, but the activities of these clubs tend to be subordinated to the joint activities of husband and wife.

MARRIAGE

In general, marriages occur at a later age than in other social classes. In Yankee City, an eastern city of 17,000, the average age for upper-upper-class marriages in the 1930's was 27.9 years, higher than for any other social class and a full five years later than the average age in the lower-lower class.[15]

As in all social classes marriages tend to occur within the class. Social isolation and close supervision of the child and young adult help to limit

[14]Lundberg, op. cit., p. 420.

[15]W. Lloyd Warner and Paul S. Lunt, The Social Life of a Modern Community (New Haven: Yale University Press, 1941), p. 423. Since this study was made the median age of marriage in the United States has declined. It may be assumed that ages given here and elsewhere by social class would all be lower now but still have the same relative position to each other, that is, highest in the upper-upper class and lowest in the lower-lower class.

his contacts, and hence choice of a spouse, to the small upper-upper class. Moreover, the emphasis on family prestige and the quality of family stock makes it unthinkable for the young person to marry outside his class, for such a marriage would necessarily be into a lower social class. The debut also serves to promote the in-class marriage. This custom originated, apparently, during a period when girls were secluded during their adolescence and had few contacts with young men and sometimes few contacts with adults beyond the kinship circle. The debut served to introduce the girl to the friends of her parents and to their sons. It brought together the young people who were expected to marry each other and provided an opportunity for parents to survey each other's offspring. Although now young people of the two sexes are not segregated during adolescence to the same extent as formerly, the practice in upper-upper-class families of sending their sons and daughters to private schools organized on a one-sex basis implies a partial separation. The debut identifies for girls and young men alike the group within which marriage is suitable.

The young person who rebels and marries according to personal choice may find his mate barred from the more important social functions even though he may be included, or he as well as his mate may be ostracized or even rejected by the immediate family. Sometimes personal attachments with those of a lower class develop but are summarily ended when the time for marriage comes; or occasionally they lead to irregular alliances. Occasionally a mature adult of upper-class status who has emancipated himself from the control of his kinship and class marries someone from a much lower class. So unusual is such an event, however, that it brings wider publicity in news magazines than does a marriage within the class.

Children in the Upper-Upper Class

For several reasons, children in the upper-upper class are not only few in number but also few in proportion to the older people. The birth rate is lower in the upper-upper class than in classes of lower status, judging from Tables 4, 5, and 6. In addition, the life expectancy has been increasing, thus increasing the proportion of older people.

FUNCTION OF SONS

Children, though few, are important. Sons are especially favored, as they carry on the family name and provide for continued control of profession or business. So important is this function of sons that when a childless couple consider adoption, they are often persuaded by the extended family to adopt a daughter rather than a son so that only those of the true blood will carry the name through adulthood and pass it on to succeeding generations.[16]

TRAINING OF CHILDREN

Children belong to the kinship; they are links in the long chain of the generations. Their education includes a strong emphasis on the culture of the upper-upper class and of the particular family. The class culture comes not only through the family but also through the private schools, camps, clubs, and restricted social groups to which the children are sent. The teachers who serve the upper-upper class are not themselves of this class; but, having familiarized themselves with the attitudes and standards of the class, they impose the class culture on the children. In the South, a Negro mammy, who has perhaps been associated with a particular family since childhood, may rear the children, impressing upon them the class and family culture. As these adult intermediaries intrude between parents and children, the parent-child ties tend to weaken, and the children may feel not only great affection but emotional dependence upon some one nurse or governess who has become a

TABLE 4

AVERAGE NUMBER OF CHILDREN EVER BORN PER WOMAN, AGED 45 AND OVER, WHO HAD EVER BEEN MARRIED, BY FAMILY INCOME, 1963

Amount of family income	Average number of children
Total population	2.7
$10,000 and over	2.2
7,500–9,999	2.4
5,000–7,499	2.4
3,000–4,999	2.6
Under 3,000	3.2

SOURCE: *Statistical Abstract of the United States, 1967* (Washington, D.C.: Government Printing Office, 1967), p. 52.

parent-substitute. Likewise, the resentment that children sometimes feel toward parents who both love and discipline them is directed toward the parent-substitute, while the parent-child relationship remains less intense but also more amicable.

The family culture is also impressed upon the child by the extended

[16]Amory, *op. cit.*, p. 21.

family, of which the upper-upper-class child remains a member throughout his life unless he definitely wrenches himself loose. Grandparents
and elderly uncles and aunts impose on the child the standards of the

TABLE 5
AVERAGE NUMBER OF CHILDREN EVER BORN PER WOMAN, AGED 45 AND OVER, WHO
HAD EVER BEEN MARRIED, BY HUSBAND'S OCCUPATION, 1964

Occupation of husband	Average number of children
Total population	2.5
Professional, technical, and kindred workers	2.1
Managers, officials, and proprietors, excluding farm	2.2
Clerical and kindred workers	2.0
Sales workers	1.9
Craftsmen, foremen, and kindred workers	2.5
Operatives and kindred workers	2.6
Service workers, including in private household	2.4
Laborers, except farm and mine	3.0
Farmers and farm managers	3.5

SOURCE: *Statistical Abstract of the United States, 1967* (Washington, D.C.: Government Printing Office, 1967), p. 52.

TABLE 6
AVERAGE NUMBER OF CHILDREN EVER BORN PER WOMAN, AGED 45 AND OVER, WHO
HAD EVER BEEN MARRIED, BY EDUCATION OF WOMAN, 1964

Education of mother	Average number of children
Total population	2.7
College	
4 or more years	1.7
1 to 3 years	2.0
High school	
4 years	2.0
1 to 3 years	2.5
Elementary school	
8 years	2.8
Less than 8 years	3.6

SOURCE: *Statistical Abstract of the United States, 1967* (Washington, D.C.: Government Printing Office, 1967), p. 52.

family and feed to his listening ears the tales and legends of the ancestors. The child becomes aware of a proud past that he must emulate in
his own life, and of the expectations of the family regarding his conduct
and achievements. Long before children are mature enough to think
logically of their future, the son knows what school and college he is

destined to attend, what occupation the family has planned for him; the girl knows the kind of training she will receive and the type of young men she will meet at her debut, one of whom will become her husband.

Family gatherings at holidays when children and adults assemble under one roof are occasions for family reminiscing and account-taking. It is especially significant that these gatherings are often held in a home that has been in the family for generations, a repository for both the family portraits and the small mementos that symbolize the personal history of past members of the family. Personal and family diaries of generations past are often open for younger members to read. On these occasions especially the child feels himself a member of the extended family and of a historical family.

Ritual, or prescribed formal procedures that acquire a sense of rightness, has more place in the upper-class family than in that of any other social class. Examples are acts of courtesy of children to all older people (rising when an older person of either sex enters the room); exclusion of children from the family dinner table except on special occasions; dressing for dinner; and prescribed acts of deference of both children and adults to the oldest generation of the extended family. These rituals emphasize the roles of the members of the family and place each in a hierarchical status with reference to the others, in terms of sex, age, and achievements. They also emphasize the family unity. In other words, they both control and restrict behavior and at the same time incorporate each member firmly into the family.

Often the rituals center around the heirlooms and symbols of the past that have already been mentioned as important in inculcating a sense of family continuity and prestige. Cherished sets of fine china or silver may be used only on certain sacred family occasions. The christening dress or wedding jewels that pass from generation to generation for appropriate use emphasize to young and old alike the identity of a particular family.[17] Such objects often attain an intangible value completely unrelated to their material value. They frequently become objects of envy among upwardly mobile families of lower status, who crave such symbols of ancestral status.

PERSONALITY OF THE CHILD

The effect on the child's personality is to give great personal and social security. The limitation of his contacts to his own social class with its unified culture eliminates comparison of his own class culture with that

[17] James H. S. Bossard and Eleanor S. Boll, *Ritual in Family Living* (Philadelphia: University of Pennsylvania Press, 1950); Bossard and Boll, "Ritual in Family Living," *American Sociological Review*, 14 (1949), 463–69.

of other classes. He therefore does not suffer from cultural conflicts and develops a unified personality. Taught that he belongs to the class with greatest prestige, treated as superior by servants, salesmen, and teachers, he tends to accept his status without question. He becomes self-confident and assured of his own worth. College education, travel, attendance at the theater, concerts, and opera equip him for a place of leadership and give him a cultural background and degree of sophistication not found in less privileged classes. Since his family is already at the top of the social scale, he has no further heights to climb. As the child matures, however, he must put forth enough effort to maintain that position; if the family is mobile in a downward direction, he may, of course, suffer great insecurity and sense of inferiority.

In terms of both economics and future life goals the upper-upper-class child is secure. Money comes from inherited sources as well as

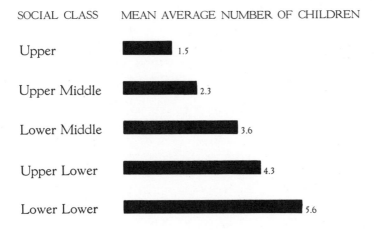

SOCIAL CLASS   MEAN AVERAGE NUMBER OF CHILDREN

Upper   1.5

Upper Middle   2.3

Lower Middle   3.6

Upper Lower   4.3

Lower Lower   5.6

FIGURE 3   *Number of Children by Social Class, Elmtown.*

Children have a different meaning in each social class: in the upper class children carry on the family name and keep the family inheritance intact; in the middle classes children are a projection of the parents' personalities into a brighter future; in the lower classes children are accepted as a natural consequence of marriage and a security against economic want. The factor of security, however, is less important than formerly because of compulsory school attendance and restrictions on employment of children.

SOURCE: A. B. Hollingshead, *Elmtown's Youth* (New York: Wiley, 1949), ch. 5.

from the present efforts of the family. Often the child's plan of life is fixed before his birth. A place awaits him in the family business, or in the professional firm of the elders. Informal family agreements may be made as to marriages between children. If the child is compliant to the family expectations, he faces a secure future without the anxiety of deciding for himself what his goals will be or of establishing himself socially or financially.

The upper-upper-class child is secure also from influences or pressures outside his class, although he is heavily burdened with the expectations and pressures of his own class and family. In his study of Yankee City, Warner discovered that only one per cent of upper-upper-class people had had their names placed on the police record, as compared with 11 per cent of the lower-lower class, and few indeed were the arrests of upper-upper-class juveniles. He states, however, that interviews revealed that upper-upper-class children had committed many of the same offenses as those for which lower-lower-class children had been arrested. The explanation lies in two factors: police are reluctant to arrest anyone with the prestige and known influence in the community of the upper-upper class; in addition, the kinship group and intimate friends either tolerate depredations of their younger members or themselves take steps to punish and control juvenile rebels.[18] In another way, also, the upper-upper-class child is secure. Although the upper-upper class is active in cultural and welfare agencies that are offered to or that impose their programs upon members of the lower classes, the upper-upper class itself is free from such movements from the outside. Thus the upper-upper-class child must conform to his own class mores, but he does not find it necessary, as do those of lower classes, to conform to the mores of official agencies or of other social classes.

Exceptions exist, of course, to the general statement that the upper-upper-class child tends to feel adequate, secure, and free from conflicts. If the immediate family becomes disorganized or disintegrates, or if the family is mobile downward, the growing child may become very insecure. The upper-upper-class child and young person also may feel inadequate and personally insecure if he cannot meet the expectations of his kinship and class. The boy who lacks ability equal to the family tasks or the girl who lacks grace and beauty may suffer great agonies. Amy Lowell, heavy-set and awkward in her girlhood, suffered despondency and self-depreciation when she compared herself to other adolescent girls whose appeal to boys far surpassed her own.[19] Her diary contains many entries to the effect that she was a fool, that no one cared for her, that she was rough, that she was a "dreadful pill." Eventually she established a reputation as a poet and also as an eccentric, but she did not achieve the marriage expected of girls of her class and generation. Individualistic as she became, she continued until her death to make her headquarters in the family home established by her

[18]Warner and Lunt, op. cit., pp. 427–28.
[19]Damon, op. cit., pp. 84–120.

father, apparently finding there security and a sense of continuity with her past.

Finally, the upper-class child may feel insecure for personal reasons, such as illness, loss of friends, deaths, or various disappointments. But even so, the upper-upper-class child often finds his situation less acute than that of a lower-class child. He is rarely alone in his emotional stress, the kinship group that surrounds him cushioning the shock.

Upper-class isolation is less complete today than formerly, and the break in the cultural wall permits contacts with those of other social classes. The trend now is for middle- and even aspiring and especially capable lower-class children to attend college and university. Although these young people may not belong to the same clubs or fraternities as upper-upper-class youths, nevertheless there is an exchange of ideas and information. Although the upper-upper-class children have more priv-ileges than those of lower groups, they often have less freedom of individual choice. Some upper-upper-class children and young people therefore attempt to throw off the restraints of their kinship and class group and seek individual freedom outside the prescribed behavior of their class. This movement may be permanent, especially if the young person moves away from the stronghold of his family and establishes himself elsewhere as an individual rather than a member of his family. Marriage outside the class is probably the final sign of rebellion. Often, however, it is temporary with an eventual return to the family pattern. Amory lists by name various young Proper Bostonians (girls as well as young men) who sought individual careers in the motion pictures or journalism, or on the stage, but after a few months or years returned to the family fold.

Many of the illustrations given of family life in the upper-upper class have been drawn from published accounts of the family histories of the truly great. In order to coordinate the various phases of family life and to present the upper-upper-class family at a less exalted level, the fol-lowing account is presented. Written by a younger member of an upper-upper-class family in one of the older cities of the East, it mirrors both the objective aspects and some of the attitudes of the class.

The Upper-Upper-Class Family in an Old Eastern City

River Boulevard is considered the most fashionable place to live in Eastern City. As the years have gone by the suburbs furthest out along River Boulevard have become the most exclusive. River

Boulevard is made up mostly of the upper class, which is divided about equally between the lower-upper and the upper-upper. Some of the suburbs have middle-class people; Oak Grove is considered the worst suburb because so many "awful people" live there, "awful people" being middle class. Many times parents in an upper-class family refuse to allow their daughters to go out with boys from Oak Grove, even though they know nothing other about them than this.

The newer houses which lie furthest from the city are larger than the old ones and each family seems to be trying to outdo the others. The houses are large and rather formidable looking; they are surrounded by many acres of land, sometimes lawn and sometimes laid out in polo fields or as pasture for riding horses.

When a baby is born into an upper-upper-class family he is taught from the beginning never to forget it. He is taught not to play with "those little children," but to play with these children. Often a group of families know each other and their children play together. Or sometimes different branches of one family live on one huge estate. All the brothers and sisters and their respective families live in houses built around the "manor house." The children on these large estates are inseparable and even after they go to school and make other friends, they remain extremely close to their cousins. The upper-class children rarely know any other children than those of their own class. They have hardly any occasion to meet middle- or lower-class children. The children usually have governesses up to the age of 12 and are carefully watched over. The governess is sometimes French, so that the children may learn to speak French at an early age. As the children become older, the governess gradually takes the role of personal maid to the girls.

There are three private girls' schools and two private boys' schools in the area. The boy usually goes to the school that his father attended and the girl to her mother's school. The friends that the child makes at these schools are all from the upper class and remain friends throughout the school years. Every party, open house, or any kind of group gathering is made up of students from these five schools. The students from the three public schools in the suburban community also stick together. The private schools and public schools do not have any activities in common. They do not even compete in sports, except for practice games and then the two groups of students part immediately after the game; they have nothing to say to each other. When the private schools play against each other, the game is always followed by a mixer where the host school serves hot chocolate and the two teams easily mix. The private schools are very particular about the children they accept. Children outside the recognized class are not accepted unless they have famous fathers and then the children often do not try to associate themselves with the upper class. When upper-class families cannot afford to send their children to these schools, they are awarded scholarships.

After the girl is graduated from this school, she is given a debut by her parents. This function serves to introduce her to the adult friends of her family and also to an eligible group of young men, somewhat older than the boys whom she had dated in school. She thus enters the upper-upper-class adult society under the guidance of her parents.[20]

Every family is proud of its heritage and talks freely about its ancestors. In almost every home on the wall in a prominent position is the family tree, appropriately framed. Many families have a crest, which is also framed, and which is used on stationery, rings, and so forth. The *Social Register*, a book containing only the names of people who are considered upper-upper class, is used as the telephone directory. Very seldom does anyone in the family find it necessary to use the regular telephone directory. Only the people whose names are in the *Social Register* own the book. Outsiders are made to see that they are not wanted. Money has *nothing* to do with getting into the *Social Register*. The criterion used is the family background. If the family dates back for many generations, if the members belong to exclusive clubs, and the daughters have always made their debut, the family is considered upper-class. "Outsiders" who suddenly make a lot of money are not readily accepted. The family background is what is important and you can't change that—you either have a good family background or you don't.

It is close to impossible to break into the upper-class on River Boulevard. There are many institutions that help to keep the class untouchable. The exclusive private schools for children have already been mentioned. Many of the men belong to the City Guards, to which their fathers and grandfathers also belonged. A few newcomers, relatives and close friends, are admitted, but only when they are acceptable to the Guard leaders. The Guards are determined to remain small and select. They go on maneuvers once a year and are the pride of the city. The men have another exclusive group—the Union League, which is in the city and provides a place for upper-class men to meet, eat lunch, or give dinner parties. Sons and grandsons of members are readily accepted into the League; only a few "outsiders" are chosen each year from the long waiting list.

The women have similar exclusive clubs, such as the Junior League, to which new members are admitted only upon recommendation of an old member and approval by the board. Certain country clubs are considered "the" clubs to belong to; prospective members are carefully screened. Informal parties are limited to members of the upper class.

The adults have many small parties, usually for members of both sexes. In addition, the women serve tea in the afternoon when women friends customarily drop in. Also, the women are together during much of the day, busy with such activities as charitable work or raising funds for some drive. The men in their leisure

[20]For a detailed account of the debut, dating, and courtship practices in this community, see Chapter 13.

play golf, ride, or go to the club. The upper class is extremely interested in sports, mainly riding, hockey, tennis, squash, and football. Evening social affairs are for husband and wife together.

Manners are thought important in some families but not in
others. In one leading family the daughter eats and dresses as
though she were a manual laborer; in another the daughter would
not be seen out of doors in her blue jeans.

The parents teach their children the manners of everyday life,
but when big issues are to be decided the oldest member of the
family is consulted. She (rarely he) is usually looked up to as a
great figure and the children must be dressed perfectly and on
their best behavior when with her. The family group usually is extremely close and large as there is a great deal of intermarriage.
For example, during one year two sisters married cousins, all
having the same surname.

The religion of this upper-class community is predominantly
Episcopalian, with Presbyterian next. There are a few upper-
upper-class Catholic families, but no Jewish families. Occupationally the men are usually professionals or business executives,
while many are just "country gentlemen," who look after their
investments, breed horses, and so on.

And so this is River Boulevard. Good, bad, prejudiced or what,
to us who live there it is heaven on earth.[21]

The Lower-Upper-Class
or Nouveau Riche *Family*

When classes in Yankee City were compared, the lower-upper resembled the upper-upper more nearly than any other class. However, dis-
similarities were sufficient to prevent acceptance of the lower-upper
family into the upper-upper class. Upper-upper-class families were
clearly aware of the identity of the lower-upper families and their efforts
to be accepted into the highest level of the hierarchy. They referred to
lower-upper families disparagingly as *nouveau riche*, social climbers,
and people whose social affairs were "too-too," or who were pushy. The
differences are sufficient that in the older eastern, southern, or middle
western communities lower-upper-class families may never be admitted
fully into the upper-upper-class group; but in the newer communities
of the Middle West and West, where the upper-upper-class families
are less securely entrenched, newcomers without a past history in the
community but with present income and cultural levels equal to those
of the upper-upper class may be admitted into that class level within
one generation.

[21]Unpublished description, about 1952.

The Family's Past

The lower-upper-class family can successfully imitate the upper-upper-class family in everything except the age of the family stock after it achieved prominence in the community. Family portraits do not include great-grandparents. Books in the library have not been inscribed by the illustrious ancestors. The valuable antiques came from the modern dealer's showroom rather than through inheritance. Legends and tales of the family are limited to a generation, as the lowly past must be wiped out and forgotten. Often the family, having no accumulated record of the family history through documents and diaries, employs a genealogist to trace the family history, hoping of course to find a link with some upper-upper-class family. Whereas the upper-upper-class family has acquired an honorable past and has accumulated its material symbols of culture over four to six generations, the newly arrived lower-upper-class family buys its past and surrounds itself with the symbols of upper-upper-class status.

Cultural Unity

There is less cultural unity among lower-upper-class families than among the upper-upper-class families. For one thing, they represent more divergent backgrounds. Some families have made wealth in the development of the West and then moved East to establish themselves and their children socially. Others stem from groups that entered from different countries of Europe within the past 75 or 100 years and may retain some elements of their ancestral culture. There is then somewhat more diversity of standards, attitudes, family traditions, and religious affiliation than among upper-upper-class families. In addition, among families actively seeking a way up, a competitive situation develops. These families do not stand together and consolidate their class position, but each seeks to remain in a fluid situation in order to identify itself when an opportunity offers with the class above.

Economic Basis

The wealth of the lower-upper-class family is less likely to be inherited than is that of the upper-upper-class family; or, if inherited, it originated only a generation or two ago. The wealth is "new money," acquired in the latter-day industrial developments rather than in the time-honored upper-upper-class occupations of shipping, cotton manufacturing, railroading, or plantation operation.

Often the amount of wealth of the lower-upper-class families exceeds that of the upper-upper class. Moreover, it is spent differently. The study of Yankee City showed that the lower-upper class spent more than the upper-upper on food, house equipment and operation, rent and shelter, automobiles, vacations, club expenses; the upper-upper-class family exceeded in expenditures for clothing, taxes, formal education, gifts, and charity.[22] The accounts of ostentatious expenditures made now or in the past by families of great wealth often refer to lower-upper-class families with newly acquired wealth unsupported by family standards of sobriety in expenditure. The first generation of a family arisen from a lower status but with large amounts of excess money to spend has no family standards to control the spending of that money. The first impulse seems to be toward extravagant and useless expenditures unrelated either to enhancing the culture and education of the family or to public welfare. Sometimes the period of a generation in a particular locality will be characterized by the extravagance of the newly wealthy.

With the passing of time and the aid of public disapproval, the family develops standards that prohibit some of the ostentatious displays of wealth, and passes the new standards on to the children. However, in families of great wealth that yields excess income, a permanent leisure group may develop, free to devote itself to whatever occupation it pleases. These leisure members may choose art, literature, or science, and contribute to art or knowledge; but in other families the leisure members focus their lives about themselves with personal pleasure as the dominating motive. Thus, breeding and racing of fine horses, near-professional polo, or boat racing may become the major occupations of some lower-upper-class individuals or families.

Residential Stability

Because of its late arrival at the upper part of the social scale, the lower-upper-class family has usually acquired a home suited to its status within the past generation, as compared with family homes in the upper-upper class that may run back to the early development of the community. In general, the lower-upper-class family lives in a "new" part of the city or in a residential suburb, whereas at least the older generation of the upper-upper-class family is likely to live in an older part of the city, bulwarked by class solidarity against the encroachments of lower social classes as the city sweeps outward. In small communities, upper-upper- and lower-upper-class families may be inter-

[22]Warner and Lunt, *op. cit.*, pp. 290, 295, 296.

mixed geographically, but are distinguishable because of the larger size and often greater age of the houses of the upper-upper class.

The homes of the lower-upper class are more likely to have modern equipment and hence to be more comfortable to live in than the old family residence of the upper-upper-class family; but, of course, they lack the aura of age and the implication of a family that has helped to found and develop the community.

FAMILY ORGANIZATION

The family unit of the lower-upper class tends to be the husband and wife and their unmarried or minor children. As the family gains status and becomes stabilized, three generations may function together; but rarely is there the large interconnected kinship group of the upper-upper class. Too often one branch of the family has pushed ahead, leaving collateral branches or parents in a lower social class. It is both advantageous to the rising family and a means of avoiding jealousy and conflict for the nuclear family unit to retain its independence. Also, the nuclear family is characteristic of the middle class from which the lower-upper-class family has arisen. Transition to a kinship group can be made only by violating ingrained values that have accrued to the nuclear family.

The lower-upper-class family tends to be paternal in organization, with the husband functioning as head of the family as well as head of his business. The wife is released by maids from too pressing household duties and finds time for active daytime participation in club life and philanthropic or community activities. One of her chief concerns is to associate herself with upper-upper-class women, first in secondary groups, later through personal invitation in their primary groups.

MARRIAGE

Marriage occurs at an only slightly earlier age than in the upper-upper class, according to the Yankee City study.[23] The age is markedly higher, however, than in the lower social classes. Marriage tends to be within the class or, preferably, upward. The unusually attractive daughter or the brilliant son may make this move. Or the son or daughter of a wealthy lower-upper-class family may be acceptable in marriage to a member of an impoverished upper-upper-class family. Marriage down-

---

[23]Warner and Lunt, *op. cit.*, p. 255; see also A. B. Hollingshead, "Selected Characteristics of Classes in a Middle Western Community," *American Sociological Review*, 12 (1947), 388.

ward into the middle class is accepted by the family but is deplored. Marriage tends to be stable; divorce is frowned upon as a blight.

CHILDREN

Children are planned for, with a limited number desired. Since the family unit is small, children belong to the parents rather than to an extended family group. Nursemaids, tutors, governesses, private schools, and private camps function in the rearing of children, although not to the same degree as in the upper-upper-class family. The private camps and schools patronized by the lower-upper-class family tend to be the same institutions to which the children of upper-upper-class families go; they form an important avenue of communication and are the source of informal friendly relationships that later may lead to adult social relationships or intermarriage between families in the two social classes.

The children of the lower-upper class have many of the same types of security as those of the upper-upper class: economic, future life goals, freedom from police or charitable interference. Socially, the child has less security unless his family has accepted its status and does not aspire to enter the upper-upper class. If the family is still upwardly mobile, the child may become insecure simply because of the pressure put upon him to conform to the standards of the upper class and to attempt to enter it either socially, or through business or marriage. If the family is slipping downward the child may be very insecure as a reflection of the family's anxiety.

Children are not an economic asset, as in some lower classes, but are an extension of the family into the future. They are the bright hope of the parents that the family may enter into the upper-upper class. Children are therefore reared with this end in view. Both boys and girls are given a good education; boys are assisted to establish themselves in business or a profession; and girls are shepherded into the proper groups for a desirable marriage.

The Negro Upper-Class Variant [24]

The upper social class of Negroes has a history that began long before the Civil War. The education, occupational level, and economic resources of this very small segment of the Negro race bore little resem-

[24]Based primarily on E. Franklin Frazier, *Negro Family in the United States* (Chicago: University of Chicago Press, 1939), chs. 10, 12, 19.

blance to those of the white upper class, but were far above those of slaves. At that time virtually no group spanned the gap between the slaves and this small upper-level group. Some writers on the Negro refer to this most favored stratum of Negroes as an upper class, with the point of reference being the slave; others, however, using the white social-class system as the standard, refer to the highest level of the Negro social hierarchy as middle class. Because a Negro middle class has developed since the Civil War whose origins are in the former slave masses, the older upper-level group is here included as a variant type of upper class.

THE HISTORICAL FREE NEGRO

The historical Negro upper class had its origin in Negroes who were free prior to the Civil War. In the early years of the slave trade some Negroes were classified with indentured servants, who were freed after a certain period of service. A few Negroes were permitted by their masters to buy their freedom and later to buy their slave-wives and children. But apparently the largest proportion of free Negroes were former slaves who had been freed by their masters. Occasionally a slave owner would provide that at his death all his slaves should be freed. Other Negroes who were freed were the children of white masters whose mothers were the slaves of these same masters. These children were freed by their fathers, sometimes after receiving an education beyond any provided for slaves. The original group of such free Negroes were mulattoes, and by further intermarriage among themselves or at times through free unions with whites (primarily a mulatto girl and a white man), some of the free Negroes became light-skinned; only a few were pure-blood Negroes.

Two basic characteristics of the pre-Civil War upper class were the fact of freedom and some white ancestry. It was a matter of pride to have some white ancestry, especially if it could be traced to some prominent individual or family. These ancestral heritages of freedom and white ancestry are still prized among upper-class Negroes, although the upper class is less likely to be limited to this group than was true prior to the Civil War. As among white upper-upper-class families, their ancestry gives Negroes a sense of family continuity and pride.

The early upper-class Negroes did not represent any special occupational strata. Occupation was less important than ancestry. The variety of occupations represented by the old upper class is seen from the list for the upper class of Athens, Georgia, around 1900: five teachers, two physicians, three employees of the United States mail service, three barbers, two tailors, one bookkeeper, two carpenters, two shoemakers, two waiters, one editor, one real estate agent, two ministers, three black-smiths, one cook, one restaurant keeper, one farmer, and one plumber.[25]

THE NEGRO FAMILY

The unit of the old upper class was the marital family, in contrast to many slave families where the stable unit was the mother and her children and where the fathers were not in a position either to head or support a family.

The Negro family looked to the upper-class white family for its model. Husband and wife were legally married and did not follow the custom on many plantations of free unions among the slaves. The father was the patriarchal head of the family and maintained control over his children. An effort was made to own a home. In the rural areas, the home was a few acres of land. However, most upper-class Negroes lived in cities, and their aspiration was to own a small house. The organized family and home ownership gave stability to the family.

The upper-class Negroes held aloof from lower-class Negroes both before and after the Civil War. They often lived in or adjacent to white neighborhoods. Although they did not mingle socially with the whites, their behavior conformed to that of the neighborhood. Members of the old upper class formed their own social community, entertaining in their own homes and thus limiting their and their children's contacts to other upper-class families. Children tended to marry within the class.

CHILDREN IN THE OLD UPPER CLASS

Children attended schools operated by missionaries from the North. These schools sought not only to give an academic education but to inculcate moral values and the virtues of industriousness and thrift.

Parents impressed upon children that they should be courteous and restrained in behavior. They attempted to give their children the values of the whites which they had acquired while working in white homes.

OLD AND NEW UPPER-CLASS NEGRO FAMILIES

Even the better educated and more prosperous of the free Negroes of the pre-Civil War period were a far cry from being upper class by white standards, but they did have some of the attributes of the white upper class: pride of ancestry, a sense of family continuity, stable family life,

[25] *Ibid.*, p. 395, from a study by W. E. B. DuBois.

and, compared with lower strata of Negroes, freedom, economic independence, and better education.

After the Civil War and a long period of adjustment, the upper class received additional members, the descendants of slaves who had secured enough education and training to lift themselves above the level of the unskilled labor of the mass of Negroes. Entrance into the old upper class of Negroes called for more than income. The proper ancestry, stability of family life, and the training of children in the old virtues were necessary. The successful upwardly mobile Negroes often had some white ancestry and hence the lighter skin prized by the upper class. Husband and wife tended to remain together and often had some service contact with whites that gave them a model for the training of their children.

As industry developed in cities, in both the North and South, and later as machinery began to replace rural labor, Negroes crowded into the cities, forming an urban lower class but also opening to their children a greater opportunity for education, which some of them grasped. The old small urban upper class rejected and withdrew from the mass of Negroes whether they were in the lower class or upwardly mobile. They moved from old areas to the edge of the city and continued to teach their children the old values. They also often tried to protect their children from contacts with whites and to build up their own little society. Although this small segment continues to exist, it has been almost overwhelmed by a rapidly growing new middle class, called by one writer the "black bourgeoisie."[26]

Symbolic Importance of Upper-Class Families

Although the two white upper classes include a very small proportion of American families, they are extremely important. They have been and still are responsible for much of the industrial development of the country; they are the custodians of great wealth and determine how that wealth shall be used, whether for themselves individually or for the benefit of science, art, or community welfare through the establishment of foundations to subsidize research, creative effort, schools for the underprivileged, pensions for the old, and many other welfare projects. Although some of this wealth and a portion of the services are now in the process of transfer to governmental agencies, industrial leadership is still linked to families.

In another way, too, the upper classes are significant. They are a

[26]E. Franklin Frazier, *Black Bourgeoisie* (Glencoe, Ill.: Free Press, 1957).

symbol of accomplishment; their wealth and prestige are regarded as rewards for astuteness and industriousness. What these families have achieved in the past by individual effort, all ambitious individuals and families believe they can accomplish in the future: "there is always room at the top," "any boy can be President," "we are as good as they," are verbalizations of this belief. A sufficient number of families have been spectacularly successful to give credence to the belief that, though not all families could achieve similar success, any family has a chance. This belief has influenced the middle-class family in its choice of activities and especially in its goals of child training.

Although the Negro upper class has not attained economic equality with the white, nevertheless within the Negro social class system it has set a standard for accomplishment.

Questions

1. What are the characteristics of the upper-upper-class family?
2. How are children trained in the upper-class pattern?
3. How does the extended family group gain its power over individual family units?
4. In what ways is the upper-class child given security?
5. How does the lower-upper-class family differ from the upper-upper one?
6. What differences are there in the roles of children in the upper-upper- and the lower-upper-class families?
7. Evaluate the definition of the type of Negro described as upper class.

Bibliography

UPPER-CLASS FAMILY LIFE

ADAMS, JAMES TRUSLOW, *The Adams Family* (Boston: Little, Brown, 1930).

AMORY, CLEVELAND, *The Proper Bostonians* (New York: Dutton, 1947).

_____, *The Last Resorts* (New York: Harper, 1952).

BALTZELL, E. D., *Philadelphia Gentlemen: The Making of a National Upper Class* (Glencoe, Ill.: Free Press, 1958).

DAVIS, ALLISON, B. B. GARDNER, and M. R. GARDNER, *Deep South* (Chicago: University of Chicago Press, 1941).

Lundberg, Ferdinand, *America's 60 Families* (New York: Vanguard, 1937).

Saveth, Edward N., "The American Patrician Class: A Field of Research," *American Quarterly*, 15 (Summer Supplement, 1963), 235–52. Reprinted in Bernard Farber, editor, *Kinship and Family Organization* (New York: John Wiley and Sons., Inc., 1966).

Warner, W. Lloyd, and Paul S. Lunt, *Social Life in a Modern Community* (New Haven: Yale University Press, 1941).

NEGRO UPPER-CLASS FAMILY LIFE

Drake, St. Clair, and H. R. Cayton, *Black Metropolis* (New York: Harcourt, Brace, 1945).

Frazier, E. Franklin, *Negro Family in Chicago* (Chicago: University of Chicago Press, 1932).

_____, *Negro Family in the United States* (Chicago: University of Chicago Press, 1939).

_____, *Negro Youth at the Crossways* (Washington, D.C.: American Council on Education, 1940).

CHAPTER 6

Middle-Class Families

THE MIDDLE CLASS, like the upper class, has a unique subculture. Among some families, which in economic status, length of residence, and degree of influence edge near the lower-upper class, the family pattern consciously follows that of the upper class. Likewise, among middle-class families with low and insecure economic and social status, the family pattern may vary little from that of the lower class. But in general the middle class has developed its own subculture, deeply rooted in the family and supported by the church and public school. Although the middle class is a feeder for the upper classes, the small proportion of families (3 per cent) in the upper classes indicates that the upward mobility at the top is limited. Within the middle class itself, however, there is ample range for mobility from lower- to upper-middle. Nevertheless the entire class has certain unifying features, including a belief in the goodness of middle-class status that helps to prevent envy of the upper classes. The lower-middle class is more mobile, seeking to achieve upper-middle-class status and using many precautions not to slip downward. Thus, faith in the middle class is accompanied in the lower ranks by an uneasy fear of downward mobility.

The discussion treats the middle class as a unit, pointing out, however, any marked differences between upper-middle-class and lower-middle-class families. This procedure seems justified inasmuch as the upper-middle class has a firmly established subculture toward which the lower-middle class aspires. Lower-middle-class families seek to shake off attachments to lower-class ancestors and to identify with the middle class.

Characteristics of the Middle-Class Family

THE FAMILY'S PAST

Historical knowledge rarely extends over more than three generations, and if the family has been socially mobile or migratory, it may be limited to two generations. Absorbed with earning a living and without adequate academic education in the past to develop an interest in journals or diaries, middle-class families as a rule do not possess written records of past generations. Family portraits and valuable heirlooms are lacking. The past possessions of the family have been consumed with daily use or lack the beauty or pecuniary value of heirlooms. If the family has been upwardly mobile, the desire may have been to forget the past; all tangible articles have been sold, given away, or destroyed; sentimental attachments to the past, even the admission of knowing a foreign language native to the parents, are rejected. Family names may be changed slightly to rid them of foreign connotations, and reluctance may be shown to admit kinship with less mobile relatives. However, if the family has its roots in a status-giving European nationality (especially English), that may generate unusual interest in the past family history. Genealogies may be compiled in the effort to find a tie with a higher social class. The true middle-class family, however, is content with its independence, with its relative freedom from the past and from collateral kinship groups, and with the opportunity for upward mobility within the class.

CULTURAL UNITY

The cultural unity of the middle-class family in general is less marked than in the upper class. In cities that have grown through immigration, the middle class has a certain proportion of members whose parents or grandparents were European-born, thus creating diversity of religion, differing standards for family life, and differing conceptions of and interest in art, music, literature, and education. Threads of the ethnic patterns run through the general fabric of middle-class culture even when the family no longer consciously identifies itself with the ethnic group. In Yankee City, in contrast with the upper-upper class, which contained only families of old Yankee stock, the upper-middle class had 23 per cent of foreign-born or ethnic stock and the lower-middle

47 per cent.[1] Religious and associational affiliations follow the ethnic pattern to some extent.

The cultural differences are reflected in families, either through the social contacts with others of the same class but different ethnic or religious groups, or through intermarriage between the subcultural groups. Even when there is no family conflict, the culture transmitted by each family must be recognized as tending to have a dual aspect— partly middle-class and partly ethnic-religious.

ECONOMIC BASIS

Unlike the wealth of the upper class, the income of the middle class is only based to slight degree on inherited wealth and that only in the upper-middle class. The savings of the lower-middle-class family usually amount to only a few thousand dollars, sufficient to tide over the old-age period. Inherited by children, the amount when divided is negligible. If a business is inherited, usually it is small, and the active daily work of the heirs is necessary for continued operation. At the lowest end of the middle-class scale money is used as it is earned, often with almost no savings for old age.

Typical occupations for the upper-middle-class men are proprietorships of small businesses, the professions, and managerial positions in the large-scale business operations of the upper class. In the rural area the upper-middle-class farmer owns a large farm upon which he does some of the work but with the help of various hired hands whom he supervises. In the lower-middle class are found clerical, skilled, and semiskilled workers, artisan proprietors, and in the rural area men who operate their own farms without outside help or who are stable tenants.

Employment of women, rare in the upper classes, becomes apparent in the middle class. In the upper-middle class the adult daughters often work before their marriage, not from actual necessity, but because of the middle-class reverence for industriousness and thrift, and abhorrence of idleness. Young married women may also work in the first few years of marriage and middle-aged women after their children are married or in college. Young children are not expected to work. For boys, however, Saturday or vacation jobs are regarded as praiseworthy attempts to establish the much-prized middle-class independence.

Within the range of occupations reserved for the middle class, each young person is free to choose the one he wishes to enter. Preferably the son should select an occupation of somewhat higher status than

[1]W. Lloyd Warner and Paul S. Lunt, *The Social Life of a Modern Community* (New Haven: Yale University Press, 1941), pp. 422, 430–31, 435, 439.

that of the father, although some sons follow the father's occupation—a doctor's son may become a doctor; a businessman's son may plan to enter his father's business. But it is conceded that each child has the right to select his own vocation. How high in the occupational scale a boy may enter and how far he may move upward are influenced both by the position his father holds and by his own education and achievement.[2]

RESIDENTIAL STABILITY

The middle-class family is freer to move its place of residence than the upper-class family, for it is not held in one place by the location of family property or family industry. Since each married couple starts life independently, they are free to remain in the city where their parents live, or to leave it. Even if they remain in the city of their childhood, they typically make several moves during the period of their married life. Each young couple, with some aid from parents, establishes itself and depends upon its own resources, which often are small during the early years of married life. The parents may live in a suburban district; but they may have started married life in a two-room furnished apartment. It is thought appropriate that their children, in turn, begin married life in a small and relatively inexpensive apartment, moving from one residential area to a better one as their resources increase until they also are able to live in the suburb. Middle-class children are not expected to begin married life "where the parents left off"; not only each generation but each child must prove its worth and establish itself anew in the middle-class status.

MARRIAGE

Marriage occurs within the subclass (or an adjacent class) at a slightly lower age than in the upper classes. Within the class, the range of choice is wider than in the upper classes. Middle-class children attend public schools, where they meet children from all ranges of the middle class and the lower classes as well as such upper-class children as do not attend private schools. The number of middle-class children, also, is much greater than the number of upper-class children, thus providing a more numerous group from which to choose. By the time dating begins, differentiation into class groups has been fairly well established.

[2]Cavan, Ruth Shonle, "Subcultural Variations and Mobility," in Harold T. Christensen, ed., *Handbook of Marriage and the Family* (Chicago: Rand McNally, 1964), ch. 14.

SOCIAL CLASS

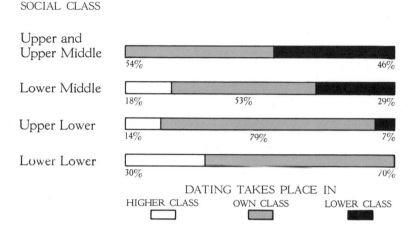

FIGURE 4   *Dating and Social Class.*

In Elmtown (7,000 population), most teenagers dated with members of their own social class. Previous friendships, control by parents, available spending money, and degree of familiarity with social-class customs are all factors in restricting dating to one's own social class. Dating activities also differ by social class, varying from the formal dances limited to country club members, through public school parties open to all pupils, to informal Coke dates, and finally to the tavern and automobile of the lower-lower-class youth.

SOURCE: A. B. Hollingshead, *Elmtown's Youth* (New York: Wiley, 1949), pp. 197–98.

Some upper-class children have been sent to private secondary schools as preparation for both college and later class position; some lower-class children have dropped out of school. In the remaining public school group, primarily middle-class, many cliques form, identifying the various gradations in social status. These cliques solidify during the three or four years of high school, with dating becoming more and more confined to the members in a given clique. Although the cliques are formed primarily on the basis of class lines, they are not formed for middle-class children on the basis of parental friendships. The boys and girls in a given clique may all be upper-middle class, but their parents may be unknown to each other or know each other only by name, unless the community is a small one. For those who attend college, the high school cliques tend to weaken, and new cliques, also largely class delimited, form in college. Again, after college, other cliques may form, as college graduates scatter to new communities, or there may be a reforming of the old cliques if they return to the home community. As young people tend to shift from dating to courtship, choices are made within the cliques—therefore within the social class—but without specific reference to parental choice or supervision. The courtship may be well advanced before the parents of the couple meet each other, a situation especially true when the young person is living in a different community from that in which the parents live. Thus there is great freedom of choice of marital partner in the middle class. Parental pressure is informal and personal; there can be no threat of disinheritance or refusal to accept the spouse into the kinship group as may occur in the upper class. The only penalty can be hurt feelings and displeasure—not too effective in a class where each marriage marks the beginning of an independent family and where the young couple are free to move to a distant community if they wish.[3]

NUCLEAR FAMILY ORGANIZATION

The middle-class family unit is the nuclear family composed of husband, wife, unmarried adult children still living at home, and minor children. The family begins with the marriage of a man and woman and ends with the death of husband and wife or sometimes with the death of one and the envelopment of the other by the family of a married son or daughter.

The family tends to be paternal (although scarcely patriarchal) in type with a trend toward an equal partnership in many areas. The husband is the economic head of the family. Usually he is the sole wage earner during the years when children are minors and often throughout the lifetime of the family. Even when other members of the family are employed, the husband typically earns by far the largest amount and is regarded as the producer of stable and dependable income. His wife and his daughter may work if they wish, but are under no compulsion to do so; consequently, they may also stop working at will, whereas it is contrary to all middle-class expectations that the husband should stop working. In the family circle, also, the husband is regarded as the head of the family, and major decisions in all except purely domestic matters are referred to him; or, in case of a family council, the final or the weighty vote comes from the husband. Nevertheless, his headship is benevolent. He is deeply concerned for the welfare and happiness of his family and hence is swayed by their opinions and their reactions to him. His decision, therefore, often is a nominal one, being merely the vocal expression of the joint opinion of the family.[4]

[3]For a detailed discussion of dating, see Chapter 13.
[4]Robert O. Blood and Donald M. Wolfe, *Husbands and Wives: The Dynamics of Married Living* (New York: Free Press, 1960).

SOCIAL CLASS	YANKEE CITY, MEDIAN AGE	ELMTOWN, USUAL AGE	
		BRIDE	GROOM
Upper Upper	27.9		
Lower Upper	26.6	Mid-Twenties	Mid-Twenties
Upper Middle	26.1		
Lower Middle	25.1	Early Twenties	Early Twenties
Upper Lower	24.4	Late Teens	Early Twenties
Lower Lower	23.2	Mid-Teens	Very Early Twenties

FIGURE 5   *Age of Marriage by Social Class.*

In Yankee City the average ages of marriage of upper-upper- and lower-lower-class people differed by almost five years. In Elmtown all classes tended to marry younger than corresponding groups in Yankee City. The early age of marriage in the lower classes is related to less emphasis on education and the early economic establishment of the men. These young people marry with less formal preparation than do those of the higher class levels. Often, however, they have gained early independence and are more aware of the problems of family life than the more closely supervised and protected youth of the upper social classes. The period of childbearing is longer, and the first child may be born while the mother is little more than a girl.

SOURCE: W. Lloyd Warner and Paul S. Lunt, *Social Life of a Modern Community* (New Haven: Yale University Press, 1941), p. 255; A. B. Hollingshead, "Selected Characteristics of Classes in a Middle Western Community," *American Sociological Review*, 12 (1947), 388, 390, 392, and 394.

Functionally, husband and wife have differentiated but strongly interlocking roles. The husband, in addition to being the chief income producer, has many duties about the home, a situation seen most clearly in the smaller city or suburb where families live in individual homes without the janitorial services found in large-city apartment buildings. He often performs such tasks as mowing the lawn, making repairs, and painting the house inside and out. At the lower end of the scale, where manual skills are part of the equipment of the male members of the family, the family may build its own house from floor to chimney.

The wife has a triple role: as wife and mother, as housekeeper, and as social arbiter. The maternal aspect of her interpersonal role tends to supersede the wifely aspect—a reversal of the situation in the upper-upper class. Only during the first childless years of marriage do husband and wife place the sexual and social phases of their own relationship above the demands and welfare of their children. The husband's interest in his home and children makes it possible for the wife to become more mother than wife during the years of her children's minority.

The middle-class wife is not only the manager of her home but its actual keeper, especially in regions where inexpensive domestic help is lacking. At the upper range of middle class, she may possibly have a full-time maid, but she more usually has a laundress or a "cleaning woman" who comes in one or two days a week or a schoolboy on Saturday to do rough work. In the lower-middle-class range, even such part-time assistance is unknown. Since the wife expends much time and energy on her home and carries out many of her own ideas of decoration and ornamentation in it, it becomes an extension of her personality. She receives much satisfaction from praise of her home from other women. The home, together with its furnishings, therefore becomes something to be preserved and cared for rather than something for the use and comfort of the family. She therefore makes many restrictions regarding the use of the home by her family. The children may play only in certain rooms (their bedrooms, the kitchen, the "family" room).[5] No one may put his feet on a chair or couch; cigarette ashes may not accidentally fall on the rug; chair arms or table tops must not be marred by wet glass rings or hot cigarette butts. Violation of these wife-made rules is an affront to the wife herself, an attack on her ego.

The social activities of the family rest largely in the hands of the wife. "My wife keeps the social calendar" is the stock reply of one husband when any question arises of social activity outside the family. This manipulation of social participation relates not only to husband-wife activities but to those of the children as well and over as long a period as the mother is able to exert control over her children. The middle-class woman tends to be very conscious of social position and exerts a deliberate effort to preserve or improve the position of the family. She passes judgment on invitations and feels free to accept or reject them in terms of their value to the family status, her husband's business opportunities, or the children's future. She also makes the list of guests invited to her home, with the husband perhaps having a veto power. She guides her children's choice of friends by all methods from subtle insinuations that a certain child is undesirable, through direct

[5]From one period to another, the everyday living space of a family and especially of children shifts from one part of the house to another and is called by different names. In the days of stove heat, when the cellar was chiefly a cold room for the storage of food, everyday living went on in the large kitchen. With central heating, a basement "rec" or rumpus room became popular. With the single-level houses of the 1950's came the family room, with a separate living room replacing the one-time parlor.

SOCIAL CLASS

Upper Upper — 52% | 48%

Lower Upper — 8% | 52% | 40%

Upper Middle — 13% | 38% | 49%

Lower Middle — 9% | 39% | 52%

Upper Lower — 13% | 65% | 22%

Lower Lower — 37% | 63%

MARRIAGE TAKES PLACE IN

HIGHER CLASS   OWN CLASS   LOWER CLASS

FIGURE 6   *Marriage and Social Class, New Haven.*

Although the tendency is strong for men to select wives from their own social class, another tendency also appears—marriage with women of less social status than their own. Only the lower-lower class does not exhibit this trend. Generally out-class marriages are between those of adjacent class status, rags to riches marriages being both unusual and socially disapproved. Marriages decline in formality and social control as social-class level declines. In the higher social classes, not only the family and kinship group tend to control the choice of mate, but the entire social class is interested in the preservation of class lines. In the middle ranks marriage tends to be a family affair only, whereas in the lower classes marriage is treated as an individual concern of the man and woman alone.

SOURCE: A. B. Hollingshead, "Cultural Factors in the Selection of Marriage Mates," *American Sociological Review,* 15 (1950), Table 4, p. 625.

statements that one child is "dirty" and another child "good fun," to outright forbidding of certain contacts and deliberate inclusion of her child in desirable groups.

Special attention has been given by some writers to the wife of the business executive, who is typically upper-middle class.[6] Her social role

[6]William H. Whyte, Jr., "The Wives of Management," *Fortune,* 44 (October, 1951), 86–88ff.; "The Corporation and the Wife," *Fortune,* 44 (November, 1951), 109–11ff.; and *Is Anybody Listening?* (New York: Simon and Schuster, 1952), ch. 8, "The Wives of Management". See also Margaret L. Helfrich, "The Generalized Role of the Executive's Wife," *Marriage and Family Living,* 23 (1961), 384–87.

has been described as subordinate to her husband's business role, but closely related to it and to her husband's success. Without intruding into his business surroundings, she tends to give him personal support and encouragement; in social activities she fits herself into the business hierarchy, not trying to force herself into association with wives of a higher level but preparing herself to move upward with each promotion of her husband. One book sums up the role of the upper-middle-class wife in these words:

> The wife considers herself more responsible for the husband's work performance and success [than in the working class]. She must be understanding and helpful when he has problems there and she must do a good job of representing him socially to work associates, clients, the boss, when that is necessary. For herself, the middle class wife often finds some knowledge of her husband's job intellectually stimulating, it helps her avoid being "just a housewife."[7]

Her community activities often extend beyond the purely social role, especially as her children mature and leave her with free time. Middle-class wives form the bulwark of the boards, committees, and volunteer groups that "run" civic and community ventures. The origin and successful operation of many welfare groups, children's agencies, recreational programs, homes for old people and the like have rested in the hands of some small group of persistent middle-class women who have brought their husbands and other men into the picture for financial and legal aid but have never relinquished their essential control of the projects.

Kinship Web

Middle-class nuclear families are bound into a loose but reciprocally functioning kinship web. So widespread is the range of types of aid that the ideal of the autonomous middle-class family is somewhat weakened by the reality of financial aid and social support given, especially between parents and children. A Cleveland study of 53 lower-middle-class families may be considered as typical for this social class.[8] All the families were voluntarily involved in a network of giving and receiving aid. Within a one-month period, all gave or received at least one of the following types of aid: help during illness, financial aid, caring for chil-

[7]Lee Rainwater, Richard P. Coleman, and Gerald Handel, *Workingman's Wife* (Dobbs Ferry, N.Y.: Oceana Publications, 1959), p. 87.

[8]Marvin B. Sussman, "The Isolated Nuclear Family: Fact or Fiction," *Social Problems*, 7 (Spring, 1959), 333–40.

dren, advice, and valuable gifts. The items are listed according to frequency, from 76 per cent of the families giving or receiving aid in illness to 22 per cent giving or receiving valuable gifts, in decreasing order.

Social relationships are also common between parents and married children in the lower-middle class. Weekly visits were common. In addition, 81 per cent of the families held large family gatherings at least once a year to celebrate some holiday or anniversary.

Interestingly, in attitude studies, both young and middle-aged married couples contend that they do not wish to receive aid from parents or children respectively. However, the reality is that aid and services flow both ways, increasing or decreasing with need, but apparently not blotting out the efforts of each nuclear family to maintain itself and practice independence.

Middle-Class Children

The middle-class family has more children than upper-class but fewer than lower-class families. In the middle-class family the children "belong" to both parents, in contrast to the upper class where they belong to the kinship and are important as links in the historical family. The family unit for the child consists of his parents, himself, and his brothers and sisters. Next in importance are the grandparents, especially if they live in the same community and are seen often or if the children are left in the care of the grandparents when their parents go to some social affair or away on a vacation. The tie to uncles, aunts, and cousins is less marked, and these relatives may be almost unknown if they live at a distance and are not visited. It is not uncommon for the middle-class child not to know the names of even first cousins if personal contacts have been allowed to lapse. This narrowing of the family circle to parents and children—and perhaps grandparents—restricts emotional ties to a small group and consequently tends to intensify them. The fact that children are relatively few in number and that the parents and especially the mother assumes personal care of the children also adds to the intensity. Children often are taken by the parents on all vacation trips, and it is not unusual for the child never to have spent a night separated from the parents from infancy to the time of college entrance or marriage. If the emotional relationship, as is usual, is one of love and dependence, the bond is very strong. Conversely, if the family relationships breed resentment, anger, and a feeling of frustration, these emotions also are strong. Unless the kinship circle is close, neither child nor parent has a wide circle of less immediate family members from which to seek substitute satisfaction or upon whom to vent resentments. Emotional satisfactions come from a small group, and emotional reactions, whether affectional or hostile, find their outlet within the nuclear family or close kinship circle.

Although there is no modified extended family (as in the upper class) to converge on the child with family ambitions, the parents and perhaps grandparents project on him their own ambitions. The situation may become more intense than in the large family grouping of the upper class, where, if one child fails, another—a cousin, perhaps—is available to carry on for the kinship. In the small family there may be only one son or one daughter to satisfy family expectations or to carry out the unfulfilled ambitions of their parents.

The middle-class child is expected to fulfill not only family ambitions but also the social-class ambitions of his parents. If they are firmly fixed in the middle class, he must see that he maintains their standard and does not slip downward. The child of upper-middle-class parents must not permit himself to become lower-middle class, and the child of the lower-middle class must not disgrace his family by slipping down into the lower class. And in many families, the child is expected to achieve greater success than did his parents, the son through entering a more highly preferred occupation, the daughter by marriage above her parents' social class. Certain anxiety is established in the child by his parents' great need that he should bring credit to them. He is exhorted by his parents, not only to get as good grades in school as his father did, but also to equal or surpass the children of middle-class neighbors. The boy must secure the quota of school honors, the type of job, and the amount of salary thought suitable to a middle-class child.

A study of successful middle-class men in a Boston suburb showed that they wished their sons to enter occupations of the level that the fathers then held—not of a lower level where the fathers may have started their careers.[9] They wished their sons to have the traits that they believed had made them successful: responsibleness, initiative, competence, aggressiveness, and the capacity to meet competition. They should be emotionally stable and capable of self-restraint.

These fathers felt less concern about their daughters. College seemed less important than personal qualities of goodness and sweetness. In general, the middle-class girl is expected to maintain the standard of dress, the fastidiousness of appearance, and the type of dating partner

[9]David F. Aberle and Kasper D. Naegele, "Middle Class Fathers' Occupational Role and Attitudes toward Children," *American Journal of Orthopsychiatry*, 22 (April, 1952), 366–78.

that other middle-class girls achieve. Her ultimate goal is marriage; her principal future roles, wife and mother.

Middle-class parents are self-consciously parents and follow the dictates of "scientific child care." They strive to be intellectual about their parenthood, reading special magazines and articles in newspapers and women's magazines written for parents by educators, physicians, and child psychologists. They compose child-study groups, listening to specialists in child training; and they are the bulwark of the Parent-Teacher Associations. Where preschool nurseries are available, they patronize them in order to give their children proper social contacts under trained supervision. They attempt not only to follow what the specialist tells them is the correct way to feed or train their children, but also to understand some of the theories that underlie the advice. Thus, they often attempt to curb their natural impulses to love and caress or to mete out swift punishment, in order to conform to the current theories of child training. In the upwardly mobile lower-middle class, the ethnic characteristics of older family members may cause the young parents to mistrust advice from the older generation. They seek to reject the past, to grasp a better future.

In general, the middle class distrusts natural impulses, and the family early imposes upon children many repressive, regulative, and ritualistic routines. The middle-class child is taught by his parents not to fight, or at most to fight only defensively. He is also taught not to annoy people, not to run over lawns or destroy flower beds, not to "swipe" fruit from orchards or back yards, not to "snitch" fruit in the grocery store, not to sneak into the movies without paying, and so on. All these activities, which employ physical and mental alertness and which give the satisfaction of victory over an opponent, are denied the middle-class child. He has certain substitutes in the nature of organized sports, playgrounds, play equipment at home, camping trips, and youth organizations, but always under adult supervision and within middle-class restrictive mores.[10]

Another traditional prohibition imposed on middle-class children forbids an open expression of interest in sex. With larger homes and the privacy of separate bedrooms for parents, the middle-class child rarely sees sexual activities by accident, as the lower-class child may do. His restricted social activities, especially in the evenings, and the middle-class refusal to tolerate houses of prostitution or looseness of behavior in their communities, further protect the child. Middle-class parents also are inhibited by their own early training from freely discussing matters of sex with their children. When they do give "sex education,"

[10]For a discussion of a developmental, permissive approach to child training, see Chapter 19.

it is often limited to biological facts and does not relate sex to the child's physical or emotional impulses. Thus the child is thrown back into his ignorance or projected into a state of anxiety. He seeks and finds information from slightly older children in his own group or from secretively talking with or observing lower-class children whose avenues of gaining knowledge and sexual experimentation are wider. The current trend of middle-class teenagers and youth is to break out of this repressive mold and to establish their own policies and practices of sex behavior.

The impressing of habits and attitudes upon a child takes place primarily through the application of penalties and rewards. These may be physical in nature, such as a slap or a stick of candy; or psychological, such as scolding or praise; or social, such as being isolated in a closet or being allowed to accompany the parents to a picnic. The relative frequency of penalties or rewards and the types used vary from one social class to another. In general, the middle-class parent tends to use rewards more than penalties; he especially uses physical penalties sparingly but may employ physical rewards. Psychological and social penalties and rewards are both used. They are longer lasting and often more devastating to the personality than physically painful but quickly ended punishments. The middle-class parent, by shaming the child, telling him the parent will not love him if he continues his disobedience, or shutting him in a room and thus refusing to associate with him, makes an attack on the child's personality and the child's conception of himself. The experience makes a rift, however small, in the emotional relationship of the child with the parent and arouses fear and anxiety that the parent will not love and protect him, and give him security.[11]

The effect of middle-class training on the future personality of the child has been debated since the 1940's, when dire predictions of neuroticism were freely made. Repetition in the 1950's of studies of the 1940's shows a reduction of repressive measures in child training, due perhaps to the cult of "permissiveness" of the later period.[12] Studies of the 1940's led to a widely quoted hypothesis that the middle-class male child was doomed to neuroticism because of the stress placed on competitiveness and certain conflicts between masculine and feminine attitudes in his upbringing.[13] However, a study published in 1958, based on a factor analysis of personality test items, showed

[11]W. Allison Davis and Robert J. Havighurst, *Father of the Man* (Boston: Houghton Mifflin, 1947).

[12]Martha Sturm White, "Social Class, Child Rearing Practices, and Child Behavior," *American Sociological Review*, 22 (1957), 704–12, discusses studies of the two periods.

[13]A. W. Green, "The Middle Class Male Child and Neurosis," *American Sociological Review*, 11 (1946), 31–41.

that lower-class children exhibited markedly more neuroticism than middle-class children.[14] The neurotic factors were concern over status, concern over achievement, rejection of family, and nervous symptoms. The authors attribute the difficulty primarily to contrasts between the lower-class values as taught at home and the middle-class values of which the child becomes conscious when he widens his contacts in school and the community.

Many of the rules of behavior and training laid down for middle-class children are compulsive and ritualistic in nature. They tend to become "right" in themselves. Rituals with attitudinal content that tend to establish principles are less used. The middle-class family does not have sufficient family history nor deep enough kinship connections to have many traditional rituals from past generations. Upwardly mobile parents, perceiving the use of rituals by upper-class families, may somewhat self-consciously impose rituals upon themselves and their children. Previous informal methods may be discarded in favor of formal methods that may not fit well into the total family pattern. After-dinner coffee in the living room may convey satisfaction to the family that a step upward has been gained, but may be at variance with breakfast in serial order in the kitchen as each member of the family snatches a bite to eat on the way to work or school at different hours of the morning. If not all members of the family accept the value of such rituals, they may become divisive rather than cohesive in the family life.

The Upper-Middle-Class Parvenu

The group termed "parvenu" by Hodges is in transition between lower- and upper-middle class.[15] A study of a California metropolitan community distinguished between a stable or core upper-middle class and an upwardly mobile or parvenu class that identified itself with the upper-middle class but lacked many of its essential qualities; although the study is not specifically centered on family life, many qualities of family life can be inferred from the discussion.

The two groups had many overlapping qualities, as one would ex-

[14]William H. Sewell and A. O. Haller, "Factors in the Relationship between Social Status and the Personality Adjustment of the Child," *American Sociological Review*, 24 (1959), 511–20.

[15]Harold M. Hodges, San Jose State College, "Is the Upper-Middle Class Really Two—a Proposal," mimeographed.

pect; nevertheless, there were distinct differences. The core class had two or more generations at the upper-middle-class level, the parvenu class was first generation: the first "inherited" its position, the second "acquired" it by its own efforts. It follows, therefore, that the core class had consolidated its position both as to status and class qualifications; the parvenu was marginal to core qualifications and retained many characteristics of the lower-middle and/or rural background from which it came. Core males more often were in the older professions of medicine, law, architecture, college teaching, or the ministry; parvenus tended more often to be in newer occupations, such as engineering, or in occupations of somewhat lower prestige, such as dentistry, high school teaching, or business. The median incomes of the two groups in 1958–60 were $15,300 and $8,900. The parvenus spent a higher proportion of their income on housing and furniture—and more often bought on the installment plan—in an apparent effort to exhibit status symbols of the core middle class.

The style of life of the parvenus resembled their rural or village origin as well as their lower-middle-class background. For leisure they favored popular television programs, gardening, do-it-yourself projects, and popular types of reading; in contrast, the core upper-middles favored artistic and intellectual pursuits (ballet, concerts, theater); they read more and preferred "intellectual" magazines. In general, they were more urbane and sophisticated than the parvenu class. More than any other class in the area studied, the parvenus valued success, striving, hard work, frugality, and saving. The parvenu believed that these and similar characteristics accounted for success, including his own. These were qualities that he wished to instill in his children, and he felt more than the father in any other class level that a father should encourage his son to climb higher, socially and occupationally, than the father had done.

Both parents subscribed strongly to moralistic values and advocated avoidance of swearing, flirtation, illicit sex affairs, heavy drinking, "fast living," and heavy smoking. The women were especially moralistic in their attitudes and felt that strict and often ritualistic moral behavior should be demanded even of preschool children.

The family ideal was thought of as organized around the father as the authority, with children giving unquestioning obedience.

Hodges concludes that the parvenus had effectively, though not completely, bridged the gap in education and occupational status between the lower-middle and the upper-middle classes. But they had not been able to achieve status mobility as signified by attitudes and life style.

They had not achieved total assimilation into the core upper-middle class, although they had pulled away to a certain extent from their childhood status and teachings. They were in a marginal or in-between position. There was evidence that they felt insecure, frustrated, and (therefore) aggressive.

One may only speculate about the effect of this social background on the position of children of the parvenu. With care on the part of their parents in choice of schools and summer camps and with instillation of the ambition to rise above their parents' position, some at least will move into the core middle class. But some almost inevitably will fail and perhaps sink back to a lower level. It is also possible that others will accept the position midway between lower- and upper-middle class and establish new values to justify that position.

The Black Bourgeoisie[16]

In the social-class structure of Negroes prior to and immediately following the Civil War few families were middle class. The great mass of Negroes were lower class; a small elite group formed an upper class. The middle class was slow to form, since it had to wait until a group with education and occupational training emerged from the newly freed slave population. When such a segment of Negroes developed they were not welcomed by the old upper class. They often were darker in skin color and lacked the claim to white ancestry and long-time status as free Negroes. Only with tremendous effort and individual success could the upwardly mobile Negroes gain acceptance into the old upper class.

The upwardly mobile Negroes also found it difficult to meet the family standards of the upper class. The family first of the slaves and later of lower-class Negroes tended to be organized around the mother or grandmother, whereas the upper class had a patriarchal type of family organization. In the lower class, men came and went, and often the unions, even when stable, rested on common-law marriage, which was accepted in the lower class but scorned by the upper class. Lower-class children also were unrestrained in behavior, and the family lacked the tradition and the skills needed to train children into an upper-class pattern or into the white middle-class pattern.

A great impetus was given to the formation of a middle class as

[16]Based primarily on E. Franklin Frazier, *Black Bourgeoisie* (New York: Free Press, 1957).

Negroes left the farms and moved into cities and especially into northern industrial cities, where opportunities for work more often brought an adequate income and where children had the same type of education as white children, often in the same classrooms. The migration to the North swelled around the time of World War I and left an enlarged permanent population of Negroes in northern cities. The present adult Negro population includes many people reared in the North, who are in a position to pass on to their children some of the values and customs of the American middle class they learned during their childhood.

The scheme of values of the upwardly mobile group differed greatly from that of the old upper class. Education, type of occupation (business or professional), and financial success became the keys to upward mobility. Some of the more successful married into the upper class, perhaps raising the financial rating of an upper-class family in return for a wife with light skin. Others bypassed the upper class and formed an ambitious and relatively prosperous middle class. The earlier members of this middle class climbed the status ladder slowly, learning the values and customs of the middle class gradually. But with the rapid growth of prosperity after World War II, many people seemed ready for middle-class status financially but without the support of middle-class values and customs.

Material symbols of success tended to outweigh the staunch character and virtues of industriousness and thrift of the older middle and upper classes. An interest in literature, cultural education, and art has been replaced by an exaggerated interest in status symbols and elaborate entertainment, beyond the reasonable ability of the middle-class person to pay for on a normal income. As a result, professional men may lower the quality of their services in order to have time also for some more lucrative form of business. One writer speaks of physicians who sell drugs and of businessmen who are affiliated with the numbers game, a form of gambling popular among lower-class Negroes and very profitable for those who operate the game.

Children are reared in this artificial atmosphere. In many Negro colleges, the chief aim of many students seems to be to establish status through an expensive make of car and elaborate social functions, rather than to secure a cultural education. Choice of a profession or occupation is motivated by the social status attached to it or the amount of income it will bring, rather than by an ideal of service or the opportunity to contribute to literature, art, science, or public life.

Adults in the new middle class do not follow or teach their children the old virtues of the upper class (really staunch middle-class virtues).

Frazier has stated that the older family values called for stability of marriage and conventional sex behavior, but that in the new middle class, divorces and scandals do not affect the person's social status; in fact, the attendant notoriety may enhance prestige. He attributes the change to the fact that many members of the new middle class have risen so rapidly from the lower class that they have not had time to acquire middle-class values. Added to this mobile group that has come up through education and occupation are actors and entertainers who exercise great influence because of personal glamor and financial success and who help to create an artificial social world for their followers and admirers. Moreover, successful underworld Negroes, whose income is derived from gambling, prostitution, the policy game, and other illegal occupations, have been accepted into the middle class.[17] With incomes greater than those of most middle-class Negroes, they tend to dominate the class whose values are based on conspicuous spending and glamorous show.

Frazier attributes the present situation to other factors in addition to the prosperity of the present and the rapid upward mobility. The history of the Negroes in the United States has tended to give them a deep feeling of inferiority that education and genuine success in professions and the arts has not erased in the face of continued rejection by whites. The quest for status and recognition has seemed to fail. The members of the old upper and middle classes tended to withdraw from the struggle for white recognition and to isolate themselves within their own social world. The new, more prosperous middle class has sought compensations in the things that money will buy. They have tried to copy what they can see of the life of upper-middle- and upper-class whites—often showy aspects of the white *nouveau riche* class. Frazier says they are trying to escape into a world of make-believe, supported by myths of a firm economic business base that the Negro community does not really possess and by exaggerated reports in Negro newspapers of social and professional success.

Children are reared within this world of make-believe as parents attempt to shield them from contacts with whites. Sometimes the words "Negro" or "colored" are never used before the children, and they may never be permitted to learn that there are restaurants or stores where they may not enter without risk of insult. Sometimes the children are sent to all-Negro private schools. Southern Negro families, on the other hand, may send their children to predominantly white northern schools where Negro students may be enrolled. However, if there are not

[17]St. Clair Drake and Horace R. Cayton, *Black Metropolis* (New York: Harcourt, Brace, 1945).

enough to form their own social group, the few Negro students may be almost completely excluded from the informal social life, even though they have equal opportunities in the more formal activities of the school or college. Negro parents differ markedly as to whether they think it is advisable to shield their children and in a sense condemn them to life within a segregated social group, or to expose them to the realities of the situation early and teach them to adjust to the hard fact of exclusion from full participation in white groups and to some extent in the full cultural wealth of the country.

In either case, Negro parents are devoted to their children, which results in their being somewhat spoiled and over-indulged. Frazier suggests that parents, through their sincere devotion to their children, may seek compensation for their sense of frustration and the artificiality of their make-believe world. Over-indulgence of children is often directed toward trying to better their chances of penetrating into areas of participation that the parents could not penetrate.[18]

Middle-Class Families as the Balance Wheel

Middle-class families form a balance wheel between the small but financially powerful upper-class families and the laboring strength of the lower-class families. Although they include fewer people than lower-class families, their dominance in the professions places them in a position of leadership not only within their own group but in the lower class. Schoolteachers, who are primarily middle class, teach the children of lower-class families. Social workers, also primarily middle class, guide the destinies of lower-class families in times of stress. Related to the quality of this leadership is the degree of adjustment made by lower-class families to their problems. Children are greatly affected by the attitudes of their middle-class teachers toward them. Thus, the influence of the middle class spreads out to affect lower-class families and children.

Middle-class families, being more mobile than upper-class families, are more subject to the tensions of mobility. They are less subject, however, than lower-class mobile families because they are usually better prepared for the move, less likely to move without some definite prospect of work, and better able financially to tide over a period of lowered income.

Of the three class levels, middle-class families are most involved in

[18]Frazier, *op. cit.*, pp. 223–24.

the issues of family life occasioned by social changes (discussed in Chapter 2). The middle position, with the possibility of upward and the threat of downward mobility, makes the middle class very conscious of social values and also very conservative. Moral injunctions are placed upon children early in life, and rigid standards are set for them. Those who deviate (the career wife, the one-child family, the divorced couple, and so on) often feel emotionally guilty even though intellectually justified in their position.

Questions

1. Discuss the attitudes of middle-class families toward family histories.
2. In a given community why do middle-class families usually have less cultural unity than upper-class families?
3. What roles does the middle-class wife play?
4. What factors contribute to the intensity of emotional relationships between the middle-class mother and her children?
5. Why does the middle-class mother depend heavily upon specialists to guide her in childrearing?
6. Discuss the position of the upper-middle-class parvenu as midway between their earlier class position and the core middle class.
7. How does the new black bourgeoisie differ from the "old" upper-middle- and upper-class Negro?
8. How does Frazier explain the difficulties of the black bourgeoisie in attaining upper-middle-class values?

Bibliography

MIDDLE-CLASS FAMILY LIFE

BLOOD, ROBERT O., and DONALD M. WOLFE, *Husbands and Wives: The Dynamics of Married Living* (New York: Free Press, 1960).

CLARK, LINCOLN H., ed., *Consumer Behavior* (New York: New York University, 1955), Vol. 2, "Careers and Consumer Behavior," pp. 1–18, by David Riesman and Howard Roseborough.

DAVIS, ALLISON, B. B. GARDNER, and M. R. GARDNER, *Deep South* (Chicago: University of Chicago Press, 1941), ch. 5

HOLLINGSHEAD, A. B., "Class Differences in Family Stability," *The Annals of the American Academy of Political and Social Science*, 272 (1950), 39–46.

———, "Selected Characteristics of Classes in a Middle Western Community," *American Sociological Review,* 12 (1947), 385–95.

KOOS, E. L., "Class Differences in Family Reactions to Crisis," *Marriage and Family Living,* 12 (1950), 77–78, 99.

———, "Middle-Class Family Crises," *Marriage and Family Living,* 10 (1948), 25, 40.

RAINWATER, LEE, RICHARD P. COLEMAN, and GERALD HANDEL, *Workingman's Wife: Her Personality, World and Life Style* (Dobbs Ferry, N.Y.: Oceana Publications, 1959).

SEELEY, JOHN R., R. A. SIM, and ELIZABETH W. LOOSLEY, *Crestwood Heights: A Study of Suburban Life* (New York: Basic Books, 1960), ch. 7, "The Family."

SUSSMAN, MARVIN B., "The Isolated Nuclear Family: Fact or Fiction," *Social Problems,* 7 (Spring, 1959), 333–40.

WHYTE, WILLIAM H., Jr., "The Corporation and the Wife," *Fortune,* 44 (November, 1951), 109–11ff.

———, *Is Anybody Listening?* (New York: Simon and Schuster, 1952), ch. 8.

———, "The Wives of Management," *Fortune,* 44 (October, 1951), 86–88ff.

CHILDREN AND ADOLESCENTS IN THE MIDDLE CLASS

DAVIS, ALLISON, *Social-Class Influence upon Learning* (Cambridge: Harvard University Press, 1949).

———, and R. J. HAVIGHURST, "Social Class and Color Differences in Child-Rearing," *American Sociological Review,* 11 (1946), 698–710.

GREEN, A. W., "The Middle Class Male Child and Neurosis," *American Sociological Review,* 11 (1946), 31–41.

HOLLINGSHEAD, AUGUST B., *Elmtown's Youth* (New York: Wiley, 1949).

NEUGARTEN, B., "Social Class and Friendship among School Children," *American Journal of Sociology,* 51 (1946), 305–14.

SEWELL, WILLIAM H., and A. O. HALLER, "Factors in the Relationship between Social Status and the Personality Adjustment of the Child," *American Sociological Review,* 24 (1959), 511–20.

WHITE, MARTHA STURM, "Social Class, Child Rearing Practices, and Child Behavior," *American Sociological Review,* 22 (1957), 704–12.

NEGRO MIDDLE-CLASS FAMILY LIFE

BERNARD, JESSIE, *Marriage and Family among Negroes* (Englewood Cliffs, N.J.: Prentice-Hall, 1966).

DAVIS, ALLISON, B. B. GARDNER, and M. R. GARDNER, *Deep South* (Chicago: University of Chicago Press, 1941).

DRAKE, ST. CLAIR, and H. R. CAYTON, *Black Metropolis* (New York: Harcourt, Brace, 1945).

FRAZIER, E. FRANKLIN, *Black Bourgeoisie* (New York: Free Press, 1957).

———, *Negro Family in Chicago* (Chicago: University of Chicago Press, 1932).

———, *Negro Family in the United States* (Chicago: University of Chicago Press, 1939), ch. 20.

———, "Negro Middle Class and Desegregation," *Social Problems,* 4 (April, 1957), 291–301.

———, *Negro Youth at the Crossways* (Washington, D.C.: American Council on Education, 1940).

CHAPTER

7

Lower-Class Families

SIMILAR TO the upper class and the middle class, the lower class also has two subdivisions—upper-lower and lower-lower. The upper-lower approaches the lower-middle in culture, so much so that in some small communities the two are thought of in conjunction with each other under the vernacular term, the Common Man.[1] The lower-lower merges into the ranks of the declassed—the vagrants, delinquents, and criminals who follow no class pattern but have their own small-group contra-cultures that are opposed to commonly accepted social values. In large industrial cities the lower-lower class may be composed largely of people with definite non-American ethnic cultures brought with them from foreign shores. Because these foreign-born or foreign-culture groups have special family situations, they are not specifically discussed in this chapter, in which the discussion of lower-lower-class families is general in nature.

The lower class is numerous in all communities, but especially so in the large industrial cities where unskilled and semiskilled labor predominates. In such a situation the lower class far outnumbers the middle class. Its contribution to community leadership is usually not marked, or, if it is marked, it is in the nature of retardation of community projects. As officers of organizations, the middle class takes the lead in community planning and enforcing the mores.

[1]W. Lloyd Warner and Associates, *Democracy in Jonesville* (New York: Harper, 1949), p. 24.

Characteristics of the Lower-Class Family

THE FAMILY'S PAST

Even more brief than the history of the middle-class family is that of the lower-class family. The European origin a generation or two ago gives a finite beginning to the American phase of the family, often within the memory of the older members. Dispersion of family members as they migrate from job to job breaks the connecting ties between related nuclear families. Correspondence is irregular, and visits are made only at long intervals. There are virtually no written family records. For a minority at the lowest range, however, stability rather than mobility is common, for an impoverished and dependent class marks the lowest status in the social hierarchy. This class is too dependent upon social institutions and too completely enmeshed in poverty even to migrate with the hope of finding work. It has a history, not in its own family possessions, but in the records of social agencies and in the legends of the community that identify certain families as permanently worthless. Some of these families have been in the active case load of social agencies off and on for two or three generations.

THE FAMILY UNIT

The family unit consists of the husband, wife, and their unmarried adult children and minor children. In some respects, the stable and continuing family unit is the mother and minor children. The death rate, especially of the men, is higher in the lower classes than in the middle or upper classes; therefore there are more widows. In addition, the marriage bond is weak; desertions, separations, and divorces destroy the family unit. Almost without exception, the mother keeps the children, and the father is the one to withdraw. New marriages—legal or common-law—bring a new man into the family as husband but rarely as a genuine replacement of the original father. Occasionally there may be a succession of husbands. Thus, even in the event of a stepfather, the core of the family remains the mother and her children.

[2]Walter B. Miller, "Implications of Urban Lower-Class Culture for Social Work," *Social Service Review*, 33 (September, 1959), 219–36.

Especially in the Negro lower-lower class, temporary liaisons and common-law marriages are practiced without feelings of guilt. The lower-lower class does not regard the children as unwanted or handicapped, since the mother assumes responsibility for their rearing and relief agencies assist financially. Sociologists and anthropologists recognize the female-based family as a subtype of the American family.[2] Another term, "matrifocal family," has been applied to Negro families in the Caribbean, emphasizing the transient character of the adult male and the stability of the mother's household, not only for children, but also for adult sons who may be between liaisons.[3] Freilich's analysis links the matrifocal family of the Caribbean with the background of slavery; a similar relationship can be seen in the lower-lower-class Negro family in the United States.

In the lower-class matrifocal family, the grandmother may be included in the household group. Otherwise, ties with grandparents and collaterals are weak, although at a time of family crisis, usually with economic implications, they strengthen, and one branch of the family gives sanctuary to a stranded branch. When the conditions change, the families separate. Inasmuch as crises fraught with economic strain are more frequent in the lower-class family than in the family of any other class, these temporary mergings and withdrawals are fairly common.

CULTURAL DIVERSITY

The lower class as a whole is a variegated group: families with a lengthy American background who somehow or other have failed to make the grade; newly arrived immigrant groups in the cities who, because of lack of vocational training and language difficulties, come into American society at the lower-class level; remnants of earlier ethnic groups who have failed to adjust to American culture at a higher level; groups that come into cities from other sections of the United States where they have been economically and culturally deprived (southern Negroes and "poor whites" from the hills of the southern border states). When the ethnic groups are included, the variations of language, culture, and religion are great. An illustration is found in Yankee City. Both upper-lower and lower-lower class contained 30 per cent who were foreign-born.[4] The upper-lower class had 28 per cent, and the lower-

[3] Morris Freilich, "Serial Polygyny, Negro Peasants, and Model Analysis," *American Anthropologist*, 63, No. 5, Pt. I (October, 1961), 955–75.

[4] W. Lloyd Warner and Paul S. Lunt, *The Social Life of a Modern Community* (New Haven: Yale University Press, 1941), pp. 209, 211.

lower class 38 per cent, who were born outside of Yankee City (although for the most part nearby or in other parts of New England). No other social class in Yankee City included as few Yankee City-born members. The ethnic and racial groups, largely concentrated in the two lower classes, consisted of nine stocks, representing many different languages, cultural values, and religions: Irish, French Canadians, Jewish, Italian, Armenian, Greek, Polish, Russian, and Negro.

Confusion and conflicts are reduced by the tendency for families with the same cultural background to cluster together, living perhaps in distinct and separate communities. Sometimes the majority of persons residing in one community work in the same industry, thus further reducing contacts. The lower classes, then, somewhat resemble a mosaic of cultural groups, each with a distinctive and group-centered life of its own. When groups meet, conflicts may arise; among adolescents and youths, especially male, physical conflicts may be sought, either in free-for-all or planned battles or on another level through competitive group sports. When marriages occur between members of different or opposed cultural groups, the conflict may be carried over into either an inter- or an intrafamily conflict.

Regardless of these differences, the general pattern of economic status and insecurity, the necessity for each member of the lower class to become self-sufficient, and the lack of community prestige and influence produce certain family similarities that characterize the lower classes.

Economic Basis

Inherited wealth is unheard-of in the lower classes. Income is primarily from wages earned through semiskilled and unskilled labor. These are the jobs that may be entered easily and that are easily refilled if the worker leaves. The workers are at the mercy of even slight changes in the market and may be laid off without ceremony because they are easily replaced. Much seasonal work is also done by lower-class workers. Income is not only low but uncertain; consequently, savings are small, and an accumulation of family wealth impossible.

The lower-class family is the one that experiences the economic life cycle observed by Rountree in his study of the English laborer.[5] In the life cycle of the family, early manhood and womanhood when courtship and marriage occur is a period of relatively adequate income; the youth is young and vigorous, the wife is able to work, and there are no children or one child. The second stage comes when the number of

[5]B. S. Rountree, *Poverty: A Study of Town Life* (London: Longmans, 1922).

children increases and the wife drops out of employment, while expenses mount; this is a period of insecurity and perhaps downright poverty. As the children come into adolescence and begin to work, comes the third stage; the family income is larger and many home improvements are made, as the accumulated moderate incomes from several workers may make a respectable total. In the fourth stage, as children marry and leave home, income decreases but so also do expenses. With old age the cycle comes to a close with the old couple again facing the poverty and insecurity they knew in their childhood. Savings are small or do not exist, and payments under Old Age Assistance or Old Age and Survivors' Insurance are often adequate only for minimum essentials.

When savings are possible, as among the more thrifty upper-lower-class families, they may go into the purchase of a small home. In some cities this home is a small frame house with a basement flat and a second-floor flat, in one of which the family lives, the other being rented for additional income. In other cities, the upper-lower-class family buys a small plot in an unincorporated area beyond the city and there, unhampered by municipal building ordinances, constructs a small house, often of second-hand materials and without plumbing, electricity, or gas, although these may be added later. But the proportion of lower-class families owning homes is small. In Elmtown, 35 per cent of the upper-lower-class families and 19 per cent of the lower-lower-class families, as compared with 66 per cent of lower-middle-class families, owned their homes.[6] In Yankee City, only 6 per cent of lower-lower-class families owned homes.[7]

Only rarely are savings sufficient to tide the family over an emergency, such as a major operation of the chief wage earner or a long-continued period of unemployment. A limited degree of security may be gained when the wage earner is eligible for unemployment insurance. Even the upper-lower-class family may have to apply for relief during an emergency, and the lower-lower-class family may be on and off relief as a permanent feature of life. Relief, therefore, is accepted as a possibility or even a probability and is sought without the deep shame and loss of self-respect with which the occasional middle-class person reluctantly approaches a welfare office. Moreover, it is sought before the family has lowered its standard of living or threatened its future security through the exhaustion of resources that typifies the middle-class family in economic distress. The lower-class family has few resources to be exhausted, and life on relief often represents only a

[6]August Hollingshead, *Elmtown's Youth* (New York: Wiley, 1949), pp. 97, 140, 116.
[7]Warner and Lunt, *op. cit.*, p. 448.

slight diminution of the customary standard of living. The attitude of realistic acceptance of economic insecurity is expressed in these words by one lower-class father: "There's never been a time when I could be sure that I could care for my family. And my father was that way before me, too."[8]

SOCIAL CLASS   OCCUPATIONS

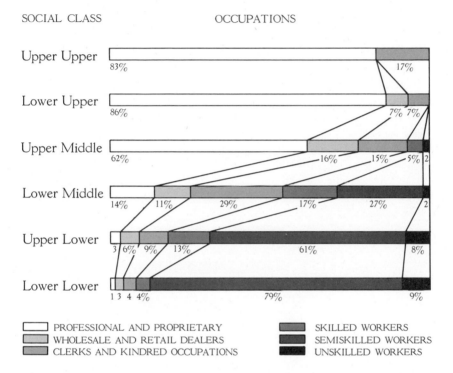

FIGURE 7   *Occupations Typical of Different Social Classes in Yankee City.*

In this New England industrial city of 17,000 inhabitants the employed members of each social class except the lower middle are heavily concentrated in one occupational classification. Occupation is one influence on family life, affecting such things as hours of rising and going to bed, kind of clothing worn, affiliation with occupational and social organizations, family expectations for the children, and amount of income. As a result social classes predominantly of one occupational type have greater uniformity of family life than has the lower-middle class with its varied occupations.

SOURCE: W. Lloyd Warner and Paul S. Lunt, *Social Life of a Modern Community* (New Haven: Yale University Press, 1941), p. 261.

[8]Earl L. Koos, "Class Differences in Family Reactions to Crisis," *Marriage and Family Living,* 12 (1950), 77. In contrast to the above is the attitude of the middle-class man, quoted by Koos: "I'd shoot myself before I'd go to the county welfare office and apply for help."

Regular or intermittent employment for all members of the family who can work is not only the common practice but is believed to be normal and necessary. It is also accepted by both husbands and wives that wives should be employed a large part of the time, even when the children are small. The necessity for women to work is increased also by the number of families in which the father is dead or has deserted either temporarily or permanently. The mother, with whatever aid she can secure from social agencies or relatives, must pick up the economic responsibility for herself and her children.

The extent of employment of lower-class mothers can be seen from a comparison of the percentage of wives who are employed, according to the income of their husbands. The figures are for wives aged 20 to

SOCIAL CLASS

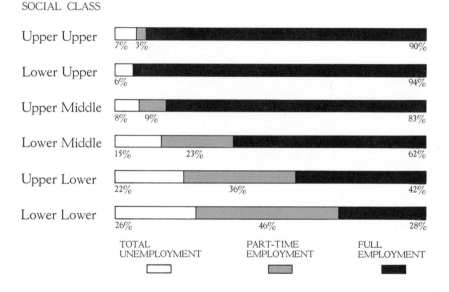

FIGURE 8   *Unemployment by Social Class, Yankee City.*

The graph shows the percentage of unemployed among the working members of each social class at one period in the early 1930's during the depression. Unemployment and partial employment create family insecurity and loss of status for the unemployed persons. Although relief agencies try to provide for basic needs, the necessity of applying for relief may bring a sense of degradation, especially to middle-class families. The percentages of all persons on public relief were as follows: lower-lower, 34; upper-lower, 10; lower-middle, 4; upper-middle, less than 1. No upper-class person received relief.

SOURCE: W. Lloyd Warner and Paul S. Lunt, *Social Life of a Modern Community* (New Haven: Yale University Press, 1941), pp. 277-79.

44 who are living with their husbands. When the husband's income was less than $1,000 per year, 43 per cent of wives worked. With increase in level of income, the percentage of working wives dropped. For example, when the husband's income was between $3,000 and $5,000 per year, 35 per cent of wives worked. The drop continued; when the husband's income was $10,000 or more, only 16 per cent of wives worked. Mothers with children under six years of age were much less likely to work than those with no children or older children. But among families in which the husband's income was less than $3,000, approximately a fourth of the mothers with children under six years old were employed.[9]

Children also work without question. Their work is not in support of an ideal of thrift and industry, as in the middle class, but from necessity. Since the educational ideals of the family usually are low, parents expect children to leave school and begin to work as soon as the law permits. Younger children are expected to secure after-school, Saturday, and vacation jobs. Moreover, the children find it difficult to relate the training they receive in the average public school to the realities of their lives and are only too ready to find a legitimate excuse for ending their formal education. Since they have neither a sound liberal education nor vocational training, they enter unskilled or semi-skilled work and thus repeat in their lives the cycle followed by their parents. In securing work, the children answer newspaper ads or approach the employment office as the only contact between adolescent and employer. Since the father's employment is on an impersonal and often impermanent basis, he is unable to provide an occupational opening for his children.

RESIDENTIAL STABILITY

Lower-class families have less residential stability than those in higher classes. Many are newcomers seeking a better living than they had in some other community—for example, rural migrants. Those who are able to build achieve a certain stability for a period of perhaps 10 to 20 years. But the house may be lost through mortgage foreclosure, or sold if a job is lost and another found in some other community, or sold as old age approaches. Those who rent move frequently, and those who do not own furniture but live in small furnished rooms or flats move most often of all. Nevertheless, in each community some lower-class

[9]*1960 Handbook on Women Workers*, Women's Bureau Bulletin No. 275 (Washington, D. C.: Government Printing Office, 1960), p. 41. The figures are for 1958–59.

families have held that status over a period of generations without rising in the social scale. In Elmtown, many lower-lower-class families have been residents of the community as long as the upper-class families, and, like the upper-class families, are linked in the public mind with the past behavior of their ancestors.[10] The legends that cling to

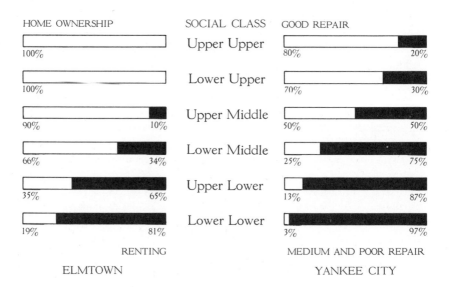

FIGURE 9   *Homes According to Social Class.*

In Elmtown, a midwestern city of 7,000, all upper-class people, but only one fifth of the lower-lower class, owned their homes. In Yankee City, 80 per cent of the upper-upper class, but only 2 per cent of the lower-lower class, lived in homes in good repair. Ownership increases stability of family life and incorporation into community life.

SOURCE: A. B. Hollingshead, *Elmtown's Youth* (New York: Wiley, 1949), ch. 5; W. Lloyd Warner and Paul S. Lunt, *Social Life of a Modern Community* (New Haven: Yale University Press, 1941), pp. 425, 432, 437, 440, and 441.

these permanent lower-lower families are notorious, however, rather than laudatory: a murder, chronic drunkenness, or family abuse on the part of the grandfather hangs over the present generation, giving a pattern for the children and lowering community expectation of achievement from them.

Although we think of home-ownership and residential stability as adding to a family's prestige, for great numbers of the lower class such stability is a handicap. For one thing, it fixes them in a class level that

[10]Hollingshead, *op. cit.*, pp. 113–14.

has little to offer them or their children. For another, it reduces their economic opportunities. The semiskilled or unskilled laborer must be a ready migrant if he is to have work all the time. Tied to one locality, he may be unemployed a much higher percentage of the time than if he is mobile.

Marriage

Young people in the lower classes marry at an earlier age than in other classes. In Yankee City the average age in the upper-lower class was 24 years and in the lower-lower 23, or four or five years younger than in the upper-upper class.[11] In Elmtown, where all the marital ages were lower than in Yankee City, men married in their twenties and girls in their late teens in the upper-lower class and in the very early twenties and middle teens in the lower-lower class.[12]

Marriages tend to occur between members of the same class, but if there is out-class marriage it is upward, since there is no lower class into which marriage may be made. Thus the attractive girl or the enterprising youth may marry into a family somewhat above his own in social status. Since each marriage starts a new and independent nuclear family, however, the decision is more or less in the hands of the couple as to whether the future family pattern follows that of the lower or the higher class.

Marriage occurs with less preliminary social contact and with less ritual as to ceremony than in the middle or upper classes. Eligible girls and men do not meet in a debut as in the upper class nor through supervised mixed-group activities as in the middle class; they do not even meet at school, for many have left school before mid- or late adolescence. The street corner, the tavern, or the factory provides the locale, and individual initiative brings youths and girls together. Courtship is short, often sexually exciting, and ends with a marriage that is announced to family and friends after it has occurred. The economic status of the husband may be low, for the criterion of selection is personal and sexual attraction rather than economic and social suitability.[13]

Family Organization

In the normal family unit of husband, wife, and children, the father is the head of the family. Lower-class families are more nearly patri-

[11]Warner and Lunt, *op. cit.*, p. 255.
[12]Hollingshead, *op. cit.*, pp. 106, 116.
[13]For a detailed discussion of preparation for marriage, see Chapter 13.

archal than families in any other class. The husband asserts his authority more thoroughly and more harshly than in higher classes, keeping
wife and children in submission by physical force if necessary. He is
the final authority and disciplinarian to whom the mother refers in her
daily training of children; except in times of stress, he is the chief wage
earner and controls the purse; he makes the final decisions for the
family.

Nevertheless, it is the mother who rears the children, and it is with
her that the children remain if the family disintegrates. The father,
however, may make rules for the rearing of the children, which the
mother enforces in his absence. The mother's role also is that of housekeeper, and the husband does not expect to participate in housekeeping
tasks after he comes from work. The roles of husband and wife are
more sharply drawn than in the middle class where there is more
sharing in planning and often in execution of the plans.

The husband and wife have a life of their own which takes precedence over the demands of their children. The bond between them is
personal and sexual in nature. Having fewer interests, husband and
wife have less of a companionship and friendship relationship than the
middle-class husband and wife achieve. Children, though important
and welcome in the lower-class family, nevertheless have less family
importance than in the middle-class family. They are definitely subordinate to the parents, who neither cater to them nor sacrifice for their
education and cultural development as middle-class parents do. Moreover, the expectation is strong that children will leave school after
fulfilling the minimum legal requirements in order to work and contribute to the family until the day of their marriage.

Although the obligations are more simple than in higher social
classes, the roles of husband and wife are specific. The husband earns
the living if he is able to do so, supports his family, is not cruel but
may be strict, and is faithful to his wife (although discreet deviations
are tolerated, especially in the lower-lower group). The wife bears
and rears the children, keeps house, earns money if her husband is
unable to earn all that is needed, and is faithful to her husband. If
these obligations are broken, the offended party may and often does
leave, opening the way for a possible divorce. As has already been
stated, the children almost without exception remain with the mother.
Since the husband may find work almost as readily in another city as
in the one where his estranged or divorced wife lives, he often leaves,
thus obstructing any attempts of the wife to secure support for herself
or their children. The wife therefore finds herself facing the roles of

both father and mother to her children. Sometimes she and the children are absorbed back into her parental family where she may serve a useful function if her parents are old; or collateral relatives may give her room and board for a time, although rarely are they able to give cash help if she lives elsewhere. The mother faces three possible solutions: to work for the support of herself and her children; to remain at home with them and apply for Aid to Dependent Children, a form of public relief; or to remarry.

The role of the second husband is a peculiar and unstable one. He is husband to his wife but not father to her children. He does not assume authority over them, nor do they recognize him as their father; however, he may be friendly with them and help support them. If he attempts to discipline his stepchildren, conflict may result, with the mother siding with her children in their rejection of his authority. Sometimes the solution is found by placing the children with relatives who are willing to accept them, or by permitting very young children to be adopted. At other times, the second marriage breaks on the rocks of family conflict.

Family life in the lower class is less stable than in the middle or upper classes. Separations, often without divorce, are frequent. The very fact that after a separation the marriage may be resumed without formality adds to the instability. One separation may follow another, often taking the form of desertion by the father who moves out, leaving the mother and children without support. With longer periods of separation, but no legal termination of the marriage through divorce, temporary alliances or more permanent common-law marriages may replace legal marriage. The death rate is higher in the lower classes than where there are more economic security and better health practices; and it is higher for men than for women. Widows, often with young children, are frequent. Another disturbing factor is the presence in the lower classes of detached men who have come into this country from abroad or have moved into certain industrial areas seeking work in proportions that disturb the natural sex ratio by providing an excess of men. Some of these men have wives and children elsewhere; other are unmarried; some are non-Caucasian. Seeking not only sexual satisfaction but the practical homemaking advantages that a woman can provide in the way of food, mending, aundry, and a homelike place to spend evenings and holidays, many of these men are willing to become partners to temporary or illicit household arrangements. As job opportunities change or the desire comes to return home, they leave with as little ceremony as they came. In many families, although illegal unions are unknown, divorce or death breaks the family, leaving a parent and perhaps children. Remarriage may follow, with the usual difficulties of adjustment.

The instability of the lower-class family is reflected in the rate of broken homes. In the upper-lower class in Elmtown, 33 per cent of the homes were broken, and in the lower-lower class 56 per cent.[14]

One may question why separations and divorces are disproportionately frequent in the lower classes. One possible answer is that stresses and strains are more frequent. The family lives closer to the thin line that lies between sufficiency and poverty. Ill health and disease are of more common occurrence. Homes are small and allow little freedom of movement or privacy.

Another plausible reason lies in personality development. As will be discussed later in this chapter, lower-class children are encouraged and openly taught by their parents to be aggressive. They are expected by their families to fight for status in their play groups, to elbow others aside in securing work, and to employ small trickery in shopping and entering movies. Life in the lower classes demands aggression for survival. These aggressive attitudes are vented not only toward the outside world but within the family circle. Brother competes with brother for clothing, food, and the most comfortable chair or bed; parents compete with children; and children with parents. Aggressive individualism, tempered by a certain practical kind of familism in time of crisis, becomes habitual. Cooperation, conciliation, and compromise, common in the middle- and upper-class family, are neither taught to the child nor demonstrated in his family. Any encroachment upon the individual or his rights as he conceives them brings an aggressive reaction inside the family as well as outside.

Another personality trait of the lower class is withdrawal when faced with overwhelming odds. The boy or girl who finds schoolwork difficult or unpleasant does not wait until the legal age to leave school, but truants and perhaps becomes adept at evading the attendance officer. Many adolescent lower-class boys and girls leave home to evade parental control, sleeping in hallways or, in the summer, in vacant lots, or securing work and renting a cheap room. Boys may tramp across the country, working and begging alternately as they go. When marriage becomes a trial, the husband tends to follow the same pattern and withdraws. The wife less often leaves as she feels emotional ties to and responsibility for her children.

[14]Hollingshead, *op. cit.*, pp. 106, 117.

Lower-Class Children

Lower-class families have a higher average number of children than any other social class. Using education of married women as a crude criterion of social-class status, Table 6 shows that in 1964 the average number of chi dren for women with less than eight years of education was 3.6 and with eight years, 2.8. However, women with one to three years of college averaged 2.0 and those with four or more years of college, 1.7. Thus the average number of children among the best educated women was less than half the average among the most poorly educated. In the small city of Elmtown in the 1940's, the average number of children was 5.6 in the lower-lower-class family and 4.3 in the upper-lower-class family.[15]

Studies show that lower-class families state that they want three or four children, spaced about two years apart. Those with larger families have more children less because they want them than because of ineffective methods of contraception.[16] One study showed that 75 per cent of the upper-lower-class families but only a third of lower-lower-class families used contraceptive techniques effectively. Their interview responses showed that they were ignorant of how contraceptives work; some women were afraid that a diaphragm inserted in the vagina might "get lost" in their bodies; some men objected to reduced pleasure when a condom was used. Even when effective types of contraceptives were used, they were often used sporadically, indicating a failure to realize that only one omission of the contraceptive might result in pregnancy.

Factors other than ignorance and carelessness also are present. By the accident of national origin, many lower-class families are descendants of recent immigrants from Catholic countries; they adhere to the Catholic prohibition against artificial control of conception. In addition, the use of contraceptives presupposes a certain degree of sophistication, self-discipline, and sometimes expenditure that are contrary to the lower-class culture. Another factor contributing to the high birth rate is that children are regarded as assets to the family in that they

[15]Hollingshead, *op. cit.*, pp. 106, 116.
[16]Lee Rainwater and Karol Kane Weinstein, "A Qualitative Exploration of Family Planning and Contraception in the Working Class," *Marriage and Family Living*, 22 (1960), 238–42.

begin to earn early in life. Also, lower-class values do not demand the heavy expenditures of middle-class families for prenatal care, hospital delivery, pediatric supervision, dental work, special educational classes in childhood, and college education. These have become routine necessities of childrearing in the middle class; they are regarded as superfluities by the lower-class family.

Another factor is the early age of marriage, especially for girls, at a time when sex drives are strong and fertility high. The early marriage also lengthens the total span for childbearing.

Finally, the general attitude in many lower-class families is that children are a natural outcome of marriage. The mother especially finds satisfaction in producing children and lavishes affection on them, particularly if her relationship with her husband is not completely satisfying to her emotionally.

The training of lower-class children differs from that of middle- and upper-class children, both in objectives and methods. The objective is to develop a tough-minded, hard-fisted individual, able to compete to the point of personal conflict in support of individual rights and privileges. When these rights are not challenged, the lower-class person is orderly and law-abiding. The little boy is not taught, as is the middle-class boy, to wait until he is struck before he fights, nor to seek the protection of parent, teacher, or policeman. He is expected to be able to take care of himself at an early age. The little girl, likewise, is taught to be self-sufficient, to protect her virtue by a sharp tongue and her fists if necessary.[17]

At an early age both boys and girls are allowed to extend their activities into the community without the supervision of parents or other adults. They play in the neighborhood at night and attend movies alone at an age when middle-class children are carefully sequestered in house or yard by their parents. They learn to ride the bus across the city, shop for their mothers, care for younger brothers and sisters, make change, avoid automobiles, earn money, and otherwise look after themselves and contribute to the utilitarian functions of the family while still well below teen age. Conversely, they are not taught certain duties and aspirations that have high value in the middle-class family and that middle-class children are urged and coerced into learning—regularity of school attendance, ambition for at least high school graduation, excessive neatness and cleanliness of both person and the child's room, and avoidance of fighting unless attacked.

As stated in the discussion of the middle-class family, the methods

---

[17]An excellent comparative statement of middle-class and lower-class child training is given in W. Allison Davis and Robert J. Havighurst, *Father of the Man* (Boston: Houghton Mifflin, 1947).

of training differ between the two classes. The lower-class mother rears her children with a combination of leniency and impulsive aggressiveness. One might say that she treats her children more naturally and more in accord with her own emotional needs than does the middle-class mother who trains her children with the child psychologist always peeping over her shoulder. The mother responds to the personal relationship between herself and each child, whereas the middle-class mother tries to do what is "best for the child," often denying her own feelings in the process. The lower-class child is less likely to view himself as a person of special value for whom parental sacrifices are justified. He plays a subordinate role in the family, gaining in status when he reaches an age to contribute financially.

Ritual is less used in the lower-class family than in the family of any other class. Nevertheless, only in the very lowest levels is ritual non-existent. The celebration of Christmas is a form of ritual if repeated year after year in characteristic fashion. Catholic families tend to follow religious rituals that reinforce in the family the teachings of the Church. However, many of the rituals that reflect leisure (as the after-dinner coffee of the middle-class family) or that regulate relations between family members (as the standing of the child when an older person enters the room) are unknown. Houses are crowded; duties crowd fast one upon another; tensions are often unresolved. The members of the family may seek avoidance of each other through outside activities rather than finding satisfaction in a closely integrated family pattern of rituals.

Upwardly Mobile Upper-Lower Class— The Nouveau Bourgeoisie

A portion of the upper-lower class is upwardly mobile into the lower-middle class. The process, observed especially since the end of World War II, rests on the high percentage of employment among upper-lower or blue-collar workers, higher incomes not only in number of dollars but in buying power, and the widespread practice of buying goods on the installment plan. The ambitious blue-collar worker therefore is able to acquire some of the material goods of the lower-middle class and to move into a lower-middle class residential area.[18] He does not so readily acquire the values and ways of behaving of the

---

[18]Robert H. Bohlke, "Social Mobility, Stratification Inconsistency, and Middle Class Delinquency," *Social Problems*, 8 (Spring, 1961), 351–63. The study reviews earlier studies and is generally applicable to upward mobility.

middle class. When an individual family makes the physical move into a middle-class area, the members may be rejected by neighbors, schools, and other institutions, which often results in feelings of insecurity, frustration, and perhaps aggression.

Another result of upward mobility involving a large amount of installment buying is the potential economic insecurity. A long period of unemployment for the chief wage-earner may send the family rapidly downward in status.

Limited upward mobility also may be carried out by a larger group than the family; for example, when families of lower status move into a newly built lower-middle-class suburb or other community, or when an industry moves and houses its blue-collar workers in a community of much better quality than the one from which they came.[19] Families then give each other support but do not quickly or automatically become middle class. The slow process of changes in values and behavior must still be accomplished.

Crises

That lower-class families are subject to many types of crisis has been implied in the preceding discussion. Frequent unemployment, the higher illness rate than in other social classes, the higher birth rate that results in the more frequent introduction of a new member into the family circle, delinquency of younger members of the family, occasional or chronic alcoholism, and aggressiveness between neighbors or relatives as well as personal clashes within the family are some of the conditions that cause a breakdown of the folkways of the lower-class family and require the family to readjust itself in some way. The lower-class family is rarely equipped by education or training to resolve a personal crisis on the verbal level. Verbal emotional explosions may relieve inner tensions but add to the disruption; and sometimes the verbal expression moves into physical aggressiveness against or between offending persons. Thus, the husband may beat his wife, or the wife may throw china at her husband; children may be beaten; neighborhood fights may occur; and occasionally, in one of these personal clashes, someone is killed. Such aggressions not only widen the breach but often serve to bring the crisis to the attention of the neighbors or the police. Crises that emanate from lack of money are also frequent and difficult to resolve because the family lacks accumulated savings and finds it impossible, or nearly so, to establish credit.

[19]For an interesting study of such a move, see Bennett M. Berger, *Working Class Suburb: A Study of Auto Workers in Suburbia* (Berkeley: University of California Press, 1960).

Lower-class crises tend to be prolonged and often result in serious damage to family unity. The family tends to disintegrate under the pressure of the crisis, although later it may re-form. The husband may desert when a new baby threatens to upset the household routine or to impose extra expense; but he may return six months or a year later. The adolescent boy or girl may run away but be sent home by some social agency or the police of another community. At other times the disintegration is permanent, and the family may appeal to official agencies for help. The wife may bring suit against her husband for nonsupport or obtain a divorce; she may ask for financial relief or aid in controlling rebellious children.

The official agency usually enters into the situation, however, after other efforts have already been made to solve the problems. The lower-class family does not keep its problems to itself. Less reticent about its problems, less proud of its status than the middle-class family, the lower-class family tends to seek outside aid, but not of a professional nature in the first instance. The druggist, the bartender, and relatives are approached for advice or financial assistance. Only when they fail are the legal and social agencies approached.[20]

Special Characteristics

The lower class as a whole abides by the common mores of our society and meets such expectations as family self-support (except, perhaps, in times of great crisis), legal monogamous marriages, conformity to laws, participation in community institutions (such as sending their children to school), and affiliations with some type of church connection.

There is a small substratum, however, that deviates from the class and family mores. These families might be illustrated by families of beggars, pauperized families that make no effort to break their dependency upon relief agencies, families that violate the sex mores through unofficial polygyny or the practice of incest or in which prostitute mothers teach their daughters to become prostitutes, and criminal families. These families may belong to small groups that have developed mores of their own and a philosophy that cushions them against a feeling of guilt or rationalizes their conduct. Other families are composed of demoralized individuals in the sense that they do not have a system of mores, have not developed a conscience or superego, but live close to their natural needs and impulses.

[20]Earl L. Koos, "Middle-Class Family Crises," *Marriage and Family Living,* 10 (1948), 25, 40.

The Lower Class as a Population Pool

The lower class forms a population pool from which higher strata—chiefly middle class—draw replacements necessitated by their lower reproductive rate. The excess members in lower-class families originate partly from the high birth rate and partly from immigrant groups, which usually enter the American social-class system as unskilled workers at the lower-class level.

Questions

1. What is the origin of lower-class families?
2. How does the lower-class family gain economic security?
3. What is the basic family unit in the lower class?
4. What role do children play in the lower-class family?
5. Does the training of children fit them for life in the lower class?
6. Contrast the families of the three social classes (upper, middle, and lower) on as many points as possible. Which class seems to have the most rigid type of family life? Which the most flexible? Is rigidity or flexibility most desirable under present social conditions?

Bibliography

BERGER, BENNETT M., *Working Class Suburb: A Study of Auto Workers in Suburbia* (Berkeley: University of California Press, 1960).

BOHLKE, ROBERT H., "Social Mobility, Stratification Inconsistency, and Middle Class Delinquency," *Social Problems*, 8 (Spring, 1961), 351–63.

CAVAN, RUTH SHONLE, *Juvenile Delinquency* (Philadelphia: Lippincott, 2d ed., 1969).

DAVIS, ALLISON, *Social-Class Influences upon Learning* (Cambridge: Harvard University Press, 1949).

———, B. B. GARDNER, and M. R. GARDNER, *Deep South* (Chicago: University of Chicago Press, 1941).

HOLLINGSHEAD, AUGUST B., *Elmtown's Youth* (New York: Wiley, 1949).

KOMAROVSKY, MIRRA, *Blue-Collar Marriage* (New York: Random House, 1962).

KOOS, EARL L., *Families in Trouble* (New York: King's Crown Press, 1946).

MILLER, WALTER B., "Implications of Urban Lower-Class Culture for Social Work," *Social Service Review*, 33 (September, 1959), 219–36.

_____, "Lower-Class Culture as a Generating Milieu of Gang Delinquency," *Journal of Social Issues*, 14, No. 3 (1958), 5–19.

RAINWATER, LEE, *Family Design: Marital Sexuality, Family Size, and Contraception* (Aldine, 1965).

_____, RICHARD P. COLEMAN, and GERALD HANDEL, *Workingman's Wife: Her Personality, World and Life Style* (Dobbs Ferry, N.Y.: Oceana Publications, 1959).

_____, and KAROL KANE WEINSTEIN, "A Qualitative Exploration of Family Planning and Contraception in the Working Class," *Marriage and Family Living*, 22 (1960), 238–42.

_____, _____, *And the Poor Get Children* (Chicago: Quadrangle Books, 1960)

CHAPTER

8

Ethnic Groups and the Process of

Horizontal Mobility

THE PROCESS of absorption of foreign-culture families into the American culture occurs chiefly on a family basis, with the children of each generation pushing on ahead of their parents, first into ethnic culture and eventually into American culture. In this process of assimilation, each foreign culture makes some contribution to American culture. However, the exchange of culture is uneven, and most of the foreign culture is lost in the process.

Cultural and Social Assimilation

An analysis of ethnic families requires a distinction between cultural and social assimilation. The struggle toward cultural assimilation usually begins during the lifetime of the original immigrants. When large foreign-born groups formed indigestible masses in American cities, a tremendous effort was made to induce them to give up their native culture and conform to American culture. The Americanization programs of the first quarter of the twentieth century rested on an active and persistent effort to persuade, almost force, the immigrant to become an American. Public schools and community centers located in foreign-born areas were especially active in this effort. If they did not succeed with the foreign-born adults, they usually succeeded in giving to their children the rudiments of American culture—so much so that children often were alienated from their parents. At the present time, unless the descendants of foreign-born groups have deliberately isolated themselves from American culture, it may safely be said that the descendants of immigrants who came prior to the restrictive laws of the 1920's are now American in culture.

While the American culture was being impressed upon foreign-born families by organized institutions, social inclusion in American groups was neglected. In fact, the pressure of informal American groups and families ran in the opposite direction, toward exclusion. Foreign-born people and their descendants were not welcomed into close association with or as participants in American institutions. They were neither elected to membership in American clubs nor invited as friends into American homes. The exclusion was also discriminatory. They were regarded by Americans as not only different but inferior. Sought as factory workers or as maids, they were rejected as social equals.[1]

The newly arrived foreign-culture group may be distinguished from the ethnic group in this way: the foreign-culture group has not adjusted either culturally or socially to American life; the ethnic group has usually adopted American culture, retaining only traces of the foreign culture, but has not been fully absorbed socially into American institutions or informal social life. In a few instances, groups long removed in time from the original immigrant forebears retain a high degree of both cultural and social distinctiveness. The Amish are an example: although they have adopted many American culture traits, they cling to many of their original traits and form their own social world. They are able to remain both culturally and socially withdrawn from American life only by forbidding contacts, assessing heavy penalties for violation of the rules of seclusion, and expelling from their community those who mingle with outsiders. The Amish therefore are an oddity in American life and do not represent the usual processes of adjustment. The majority of foreign-culture groups, at least in the second generation, have been willing, even eager, to become a part of American life, but may fail when social pressures are opposed to their participation as equals in American institutions and informal groups.

Racial groups may also be fitted into the same conceptual framework. A newly arrived racial group, such as the Negro Puerto Ricans who entered New York City in the 1940's, experiences both cultural and social nonadjustment. In contrast, Negro Americans whose ancestors

[1] The distinction between cultural and social assimilation is interestingly stated in Peter A. Munch, "Social Adjustment among Wisconsin Norwegians," *American Sociological Review*, 14 (1949), 780–81.

have lived in the United States for generations share American culture with white Americans, but often are excluded socially from all except formal participation in certain institutions and activities. They are assimilated culturally but not socially. The speed of social absorption of Negroes or other nonwhite racial groups is much slower than that of eventual social absorption of the white ethnic groups.

The degree of cultural and social assimilation of an ethnic group affects the organization and interaction within the family as well as between the family and the community.

The Culturally and Socially
Unassimilated Family

Culturally, the basic problem of the foreign-culture family that comes to the United States to live is the same problem faced by the unprepared rural American family that migrates to the large city. A family that has adjusted itself to one type of physical and cultural environment through accepting the coordinated folkways and mores of that environment moves into a different environment where the old patterns of family life are not applicable. However, the foreign-culture family has a much more difficult time than the rural family, which, after all, speaks the American language and shares with other Americans certain concepts and ideals both of family and community living.

THE CONTROLLING UNIT IN IMMIGRATION

Immigrants come as individuals or small-family units. Often the husband comes alone and later sends for his wife and children, using money earned and saved in this country. Many young unmarried men immigrate and later send back to their native village or city for a girl already selected, or they ask their parents to select a wife for them; sometimes a fellow immigrant will arrange to send for a niece or sister who becomes the bride of his friend. As men become adjusted they may marry the American-born girls whose parents are of their own nationality, or may marry outside their ethnic group. Thus, many of those who enter the United States as individuals soon establish families.

Although immigrants rarely come in as community groups, they tend to establish themselves in this country in areas limited to their own nationality. Newly arrived immigrants are taken for a season into the home of a relative or family friend, who usually lives in a colony of his countrymen. In large northern cities these colonies are easily distinguishable, not by political boundaries or artificial barriers but by the physical characteristics, dress, spoken language, and names on stores that designate one block as belonging to, let us say, Italians, and the next to Greeks.

The individual and the family, therefore, are incorporated into a little community that perpetuates as much of the native culture as is possible in the changed environment. The colony also provides social life, institutional participation, and an opportunity to choose a spouse of the same national origin. The colony impedes both cultural and social assimilation, but it gives security and companionship and no doubt reduces personal and family disorganization, which, at best, often are concomitants of the process of readjustment.

DEGREE OF CULTURAL CHANGE

For all foreign-culture groups the degree of cultural change is great. The Englishman, educated and urban-adjusted, lives through a period of strangeness, in which he learns new meanings for old words, finds that the brashness of American children is normal and admired, and that Americans do not always share his national attitudes and ideals. Foreign-language groups have a more difficult problem, although, nestled in their little urban colonies, they try to reproduce their native culture completely. In this project they never succeed, for the impact of American institutions and mores is immediately felt. The change in environment is greatest when the immigrant comes from a rural area in his native land to urban America, but even the urban-to-urban and the rural-to-rural immigrants find much that is strange.

READINESS OF THE COMMUNITY
TO RECEIVE IMMIGRANTS

The deliberate attempt to make Americans out of foreign-culture people has already been mentioned. Too often only superficial American qualities have been adopted by the immigrants, without a corresponding change in attitudes. The result has often been family disorganization and violent conflicts between the parents who tend to retain the native culture and their American-educated children who have a muddled conception of both the native and the American standards.

Degree of Family Adjustment

The processes of family adjustment are closely related to the preceding factors. Many of the immigrant groups entering the United States have two characteristics: patriarchal family organization and rural peasant background. This combination was true for the foreign-culture groups studied in Yankee City—Irish, Polish, Greek, and Armenian—as well as for other groups entering the East, Middle West, and Southwest, such as the Puerto Rican, Italian, Norwegian, Finnish, and Mexican.[2] The patriarchal organization and the rural background are related and reinforce each other.

When such a family settles in an American city, the family organization is immediately broken. The father finds work in a factory and therefore is absent from home all day. Wife and children are freed from his personal supervision, although the wife may attempt to act as a surrogate for him. Moreover, the father is no longer a free agent who can control his own time and activities in the interest of the family. He is subject to the demands of his job and comes under the supervision of a foreman or employer. His status and prestige are therefore decreased. As soon as the older children begin to learn American culture at school, they assume a new role in the family as interpreters of the American culture to their parents and often as linguistic contacts between the parents, especially the mother, and outside agencies, such as stores or social agencies. In their own eyes their status has increased, and often they compete with their parents for control of the family and in particular of the younger children.

When the children begin to earn money, the gap between status of father and children narrows. The father often expects children to turn their pay over to him intact to be used for the family good, with the father making decisions as to expenditures. An example is the Polish father in Yankee City who had been unemployed for several years without making an effort to find work. His daughters, all over 18 years of age, gave him their earnings, which he accepted as his due. He saved some of the money, bought what he thought the family needed, and gave or withheld small sums that the daughters might wish to have. He saw nothing unjust in this procedure; in his native land the elderly father had lightened his work on the farm as children came to maturity

[2]W. Lloyd Warner and Leo Srole, *The Social Systems of American Ethnic Groups* (New Haven: Yale University Press, 1945), ch. 6, "The Family."

but had still supervised their work and handled the family finances.[3] Often the children object to such complete dominance by the father. They wish to handle their own money. Sometimes they pay a fixed amount to the parents but in other cases withdraw completely from the family, or remain in the family home but do not contribute and perhaps do not work regularly. Neither parents nor children are fully aware of adjustments made by American families whereby the children normally contribute an agreed-upon sum to the parents and control the remainder of their earnings themselves, a procedure usually preceded by years of careful training by parents in the handling of small sums of money, budgeting, and saving. The immigrant family has no pattern in its background for the individual management of income by members of the family.

In other aspects, also, the immigrant family lacks behavior patterns for a family organized on any other than a patriarchal system. When the authority of the father breaks down, as it almost always does in the urban situation, there is no alternative system of compromise, family counseling, and the like such as characterizes many American families. The parents do not know how to strike that fine line between freedom versus self-control for their children that marks the adolescent period of the American child.

Moreover, other agencies supplement or replace the family, assuming functions once the prerogative of the parents. Recreational and educational agencies compete with the parents in supplying the needs of the children and often of the wife, sometimes with contrary teachings that tear down rather than give support to parental status. Sometimes the parents find aid in ethnic institutions—clubs or church— provided that they do not simply try to reestablish the ethnic culture intact but recognize the necessity for adaptation to the new social situation.

The family therefore faces the problem of changing its old culture to meet the new social situation, a change that involves not merely external skills and a different physical environment but deeply seated traditions and highly valued ideals about which personality has been constructed.

New social contacts also give little help to the immigrant family. Each member of the family meets different social groups—the father at his place of employment, the children at school and settlement, the mother in her immediate neighborhood. Unaccustomed to these divi-

[3]*Ibid.*, pp. 128–29.

sive social contacts, unlearned in the skills of sharing them with each other, the family tends toward disintegration. Sometimes, also, the social groups that are willing to accept the recent immigrant are ones that do not represent the best of American culture—the boys' gang, the streetcorner boys, the unsupervised girls' clique.

The shifting of roles, the declining status of parents and increasing status of children, the inadequacy of the old family organization, and the need to change personal conceptions and standards of conduct all tend toward family disorganization and personal demoralization. This phase of adjustment, however, is usually a transitory one, and in time increased familiarity with American culture and enlarged participation in American social groups bring about new family orientation.

Several illustrations are given of foreign-culture families still in the process of adjustment. If repetition seems marked, it is only because a similarity of backgrounds and present situations creates much the same process in different groups. Each case, however, shows a somewhat different stage of adjustment.

THE MEXICAN PEASANT FAMILY

Mexican peasant-family life developed in a rural village, where families are held together by intermarriage and the sharing of a common body of traditions. Roles are predetermined by custom, and public opinion is a potent force in the regulation of conduct. The family is organized on a bilateral basis, the children bearing both family names. After marriage husband and wife remain members of their parental families, which are bound together through the marriage. In this larger kinship family the father or oldest wage earner is head; he controls finances, exercises authority over the younger members, and protects his wife and daughters from unwelcome attentions of other men. Respect for the mother gives her a status above her children but below her husband; the son outranks the daughter. Marriages are made with the interest of the kinship family uppermost, and divorces are almost unknown. The family is further extended and strengthened by the godparents, chosen as sponsors of the children. The tie between godparents and children is strong, with the godparents assuming responsibility for the children if the parents die, and the children giving respect and love to the godparents. Thus family life is controlled by the traditions of the village and large family group, and marriage is stable.

The roles of family members are well defined, with a definite separation between men and women. Women work in the home and find their function in life through the care of home and children, whereas it is not seemly for the father to work in the home. Young unmarried men and women do not associate freely with each other, their contacts being closely supervised by older members of the family.[4]

The migrant Mexican family in the northern industrial city finds that the roles, family organization, and system of controls that worked very well in the Mexican village are not applicable.[5] Very serious indeed is the change in the role and status of the father. As an unskilled laborer, the father often has temporary periods of unemployment when he is unable to provide for his family. He loses status, both in the eyes of his family and in his conception of himself. Sometimes he deserts temporarily, either to seek work elsewhere or to escape the censure of wife and children. As his status declines, his authority over his family also diminishes and family unity gives way to individualism.

If the wife remains in her secluded position in the home, she often does not learn that in America wives have a relatively high status; therefore she does not threaten her husband's position. But if she assimilates American attitudes and especially if she begins to work, she does threaten the status of her husband. Likewise, if she extends her social life beyond the home, the husband feels that his exclusive possession of his wife is endangered. He may object to his wife's talking impersonally with another man or attending motion pictures with a woman friend. Quarrels between husband and wife and with neighbors follow.

It is difficult for the father to fulfill his traditional role in other ways. He may not be able to care for aged parents as he did in Mexico; his daughters may resist and evade his protective supervision over them.

The children, and especially the oldest son, play different roles than in Mexico. The oldest son, first to attend an American school, often is the first one in the family to learn American customs and accept American attitudes. He directs and guides the younger children, thus assuming some of the traditional parental obligations. When sons begin to work, they oppose the father's demand that their money should go into the family fund to be used for the family as a whole. This withholding of money is an attack upon the unity and integration

[4]R. C. Jones, "Ethnic Family Patterns: The Mexican Family in the United States," *American Journal of Sociology,* 53 (1948), 450–51.

[5]Oscar Lewis, *Five Families: Mexican Case Studies in the Culture of Poverty* (New York: Basic Books, 1959). The analysis of the first family gives the Mexican rural village background, with only slight traces of diffused urban culture. The other four cases show different degrees of adjustment to Mexico City. The strains on the traditional family are severe but are less disruptive than those experienced in the adjustment of the rural Mexican to American urban life.

of the family and upon the headship of the father who in Mexico controlled the family finances. To the employed sons, such relinquishment of their earnings seems absurd; they wish to function as individuals rather than as family members. Daughters become restive under the prohibition upon mixed social affairs and are eager to follow the American custom of social activities between unmarried adolescent girls and boys. Parties and dating are open to many misinterpretations by Mexican parents who believe their daughters to be either lewd or about to launch upon an unsuitable marriage disapproved by the family.

Gradually the roles of the family change. The sons gain a position equal to that of the father and above that of the mother, while daughters secure a status equal to that of the home-staying mother. The old family organization therefore breaks down, often before a stable organization on a more equalitarian basis has developed.

Kin and godparents are usually not present to support the old family organization. Mexican clubs and the Catholic Church provide some semblance of community control, but attendance is irregular, especially on the part of the older children.

Gradually individualism within the family and competition between families, fostered by the urban situation, replace the older close family unity and community integration of the Mexican rural community. In time, the family tends to become reorganized, with greater freedom and higher status for the wife and children and less responsibility resting on the father; but this change usually does not affect the original migrating marital pair so much as their children.[6]

In summary, the process of cultural change in the Mexican family is slow and is attended by conflicts within the family. During the initial stages of the process the Mexican family usually lives in a community of other Mexican families, in which such institutions as Mexican clubs and the Catholic Church function. Mexicans are hindered in participating socially with Americans because of their non-American ways, and also because Americans are often prejudiced against their skin color inherited from Indian ancestors.

THE PUERTO RICAN FAMILY

The Puerto Rican family in New York City is in the early stages of both acculturation and social acceptance. Since Puerto Rico is a part of the United States, its citizens are free to enter New York City with-

[6]N. D. Humphrey, "The Changing Structure of the Detroit Mexican Family: An Index of Acculturation," *American Sociological Review*, 9 (1944), 622–26.

out restriction. During the 1940's many Puerto Ricans entered New York, crowding into limited geographic areas.

Although Puerto Ricans are United States citizens, their language and culture are foreign to American ways. Originally inhabited by Indians, the island was settled by Spaniards in the sixteenth century and received an early influx of Negro slaves. The three races interbred, until now in lower-class families all degrees of hybrids are found, with little or no prejudice on the basis of color. Upper-class Puerto Ricans proudly proclaim their pure Spanish ancestry. Spanish is the native language, and Spanish culture is followed by the upper class and is a factor in lower-class mores. The migrants to New York are from the lower or working class, and range in color and physical characteristics from white to Negro; the Indian ancestry has been obscured. In the Bronx settlement, about 75 per cent are white; in Manhattan, 43 per cent.[7]

Although Puerto Rico is primarily an agricultural island, most of the migrants have come from the cities with island occupations classified as manufacturing, trade and transportation, and services; only 9 per cent of the male migrants worked in agriculture. Nevertheless, they have not been fitted for the transfer to New York industry. The island cities are small, work is done by hand rather than machines, there is no time clock to be punched, and no intricate transportation system to be mastered in going to and from work. Although these migrants have lived in poor areas of their native cities, they were not in overcrowded tenements, and the warm climate made it possible for them to spend much time out of doors. All in all, their way of life was more rural than urban.

The family in Puerto Rico reflects the Spanish influence; the dominant pattern of organization is patriarchal. The father exercises strict control over wife and children, and especially over unmarried daughters. The family of husband, wife, and children is part of an extended or kinship family, which sometimes includes a close relationship with the godparents of the children. Orphan children and old people are

[7]This discussion of Puerto Rican adjustment is based upon the following sources: *The Puerto Ricans of New York City* (Puerto Rican Department of Labor, New York Office, Employment and Migration Bureau, 1881 Broadway, New York City, mimeographed, undated); C. Wright Mills, Clarence Senior, and Rose Kohn Goldsen, *The Puerto Rican Journey* (New York: Harper, 1950), which reports a study based upon interviews with 714 Puerto Ricans in Spanish Harlem and 399 in the Bronx, two areas of highly concentrated settlement: *Resume of Dr. Clarence Senior's Study of the Puerto Ricans of New York City* (Welfare Council of New York City, 44 East 23d Street, New York City, mimeographed, 1949); *Puerto Rican Children: Some Aspects of Their Needs and Related Services* (Welfare Council of New York City, 44 East 23d Street, New York City, mimeographed, 1949).

cared for within the kinship unit, and in the small family children contribute their earnings to the family pool.

The migrant unit often is only a small segment of this family group. Contrary to most migrations, more Puerto Rican women than men entered New York. In the island the sex ratio is 100 (equal numbers of men and women), but in the New York colonies there are only 63 males to 100 females, and among Negro Puerto Ricans only 30 males to 100 females. The percentage of divorced and widowed is higher than on the island, representing people already somewhat separated from the family before migrating. Almost two-thirds of the migrants are between the ages of 18 and 39, and came without the older relatives who control the kinship family. The marriage rate is high among the migrants, and the firstcomers often send for family members and relatives, all of whom may be hospitably received into the small tenement flat. Thus in some cases the extended family appears in the New York colonies, and unmarried people are included in loose family groups.

The first tendency of the migrant family is to carry over the family organization and roles of the island. The father asserts his headship and finds a job, which usually is some form of unskilled labor regardless of the type of work he did on the island; he does not work around the home. The mother remains in the home, limiting her contacts to other families in the tenement building. Children are kept under close supervision. All employed members contribute their earnings to a common family purse. But this high development of familism is unsuited to the city and soon begins to break down. The excess of women sets a new pattern of work outside the home; while the newly arrived husband's earnings are low and in periods of unemployment, wives begin to work, finding in New York many opportunities not available on the island. The earning by women undermines the husband's position of authority and increases the status of the women. Children also are soon evading or opposing their father's authority, either because they are earning their own money or because they come in contact with the greater freedom of American children in school or some local community center. Girls especially have a difficult adjustment to make, being torn between habitual obedience to the father and the desire to share in mixed social activities of American adolescents. Attendance at an evening party at the local center may be followed by a beating at the hands of the father, which is accepted by the daughter as justified.

New courtship and marriage practices beyond family control appeal to young people but dismay their parents. In the lower class in Puerto Rico girls are not given the close chaperonage found in the middle and upper classes. They marry at a young age, often in a common-law union without the expense of a civil or religious ceremony. In the compact island community such alliances are controlled by the extended families who usually know the man; therefore they tend to be as stable as legal marriages. Fifty per cent of the unskilled class and 25 per cent of the skilled have contracted common-law marriages. The children born are not considered illegitimate and have the usual care of both parents. In New York such children are classed as illegitimate. Without the stabilizing influence of the extended families and with many opportunities for chance meetings with strangers, nonlegal unions are unstable and afford little protection to the wife or children.

Courtship on the island is carried on with some degree of dignity. Adult Puerto Ricans are shocked by the open love-making of the American city and read into handholding and kissing immoral connotations.[8] Their adolescent children are eager to enter into American life, but often have not learned the codes of control followed by American adolescents.

With the loss of integration of the large family and the inability of parents and older relatives to guide younger people in the strange urban ways, official agencies come onto the scene. Too often, however, they further undermine the family. Parents, brought into court on a charge of child beating, feel that the judge is upholding the child's rebellion. Accustomed to having dependents cared for within the kinship of the family, the family in need of help either leans too heavily upon the social agency as a substitute for the kinship group, or resents the authority exercised by the agency over family members, especially so when an attempt is made to place a child in a foster home. Schools and community centers, perhaps overly eager to Americanize the children, estrange them from their parents and inadvertently contribute to family disorganization.

Negro Puerto Ricans have an especially difficult adjustment to make. In the island, dark members of families are accepted as equals, whereas in New York whites discriminate against the dark-skinned Puerto Ricans. These Negroes tend to withdraw into the Puerto Rican colony rather than yield to the discriminatory American treatment. Sometimes the white Puerto Ricans adopt the American attitude and reject them. They are then in a no-man's-land, both culturally and socially.

The Puerto Rican family, in its first stages of adjustment to a new culture and social world, is undergoing the family disorganization that attends the failure of old roles to fit the new situation, the clinging of older members of the family to their old position of status, duties, and

[8]Reuben Hill, "Courtship in Puerto Rico: An Institution in Transition," *Marriage and Family Living*, 17 (1955), 26–35.

privileges, and the eager rushing of younger members into the superficial patterns of American life without, however, grasping the underlying ideals and codes. In time the Puerto Ricans, as other foreign-culture groups before them, will make an adjustment.

The Culturally Assimilated
But Socially Unassimilated Family

With the passage of time and continued exposure to American culture, the foreign-culture group becomes tolerant of or openly accepts some elements of American culture. As rebelling children, marginal to both the native and the American cultures, marry and establish themselves creditably, parents have many of their fears eased. The period of stress between the generations is followed by a decline in assertiveness of parents as they grow old and by an increase in dominance of the adult children. Sometimes the children pass quickly as individuals into the American community. Often, however, they ally themselves with others of the same background to form the typical ethnic group—culturally more American than foreign but socially exclusive. The family is one of the chief agencies through which ethnic affiliation is maintained.

THE ITALIAN FAMILY

A study of the American-Italian family made in the 1940's carries the process of assimilation further on the way toward complete social assimilation and loss of ethnic identity.[9] In the 1960's—almost a generation later—social assimilation is complete for many Italian families; others are still ethnic in their culture. The study in question traces changes in the Italian family in America over a period of 50 years and three generations. Three stages appear as the immigrant family becomes the ethnic family. (1) The original Italian families upon entering the United States attempt to continue the type of family life learned in the Italian rural village. (2) Finding it unsuited to the American city and their growing children opposed to Italian ways and

[9]The discussion of the Italian family is based primarily on Paul J. Campisi, "Ethnic Family Patterns: The Italian Family in the United States," *American Journal of Sociology*, 53 (1948), 443–49. A later study of an Italian community in an eastern city corroborates many of Campisi's findings and adds a wealth of detail: Herbert J Gans, *The Urban Villagers, Group and Class in the Life of Italian Americans* (New York: Free Press, 1962).

drawn to the American, the Italian parents gradually yield to the pressures but not according to a consistent plan. The old coordination of roles and functions is disturbed, and family solidarity is weakened. (3) As the children become adult and in their turn marry and rear families, they are able to reorganize their family life on a pattern that is compatible with urban life and American social norms, but with definite ethnic traces. Table 7 summarizes the changes in significant areas of family life.

The relation of the Italian family to the community also changes with immigration. In Italy the family owns its home and land and has little residential mobility. It has become well integrated into the community, carrying on many community activities and sharing feasts and holidays with others in the community. The family is fully developed and performs many functions usually carried out by institutions in America. In the American city the family finds itself living in a rented flat, moving often, somewhat active in the Italian colony but not participating in American activities. The family tries to transmit the Italian culture to its children but often finds its teachings in conflict with American culture taught by the public schools and other agencies with which the children make contact. The Catholic Church, a dominant institution in Italy, remains relatively strong, but it also loses some of its influence. In Italy, for instance, marriage is always a religious ceremony, but in America marriages increasingly occur outside the religion and marriage may involve simply a legal ceremony. Divorce, forbidden by the Catholic religion and absent from the Italian family, now occurs, although less frequently than among non-Catholics. Dating and courtship patterns change with each generation on American soil; from an adult-controlled process of mate selection in Italy, the movement has been toward the American pattern characteristic of the social class with which the Italian family has become affiliated. In the upper-middle and upper class, teenagers of Italian ancestry tend to be American in values and behavior; in the lower classes, they tend to be ethnic.[10]

RESIDENTIAL MIGRATION

With increasing absorption of American culture, the Italian family moves also toward social assimilation into the American community.[11]

[10]Francis A. J. Ianni, "The Italo-American Teen-ager," *Annals of the American Academy of Political and Social Science*, 338 (November, 1961), 70–78. See also this book, Chapter 12.

[11]Campisi, *op. cit.*, p. 447; J. K. Myers, "Assimilation to the Ecological and Social Systems of a Community," *American Sociological Review*, 15 (1950), 370–72.

TABLE 7

THE ITALIAN-AMERICAN FAMILY MOVES FROM ITALIAN TOWARD AMERICAN CULTURE

The family culture of the peasant immigrant from southern Italy	Adaptations made to American culture by immigrants and their children	American-Italian family culture of adult children in their marriages and with their children
ORGANIZATION		
Large-family system including kin and godparents; 10 children not unusual.	Relation to kin close, but godparent bond is weakened; migration has broken the kinship pattern, although it is still the ideal; fewer children.	Small-family system; few children; godparents not considered in the kinship.
MARRIAGE		
Parents select mate from same village and provide dowry; marriage in early teens.	Individual selects mate but with parental consent; parents urge marriage to someone from same province and oppose any marriage into another religion. No dowry. Marriage in late teens or early twenties.	Individual selects mate regardless of parental wishes; increasing number of unions with other nationality and religion. Marriage in early or middle twenties.
ROLES AND STATUS		
Father the patriarch with highest status; primogeniture gives eldest son high status; mother the center of the home and educated only for marriage. Individuals subordinate to the family with father enforcing his authority by force if necessary.	Father's status lowered or fictitiously maintained; mother relatively higher status and some outside activities; girls given wider education; sons less dominated by father; severe punishments avoided to prevent clashes with the law.	Trend toward equalitarian status of all members; education emphasizes personality; sons expected to do well in school but not to contribute to family finances. Family subordinate to individuals.
INTERPERSONAL RELATIONS		
Premarital kissing and petting not allowed; husband and wife show no	Husband and wife maintain old relationship but tolerate show of affec-	Husband and wife may show affection in family or public; premarital

TABLE 7

THE ITALIAN-AMERICAN FAMILY MOVES FROM ITALIAN TOWARD
AMERICAN CULTURE (*cont.*)

The family culture of the peasant immigrant from southern Italy	*Adaptations made to American culture by immigrants and their children*	*American-Italian family culture of adult children in their marriages and with their children*
INTERPERSONAL RELATIONS (*cont.*)		
demonstration of affection before the family or in public.	tion between married child and spouse; premarital love-making not openly allowed.	love-making openly practiced.
DIVORCE AND SEPARATION		
Divorce not allowed and desertion rare.	Occasional divorces but contrary to belief; desertion rare.	Religion forbids divorce, but it occurs; desertion rare.

SOURCE: Summarized from Paul J. Campisi, "Ethnic Family Patterns: The Italian Family in the United States," *American Journal of Sociology*, 53 (1948), 444–46.

It may Americanize the family name, move away from the Italian neighborhood into a completely American area, and have as few contacts as possible with the Italian-born parents. This complete rejection of both Italian culture and social participation may aid the family to gain acceptance in an American community. It is, however, of rare occurrence. Other families reject the Americans culturally and socially, clinging in the second and third generations to the parental group, the old Italian colony, and Italian ways. This tendency too is a minor one. The most typical trend is a slow migration of second-generation families that have established themselves economically. Leaving the original Italian colony, they do not disperse widely in the city but infiltrate into certain areas according to their economic standing and social aspirations. Thus the most successful may penetrate an upper-middle-class area, buying or building homes along one or two streets, and in time creating a little American-Italian colony. They and their Italian parents and older relatives in the older colony visit back and forth, and no effort is made to conceal their Italian ancestry and allegiance. Often they are regarded with curiosity or suspicion by their American neighbors, and social acceptance is slow. This group, culturally more American than Italian and socially tolerated but not accepted, becomes the ethnic group until such time as it becomes still more American and is accepted freely by the American group, when it will break up and disperse into the American society as individuals or small-family groups, finally intermarrying with Americans and losing its ethnic identity entirely.[12]

This process of residential migration, illustrated by the Italians, is not peculiar to them. Another example is the Norwegian colony that first settled in lower Manhattan in 1830.[13] From the coastal district of Norway, the immigrants were adjusted to a combination of seafaring, fishing, and agriculture, living in and loving the open green spaces of land. Their first settlement in Manhattan was near the loading docks and drydocks for ship repairs. As shipyards were opened in Brooklyn—and as Manhattan became more densely settled—families moved to Red Hook, the section of Brooklyn that lay across from the Battery. Here from about 1850 to 1890 the colony was massed. Again increasing density of population and the inroads of other ethnic groups pushed the Norwegians out further, until in succession three additional areas were occupied by them. Each move carried them to an area that was not closely built up and was somewhat secluded from other ethnic groups. New arrivals from Norway joined the older Norwegian ethnic group. Churches and a foreign-language newspaper followed them. Thus for more than 100 years, this ethnic group has maintained a distinctive group life through a process of residential migration. During the process new increments of Norwegian population have been added and others have been left behind or have dispersed into the general population.

The residential migration of ethnic families as they merge into the culture and social life of the American city is not haphazard. In general, the first colonies established by immigrant families in American cities have been in lower-class areas. Only as they become adjusted, earn more money, and accumulate some savings are they able to move away. Although in specific instances their movement may be to a remote area, in general a progressive migration occurs from the inner part of the city where they typically make their first settlement outward toward the edge of the city along some main line of transportation. Thus, a certain amount of concentration of each ethnic group in one sector is characteristic. Also, since a residue is left behind in each area of settlement, after a period of years members of the ethnic group representing several

[12]Residential mobility and its relation to the transition from foreign-culture to ethnic status for Italians in Boston is analyzed in Walter Firey, "Sentiment and Symbolism as Ecological Variables," *American Sociological Review*, 10 (1945), 146–48.

[13]Christen T. Jonassen, "Cultural Variables in the Ecology of an Ethnic Group," *American Sociological Review*, 14 (1949), 32–41.

generations and several levels of success are found along the line from the center of the city to the suburbs. They often also represent degrees of assimilation into American culture and social groupings, with the least assimilated in the interior areas, the most in the outer areas. As the ethnic families infiltrate these outer areas, they come into contact with American families and along the edges with members of other advancing ethnic groups. These contacts decrease the ingrown character of each ethnic group and promote inclusion in the American social world. In time the family no longer thinks of itself as belonging to some specific ethnic group and does not teach the children the old songs and legends, the old glory and pride of the ancestral group. When the family thinks of itself as American and affiliates itself on a social-class basis with other families of whatever ethnic origin, the stage of ethnic affiliation has passed and the family is American.[14]

RELIGIOUS AFFILIATION

One phase of ethnic culture that is influential in family life clings after most other aspects have faded—religion. So tenacious is religious affiliation that in the later stages of the transition from ethnic to American culture, religion may become the chief symbol of ethnic loyalty. For example, in Viroqua, a small mixed Norwegian-American city in Wisconsin, in which the Norwegians have adopted the American culture but maintain an ethnic loyalty, Norwegian and Lutheran are almost synonymous.[15] When a Norwegian leaves the Lutheran Church to affiliate himself with some other church, he is no longer considered a Norwegian. Lutheran women sometimes join the Ladies Aid in some other church, but non-Norwegians do not participate in Lutheran activities and indeed are not accepted socially in these activities unless they have married Norwegians. In Jonesville, another small Midwestern city, the Norwegian group, still holding itself aloof after 80 years, has taken on the characteristics of a Lutheran sect and is referred to locally as the Norwegian-Lutheran population. The group no longer follows the Norwegian culture but adheres closely to the ideals, standards, and codes of conduct of the Lutheran Church and in so doing opposes itself to the American groups in the community.[16]

[14]For graphic illustrations of the outward advance of ethnic groups in Chicago from 1898 to 1940, see R. G. Ford, "Population Succession in Chicago," *American Journal of Sociology*, 54 (1950), 156–60.

[15]Munch, *op. cit.*, pp. 785–86.

[16]W. Lloyd Warner and Associates, *Democracy in Jonesville* (New York: Harper, 1949), pp. 168–92.

Religious affiliation shows strongly when marital partners are selected. In New Haven, Connecticut, when members of an ethnic group begin to marry outside the group, they show a strong tendency to marry into another ethnic group with the same religion. [17] Irish, Italians, and Poles (all Catholic) tend to intermarry; British-Americans, Germans, and Scandinavians (all Protestant) likewise tend to intermarry; Jews are most likely to marry other Jews. Thus, as general ethnic affiliation dies out, it is replaced by loyalty to the religion of the ethnic background.

Marriage within or outside the ethnic religion is significant for family life, for each major religion has extended its ideals into a definite conception of marital relationships and family life. Marriage within the religion assures unity of ideals to the family and their transmission to the children by both family and religious institutions. Marrying outside the religion may mean that one religion is discarded, and the children are reared in the other; but it may also mean that both parents give up close allegiance to religion with the result that children are reared without the support that a common religious affiliation typically gives to family stability.[18]

THE FAMILY AS THE SEEDBED OF ETHNIC CULTURE

The disorganization of the family in the early adjustment period of the foreign-culture group has been discussed. As the group passes beyond the conflict stage into the ethnic classification, the family becomes one of the strongest carriers of the ethnic culture, aided by the ethnic church or other religious institutions and perhaps by one or two ethnic clubs. It is in the family that the correlation of the old and new cultures is made, and that children receive their first and much of their later ethnic training. Many of the European immigrants came from societies in which the family was the extended or kinship family. That pattern is broken by the migration but remains in the memory of the immigrants and often is at least partially re-established as children and grandchildren are added to the original family. The extended family with close ties of affection binding the foreign-born grandparents and the American-born parents and their children again functions, although not necessarily just as it did in Europe. Perhaps the extended family is more characteristic of the rural ethnic settlements than of urban com-

[17]Ruby Jo Reeves Kennedy, "Single or Triple Melting-Pot? Intermarriage Trends in New Haven, 1870–1940," *American Journal of Sociology*, 49 (1944), 331–39.
[18]For a further discussion of religious intermarriages, see Chapter 10.

munities. In Middle Western Norwegian settlements it helps to per-petuate the ethnic culture. Among Wisconsin small-city Norwegians:

> Another important focus of loyalty among the Norwegians . . . is the family, especially the extended family which is often referred to as the "clan." Here is where another important part of the social life of the Norwegian group takes place in the form of visit-ing, celebrations, and regular family reunions. Of course, this is again a social activity from which non-Norwegians are ex-cluded although they are freely accepted in case they are married in the clan—which happens quite frequently—and assume a certain loyalty to the clan.[19]

Among Norwegians in western Iowa and South Dakota the family and the Lutheran Church are the two institutions that preserve the Norwegian culture into the third generation. The ethnic culture is retained longer in the rural areas than in the small cities, for in the farm families Norwegian is spoken; daily customs, such as afternoon coffee, are preserved; and children and grandchildren alike have been taught the old Norwegian legends.[20] It is the family expectation that children will marry within the Norwegian group and the Lutheran Church, thus automatically preserving much of the culture for the next generation. Nevertheless, the culture thins out even in the rural areas, for careful study shows that fewer of the American-born children than of the foreign-born parents adhere to Norwegian customs and concepts. In the small city deviation is more marked, although loyalty to the Nor-wegian culture is strong and is reinforced by ritualistic celebrations of outstanding events in Norwegian history.

It is significant to note that in many rural and semirural communi-ties, where one ethnic group is relatively strong and the formal pressures toward Americanization found in cities are weak, the foreign-culture family passes into the ethnic family with a minimum of conflict and family disorganization.

From Foreign Culture to Ethnic to American—A Finnish Family

The account of a Finnish family written by a daughter shows the cul-tural and social adjustment of the foreign-born parents and their Ameri-

---

[19]Munch, *op. cit.*, p. 785.

[20]Lieutenant John Useem, U.S.N.R., and Ruth Hill Useem, "Minority-Group Pat-tern in Prairie Society," *American Journal of Sociology*, 50 (1945), 377–85.

canized children. It also shows the interpersonal tensions and conflicts not only between parents and children but also between husband and wife arising from cultural factors.

THE RURAL FAMILY IN FINLAND

Mary and John (to use American versions of their names) were born and reared on a farm in Finland. Mary's father owned the land, which had been in the family for several generations, while John's father was a tenant. Economically interdependent, socially landowner and tenant lived in different worlds. The tenant was not, however, of the lowest class, for farm laborers occupied a still lower position.

With many lakes running through and between the large farms, each farm had a high degree of self-sufficiency, and the family was dependent upon its own members for utilitarian functions and social life. With a patriarchal organization, the eldest male, grandfather or father, was head both of his farm and his family. He supervised the work of tenants and laborers and carried out many duties himself. He arranged for the annual visit of cobbler, harnessmaker, tailor, and saddler to repair and replace worn equipment and clothing. He trained his sons, one of whom would inherit the farm. The mother's duties were also well fixed in the rural culture. She had charge of the household duties, training her daughters in them. She supervised and helped to carry out spinning, weaving, knitting, and dyeing cloth. Often she made her own potato flour and candles. She also had farm tasks—the dairy, poultry, and vegetable garden were in her care. At times she aided in heavier work. The daughters—lowest in the family hierarchy—were assigned tasks according to their age and strength. The old and ill were cared for at home, a special bunk being constructed near the fireplace for their comfort. The farm home often housed three generations.

Social life was confined almost entirely to the family group, especially during the winter. The children had an outside contact in the school, rural children often attending for only four years between the ages of 9 and 13. The Lutheran Church also offered educational services and exerted strict control over the conduct of its members.

Marriage was arranged by the family with due regard to social status, property, and potential service to the family. Divorce, provided by law, was nevertheless a scandal. An illegitimate child was protected by law; he was entitled to the use of his father's name and to inheritance from both parents equal with that of legitimate children. Little social stigma was attached to illegitimacy.

A special phase of family life was the steam bath, with which the

Finns purged their bodies prior to Sunday church services; these ritualistic and cleansing baths were carried out by both sexes simultaneously in a special bath house or sauna. This was the occasion when nudity was socially accepted.

TRANSITION TO AMERICA

From such a background John immigrated to the United States and settled in a small city, Milltown, where there was a Finnish colony. He left behind his status as farm tenant and was free to establish himself on whatever level he could; nevertheless, he brought with him some of the attitudes of a subordinate class. Mary rebelled against the marriage arranged by her family and against their wishes borrowed money and came to the United States with John's sister. Her plan was to save enough money to return to Finland and establish a small business. The two young women settled in the city where John was working. The remainder of the story is in the words of the daughter of John and Mary; the italicized statements in brackets call attention to crises and stages in the adjustment process.

[*Employment was easy to find, with Mary using her household skills and John finding unskilled work.*] My mother found a position in a household as cook, housekeeper, and nurse. From her small salary she was able to pay her debt in Finland. My father worked in a local steel mill.

[*The Finnish colony provided social life; some American culture was learned in night school. The thrift and industry of early training are apparent in the home ownership.*] Their culture conflicts in Milltown were minimal. They established friendships with other Finnish immigrants who had organized a self-sufficient neighborhood. About two years after my mother's arrival, she and my father were married. [*This marriage was in violation of the Finnish mores. In Finland a marriage between the daughter of a landowner and the son of one of his tenants would have been socially impossible. Mary thus continues the rebellion toward her family that was evident in her rejection of their choice of a husband and in her migration to America. Later portions of the story suggest that her rebellion was against her family rather than the Finnish culture.*]

Their combined earnings made it possible for them to buy a house in the Finnish neighborhood. Three children were born. The family organization was semipatriarchal. The greater part of social, religious, and political activities were confined to their ethnic group. My father went to night school and subsequently gained his citizenship.

[*In the rural setting, the Finnish family patterns of their youth were more closely followed.*] Eight years later my father's health began to fail. The house in Milltown was sold and a ten-acre farm seven miles from the city was purchased. During the years of the 1920 boom and the depression that followed the farm was relatively self-supporting; more land was rented. Three more children were born. The roles of family members followed closely the patterns learned by my father and mother in Finland. They did not conflict to any degree with the rural patterns of behavior practiced by the surrounding farm families. The semipatriarchal family organization continued. Father was the authority and administrator, but he found the role difficult as he had not learned it in Finland where he was a member of a tenant family. [*The father was adjusting not only to a new culture but also to a new social-class position in America—an adjustment that he would not have been called upon to make in Finland.*] He tended to cling to the old country methods of farming. The fields were plowed with a single horse and plow at a time when nearby farms were becoming mechanized and others were accepting federal subsidies that he refused as "charity."

Mother assumed the role she had learned in Finland. She made her own bread, canned, worked in the gardens and fields, and milked and cared for the cow [*always the woman's task in Finland*]. She later acquired a loom and made her own rugs. She frequently expressed a desire for a spinning wheel and some sheep.

The roles of the children were clearly defined. The boys enjoyed higher status than the girls. Early in life we learned that we were expected to carry out certain "duties." Earnings were pooled and thrift was emphasized.

The children were taught to be clean [*the "sauna" was frequented on Saturday night and on the eve of church holidays*], religious, and thrifty, and to abstain from intoxicating drink, tobacco, and other "sinful" activities. We must work hard and love our parents above all except God. The aims of my parents were: to perpetuate the family name, to rear all of us so that we could support them in their old age, to teach us the moralistic attitudes and values of the Finns, to marry us into the ethnic group, and to provide us with better educations than they had. Their ultimate goal was to turn the farm over to the youngest son; they would build a house on the hill.

[*The ethnic group provided social contacts. This circumstance was a limiting factor so far as ultimate social adjustment was concerned but gave support to the family ethnic pattern.*] Religious, social, and business activities were confined to the ethnic group in Milltown. In the home, Finnish was spoken.

[*As the children entered adolescence, when the American culture calls for mixed activities and considerable freedom from parental supervision, family unity was strained. The parents supported the Finnish folkways and mores, the children defended the American. It is significant that the tensions and conflicts did not result in open family disintegration; later the children dispersed and established individual small-family units as opposed to the Finnish extended family.*]

From our schools we brought an increasing number of conflicting ideas and behavior patterns into the family. Also, the countryside was provided with a long-awaited public service—electricity. We had a radio, a car, and a telephone. My brothers and sister who had graduated from high school were employed in Milltown and brought friends into the home who were outside the Finnish circle of friends.

Quarrels took place between my father and brothers, and my father beat the children for their defiance of his authority. The following are the most typical areas of conflict that contributed to the disorganization of the semipatriarchal family that my parents had established in America: (1) language conflicts; we children spoke English and were embarrassed when the Finnish language was used in the presence of English-speaking guests; (2) dating, which was defined as courtship by our parents; we wanted to carry out the dating patterns of our schoolmates; (3) socially acceptable behavior; we wanted to drink and smoke if we chose; (4) sex education; we wanted to learn more about the facts of sex; (5) earnings; we wanted to keep our individual earnings for personal use instead of turning them over to our father for family use; (6) political attitudes; we could not understand why our relatives in Finland were fighting on the side of the Germans when we learned in civics classes that the Germans were "bad"; (7) class status; we were unaware of the class structure in Finland and could not understand the tension between our parents that grew from their difference in status there.

[*As more of the children came to maturity, gained status in the non-Finnish community, and passed beyond the age where they could be beaten into submission, the family reorganized on a compromise basis. Although the parents did not approve of their children's American behavior, they learned to tolerate it. The children either compromised in their turn or withdrew from the family either through marriage or by moving to another city. Such withdrawal is regarded as normal in American culture, although not in Finnish.*]

Reorganization in some areas occurred even as disorganization began and often continued in other areas. Concessions were made on both sides. Eventually the family spoke only English when guests were present. Each child, down the age scale, found it easier to obtain greater freedom in his personal life. My parents learned that other patterns of behavior did not necessarily end in "sin." As a larger number of children found employment, the contribution that each needed to make to the family pool became smaller and was therefore less grudgingly given. Misunderstandings and grumbling continued, and complete approval of the children's behavior has not been reached even to this day. Social drinking, even in minimal amounts, smoking, and irregular church attendance are consistently denounced by my father. He recognizes, however, that his position of authority is now merely nominal.

[*The children in adulthood found it possible to enter fully into American life only by a decisive withdrawal from the family. There is a suggestion that the nonethnic marriages, the elopements, and the conversion to another religion may contain some element of revolt against the parents.]*

Three children eventually moved away from the home area entirely in order to fulfill their individual ambitions. No child married into the ethnic group. Two children eloped since they knew their marriages would not be approved. One son—the potential heir—joined the Catholic Church prior to his marriage to a Catholic girl. Another son was divorced and remarried.

After four children had left the farm and withdrawn from close affiliation with the patriarchal family, mother died after an illness of two years. The farm was sold [*symptomatic of the break-up of the patriarchal family*], and father, my brother, and sister moved to Milltown. For a time father tried living with one of his daughters whose home and family were completely Americanized. But he was unhappy and there were many conflicts. At the age of 64 he married a widow of 60, a woman who had been born in Finland but reared in America. She had adjusted to both cultures but has her social activities in the Finnish community in Milltown [*the true ethnic type*]. She does not attach any social stigma to my father's status in Finland as a youth. She is cheerful, enjoys father's witticisms, admires his "good mind," is demonstrative in her affections, and takes a commonsense attitude toward his emotional and physical needs. Father in turn is proud of her participation in social and religious activities.[21]

In summary, the family in its earlier years on the farm was able to maintain many elements of Finnish culture and to confine social contacts to the Finnish community and institutions; as the children grew to adulthood, the parents attempted to remain in this exclusive social world, whereas the children learned the American culture and expanded their contacts to the American social groups and institutions, living for a time in both the Finnish and the American cultural and social worlds; their marriages and new places of residence, made on the basis of individual rather than family choice, marked the point of transition from the Finnish to American cultural and social adjustment. The father, unable to follow them into the American world, made his adjustment to a Finnish ethnic community through his removal from the farm to the city and his second marriage to a woman in the ethnic community.

The Ethnic Family and Social Mobility

The transition of families from ethnic to American culture and social participation has been a common phase of family life in our society for

[21]Unpublished record.

several generations. The presence of many families, always turning away from and rejecting the culture of the past, has influenced our general patterns and values of family life. In these families, the parents and grandparents have been unable to serve as models or to pass on to their descendants values and customs compatible with the American situation. Individualism has been fostered, beyond that which urbanism normally produces. Young people have had to make their own decisions in courtship; they have experimented with new types of family organization; and child training has been learned from books and study groups. The integration of the original family stock (usually based on patriarchal kinship organization) has been lost, and the younger people have formed small nuclear families. With the passage of time, the nuclear families formed by brothers, sisters, and cousins form collateral kinship groups of the same level of assimilation, which maintain friendly contacts.

As families have made the cultural transition, they usually have also passed from one social-class level into another. Barriers of language, confusion of cultures, and lack of training in urban skills have handicapped the original immigrants. Their children and grandchildren, reared in American schools, have better economic opportunities. They move from the original, lower-class residential areas into neighborhoods with better housing and a higher standard of living. This movement from class to class is vertical mobility, the subject of the next chapter.

Questions

1. Distinguish between foreign-culture, ethnic, and American families.
2. What is the difference between cultural assimilation and social assimilation?
3. Discuss the adjustment problems of the foreign-culture (immigrant) family in the United States. Would adjustment problems be less or greater if immigrants settled in rural areas instead of in cities?
4. Compare the adjustment problems of Mexican and Puerto Rican families.
5. Discuss the relation of residential migration to the process of social assimilation; of religious affiliation to assimilation.
6. From personal experience, observation, or original investigation trace the adjustment process of an individual family.
7. What might schools, churches, and other community agencies do

to assist foreign-culture families to adjust with a minimum of family disorganization?

Bibliography

BARRABEE, PAUL, "How Cultural Factors Affect Family Life," *Social Welfare Forum* (New York: Columbia University Press, 1954), pp. 17–30.

CAMPISI, PAUL J., "Ethnic Family Patterns: The Italian Family in the United States," *American Journal of Sociology*, 53 (1948), 443–49.

GANS, HERBERT J., *The Urban Villagers, Group and Class in the Life of Italian-Americans* (New York: Free Press, 1962).

HANDLIN, OSCAR, *The Newcomers: Negroes and Puerto Ricans in a Changing Metropolis* (Cambridge: Harvard University Press, 1959).

HOFFMAN, O. F., "Cultural Changes in a Rural Wisconsin Ethnic Island," *Rural Sociology*, 14 (1949), 39–50.

HUMPHREY, N. D., "The Changing Structure of the Detroit Mexican Family: An Index of Acculturation," *American Sociological Review*, 9 (1944), 622–26.

IANNI, FRANCIS A. J., "The Italo-American Teen-ager," *Annals of the American Academy of Political and Social Science*, 338 (November, 1961), 70–78.

JONES, R. C., "Ethnic Family Patterns: The Mexican Family in the United States," *American Journal of Sociology*, 53 (1948), 450–51.

LEWIS, OSCAR, *Five Families: Mexican Case Studies in the Culture of Poverty* (New York: Basic Books, 1959).

MILLS, C. WRIGHT, CLARENCE SENIOR, and ROSE KOHN GOLDSEN, *The Puerto Rican Journey* (New York: Harper, 1950).

MUNCH, PETER A., "Social Adjustment among Wisconsin Norwegians," *American Sociological Review*, 14 (1949), 780–81.

NEW, MARY L., and PETER KONG-MING NEW, " 'Life Style' of Chinatowners in San Francisco and Oakland," *Midwest Sociologist*, 17 (Spring, 1956), 29–33.

OPLER, MARVIN K., "The Influence of Ethnic and Class Subcultures on Child Care," *Social Problems*, 3 (July, 1955), 12–21.

RAND, CHRISTOPHER, *The Puerto Ricans* (New York: Oxford University Press, 1958).

THOMAS, J. L., "Marriage Prediction in *The Polish Peasant*," with comment by Florian Znaniecki, *American Journal of Sociology*, 55 (1950), 572–78.

THOMAS, W. I., and F. ZNANIECKI, *The Polish Peasant in Europe and America* (New York: Knopf, 1927), Vol. II, Parts III and IV.

WARNER, W. LLOYD, and LEO SROLE, *The Social Systems of American Ethnic Groups* (New Haven: Yale University Press, 1945), especially ch. 6,"The Family."

WESSEL, B. B., "Ethnic Family Patterns: The American Jewish Family," *American Journal of Sociology*, 53 (1948), 439–42.

YOUNG, PAULINE V., *The Pilgrims of Russian-Town* (Chicago: University of Chicago Press, 1932).

$$9$$

Vertical Mobility of Families

IN THE United States two trends, one toward continuity of family social-class placement, the other toward discontinuity and change, operate simultaneously. A number of studies indicate that about 30 per cent of people occupy a different class position than that of their parents, as judged primarily by differences in the occupational ranking of fathers and sons.[1] The majority of people—about 70 per cent—remain in the same occupational level (or social class) as their fathers, and such stability of class placement may continue through a number of generations. Examples of specific upper-class families cited in Chapter 5 referred to families that had held this status for several centuries. At the opposite end of the class hierarchy are lower-class families with great stability; for example, in Elmtown in the 1940's 60 per cent of lower-lower-class families had held this position since before the Civil War.[2] The majority of families, therefore, are stable in class position, the minority mobile.

Mobility may be upward or downward, depending upon a number of factors. In the United States, the major movement usually is upward, but there is also a downward movement; in other words, an exchange of positions.

[1]Richard Centers, "Occupational Mobility of Urban Occupational Strata," *American Sociological Review*, 13 (1948), 200; Seymour M. Lipset and Hans L. Zetterberg, "A Theory of Social Mobility," *Transactions of the Third World Congress of Sociology*, 2 (1956), 155–77; Carson McGuire, "Social Stratification and Mobility Patterns," *American Sociological Review*, 15 (1950), 195–204.

[2]August B. Hollingshead, *Elmtown's Youth* (New York: Wiley, 1949).

Mobility may be by individuals, families, or communities. An entire community or region may shift in social-class status when some cataclysmic event occurs that affects all families. Widespread and prolonged drought, war that destroys the economic means of a region, the movement of a large industry into another part of the country, or a depression may simultaneously affect large numbers of families. All these events, external to the family, have happened in the United States, causing marked downward mobility of families. Full employment and prosperity carry many people upward. In addition to these community or mass movements, individuals and families under normal conditions shift up or down in position.

This chapter is concerned with the relationship of mobility to families. Therefore, after a brief résumé of factors influencing stability and upward and downward mobility, the discussion will be limited to the processes by which families as units or individuals as family members change social-class position.

Factors That Favor Stability of Family Placement

Generally speaking, stabilizing factors are ones that segregate families into groups in which subculture is emphasized, and isolate them from contacts with other groups.

RESIDENTIAL SEGREGATION

The discussion of city and suburban areas has already pointed out the existence of intracity communities and individual suburbs whose inhabitants differ as to national background or occupational orientation. They differ also as to social class. Many of these areas are separated from adjacent areas by such physical barriers as railroad tracks, parks, or heavy traffic streets. Other barriers to intrusion are regulations as to the type and cost of housing that must be built in certain areas, which tend to exclude families of low income. Self-segregation is also sought through formal regulations and informal agreements of homeowners or builders not to sell housing to people of a specified nationality, religion, or race. Equally strong is discrimination against an intruder, who may be harassed by vandalism or nuisance telephone calls until he moves from the area. Other factors cause people to huddle together and resist moving, especially when a foreign language opens the way for easy communication among residents who would find themselves linguistically isolated in some other area.

Within each such area some type of communal life that emphasizes the special subculture of the group and provides for many of their needs tends to develop. Children and unemployed wives especially find their lives circumscribed by the communal life. Adolescents and employed members live to some extent a double life—partly in the community and partly in the wider contacts of the city. As cities grow and change, the residents of one area move into another area, but they tend to retain a uniform class, ethnic, and racial pattern in the new areas as in the old.[3] To the extent that these patterns of residential segregation are perpetuated, the subculture of the group tends also to be perpetuated.

INSTITUTIONS THAT SERVE ONE CLASS OR ETHNIC GROUP

In the different communities institutions develop that are specifically designed to serve the local group. These include special shopping centers that stock the goods desired by the group, parochial or foreign-language schools, churches with which the group is affiliated, and clubs and private schools with carefully selected membership. These institutions, which preserve and transmit to their members and clients the in-group subculture, are especially important when they serve the children of the community.

FAMILY TEACHING OF THE CLASS OR ETHNIC SUBCULTURE

Segregation based on physical or social barriers is reinforced by the teaching of parents. At birth each child automatically receives the social-class and ethnic status of his parents. Whatever he may become in later life, the baby has no individual status but takes his status from his parents. The family immediately begins to induct the child into the class or ethnic subculture.

[3]Walter Firey, "Sentiment and Symbolism as Ecological Variables," *American Sociological Review*, 10 (1945), 140–48.

The teaching of class position is not carried on formally but through the daily supervision by parents of their young children's play contacts. The child is encouraged to invite certain children to his home and is called into the house when seen playing with some other, less desirable child. If children of several social-class levels are playing together in the home, the mother selects certain ones for attention and praise and ignores others, although she will not ask the children of lower-class level to leave the home. Her own child, wishing to please his mother and responsive to her behavior and tone of voice, unthinkingly follows her lead in selecting his playmates. Also, the visiting child who is ignored is equally responsive and soon feels that he is not wanted, whereas the child who is selected for favorable attention responds to the praise and accepts the valuation placed upon him by his playmate's mother. Thus the mother, by selecting her child's playmates, gives him his class identification of other children, which they in turn are receiving from their parents. By the time children are in the fifth grade they are well aware of their own and other children's social-class placement.[4]

The family also is responsible for the first inculcation of class or ethnic subculture. The differences in family organization and standards in the various social classes have already been discussed. The mother encourages, praises, punishes, as the child conforms to or rebels against the behavior that she demands of him. In time, the child accepts not only the behavior but also the rationalizations that support the behavior. He believes in the cultural peculiarities of his class or ethnic group. The exception to this statement is found in situations in which the child's contacts are not confined to his own class or ethnic group; then other contacts compete with the family, and the child may come to identify himself wholly or partially with some other group.

Community Expectations

The stability of family subculture is bulwarked from without by the community expectations of how certain families will behave. In Plainville, the little Missouri town studied by West, certain breaches of conventions and laws that would not have been tolerated if committed by middle-class families were regarded with tolerance when they occurred in the lower class.[5] It was assumed that the lower-class families did not

---

[4]W. Lloyd Warner and Associates, *Democracy in Jonesville* (New York: Harper, 1949), ch. 5.

[5]James West, *Plainville, U.S.A.* (New York: Columbia University Press, 1945), pp. 123–26.

know any better. Thus, when a man and woman lived together without marriage, the situation was regarded as amusing rather than immoral. Lower-class men who stole chickens or corn were treated as though they were children, by scolding or scaring through a pretense of shooting.

Shiftlessness and lack of ambition are expected by the middle class of lower-class families. Likewise, the lower class looks to the classes above them for leadership in community activities and often for direct assistance in finances. Sometimes a lower-class family will look to some particular upper-class family with whom there is a close tie, perhaps through years of employment, for assistance or protection in case of lawbreaking. In general, however, serious delinquent and criminal behavior is regarded as typical and to be expected of lower-class people, and the tendency is to allow the processes of the law to operate in order to teach the offender and his class what may be anticipated if such behavior continues. Similar behavior from members of the upper classes is regarded as more or less incidental and settlement is made outside of legal processes. Such differential attitudes toward and treatment of similar behavior help to set the limits of acceptable behavior for children growing up in any one of the classes.

Thus, stability of family placement rests upon some type of physical or cultural segregation, whether enforced from the outside (as in some racial areas) or by the wish of the group itself. In this in-grown social situation the group subculture is perpetuated and taught to the children by institutions, parents, and community expectations.

Factors Fostering Upward Mobility

A different set of factors fosters upward mobility.

PHILOSOPHY OF THE OPEN-CLASS SYSTEM

The dictum that "all men are created free and equal," the right of all adult citizens to vote, the selection from any social level of a candidate for President and other positions of political leadership, the opportunities for individual wealth, the system of free education and, at the college level, low-cost education, all support the philosophy of the open-class system. Theoretically, any individual or family may climb as high in the socioeconomic scale as ability warrants. There is no categorical selection of the families that are privileged to climb. Actually, also, enough spectacular successes have occurred to give credence to the theory. The fact that the proportion of any one class that reaches a higher level is small does not detract from the belief.

DIFFERENTIAL BIRTH RATE BY SOCIAL CLASSES

Table 6 in Chapter 5 showed that college-educated married women were producing on the average less than the two children needed to replace husband and wife, whereas women of less education produced more than enough children for replacement. It may be assumed then that there are some "vacancies" in the higher level classes that may be filled by specially trained or apt members from lower classes.[6]

THE EXPANDING PRODUCTION OF THE UNITED STATES

The development of the United States accounts for much upward mobility of families and individuals. The history of the United States has offered a series of expanding economic opportunities. The vast expanse of land to be cultivated and the abundance of natural resources— timber to be cut, metals and coal to be mined, oil to be drained from the depths of the earth—offered opportunity for wealth and economic prestige to the capable of any social class. In point of numbers alone, the upper class could not supply the need. Moreover, many of the upper-class families had become entrenched in their class position and a fixed mode of life before the greatest industrial development of the country began. Supervision of their inherited wealth, whether in investments or a family business, preoccupation with the arts, a family tradition of certain professions as appropriate for their sons, all deterred upper-class families from exploiting the resources of the expanding frontier.

Although there is some indication that the making of great fortunes, which start families on the upward social trek, is a thing of the past, industrial booms (such as those which accompanied World War II), the opening of some new area for development, or a new invention pave the way for upward economic mobility that in time will result in higher social-class placement.

[6]For a detailed discussion of the process, see McGuire, *op. cit.*

SPATIAL MOBILITY

Migrations into new communities, both in the pioneer period and more recently, are conducive to social mobility. Freed from the ties to the home community, each family may make an individual effort to raise its social status. Not all succeed: some remain at the same level; others move downward permanently or as a temporary stage in the process of readjustment.

INSTITUTIONS THAT SERVE SEVERAL OR ALL CLASSES AND ETHNIC GROUPS

Any institution that brings together people of different social classes or ethnic groups breaks down isolation and makes it possible for individuals from different cultural groups to become personally acquainted. They come to regard each other as individuals rather than as members of a specific class or ethnic group. Each receives something of the culture of the other and in return gives some of his culture. This interchange of culture not only develops an appreciation of the other group but permits the ambitious person to gain a toehold on the social ladder.

In the realm of social heritage as well as the learning of skills, public schools may serve to bring individuals of different social classes and ethnic groups together. The schools are free, open to everyone, and operate under state laws that require all children to attend until they reach a certain age. It is true that the schools are not completely free from class affiliation. In a large city, all the children in the district may represent one class level or one ethnic group; then only the teachers may bring to the children the culture of another group. In other schools, teachers, administrative officers, and the school board may represent the same subcultural group and may favor children of their own group. Nevertheless, the persistent individual can continue in school, slowly absorbing the folkways and mores of other groups represented and making easier his eventual transition to another social class or from the ethnic group into the American culture.

Public libraries, art museums, and public concerts are other such agencies that are open to all without restriction.

Family mobility therefore is related to factors that destroy fixed social systems and encourage wider contacts, such as easy entrance into new occupations or new geographic areas, or inclusion in institutions that cut across class and ethnic barriers. Another factor is the abiding American faith in the right and the potential ability of any person or family to improve their social position.

Factors Fostering Downward Mobility

Downward mobility is not an objective for which people strive, but is indicative of failure to maintain a given class position or to achieve an attempted upward mobility. Factors involved are ones that destroy a previously held position.

COMMUNITY FACTORS

Earlier in this chapter, various external catastrophes were listed that destroy class positions and abruptly force families into lower positions: natural catastrophes, movements of industry and the introduction of new inventions that leave workers stranded, severe depressions, and wars. Sometimes the downward movement is temporary, and families regain their lost position. Sometimes, while many suffer a major downward movement, others may gain status by the same event. For example, a major invention may displace some workers but open new opportunities to others.

PERSONAL FACTORS

People who are content with their social-class position cannot be said to have failed. It is only those who lose position or who have attempted upward mobility and failed who can be thought of as being downwardly mobile. Lack of capacity, education, or technical and social training may lead to downward mobility, either from a previously stable position or from attempted upward mobility. Personal habits, such as excessive drinking or drug addiction, may prevent a person from meeting the expectations of a given social-class position, and may lead to a decline in status for the individual and perhaps for his entire family if he is the one upon whom they depend for income. Violation of the mores of a person's class or the commission of a serious crime may also lower class status.

The characteristics that cause downward mobi'ity differ from one social class to another. The chronic drunkard in the middle class may quickly be rejected and lose status, whereas the chronic drunkard in the lower class may be tolerated. The social-class definition of a crime is more important than the legal definition in fixing status. Some middle-class white-collar crimes are regarded as misfortunes rather than real crimes, and after imprisonment the offender may be received back by family, friends, and business associates. However, rape by a middle-class man might readily lead to complete rejection.

The Process of Upward Mobility

When the family or some of its members are upwardly mobile, they must pass through a certain process with both sociological and psychological components.[7]

Rarely does an entire family achieve upward mobility. Instead, one or two members may forge ahead and gradually establish themselves in a class one or, more rarely, two or more ranks ahead of the general family status. The advancing individual is often a son or daughter, but sometimes husband or wife will move ahead while the spouse clings to the original class status. The most frequent advances are made by those in the lower-middle and upper-lower classes. It will be recalled that in these classes the family unit tends to be the husband and wife and their children. When the son or daughter marries, he or she tends to withdraw from close incorporation in the parental family and to establish an independent family unit with separate living quarters. The movement of son or daughter into a higher social class therefore accentuates a process already accepted as normal. Nevertheless, upward mobility widens the breach between related family units, even when the parents have encouraged and financially aided the son or daughter to fit himself or herself for entrance into a higher class. The desire of the middle-class parent to give his son or daughter the "advantages" he did not have in youth is linked with the pain of estrangement after the son or daughter has achieved the parent's goal.

The process of upward mobility typically includes the following steps:

1. The person or family goes through some anticipatory socialization, secured through reading, motion pictures, television programs, or

----

[7]For a slightly different formulation of the mobility process, see Warner and Associates, *op. cit.*, pp. 55–76. An excellent case of a Negro family that was first upwardly mobile and then downwardly mobile, with the exception of one son, is given in Allison Davis and John Dollard, *Children of Bondage* (Washington, D.C.: American Council on Education, 1940), pp. 99–126.

observation of the behavior of higher classes in public. What is learned is often limited to external characteristics of behavior or to knowledge of material symbols of the class.

2. He associates himself with the higher class in whatever way he can.
3. Through the association he absorbs some of the subtle and intangible attitudes and values of the class.
4. Psychologically he strives to identify himself with the higher class and to destroy his identification with the class he is leaving.
5. The process is complete when he is accepted by the higher class as a member.

Each step merits further discussion in relation to family interaction.

Acquiring Characteristics of a Higher Class

Certain external class characteristics can be acquired by those of a lower class without the direct aid or permission of individual members of the higher class. These external characteristics include amount of education, to some extent selection of schools attended, preparation for special occupations typical of the higher class, cultural attainments, manners, and style of dress. Preparation begins as a rule in childhood and may be initiated by parents or by a schoolteacher who is attracted by a child's mental ability or personal characteristics that seem to set him apart. Thus, the lower-class child who is being steered toward the middle class may be provided with a piano and given music lessons perhaps at some sacrifice to his parents and other members of the family. He will be provided with better clothing than other children of his class, and may be sent to the Sunday school of the middle class, although the parents may not be affiliated with the denomination. The community center that he attends may respond to his better appearance and achievements by making summer camp possible for him. The schoolteacher will single him out for inclusion in activities usually reserved for the middle-class children; he may appear in programs or serve on school committees to which other lower-class children are not appointed. Later, teachers will advise him to enroll for high school courses that lead into middle-class occupations and perhaps will help him to secure a scholarship which makes some college or specialized training possible.

In like manner, the child of ambitious middle-class parents will be given some of the outer characteristics of the upper-class child. He will be enrolled in a dancing class patronized by the upper class, sent to a private summer camp, entered at the correct college, advised to prepare for some profession. His social life will be guided away from those of his own class, and every opportunity will be seized to associate him with those of the next higher class.

The normal process by which parents pass on to their children the culture of their class is destroyed. Slowly the child is alienated from his class and from his family as a part of that class. He is no longer able to identify completely with his parents nor to take them for his models; rather, he must take as models the idealized conceptions of the higher class that the parents present to him by word of mouth, by story or legend, by the remote figure pointed out at public functions. The more successful the parents are in preparing their child for advancement into the higher class, the greater is the alienation.

ASSOCIATION WITH THE HIGHER CLASS

In all communities certain organizations cater to one special class; other associations, however, cut across class lines, at least to the inclusion of two or three adjacent classes. Organizations based on a non-class characteristic (such as the American Legion or the League of Women Voters), although they may be dominated by one social class, nevertheless are open to the aspiring climber from below. Among children, the public school serves this purpose to some extent. Junior and senior high schools, with larger districts than elementary schools, are more likely to include several social-class areas and thus bring together children of different classes. Freedom of entrance into cross-class organizations does not imply, however, that the child from the lower class is necessarily welcomed or made to feel at home. He may be ignored, shunned, or ridiculed as the children of the higher class seek to preserve their own status by excluding a child of lower status. Nevertheless, the persistent parent and child can find a few situations in which the child can be brought into contact with the children of the higher class. In many organizations there are unwelcome tasks that may fall to the lot of the intruding child—the clean-up committee, the ticket sellers. The willing child who accepts these tasks and is able to overlook personal rebuffs may gradually establish himself on the fringe of the higher group in institutional and organizational settings, although he probably will not be invited into the homes of the children. The following experience of a girl is pertinent.

> One year when my middle-class parents found it necessary to spend the winter in the South, I attended a private school as my parents were unfamiliar with the different parts of the city or the quality of the public schools. This school catered to upper-class children. I made some friends at school and was invited by

a little girl to spend Saturday at her home. Her mother carefully
led me to talk about my parents, where we lived, what my father's
business was, and so on. I was treated with courtesy but I was
never invited to come again.

At a later period in life, the young man who has prepared himself
for an occupation of a higher social class may find himself a valued
member of a business or professional association; his wife may be prominent in civic groups; yet neither may be invited to the homes of their
business or club associates. Nevertheless, these nonpersonal contacts
are a part of the preparation for the higher social class, for they permit
absorption of the manners, speech, slang, jokes, attitudes, and values
of the higher class. As these associations strengthen, the child or couple
is drawn further and further away from the original class and family
connections. For a time the individual or couple may lead a very isolated existence in so far as personal contacts are concerned. Secondary
contacts may be many but may not include those on a primary level.

ABSORPTION OF ATTITUDES AND VALUES

The beginning of the process of changing classes may be in anticipatory
socialization, that is, learning in advance some of the skills and attitudes
appropriate to the prospective new class. The total process goes beyond
that of socialization into acculturation, that is, the person must
abandon one subculture and adopt another. Mentally, he probably
faces many conflicts, for his affiliation for a time is to both classes. If
his original socialization has been in the lower class, he will have to
abandon the idea of masculine superiority as well as learn to accept
intermittent financial aid from outside sources while children are small;
he will have to remold his extramarital behavior with regard to sex;
he will have to avoid dependence upon public agencies. These attitudes
and acts are frowned upon by the middle class.

Small and often subtle qualities that are class-marked have to be
changed. The pronunciation of a word, the quality of laughter, the
mode of greeting a stranger, the connotations of a joke must conform
to the practices of the higher class.

IDENTIFICATION

Identification with the parents during childhood is a normal part of
the process of maturing in our culture. Chapter 12 elaborates upon

the value of such identification to the child in the development of feminine and masculine roles. Typically the parental identification is paralleled by social-class identification, exemplified first in the parents and, as the child widens his contacts, in playmates and neighbors. In freeing himself from parental identification, the adolescent often vacillates between burying himself deep in the security of parental identification and defying his parents in the attempt to free himself. He suffers from conflicting impulses and opposed needs. Eventually he succeeds in identifying himself not with any one person but with the mores of his own generation. In changing identification from one social class to another, the person undergoes similar difficulties. If the shift comes during adolescence, it may involve the denial of both parental and social-class identification. If it comes during young adulthood, after the parental identification has been broken, it will still be difficult and will also involve a still further withdrawal from the parental family.

In class identification, the individual accepts the values and responsibilities of his social class as his own. He tends to be somewhat ethnocentric about his class culture and to believe in it and rationalize its deficiencies. He is aware of the errors and shortcomings of other social classes but regards his own social class as most adequate. In affiliating himself with the culture of another social class he must reverse his attitudes; he must accept the new social class as best and be able to accept and believe in the criticisms made by this class of his original class. Implied is criticism of his parents, siblings, and friends of the old class.

Before his new identification is complete, he typically will vacillate, as does the adolescent, between the two classes. At times he will feel that the old class is best, that he will never be accepted by the new class, that the prize of higher status is not worth the struggle and denial of family and friends necessary to attain it. At times he will feel guilty that his success is greater than theirs and perhaps will seek to assuage his guilt by buying a new home for his parents or financing a niece or nephew through school. He may try to pull his entire family up with him, moving parents or siblings to the residential area of the higher class. But parents are usually too deeply imbedded in the old class subculture to make the transition and only serve to impede him. Gradually he will move toward a more secure position in the higher class.

The desire for full upper-class inclusion, which he may never attain, he will project upon his children, giving them full entrance into the higher class through their attendance at the proper schools and camps.

As he withdraws from his old social class, his family and friends, although proud of him and their early contacts with him ("I knew him when—"), also are secretly envious and often openly critical. At best they recognize that he has grown away from them and is no longer one of them. When more critical, they say that he is "high hat," or extravagant, or has a "swelled head." Gently or ruthlessly, the social class and his own family reject him, and the ranks of his original class subculture close behind him as the new class opens before him.

ACCEPTANCE BY THE HIGHER CLASS

The final step of acculturation into a higher class comes with acceptance of the aspiring individual and his family into the primary groups of the higher class. He is elected to membership in exclusive clubs where a unanimous vote is necessary for membership; he is invited to the homes of his new friends; he is welcomed as a neighbor in the proper residential area. He is accepted now not only because of his occupational standing and his willingness to serve on committees and contribute to the right causes, but as a person who understands the class connotations of words spoken as well as the dictionary definition and who laughs at a joke not because of its obvious humor but because of its subtle class meanings. Sometimes the person who starts the upward climb is never fully accepted, this last reward going to his children or even grandchildren. In small cities and the more recently developed regions acceptance requires less time than in the older cities of the East and South where the upper class counts its existence not in years but in generations. The final mark of acceptance comes when he, or his child, is able to marry into the new class.

The Process of Downward Mobility

In some ways the process of downward mobility is the opposite of the upward process. The downwardly mobile person or family must give up many of the things that the upwardly mobile person is striving very hard to achieve. He is not concerned with identifying himself with a lower class nor with gaining their acceptance, but is struggling to retain his identification with and membership in the higher class. The final adjustment is not his acceptance into the lower class but his personal acceptance of himself as a lower-class member, the mellowing of his discontent.

The family adjustment to the economic depression of the 1930's will serve to illustrate one type of downward mobility.[8]

ECONOMIC VULNERABILITY

Social classes differed in their vulnerability to the effects of the depression.[9] Upper-class and upper-middle-class families were least affected. As income was reduced, these families curtailed certain expenditures but usually did not have to give up their homes or lose their social-class position. When the reduction was severe, or the husband lost his position, traumatic internal adjustments within the family sometimes were necessary. At the opposite extreme of the class hierarchy, the lower-lower-class family suffered little change in class status, since there was little change that it could make. Many of these families accepted periodic or complete unemployment as a way of life. They were not embarrassed by applying for relief and, in fact, felt a certain amount of security when they were on the relief list.

The working-class family was most deeply affected both in downward mobility and emotionally as the members tried to avoid acceptance of their new status.[10] The following brief case summaries are of lower-middle-class families that experienced great losses in the depression.

> The Linds had been comfortably self-supporting for years and never had a debt. When the father was no longer able to meet their needs and began to accumulate moderate debts (the interest on a $1,000 mortgage and $50 for milk), he worried excessively. It seemed impossible to him that he should not be able to meet his obligations. He cried at the relief office in telling of these debts; he walked the floor at night and felt "sort of desperate." At one period he drank, until his wife "put her foot down."

[8]The depression was chosen to illustrate downward mobility for two reasons. First, in the history of the United States some type of depression has occurred about once every five years, the most severe and prolonged being the depression of the 1930's, when for a time a third of the regularly employed labor force was without work. Depressions, therefore, are a recurring cause of downward mobility. The second reason is that at least seven major studies were made and published, analyzing the effect on family life of the depression of the thirties. See bibliography for references.

[9]For a detailed analysis of the effect of the depression on different social classes, see Ruth Shonle Cavan, "Unemployment—Crisis of the Common Man," *Marriage and Family Living*, 21 (1959), 139–46.

[10]Ruth Shonle Cavan and Katherine H. Ranck, *The Family and the Depression* (Chicago: University of Chicago Press, 1938), pp. 60–61.

Mrs. Lind likewise worried until she thought "the top of her head would come off with severe headaches." For two years the family struggled along, applying three times for relief before it was finally granted. They felt humiliated in asking for relief, but were desperate.

In the Garfinkel family, the father was described in 1928 as a quiet man, colorless, healthy, with no bad habits. He disliked to spend money but was generous with the mother. Each year he saved for periods of unemployment. The mother at this time was an emotional woman with little poise, given to loud, embarrassed laughter. The family seemed to be fairly happy except for the mother's tendency to over-protect her children. When the father's income was reduced from $40 to a few dollars a week, the relief agency helped intermittently whenever the income was less than $17 per week. For a year or more the family lived with this uncertain status, neither on relief nor completely self-supporting. The father's reaction to his economic insecurity was to develop physical fears. Spots on his body burned; he had headaches; he feared cancer. He spent much time going from clinic to clinic, where no physical basis for his ailments could be found. The mother, her condition complicated by high blood pressure, developed a very excited state. At times her chief social interaction was excessive giggling. The relief agency finally assumed full responsibility; and when the father was placed on work relief, most of these difficulties in both father and mother disappeared.

Clinging to Customary Status

When the employed person, usually the husband, was first laid off, the family accepted it as a normal short lay-off. Men spoke of deserving a short vacation. Even prolonged unemployment was met with disbelief that unemployment was anything except temporary. When no recall came, the man was forced to look for other work, at first, in his special skill. If such a job was not found, he later sought for a less specialized and less well-paid type of work, and eventually for anything, even odd jobs. This was a long-drawn-out process. Skilled workers sometimes delayed taking a job with lower pay or less prestige for as long as six months. Other members of the family, unaccustomed to work, looked for jobs; if they found them the financial strain was eased, but often at the expense of loss of face for the husband.

Loss of Status Symbols

Most of the working-class families were not securely rooted in the middle class; they were lower-middle and upper-lower. Symbols of middle-class status therefore were precious. Financial resources were slowly consumed in the following order: credit was used to the limit; small savings were used; loans were made; goods were sold or pawned; and insurance policies were cashed. Families gave up the telephone, summer vacations, club memberships, and so forth. As long as possible, these adjustments were concealed from neighbors and friends.

A more obvious symbol of loss of status was loss of a house upon which payments could no longer be made. Some families moved in with relatives. The final degradation was application for relief. For these normally self-supporting and often upwardly mobile families, relief was regarded as a personal disgrace. It meant the loss of all their aspirations for a secure social position or perhaps a better one than that of their parents. The fact of downward mobility could no longer be denied or hidden.

LOSS OF PLANS FOR THE FUTURE

As members of the lower-middle class, many workingmen's families had specific plans for the future, of which home ownership was only one. Special or college education for their children was another, toward which money was saved. Savings for emergencies or for old age were also a part of middle-class subculture. (The depression began prior to the Social Security Act with its various forms of aid for old people.) With the loss of money, the working-class family again faced the hand-to-mouth existence of the lower-lower class.

CHANGE OF PERSONAL ROLE

In these working-class families the father held the superior role as chief or sole wage earner and head of the family. Only with great emotional turmoil could he change this conception of himself and face the fact that he could not function as the head—that his depression role resembled that of the irresponsible or incapable lower-lower-class husband. If one or more of the older children found work, he saw himself displaced in the family organization by a subordinate. If his wife (formerly unemployed) found work, he felt that the male and female roles were reversed. The social worker, usually a young woman, only added further to his sense of defeat. As the husband's role declined, and the roles of other family members increased in relative importance, wife and children often lost respect for him. They began to assume his former functions of authority and decision-making.

However, it should not be thought that the husband was the only one to suffer some degree of personal disorganization. When no one could find work, all suffered a sense of failure. Teenage boys left home and wandered in groups across the country, living from hand to mouth, often by petty thievery.

ACCEPTANCE OF LOWER STATUS

The family was able to reorganize only after it had accepted its lowered social-class placement and had stopped comparing its current status with the more comfortable past.[11] It found rationalizations to justify unemployment, lowered income, and loss of status. The family members began to function together as a unit, to accept new roles for themselves and others, and to enter into new activities commensurate with their new status.

With the improvement in economic conditions in the 1940's, some families resumed upward mobility. In some instances, men on relief for a decade found employment; for other families, only the younger members again became upwardly mobile.

SPECIAL FACTORS

Various special factors eased or increased the difficulties of adjustment. For some families intrafamily contacts increased and intensified. The family spent its time at home because money was lacking for other types of activities. Unemployed members were at home when formerly they would have been working. Out-of-school children were at home because they could not find work. The family often found itself cramped into smaller quarters than usual, often because they had moved to a smaller apartment or house to save rent, but sometimes because they had enough money to heat only one or two rooms of the house, into which the whole family must crowd and within which all activities must be carried on. When the family was well integrated, this overcrowding seemed to create little ill-will; but when tension already existed, friction was common.

Family integration or unity was of great importance in carrying the family through the depression.[12] When common interests, affection, and a sense of economic interdependence were present, the family had a strong bulwark against disorganization. The omission of any of these

[11] E. Wight Bakke, *Citizens without Work* (New Haven: Yale University Press, 1940); an eight-year study of 24 families who endured prolonged unemployment.
[12] R. C. Angell, *The Family Encounters the Depression* (New York: Scribner, 1936).

elements from family life tended to weaken the stability of the family.

Previous habits of adaptability of the family also helped it to adjust to the depression.[13] Three elements contributed to the necessary flexibility. A nonmaterialistic philosophy of life was important; this philosophy placed greater emphasis upon cultural values than upon material possessions. Freedom from traditionalism also aided the family to accept new conditions. Habits of responsibility also strengthened the family, in that each member was vitally interested in the welfare of the entire group.

Previous experiences in meeting crises set a precedent for adjustment to the depression. The family pattern established before the depression tended to continue after unemployment, but in intensified form. Thus the family that had been able to adjust to earlier crises tended to adjust well to the depression, but the family that had not adjusted to prior crises, but instead had tended to disintegrate or fall back upon relatives or relief agencies, or in some other way had failed to revamp its customary ways to meet a crisis, was unable to meet the depression in adequate fashion.

Thus the effect of a depression was not merely a matter of dollars and cents or even of loss of social status in the community; it was also closely related to the type of family organization that existed prior to the depression. The integrated, adaptable family, with an adequate pattern of adjustment already developed, met the depression with less emotional turmoil and less loss of family strength than the family that was lacking in unity, that was rigid in family pattern, and that had an inadequate method of adjusting to changes.

Family Reactions to the Downwardly Mobile Individual

The downwardly mobile individual often is unable to meet some of the social-class expectations or mores. A part of his adjustment is to his lowered status; equally important is his relationship with his family.

The upper-class person who becomes alcoholic or a recognized philanderer, the middle-class man who refuses to support his family or who becomes a day laborer, and the lower-class person who becomes a habitual criminal are all examples of those who repudiate their class mores. Many, although not all, of the residents of "homeless men" areas

---

[13] *Ibid.*

in cities once were members of the middle class or occasionally of the upper class. Not all downward mobility carries the individual or family to such low levels, however. The upper-class deviant may slip to middle class, the upper-middle to lower-middle, the upper-lower to lower-lower; the lower-lower can move downward only a short distance, but he may sink to the level of those who disregard all social rules.

Upper-class families often protect their deviants, their ne'er-do-wells, alcoholics, feeble-minded, and criminals through the power given by social prestige and wealth. A companion for the wayward girl, a body-guard for the alcoholic, private sanitariums for the feeble-minded, a life abroad for the philanderer, financial restitution for crimes and other misdeeds all help prevent the downward journey of the upper-class person who fails to meet family and class expectations. In any other class the family would be unable to provide so impregnable a shield. In the upper class the coordinated family stands supreme, and only by a persistent effort can the individual escape from it.

The middle-class family, eager to protect the family's good name and unable to help the deviant, often repudiates the erring one, and thus saves the family name by denying responsibility for the deviant or even denying the relationship. Thus, a family may say of a related nonconforming family or person with the same name, "We don't claim them," or "They are very distantly related." The lower-class family may use the same device, especially if it is upwardly mobile and wishes to shake off entanglements with lower-lower-class members or relatives. If the relationship cannot be wiped out by denial, the family may assume a fatalistic attitude—"Every family has one black sheep." In the more religious families the attitude is resignation over a trial sent to test their faith.

The attitude of the downwardly mobile person cannot be stated categorically. He may feel guilty that he has not upheld the class standards; or relieved to be no longer subject to expectations and demands that he is not fitted to meet.

Social Mobility and Family Disunity

In earlier chapters the disorganizing effects of spatial mobility were discussed. Social mobility likewise breaks down the unity of families as some members rise or fall, identifying themselves with a new class subculture and rejecting the old. Like migrations, social mobility is part of the fluid social and economic condition of our society—a part of the social background to which families must adjust.

Questions

1. What is the extent of vertical mobility?
2. How does residential segregation serve to stabilize family class placement?
3. What is the difference between a country club and a veterans organization as an agency to promote social mobility?
4. What difference in methods of training must a family use to promote stability or mobility among its children?
5. How much of an incentive to upward mobility is our philosophy of the open-class system?
6. How did the pioneer period promote upward mobility? Now that the frontier is closed, will upward mobility gradually stop?
7. Why doesn't everyone strive for upward mobility?
8. Think of some family you know that is upwardly mobile. How well do the steps given in the text for the process of upward mobility fit this case?
9. What two types of factors foster downward mobility?
10. Why was the working-class family especially vulnerable to downward mobility in the 1930's?
11. What is the difference between the way the upper-upper-class family and the middle-class family treats a downwardly mobile member? Why is there a difference?

Bibliography

SOCIAL MOBILITY

CENTERS, RICHARD, "Occupational Mobility of Urban Occupational Strata," *American Sociological Review*, 13 (1948), 197–203.

HOLLINGSHEAD, AUGUST B., *Elmtown's Youth* (New York: Wiley, 1949).

JANOWITZ, MORRIS, "Some Consequences of Social Mobility in the United States," *Transactions of the Third World Congress of Sociology*, 3 (1956); also in Reprint Series in the Social Sciences, No. 135 (Indianapolis: Bobbs-Merrill).

LIPSET, SEYMOUR M., and REINHARD BENDIX, *Social Mobility in Industrial Society* (Berkeley: University of California Press, 1959).

———, and HANS L. ZETTERBERG, "A Theory of Social Mobility," *Transactions of the Third World Congress of Sociology*, 2 (1956); also in Reprint Series in the Social Sciences, No. 176 (Indianapolis: Bobbs-Merrill).

McGUIRE, CARSON, "Social Stratification and Mobility Patterns," *American Sociological Review*, 15 (1950), 195–204.

WARNER, W. LLOYD, and J. C. ABEGGLEN, *Big Business Leaders in America* (New York: Harper, 1955).

———, ———, *Occupational Mobility in American Business and Industry, 1928–1952* (Minneapolis: University of Minnesota Press, 1955).

———, and Associates, *Democracy in Jonesville* (New York: Harper, 1949).

WEST, JAMES, *Plainville, U.S.A.* (New York: Columbia University Press, 1945).

EFFECT OF THE DEPRESSION OF THE 1930's

ANGELL, ROBERT C., *The Family Encounters the Depression* (New York: Scribner's, 1936).

BAKKE, E. WIGHT, *Citizens without Work* (New Haven: Yale University Press, 1940).

———, *The Unemployed Worker: A Study of the Task of Making a Living without a Job* (New Haven: Yale University Press, 1940).

CAVAN, RUTH SHONLE, "Unemployment—Crisis of the Common Man," *Marriage and Family Living*, 21 (1959), 139–46; reprinted in Cavan, ed., *Marriage and Family in the Modern World* (New York: Crowell, 1969).

———, and KATHERINE HOWLAND RANCK, *The Family and the Depression* (Chicago: University of Chicago Press, 1938).

GINSBERG, ELI, and Associates, *The Unemployed* (New York: Harper, 1943).

KOMAROVSKY, MIRRA, *The Unemployed Man and His Family* (New York: Dryden Press, 1940).

MORGAN, WINONA L., *The Family Meets the Depression* (Minneapolis: University of Minnesota Press, 1939).

IO

Cross-Cultural Marriages

NEW ALIGNMENT of families in the social struc-
ture takes place not only through vertical mobility but also through
change in family affiliation from one race or ethnic group to another.
Such transitions are shown by interracial, interreligious, interethnic,
and interclass marriages. Two trends are discernible in all four types
of intermarriage—a major trend to marry within one's own subculture,
and a minor trend to marry into another subculture. The major trend
is supported by the feelings of ethnocentrism that all the groups possess—feelings clearly evidenced by their high evaluation of their own
way of life, the tendency to cluster together residentially, and to resist
the intrusion residentially or socially of other groups. The minor trend
is shown by the vertical and horizontal mobility that carries some
individuals and families away from their original subculture into
another and seemingly more favored subculture. A part of the resistance to intrusion is a philosophy of endogamy that positively seeks to
contain marriages within the subculture, and as positively resists the
minor trend toward exogamy both as philosophy and as practice.

In general, the major trend toward endogamous marriages represents the official stand of the subculture. The minor, exogamous trend
is linked with individualistic and romantic attitudes that support the
right of each individual to select his own mate regardless of the official
stand of his subcultural group.

When the principle of endogamy is violated, disapproval varies
according to type of intermarriage that takes place. None of the types
of intermarriage under discussion is illegal. The pressure against intermarriage and the forms of disapproval are embodied in institutional

rules and in the mores. The greatest disapproval comes from the specific subculture that feels threatened by intermarriages that would carry its members into another group or that would introduce a stranger into the subculture. Since some types of intermarriage are regarded as more threatening than others, attitudes toward intermarriage differ. Studies indicate that the greatest opposition exists toward interracial marriages. Lines between the major religious groups are next to race in rigidity, reflecting a strong tendency for marriages to occur within the religious group. Ethnic affiliations, often related to religion, rank third in determination of intermarriages. Finally, some opposition is aroused by interclass marriages.[1] Each of these types of intermarriage is discussed as to frequency, related factors, and effect on family life.

Interracial Marriage

The type of endogamous marriage most strictly adhered to is that within one race. Until the early 1960's the laws of twenty-nine states forbade certain types of interracial marriages. Under the impact of the growing opposition to discrimination between races, one state after another modified its laws. By 1967, only sixteen states made interracial marriages illegal. In June, 1967, the United States Supreme Court ruled unanimously that states cannot forbid marriages between people of different races. The decision resulted from a Virginia case but applies to all states.[2]

Even in the states that did not forbid Negro-white or other interracial marriages, few such marriages occurred relative to the total number of either Negro or white marriages. A study of interracial marriages recorded in Boston from 1914 through 1938 shows that Negro-white marriages equaled from 3.1 to 5.2 per cent of all Negro marriages when the percentages were computed by five-year periods. The total percentage for the full period was 3.9 per cent. Since there are many more white marriages than Negro marriages in a northern city, the percentage of white marriages in which one partner was a Negro was

[1] Ruby Jo Reeves Kennedy, "Single or Triple Melting-Pot? Intermarriage Trends in New Haven, 1870–1940," *American Journal of Sociology*, 49 (1944), 331–39; August B. Hollingshead, "Cultural Factors in the Selection of Marriage Mates," *American Sociological Review*, 15 (1950), 619–27. For a summary of research on various types of intermarriage, see Larry D. Barnett, "Research on International and Interracial Marriages," *Marriage and Family Living*, 25 (1963), 105–107.

[2] "Justices Upset All Banson Interracial Marriage, 9 to 0 Decision Rules Out Virginia Law—15 Other States Are Affected," *New York Times*, 116, no. 39,952 (June 13, 1967), p. 1, col. 1; also p. 29, col. 4.

very low. For the five-year periods the percentages varied from 0.10 to 0.18 with a percentage of 0.12 for the entire period. For the period 1916 through 1937, Negro-white marriages in New York State exclusive of New York City varied from 1.7 to 4.8 per cent of all marriages involving Negroes; the corresponding percentage of white marriages is not given but, as in Boston, would be very low.

In California, with its medley of races, various laws forbidding certain types of interracial marriages were repealed in 1948, thus opening the way for many types of legal interracial unions.[3] An analysis of all marriage licenses issued in Los Angeles County in the 30 months following the repeal uncovered very few marriages between whites and those of other races. Out of a total of 78,266 licenses, only 455, or 0.56 per cent, were issued to couples of whom one was white and the other of some other race.[4] A later study for the whole of California showed that of a total of 81,939 marriages, 944 were interracial, or 1.2 per cent; in 1959, the percentage was 1.4.[5] The figures include among nonwhites Orientals and American Indians as well as Negroes. Since the first set of figures was for Los Angeles County and the second for the entire state of California, a direct comparison cannot be made. The figures suggest that an increase in white-nonwhite marriages has occurred, but also that they constitute a very small proportion of all marriages.

DEGREE OF SOCIAL INTEGRATION

The study of Boston interracial marriages suggested that Negroes and whites entering into such marriages were not well integrated into racial social structures. The whites of long American affiliation have a social-class structure, described in Chapters 5–7. Ethnic groups usually have a social structure of their own, which may also include a class structure. Negroes likewise, because of their exclusion from American white social organization, have developed since the Civil War a class structure resembling that of the whites with institutions and informal

---

[3]Prior to the repeal, California laws forbade the marriage of whites to Negroes, Chinese, Japanese, and (after 1933) Filipinos. Whites could marry Mexicans and American Indians. Other racial groups than the whites could intermarry. The laws were repealed following a suit brought by two Catholics, a Negro and a white, who argued that their religious freedom was denied by the laws: they were able to receive all religious sacraments except that of marriage, which was unconstitutionally denied to them.

[4]John H. Burma, "Research Note on the Measurement of Interracial Marriage," *American Journal of Sociology*, 57 (1952), 587–88.

[5]Larry D. Barnett, "Interracial Marriage in California," *Marriage and Family Living*, 25 (1963), 424–27.

groups, business and recreation, churches and clubs, that meet the needs of their members. The person, whether old-line white, ethnic, or Negro, who is well incorporated into his social structure is unlikely to intermarry, since his contacts tend to be within his own social unit where his needs are adequately met. He marries within his social structure not only because of an abstract belief that he should do so but because his contacts since childhood, his memories, his deepening adult friendships, and his dependencies and securities are within this structure. It is natural for him to fall in love with a member of his cultural and social group. An interracial marriage therefore indicates either that the person has not been thoroughly integrated into his social group or has withdrawn from it for some reason. His needs are not met there; he seeks elsewhere for contacts, friendship, and marriage. He tends to be either somewhat disorganized or a cosmopolitan person who makes friendships on a personal rather than cultural basis.

The emancipation of the interracial couple from social ties may be at the basis of the finding in an Indiana study that less than 60 per cent of such marriages had religious ceremonies as compared with 85.8 per cent of white marriages and 73.7 per cent of Negro marriages.[6]

Such failure to find incorporation in the race structure may result from unbalanced sex ratios that prevent marriage of all members of a race within the race. This was the situation in California in the 1920's and 1930's, when there were approximately 2,400 Filipino males to each female. Between 1924 and 1933, out of every 100 marriages involving a Filipino, only 30 were within the Filipino group: the other 70 were with whites, Mexicans, or other Orientals.[7] So frequent did marriages between Filipino men and white women become that California passed a law in 1933 forbidding Filipino-white marriages. Since the repeal of the law in 1948, the most frequent type of intermarriage has been between a Filipino man and a white woman, with the combination of Filipino man and Mexican woman ranking second.[8]

When nonwhites intermarry with whites, the white person often is foreign-born, a situation true in Negro-white marriages in Boston and elsewhere.[9] Foreign-born whites as a rule have less color prejudice than native-born Americans; moreover, the sex ratio of foreign-born groups often is unbalanced, usually with an excess of men. These men seek

[6]Todd H. Pavela, "An Exploratory Study of Negro-White Intermarriage in Indiana," *Journal of Marriage and the Family*, 26 (1964), pp. 209–10.
[7]Constantine Panunzio, "Intermarriage in Los Angeles, 1924–1933," *American Journal of Sociology*, 47 (1942), 690–701.
[8]Burma, *op. cit.*, pp. 587–88.
[9]Otto Klineberg, ed., *Characteristics of The American Negro* (New York: Harper, 1944), pp. 283-300.

brides in other cultural and sometimes other racial groups, occasionally competing with the racial males even when the number of women is too few to supply wives for the men of the race. The status of a white person and perhaps a higher income may make the foreign-born white man attractive to the nonwhite woman.

Not all interracial marriages, however, occur between white men and nonwhite women. The Filipino-white marriages of California illustrate the reverse situation. New York and Boston studies show that Negro men married white women almost five times as often as white men acquired Negro wives; in New York State (exclusive of New York City) the Negro man-white woman marriage occurred almost three times as frequently as the reverse combination.[10] These Negro grooms tend to come from higher occupational strata than Negro men in general; when they do not marry white women of their own approximate occupational strata, they turn to unskilled white women who perhaps find satisfaction in the comforts that the Negro husband can provide, while the husband values his wife for her race. The white brides, unlike the white grooms, do not, however, include an over-proportion of foreign-born. Both Negro grooms and white brides include a higher proportion of divorced persons than does the general population.

Often the initial contacts that lead to interracial marriages are made in the course of work.[11] Negro brides, for instance, have an unusually high representation of servants. Accustomed to working for white families, these women are not closely integrated into the Negro community and have become adjusted to association with whites. Negro grooms in interracial marriages also have a disproportionately high number whose work provides contacts with whites, as chauffeurs, porters, waiters, and cooks. They have, to some extent, been living within the white community.

A study of limited proportions of interracial marriages in Indiana challenges some of these findings.[12] Based on 95 interracial marriages of 1958–59, the study showed that brides and grooms were of approximately the same occupational status, thus calling into question the idea that the white wife values her non-white husband for his higher occupational status. The study confirmed other findings, however: the combination of Negro groom with white bride outnumbered the reverse combination by a ratio of about 2.5 to one; the divorce rate was somewhat higher than in endogamous marriages of either whites or Negroes; the interracial couples were slightly older than endogamous couples.

[10] *Ibid.*
[11] *Ibid.*
[12] Pavela, *op. cit.*, p. 209.

ADJUSTMENT IN INTERRACIAL MARRIAGES

Because of the social disapproval, and sometimes cultural differences as well, marital adjustment often is difficult. Since Negro-white marriages have been more thoroughly studied than other types of interracial marriages, the discussion that follows applies specifically to them.

In entering into an interracial marriage—or even friendship—both the man and the woman must defy their racial mores and meet the disapproval and perhaps ostracism of their friends. Flirtations and romances between Negroes and whites who work together, of a type that within one race would naturally lead on to marriage, are stopped at a casual level or, if they lead to more intimacy, are kept secret. When deep affection develops, marriage often is not the outcome, or a secret marriage is consummated. For an open courtship and married life the couple must be well withdrawn from dependence upon the approval of their respective racial groups and prepared to stand as an isolated couple withdrawn from both racial social structures.

A summarization made by Drake and Cayton of types of Chicago Negroes who intermarry with whites includes intellectuals and Bohemians, who are not responsive to social controls, or members of certain cults that include disregard of racial differences as part of their social philosophy.[13] Lower-class Negroes, without pride of race, also intermarried. Well-established upper-class and middle-class Negroes and the respectable lower class did not intermarry, although at an earlier period in Chicago relatively stable working-class Negroes did intermarry.

The degree to which the couple tends to be isolated is indicated by the following restrictions laid upon them:

They often lose their jobs if the intermarriage becomes known.

They have difficulty in finding a place to live and usually must find it within the Negro community; even here there is difficulty, as it is often assumed that they are not married and hence not "respectable."

The families, especially the family of the white partner, almost always disapprove; the couple therefore keep the marriage secret or "lose" themselves in the Negro community and break off all contacts with the white family.

Friends usually refuse to accept the partner of the other race, al-

---

[13]See St. Clair Drake and Horace R. Cayton, *Black Metropolis* (New York: Harcourt, Brace, 1945), pp. 137–39.

though they may continue to meet the partner of the same race.

Family and friends cannot be counted upon to help the couple in time of crisis.

The white partner (who usually is the wife) is branded by both whites and Negroes as not respectable no matter how circumspect her behavior.

The couple must continuously defend and rationalize their marriage.[14]

As a consequence, mixed couples tend to band together for social contacts and practical assistance. At one time in Chicago such couples organized a club, called the Manasseh club, which was both a fraternal benefit society owning a cemetery plot and a social organization that met for dances and picnics. The club no longer exists, but mixed couples still tend to associate with each other or with other tolerant groups. To the extent that the couple can withdraw from both racial groups into a mixed racial group they are saved many strains upon their relationship and are given needed primary-group contacts and secondary-group associations that tend to support the marriage, give security, and provide justifications.

INTERRACIAL MARRIAGES OF AMERICANS IN THE ARMED FORCES

Service in foreign lands and especially the residence of occupation troops after active warfare has ceased have led, as a by-product, to many marriages between American servicemen and local women. From time to time, the United States government has made arrangements for the entrance of wives from other nations into the United States. When the wives are Australian or European, the adjustment that they make is cultural and social; they meet a minimum of prejudice. The Oriental wife, however, faces not only the cultural and social adjustment but also the barrier of racial prejudice. Early fears for the success of American-Japanese marriages were not borne out, according to several studies made in the mid-1950's.[15] The marriages themselves

[14] *Ibid.*, pp. 140–53. Accounts of specific marriages sometimes reveal the attitudes of the couple and their relatives; see, for example, "My Daughter Married a Negro," *Harper's Magazine*, 203 (July, 1951), 36–40; R. L. Williams, "He Wouldn't Cross the Color Line," *Life*, 31 (September 3, 1951), 81–94.

[15] Gerald J. Schnepp and Agnes Masako Yui, "Cultural and Marital Adjustment of Japanese War Brides," *American Journal of Sociology*, 61 (1955), 48–50; Anselm L. Strauss, "Strain and Harmony in American-Japanese War-Bride Marriages," *Marriage and Family Living*, 16 (1954), 99–106.

had certain elements conducive to stability. A screening process by Japanese authorities weeded out known prostitutes and criminals among brides. The serviceman was required to prove that he was not already married and could support a wife; he had to secure the permission of his commanding officer. His chaplain interviewed him and usually discouraged the idea of marriage. Nevertheless, marriages occurred, although they were few in comparison with the temporary or semipermanent free liaisons.

In age, brides and grooms were mature: the average age of brides was between 22 and 24, according to two studies, and of grooms 24 to 27. The girls came from both city and rural backgrounds, but most of them lived and worked in cities. Few were living with their parents. The couples often met at the place where the girl worked or through friends. They dated an average of slightly over two years, according to one study, sometimes living together during a part of this time, especially during a period when servicemen were not permitted to marry Japanese women. After marriage, the couple lived an average of several years in Japan before removing to the United States. It seems probable that only the couples with the most satisfying relationships changed their status from a free union to marriage.

Studies of couples made after they had lived in the United States for several years showed that the brides were adaptable to American culture. They prepared and ate American foods and rejoiced in the use of American household appliances. They observed American holidays and did not try to introduce Japanese festivals. Even when the wife, as occasionally happened, came from a slightly higher social class than her husband, the higher standard of living of the working-class in the United States with home ownership and a car compensated for the difference in class status.

Wives seemed well received by the husband's family. Many couples, however, settled in cities and had only infrequent contacts with the husband's family. In cities they found other American-Japanese couples with whom they became friends. Usually they had entered marriage with few religious ties and the husband with few aspirations for occupational improvement. They were, therefore, relatively free from family or social pressures.

In her domestic role, the Japanese wife did not compete with her husband. The Japanese girl is reared to regard her chief function as that of making her husband comfortable and happy; even though she may have worked in Japan, employment outside the home was secondary to fulfillment of her domestic role.

In individual cases, interpersonal strains existed, similar to those found in racially homogeneous marriages; or the Japanese wife was not well accepted by the husband's intimate groups. However, since the returning husband could select his place of residence, the couple had an opportunity to avoid locales where they would have been rejected.

The above comments are based primarily on two studies of a limited number of urban couples. They show that in the early years of American-Japanese marriages the fact of differences in race, language, and culture do not automatically cause the marriage to disintegrate. Two factors seem important in creating stability. Neither husbands nor wives were closely integrated into their families nor into institutional groups; they acted to some extent as individuals detached from strict social controls. However, the screening process undoubtedly prevented some of the most unlikely marriages. It also happened that some cultural elements offset each other: for example, the husband's desire to be head of his family was complemented by the Japanese woman's training to fulfill a secondary role.

CHILDREN

Children of white-nonwhite marriages usually resemble the nonwhite parent in skin color and therefore popularly are classified as nonwhite. Often, also, they are legally designated as nonwhite and subject to any restrictions placed upon the nonwhite group. Nevertheless, with one white parent, the child may not have the same status as a child with both parents of the same race. Since more is known about Negro-white children than children from other racial mixtures, their situation alone is discussed.

Since the interracial couple lives as a rule in the Negro community and since the tendency is to classify all hybrids as Negroes, the interracial character of the family is a transitory affair lasting only one generation. Children of the marriage, usually showing their Negro inheritance, are accepted by both Negroes and whites as Negroes. Their contacts are with other Negroes, and they are readily accepted into Negro social groups. They become psychologically and socially Negroes; the process is furthered by the fact that the white parent often does not inform her parents or relatives of the birth of a child and the child therefore does not have contacts with or emotional disturbances over disapproving and emotionally disturbed grandparents, uncles, and aunts. When the white parent attempts to force her colored children into contacts with whites, she helps to create emotional conflicts for them. Perhaps the most trying situation arises when the child is very light and in a position to identify with either race. He has emotional ties through his parents with both races, but eventually tends to identify with one or the other. If very light, he may "pass" into the white group and sever contacts with his parents and childhood associates. In some cases the child is unable to identify with either race and is torn between the two, sometimes isolating himself from both. He may wish to identify himself with the whites, but his color or the knowledge that he is colored may cause the whites to reject him. Toward the Negroes who would accept him he develops a feeling of aversion or hostility. Most children, however, adjust successfully in the Negro group.[16]

Religious Intermarriage

The percentage of interfaith marriages varies from one religion to another; it is also related to community conditions. Catholics and Jews who marry outside their faith tend to marry Protestants rather than each other. The percentages may overemphasize the problem. Only a few studies of interfaith marriage attempt to measure the degree to which the person is identified with a designated religion. When one member or both members of a marriage are only nominally affiliated with a religious group, religion may not be significant in the marriage.

CATHOLIC INTERFAITH MARRIAGES

An estimate for the United States made by John L. Thomas, S.J. states that 25 to 30 per cent of all marriages sanctioned by the Catholic Church are intermarriages.[17] Mixed marriages not sanctioned by the Church would increase the percentage. For example, in Connecticut in 1949, mixed marriages sanctioned by the Church equaled 40.2 per cent of all Catholic marriages; with the addition of mixed marriages not sanctioned by the Church, the percentage would probably approximate 50 per cent.[18] In Iowa in 1953, among all marriages involving a Catholic, 42 per cent were mixed; this figure includes both those sanctioned by the Church and others.[19]

---

[16]Drake and Cayton, op. cit., pp. 154–59.

[17]John L. Thomas, The American Catholic Family (Englewood Cliffs, N.J.: Prentice-Hall, 1956), pp. 154, 166.

[18]John L. Thomas, "The Factor of Religion in the Selection of Marriage Mates," American Sociological Review, 16 (1951), 487–91.

[19]Loren E. Chancellor and Thomas P. Monahan, "Religious Preferences and Interreligious Mixtures in Marriages and Divorces in Iowa," American Journal of Sociology, 61 (1955), 233–39.

JEWISH INTERFAITH MARRIAGES

All studies of Jewish intermarriages in the United States report low percentages.[20] Pressure for in-group marriages comes from both within and without. Jewish principles are unalterably opposed to mixed marriages. Rabbis refuse to perform the marriage ceremony, and parents are distressed and sometimes refuse to have further contact with a son or daughter who marries outside the faith. The vigilance of parents extends to heterosexual friendships between boys and girls, since these might lead into dating and courtship. The situation in Derby, a Connecticut city of 10,000, is described as follows:

> . . . although it is quite common for a Jewish boy in Derby to have friends of his own sex among gentiles, it is only rarely that he will have a gentile "girl friend." One or two "dates" of this sort are sufficient for the relationship to become a topic of gossip in the community. In such cases, word usually reaches Jewish parents quite rapidly and they plead with their wayward sons to "stop bothering with 'Shikses' because there are plenty of fine Jewish girls in town."
> More or less the same is true of Jewish girls. In fact, it is even more difficult for them than for unmarried Jewish males to cross the religious line heterosexually. The male friends of Jewish girls are very carefully checked, more so than in the case of gentile girls.[21]

PROTESTANT INTERFAITH MARRIAGES

Most of the studies on interfaith marriage combine all Protestants into one group. Some Protestant denominations are deeply opposed to having their members marry outside the denomination. One such denomination is Lutheran. A study sponsored by the United Lutheran Church showed that 58 per cent of Lutherans who married between 1948 and 1950 chose a spouse from some other church, usually (57 per cent) some other Protestant denomination.[22] However, 20 per cent of individuals marrying out were married to Catholics, 1 per cent to

[20]M. L. Barron, "The Incidence of Jewish Intermarriage in Europe and America," *American Sociological Review*, 11 (1946), 6–13. A summary of studies is given. Also Albert I. Gordon, *Intermarriage, Interfaith, Interracial, Interethnic* (Boston: Beacon Press, 1964), ch. 7.

[21]*Ibid.*, p. 8

[22]James H. S. Bossard and Harold C. Letts, "Mixed Marriages Involving Lutherans," *Marriage and Family Living*, 18 (1956), 308–10.

Jews, 3 per cent to other non-Protestants, and 19 per cent to persons with no church affiliation.

CONDITIONS INFLUENCING INTERRELIGIOUS MARRIAGES

Certain social conditions affect the proportion of interreligious marriages.[23] For example, when one religious group has few representatives in a community, many exogamous marriages occur. Rates of mixed Catholic-Protestant marriages are high in areas where there is a low proportion of Catholics in the population, thus reducing the number of persons from which individual selection of a spouse may be made. For example, as many as 70 per cent of the sanctioned marriages in the dioceses of Raleigh, Charleston, and Savannah-Atlanta, where Catholics form a small proportion of the population, were mixed, according to one study. In contrast, in the dioceses of El Paso, Corpus Christi, and Santa Fe, with a high proportion of Catholics, the intermarriage rate was less than 10 per cent of sanctioned marriages.[24] One factor in the low rate of intermarriage of Derby Jews is that the young people of this small city have contacts with the larger Jewish communities in nearby New Haven and Bridgeport. The area of choice is thus greatly widened so that someone of compatible personality as well as Jewish religion is more likely to be found than if selection of the spouse were limited to the smaller community.[25]

In the Far West, where many people belong to the Mormon Church, studies have been made of Mormon-non-Mormon marriages.[26] In Salt Lake City (1937), where Mormons constituted almost three-fourths of the population, only 7 per cent of Mormons married non-Mormons. In Oakland and Berkeley, however, where Mormons make up less than 5 per cent of the population, the percentages of Mormons marrying non-Mormons were 47 and 30 respectively.

Mixed marriages of Catholics also occur more frequently in upper social classes than lower, as measured by rental areas in one city. Among 51,671 families in one large city, the percentages of families living in different areas that were based on mixed marriages increased regularly from 8.5 per cent in the lowest rental area to 17.9 in the

---

[23]For a general discussion of conditions, see Gordon, *op. cit.*, ch. 3.

[24]Thomas, "The Factor of Religion in the Selection of Marriage Mates," p. 489.

[25]Barron, *op. cit.*, p. 8.

[26]Clark E. Vincent, "Interfaith Marriages: Problem or Symptom?" in Jane C. Zahn, ed., *Religion and the Face of America* (Berkeley: University Extension, University of California, 1959), pp. 67–87, quoting unpublished studies.

highest, with 19.3 per cent among suburban families.[27] Although the study in question did not venture an explanation, it seems probable that persons in the higher rental areas were also those with less ethnic affiliation and with higher education. Both of these factors would tend to increase their contacts in both number and variety with persons of other religious faiths and to free them from strict compliance with religious rules. Right of individual selection of the spouse would tend to direct the choice.

A social situation that reduces out-marriages is the coincidence of religious faith and ethnic culture.[28] As long as the ethnic culture is strong, marriages tend to occur within the ethnic group. When the ethnic group represents only one religion, marriages are automatically within the religion as well. Ethnic and religious affiliation strongly reinforce each other in determining marital selection.

The emergence of young people from family control and from segregated ethnic groups also encourages interfaith marriages. In work, at college, and in places of public recreation, young people meet as individuals rather than as representatives of a religious faith. They do not, however, abandon all their early teaching and loyalties. But they are in a position to meet, date, and become close friends with people of unlike faith. Sometimes the process has moved close to love and marriage before they face the differences in their religious beliefs; sometimes the differences add piquancy to their friendship. Studies of samples of students at the University of Idaho and at Iowa State University both showed that 97 per cent of students would date those of another faith.[29] The percentage willing to marry outside their faith was smaller (59 and 32 per cent respectively), but nevertheless exceeded or was equal to the percentages of interfaith marriages that occur in various communities.

RELIGIOUS AFFILIATION AFTER MARRIAGE

Religious groups are not interested in becoming assimilated into one common faith, but desire to retain their separateness and individual identity. In their attempt to do so, different religions try to prevent out-marriages of their members. The Jews are the most forthright in

[27]Thomas, "The Factor of Religion in the Selection of Marriage Mates," pp. 489–90.
[28]*Ibid.*
[29]Alfred J. Prince, "Attitudes of College Students Toward Inter-Faith Marriages," *The Coordinator*, 5 (1956), 11–23; Lee G. Burchinal, "College Students' Attitudes Toward Cross-Religious Dating and Marriage," paper read at the annual meeting of the Midwest Sociological Society, April, 1958.

their efforts; the official policy of the orthodox and conservative branches of Judaism is to refuse to recognize the marriage of a Jew and a non-Jew. The reform branch—the most liberal of the three—rests its policy on a statement made in 1909 by the Central Conference of American Rabbis, which says that "... mixed marriages are contrary to the tradition of the Jewish religion and should therefore be discouraged by the American Rabbinate."[30] According to traditional orthodox principles, the Jew who married outside the faith was considered dead; the death ceremony was held, and he was no longer accepted by family or synagogue. Although this extreme measure of social annihilation is not followed in most American Jewish communities, rabbis of all three branches refuse to perform the marriage ceremony for a Jew and a non-Jew. It is possible, however, for the non-Jew to take a course of instruction and accept the Jewish religion prior to marriage. The couple may have a civil ceremony or perhaps be married by a minister in some other religion; in either case, the Jew has cut himself off from his religion and sometimes from his family and friends.

The Catholics follow a compromise policy by recognizing marriage between a Catholic and a non-Catholic, provided the non-Catholic takes a course of instruction and agrees to observe certain safeguards erected by the Church to preserve the religion of the Catholic member and to assure that the couple's children are trained in Catholicism. The non-Catholic typically agrees to the following points:

He marries with the understanding that the marriage can be dissolved only by death (that is, not by divorce). He agrees that all children of either sex born of the marriage shall be baptized and educated in the Catholic religion alone; that he will not in any way hinder the Catholic member from practicing freely and faithfully the Catholic religion; and that in the performance of his marriage there will be only the Catholic ceremony.

The Catholic promises to rear the children as Catholics and to have only the Catholic ceremony.

Until 1966, even with these agreements the couple could not be married in the sanctuary, the nuptial blessing was not given, and Mass could not be celebrated as part of the marriage ceremony. The couple could be married in the church rectory or before the altar rail.

In 1966, the Pope issued a document entitled the Sacrament of Marriage, which retained the concessions by the non-Catholic member of a mixed marriage but added concessions on the part of the Church to the

[30] *Yearbook* of the Central Conference of American Rabbis, XIX, pp. 170, 174–84. The position of the orthodox and conservative branches was stated by officers of the Rabbinical Council of America and the Rabbinical Assembly of America in personal correspondence.

non-Catholic as well as the Catholic member.[31] The modified regulations do not require that the agreement on education of children should
be a written document signed by the non-Catholic; the non-Catholic
makes a verbal promise not to interfere, with the responsibility for the
children's education falling on the shoulders of the Catholic member.
Mixed marriages may be performed in the sanctuary with full Catholic
rites and benediction. Although a non-Catholic clergyman may not
participate in the actual marriage rite, he may be present and after the
marriage may participate in joint prayers and address the marriage
party. The rule on excommunication of a Catholic who marries a non-
Catholic without following Catholic regulations has been abrogated
and this new ruling is retroactive. Catholics who engage in such marriages are still considered to be in a state of grave sin of disobedience
but they are not placed outside the Church. Bishops have some authority to modify some of the regulations and others may be appealed to
the Pope.

When the above requirements are met, the mixed marriage is considered valid. When they are not met, the couple cannot be married
by a priest; they may have a civil marriage or have the ceremony performed by a minister of some other faith that does not place restrictions
on its ministers. Such a marriage is considered invalid by the Catholic
Church.

Although the valid marriage presumably protects the Catholic religion, not all Catholic members of such marriages continue to practice
their faith. One study showed that approximately 25 per cent of Catholic members had stopped their religious practices and another 20 per
cent became irregular church attendants.[32] However, 55 per cent remained faithful to their religion. Comparative figures are not given
for the religious observances of members of all-Catholic marriages.
Apparently studies have not been made of the religious life of the non-
Catholic member of a valid mixed marriage. He has a choice of three
alternatives: he may become a convert to Catholicism, a step that
closes the religious schism within the marriage; he may continue to
practice his own religion, thus creating a family divided in religious
belief and practices; or he may already be or become indifferent to
religion. In the last two types, one avenue for religious unity of the
family is lost.

There is a general feeling that Catholic-Protestant marriages are

[31]"Excerpts from Vatican Document on Mixed Marriage," *New York Times*, CXV,
No. 39, 501 (Mar. 19, 1966), p. 9, col. 3ff.; "Pope Eases Intermarriage Rules,"
Ibid., p. 1, col. 5 and p. 9, col. 2; "The Pope on Mixed Marriage," *Ibid.*, p. 28,
col. 2.
[32]Thomas, *The American Catholic Family*, pp. 152–53.

less happy than those in which husband and wife have the same religious affiliation. Sometimes comparative divorce rates have been used to try to establish the truth of this supposition. Among various combinations of religious affiliation, Catholic-Catholic marriages usually have the lowest divorce rates; intramarriage among Jews and among certain Protestant denominations have only slightly higher divorce rates. Divorce rates in such religiously homogamous marriages run from about 4 to 10 per cent of marriages of each type. In general, interreligious marriages have higher divorce rates, but these differ with the specific combination and are not sharply divided from the rates of homogamous marriages. In other words, there is somewhat greater probability of divorce in the mixed marriage than in the religiously homogamous marriage, but for all types the great majority (78 to 94 per cent) remain married at least during the early years of marriage when the divorce rate is highest.[33]

Divorce rates are not merely a matter of religious affiliation. Other factors that affect rates include youthfulness of marriage (higher rates) and class status. Here low status exceeds high status in rate.

The tendency of religiously homogamous marriages to have low divorce rates cannot be entirely attributed to contentment in marriage. The Catholic Church does not recognize divorce as a way to end marriage, a principle that tends to prevent divorce regardless of unhappiness. According to one study, Catholic families had more than their share of desertions.[34] It is therefore necessary to be cautious in using low divorce rates as an indication of success in homogamous marriages, whether Catholic or Protestant.

Effect on Family Interaction

The aversion to interreligious marriages has been great enough that most studies have emphasized the hazards of such marriages rather than the characteristics of successful marriages. It has been pointed out that it is difficult for either partner to the marriage to foresee the feel-

[33]The most detailed study has been made by Lee G. Burchinal and Loren E. Chancellor, "Survival Rates among Religiously Homogamous and Interreligious Marriages," *Social Forces*, 41 (1963), 353–62. Published studies include H. Ashley Weeks, "Differential Divorce Rates by Occupation," *Social Forces*, 21 (1943), 334–37; Judson T. Landis, "Marriages of Mixed and Non-Mixed Religious Faith," *American Sociological Review*, 14 (1949), 401–7; and Loren E. Chancellor and Thomas P. Monahan, *op. cit.*

[34]Thomas P. Monahan and William M. Kephart, "Divorce and Desertion by Religious and Mixed-religious Groups," *American Journal of Sociology*, 59 (1954), 454–65.

ings of frustration that they will have if they are unable to carry out religious rituals in the home or to have prescribed foods because of the disbelief or lack of cooperation of the partner of the other faith. Few young people are so thoroughly independent of their parents and relatives that their disapproval will not mar the marriage relationship. And many husbands and wives find a new source of disagreement when children are born, even though they have agreed before the marriage into which religion the child is to be inducted. Religious beliefs are deeply ingrained and are supported by many auxiliary beliefs and customs as to the relationship of husband and wife, the functions of the family, and the relation of the family to the church. Even those who are "indifferent" to religion find under stress of some crisis that belief in their own religion and dislike or actual scorn of the religion of the spouse come into overt expression.[35]

CHILDREN

What of the children of mixed marriages? A study by Landis of the middle-class parents of college students throws some light on the religious training received by children of mixed marriages.[36] The children were reared in the mother's faith from two or three times as often as in the father's faith, regardless of whether the mother was Catholic or Protestant. (Too few Jewish mixed marriages were found to make possible a similar comparison for them.) This finding is in line with our general knowledge that the mother in the middle class takes more responsibility for rearing the children than does the father. Regardless of agreements made before marriage, she wishes to rear her children in her own faith. In some instances the parents solved the dilemma by acquainting the children with both faiths and permitting them to choose for themselves; in others some children attended the father's church and some the mother's; in only a small percentage of cases were the children reared without religious affiliation. Children also sometimes fanned the flame of antagonism on the part of relatives who had reconciled themselves to the out-religious marriage of their sons or daughters but opposed the training of grandchildren in any except their own religious faith. So potent a cause of quarreling and tension is the question of the religious training of children that Landis concludes that in childless mixed marriages there would be small cause for conflict, but

[35]Ray Baber, "A Study of 325 Mixed Marriages," *American Sociological Review*, 2 (1937), 705–16.
[36]Landis, *op. cit.*

that the birth of a child revives old religious loyalties and pits husband against wife. In other families, and especially if one parent is more or less indifferent to religion, amicable agreements are reached as to the training of children.

Ethnic Endogamy

Ethnic endogamy is related to religion. Each major religious group includes several ethnic groups. Among ethnic groups represented in the United States, Catholics include Irish, Italian, Polish, French, and French-Canadian; Protestants include British, Scandinavian, and German; Jews include German, Russian, Spanish, and Portuguese. In marriages there is a strong tendency toward endogamous ethnic marriages. As the ethnics with continued residence in the United States lose some of their distinguishing characteristics (such as language, native clothing, and political ideals) and become more alike in culture, the tendency toward ethnic exogamy begins, but religious endogamy tends to continue. For example, Irish tend to marry Irish, but among those Irish who marry outside the ethnic group the tendency is strong to marry into another Catholic ethnic group rather than into a Protestant ethnic group.

The first trend, toward ethnic intramarriage, is shown for New Haven in Table 8. The decreasing percentages of endogamy from 1870 through 1900 to 1940 are due to increasing loss of divisive characteristics and increasing uniformity of culture among the once foreign-culture groups. The Jews are included in this table, although they are

TABLE 8
INTRAMARRIAGE BY NATIONAL-ORIGIN GROUPS, NEW HAVEN

	1870	*1900*	*1940*
Jewish	100.0 %	98.92%	93.70%
Italian	—*	97.71	81.89
British-American	92.31	72.00	54.56
Irish	93.05	74.75	45.06
Polish	—*	100.00	52.78
German	86.67	55.26	27.19
Scandinavian	40.00	82.76	18.46
ALL NATIONALITIES	91.20	75.93	63.64

*In 1870 almost no Italians or Poles resided in New Haven.

SOURCE: Ruby Jo Kennedy, "Single or Triple Melting-Pot? Intermarriage Trends in New Haven, 1870–1940," *American Journal of Sociology*, 49 (1944), 333.

not, strictly speaking, an ethnic group in the same sense that the nationality groups are; they are in reality a religious group originating from several national backgrounds and with mixed religious-ethnic characteristics. In the purely ethnic groups, the Italians have shown the greatest persistence of endogamy, whereas Germans and Scandinavians marry more often outside the ethnic group than within it. The Italian trend may be related to the recency of arrival of the Italian group and its relatively low social prestige as compared with ethnic groups that have become better adjusted to American life. Germans and Scandinavians have a longer history in New Haven and are less clearly marked as an ethnic group. In earlier sections of this book the pressure toward ethnic endogamy in groups not represented in New Haven has been discussed—for example, among the Norwegians and the Finns.

Although religious endogamy tends to preserve certain family ideals and institutional associations in exogamous ethnic marriages, other issues may arise based on differences in culture. These may concern such simple things as food habits and manners or vital ideals and relationships, such as the relative status of husband and wife, ideals of educational level for children, and moral standards.

Interclass Marriage

Less disapproval is felt toward interclass marriages than toward interracial, interreligious, or interethnic marriages. Nevertheless, the major tendency is to marry within one's own social class or in an adjacent class.

Measuring social class according to the previously classified areas in which the families of the marital couple lived, Hollingshead found that in New Haven 58.2 per cent of marriages occurred between people living in areas of the same social stratum (not necessarily the same area), and an additional 24.6 per cent between those from areas of adjacent class level.[37] Table 9 shows for each social class the percentage of both husbands and wives who married in the same, a higher, or a lower social class. The amount and dominant direction of mobility vary from one class to another.

Elmtown, the small Midwestern city studied by Hollingshead, showed a marked tendency for people to marry within their own social class.[38] Through a study of 489 adolescents and their relatives, Hol-

---

[37]Hollingshead, *op. cit.* The study was based on all 1948 marriages in which the couple was still living in New Haven in February, 1949.

[38]A. B. Hollingshead, "Class and Kinship in a Middle Western Community," *American Sociological Review*, 14 (1949), 469–75.

TABLE 9

DIRECTION OF MARRIAGE OF MEN AND WOMEN IN DIFFERENT SOCIAL
CLASSES, NEW HAVEN, 1948

Social class of husband	Class position of wife			Total Number	Per cent and Direction of net mobility
	Higher	Same	Lower		
I	0.0	52.0	48.0	25	48.0 downward
II	7.6	53.3	39.1	105	31.5 downward
III	12.9	38.4	48.7	39	35.8 downward
IV	8.6	39.3	52.1	140	43.5 downward
V	12.8	64.8	22.4	389	9.6 downward
VI	36.8	63.2	0.0	310	36.8 upward

Social class of wife	Class position of husband				
I	0.0	59.1	40.9	22	40.9 downward
II	7.6	60.8	31.6	92	24.0 downward
III	20.0	33.3	46.7	45	26.7 downward
IV	12.0	38.7	49.3	142	37.3 downward
V	15.7	68.1	16.2	370	0.5 downward
VI	41.8	58.2	0.0	337	41.8 upward

SOURCE: Based on Table 4 in August B. Hollingshead, "Cultural Factors in the Selection of Marriage Mates," *American Sociological Review*, 15 (1950), 625.

lingshead determined that members of kinship groups tend to belong to identical social classes or to the next adjacent social class. For example, among 354 middle-class adolescents, 184 relatives were also in the middle class and 132 in the next class lower. Only 38 relatives fell outside this narrow range. He concluded that in past generations marriages had occurred within the social class, thus building up a kinship group that exemplified the class culture and that not only trained the oncoming adolescent in the class culture but guided him into marriage within that class by emphasizing such characteristics in a suitable partner as occupation, amount of income, degree of education, religious affiliation, place of residence, family background, ethnic origin, and reputation—in all instances placing high value on the characteristics as found in the social class of the kinship group and devaluing the characteristics of other social classes.

Interclass mobility has also been measured by comparing marriages between members of the same occupational class with marriages between members of different occupational classes. A cross-sectional study of males, whose marriages occurred between 1885 and 1945, shows that although many men marry women from their own occupational level, a larger proportion marry outside their level (Figure 10).

The tendency is strong in the higher occupational levels for men to marry into a lower level, whereas lower-level men tend to marry into higher classes. Both stability and mobility are shown at each level.

In interclass marriages two people reared in somewhat different culture patterns come together into an intimate daily association where adjustment rests in part upon consensus of ideals and similarity of behavior patterns. Although a thorough study of degree of adjustment in interclass marriages has not been made, some evidence exists that they less often lead to satisfactory and more often to unsatisfactory adjustment than do marriages between members of the same social class. This statement rests upon a study that utilized the schedules of 428 husbands and 417 wives secured for an earlier study of prediction of degree of marital adjustment. From the original schedules Roth and Peck were able to give a social-class placement to each husband and wife and then to compare marital adjustment by social class and by mobility. A direct relationship was found between social class and adjustment score, with better adjustment correlated with higher social-class placement. Our interest here, however, is with cross-class marriages. Figure 11 shows that intraclass marriages are preponderantly characterized by fair or good adjustment; marriages with one class difference between husband and wife are about equally divided between good, fair, and poor adjustment; and marriages with husband and wife more widely separated in social-class placement have almost half showing poor adjustment and a very low percentage with good adjustment.

A slight difference was found according to whether husband or wife occupied the higher social position. Marital adjustment was more often good, less often poor, if the husband occupied the higher status than when the wife had the higher position. The difference is not marked, but it is in keeping with general trends whereby men tend to marry women with slightly less education or occupational status, and women prefer men superior to themselves in these respects. The higher position of the wife is a violation of deep-seated traditions of husband-superiority and therefore may add to the difficulty of adjustment.

Trend Toward Stability

Each of the measures of social mobility and transition shows a fairly high degree of mobility, but also shows that stability is more common than mobility. From the point of view of the family the significant fact seems to be that our ideals and patterns of training the young

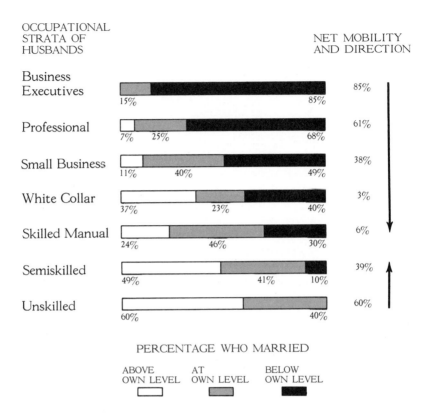

FIGURE 10   *Marriages Within and Across Occupational Lines.*

The distribution of marriages by occupational strata shown here bears a striking similarity to the distribution by social classes in New Haven illustrated in Table 9. Moreover, the interoccupational marriages classified here also tended to be among members of adjacent levels. The occupational classification of wives is based upon the occupations of their fathers.

SOURCE: Richard Centers, "Marital Selection and Occupational Strata," *American Journal of Sociology*, 44 (1949), 533. An earlier study of marriages by occupational levels (T. C. Hunt, "Occupational Status and Marriage Selection," *American Sociological Review*, 5 [1940], 494–504) used the woman's own occupational status rather than her father's and included a classification "at home." Since women follow somewhat different occupations than men, the correlation between men's and women's occupations is less clear than when the woman is classified according to her father's occupation. On the other hand, Hunt's method made allowance for cases in which the woman had a higher occupational status than her father had. He found very high percentages of intraoccupational marriages at some levels; for instance, 52 per cent of professional men married professional women, and 36 per cent of white collar workers married white collar workers.

tend primarily to maintain stability of individual and family placement. Only among some socially ambitious families do we find definite attempts to train children for entrance into a higher social class, through family training and provision for education beyond that of their parents. The desire of families, ethnic groups, and religious organizations is to perpetuate themselves in essentially the patterns of the past or at least of the present. Change is deplored, and eyes are closed to the fact that a high proportion of children will move away

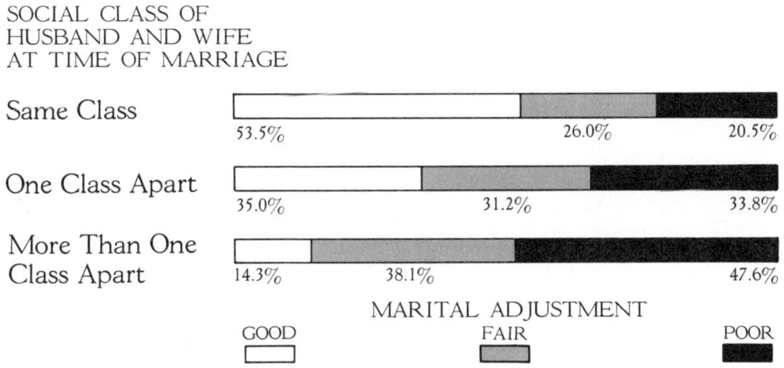

SOCIAL CLASS OF
HUSBAND AND WIFE
AT TIME OF MARRIAGE

FIGURE 11 *Marital Adjustment and Social Class.*

A striking decline in good marital adjustment is shown with increase in social-class dissimilarity. This graph is based upon an analysis of questionnaires from 428 husbands and 417 wives. The criteria of adjustment were agreements and disagreements between husband and wife, common interests and activities, demonstration of affection, confiding, expressions of satisfaction or dissatisfaction, and feelings of unhappiness and lonesomeness. These criteria were scored in such a way that a total score was secured indicating marital adjustment.

SOURCE: Julius Roth and R. F. Peck, "Social Class and Social Mobility Factors Related to Marital Adjustment," *American Sociological Review*, 16 (1951), 481. Roth and Peck analyzed by social class and marital adjustment the schedules originally used by E. W. Burgess and L. S. Cottrell in *Predicting Success or Failure in Marriage* (New York: Prentice-Hall, 1939).

from the family pattern in some respect, either through entering a different occupational and social-class level or by intermarriage into another racial, ethnic, or religious group. The young people who make the change often have little preparation for it, and when, as in intermarriage, each comes from a distinctive background of culture that has been taught to him as right, the probability is high that tensions and conflict will occur, on the one hand with the parental group and on the other between husband and wife.

Nevertheless, not all social mobility and transition end in disaster to the personality or to marriage. The probability is increased, but in most instances adjustment is achieved. The successful cases are the ones in which the change helps the person to fulfill his needs. Upward social mobility gives prestige and certain types of security; marriage between the ethnic and American may aid the ethnic to learn and accept the American culture. Concentration of research on failures of intermarriage has tended to obscure the fact that most such marriages seem to succeed. Studies of successful intermarriages would add to theoretical knowledge of the processes of interaction and would also be of practical use.

Questions

1. How do you account for the low proportion of interracial marriages, even though they are not illegal?
2. What are the special problems of adjustment that interracial couples are called upon to make?
3. What special adjustment problems confront the children of interracial marriages?
4. Discuss the marital adjustment of white veterans who have married nonwhites abroad.
5. Compare the policies of Protestants, Jews, and Catholics with reference to interreligious marriages. Is the member of the outgroup rejected or accepted? What is the status of children of the mixed marriage?
6. How could the handicaps of interreligious marriages be reduced?
7. How is ethnic endogamy related to religion?
8. What types of interclass marriage seem to lead to the greatest marital satisfaction?
9. What is your conclusion regarding intermarriage as a type of cultural and social mobility?

Bibliography

THEORETICAL CONCEPTS RELATED TO INTERMARRIAGE

GORDON, ALBERT I., *Intermarriage: Interfaith, Interracial, Interethnic* (Boston: Beacon Press, 1964).

MARCSON, S., "A Theory of Intermarriage and Assimilation," *Social Forces*, 29 (1950), 75–78.

MERTON, R. K., "Intermarriage and the Social Structure," *Psychiatry*, 4 (1941), 371–74.

STONEQUIST, EVERETT V., *The Marginal Man* (New York: Scribner's, 1931).

INTERRACIAL MARRIAGE

ADAMS, ROMANZO, *Interracial Marriage in Hawaii* (New York: Macmillan, 1937).

BARNETT, LARRY D., "Interracial Marriage in California," *Marriage and Family Living*, 25 (1963), 424–27.

_____, "Research on International and Interracial Marriages," *Marriage and Family Living*, 25 (1963), 105–107.

DRAKE, ST. CLAIR, and H. R. CAYTON, *Black Metropolis* (New York: Harcourt, Brace, 1945), ch. 7.

GOLDEN, JOSEPH, "Characteristics of the Negro-White Intermarried in Philadelphia," *American Sociological Review*, 18 (1953), 177–83.

_____, "Patterns of Negro-White Intermarriage," *American Sociological Review*, 19 (1954), 144–47.

PAVELA, TODD H., "An Exploratory Study of Negro-White Intermarriage in Indiana," *Journal of Marriage and the Family*, 26 (1964), 209–11.

SCHNEPP, GERALD J., and AGNES MASAKO YUI, "Cultural and Marital Adjustment of Japanese War Brides," *American Journal of Sociology*, 61 (1955), 48–50.

STRAUSS, ANSELM L., "Strain and Harmony in American-Japanese War-Bride Marriages," *Marriage and Family Living*, 16 (1954), 99–106.

INTERRELIGIOUS MARRIAGE

BARRON, M. L., "The Incidence of Jewish Intermarriage in Europe and America," *American Sociological Review*, 11 (1946), 6–13.

_____, *People Who Intermarry* (Syracuse: Syracuse University Press, 1946).

BOSSARD, JAMES H. S., and HAROLD C. LETTS, "Mixed Marriages Involving Lutherans," *Marriage and Family Living*, 18 (1956), 308–10.

BURCHINAL, LEE G., "Membership Groups and Attitudes Toward Cross-Religious Dating and Marriage," *Marriage and Family Living*, 22 (1960), 248–53.

_____, "Premarital Dyad and Love Involvement," in Harold T. Christensen, ed., *Handbook of Marriage and the Family* (Chicago: Rand McNally, 1964), ch. 16.

_____, and LOREN E. CHANDLER, "Survival Rates among Religiously Homogamous and Interreligious Marriages," *Social Forces*, 41 (1963), 353–62.

CAVAN, RUTH SHONLE, *American Marriage* (New York: Crowell, 1959), ch. 8.

CHANCELLOR, LOREN E., and THOMAS P. MONAHAN, "Religious Preferences and Interreligious Mixtures in Marriages and Divorces in Iowa," *American Journal of Sociology*, 61 (1955), 233–39.

LANDIS, J. T., "Marriages of Mixed and Non-Mixed Religious Faiths," *American Sociological Review*, 14 (1949), 401–15.

PRINCE, ALFRED J., "Attitudes of College Students Toward Inter-Faith Marriages," *The Coordinator*, 5 (1956), 11–23.

SLOTKIN, J. S., "Jewish-Gentile Intermarriage in Chicago," *American Sociological Review*, 7 (1942), 34–39.

_____, "Social Factors in Amalgamation; Based on a Study of Jewish-Gentile Intermarriage in Chicago," *Sociology and Social Research*, 26 (1942), 346–51.

THOMAS, JOHN L., *The American Catholic Family* (Englewood Cliffs, N.J.: Prentice-Hall, 1956).

———, "The Factor of Religion in the Selection of Marriage Mates," *American Sociological Review*, 16 (1951), 487–91.

ZAHN, JANE C., ed., *Religion and the Face of America* (Berkeley: University Extension, University of California, 1959), chapter by Clark E. Vincent, "Interfaith Marriages: Problem or Symptom?" pp. 67–87.

INTERETHNIC MARRIAGE

HOLLINGSHEAD, A. B., "Cultural Factors in the Selection of Marriage Mates," *American Sociological Review*, 15 (1950), 619–27.

KENNEDY, R. J. R., "Premarital Residential Propinquity and Ethnic Endogamy," *American Journal of Sociology*, 48 (1943), 580–84.

———, "Single or Triple Melting Pot? Intermarriage Trends in New Haven, 1870–1940," *American Journal of Sociology*, 49 (1944), 331–39.

INTERCLASS MARRIAGE

CENTERS, RICHARD, "Marital Selection and Occupational Strata," *American Journal of Sociology*, 44 (1949), 530–35.

HOLLINGSHEAD, A. B., "Class and Kinship in a Middle Western Community," *American Sociological Review*, 14 (1949), 469–75.

ROTH, J., and R. F. PECK, "Social Class and Social Mobility Factors Related to Marital Adjustment," *American Sociological Review*, 16 (1951), 478–87.

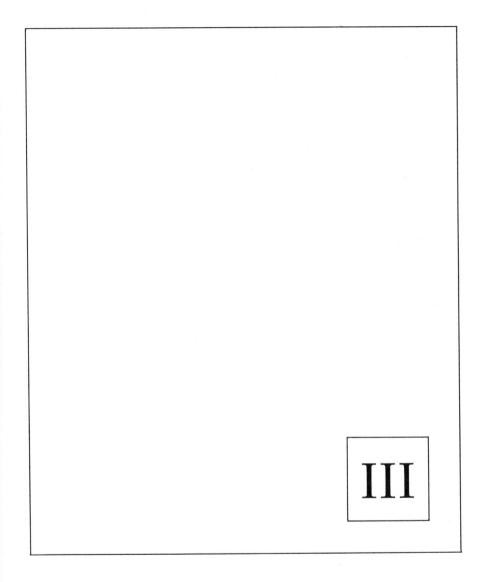

III

The Cycle of Family Life

II

The Family Life Cycle

FROM THE total stream of family life, specific sets of relationships or age periods have been selected for close scrutiny in the following chapters, such as adolescence, the dating and engagement period, early marriage, and so on. However, the pattern of family life is not a series of disjointed segments, even though changes may sometimes be abrupt and an occasional family may be shattered. Family life flows on, losing itself in the past and reaching toward the future—a long river of experience that begins at birth, already loaded with heredity from the past, that flows on until the end of life, passing along in its turn hereditary factors and learned values to younger lives in the early stages of the process of living. Figure 12 shows the marital status of the population throughout the family life cycle. Families begin when youth are in the late teens and early twenties, skyrocket through the twenties, finally encompass 90 per cent of the population, and then begin to decline as death creates widows and widowers.

Family Life Cycle as a Series of Developing Stages

The cycle of the family can be divided into a number of segments for study. Eight are used in this discussion, the transition from one stage to another being made on the basis of age, additions to or loss of members, and changes in central roles, three indicators of change that are closely related. Table 10 brings these three measures of family life into juxtaposition with each other, using the average family of two or three children for the model. It shows the relation between number in the family at any given period of family life, the age of the members, and the duration of each period.

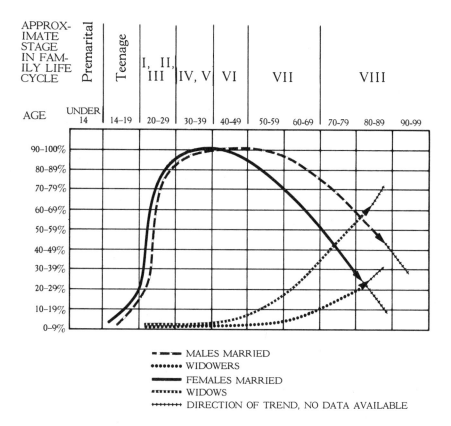

APPROX-
IMATE
STAGE
IN FAM-
ILY LIFE
CYCLE

Premarital · Teenage · I, II, III · IV, V · VI · VII · VIII

AGE   UNDER 14 · 14–19 · 20–29 · 30–39 · 40–49 · 50–59 · 60–69 · 70–79 · 80–89 · 90–99

90–100%
80–89%
70–79%
60–69%
50–59%
40–49%
30–39%
20–29%
10–19%
0–9%

- - - MALES MARRIED
••••••• WIDOWERS
——— FEMALES MARRIED
•••••••• WIDOWS
++++++++ DIRECTION OF TREND, NO DATA AVAILABLE

FIGURE 12   *Percentage at Each Age Who Were Married or Widowed, by Sex, for 1966.*
Divorced people are not shown; the percentage never rises above 4.9.

SOURCE: *Statistical Abstract of the United States, 1967* (Washington, D. C.: Government Printing Office, 1967), p. 33.

The stages fall into a developmental pattern in which family life expands, holds steady for a period during which children are reared to maturity, and then contracts. The concept of family development came

TABLE 10

EIGHT STAGES IN THE FAMILY LIFE CYCLE

Stage	Approximate age of wife	Approximate age of husband	Approximate duration of stage in years	Generational periods
Premarital, corresponding to Stages I–V below for children				
Birth	0	0		Family
Preschool	0–5	0–5	5	of
Preadolescent	6–12	6–13	7–8	Orientation
Dating adolescent	13–16	14–17	4	
Seriously dating or engaged	17–19	18–22	3–5	
Marriage	20	23		
I. Beginning family	20–21	23–24	2	
II. Childbearing family, 2 or 3 children	22–25	25–28	4	
III. Additional years with preschool children	26–28	29–31	3	Family
IV. With preadolescent children	29–35	32–38	7	of Procreation
V. With dating adolescents	36–41	39–44	6	
VI. Middle-aged, with seriously dating or engaged children; "launching" period	42–47	45–50	6	
VII. Postparental middle age; grandparenthood	48–63	51–65	15–16	
VIII. Postmarital: wife becomes widow	64		11	Family
wife dies	74			of
or husband becomes widower		66	7	Gerontation
husband dies		72		

SOURCE: Based primarily on Evelyn Millis Duvall, *Family Development* (Philadelphia: Lippincott, 1967), pp. 13, 15, 18; Paul C. Glick, *American Families* (New York: Wiley, 1957), and "The Life Cycle of the Family," *Marriage and Family Living*, 17 (1955), 3–9.

from the concept of a developmental individual life cycle, at each stage of which the person faces certain tasks of learning and adaptation. These tasks help him to adjust to the present and at the same time prepare him for the new situations that emerge with each succeeding

stage.[1] A developmental task, according to Havighurst, who is referring to the individual, "is a task which arises at or about a certain period in the life of the individual, successful achievement of which leads
to his happiness and to success with later tasks, while failure leads to
unhappiness in the individual, disapproval by society, and difficulty
with later tasks." Duvall adapted this definition to family life.[2]

For the individual, developmental progress rests on three factors,
according to Havighurst and Duvall: the person's physical readiness
to undertake the tasks of each succeeding stage; the expectations of
society that certain tasks of development will be accomplished at each
period; and the individual's aspirations and values that motivate him
to move on to the next stage.

These three factors can be applied to the family, as the following
illustrations suggest. 1) Physical maturity is necessary for parenthood;
2) social expectations are that marriage will be delayed until physical
maturity, but that marriage will be accomplished by the early twenties;
3) families create definite goals and aspirations that motivate many
activities.

GENERATIONAL STAGES

The specific stages shown in Table 10 may be conveniently grouped on
a generational level.[3] The family of orientation is shown in Table 10
for the period when the person has not yet married. The family of procreation is the counterpart of the family of orientation, viewed from
the position of the parents. In Table 10 the family of procreation is
linked with the family life stage when there are children in the family.
The family of gerontation, centering in the older couple whose children
are no longer at home, is identified in Table 10 as the postparental and
postmarital family. It is evident that each married person passes
through the stages of orientation, procreation, and gerontation, and
that the three types of family coexist in one kinship group if three generations are present. Along with the affinal family of in-laws, these four
types of family form the kinship web of the American family system.

[1] Robert J. Havighurst, *Human Development and Education* (New York: Longmans,
Green and Co., 1953).

[2] Evelyn Millis Duvall, *Family Development* (Philadelphia: J. B. Lippincott Co.,
1967).

[3] Marvin B. Sussman, "Relationships of Adult Children with their Parents in the
United States," in Ethel Shanas and Gordon F. Streib, eds., *Social Structure and
the Family: Generational Relations* (Englewood Cliffs, N.J.: Prentice-Hall, 1965),
p. 74.

Differing Patterns of Change

Not all kinds of change fall into the same longitudinal pattern. Some elements of family life have their most intense development in early marriage, others at middle age, still others in old age. Thus the family is not forced to adjust to all changes and potential crises at one time. Changes are met as they arise, and (as with the individual) success in meeting one change or crisis lays the foundation for success in meeting the next, through developmental patterns that may be repeated and through increased personal competence. Similarly, failure in meeting one change lays the foundation for failure with the next.

Some changes are closely related and cause a concentration of needed adjustments at certain points in the family life cycle. At other periods, few major changes occur.

The normal rhythm of change may be shattered by unexpected crises, such as the death of a child or young adult, which is of a different quality than the death of an older person, which must be anticipated as normal. Financial losses, wars, or natural catastrophes are of this unpredictable nature.

The graphs that follow show some of the normal changes and the periods in the family cycle when they loom as major concerns.

Employment and Money

Employment and money are two underlying elements, sometimes beyond the control of the family, that set the stage for many features of family life. Employment of males has two expected periods of major change, as Figure 13 shows. One is in the late teens and early twenties when the youth or man is settling himself into employment. He often sets his entire life-pattern of work at this period. The other major change comes in the sixties when desired or enforced retirement removes him from the labor market. Both periods of major change call for adjustment of roles and personal routines. They differ in that, during the first, the male looks forward to and hopes for expanded opportunities and income. In contrast, with retirement, expectations are diminished or lost and customary work roles no longer give structure to the man's life. Often physically able and desirous of working, socially expected retirement forces him out of his job.

The woman's work cycle follows a different pattern. Fewer married

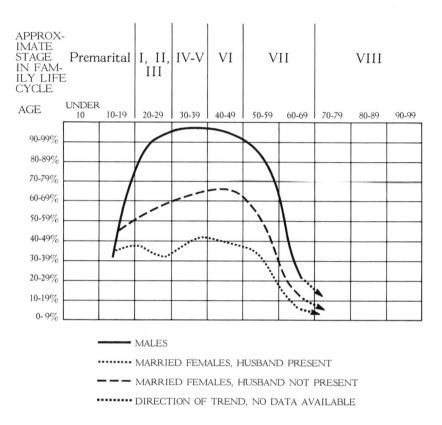

FIGURE 13   *Percentage of Males and Females (by Marital Status) Who Are Employed at Each Age Level, 1966.*

SOURCE: *Statistical Abstract of the United States, 1967* (Washington, D. C.: Government Printing Office, 1967), pp. 222, 229.

women work than their husbands, and they are more free to choose whether or not they will work. Whereas employment in and of itself is socially expected of all able men under age 65, it is not a positive independent value for women. It competes with production and care of children, homemaking, and the desire of some husbands to provide completely for their wives. The curve of employment for women living with their husbands never reaches much over 40 per cent at any time. It declines during the family cycle in periods I, II, III, and IV, when there are preschool and other young children at home. These women may return to work but they retire earlier than do their husbands. The trend of employment for women not living with their husbands (widowed, divorced, separated) does not show a drop during the preschool period (perhaps there are fewer children or the need for money is greater) and does not indicate early retirement.

The employment cycle may be compared with trends in disagreements over money. Figure 14 is based on a study of Michigan urban (Detroit) and rural wives.[4] In stages II and III, when infants and preschool children create many demands for additional expenditures, dis-

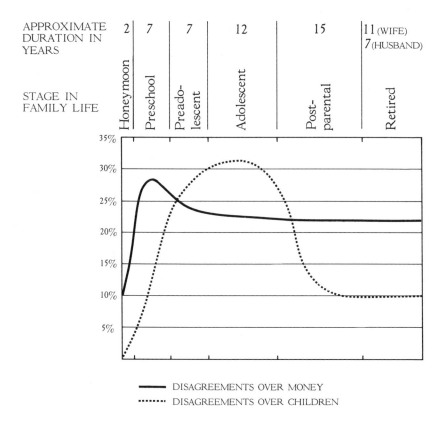

FIGURE 14 *Percentage of Wives Admitting Disagreements with Their Husbands over Money and Children, Michigan Study (15 percent of Michigan wives had no disagreements). Blood and Wolfe use a slightly different terminology and division points for the family life cycle than those shown in Figures 12 and 13.*

SOURCE: Robert O. Blood and Donald Wolfe, *Husbands and Wives: The Dynamics of Married Living* (New York: Free Press, 1960), p. 247.

[4] Robert O. Blood and Donald M. Wolfe, *Husbands and Wives: Dynamics of Married Living* (New York: Free Press, 1960).

agreements over money reach their highest proportion among all disagreements, and never fall as low as the 10 per cent of the first few years of marriage. The years of disagreements coincide with low salaries of husbands who are still establishing themselves vocationally and with the decline of employment of young mothers. The peak of expenses probably comes later when children are adolescent (and disagreements over children are at a peak). By that time husbands are earning near their peak income and many wives have returned to work. The squeeze on income seems greatest in the early years of marriage.

While income after retirement is low, disagreements over income remain at the level they reached years before. Needs are fewer and perhaps the couple has anticipated retirement and succeeded in making adequate plans to bring reduced income and needs into balance.

Interpersonal Relationships

Interpersonal relationships rest on the number in the family and their role relationships. Figure 15 shows the increase and decrease in membership and relationships in a nuclear family of two parents and three children. Each child is a new member who enters into a socially determined role based on sex, his sibling position, and the social class culture of his parents. Interpersonal relationships increase faster than number of persons. Husband and wife have only one interpersonal relationship between themselves. The first child has a relationship to each parent, the total of relationships then becoming three. When the family of five is complete, the interpersonal relationships total ten. Once attained, these ten are maintained, but with shifting emphasis until children begin to leave home. The number of relationships decreases and eventually vanishes when the parents die.

If close relatives are in frequent contact with the nuclear family, the number of interpersonal relationships increases tremendously. Assuming four grandparents and the family of five, the total number of interpersonal relationships reaches thirty, increasing in the early part of the family life cycle, and decreasing later as children leave home. Actually, the rate of decrease is often increased by the deaths of some of the grandparents.

With so many interpersonal relationships, the opportunities for tensions and conflicts are numerous. To reduce tensions or their potentiality, the mother may maneuver her children or the grandparents—even her husband—in order to reduce opportunities for tensions. Chil-

dren may be settled into quiet play before their father comes home; the
child who rubs one set of grandparents the wrong way may be given
permission to visit a friend while the grandparents are in the home.
Thus the mother is often the pivot about which the complex set of interpersonal relationships revolves. Because of the complexity, the pe-

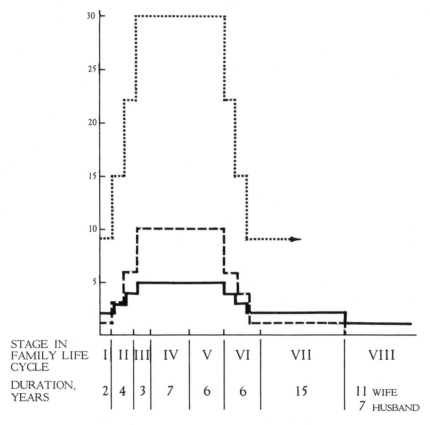

STAGE IN FAMILY LIFE CYCLE	I	II	III	IV	V	VI	VII	VIII
DURATION, YEARS	2	4	3	7	6	6	15	11 WIFE 7 HUSBAND

——— NUMBER IN NUCLEAR FAMILY OF PARENTS AND THREE CHILDREN.

– – – NUMBER OF INTERPERSONAL CONTACTS AMONG PARENTS AND CHILDREN.
MAXIMUM IS 10.

········· NUMBER OF INTERPERSONAL CONTACTS AMONG PARENTS, CHILDREN
AND FOUR GRANDPARENTS. AS GRANDPARENTS DIE, THE CONTACTS
ARE FURTHER DECREASED. MAXIMUM IS 30 CONTACTS WITH ALL
COMBINATIONS.

FIGURE 15   *Number of Persons in the Nuclear Family and Possible Number of Interpersonal Contacts at Different Stages of the Family Life Cycle, in the Nuclear Family and When
Grandparents Are Included.*

riod when children are growing up is often regarded as the most intense of family life.

The complexity of interpersonal relationships has another aspect besides the creation of tensions. Help may be given within the kin system. Also, an informal but powerful system of social control often holds erring family members in line.

HUSBAND AND WIFE DISAGREEMENTS IN INTERPERSONAL RELATIONSHIPS

Specific interpersonal tensions arise at different periods in the family life cycle. A crucial set of relationships concerns the husband and wife. Among the Michigan families disagreements over personality differences were most frequent in the beginning years of marriage (Figure 16). They decreased rapidly, only to increase slightly during the period when children were preadolescent. Adolescence and the departure of the children from home found personality disagreements at their lowest point. With husband and wife alone in the postparental and retirement periods, a relatively high point in disagreements was reached. The high points coincide with periods of role change: early marriage when single life gives way to pair relationships; when the preadolescent is passing from childhood to adolescence; and when the family group shrinks to the elderly couple.

Disagreements over roles were not reported at all by the very newly married, rose during the preschool period, and then leveled out for the remainder of the cycle (Figure 16). Role disagreements never accounted for more than 5 per cent among all disagreements. Although Blood and Wolfe do not specifically define their use of the term role, it apparently refers to functions performed by husband and wife.[5] They interpret the trend as follows: the newly married couple enjoy joint activities; housekeeping offers a new field of activity to be shared and enjoyed. By the time the novelty wears off, children present a new area for sharing. Early marriage is also a time for sorting out specialized roles. This stage coincides with the period of increase of disagreements (preschool). Thereafter specialization of roles increases, but disagreements remain stable at a low level. Increased specialization when husband and wife adopt separate but coordinated roles may be thought of as conducive to stability. It also indicates that the newness of married life and delight in sharing the same tasks has given way to appreciation

[5] *Ibid.*, pp. 68–71.

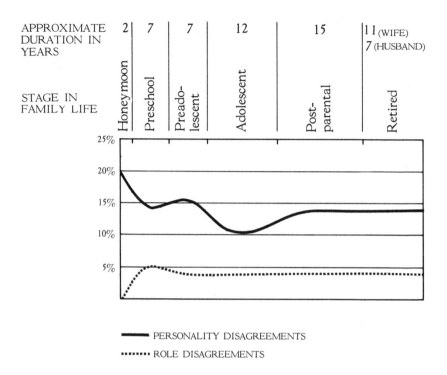

APPROXIMATE DURATION IN YEARS	2	7	7	12	15	11 (WIFE) 7 (HUSBAND)

FIGURE 16 *Disagreements over Personality Differences and Roles, as Percentage among Total Disagreements, during the Family Life Cycle, for Michigan Couples (15 percent of the couples had no disagreements).*

SOURCE: Robert O. Blood and Donald Wolfe, *Husbands and Wives: The Dynamics of Married Living* (New York: Free Press, 1960), p. 247.

of an efficient, well-run household, where each performs his tasks to create a satisfying whole.

Michigan wives reported on disagreements in shared activities (Figure 17).[6] Recreational interests and amounts of recreation created many disagreements in the early married years, which dropped during the period when young children absorbed much time and perhaps temporarily helped to fulfill the need for recreation. Disagreements increased as children began to leave the family and remained moderately high throughout the rest of the cycle.

Disagreements over religion—politics—sex were never high in the

[6]*Ibid.*, p. 247.

Michigan study, but show the characteristic cycle of decrease in early married life (Figure 17). The investigators did not ask specifically about these subjects and comment that the reports are based simply on information volunteered by the wives. They feel that, especially with reference to sex, the disagreements are underreported.

INTERPERSONAL RELATIONSHIPS BETWEEN PARENTS AND CHILDREN

A second crucial set of interpersonal relationships is between parents and children. According to the Michigan study, disagreements of hus-

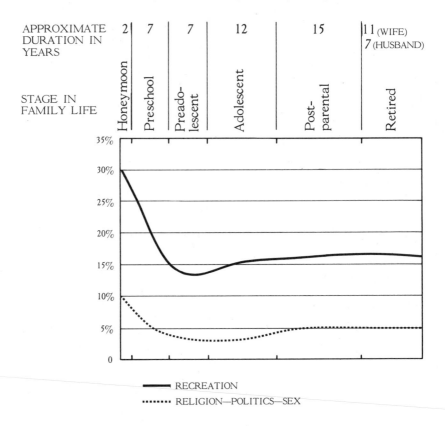

FIGURE 17   *Disagreements over Recreation and Religion–Politics–Sex, as Percentages among Total Disagreements, during the Family Life Cycle, for Michigan Couples (15 percent of the couples had no disagreements).*

SOURCE: Robert O. Blood and Donald Wolfe, *Husbands and Wives: The Dynamics of Married Living* (New York: Free Press, 1960), p. 247.

band and wife over children reaches its peak in the adolescent years, when adolescents are straining for independence and parents are most concerned about the children's current conduct and their future (Figure 14). When this difficult period ends with adulthood of children and their final departure from parental care into jobs and marriage, this source of disagreements diminishes abruptly, although it never disappears.

KINSHIP TENSIONS AND HELP

A third area of interrelationships is based on kinship rather than on the nuclear household. Among the Michigan families, disagreements over in-laws are relatively high at the beginning of marriage, when many young people make their final wrench to free themselves from their parents and at the same time establish a workable relationship with parents-in-law.[7] The in-law relationships are complicated since they involve both the husband's and the wife's families of orientation. Disagreements may arise between the generations or between the two sets of parents. Brothers- and sisters-in-law may complicate the situation.

The Michigan study does not indicate that the in-law problems of young married people may have their counterpart in similar problems on the part of the parents-in-law, who would be in the postparental period of the family life cycle.

From another source and locality—Minneapolis-St. Paul—comes a different view of in-law relationships, based on exchange of types of aid among three generations of the same families.[8] These correspond to the in-law groups of the Blood and Wolfe study. Figures 18, 19, and 20 show the flow of different kinds of aid given and received between married children with preadolescent children, middle-aged parents, and grandparents, two-thirds of whom were in the 71–80 age bracket. Families with adolescents and young adults still living at home were omitted from the study. The families were studied over a twelve-month period as to numerous types of aid, between the generations, along horizontal lines (siblings, cousins), and from outside agencies. A vast network was uncovered. Only the generational pattern is discussed here.

Generally, the grandparents give least aid to the other two generations and receive the most from them. The discrepancy is especially great for care in case of illness and for household management. The parent generation gives more than it receives in every area except ser-

[7]Ibid.

[8]Reuben Hill, "Decision Making and the Family Life Cycle," in Shanas and Streib, op. cit., pp. 113–39.

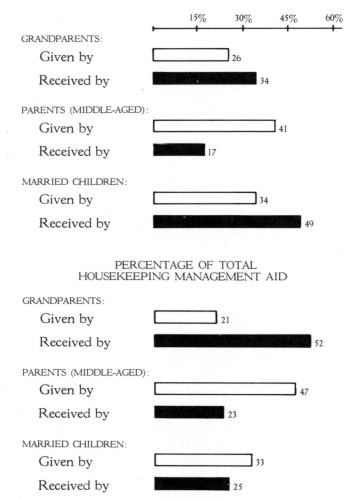

FIGURE 18 *Percentages of Instances of Economic Aid and of Housekeeping Management Aid Given and Received by Each of Three Generations in the Same Families in a 12-Month Period (These are practical types of aid.)*

SOURCE: Reuben Hill, "Decision Making and the Family Life Cycle," in Ethel Shanas and Gordon F. Streib, eds., *Social Structure and the Family: Generational Relations* (Englewood Cliffs, N. J.: Prentice-Hall, Inc., 1965), p. 125.

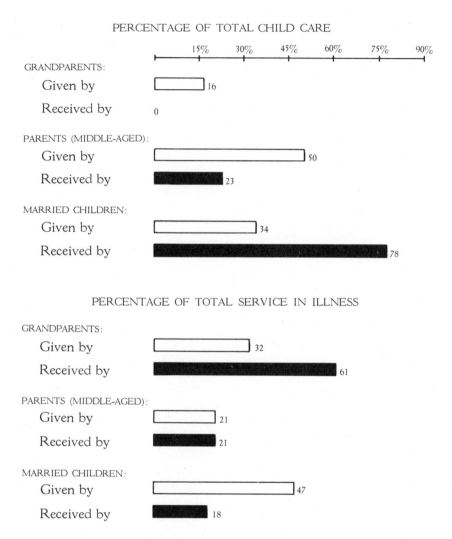

PERCENTAGE OF TOTAL CHILD CARE

FIGURE 19   *Percentages of Instances of Child Care and of Service in Illness Given and Received by Each of Three Generations in the Same Families in a 12-Month Period (These are service types of aid.)*

SOURCE: Reuben Hill, "Decision Making and the Family Life Cycle," in Ethel Shanas and Gordon F. Streib, eds., *Social Structure and the Family: Generational Relations* (Englewood Cliffs, N. J.: Prentice-Hall, 1965), p. 125.

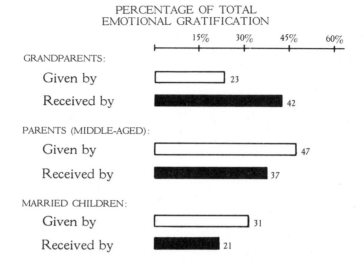

PERCENTAGE OF TOTAL
EMOTIONAL GRATIFICATION

GRANDPARENTS:
 Given by   23
 Received by   42

PARENTS (MIDDLE-AGED):
 Given by   47
 Received by   37

MARRIED CHILDREN:
 Given by   31
 Received by   21

FIGURE 20 *Percentage of Instances of Emotional Gratification Given and Received by Each of Three Generations in the Same Families in a 12-Month Period.*

SOURCE: Reuben Hill, "Decision Making and the Family Life Cycle," in Ethel Shanas and Gordon F. Streib, eds., *Social Structure and the Family: Generational Relations* (Englewood Cliffs, N. J.: Prentice-Hall, Inc., 1965), p. 125.

vice in illness (where giving and receiving are equal). The married child generation both gives and receives. It ranks highest, as would be expected, on receipt of child care, primarily from parents. It also ranks high on receipt of financial help, also primarily from parents. But married children give in excess of receipts in service in illness, housekeeping management, and emotional gratification.

If the three generations are viewed as stages in the family life cycle, the married child generation (in the stage of in-law role adjustment, according to the Michigan study) receives more than it gives in crucial areas of need (child care and finances), but it also builds up patterns of giving that come to full bloom in the middle-aged period, when the couple are most affluent, relieved of many child-care problems, and most experienced in family relationships. The grandparent generation has lost some of its competence and has experienced an increase in needs. It receives specialized types of help, having earlier given help generously to others.

The exchange of emotional gratification is of special interest. The grandparent generation receives the largest portion of emotional gratification—an indication of its failing sense of personal competence and perhaps of its decline in non-family contacts which supported it in earlier years. The parent generation receives a higher proportion of emotional gratification than any other kind of aid, perhaps because it gives the most aid and is in a position to receive emotional gratification from both old parents and adult children. Married children apparently are satisfied with emotional gratification within their own nuclear families. They give more than they receive.

The author of the study comments on the interrelationships, as showing a well-developed pattern of interdependence, lasting throughout the family life cycle, but with changed focus from stage to stage. In the beginning of the cycle the married child generation is willing to receive help, chiefly economic and child-care, giving in exchange a variety of forms of aid and no doubt seeing its future role as major givers. Hill states that this generation apparently "perceived itself more or less in equilibrium in its giving and receiving." The grandparents are almost in a dependency status, receiving more than they give, but in the preceding stage as parents having given more than they received. The parent generation is high in giving and modest in receiving, a patron-type status. Earlier, when the parents were in the child-rearing stage, they no doubt received generously, and no doubt already foresaw the near-dependency stage of old age.

The Climax of Disagreements and Tensions: Divorce

Some of the wives interviewed by Blood and Wolfe had been divorced and remarried. Divorces, whether or not followed by remarriage, are linked to the family life cycle. Figure 21 shows, for six selected states, all divorces granted in 1963 according to the ages of husband and wife. The highest proportion of divorce decrees is granted when the husband and wife are in their twenties—the period of early marriage adjustment and childbearing. For a true picture of divorce it is necessary to consider divorces at each age level in comparison with the proportion of married people at each age level. Figure 21 shows the proportion of married people who fall into each age level. In the younger ages the proportion of divorces exceeds the proportion of married people; in the older age levels the reverse is true: there are proportionately fewer divorces than there are married people. Thus, in the early years of marriage, divorces not only exceed any other period numerically, but, in relation to the group at risk (the married population), they are far out of line.

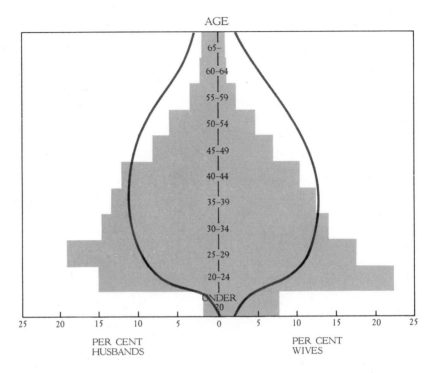

FIGURE 21 *Percentage of Divorces and Annulments, by Age of Husband and of Wife at Time of Decree; Total of Six Selected States, 1963; also Percentage of the Married Population, by Age and Sex.*

The pyramid shows the percentage of the total number of divorces, by sex, that falls into each age category.

SOURCE: *Divorce Statistics Analysis, United States, 1963.* Public Health Service Publication No. 1000—Series 21—No. 13 (Washington, D. C.: U. S. Government Printing Office, 1967), p. 12. The heavy line shows the approximate percentage of the married total population, by sex, that falls into each age category.
Statistical Abstract of the United States, 1967 (Washington, D. C.: Government Printing Office, 1967), p. 33.

Overall View of Satisfaction in Marriage

Disagreements in specific areas and at specific periods are offset by satisfactions. Three measures were used by Blood and Wolfe to trace marital satisfaction: satisfaction of the wife with her husband's understanding, satisfaction with his love, and absence of disagreements between the two. For the first two measures a simple five-item scale was used, for the third the percentage of wives who reported no disagreements. The trends of the three measures during the family life cycle are shown in Figure 22. Each measure has a distinctive trend. Virtually no generalization can be made except that the highest degree of satisfaction, by two measures, tends to come near the beginning of marriage, although not at exactly the same stage of the cycle. Two measures show some decline toward later life; one shows an improvement in satisfaction. The period of least satisfaction, by two measures, comes when the children are growing up.

Blood and Wolfe link love with ease and amount of communication. It may also be compared with the frequency of coitus, not for the Michigan wives, from whom such information was not secured, but from the Kinsey report, which is based on a large and widespread number of women. Whereas love shows only a slight decrease from honeymoon to old age, frequency of coitus declines regularly and rapidly. This decrease is related to a decrease in physical sexual drive (especially on the part of the male) and perhaps by a diversion of energy to other interests. A significant aspect of Figure 22 is that love and sex are only loosely related. Given a rather high satisfaction with love, the decrease in sexual drive and impulse does not destroy love. Love is sustained by satisfactions other than sex.

SATISFACTIONS IN INTERPERSONAL RELATIONSHIPS OF HUSBAND AND WIFE

One satisfaction given by marriage is companionship, which "is more than just a habit made possible by the existence of leisure time. Companionship fulfills a basic human need—the need for response from another person, for what sociologists call 'primary relations'."[9] Significant for the family life cycle is the association of different types of companionship with different stages in the cycle.

Informative companionship is the dominant type throughout the family life cycle and in the "honeymoon" stage far outranks all other types (Table 11). This kind of companionship is a sharing with each other of things that happened as husband and wife went about their separate activities during the day. The sharing is interpreted as giving to each a sense of participation in the individualized role that the other plays. The decline with age may be related to the narrowing of personal roles or perhaps to familiarity over the years with roles so that there is less that is new to relate.

[9]Blood and Wolfe, *op. cit.*, ch. 6.

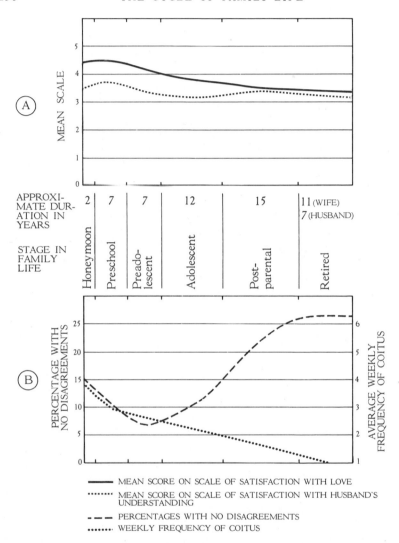

FIGURE 22–A *Trend of Love Satisfaction and of Satisfaction with Husband's Understanding, by Stages in the Family Life Cycle, for Michigan Wives.*

SOURCE: Robert O. Blood and Donald Wolfe, *Husbands and Wives: The Dynamics of Married Living* (New York: Free Press, 1960), pp. 232, 247.

FIGURE 22–B *Percentage of Michigan Couples with No Disagreements and Frequency of Coitus, by Stages in the Family Life Cycle.*

SOURCE: Blood and Wolfe, *op. cit.*, p. 247.
Alfred C. Kinsey, *et al.*, *Sex Behavior in the Human Female* (Philadelphia: Saunders, 1953), p. 77.

Colleague companionship refers to social contacts of the wife with the husband's work colleagues, a type of companionship that must be deliberately sought or initiated. It is infrequent, builds up to the pre-adolescent period, and then declines. The wife shares little in her husband's work life through actual acquaintance or friendship. Her sharing is vicarious through informative companionship.

Another type of companionship is through joint participation in organizations. It is not a dominant type of companionship, and is espe-

TABLE 11

TYPES OF HUSBAND-WIFE COMPANIONSHIP AND THE FAMILY LIFE CYCLE*

			Period			
		Honey-moon	Pre-school	Pre-adoles-cent	Adoles-cent	Post-paren-tal	Retire-ment
1.	Mean informative companionship	3.60	3.19	3.10	3.15	2.77	2.00
2.	Mean colleague companionship	0.84	1.20	1.44	1.10	0.99	0.55
3.	Mean organizational companionship	1.10	0.65	1.13	1.35	1.35	0.73
4.	Mean friendship companionship	1.68	2.32	2.24	2.38	2.42	2.64

1. Based on the question, "When your husband comes home from work, how often does he tell you about things that happened there?" The numerical classification used was: 0—never   1—occasionally   2—monthly   3—weekly   4—daily

2. "How often do you folks get together outside of work with any of the people you or your husband work with?" Same classification as for No. 1.

3. Based on a question about kinds of organization, e.g., labor unions, church, business or civic groups, etc. Classified by types of organizations rather than total number.

4. "About how many of your husband's friends are men that you personally know quite well?" The numerical classification used was: 0—none   1—some   2—about half   3—most   4—all

SOURCE: Robert O. Blood, Jr., and Donald M. Wolfe, Husbands and Wives, The Dynamics of Married Living (New York: Free Press, 1960), pp. 157–60, 281–84.

cially low when young children demand personal care. It builds up during the adolescent and postparental period, only to reach another low point in old age.

Friendship companionship was narrowly defined as the proportion of the husband's friends the wife knew well. This definition omits many other types of friendship which might also have given great satisfaction to the wife, such as with neighbors, kin, or women's clubs. Friendship companionship increases regularly over the family life cycle; apparently the wife comes to know more and more of her husband's friends. Also, according to Blood and Wolfe, with the passing years the husband's associates become fewer in number and hence a larger proportion may be known to the wife.

An overall view shows that the period when children are adolescent ranks highest in companionship, with the preadolescent and postparental periods standing next. The period of retirement has the least companionship, except for sharing by the wife of her husband's business friendships.

The preceding discussion shows the continuity of family life; it also shows that each stage has its own new situations and crises as well as its own satisfactions. As adjustments are made at one stage, the transition to the next stage is already in sight. The family life cycle calls for a dynamic process whereby different numbers of people, of both sexes, and changing age and roles are first socialized into the family and general culture, only to be released later to repeat the process with another generation.

The discussion of different stages and phases of the family life cycle which follows begins with adolescence.

Questions

1. What is meant by family life cycle?
2. What is the relation between the families of orientation, procreation, and gerontation? What is the affinal family?
3. Summarize the chief characteristics of each of the eight stages of the family life cycle.
4. How can adjustment in specific phases of the early stages of the cycle contribute to adjustment in later stages?
5. In reciprocal aid-giving between the generations, discuss the relation of the parental generation to both the young married and the grandparent generations.
6. In addition to changing aspects here discussed, what other aspects of family life do you think might change during the family life cycle? Look up data to confirm or refute your suggestions.
7. What changing characteristics of the individual's life cycle might affect the family life cycle? See reference in the Bibliography to Pressey and Kuhlen.

Bibliography

BLOOD, ROBERT O., and DONALD M. WOLFE, *Husbands and Wives, The Dynamics of Married Living* (New York: Free Press, 1960).

CAVAN, RUTH SHONLE, ed., *Marriage and Family in the Modern World* (New York: Crowell, 1969), ch. 5.

DUVALL, EVELYN MILLIS, *Family Development* (Philadelphia: Lippincott, 1967).

HILL, REUBEN, "Decision Making and the Family Life Cycle," in Ethel Shanas and Gordon F. Streib, eds., *Social Structure and the Family: Generational Relations* (Englewood Cliffs, N.J.: Prentice-Hall, 1965), pp. 113–39.

PRESSEY, SIDNEY L., and RAYMOND G. Kuhlen, *Psychological Development Through the Life Span* (New York: Harper and Row, 1957).

SUSSMAN, MARVIN B., "Relationships of Adult Children with Their Parents in the United States," in Ethel Shanas and Gordon F. Streib, eds., *Social Structure and the Family: Generational Relations* (Englewood Cliffs, N.J.: Prentice-Hall, 1965), pp. 62–92.

I2

The Adolescent Personality

LEGALLY, marriage begins with the wedding ceremony. It is preceded, however, by many years of preparation, including personality growth from infancy on and, during adolescence, more specific adjustments between boys and girls and the development of adult roles. Also, the reading of the marriage service does not guarantee that the couple will "live happily ever after." The wedding simply marks an important step in a process that begins in infancy and ends with death.

The Parents' Relation to Personality Development

A major social expectation in American society is that parents will care for, love, and socialize their children during childhood and early adolescence.[1] Equally firm is the expectation that during these years children will be prepared for adulthood and will be set free during later adolescence.

[1]Comprehensive discussions of child and adolescent development may be found in the following: Clyde Kluckhohn, Henry A. Murray, and David M. Schneider, eds., *Personality in Nature, Society, and Culture* (New York: Knopf, 1955); L. Joseph Stone and Joseph Church, *Childhood and Adolescence: A Psychology of the Growing Person* (New York: Random House, 1957).

Three Phases of the Parent-Child Relationship

1. That dependence of the baby upon the parent is a necessity of physical survival has long been recognized. Such dependence is also the basis for a secure child who gradually gains the self-reliance to become an independent personality as he comes into adolescence. Dependence therefore is not limited to the parents' provision for physical needs but also includes their love. From this relationship the child develops a conception of himself as worthy of love, as approved, as meeting the standards of his little society. When he enters the larger society of the adolescent, he confidently expects approval.

2. Closely related to the child's dependence upon the parent is his identification with the parent. Seeking the love and approval of the parent, the child comes to admire the parent and to seek to be like him. Most obvious is the imitative play of the child. More important is the acceptance by the child of the parents' standard of right and wrong, methods of meeting problems, and attitudes toward hundreds of situations. In fact, the parent's personality is the model for the child's own personality. This identification with the parent is the basis for the child's conception of himself and of his role. In attitudinal form, it provides his personal ideals or conscience, and in behavior it gives him the patterns of conduct for certain roles that he will play in adult life. By the time adolescence is reached, the child should be well on his way to being able to accept responsibility for his own decisions and conduct.

3. The basis for the parent's love and approval is also important in preparing the child for independence. If the parent lavishes love and approval without merit on the part of the child, a weak personality will develop. The child will continue to be dependent upon someone who will protect and praise him without effort on his part to earn these rewards. But if the parent has given love and approval in relation to the child's attempts to control and modify his conduct to meet parental standards, then the child will not expect approval in the larger society unless he makes some effort to earn it. This transition from the unearned love given the helpless baby to love and approval based upon contributing to the happiness and

welfare of others is necessary before the adolescent can free himself from dependence upon his parents.[2]

Thus the child ideally should come into adolescence after passing through three phases in his relation to his parents: an early dependence that has given him security and self-confidence with which to meet the larger world; identification with the parents who have provided him with generalized principles of conduct; and the acceptance of social and personal ideals as the basis for love and approval.

THE PARENT OF THE OPPOSITE SEX

The parent with whom the child has most closely identified himself may affect his capacity to free himself. Usually, boys and girls make their earliest close identifications with the mother, who has the major care of both in the typical American family. If the mother's conception of her own self and role are harmonious with the demands of her society, she provides a clear model for her daughter. But she also presents the same feminine role to her son. The boy therefore needs another model, an adult male, typically the father, to provide the masculine self and role that complement the feminine self and role.

In many rural areas or in the working-class group where the son begins early to share in the father's work as an apprentice, the son's identification with the father is more easily accomplished than in the upper social classes in cities, where absence of the father from home for nine or ten hours a day and his absorption in complex professional work make identification by the son difficult. The son may then tend to identify with his mother, acquiring admirable personality traits perhaps, but ones not necessarily suited to the masculine role. The fact that teachers, even in high school, often are female adds to the boy's difficulty. The adolescent boy is often catapulted from adult feminine models into a peer society of adolescent boys without having made an adequate identification with any adult male.

The girl less often has a similar problem; in some cases, however, the girl identifies herself with her father rather than her mother. The mother for some reason may have rejected the girl; or the father may have encouraged her identification with him, as sometimes happens when the father who desired a son attempts to convert his daughter into one.

Although close identification with the parent of the opposite sex is a

[2]For a discussion of effects of extreme maternal dominance or indulgence, see David M. Levy, *Maternal Overprotection* (New York: Columbia University Press, 1943).

hindrance to the child as he matures, this parent has the important function of teaching the child the complement to his own role.

The father through his daily contacts with his daughter gives her an idea of how a man may be expected to treat her as a girl and woman. The father who is too exclusively only a parent to his daughter fails to give her a standard by which to measure boys and men. The father who admires his daughter's appearance, who shows her the small courtesies of opening a door or holding her coat, who respects her opinions, in short who treats her like a young woman as well as a daughter, gives her both a conception of herself as a woman and also a model against which to measure boys and men whom she meets. Likewise, the mother provides for her son his first experience with a woman, and from her the son will learn what his own role is with reference to women and also what to expect of women. The mother, therefore, who encourages her son to be attentive to her, to hold her coat and to give her a seat, is helping him to learn his role as a young man. Her respect for his judgment and her willingness to help and encourage him in his hobbies will teach him what to expect of the girls and young women whom he meets.

DIFFICULTIES OF EMANCIPATION FROM THE PARENT

After the loving, dependent childhood, the adolescent in our society is expected to free himself from his dependence upon his parents, but the way is often made difficult for him.

The small size of the present-day family tends to concentrate all close emotional ties within a very small number of people. The child's dependency needs are met almost exclusively by the mother. The one or two brothers or sisters are too near the child's own age to serve him; in fact, they may be competitors for the mother's attention. The father is absent from the home many hours of the day and grandparents often live at a distance. The mother-child ties therefore often become intense.

Parents and child may be reluctant to break their mutually satisfying emotional relationship. Parents may cherish the identification of the child and indeed may identify themselves with the child, responding as intensely as the child to every joy and sorrow. Parents receive many satisfactions: pride if the child is clever or mannerly or handsome; compensation for early deprivations if the parents are able to give the child privileges that they did not have at an early age; love and affection. Parents may see nothing with which to replace the satisfactions, especially if the child is the only one in the family, the last child, or the only child of the parent's own sex.

The child, on his part, may wish with part of his personality to become more independent, but at the same time feel insecure and inadequate in the face of the new demands made upon him by other adolescents and adults alike. In a contest between parental standards and those of his own age-sex group, the parents' standards are followed, even though they may be less appropriate to the situation than those of the adolescent group or may involve alienation from the peer group. The parents continue to be the chief source of love and approval.

The adolescent who has been unable to free himself from his parents faces two difficulties. First, he may continue to conceive of himself as a child and therefore be unable to make satisfactory relationships with members of the opposite sex. This is especially true if the adolescent is dependent upon the parent of his own sex. Second, other dependent adolescents seek friends of the opposite sex but only those who remind them of the parent with whom they remain identified. Thus, the boy who is closely attached to his mother may enjoy dating only girls who in some way resemble her; girls who still idealize the father may look for a minor image of the father in every boy. Parents sometimes are flattered by this tendency or are made to feel secure in their child's choice of friends since in the friends they recognize some of their own qualities. They overlook the fact that the entire relationship may be colored by an effort on the part of the son or daughter to play an immature dependent-child role to the girl friend or boy friend rather than the mature masculine or feminine role of equality.

THE PROCESS OF EMANCIPATION

As has been stated, in the process of identification the child comes in time to internalize the precepts of his parents and to have a set of abstract principles to guide his behavior. These principles have been formed, however, in a particular milieu, that of the parental family and immediate neighborhood of the child. As the adolescent's milieu widens with entrance into high school, these principles must be tested against the standards of new groups. The adolescent usually has not acquired a sufficiently firm set to his personality to be able to discard his identification and dependence upon personal approval. Therefore he tends to seek new models, either to replace the parents or to supplement them.

Ideally, the transition is not accomplished by breaking the ties with the parent and then finding new ties, but by a gradual replacement of parental identification with other types. The parent may be replaced by a teacher or adult friend, who for a time may be openly imitated by the adolescent in manner and dress and invited to share his problems and exultations. Or the adolescent may retain his allegiance to the parent in some respects but emulate new traits in other models. Another variant is identification not with an adult but with some friend or small group of the same age and sex, which usually is a step toward adulthood in that the age-sex group is the one in which the adolescent must eventually form his closest attachments. So long, however, as the adolescent feels that he must attach himself to specific persons who form his models and from whom he receives approval, he has not achieved full independence.

If the parent-child identification has been too complete, the adolescent may be unable to free himself gradually. In that case he may wrench himself free with a violent show of rebellion. His attitude toward his parents may be one of marked hostility with rejection of their every suggestion or wish. Or he may vacillate between rebellion and dependence. The rebellious boy or girl usually has no substitute models for the parents and has not achieved independent principles. Therefore he flounders, confused and insecure, following first this chance group and then that, and often feeling guilty over violations of his parents' standards. Therefore, from time to time, when insecurity or guilt overcomes him, he returns to the status of dependent child seeking protection from the parents or from parent-substitutes.

IMPORTANCE OF PARENT-CHILD IDENTIFICATION

Identification with the parents as well as the achievement of freedom from that identification during adolescence are important in preparation for marriage. Since the parents do offer the basic models, the roles that the parents fill as husband and wife and as father and mother are extremely important in determining the conception that sons or daughters will have of their future roles. The most advantageous situation exists when the parents are consonant with the social situations that the child faces; then the modifications that the adolescent inevitably must make will not destroy the basic conceptions gained from the parents. Parents who are elderly and therefore far removed from their own adolescence, or who were reared under different social conditions, often present to their children models that cannot be fitted into the current social situation. Similar difficulty besets the parents in a socially mobile family, whose conceptions of family roles, learned in their childhood in a different social class, are not suitable for their children. Parents of foreign culture or rural origin now in urban settings also are handicapped in setting models for their children.

In one important phase of adolescent life, almost all parents are unable to supply their children with a suitable pattern of conduct. Adolescents invariably see their parents only as parents and mature married people. The parents, long past their own dating and courtship experience, cannot provide their children with an adequate model for dating and courtship. In fact, so firmly fixed in the adolescent's mind is the picture of the father and mother as settled middle-aged parents that he often cannot conceive of his parents as having moments of passion or as enjoying a movie hand in hand; much less can he visualize his parents as young and in love. If the parents insist that they too have lived through the emotional ups and downs of dating and courtship and understand the problems of that period, the children are incredulous and believe that times have changed, even that human nature has changed. Nevertheless, present-day parents were the "lost youth" of the 1920's or 1930's who cast aside many of the restraining mores of an earlier generation. Because of the inability of parents to provide a model for dating and courtship, adolescents necessarily turn to those of their own age or recently married youths for their models.

Physical Changes and Adolescent Interpretations

Many internal and external bodily changes occur during adolescence that seem to the boy or girl quite incongruous with earlier changes, which to the child appeared to consist of gaining height and weight in predictable and desirable fashion. With adolescence come more radical changes to which the youth must adjust. Of great importance also are the ways in which the changes are defined and the alteration they make in the adolescent's conception of himself.

PHYSICAL CHANGES

Obvious physical changes make it impossible for the adolescent to take his body for granted as do the child and the adult. The appearance of hair on various parts of the body may arouse anxiety if the adolescent is shrinking from maturity, or give pride as a symbol of maturity; in either case, it almost certainly brings self-consciousness. Rapid growth in unequal rates for different parts of the body causes the awkward and clumsy adolescent to stumble over chairs and upset cups and glasses. The actual physical awareness by the child is emphasized by the reaction of family and friends to the changes. Outgrown clothes become the occasion for comment and perhaps argument in the family. Kindly friends of the parents comment on how much the adolescent has grown since they saw him last. Mothers become concerned if puberty comes too early—or too late. Friends ridicule in envy the boy or girl who matures earliest, and condole with the ones who lag in their development. Thus the adolescent is made conscious of his physical condition both by his inner awareness of change and by the reactions of other people.

Physical defects assume a new meaning. Some unusual facial formation, extreme but not abnormal height, or smallness of size creates a bitter problem. Very minor and sometimes temporary defects, such as birthmarks, moles, uneven teeth, or acne, are only less worrisome to the adolescent. Especially difficult for the adolescent to accept are features that cause a boy to appear feminine (curly hair or lack of a beard) or a girl to seem masculine (muscular physique or a deep voice). These defects not only affect the social acceptability of the adolescent but help to shape his personality and perhaps contribute to traits incompatible with later marital happiness.

The age of sexual maturity is important. For instance, the girl who experiences the menarche at the age of 10 may become extremely self-conscious and feel herself set apart in some discriminatory way from other girls of her age. Failure to develop secondary sex characteristics at the proper time—the girl's flat chest, the boy's treble voice—may cause extreme self-consciousness and anxiety.[3]

These physical features affect the adolescent in several ways, related to marital adjustments.

1. SOCIAL PARTICIPATION. Although activities for adolescents are varied, certain ones are highly valued. Athletics for boys are of extreme value, not only for the boy's standing among boys but for the girls' evaluation of the boy. The girl who dates the football or basketball star, the fastest man in track, or the swimming champion has the envy of her girl friends. And almost any boy who makes a varsity team has higher status than the boy who tries out and fails, unless the latter achieves in another field. The girl gains status by her ability to dance; to engage in mixed outdoor activities, such as hiking, picnics, and swimming; and to participate in club and social activities.

    Any physical condition that prevents social participation is a

[3]"Physical and Physiological Changes in Adolescence," *The 43d Yearbook of the National Society for the Study of Education*, Part I, "Adolescence" (Chicago: University of Chicago Press, 1944), Sec. I; H. H. Remmers and D. H. Radler, *The American Teenager* (Indianapolis: Bobbs-Merrill, 1957).

serious handicap in that it shuts off the normal contacts with those of the other sex.

2. PERSONALITY ADJUSTMENT. The boy who cannot meet the ideal physical standard of masculine attractiveness or the girl who fails to approximate the feminine ideal often develops a feeling of inadequacy and tends to withdraw from social contacts. Withdrawal tends further to decrease social contacts. The young person attributes his isolation solely to the physical shortcoming, failing to see that much of the difficulty may arise from his own self-attitude. Thus he may come into maturity and the period for marriage with inadequate social experience and with a conception of himself as being unattractive to the opposite sex. His expectation of marriage is affected, as well as his standard for a mate, since he may be willing to lower his standard in the belief that he cannot otherwise secure a mate.

The rate of growth also has sociological and psychological effects. The boy or girl who grows to full adult size in the early teens may be expected by those who do not know his true age to conduct himself as an older adolescent. The tall young girl may be sought for dates by mature young men, at a time when she is not prepared by either knowledge or acceptance of the adult feminine role to control the social interaction of dating on an adult level. Both flattered and frightened, she may easily fall into a pattern of dating and sexual behavior that is unrelated to her little-girl personality. Among her own age-group such a girl may feel awkward and conspicuous. The tall boy faces somewhat similar problems. The small girl who finds herself still resembling a junior high school girl when she is in the last year of high school may continue to play a childish role, seeking indulgence and protection from her larger companions. The undersized boy, on the other hand, often hesitates to approach girls for dates for fear they will laugh at him or summarily refuse his request.

These peculiarities also have more lasting effects. The boy or girl who does not date during adolescence comes into young adulthood without the normal experience of adjusting to varied personalities, of verbal fencing, or of making frank expressions of friendship. He then either goes through a delayed period of dating or enters marriage without the dating experience that has come to be an expected part of the marital process in the United States. Also, the conception of personality built up during adolescence carries on into the more mature years. The little girl, the athletic girl, or the prematurely tall sophisticated girl continues into adulthood to act childish, athletic, or sophisticated, even though growth and circumstances indicate the greater appropriateness of other roles.

Sexual Development

Although it is now known that sexual drives are operative to some extent from early childhood, perhaps from infancy, the actual maturing of the sex organs and our cultural definition of sex make this drive one of the special problems of adolescence.

Early childhood manifestations of sex are physical in nature and are related to the little child's general interest in pleasant physical sensations and curiosity about his body. Sucking, being cuddled or patted, and playing with toes or fingers are examples of this hedonistic interest and curiosity just as much as is the more obviously sexual manipulation of the sex organs and inspection of the sex organs of children of the opposite sex. These tendencies of the young child seem to be as natural and untaught as the tendency to eat, play with toys, or explore. The reaction of adults to interest in or curiosity about the sex organs is entirely different, however, from their reaction to other pleasure-seeking or curiosity-satisfying activities. The child is placed in a sleeping position that makes touching the sex organs difficult or impossible; a hand that strays toward the sex organs in the daytime is pulled away with a scolding or a slap; clothing is designed to prevent a view of sex organs; at an early age most children are prevented from bathing, toileting, or undressing before those of the opposite sex, even siblings.[4] The good child, who meets the mother's approval, is the sexless child. The child therefore learns habits that prevent sexual exploration, and he learns to conceal much of his curiosity about sex. When his questions are answered, he recognizes a reluctance or self-consciousness on the part of his parents. Rarely do parents voluntarily give information on sex, although they instruct the child on other subjects whether or not he is interested in receiving the information. The entire attitude and habit training with reference to sex tends to be repressive and to assume that the child has no sexual impulses or needs. His desire for physical pleasure is diverted into other channels, and his need for love is satisfied through nonsexual contacts. His curiosity is met with evasive or partial answers.

[4]The protection of sex organs is especially dominant in the American middle class, whereas some ethnic groups follow other practices. For example, in the sauna or bath house, all members of Finnish families bathe together. In some Mexican families children up to the age of five play around the house in the nude. American lower-class little girls in the warmer parts of the United States may not wear underclothing; their bodies are freely exposed when they play. Lower-class children and often adults in large cities freely urinate in alleys or at the curb of streets without causing comment.

Many studies show, however, that children are not the sexless creatures that their parents assume. Children who are restrained at home because of disapproval of the parents exhibit considerable curiosity in a more permissive situation. Writing of a school that provided a free environment, Augusta Alpert says that the six-year-olds exhibited more curiosity about sex than the pre-school age, evidenced by questions about body structure and mating and attempts at mutual exploration of each other's bodies.[5] By the age of seven, home repressions were beginning to affect their behavior, even in a free environment, and curiosity was expressed more secretively. Bodily explorations, peeping, obscene language, smutty jokes, lifting of girls' dresses by the boys, and some masturbation carried the children to puberty, when interest centered on the opposite sex in a more personal and social manner.

Kinsey, in his mammoth report on sexual activities of males, states that 57 per cent of older boys and adults recall some sort of preadolescent sex play, while 70 per cent of preadolescent boys admitted such play.[6] Sex play includes kissing and caressing but not intercourse. The sex play, which might be limited to a single experience, usually occurred between the ages of 8 and 13 and typically was with a companion of the boy's own age or a girl slightly older who served as teacher. With the advent of adolescence about half of the boys gave up sex play, whereas the other half continued it until complete sex relations replaced it.

Preadolescent girls also have sexual interests, shown by sex play with boys and girls usually from curiosity or as incidental to other types of play. According to the Kinsey study, 15 per cent of adult women could recall sex play with boys, 18 per cent with girls, and 15 per cent with both in their preadolescent years.[7] Kinsey believed that the high percentage of girl companions resulted from the restrictions on little girls in playing with boys. He also thought that many more women probably had had sex play but could not recall it.

INADEQUACY OF SEX EDUCATION

The great importance of early sex education, preferably given by parents, is agreed upon by educators, psychologists, and sociologists. The

---

[5]"The Latency Period," *American Journal of Orthopsychiatry*, 11 (1941), 126–33. Alpert's conclusion was that there is no latency period, or period between age five and puberty, when organic and functional sex development is arrested. Seeming latency is due to adult disapproval that drives sex interests into hidden channels.

[6]Alfred C. Kinsey, *et al.*, *Sexual Behavior in the Human Male* (Philadelphia: Saunders, 1948), pp. 165–66.

[7]Alfred C. Kinsey, *et al.*, *Sexual Behavior in the Human Female* (Philadelphia: Saunders, 1953), pp. 107–14.

inadequacy of sex education is attested to by the unanswered questions of adolescents, if one may judge from questions written anonymously by one class of eighth grade girls in a California school.[8] Approximately half of the class of 47 girls responded to an invitation to hand in unsigned questions about boy-girl relationships. The questions fell into several categories that were made the basis for later discussion with the class.

Questions on sexual intercourse included the following among others. What happens when you are seduced? What is intercourse? Does it hurt when you have intercourse? What happens when a boy rapes you? What is the satisfaction obtained from sexual relations?

Others were classified as dealing with abortion. How do you keep from having a baby after you are pregnant? Is it safe for young girls to have an abortion? And others.

Some questions concerned sexual functioning and behavior of males, such as: Do boys do something like menstruation? Why can't men have babies? What do you do when a boy starts getting fresh? Why are men so eager?

Another group of questions concerned functioning of the female. What enables women to have babies? What is laboring and does it hurt? How long do women have babies? And similar questions.

In a miscellaneous classification were such questions as the following. What is petting? What happens on your wedding night? How can you keep from getting pregnant?

The author of the articles from which these questions are drawn points out that giving sex information to their children is a difficult task for most parents. This opinion is supported by Kirkendall, who has made numerous studies of premarital sexual behavior and related problems.[9] He states that there is a great need for sex education for adults, to aid them both in dealing with their own problems and in working effectively with children and youth. His conception of sex education at whatever level goes far beyond factual information (although this also is needed) to include "the development of a positive approach to the direction and regulation of the sexual impulse."

The inadequacy of sex education is attested to by the curiosity and ignorance that continue into young adulthood. A traveling lecture team on "Sex: Fallacies, Facts, and Problems," which visited the occupation forces in Europe, secured 1,127 questions from 20,000 troops (about

[8]Thomas Poffenberger, "Family Life Education in This Scientific Age," *Marriage and Family Living*, 21 (1959), 150–54; Poffenberger, "Responses of Eighth Grade Girls to a Talk on Sex," *Marriage and Family Living*, 22 (1960), 38–44.

[9]Lester A. Kirkendall, "Where Should We Go in Sex Education?" *The Coordinator*, 6 (December, 1957), 19–23.

one question for every 20 men) that revealed great ignorance and many unsound folk beliefs.[10] A similar situation exists among young women. The director of a mental hygiene clinic in discussions with senior nursing students collected 1,908 questions, 31 per cent of which related directly to sexual topics.[11] Many of these poorly informed young people would be parents of the 1960's, struggling with the questions of their own children.

An important advantage of parental sex education is the relationship of confidence that is set up between the parent who gives information in a straightforward and sympathetic manner and the child who receives it. Refusals and evasions give the child a feeling of rejection. If the child has secured his first information from other and secret sources he may feel guilty, especially if the parent has made him feel that sex is a subject about which he should remain ignorant. In either case, the child is thereafter reluctant to ask questions of the parent. Identification of parent and child in an important area of experience has failed to occur. If this confidential contact is not established when the child is young, it is almost impossible to establish later. Once developed, however, it may be continued as long as the adolescent feels the need for adult guidance.

The failure of fathers to enlighten their sons leads to a hazardous situation. Mothers who attempt to give their sons information speak from ignorance of the actual situations in which their sons will be placed when other and perhaps older boys confront them with sex information or practices in their crudest forms. The fathers, having been through similar experiences as boys, could help their sons but are prevented by feelings of guilt or embarrassment.

THE ADOLESCENT BOY'S ACCEPTANCE OF SEX

As the boy comes into adolescence, he cannot avoid consciousness of sexual tensions and their natural release through involuntary nocturnal emissions. This experience is so closely related to the actual role of the male in sex relations that the boy is literally forced to accept the fact of his physical masculinity. Moreover, as we have already seen, before

[10]Fred Brown, "What American Men Want to Know about Sex," *Journal of Social Psychology*, 27 (1948), 119–25. A book containing the questions and answers to them has been published: Fred Brown and Rudolph T. Kempton, *Sex Questions and Answers: A Guide to Happy Marriage* (New York: McGraw-Hill, 1950).

[11]Albert Ellis and Earl W. Fuller, "The Sex, Love, and Marriage Questions of Senior Nursing Students," *Journal of Social Psychology*, 31 (1950), 209–16,

adolescence most boys have acquired a varied knowledge of sex and perhaps some type of experience through masturbation or sex play.

Because of the dual sources of sex information for the boy (adults on one hand, boys on the other), sex often comes to have two connotations for him. From adults he learns that sex is a responsibility, something to be conserved until marriage, and that it is related to the birth and upbringing of children. From his own age group he learns of sex as pleasurable, exciting, and stimulating, with possibilities for experimentation in the present. The second interpretation often is more acceptable to the boy, not only because it promises immediate gratification but because it is compatible with other traits of the adolescent personality. The adolescent is still essentially self-centered, seeking satisfaction for his inner needs and unable to accept altruistic obligations to other people. The adult conception of sex as related to marriage and children contains a large element of altruism, of giving and compromise, as well as an element of personal pleasure. The adolescent finds it difficult to accept this conception of sex inasmuch as his personality as a whole has not developed to an altruistic stage.

Even when the boy accepts an adult interpretation of sex, he may find it difficult to apply it to his own conduct during adolescence. A gap of five to ten years intervenes between the onset of puberty and the time when the boy may expect to be sufficiently well established socially and economically to marry. Although postponement of immediate pleasures for the achievement of future goals is part of the growing-up process, especially in the middle class, the long delay combined with the self-centered aspect of the young adolescent's personality poses an almost insuperable problem for many boys. This situation gives rise to a tendency for boys to separate sex as a pleasurable physical reaction from sex as a responsible part of marriage. They accept marital sex for the future, physical sex for the present. Whether a boy represses, expresses directly, or sublimates sex during adolescence depends upon the individual boy and his background of training and experience.

The boy whose early training has been very restrictive and repressive, who associates sex with sinfulness or disgust, may continue to repress sex—to deny its existence in himself as a motivating force.

Direct expression of sex does not necessarily mean sex relations with women. Many adolescents indulge in masturbation and contain their sexual pleasures within their own activities. The practice, however, is simply a stopgap—a temporary adjustment on the way to a completely adult adjustment.

The Adolescent Girl's Acceptance of Sex

Acceptance of the role of female is difficult for some girls. Since sex interests have been repressed in childhood, the girl has had little preparation for conceiving of herself as a potential woman. Whereas the boy's first introduction to sexual changes in himself is with a function directly connected with future intercourse that gives a pleasurable anticipation, the girl's first personal experience usually is with menstruation. If the girl is unprepared for the menarche, or if she associates it with elimination, her emotional reactions may be of a negative nature. Fear, a feeling of guilt (this is some strange punishment), consternation, or disgust are common reactions. She may be embarrassed by the extra sanitary measures that are necessary or resent restrictions on her activities. Pain may further antagonize her. The young girl's knowledge of the relation of menstruation to maternity tends to remain purely on the intellectual level. She cannot conceive of herself as a mother, and the time of marriage is in the dim future. Nature, she often feels, was very stupid in its construction of women and menstruation is regarded as a nuisance. Thus, whereas the boy's early association with puberty includes the idea of pleasure, the girl's attitude at best is neutral and often distinctly negative.

The girl's conception of sexual experience, therefore, does not come directly by way of maturing of her sex organs but through verbalization. She is partially informed and warned by her mother, she reads about sex experience, or she listens to more knowing girls repeat hearsay events or jokes. Intercourse is something that can and does happen to girls and women, but she may have difficulty believing that it can ever happen to her, much less that she can secure enjoyment from it.

Nevertheless, the girl shows indirect interest in sex. She spends much time on her personal appearance; she copies alluring gestures and tricks of speech from older girls or motion-picture actresses and tries them out on boys of her social group. She is greatly interested in romanticized love—in love movies, in an endless succession of popular love songs, and in newspaper accounts of weddings and photographs of brides. More directly, the girl may express sexual interest in masturbation, although not to the extent that boys do. Only slightly more than half as many girls as boys masturbate.[12] Girls also often have crushes that they define as platonic and do not relate to sex but rather to a deep

[12]Georgene H. Seward, *Sex and the Social Order* (New York: McGraw-Hill, 1946), pp. 171–74.

friendship. The crush may be on another girl, in which case the girls would furiously deny any sexual components; or with a boy, but again without recognition by the girl of sexual drives.

With the entrance into dating, the girl recognizes that her interest in boys has a distinctive quality. She may still, however, avoid a realistic admission of sex in herself. She may think of love-making as a symbol of friendship and without sexual implications, at the same time that the boy of her own age recognizes clearly the relationship between kissing and embracing and his own sexual impulses. She may think of sex as something that she will assume at marriage along with the wedding ring.

Social Adjustment of Boys and Girls to Each Other

The social adjustment of boys and girls to each other on a personal basis is primarily carried out during adolescence.

PREADOLESCENT DIFFERENTIATION OF SEXES

Prior to adolescence, differentiation of boys and girls is made within the family. Boys are more often encouraged to disregard minor injuries than are girls, to be more venturesome and unafraid, and to compete with other boys by earning money or in sports. Roughness and crudities are overlooked as the prerogatives or natural tendencies of the "real boy." Girls are encouraged to remain more closely under parental supervision and hence to retain dependence longer; they are praised for having nice manners and scolded for roughness that would merely bring an indulgent smile if performed by their brothers. Fathers may take their young sons fishing or hunting; mothers take their daughters to teas and on shopping expeditions for clothing or household supplies. Thus, early in life boys and girls are given a realization of expected differences in masculine and feminine ideals and conduct—or conceptions of the self and role.

Children are hampered in making childhood social adjustments to the other sex. In many ways children's activities are deliberately organized on a one-sex basis. Parochial and some public schools, Scouts, Sunday school classes, children's parties, and physical education classes in coeducational schools tend to cater to boys or to girls but not to both.

Adult leaders of these activities give several reasons for the separation, chiefly that the needs of boys and girls differ and separation makes possible specialization, and that discipline is easier in the one-sex group. The first reason emphasizes a tendency to prepare the boys and girls for masculine or feminine roles; the second implicitly recognizes an early interest between the sexes, which is met by avoidance or repression rather than by acceptance and guidance.

As a result of this situation, children tend to build their closest associations with those of their own sex. The repressed natural interest in the other sex is expressed through antagonism and hostility as well as through the occasional sex play already described. Boys chase girls home from school, throw snowballs at them, and otherwise express their interest and hostility. Girls scream and call names, run from the boys, or maintain a scornful silence. Boys linger on the edge of the backyard play group of girls, while the girls giggle and whisper secrets. Each sex believes strongly in its own superiority and devalues the opposite sex.

Within their own groups, both boys and girls may express initiative, leadership, and acceptable aggressive activities through competition— personality traits that are considered masculine in our society. Thus, the separation of boys and girls tends to develop in girls masculine traits that later interfere with their heterosexual adjustment.

When boys and girls are included in the same groups, they are encouraged to share equally in initiative and activities. Coeducational schools pride themselves on making no discrimination. Also, in such situations, stimulation and response based on sex differences are discouraged. The boy who teases a girl in the classroom is punished; the girl who flirts with the boy seated behind her has her seat changed. Openly expressed interest in the opposite sex is reduced to a minimum.

With the approach of adolescence, however, adults tend to face in the opposite direction and expect boys and girls also to make a right-about-face in attitude and associations. Just as separation of boys and girls prior to adolescence is defended, so heterosexual adjustment during adolescence is accepted as right and necessary. In the 1950's, dating slipped down to the junior high school and even to the upper grades of elementary school. Whether this lowering of the age for dating is episodic and limited to certain communities or social classes or is the beginning of a long-term trend, it is not possible to say. If it becomes an established practice, it seems probable that it will be followed by a further reduction in the age of marriage.

Abruptly, instead of enforced separation and tolerance of aggressive antagonism, adults place before the young adolescent a wide array of mixed activities and are worried if boys and girls do not eagerly enter into them. Senior and junior high schools plan many mixed activities; churches invite attendance at mixed young people's meetings; parents plan mixed parties. Everything is done to bring boys and girls together. Children do not always accept these offerings quickly, for they call for readjustments of the one-sex attitudes and habits established in pre-adolescence.

THE MASCULINE SELF AND ROLE

The adolescent boy faces the task of coordinating his earlier conceptions of himself and relating them to his relationship to girls of his own age and social class.

Although the boy has been allowed and even encouraged to be aggressive in his own age and sex group, at the same time he has been taught to be compliant and obedient to his parents and to accept their leadership and authority. It is necessary for him to bring together these two conceptions of himself with respect to the adolescent and the adult worlds. In general, the adult masculine role demands aggressiveness from the adult male, directed, however, in certain channels and modified by considerations of fair play and sympathy for others. Obedience sinks to secondary importance, but functions in certain situations, for instance in obedience to laws and to occupational superiors. The coordination of the two conceptions of aggressiveness and submission is usually accomplished by the boy without serious difficulty.

More serious is the fact that childhood obedience has been primarily to women—to his mother and to women teachers. The adolescent boy therefore has a conception of himself as docile where older women are concerned. In achieving adulthood, he must change his attitude toward older women in order to become the aggressive dominant male of our culture. Although some boys go through a period of expressing rebellion, ridicule, and scorn for older women, in time most accept the approved attitude of kindly deference to them—a kind of lip service of obedience combined with actual aggressiveness and protectiveness.

The submission to women creates a conflict in early adolescence in the boy's relationships with girls. Girls mature some two or three years earlier than boys, and often are taller than boys of the same age. They have experienced the menarche, and their interest is directed toward boys as different from themselves and the source of new and exciting emotional and social experiences. If they have received attention from older boys, they have a sophistication unknown to the boys of their own age. In early social relationships, girls often are the aggressors, with boys behaving in a shy and feminine way. At school mixers, the boys stand in little clusters while the girls approach them, forcing conversation and sometimes openly inviting boys to dance with them. A girl may make tentative physical approaches—patting the boy's cheek or leaning her shoulder against his in an automobile—before the boy is bold enough to do so. Boys, unsure of themselves and accustomed to feminine dominance, accept this situation for a period of time. It increases the difficulty of adjustment between boys and girls, for the girl thus reinforces the dominant tendencies nourished in her childhood group, and the boy reinforces his dependence and obedience tendencies learned in his relationship to mother and teachers.

When the boy becomes pubescent, shoots ahead of the girl in height, surpasses her in muscular strength, exhibits such secondary sex characteristics as a beard and deepened voice, a struggle follows between boy and girl. This struggle exhibits itself in quarrels over which movie a couple will attend, in futile arguments over facts or opinions, in betting who is right about some inconsequential fact, and among younger adolescents sometimes in physical tussles of strength. Gradually, the boy asserts his dominance, both physically and in his control of social situations. The mores give assistance: for instance, boys are encouraged to display their physical strength publicly in sports that demand a degree of endurance that girls in time recognize they could not equal. Also the mores decree that the boy shall invite the girl on dates, pay for the entertainment, provide and drive the automobile, and lead in dancing. He is in a superior position with reference to his choice of a girl and where he wishes to take her. He may drop a dominative girl after one date.

At the same time the boy succeeds in establishing his dominance over his girl friends, he learns to curb that dominance and to confine it to certain types of relationship. After the tussles of early adolescence have been outgrown, physical struggles are frowned upon and are given a connotation of sex by adults. Sexual dominance is forbidden by the mores, and a willingness to refrain from such dominance is a part of the masculine conception.

The Feminine Self and Role

The adolescent girl enters a process that parallels and complements that of the boy—she redefines her conception of herself and relates her new conception and role to boys of her own age.

One of the earliest readjustments of the adolescent girl is the harmonizing of aggressive and docile roles. Obedience by the girl is taught at home and is emphasized for the girl more than for the boy. This attitude is compatible with the later subordinate role that she will be expected to play with reference to boys. However, the role is not clear-cut for the modern girl. In her own sex-group as a child she may express leadership and initiative; in other girls' groups, such as a school that enrolls only girls, Girl Scouts, girls' clubs, and Sunday school classes, she is encouraged to be socially aggressive. The fact that many girls are employed between graduation and marriage and may compete with men again emphasizes aggressiveness in girls. Thus, the girl finds two conflicting but socially approved patterns—aggressiveness and docility. Whereas the mature woman in our society retains both elements but directs each to selected relationships and activities, the adolescent girl finds herself exercising first one, then the other, tendency in identical situations, sometimes with unpleasant results.

The situation is further complicated by the uneven maturing of boys and girls, already discussed with reference to boys. The girl in her early adolescence regards boys of her own age as backward, clumsy, and lacking in initiative; she therefore tends to prod them into mixed activities by direct and aggressive methods. She may be helped to gain social compliance by association with older boys whom she admires and whose leadership she will follow. Otherwise, she becomes involved in a long struggle with boys of her own age but of less maturity. As boys come into dominance through physical growth and social prerogatives, she may withdraw from contacts with boys (as a few "man-haters" do), or she may comply. Often she does not so much change her evaluation of herself and her sex as find new ways of exhibiting her initiative and desire to dominate. Glamor, charm, and flattery are methods by which girls continue to dominate boys. Often the girl identifies herself with an outstanding boy and in her imagination shares some of the satisfaction of his initiative and aggressiveness. She is enabled to do this more satisfactorily if the boy meets the adolescent standards for outstanding ability so that she, as the boy's chosen girl friend, receives the admiration and envy of her girl friends and the attention of boys who admire the outstanding youth. Again, she may exhibit a docile attitude toward boys but become aggressive in her relationships with her family or girl friends.

The girl learns that compliance to boys is limited to certain areas of experience. She is expected to assume initiative and resistance with reference to sex. This area of feminine control includes personal talk about sex, sex jokes, ardent petting, and direct sex experience. Girls are taught and early accept for themselves the dictum that the girl is responsible for setting the limit to verbal or physical sexual experience. In this area alone the contest for dominance between boys and girls may continue after the girl has adjusted herself to a subordinate role in school and social activities.

Adolescent Peer Groups and Teenage Subculture

The peer group, already in evidence during childhood, becomes a dominant aspect of the social world of the adolescent.

ONE-SEX PEER GROUP[13]

"Peer group" is a term used by psychologists, sociologists, and educators to identify informal friendship groups of teenagers. Boys speak of their club or gang; girls speak of their bunch or, if they meet for lunch, their potluck group.

The essence of a peer group is its independence from adult supervision. As the adolescent seeks freedom from family control, he finds himself in an anomalous position. He desires complete independence but is not yet ready for it. He still needs support from others, approval, advice, and joint participation in new ventures, needs that the peer group of his own sex supplies.

The peer group acts as an agency of control over its members. It has its own system of values and expectations, imposed on members through group approval or disapproval. The person who exceeds the expectations (who is too good) as well as the one who fails to meet them is disapproved or penalized.

The peer group acts as a buffer between the teenager and adults. It permits minor deviations, but it controls their extent, and in general, urges its members on toward adulthood. The peer group protects the individual members in their experimentations with new and more adult forms of behavior. Some of these activities are approved by adults, for example, camping trips or travel that a protective parent would not want a boy to undertake alone; or double or triple dates for the girl as a prelude to pair dating. Other types of behavior might not receive approval, although sometimes avoidance of the issue by parents tacitly condones it. The adolescent boy's first experiments with sexual behavior are often carried out in company with other boys. The peer group

[13]Jesse Pitts, "The Family and Peer Group," ch. 21 in Norman W. Bell and Ezra F. Vogel, eds., *A Modern Introduction to the Family* (New York: Free Press, 1960); Caroline M. Tryon, "The Adolescent Peer Culture," *The 43d Yearbook of the National Society for the Study of Education*, Part 1, "Adolescence" (Chicago: University of Chicago Press, 1944), Sec. 3, ch. 12.

decrees the type and circumstances of sexual experimentation suitable for a given age—masturbation at an early teen age and heavy petting or intercourse by mid- or late adolescence. The adolescent gains courage through his peer group for behavior that is new and somewhat fearful to him, and finds in the peer group an audience to admire his prowess in what is defined as adult masculine behavior. Girls use their peer groups for an exchange of information on menstruation and boys. The peer group also provides a critical panel for evaluating indirect means of attracting boys through style of dress, hair-do, and behavior.

As both boys and girls begin dating, the peer group of the same sex serves both as a sounding board for dating experiences too personal to relate to parents and as a means of establishing and enforcing dating and sex codes.

Extreme dependence upon the peer group for approval and friendship is a passing phase of adolescence. As maturity approaches and the boy (or girl) gains a feeling of self-adequacy, he tends to free himself from this dependence just as at an earlier period he freed himself from too dependent an inclusion in the family. If the processes of family life and of peer-group life have on the one hand satisfied the current needs of the boy or girl and on the other added to his self-confidence, he will grow into a competent, self-reliant adulthood, with the ability to manage his own life realistically, to accept his responsibilities, and to find types of relationship with parents, husband or wife, and friends that meet both his and their normal needs in a mutually sympathetic and responsible way.

HETEROSEXUAL PEER GROUPS

Although the family and the one-sex peer group are never entirely lost, the heterosexual social group tends to supplement and finally to replace them as the most important type of association. The membership of heterosexual groups tends to decrease in number as "playing the field" within an acceptable group gives way to steady dating, and this in turn to engagement and marriage. These types of association are discussed in forthcoming chapters.

FAILURE TO MAKE HETEROSEXUAL ADJUSTMENT

That some adolescents fail to make an easy heterosexual adjustment is clear from the behavior of certain young people. The excessively shy boy or girl fails at the social level. The hoydenish girl and the "sissy" among boys have failed to find clear conceptions of their feminine or masculine selves and roles. The boy or girl eager to fling himself into early sex relations has stopped at the self-centered stage and is not developing the cooperative attitude of the adult. The boy or girl whose sexual interests are turned in upon himself or are diverted explosively to others of the same sex has also failed to make a heterosexual adjustment. Many of these phases are typical of certain stages of personality development, but long continuance means a fixation at a level that is immature and that may prevent growth toward maturity. Since our society encourages heterosexual activities during adolescence and holds out the bright goal of marriage with beginning adulthood, explanations must be found for failure to follow the accepted path.

Heterosexual adjustment implies entering new groups and gaining approval and status for oneself not only among new people but with the opposite sex. Therefore it creates tension and anxiety. As with any new venture, the secure person makes the adjustment more easily and quickly than the insecure person. The boy or girl who enters adolescence feeling more insecure, inferior, or inadequate than the average adolescent is handicapped.

Often when the adolescent enters high school he also enters a new social group. In some areas, for instance, the rural or suburban schools carry the student only through the eighth grade; thereafter the student commutes to some nearby urban high school. The patterns of social life change from rural to urban with an increased degree of sophistication, symbolized by later evening hours for social events, the substitution of formal for informal parties, and availability of public dances. The rural student may have to modify his ideals of social usage and perhaps some of his moral concepts. Otherwise, he may find himself without many friends or ill at ease in social groups. Also, city students may be able to identify the rural students by mannerisms of speech or style of dress and may exclude them from social activities.

Somewhat similar is the situation of the student of ethnic background. He may have attended elementary and junior high school in an ethnic community, where all his friends were reared in families like his own, with distinctive cultural traits. If the ethnic community is not large enough to support a high school, students may commute to another community where they may represent a minority group distinguishable from the majority group by appearance, name, and mannerisms. If they are not actively excluded from social groups, they may nevertheless feel ill at ease and may segregate themselves.

Although both rural and ethnic students may form their own social groups, they often fail to do so, and yearn for inclusion in the dominant group with its greater prestige and perhaps control of social events.

Thus, they may go through adolescence on the fringe of a group that they are too insecure to enter.

Insecurity also may be the result of an insecure childhood. If a child has been unwanted and unloved at home or if for some reason early friendship groups have ostracized him, the child grows up feeling rejected or socially "lost." Some children resent such exclusion and make aggressive attacks either on those who have excluded them or displace their hostility on other social groups. Sometimes this displacement is directly related to later difficult heterosexual adjustment. Thus the girl who feels that her father does not love her may turn her resentment from her father to all men or to all males. She may be aggressive and bitter against all boys, showing her feeling in sarcasm, scorn, and belittling remarks.[14] Similarly, the boy who feels that his mother has failed him may despise or doubt the sincerity of all girls and women.

In other cases, rejection by the parents breeds a general feeling of doubt and insecurity. The child may come to believe that he is unlovable, that something within his own personality or his appearance makes it impossible for others to like him. Some of these children turn in upon themselves and, never having received love, are never able to give it. If friendship is offered to them they fear to accept it. They do not know how to respond, and their early experience makes them fearful of even tentative response for fear the friendship will be withdrawn and they will be hurt further. Such insecurity may manifest itself in friendships with those of the adolescent's own sex, but is perhaps even more likely to occur in connection with the opposite sex, since here the relationships are new and uncertain, and greater show of friendliness is necessary to appeal to the would-be friend. Heterosexual adjustment may therefore be delayed until the adolescent overcomes his insecurity through a series of mild or tentative friendships or through personal achievements that give self-confidence and a feeling of adequacy.

The adolescent may repudiate close friendships of all types, both with the same sex and with the opposite, because of an unwillingness to accept the responsibility of a steady relationship in which something must be given as well as something received. This attitude may result from an earlier family situation in which the parents have placed too much responsibility on the child. In the absence of the father, the son may have been expected to act the role of the husband and father before he was ready for an adult role. Or parents may have held the child to standards beyond his possibility of attainment. With the greater freedom of adolescence, the boy or girl may shake off responsibilities and

[14] J. L. Despart, "Resistance to Change in the Adolescent Girl," *Nervous Child*, 4 (1944–45), 8–16.

seek complete freedom. He then may continue into later adolescence the status of exploitative, self-centered personality that may be normal for the young adolescent but not for the one who is approaching maturity.

Too great dependence on parents may also unfit the adolescent for deeper emotional bonds with those of his own age. Parents necessarily give young children unstinted love and physical care without receiving anything in return. As the child develops the parents may continue to cater to the child's selfish wishes rather than to encourage a cooperative relationship where child and parent exchange tasks and obligations as well as love. Such a child enters adolescence with the expectation that others, even those of his own age, will cater to him as his parents have done. This attitude may carry over to heterosexual relationships. If the mother has been the one to pamper the son, the boy expects other women and girl friends to do likewise. If the father has been the indulgent one toward his daughter, the girl will expect her boy friends to carry the burden of their friendship.

Occasionally, a child has been reared in a family where all show of emotion has been suppressed. The family may have an underlying loyalty and unity, but tender words and caresses even of the mildest sort may never be exchanged between members of the family. The situation may extend to the point where giving of presents except on conventional occasions or doing small favors may be avoided as displaying some weakness of personality or sentimentality. Such a child finds it difficult to make friendships outside the family. His repressed behavior is interpreted by boys and girls alike as unfriendliness, and he is ignored or his tentative approaches are repulsed.

TEENAGE SUBCULTURE

Since World War II, researchers and lay writers have been intrigued with the possibility that an adolescent or, as it is usually called, teenage subculture exists and that it extends beyond the local scene to include the entire nation, uniting teenagers and their peer groups in a common compact that differs from and at times opposes adult culture.[15] Early formulations identified this subculture as both a reaction to the tensions (storm and stress) then thought to be inherent in adolescent

[15]For a scientific approach, see Jessie Bernard, ed., "Teen-Age Culture," *Annals of the American Academy of Political and Social Science*, 338 (November, 1961); for a layman's report, see Dwight MacDonald, "Profiles: A Caste, A Culture, A Market," *New Yorker*, 34, Part I (November 22, 1958), 57–94; Part II (November 29, 1958), 57–107.

development, and as a form of rebellion toward adult authorities as adolescents strove to achieve independence.[16]

Empirical studies of the 1940's and 1950's indicated that any rebellion that existed was limited to certain frustrating situations and was sporadic in nature. The similarities among teenagers the country over seem to be of a superficial nature, geared to leisure activities, and both created and promoted by manufacturers and retailers who have discovered in adolescents a new market for specialized goods. The teenagers of the 1950's and 1960's have more money to spend, not only in amount but in buying power, than any previous generation. It has been estimated that when allowances from parents and earnings are combined, the amount of "free" money that teenagers have to spend increased from $2.50 weekly in 1944 to $10 in 1958, or a total of $9.5 billion per year. Except for school lunches, this money is uncommitted so far as necessities are concerned. Even when teenagers spend some of it for clothing, the choice is in their hands, with little parental advice. Manufacturers and retailers have discovered this market that did not exist before World War II and aim advertising directly at it.

The impact on teenagers comes through mass media—the radio and records (music), television (a variety of approaches to teen interests and fads, such as extravagant types of dancing), motion pictures (romance and sex behavior), and a number of magazines designed specifically for teenagers, ranging from the rather sophisticated *Seventeen* and *Mademoiselle*, popular with middle-class girls, to at least one for boys catering to hot rod devotees. Some of the magazines encourage teenagers to write about their problems. These letters are published and readers are then requested to give advice to each other via the magazine. Clubs and pen pals are sponsored. In these ways lonely teenagers are brought into a kind of peer group without face-to-face contacts among the members.

The effect of the mass media is that adolescents across the country tend to dress alike, talk alike, think alike, listen to the same music, dance the same latest fads, and read the same youth magazines. To the extent that this is true, the mass media programs serve a socialization process whereby rural, urban, ethnic, and social-class adolescents smooth out their differences. Such a socialization process undoubtedly

[16]See especially Kingsley Davis, "Adolescence and the Social Structure," *Annals of the American Academy of Political and Social Science*, 236 (November, 1944), 8–16. The views of Davis and other writers are briefly summarized by Frederick Elkin and William A. Westley, "The Myth of Adolescent Culture," *American Sociological Review*, 20 (1955), 680–84.

goes on, but it is not clear to what extent the mass media are influential. Other agencies also promote a general process of socialization toward uniformity, for example, schools and colleges, community centers, and jobs. Regardless of the effect of all these agencies, differences remain, reflecting the family and neighborhood folkways and mores of different subcultural groups.[17]

The mass media are probably influential in forming standards for personal behavior, especially in the area of dating and sexual behavior. At one time, radio and television programs that glamorized delinquency and crime were popular and led to criticism by adults who feared that they would motivate children and adolescents to commit crimes. Some types of mass media (motion pictures and crime comic books, for example) have set their own limits on stories focused on crime. On many types of programs, sexual behavior continues to be portrayed in a very alluring and permissive manner. Discussions in magazines for both youth and adults also follow this trend, with perhaps a mild admonition at the end. Whether these permissive approaches are a way of catering to already existing attitudes or whether they promote them is a moot question. It may be that a circular reaction has been established.

The earlier attitude of writers that adolescents were leagued in rebellion against their parents and other figures of authority seems to have been supplanted with the attitude that adolescents (and perhaps their parents and teachers) are simply in a state of confusion about what standards of sexual conduct are desirable and expected by adult society.[18] Since a permissive rather than a firm stand is characteristic of adults on matters of sexual behavior, adolescents turn to other adolescents for formulation of a more specific code, which is then passed down from older to younger adolescents. It seems probable that the peer group is more influential than a nationwide youth culture in setting standards. Personal face-to-face groups, typically, are more influential than secondary groups that communicate indirectly through letters to magazines and correspondence. Peer groups permit a quick exchange of opinion, an immediate judgment of behavior, and on-the-spot penalizing or rewarding of conduct. Moreover, they provide companionship and security to teenagers, who act as the local group of peers decrees. The peer group may be influenced by a nationwide teenage subculture,

[17]See the excellent discussions of Italo-American, Jewish, and Negro teenage culture by Francis A. J. Ianni, David Boroff, and Joseph S. Himes, respectively, in Bernard, op. cit.; also Chapters 10 and 13 in this text.

[18]Robert R. Bell, Premarital Sex in a Changing Society (Englewood Cliffs, N. J.: Prentice-Hall, 1966), 42–43, 162–163.

adapted, however, to the local situation, the ethnic and class culture, and the influence of parents.[19]

Whatever the effect of a teenage subculture may be, it is temporary in nature. By the middle teens, adolescents in increasing numbers are thinking seriously of college; others, not college-bound, are beginning to plan on marriage and jobs; and boys face the experience of military service.

Although studies of the 1940's and 1950's tended to emphasize the generally conforming attitudes and behavior of the majority of teenagers and the nonserious aspects of the adolescent subculture, studies of the 1960's call attention to various types of organized youth movements. The stated objectives of these movements are many: the promotion of peace or civil rights; the defeat of poverty; better mental health; support of political candidates with whose platform they can identify. Underneath may be the struggle to escape from traditional values or from the close supervision of parents, or, among college students, from administrative controls of personal behavior. The various movements organize marches and other demonstrations such as blocking entrances to buildings, make public speeches, and distribute pamphlets. Vandalism is sometimes an end result. Other youth become affiliated with adult-controlled projects through which they can express their values, such as the Peace Corps or the anti-poverty programs. This seemingly new interest in public affairs and welfare begins to crystallize at about age twelve to fifteen but reaches its full flowering in the late teens or early twenties, when it becomes especially appealing to college students.[20]

It is impossible to say whether these movements and activities will affect marriage and the family, into which the young people will enter. The greater freedom of premarital sexual intimacy may be supported by some of the movements, not necessarily directly, but as part of the total effort to find new paths of self-expression.

The Mature Personality

Failure to mature poses a serious problem for the person and society. Adult in years, prodded by social expectations of adult achievement,

[19]For a study showing that teenagers are not in rebellion against parents, see Elkin and Westley, *op. cit.*

[20]Jacob R. Fishman and Fredric Solomon, "Youth and Social Action: An Introduction," and Solomon and Fishman, "Youth and Peace: A Psychosocial Study of Student Peace Demonstrators in Washington, D. C." *Journal of Social Issues,* 20 (October, 1964), 1–29 and 54–73 respectively.

the immature adult is in reality an adolescent trying to live in an adult world. Adolescence is therefore a period of personality maturing.

Although all the traits of the mature, well-adjusted person are important in marriage, certain of these traits may be emphasized in relation to the emerging personality of the adolescent.

INTEGRATION OF ATTITUDES AND DESIRES

The preceding discussion has mentioned the ambivalent attitudes and tendencies of the adolescent: his desire to remain under the protective wing of his parents and at the same time his desire for freedom; his self-centeredness and his desire for friendships; his fear of sex and his pride in maturity; his urge for physical sexual satisfaction and his desire for social approval. During adolescence these incompatible and often conflicting tendencies are slowly welded into an integrated pattern. Certain tendencies carried over from childhood disappear as the boy or girl finds new ways of securing satisfactions; for instance, he no longer needs to demand favors from his parents to prove that he is worthy of adult consideration; he receives his friendly approval by actual successes in school or in the community. Other drives are redirected into channels that do not conflict with the basic personality pattern.

The many digressive interests that seem to pull the adolescent first into this immediate activity and then into that are screened through a selective process whereby some are dropped and others become the basis for continuing hobbies or vocational interest, often with a distant and planned goal to be attained in the future. Discordant attitudes also undergo a pruning and training process whereby consistency and dependability develop so that the person's actions may be more or less predicted regardless of the situation.

SELECTION IN HETEROSEXUAL FRIENDSHIPS

This integrating process whereby balance is achieved and conflicts eliminated applies to boy-girl ties as well as to other phases of life. The adolescent gradually finds the type of person to whom he is most closely attracted—and eventually the one person. His activities with those of the opposite sex also tend to stabilize. Many boys who have had one girl for secret sex relationships and another girl for more conventional social activities are able to modify and control their drives sufficiently to find all their satisfactions in one girl.

Development of Self-Reliance

Not only integration of traits but development of self-reliance is usually achieved during adolescence. The adult culture pattern expects self-reliance—that the person will be able to support himself, accept normal frustrations without permanent maladjustment of the personality, make his own decisions and hold to them over a period of time, and control his own behavior in conformity with the mores. The minimum requirement of this sort is acceptance of responsibility for oneself; the normal requirement, in addition, calls for partial responsibility for husband or wife and complete responsibility for children. Self-reliance not only makes the person a functioning member of society but it also frees the person from preoccupation with self-centered attitudes. Since he has met the expectations of society sufficiently well that he feels secure and able to meet his normal problems, his energies are released from the effort that occupies so much of the attention of the young adolescent—to offset his feeling of inadequacy and inferiority. He accepts himself for what he is, with all his limitations but also with all his capacities.

Mature Selection of Friends

The integrated, self-reliant person is able to turn his energies outward toward building satisfactory relationships with other people. One such relationship is with the opposite sex. Early friends of the opposite sex were sometimes chosen because they resembled the protective parent and catered to the adolescent's need for someone to lean on or because in some way they bolstered the adolescent's self-esteem. With the self-reliant older adolescent or adult, the person seeks only moderately to satisfy his personal needs; he also seeks the more unselfish satisfaction of making another person happy. Thus, the love that once was turned in upon himself may now be turned outward to become focused upon another person. Through this process the individualistic exploitative love of two adolescents becomes the mutually supportive love of two adults.

Questions

1. Describe the process whereby the child's conception of himself is formed.

2. How can the parent of the opposite sex assist the child to define his roles?
3. What is the normal process by which the American child emancipates himself from his parents?
4. Discuss the idea that young children have no interest in sex.
5. In what ways does the boy find it necessary to redefine his role during adolescence? The girl?
6. What conflicting attitudes toward sex does the adolescent boy have? The adolescent girl?
7. Devise practical plans whereby adolescent adjustment problems could be eased or avoided.
8. Is the peer group more important to the adolescent now than in the past? Discuss.
9. What evidence is there of a teenage culture? If one exists what are its limitations?

Bibliography

"American Adolescents in the Mid-Sixties," *Journal of Marriage and the Family*, 27 (1965), entire issue.

BELL, NORMAN W., and EZRA F. VOGEL, eds., *A Modern Introduction to the Family* (New York: Free Press, 1960), ch. 21, "The Family and Peer Groups."

BERNARD, JESSIE, ed., "Teen-Age Culture," *Annals of the American Academy of Political and Social Science*, 338 (1961), entire issue.

DAGER, EDWARD Z., "Socialization and Personality Development in the Child," in Harold T. Christensen, ed., *Handbook of Marriage and the Family* (Chicago: Rand McNally, 1964), ch. 18.

DAVIS, KINGSLEY, "Adolescence and the Social Structure," *Annals of the American Academy of Political and Social Science*, 236 (1944), 8–16.

———, "The Sociology of Parent-Youth Conflict," *American Sociological Review*, 5 (1940), 523–35.

DEUTSCH, HELENE, *The Psychology of Women: A Psychoanalytic Interpretation* (New York: Grune and Stratton, 1944), Vol. I.

ELKIN, FREDERICK, and WILLIAM A. WESTLEY, "The Myth of Adolescent Culture," *American Sociological Review*, 20 (1955), 680–84.

ERIKSON, ERIK H., *Childhood and Society* (New York: Norton, 1950).

GOLDFARB, ALVIN I., "Psychodynamics and the Three-Generation Family," in Ethel Shanas and Gordon F. Streib, eds., *Social Structure and the Family: Three Generational Relations* (Englewood Cliffs, N. J.: Prentice-Hall, 1965), ch. 2.

KLUCKHOHN, CLYDE, HENRY A. MURRAY, and DAVID M. SCHNEIDER, eds., *Personality in Nature, Society, and Culture* (New York: Knopf, 1955).

REMMERS, H. H., and D. H. RADLER, *The American Teenager* (Indianapolis: Bobbs-Merrill, 1957).

STONE, L. JOSEPH, and JOSEPH CHURCH, *Childhood and Adolescence: A Psychology of the Growing Person* (New York: Random House, 1957).

CHAPTER $I3$

Social Relationships Preparatory to Marriage

THE SOCIAL preparation for marriage falls into two main divisions: dating without commitments; and serious dating, oriented toward marriage and leading into engagement. Much of the heterosexual adjustment discussed in the preceding chapter is accomplished through non-committal dating, whereas the selection of a spouse, is achieved through serious dating.

Various writers use somewhat different terminology for types of dating, although all writers in this field recognize a progressive series of dating types, from the casual to the emotional, exclusive dating of the engaged couple. The types used here are (1) casual and random dating or playing the field; (2) going steady, including serious dating; (3) engagement (discussed in the following chapter).

Two other types of association between men and women are also discussed, although neither can actually be termed dating: association of men with prostitutes and with pick-up girls. They have a definite significance for dating and are discussed in this context.

For each kind of dating the discussion covers the typical age of the participants, functions of the type, characteristic behavior patterns, values and codes, and types of interaction between the pair. Physical intimacies and sexual relations are included, inasmuch as they are well integrated into the different types of association. Differences in values and behavior of men from women are noted.

The discussion is presented first in terms of the middle class, where the dating system has had its highest development. This discussion will be followed by a briefer discussion for the upper and lower classes.

Casual and Random Dating

Casual and random dating is above all an episodic type of social activity, in which each dating event is complete in itself. If the experience has been pleasant, other casual dates with the same partner may follow and in time a more continuous type of dating may develop. However, there is no obligation, implicit or expressed, that a given casual date will lead to more dates. It follows, therefore, that a person whose whole dating life is composed of casual or random dates may have a different partner for each date.

Examples of casual dates are the dates of inexperienced teenagers who are still learning the techniques of dating and are not yet ready for a sustained relationship with one person. Casual dating is also an interim type of dating for the older person who has broken up one steady dating arrangement and is seeking a new steady partner. The person who does not wish to become involved in steady dating with its possibility of marriage may engage deliberately in casual dating. Strangers in a new social situation or transients in a city may seek casual dates.

Another type of casual contact, with prostitutes or pick-ups, is not included in this definition of casual or random dates. These contacts meet one requirement of casual dating: they are episodic in nature. However, their purpose is limited to sexual contacts and their duration is often very limited. Casual dating as used here is a social engagement lasting for the duration of a social event, for example, a motion picture, dance, or other form of entertainment, together with informal social activities that may follow, such as eating, drinking, conversation, or parking and intimacies.

AGE OF PARTNERS

Although casual dating may occur in various situations, it is most typical of the young teenager, who is still working out his self-conceptions and roles as male or female. Dating begins in early adolescence, sometimes before puberty. By the 1940's youthful dating was well established, according to reports on their dating history made by college students. At an eastern coeducational college, 60 per cent of students said they were dating in their freshman year in high school, when they would have been about 14 years old.[1] In an eastern state college, 16 per cent of men students and 22 per cent of women reported that they had their first dates at age 12 or under. Ages 13 through 15 found dating in full swing, with 51 per cent of boys and 61 per cent of girls starting dating during these years. Late daters who had their first date at age 16 or later accounted for 25 per cent of men and 14 per cent of women. (Eight per cent of men and 3 per cent of women did not reply to the question.)[2] A 1958 study made at "Alpha" College, a small midwestern coeducational college, yielded the following results: by the time they were in the seventh grade, 19 per cent of the men and 16 per cent of the women had begun to date; during the eighth, ninth, and tenth grades, 50 per cent of the men and 58 per cent of the women began to date, leaving 17 per cent of the men and 12 per cent of the women who did not begin dating until their junior or senior year in high school. Eight per cent of each sex reported no dating in high school and 6 per cent failed to reply to the question.[3]

Two other studies of 1958 and 1959 show the same tendency for dating to begin in elementary school. In a southern upper-lower and middle-class community, 45 per cent of fifth grade boys and 36 per cent of girls claimed to have dated; by the seventh grade the percentages were 69 for boys and 53 for girls.[4] The study does not record the type of dates but shows that even larger percentages of boys and girls claimed kissing. A study of dating in an Iowa city of 70,000 placed the beginning of dating at age 13 or younger.[5] The median age for both boys and girls was 14. As other studies show, dating was infrequent during the freshman year in high school and gained in frequency until 85 per cent of boys and 89 per cent of girls in the senior class recorded at least one date during the year.

Preteen dating often is not dating in the sense of a couple going alone to a social event. Parents or institutions may give a party to which girls and boys come alone, their association with a favorite friend of

---

[1]M. F. Nimkoff and A. L. Wood, "Courtship and Personality," *American Journal of Sociology*, 53 (1948), 263–69. Based on 517 students.

[2]William M. Smith, Jr., "Rating and Dating: A Re-Study," *Marriage and Family Living*, 14 (1952), 312–17. Based on 344 men and 258 women.

[3]Ruth Shonle Cavan, "Dating in High School and College," in Cavan, ed., *Marriage and Family in the Modern World* (New York: Crowell, 1965). Based on 146 men and 143 women, 66 and 73 per cent respectively of the two sexes in the student body.

[4]Carlfred B. Broderick and Stanley E. Fowler, "New Patterns of Relationship between the Sexes among Preadolescents," *Marriage and Family Living*, 23 (1961), 27–30.

[5]William J. Cameron and William F. Kenkel, "High School Dating: A Study in Variation," *Marriage and Family Living*, 22 (1960), 74–76.

the opposite sex being limited to the duration of the party. Girls then leave together and boys together. Parents often bring a group of girls or boys in their cars. Adolescents speak of such association as dating. At school, a boy or girl may spend free time together, in the midst of other students. In these associations the important thing is that a girl has a boy-friend and the boy a girl-friend. They are regarded as a couple by their friends. The association may not last long but for the time being it gives status among friends.

Dating in early or midteens tends to be casual, random, or intermittent. When there is continuity it is more often of the "dating steadily" type, that is, preference for one partner but not exclusive dating, rather than steady or serious (marriage-oriented) dating. For students anticipating college, the intermittent type of dating seems especially prevalent. As late as the senior year in high school, 61 per cent of boys and 57 per cent of girls at Alpha College played the field. In view of the early age for marriage, it seems probable that persons (especially girls) not planning to attend college or not completing high school did not prolong casual dating into the late teens, but at some earlier age had begun steady or serious dating.

FUNCTIONS OF CASUAL DATING

Although casual dating is usually thought of solely in social terms, it is also one of the means by which adolescents establish their masculine or feminine roles. Boys learn through dating what their own reactions are to girls, as well as the traits and types of behavior that are pleasing to them. The horseplay and crudities typical of the boys' clique usually are not tolerated by girls. The reaction to a member of the other sex— whether shyness, desire to have some physical contact, or a comradely feeling—is worked through in a relationship that does not entail great or lasting responsibilities and that may be repeated endlessly as the boy learns the range and control of his reactions to girls of different types. The girl goes through a similar experience of adjustment. She learns to control her aggressiveness or shyness, as the case may be, and to replace competitiveness with other girls by solidarity with a girls' clique that helps her set and maintain standards of dating. She explores her reactions to mild physical contacts, and she finds out the type of boy who repels and the type who appeals to her. In a period when great emphasis is placed on the personal relationship in marriage, dating no doubt serves a useful purpose in this respect. At any rate, in American society it is the approved testing ground for the maturing masculine and feminine traits, both physical and psychological.

On the social side, dating gives experience in adjusting to the etiquette of social interaction between the sexes. Because the adolescent's ego is involved in dating, the social standards set both for self and the dating partner are high. The girl is more concerned than ever before to make a pleasing appearance; she also demands of the boy a higher degree of meticulous dress and nicety of manners than she would expect of her father or brother. The boy is equally critical of the girl.

Dating also provides an opportunity to meet many members of the opposite sex and is often justified by adolescents and adults alike on this basis alone. With abandonment of parental selection of friends, parents concede that wide opportunities are necessary to give the adolescent a chance to find unaided the type of friend he needs.

CHARACTERISTIC BEHAVIOR

The typical casual or random date is with another person of the same social class. The typical occasion of the date is whatever type of social event is popular with the age group—motion pictures, dances, sports, and so on. The dress and behavior are those approved for the age and sex group in the adolescent subculture of the community. In other words, the casual date is primarily a social occasion.

A troublesome question for many teenagers is how much intimacy is permissible during casual dating. Several surveys of college student opinion throw some light on what they regard as suitable. Table 12 shows the opinions of students at a midwestern university.

A preliminary view of the entire table shows two distinct patterns. Both men and women approve of increasing intimacy as dating moves from the first date to engagement; however, at each stage there is a majority and a minority group, often with a few students who either hold back or push ahead of the central patterns. The second pattern is the difference between men and women, with men approving of greater intimacy than women at each stage of dating.

Our interest at the moment is with the first date and infrequent or casual dating. With the first date about a fifth of both men and women disapprove of any intimacy; more than half approve of a goodnight kiss, which is the standard pattern. Very few women would go beyond the goodnight kiss. A number of men, however, deviate from the standard pattern and would approve of immediately moving into heavy petting or intercourse.

With infrequent or casual dating, the majority of women would stop with the goodnight kiss, with a minority group approving of necking. The pattern for men is vastly different: more than half of the men approve of necking at this stage of the dating sequence and 17 per cent would seek heavy petting or intercourse.

TABLE 12

DEGREE OF INTIMACY THOUGHT SUITABLE FOR DIFFERENT STAGES OF
DATING, MIDWESTERN UNIVERSITY STUDENTS, 1968

Degree of intimacy	Different stages of dating			
	First date	In-frequent or casual dating	Going steady	Engaged
Opinions of men	%	%	%	%
No intimacy	21.2	1.9	–	–
Goodnight kiss	57.7	26.9	1.9	4.0
Necking	3.8	53.9	25.0	10.0
Heavy petting (fondling of body, "making out")	13.5	11.5	65.4	38.0
Sexual intercourse	3.8	5.8	7.7	48.0
TOTAL NUMBER	52	52	52	50
Opinions of women	%	%	%	%
No intimacy	20.7	–	–	–
Goodnight kiss	75.3	60.8	1.3	0.7
Necking	3.9	39.2	65.1	18.5
Heavy petting (fondling of body, "making out")	–	–	33.0	60.3
Sexual intercourse	–	–	0.6	20.5
TOTAL NUMBER	154	153	155	151

SOURCE: Questionnaires distributed to all students enrolled in a junior level course on marriage and the family in a midwestern state university, at the beginning of the course. Students differed widely in their choice of major. All had previously had an introductory course in sociology.

The difference between the first date and casual date is marked, but of still more significance is the difference in approval between men and women. The woman faces a dilemma if she wishes to end the date with a goodnight kiss but finds her companion wishes to move into heavy petting or intercourse. Accounts written by many students reflect this situation. Women students comment that if they do not go along with the wishes of the man, he does not ask for another date. Since men are the ones who take the initiative in arranging dates, the women are at a disadvantage and according to their accounts of dating experience may find themselves unable to participate in many social activities unless they are willing to modify their personal standards regarding intimacy.

Another study is confined to opinions on intercourse at several dating stages. For random or casual dates, assuming desire on the part of both man and woman, approval of intercourse runs higher than in the previous study. Among a western intermountain sample of college students, 6.4 per cent of men and 1.4 per cent of women approved of intercourse for casual or random dating; in a midwestern sample, 17.4 per cent of males and 2.8 per cent of females approved.[6] A part of the difference between the intermountain and the midwestern samples, according to the authors, is that the intermountain sample was primarily Mormon, and, as is usually true of young people with strong church affiliations, these students were nonpermissive regarding intercourse. The difference in permissiveness between this midwestern sample and that reported in Table 12 (from different universities) may be the qualification of "assuming mutual desire."

Although the proportion of students who would approve of intercourse as part of casual dating is small, this group merits some discussion as a deviant subtype to the majority who favor only minor degrees of intimacy.

SEXUAL RELATIONS IN CASUAL DATING

Several studies devoted exclusively to premarital sexual behavior make it possible to distinguish that which takes place during casual dating from intercourse in other types of dating. Since casual dating is not on a continuous basis between two people but implies a succession of partners, sexual relations with casual dating partners become promiscuous. When partners are changed rapidly, affection and emotional attachment do not develop. Sexual relations tend to be for individual physical pleasure. Reiss refers to permissiveness-without-affection as the basis for promiscuous intercourse, which he calls body-centered.[7] The young teenager may seek intercourse on this level out of curiosity or to test his masculinity or to gain status among his male peers. He is not concerned with affection, love, a personal relationship with a girl, or marriage. His motive is experience with sex as such. As was pointed out in the preceding chapter, a boy's early sex experience is often on a casual basis with a more experienced girl near his own age or somewhat older, who may live in his neighborhood.

The older, more experienced teenager or young adult may seek some casual dates with the primary motive of intercourse or may be ready

---

[6]Harold T. Christensen and George R. Carpenter, "Timing Patterns in the Development of Sexual Intimacy: An Attitudinal Report on Three Modern Western Societies," *Marriage and Family Living*, 24 (1962), 30–35. Based on 94 men and 74 women in the intermountain sample and 213 men and 142 women in the midwestern sample.

[7]Ira L. Reiss, *Premarital Sexual Standards in America* (New York: Free Press, 1960), ch. 5.

to seize the opportunity if it arises on a casual social date. Kirkendall distinguishes two types of casual dates that involve the certainty or possibility of intercourse.[8] In one (his Level III), dates are made with a casual acquaintance for the express purpose of obtaining intercourse. The man has no emotional attachment to the girl and feels little responsibility for her. Usually the couple have known each other less than two months when the relationship moves into intercourse, apparently without protest on the part of the girl. The second type (Level IV) Kirkendall calls dating an acquaintance or friend. Intercourse is not the prime motive in making the date but grows out of the dating situation. This stage develops for most couples with a dating period of less than six months. There is slight emotional attachment, and the interest in intercourse is primarily self- or body-centered. The relationship does not tend to develop into a love relationship and may be quickly broken by either party, apparently without emotional damage.

The Level III relationship, with sex as the motive, is closely allied with a pick-up relationship, in which a boy or small group of boys invite a girl or two to accompany them perhaps in a car, with the purpose of intercourse tacitly recognized to be the objective by all concerned. These episodes are usually brief and entail very little conversation, since all members usually are experienced in intercourse. After the episode, the boys return the girls to the place where they found them. Sometimes there may be an exchange of money in a marginal form of prostitution, or a stop for food or drink. The participants may never see each other again and in fact often do not wish to, since the experience afforded little beyond the release of physical tensions.

VALUES AND CODES

For the majority of girls and boys alike, the traditional value of abstinence from intercourse and from other types of close intimacy applies to casual dating. Boys more often than girls are willing to include necking; few of either sex would go beyond this point. Implicit in the value is the fact that in our culture, affection or love is needed to justify close intimacy. Middle-class girls especially seek this justification.

In casual dating boys exhibit a double standard of behavior that becomes more pronounced with steady dating. On the one hand, they adhere to the value held by the girls of their own class—little intimacy without love. On the other, for themselves but not for their own class of girls, they accept a very old value of sex relations for the physical satisfaction it will give.

[8]Lester A. Kirkendall, *Premarital Intercourse and Interpersonal Relations* (New York: Julian Press, 1961), chs. 4 and 5.

The codes that uphold abstinence are relatively simple. "No kissing before the third date" is a rule that girls may apply. "There is safety in numbers" leads to double dating as a way of controlling the degree of intimacy. "No parking" is another rule that girls (or their parents) may make.

Boys may also accept such rules for casual dates. They also accept another one: the girl is to draw the line at the degree of intimacy she will permit. The boy may try to persuade, but it is contrary to the code that he should overpersuade or become physically abusive. This rule is part of the general code of dating and is presumed to hold at all levels of dating. It operates most completely between boys and girls who accept the same fundamental values about the type of intimacy suitable to each type of dating. When there is a difference of opinion, a difficult situation may arise. Even with infrequent dating (Table 12), many young men and women do not have the same policy as to the limits of intimacy.

TYPES OF INTERACTION

The interaction on a casual date is likely to be on a superficial social level. The partners do not know each other well, and if first impressions are not favorable they may not wish to become further acquainted. They may be willing to settle for one pleasant social event and then terminate the relationship. Even a succession of casual dates may not lead to any revelation of personal interests or thoughts.

Kirkendall's study of sex relations at this level of dating showed little emotional involvement, little concern on the part of the man for the pleasure or well-being of the girl (his study is limited to interviews with men), and very little if any verbal communication regarding the experience either before or after it occurred. Often the communication leading to intercourse was carried on by gestures and double-talk indicating only the willingness of both to participate.

It should be emphasized that most casual dating is of the social type, especially among teenagers, although upon occasion intercourse may grow out of a particular dating situation.

Steady Dating

In the course of casual dating or through other social contacts, a boy and girl, or a man and woman, are attracted to each other and seek a more firm basis of contact than the casual dating arrangement. Such

attraction may lead to steady dating, or exclusive dating with one partner, for an indefinite or an agreed-upon period of time. Various gradations usually intervene between casual dating and steady dating, each
showing increasing preference for one partner until the exclusive dating is reached. Occasionally a couple may start to steady-date without
the preliminary experience of having played the field with a number
of partners, but this is not the usual procedure.

In surveys, steady dating is often divided into two types. One type
has been called dalliance dating, in which the participants do not regard
the dating as a step toward marriage. It often develops among young
people who expect to continue their education for some time to come
and hence do not regard marriage as the next phase of their life experience. The second type has been called marriage-oriented or serious
dating and perhaps is akin to the older experience of courtship.[9] So far
as it is possible to do so, a distinction between the two types is made in
the discussion in this section.

AGE FOR STEADY DATING

Steady dating runs concurrently with casual dating throughout the
teens and early adulthood. However, the tendency is for the percentage
of persons engaged primarily in casual dating to decrease and those engaged in steady dating to increase as they approach adulthood. For
example, a study of the most prevalent type of dating college students
had engaged in during each year in high school clearly showed the
tendency to move from casual dating in the freshman year to steady
dating in the senior.[10] In the freshman year, 66 per cent of the students
stated that their most prevalent type of dating had been casual or playing the field; by the senior year, only 17 per cent still engaged primarily
in this type of dating. Intermediate types showed that dating with one
person increased from 28 per cent of students in the freshman year
to 41 per cent in the senior year. Only 6 per cent of students felt that
steady dating was the most characteristic type during their freshman
year in high school; 42 per cent felt that it was typical of their senior
year. The study of Alpha College, previously referred to, also showed
that 40 per cent of college students had steady-dated during their senior
year in high school. These are reports from college students. It is probable that high school students not planning on college moved into
steady dating earlier and with greater frequency.

[9]Robert D. Herman, "The 'Going Steady' Complex: A Re-Examination," *Marriage
and Family Living*, 17 (1955), 36–47.
[10]*Ibid.*

Pair or steady dating is closely related to the age at which a boy secures a driver's license and an available car. Parents are no longer needed as drivers. The area within which dating may take place and the freedom from adult supervision are greatly increased. Boys in the first few years of high school may be too young for a driver's license. Girls of that age may seek dates with upperclassmen who have available cars. This creates an age difference that continues on to choice of a marriage partner, when typically the husband is three years older than his wife.

College dating shows very much the same pattern of dating as takes place among high school seniors. In "Pioneer College," a small institution with two men for every woman, 25 per cent of the men were steady daters, while the remaining 75 per cent played the field.[11] Among the women, 44 per cent were steady daters and 56 per cent played the field. In a large state university with five men to every four women, 30 per cent of the men went steady, with the remainder playing the field or not dating at all. Among the women, 37 per cent went steady and most of the remainder played the field.[12]

Since college students are of marriageable age, certain questions arise regarding the continuance of random dating. The percentages given do not distinguish among college classes. Freshmen, even though they may have steady-dated regularly in high school, may drop back to a period of casual dating until they establish social contacts on the campus. In the artificial world of the campus some students may not find members of the opposite sex whom they regard as datable. If the sex ratio in special groups is unbalanced, students of minority racial or ethnic groups may find steady dating impossible, although they may have occasional casual-dating partners. Likewise, students who wish to steady-date only those of their own religion may be handicapped by lack of partners. Upperclassmen who are anticipating several years in a professional school often hold off from steady dating to avoid involvement. Upperclasswomen who desire a husband already established in a business or profession likewise may wish to avoid involvement with a classmate. Also, some account must be taken of the number of students who had steady-dated, become engaged, and withdrawn from college to be married. These students were probably more inclined to steady-date than the ones who remained to complete their college education.

[11]E. A. Smith, "Dating and Courtship at Pioneer College," *Sociology and Social Research*, 40 (1955–56), 92–98.

[12]S. H. Lowrie, "Factors Involved in the Frequency of Dating," *Marriage and Family Living*, 18 (1956), 46–51.

Functions of Steady Dating

The motives of going steady are partly personal and partly social. On the personal side is a greater enjoyment in the other's companionship than in that of anyone else—for the time being. Often a high degree of emotional fervor wells up, and the two believe themselves in love, destined for each other. This crush, infatuation, or "puppy love" is powerful while it lasts. It is a natural phase of the process of maturing and of the inability of the adolescent to integrate or counterbalance his emotional reactions with other considerations. All of his reactions tend to be strong. He hates some things, can't stand others, just loves still others. His feelings toward people are strong and unrestrained by other considerations. Therefore, his interest in one of the opposite sex also tends to be strong and one-sided. During college going steady may assume new meaning and become the beginning of courtship.

In steady dating young people are meeting the expectations of their peer groups. Pressure from others to steady-date may be strong, as the following statements from high school students show.

> There are few boys and girls in high school who do not conform to the going steady formula. If they do not conform they are regarded as queer and are left out of social gatherings and functions —not because of unpopularity but because couples are essential to the gatherings.
>
> You just weren't accepted by the majority if you didn't have someone to give your undivided attention to. It didn't matter really how often you switched from one person to another; the only essential was that at all times you had to have a "steady."
>
> When a girl and a boy are seen together about five times people begin talking about the fact that they are going steady. They then are expected to be seen together. If they aren't, it is a mild scandal all over school.
>
> Gradually, and it is almost inevitable, a certain couple are often seen together at high school functions. Whether they like it or not they are looked upon as going steady and it is taboo to date another fellow's steady. The girl is stuck. However, there is compensation. It is a big moment to be asked to go steady; wearing the boy's class ring and his letters gives the girl a great deal of prestige. Going steady is one of the most highly accepted statuses of the high school student.

Going steady gives a sense of security to both boy and girl. The girl is assured of an escort, and the boy is saved the painful procedure of approaching a new girl or one who plays the field, with the risk of being turned down.

There is prestige in going steady and especially so if the partner is admired by the friends of one's own sex. Many girls maneuver boys into asking them to go steady so that they may display the boy's ring or pin. Going steady therefore contributes greatly to the boy's or girl's sense of self-esteem and self-confidence. The arrangement is proof of desirability of the person.

Socially, new avenues are opened to the couple going steady. On one hand, parental anxiety relaxes a little if the partnership is approved. It is possible to establish general rules with the couple and to know what to expect in the way of compliance with the rules.

At the same time, going steady creates new tensions. Parents, glad of the greater stability of the relationship, at the same time are opposed on the basis that the boy or girl is limiting his social experiences, and also that the dating may (as it occasionally does at the high school level) lead into an early courtship. The boy and girl, who eagerly leap into the intensity of going steady, soon find it a burden and long for greater freedom in companionship with a variety of persons. The girl, especially, may feel uneasy over the expectation of more petting than she has previously permitted.

It is not surprising, therefore, that agreements to go steady are of short duration. If the prestige motive is uppermost, every few weeks may find a new pairing off, with the girl wearing the pin or ring of a new boy. This frequent shifting is accepted as proof of the girl's popularity. The boy, in his turn, may desire to move from girl to girl, seeking ever more glamorous partners. If the boy or girl is not sure of securing another partner, security may be the dominant motive and the arrangement may last longer—in fact it may become worn out so far as mutual enjoyment is concerned but continue because each dreads the necessity of making other contacts.

CHARACTERISTIC BEHAVIOR

Certain customs and rules have developed that protect the couple from encroachments by other persons who might wish to date one of the couple. For example: No boy other than the chosen one will ask the girl for a date; this rule is highly respected and rigidly followed. The girl, for her part, may not entice any other boy or show him favors. The couple are always invited together to social functions; if one cannot attend, the other may not attend. They have become a social unit.

Other customs tend to bind the partners together and give them a feeling of identification. Symbols are exchanged, such as rings, class pins, club pins, bracelets with the owner's name inscribed, or sweaters. These symbols are not gifts; ownership remains with the original owner, the symbols being returned when the arrangement of going steady breaks up. In fact, the absence of the pin or ring signifies to the peer group that the two are no longer going steady. Nonmaterial symbols are cultivated between the two. They may have a favorite song, a favorite seat in the motion-picture house, or a favorite place to park. They thrill to the sound of "our song," and resent the innocent intrusion of another couple who happen to occupy the favorite seat or parking spot.

Steady dating also carries the implication of more permissiveness in intimacies. Table 12, which does not distinguish between dalliance dating and the more serious or marriage-oriented type, indicates a very different type of attitude toward intimacies than those commonly accepted for casual (infrequent) dating. Two-thirds of the boys and a third of girls approve of heavy petting. Small percentages give approval to sexual intercourse. This is the first stage of dating at which heavy petting has been approved by women students or approved with any degree of frequency by men. The change in attitude between casual or various intermittent types of dating and steady dating is significant when one considers the marked sexual quality of heavy petting as distinct from the effects of necking. Necking is usually thought of as kissing, embracing, and fondling through the clothing, without obvious intent to arouse specific sexual desires or responses. Petting is more intimate than necking, and heavy petting quite definitely has as its purpose the arousal and partial satisfaction of sexual drives. It includes fondling the erogeneous areas—breasts and thighs—sometimes without the protecting covering of clothing. Intensive heavy petting may lead to complete physical release in orgasm. Intercourse is not included in the term; however, if the couple do not have complete control of their emotions, heavy petting may very readily end in unplanned intercourse.

It may be concluded then that one-third to two-thirds of young people in this college sample approve of sexual arousal and satisfaction, although by a method that permits them to remain "technically" virgins. When intercourse is added to heavy petting, three-fourths of the men approved of some degree of sexual arousal and satisfaction as a part of going steady.

IMPLICATIONS OF HEAVY PETTING AND INTERCOURSE IN STEADY DATING

Steady daters, especially those who are marriage-oriented, tend to have a basis of friendship and affection for their sexual relationship. Girls, especially, justify intimacies as an expression of affection and love. Reiss refers to this relationship as permissiveness with affection.[13] For

[13]Reiss, *op. cit.*, ch. 6.

all except a few older, sophisticated middle-class women, affection usually is considered the only justification for sexual arousal and satisfaction, whether through heavy petting or intercourse. Especially if the girl or woman stops short of intercourse, she can feel that she has observed the traditional moral standard of abstinence—that she is "good," "pure," a virgin. At the same time she has satisfied her urge for sexual satisfaction, her curiosity, or her desire to please or hold a male friend. The division between what is acceptable and not acceptable is not made on the basis of sexual experience but on the basis of what is perhaps a rather artificial boundary—whether there has actually been physical contact of the genital organs and penetration in intercourse.

The man has a somewhat different attitude. As has been pointed out, one phase of his interest in sex is physical pleasure, about which many men have no feelings of guilt, provided they secure the pleasure from girls who are experienced and who also attach no moral significance to intercourse. With steady dating, based on affection, a new element enters the picture. In this relationship, usually with a girl of his own social class and therefore marriageable, the man shares the girl's attitude that heavy petting and intercourse are justified by affection and not alone by physical desire. However, the man cannot lay aside his previous attitude nor neglect the urge that necking and petting may arouse in him for full sexual satisfaction. On the one hand, he does not wish to offend his steady-dating partner; on the other, he does wish sexual satisfaction.

Where intercourse is concerned, Kirkendall's study brings out the difference between intimacy with affection as found in steady dating and crass physical relationships as found in temporary contacts whose primary purpose is intercourse.[14] In the dating situation, 61 per cent of men who had intercourse did not reach this degree of intimacy until they had been dating for more than a year, and almost none had intercourse under two months. There was a high degree of emotional involvement and more concern for the partner's reaction than in more impersonal relationships. The man could not approach intercourse rapidly; he often had to persuade and cajole the girl into agreeing. Girls were easily offended when the men applied some of the techniques they had learned in sexual behavior with casual contacts, pick-up girls, or prostitutes.[15]

[14]Kirkendall, op. cit., various references.

[15]Clifford Kirkpatrick and Eugene Kanin, "Male Sex Aggression on a University Campus," American Sociological Review, 22 (1957), 52–58. Fifty-eight per cent of 291 university girls on one campus were offended in the course of a year by their dating partner's behavior. Most of the incidents grew out of necking and petting; however, 8 per cent consisted of attempted intercourse to which the girl was opposed.

At the same time that men agree with the girl, or at least follow her wishes, at least some of them also seek sexual contacts elsewhere. Thus, they are saved from feelings of insincerity or duplicity by equating abstinence with their conduct toward "good" girls—the old traditional double standard—and equating physical sexual satisfaction through intercourse with "bad" girls.

This discussion of heavy petting and intercourse should not blind the reader to the fact that among college students a fourth of men and two-thirds of women approve of stopping short with necking as the appropriate limit of intimacy for going steady.

However, neither should the reader avoid recognizing that steady dating is a temporary arrangement, even when the couple have not set arbitrary limits to its duration. A kind of serial promiscuity is therefore possible.[16] The survey of dating at Alpha College in 1958 showed that 52 per cent of the men and 51 per cent of the women had broken one or more steady-dating, pinning, or engagement agreements.

The shifting of partners has led to the comment that the dating system is one of "kissing promiscuity."[17] Another view would emphasize the fact that whatever is learned in one relationship is carried over to the next one, making the person more wary and cautious, if the learning has been unpleasant, or more ready to proceed quickly to the more advanced types of intimacy, if the learning has been pleasant and in accord with the person's standards of what is suitable.

VALUES AND CODES OF STEADY DATING

Steady dating is usually regarded as a strictly modern American way in which young people traverse the road to marriage, carrying out the procedure under their own control and with a minimum of formal guidance from adults. During the adolescent period, parents, teachers, and youth leaders arrange and carefully supervise mixed-group parties and dances, but they are unable to follow the boy and girl into the date that follows the dance. The folkways and mores of dating, therefore, represent two types of group influences—adult and peer group. In general, the adult folkways and mores are in control of social affairs sponsored by churches, schools, clubs, or carried out in the adolescent's home with some form of chaperonage, whereas the personal relationship between the boy and girl and conduct on affairs carried out by

[16]Cavan, *op. cit.*

[17]William Simenson and Gilbert Geis, "Courtship Patterns of Norwegian and American University Students," *Marriage and Family Living*, 18 (1956), 334–38.

adolescents themselves (movie dates, car dates, picnics, dates in lunch rooms and taverns) represent the peer culture. The peer culture is relatively independent of adult control, but never completely so. Although adolescents may adopt types of conduct not learned from their parents, they must always reconcile this conduct in some way with the earlier teaching of the parents. Many go through a period of conflict and confusion, with feelings of guilt, until a pattern that is acceptable to the adolescent's standards is attained. In a changing society with new social conditions to adjust to that are unlike those of the parent's youth, the peer culture is never quite the same as the adult culture. Moreover, the peer culture also is influenced by the need of the adolescent to achieve independence; thus, for a time, disregard or even defiance of adult standards may have a positive meaning to the adolescent and contribute to his feeling of independence and self-reliance.

Only in the case of rebellious youth, however, does the boy or girl follow his own impulses in the conduct of the date. Peer culture implies group-accepted patterns of behavior. In informal "bull sessions" a code is achieved. These sessions are not as a rule heterosexual. Girls develop their codes; boys, theirs. But the codes are always being tried out on dates and hence move toward coordination. Also the code of the opposite sex, as revealed on dates, is discussed, and those who violate the code of their sex or refuse to respect the code of the other are ruled out as undesirable dating partners.

College students bring their high school codes to the campus, where in further "bull sessions" codes are coordinated and modified to fit the new situation. The chief area in which codes fail to correspond between men and women college students is in the degree of intimacy desired. According to one study, men placed greater emphasis on affection, romantic appeal, attractive appearance, and willingness to pet in their dating partners; women liked a date who had conventional sex standards and who did not have a reputation for necking or petting.[18] Moreover, men did not understand what women wanted most in a date, nor did women understand what men wanted most. The codes, then, developing without adequate communication between the two sexes, often worked at cross purposes.

The values of dating are related to whether the dating is of the dalliance or the marriage-oriented type. In dalliance dating, the chief values seem to be the social possibilities opened, since many adolescent and youth activities are planned on the basis of couples; prestige of having achieved a dating status; added prestige if the partner has high

[18]Robert O. Blood, Jr., "Uniformities and Diversities in Campus Dating Preferences," *Marriage and Family Living*, 18 (1956), 37–45.

status in the youth group; and pleasure without complete responsibility, including necking and to some extent petting. The dater continues the education in heterosexual social relationships begun in casual and random dating and moves toward maturity in this respect. He makes these achievements under conditions of limited responsibility and with the privilege of abandoning one relationship for another as part of the normal process of dating.

The serious dater who is looking forward to marriage uses dating not only for the above purposes but also as a means toward mate selection and formal engagement.

Type of Interaction

Interaction in steady dating conforms in part to the customs and codes of the couple's peer group, but this conformity is modified by personal interaction and adjustment to each other on a personal basis. Respect for each other as persons and mutual affection are strong motivating factors in conduct. Also, since the relationship extends through a period of time, the interaction changes. What happens on one date, what each said and did, helps to determine future interaction. Dates are no longer events or episodes, as when playing the field, but are parts of a continuing process.

Friendship and affection develop but often on a rather superficial and temporary basis, a fact that probably accounts for the many dating relationships that break up. One-half or more serious dating affairs go through a fairly uniform pattern. Beginning with indifference or slight attraction, the relationship rises to strong attraction or love, and then declines again to indifference. The peak of attraction may come early in the affair, toward the middle, or in a few cases toward the end. This was the pattern for the course of serious dating for 76 per cent of male love affairs and 68 per cent of the love affairs of women in a University of Minnesota study.[19] In this study, 141 men reported on 314 broken affairs and 258 women on 582, in each case tracing the progress from beginning to end. A similar study made at Alpha College covering the fate of only the most recent broken dating affair showed that 47 per cent of the dating affairs of men and 51 per cent of those of women followed this smooth path of development and decline of attraction. In both the Minnesota and the Alpha studies, the remainder of the

[19]Clifford Kirkpatrick and Theodore Caplow, "Emotional Trends in the Courtship Experience of College Students as Expressed by Graphs with Some Observations on Methodological Implications," *American Sociological Review*, 10 (1945), 619–26.

affairs followed a rough and violent course with many ups and downs of emotion, sometimes running rapidly from dislike to love and the reverse. Some ended while the student giving the information was still in love, others on a note of dislike.

The final emotional adjustment of the individual after experiencing a break is important for the light it throws on the intensity of the affair and also on the resumption of dating with another partner. Among the Minnesota students, in 61 per cent of the male cases and 56 per cent of the women's cases, the indifference with which the affair broke was continued; there were no emotional repercussions. The remainder, with few exceptions, experienced some emotional ups and downs immediately following the break and then reached a state of indifference. The exceptions consisted of 10 per cent of the men's affairs and 13 per cent of the women's affairs, for which the residual reaction was dislike of the former partner. Among Alpha students, various reactions followed the break, but within a month approximately four-fifths of both men and women had reached a state of indifference.

The process of interaction may indicate the superficial nature of the relationship for some students; for others a brief genuine love relationship that did not endure. The affairs with violent swings of emotion may indicate strong attraction coupled with aversion, or unequal degrees of love on the part of the man and woman.

Upper-Class Dating

The contrast of middle-class dating with dating in well-established upper-class groups reveals the prevalence in upper-class groups of a formal, adult-controlled pattern within which the boy and girl work out their personal relationships. The following account refers to an eastern city in which the upper class has its roots in past centuries.[20]

> Dating begins at the age of 14 years and consists of Friday night movie dates, a quick trip to the favorite Coke bar, and home by 11:30 o'clock. This age also means the beginning of dances every other Saturday night at the country club. These dances are a step higher than dancing schools, as nothing is taught and it is conducted like a regular dance. Only certain people are invited to these dances, namely, students from the boys' and girls' private schools. The boys and girls who meet at these dances become dating partners until the senior year in high school.

[20]The account refers to the period around 1950.

The cut-in system is used and a girl is a downright flop if she is not cut in on at least twice during one number. This type of dancing is used at all the dances of this group of people—the system of a couple dancing only with each other is not used. The cut-in system shows the preference for not going steady. I should say that not one per cent of the private school students go steady. In fact the very word is thought "common" among the group. The idea is for a girl to go out with just as many boys as she can, and being seen with one boy more than three times in succession is embarrassing rather than being in a girl's favor.

At the age of 16 years young people graduate into dances at the country club that are for the older group and alternate with the dances for the younger boys and girls. A boy takes a girl to the dance and takes her home, but during the evening they scarcely see each other.

Sex begins to play a small part in the relationship. Dates for dances, movies, and so forth are usually terminated by a kiss and occasionally a necking session. However, since the clique is relatively small, a bad reputation spreads like fire and so the girl hesitates before even kissing a boy goodnight. Falling in love at this age is popular, but even if it is mutual the two rarely go steady. They may go a little farther in their love-making but since they are in love it is kept pretty quiet.

When girls reach their senior year at high school they feel too old for the country club dances and also for the senior boys. Dating college men becomes frequent. Week ends at the Eastern men's colleges are a must. It is at this time that the girls narrow their field down to two or three boys, but they are usually conveniently scattered at different colleges to make the girl appear more popular. These two or three boys very rarely include the one the girl eventually marries.

One of the nicest traditions of the upper class is the girl's debut, which occurs after she graduates from school. Since many derogatory remarks are made about coming-out parties, I will try to explain the debut. The debut is a beautiful tradition in these families, as the girl is following the pattern set by her mother and grandmother. The idea of a debut is to give the girl a chance to meet the friends of the family. Some she has known all her life, but others she has scarcely met, especially if they are from out of town. The debutante has become of age and is now considered a grownup. The parents are giving the party to celebrate this fact and to launch their daughter into the new group. Life is very different for the girl after her debut. The grownups that she meets will ask her to be on committees for charitable purposes or to join certain clubs. They have come to the party to welcome her into the adult group. Another purpose of the debut is to introduce the girl to a group of young men considered eligible as husbands. Up until the girl makes her debut she has usually dated only boys of her own age from the private schools. If she has attended boarding school she has scarcely dated at all. At the debut young men of

25–35 years old are invited. The parents explain to their daughter that she does not have to marry, but if she does here is a group of men that the parents consider acceptable. The young men have grown up in the same social class as the girl, they have mutual friends, likes and dislikes, and so, invariably, the girl does marry one of them. She wouldn't be happy marrying out of her class. She has been taught from childhood the values of her class position and the average girl wouldn't be able to accommodate herself to anything below at least an upper-middle-class position. The upper-class families do not regard the debut as a waste of money. They derive pleasure from the party and satisfaction in knowing that, according to their standards, they are doing what is right for their daughters, by introducing them to the people they will live and associate with for the rest of their lives. After the debut, couples tend to pair off. This pairing off does not mean that the couple remove themselves from the group, but means that they are pretty sure of each other. Two or three couples usually form groups within the larger social group and go almost everywhere together. Practically all the debutantes are married at least four years after they come out.

Families have a great deal to do with selection of a husband or wife by the daughter or son. Name and social position are very important and are usually determining factors. It would be almost impossible to fall in love with someone who isn't "accepted." If a boy or girl does fall in love with someone of this type, pressure from the family is usually successful in breaking it up. These relationships often develop while the boy or girl is at college. The outsiders don't know your families or social group at home and so won't tell of indiscretions. The student is away from the pressure of home and may be inclined to go wild. This tendency is true of girls as well as boys. However, the influence of home is always in the back of one's mind and few students think of marriage to these outsiders. After college the boys and girls return home, marry an old flame, and get back into their old clique.

Lower-Class Dating

Lower-class dating is carried on primarily through commercial places of recreation, such as dance halls, a drugstore or restaurant with a juke box, or taverns. Lower-middle- and lower-class children from families with a strong church affiliation may find much of their recreation through the church or church mission. In cities a certain proportion regularly attend club and mixed-group activities at settlements and community centers.

The failure of lower-class boys and girls to patronize school affairs is partly for financial and partly for social reasons. Although many school recreational occasions may not entail any great expense, the outstanding events—the formal dances—necessitate an evening dress for the girl, a presentable suit (usually not a tuxedo or formal at the high school level) for the boy, money to buy the girl a corsage and provide refreshments after the dance, and some provision for a car or taxi. Even when lower-class boys and girls are able to provide these necessary trappings for the formal school dance, they are often cold-shouldered by the middle-class students and made to feel unwanted; or they feel embarrassed and conspicuous because they are not familiar with the rituals and manners of the middle-class students. They tend, therefore, to turn to less expensive and less exacting forms of entertainment.

LOWER-CLASS DATING IN A SMALL CITY, ELMTOWN

Dating in the lower class has several distinguishing characteristics.[21] It is limited within the social class, except as some girls sporadically date boys one or two class levels above themselves; there is little playing of the field during the teenage period and much concentration upon a few dating partners, symptomatic no doubt of the early age of marriage in this class; and there is great freedom of the individual in choice of partner and place of the date. These characteristics are related to the early age at which lower-class youth leave school.

Among Elmtown youth of high school age it was estimated that, whereas no upper- and only 7.6 per cent of the middle-class boys and girls had withdrawn from school, 41 per cent of the upper-lower- and 89 per cent of the lower-lower-class boys and girls had dropped out of school without graduation. Many of these children leave school a year or two before the legal age for the state and (because many have been disciplinary problems in school) are not forced to return. Most of them have completed not more than the eighth grade. School has not been a pleasant experience, for they have met many discriminations at the hands of upper-status students and teachers; at home they have been associated with parents, brothers, and sisters who did not complete high school and who value ability to earn money more than continued academic attainments. Thus at mid-adolescence many lower-class boys and girls find themselves out of school, working at low-paid temporary jobs, and eligible for the status and responsibilities of adulthood, although still living at home, whereas boys and girls of their own age but a higher social class are still regarded by parents, school, and legal

[21]Based on A. B. Hollingshead, *Elmtown's Youth* (New York: Wiley, 1949), chs. 9, 12, 15, and 16.

authorities as children, to be supported by their parents, protected from hardships, and condoned in their misdeeds by school authorities and courts. The types of work open to lower-class boys and girls are menial in nature; the boys work on farms or do unskilled factory work; the girls are employed as maids, waitresses, or petty clerks. The work of both is monotonous, lacks prestige, and merits very low pay. With no plans for future training, both boys and girls soon realize that they are in a rut. They frequently change jobs and gradually acquire sufficient maturity to find steady employment. By late adolescence the boys have found the general type of work they will continue to do, and by mid-adolescence the girls are ready to leave their jobs for marriage.

Because of this tendency to leave school and find work, the out-of-school lower-class adolescent assumes the role of an adult from one to five years earlier than do boys and girls who finish high school. He is accepted as adult by the community and is expected to assume adult responsibilities. The adolescents themselves are quite willing to be regarded as adults, but their emphasis is upon the freedom from adult control that they thus secure.

This early adult status of the lower-class boy and girl affects their dating and courtship roles. Whereas adolescents of their age still attending school find much of their social life in school- or church-sponsored parties or in parties given by their families or private clubs, the lower-class youth spend most of their free time outside their homes with small cliques of their own age and sex composed of other nonschool youths, or in dating. One of the first expenditures of the boy after he secures a job is for a broken-down automobile that can be repaired by himself and his pals. In such a car two or three boys tour the town in the evening, stop here and there for a Coke, a beer, or to play the pinball machine, or drive to a nearby town hoping to pick up some girl who is willing to ride with them, park, and pet. The girls in Elmtown, even of lower-class status, are sufficiently protective of their status not to allow themselves to be picked up by boys who recognize them, although some may ride with boys from another town as pick-up dates. Sometimes the boys visit a local prostitute if they have sufficient money; otherwise, the evening may end with destruction of highway signs in the rural area, more stops for Coke or beer, or hanging around a skating rink or some other public place of amusement. Both boys and girls hope to preserve a certain amount of anonymity about petting or casual sex relations, except from their pals. This desire accounts for the boys' picking up girls in another town, and the girls' allowing themselves to be picked up only by out-of-town boys. Thus, each group hopes to keep its reputation clean in the home town.

At other times, especially Saturday nights, lower-class boys and girls congregate in restaurants or taverns that cater to young people, the lower-class youths going to places that are considered not quite respectable by the middle- and upper-class groups. Here boys and girls may meet without the formality of making prearranged dates. They often come in cliques of their own sex, thus having security until maneuvers between boys' and girls' cliques result in pairing off. The skating rink, certain motion-picture houses, and a few dance halls are also gathering places for the lower-class adolescents. Gradually boys and girls pair off, sometimes after a preliminary fight between two boys for a girl—an attention that enhances the girl's ego—and around midnight the boys take the girls home, stopping in tavern or café, and delaying on the way home for petting or sex play. This casual milling around and dating after an evening of skating, dancing, fighting, and drinking continues for several years before pair dating is established.

Sex is accepted more naturally by lower-class than by middle- and upper-class youth; the distinction is especially marked as between the girls of the different class levels. Lower-class families are large, and their homes are small; sex activities of parents are less easily kept secret. The greater sex activity of unmarried older youths and extramarital activities of some married people also gradually become known to the adolescent group. The assumption should not be made that sex is openly flaunted even in the lower-lower class, for the mores against open talking about sex prevail, and children are punished by their parents for displaying too much knowledge. Hence children learn to conceal their knowledge from their parents, although they talk of it freely in their own sex and age groups. Control of sex tensions thus becomes a problem to lower-class boys and girls while they are still preadolescent, and by the time of adolescence they have experimented with masturbation and occasionally homosexual activities. By the time dating begins, therefore, the lower-class youth has definitely developed sex tensions and is ready for experimentation with heterosexual activities.[22] Also, girls have learned from older girls, and boys from their seniors, the techniques by which the sex game is played. The procedure is for the boy to pro-

[22]The Kinsey report for males showed that among males not going beyond grade school, 85 per cent were having premarital intercourse by the later teens, compared with 75 per cent of the high school educated and 42 per cent of the college educated. Moreover, the lower the final educational level achieved, the more numerous were the males who reported intercourse. Alfred C. Kinsey, *et al.*, *Sexual Behavior in the Human Male* (Philadelphia: Saunders, 1948), p. 347. Girls whose education ended with grade school experienced intercourse by age 20 in 38 per cent of the cases; with high school, 32 per cent; and with college, 17 per cent. Alfred C. Kinsey, *et al.*, *Sexual Behavior in the Human Female* (Philadelphia: Saunders, 1953), p. 295.

vide a car, and make a romantic or exciting occasion by driving around and providing food, candy, or some gift. The girl, in accepting these favors, knows what is expected of her and must follow through with permitting the boy to have sex relations with her. Both are then expected to maintain a discreet silence about the affair, for neither boy nor girl wants to have a bad reputation. The boy may brag about having a "woman" but not mention any girl specifically; the girl must guard against being too easy with too many boys or men. Although it is known that both boys and girls are experimenting with sex, if the procedure is carried out discreetly, it is not an obstacle to marriage. It is accepted as natural for the girl to have sexual tensions and to desire this experience (as contrasted with upper-middle- and upper-class attitudes that boys but not girls have sexual desires).

A typical example is given in the discussion of Elmtown of a girl, Mary, who left high school in her sophomore year because she was criticized for dating older youths from neighboring towns. She began to date a local boy and after some weeks had her first sex experience with him. This affair continued for several months before a quarrel separated them. Her next affair was with a boy of the next higher social class, followed by affairs with four other young men.[23] She avoided the designation of "common property" by not permitting sex intimacies until after the fourth date.[24] At the age of 18 she married and settled down. None of the young men with whom she had been intimate had talked about her.

The casual dating and picking up of girls is followed by more regularized dating, which absorbs three or four evenings a week. Parents and friends assume that the couple will soon marry, although no formal announcement is made by a party or through the newspaper (as occurs with middle- and upper-class engagements). Since sexual experiences are already a part of the dating patterns of most boys and many girls, intercourse is accepted as a normal part of dating between engaged couples. When the girl becomes pregnant, marriage is the next step, and usually occurs through the offices of a justice of the peace or perhaps a minister, but without a formal wedding. The couple normally

[23]The tendency of some lower-class girls to date middle- or upper-class men is the counterpart of the middle-class youth's activity in picking up girls or seeking sexual dates with girls of a lower social class than his own. In a study of dating by college men, Ehrmann found that in dates with girls of their own class, men went to the point of intercourse on 26 per cent of their dates, but with girls of a lower class than their own they reached intercourse on 63 per cent of their dates. Winston Ehrmann, *Premarital Dating Behavior* (New York: Bantam Books, 1960), 181–86. (Originally published by Holt in New York, 1959.)

[24]Compare this statement with the middle-class restriction in the girl's code of no kiss until the third date.

secure a license, become married, and tell parents and friends afterward. Typically, the lower-class girl is in her middle or late teens at the time of marriage, and her husband in the early twenties.

Ethnic Dating

Dating in ethnic groups falls into the same general patterns of adjustment to American culture as that found for ethnic families, already discussed in Chapter 8. The first adjustment tends to be to the social-class level into which the ethnic family first entered, with the family following a mixture of ethnic and American patterns. When many of the ethnic characteristics have been replaced by American attitudes and customs, the family typically enters into the process of upward mobility. Dating of ethnic young people is adapted to the stage in the adjustment or mobility process that the family has achieved.

Dating in the Italian group may be used as one example. The general adjustment process of the Italian family was described in Chapter 8. Adolescent adjustment between the sexes and mate selection follow the same pattern, as briefly indicated in Chapter 8 and more completely delineated in specific studies of youth. The traditional Italian pattern of close supervision of mate selection by the parents (common in rural areas, from which the great mass of immigrants of 1900–1914 came) soon gave way to an adaptation that allowed one pattern for boys and another for girls. A pertinent study published in 1943 describes the social and sexual relationships of young people in an Italian slum in an eastern city, peopled by a lower-class group of peasant origin, in which the parents represented the old-world culture.[25]

The free heterosexual social relationships found in the American group were unknown. In other words, there was no dating and little courtship. Contacts of men were of two types: those with "good" girls (virgins), which eventually led to marriage; and those with girls who permitted sex relations, a situation without obligations. The Italian peasant folkways and mores governed the social activities of the good girls. As long as parental control remained intact, these girls were never alone with young men in unsupervised situations, unless they were going steady with implications of early marriage. The young man might call upon the good girl in her home; this procedure was interpreted by parents, relatives, and the girl herself to indicate that the man was her

[25]Based upon a three-and-a-half-year study of an Italian slum made by William Foote Whyte, "A Slum Sex Code," *American Journal of Sociology*, 49 (1943), 24–31.

suitor. Until the man was ready for this serious step, he therefore confined himself to contacts outside the home, such as club dances, picnics, parties in some girl's home, or evenings at bowling alleys. To these affairs girls and men came separately in groups. Each man chose his partner for a dance or other activity, at the end of which he returned her to her group of girl friends.

At the end of the evening, the girls returned home unescorted by the men. These affairs were a blend of Italian and American customs, with breaking away from the home on the part of the girl but an avoidance of pairing off between boys and girls. If the girl was further emancipated from parental control, usually possible only for girls who were employed, she might meet a young man by appointment on some street corner, but not allow herself to be picked up; if she worked outside the Italian district, she attained still greater freedom in contacts with non-Italians. Usually, however, the girl did not seek pair dating because of parental disapproval and the implication that she might not be a virgin.

When the young man reached the degree of maturity and economic competence that made marriage possible, he selected his wife from the Italian group, for he desired a wife who understood his ways, prepared the food that he was accustomed to, and accepted the subordinate position of the Italian wife.

Although the social contacts of the respectable Italian girl were thus strictly limited, not so with the contacts of the boy and young man of equal social status. The dictum that sexual relations were necessary for a boy's health and virility was accepted, and boys, therefore, early in adolescence established contacts with another type of girl. The girls who permitted intimacy fell into three categories: one-man girls who for a period confined themselves to one man but without implication of permanency or marriage; promiscuous girls who submitted to a man on casual acquaintance who had provided a social evening including food, drink, and a ride; and prostitutes with whom a purely business arrangement was made. In the order given there was a decreasing desirability of the women, a decreasing responsibility on the part of the man in case of discovery or pregnancy, and a decreasing degree of ego-satisfaction to the man. These girls often came from outside the district, for the boys—theoretically at least—prided themselves upon not destroying the virginity of girls of their own social group (from among whom they would later select a wife). The boys also preferred beautiful girls, particularly blondes, and if possible someone of a social class above their own. They did not maintain continued contacts with one girl, for they wished to avoid falling in love or arousing an assumption of marriage on the part of the girl.

This description shows clearly the different motivations in the two situations. For marriage, in-group solidarity and personal security were uppermost. The young man wanted some girl known to his family and friends, familiar with the group customs, and compliant to the mores. He wanted exclusive possession of the girl with no hint of allegiance with some other man. He could then feel socially and personally secure. In his sexual contacts, he sought adventure with someone beyond his social group, freedom from obligations, and prestige among other boys through attainment of a desired type of companion as well as sexual experience.

The control of the contacts between young men and nonvirgins was governed by well-developed folkways and mores that had grown out of the situation over a period of time and were accepted by men and girls alike, and, also, tacitly by good girls and parents, although not with approval. The boys accepted the responsibility of not molesting a virgin of their own ethnic group, of conforming to the group mores where marriage was concerned, and limited degrees of responsibility for paternity among one-man girls. These were peer mores, growing out of the activities of the boys and accepted by them and enforced by disapproval of the group itself.

Almost a generation later, in 1961, another article appeared that touched on the later stages of adjustment of Italian youth.[26] By this time the Italian colonies had both changed in culture and shrunk in size; Italians who had migrated from Italy were few in number. The minority of Italians who sought security in the remnants of the old Italian traditions followed a mixture of Italian and American culture, with some young people not greatly changed from those of around 1940. Most members of this minority, however, had become sufficiently adjusted to American ways that they fell into a generalized lower-class type of culture, with only a flavor of Italian culture, often signified primarily by the surname. Dating and courtship customs followed the general lower-class pattern already described. Other Italian families had entered into the mainstream of upward mobility characteristic of American families. They moved away from the Italian community, sometimes translated their name into English (Capobianco became Whitehead), and mingled with people of other ethnic backgrounds. They remained Catholic. Dating and courtship patterns came to resemble the American-Catholic system rather than the ancestral Italian. The social-class distribution spread out and moved away from the earlier concentration in the lower class. In one eastern city, in 1910,

[26]Francis A. J. Ianni, "The Italo-American Teen-Ager," in Jessie Bernard, ed., "Teen-Age Culture," *Annals of the American Academy of Political and Social Science*, 338 (November, 1961), 70–78.

77 per cent of the Italo-American males in the labor force worked as laborers; in 1930, the proportion was 55.5 per cent; and in 1950, 38.9 per cent.[27] It may be assumed that by 1960 the proportion was still less. Place of residence changed with the upward mobility, leading at least the vanguard of each generation away from the original Italian settlement in the city and into diversified neighborhoods. Each stage of upward mobility—each generation—carries the person of Italian ancestry away from the traditional Italian pattern of adolescent associations and into the American type of dating and courtship at whatever social-class level the adolescent and his family find themselves.

Jewish teenagers also represent the different stages of adjustment to American social-class culture as do the Italians. The Orthodox group, closest to the old traditional patterns, carries on social life within the Orthodox community.[28] Many Orthodox girls will not dance with boys, and some still wait for their parents to arrange suitable marriages for them. Marriage outside the Orthodox community is unthinkable, and leads to rejection by family and synagogue.

In the Jewish lower-middle class, whose families tend to live in compact urban communities, girls have greater freedom. Higher education for Jewish boys is an old tradition; for girls, it is not part of the Orthodox culture, but among non-Orthodox Jews, especially in the middle class, girls attend college and combine it with dating and mate-selection activities. Typically, lower-middle-class girls attend college in their own urban community, continuing to live at home; bright boys from the same families more often attend an out-of-town school. When the daughter lives at home she remains within the family and religious community group, where she can be sheltered in her social contacts and can be taught the values and customs of the Jewish wife and mother. Marriage is the openly avowed goal of the lower-middle-class Jewish girl. The boy attends college to secure training in business methods or a profession. The girl's objective is to make desirable social contacts and to develop culturally. Scarcely concealed is the objective of finding a suitable husband. Girls whose families are sufficiently affluent to send them away to college—who are perhaps moving into upper-middle class—may leave college at the end of two or three years if they have not succeeded in becoming engaged. They have failed of their main objective.

Lower-middle-class girls dress and use cosmetics in a way to attract male attention, but are restrained in their sexual behavior. They may dance and pet in a manner to suggest great freedom of sex behavior, but

[27]*Ibid.*
[28]David Boroff, "Jewish Teen-Age Culture," in Bernard, *op. cit.,* pp. 79–90.

actually place restrictions on how much freedom they will permit. The value of virginity at marriage is not easily sacrificed to immediate sexual satisfactions.

Upper-middle and upper-class Jews who attend eastern prestige colleges (Ivy League schools for men and the Big Seven for girls) have reversed the status of college student and Jewish affiliate. Whereas the lower-middle-class student places the Jewish religion and traditional values above immersion in the college folkways and mores, students in the prestige colleges are first exponents of the local college culture and secondly Jews. They regard their Jewish affiliation as a historical matter and not as setting them apart in a different religious, social, and cultural world. Dating and courtship customs are those of the upper-middle or upper class as represented on their particular campus.

As the young Italians and Jews, and descendants of other older immigrant groups, pass into the American culture, their places both residentially and in the lower social class are filled by yet newer groups (for example, Puerto Ricans and Mexicans) who are in the earlier stages of ethnic adjustment, but who will in time traverse the boundaries into American culture and enter into the social class structure. Dating customs keep in step with the trend.

Societal Integration of Dating

As often happens when changed social conditions call forth a new activity, such as dating, the new activity creates problems.

If mixed recreation and dating are advantageous as preparation for marriage, what of the high school boys and girls and the college men and women who do not participate?

Studies already cited show that among both high school and college students are many for whom dating is an occasional event and a few who do not date at all. Among a sample of Minnesota college students, 45 per cent of the men and 34 per cent of the women participated little or not at all in formal social activities.[29] Two-thirds of the men and more than half of the women felt that they had inadequate opportunities to meet members of the opposite sex. The men felt that their failure to meet women was most often because of lack of money and time, or they met the "wrong kind" of women. Lack of social contacts and lack of time were the reasons given by women.

[29]Clifford Kirkpatrick and Theodore Caplow, "Courtship in a Group of Minnesota Students," *American Journal of Sociology,* 51 (1945), 114–25.

Dating, then, appears to be poorly integrated into the activities of high school and college students. Unaided, many students are not able to manage the time, expense, and social training needed for successful dating.

The theoretical justification for dating is that it enables young people to meet those of the opposite sex and adjust their attitudes and activities to each other. However, the area of adjustment that dating encompasses is confined to recreation; cooperative work between boys and girls on serious projects is neglected. Can heterosexual relations on a recreational level alone prepare the adolescent for adult heterosexual cooperation in such endeavors as managing a home or rearing children?

Another questionable phase of dating is the way in which adolescents have been permitted—in fact, given an open field—to create a little exclusive social world of their own that tends to separate them from, rather than integrate them into, the adult world and mature societal activities. Might not participation in mixed groups of all ages prepare them more adequately for maturity?

Finally, genuine concern is felt by many young people as well as adults over the tendency for dating to take its cue from courtship and to include a code that approves or at least tolerates necking and petting up to and sometimes including sexual intercourse on a casual basis.[30]

Questions

1. What seem to you to be the most important functions of casual dating? Of steady dating?

2. Discuss preadolescent dating. Is it simply a fad? Has it social value? Has it positive or negative values for future marriage?

3. What is the effect on the individual of a double standard of sex behavior, one for men and another for women?

4. Discuss the pros and cons of intercourse at each dating level, in terms of the effect on the persons involved and on future choice of a spouse and marriage.

5. How does the peer group control dating? How is this code related to adult mores on sexual behavior?

6. In what ways are middle- and lower-class dating customs an outgrowth of the general class culture?

[30]For a further discussion of premarital sex relations, see Chapter 15.

7. Discuss ethnic dating at different stages of cultural and social assimilation of the ethnic group.
8. Would it be advisable to give more adult guidance to dating? If you think so, how could such guidance be given?

Bibliography

BERNARD, JESSIE, ed., "Teen-Age Culture," *Annals of the American Academy of Political and Social Science*, 338 (November, 1961), 70–78.

———, HELEN E. BUCHANAN, and WILLIAM M. SMITH, JR., *Dating, Mating and Marriage: A Documentary-Case Approach* (Cleveland: Howard Allen, Inc., 1958).

BLOOD, ROBERT O., JR., "Uniformities and Diversities in Campus Dating Preferences," *Marriage and Family Living*, 18 (1956), 37–45.

CAVAN, RUTH SHONLE, ed., *Marriage and Family in the Modern World* (New York: Crowell, 1969), ch. 6.

EHRMANN, WINSTON W., *Premarital Dating Behavior* (New York: Holt, 1959; New York: Bantam Books, 1960).

HERMAN, ROBERT D., "The 'Going Steady' Complex: A Re-Examination," *Marriage and Family Living*, 17 (1955), 36–47.

HOLLINGSHEAD, AUGUST B., *Elmtown's Youth* (New York: Wiley, 1949), chs. 9, 12, 15, and 16.

KIRKENDALL, LESTER A., *Premarital Intercourse and Interpersonal Relations* (New York: Julian Press, 1961).

KIRKPATRICK, CLIFFORD, and THEODORE CAPLOW, "Courtship in a Group of Minnesota Students," *American Journal of Sociology*, 51 (1945), 114–25.

——— ,———, "Emotional Trends in the Courtship Experience of College Students as Expressed by Graphs with Some Observations on Methodological Implications," *American Sociological Review*, 10 (1945), 619–26.

———, and EUGENE KANIN, "Male Sex Aggression on a University Campus," *American Sociological Review*, 22 (1957), 52–58.

LOWRIE, S. H., "Dating, a Neglected Field of Study," *Marriage and Family Living*, 10 (1948), 90–91, 95.

———, "Dating Theories and Student Responses," *American Sociological Review*, 16 (1951), 334–40.

———, "Factors Involved in the Frequency of Dating," *Marriage and Family Living*, 18 (1956), 46–51.

REISS, IRA L., *Premarital Sexual Standards in America* (New York: Free Press, 1960), chs. 3–6.

SIMENSON, WILLIAM, and GILBERT GEIS, "Courtship Patterns of Norwegian and American University Students," *Marriage and Family Living*, 18 (1956), 334–38.

SMITH, E. A., "Dating and Courtship at Pioneer College," *Sociology and Social Research*, 40 (1955–56), 92–98.

14

Mate Selection and Engagement

AT SOME point in the dating process the quality of the relationship changes. Outwardly, the same social rituals may be observed, but subjectively the dating couple find their attitudes toward each other changing. They wish to date only each other and begin to discuss, first tentatively and then seriously, the possibility of marriage. This period of serious dating that looks to a continued association with each other is courtship; when the intention of the couple to marry is announced, engagement begins. Courtship, an honorable word in the past, is not used currently by young people to describe the transition from dating to engagement. Young people recognize that "going steady" has lost its old meaning as a folk synonym for courtship; they may ask if a certain couple are "in love" or "serious" about each other. The step beyond "seriousness" is engagement.

The Dating-Engagement Sequence

It is possible to view random, steady, and serious dating and engagement as parts of a continuous process that, once started, tends to proceed to summation in marriage, although rarely between the original dating partners. As young people pass through this process, some aspects increase in intensity while others decrease.

1. MATURITY. In the average case, mixed group activities begin at about age 12, and engagement anywhere from 17 to 22, depending

upon the social class of the participants. The change in age roughly indicates increase in maturity and independence, both in decision-making and economically.

2. PARENTAL CONCERN. Parents are eager to launch their children into mixed activities and dating. Their concern for placing their children in the right social groups and supervising their conduct is high at the beginning of the dating period, declines as their children gain in ability to manage their own social affairs, but wells up again with courtship and the imminence of marriage. A conflict therefore may exist between the increasing maturity of son or daughter and the increased drive of the parents to guide or control the courtship.

3. NUMBER OF PARTNERS. Number of dating partners decreases throughout the process, from many at the beginning to one at the end. Moreover, this change is generally approved by both adults and young people. In the early stages many partners are regarded as a safeguard against too early emotional involvement and also as a way of enabling the boy or girl to formulate his attitudes regarding the type of partner he eventually wants in marriage. Failure to decrease the partners to one during courtship and engagement is an offense against the mores and a threat to the future marriage.

4. DEGREE OF MUTUAL RESPONSIBILITY. Carefree lack of responsibility or responsibility only for each date as it comes is the hallmark of the early date. Increasing responsibility reaches a climax in engagement when each feels deeply obligated to provide for the happiness and welfare of the other.

5. DEGREE OF EMOTIONAL INVOLVEMENT. A transition from a very low degree of emotional attachment in the early stages of dating to a high degree in engagement is the normal process. The young casual dater likes the partner for superficial social qualities; the engaged person gives love and receives love in return. Mutual dependence for response therefore becomes part of the relationship. When one participant in the engagement exceeds the other in emotional involvement or when one ceases to love the other, the engagement is threatened.

6. DEGREE OF EGO INVOLVEMENT. Interest in one's own status and the admiration or envy of others because of the high rating of the dating partner declines. Ego involvement is never entirely lost; it seems relatively less important as courtship and engagement progress because it is satisfied in part by identification with the partner, and enhancement of the partner's status becomes a round-about way of enhancing one's own status.

7. DEGREE OF IDENTIFICATION. The dating couple have little if any

identification. For a time a few interests may coincide, but deeper psychological merging is lacking. Identification increases with the dating-engagement sequence until the two partners tend to seem as one in interests, likes, dislikes, and the ability to find mutual satisfactions in each other.

8. DEGREE OF SOCIAL ASSIMILATION. In dating, young people are more likely to cross social-class, religious, and racial lines than in engagement and marriage. Typically, the engaged couple come from a somewhat similar cultural and social background and tend to pull their immediate social worlds of family and friends into a jointly shared social relationship.

9. IMPORTANCE OF PERSONALITY NEEDS. As the young person detaches himself from his family, which in the past has satisfied many personality needs, and narrows his dating down to one person, the complementing of personality needs becomes increasingly important. The casual date might satisfy only one need and still be regarded as a valuable dating partner because other needs might be met through other contacts. Courtship and engagement, because of their exclusiveness, place heavy responsibilities upon the partner.

10. EXPECTATION OF MARRIAGE. The early stages of dating are regarded as a social relationship; serious dating and engagements are oriented toward marriage. Family and community expectations, therefore, are that a marriage will occur; and once the courtship is well advanced or the engagement made known, a social process is set in motion that reinforces the personal expectation of marriage. A newspaper announcement, an announcement party, "showers" for the bride, family parties, and inquiries of friends as to the date for the wedding all serve as social pressures on the engaged couple to marry. A broken engagement, therefore, is not wholly a personal matter but an affair of the families and the community.

The general movement is away from individualism and independence, toward identification of attitudes, integration of social patterns, mutual responsiveness, and unity of interests and goals.

Duration of Acquaintance, Dating, and Engagement

The most effective length of acquaintance, serious dating, and engagement between couples has become the subject of research. We know that in our own frontier past many marriages rested on brief acquaintance, and that in other cultures, where marriages are arranged by the parents, bride and groom may not see each other until the wedding day. According to our present philosophy of marriage, however, young people must find congenial mates largely by their own efforts and often in a social situation where first acquaintance is sought because one is attracted by the other's personal appearance. The emphasis upon personal happiness necessitates that, after acquaintance is achieved, the couple shall have time to explore each other's personalities before marriage. How much time is needed for the matching of personalities and the beginning stages of adjustment to take place? What criterion can be used to judge the most advantageous length of acquaintance, serious dating, and engagement?

College students take their time about moving from casual dating to marriage, according to a study of 200 students made in 1957. The average period for casual dating with each other was 4.5 months, dating steadily eight months, having an "understanding" 10 months, and engagement at the time of the study 6 months. On the average they planned to wait another six months before marriage. Thus the average period of time between first date and marriage would be about three years.[1] Many students of course consumed less time and many more.

Studies of people married for a number of years show that long periods of acquaintance and engagement are more closely associated with successful adjustment in marriage than are short periods. In these studies, married couples were first classified as to success in marriage, and the degree of success was related to the length of acquaintance, courtship, and engagement that each couple had had.

A detailed study of 526 cases was made by Burgess and Cottrell, sociologists, for three stages of intimacy: acquaintance, courtship (serious dating), and engagement.[2] The criterion of successful marriage used was marital adjustment as measured by a self-rating scale covering various items of agreement or disagreement, common interests and activities, demonstration of affection, confiding, and feeling of satisfaction and happiness. Long acquaintance, courtship, and engagement were associated with later good adjustment in marriage. Persons married with an acquaintance of less than six months achieved good adjustment in only 22.4 per cent of the cases; with acquaintance of five or more years, 52.3 per cent had good adjustment. The percentage with

[1]Judson T. and Mary G. Landis, *Building a Successful Marriage* (Englewood Cliffs, N. J.: Prentice-Hall, 1958), 272–73.

[2]E. W. Burgess and L. S. Cottrell, *Predicting Success or Failure in Marriage* (New York: Prentice-Hall, 1939), pp. 406–7.

good adjustment increased with length of courtship: of those who courted under one year, about one-third were well adjusted in marriage; in contrast, among those who courted three or more years, over half were well adjusted. Long engagements likewise were associated with good adjustment in marriage: only 37 per cent of those not engaged at all and 25.7 per cent of those with engagements of less than three months adjusted well in marriage. In contrast is the group engaged for two or more years, 62.6 per cent of whom were happily married.

Another sociologist, Locke, found that his sample of happily married couples tended to have had longer engagements than his sample of divorced couples.[3] The average length of engagement of happily married men was ten months, compared with seven months for the divorced men. Among women, the happily married had an average length of engagement of twelve months as compared with seven months for divorced women.

Terman, a psychologist, also found a similar relation between long engagements and marital success.[4] For the criterion of success he used the person's own estimate of marital happiness. For both husband and wife the highest mean score of marital happiness was found among those whose engagements had endured five or more years.

All three of the studies cited refer primarily to urban middle-class marriages. Upper- and lower-class marriages and rural marriages have not been studied with respect to length of prior association.

Although these studies show that a higher percentage of successful marriages have grown out of long than short courtship, the correlation between length of serious dating or courtship and degree of good marital adjustment is far from perfect. Other factors beside length of courtship also operate.

The significance of length of courtship is not in the exact number of months, but in provision for sufficient time in which the psychological and sociological processes of courtship may come to summation. The interaction by which these processes are carried on cannot take place in an evening or a month. Identification involves changes in the attitudes and habits of two people. Sometimes, as in conversion, attitudes and habits change quickly; but usually changes are made slowly, a step at a time. The change is especially likely to be slow when previous attitudes and habits have to be broken down and replaced by new ones.

The courting couple do not build up the desirable attitudes and

[3]Harvey J. Locke, *Predicting Adjustment in Marriage* (New York: Holt, 1951), p. 94.

[4]L. M. Terman, *Psychological Factors in Marital Happiness* (New York: McGraw-Hill, 1938), pp. 197–201.

habits from a blank background of nonheterosexual relations. For five to ten years they have assiduously practiced the arts of random or steady dating as previously discussed. Many of the attitudes and habits of dating must be modified or even reversed. The individual and his pleasure are no longer central to the association; the couple and mutual satisfactions are all-important.

Another circumstance in modern America that requires a lengthy period of serious dating if happy marriage is to result is the lack of long friendship on a casual level or of acquaintance between the families of the interested couple. On the college campus or in the office or factory of a city, men and women meet as individuals rather than as bearers of family, class, and ethnic culture. A romantic interest or an infatuation may easily develop between two people of diverse attitudes and cultural background, who may even be drawn to each other because of their personal differences or because one forms a striking contrast to the customary social group of the other. Under these circumstances, the process of social identification is especially slow. The lower-class boy who has pushed his way into the middle-class milieu of the typical college can only slowly adapt himself to the expectations and folkways of the middle-class girl, and the girl in turn will require time in which to revise her estimates of what she expects from a husband to make allowances for the deficiencies of her husband as viewed by middle-class standards. Even when the two are from the same social class, often neither has seen the other in a familial situation. The young man has no way of knowing what the girl's response is to a sink full of dirty dishes, nor does the girl know the man's attitude about shaving on a Sunday at home. Love unfolds before the pair are familiar with each other's personalities and backgrounds. Time is the safeguard that prevents a transition from early dating to marriage without the needed courtship processes.

A long period of serious dating and engagement is not always easy to attain, however. Graduation from college, migration of young people from rural areas to cities or from one region to another, and military service are some of the types of mobility that tear young people apart before the adjustment process has run its course. Faced with separation and knowing from their dating experience of the past how tenuous a pair relationship may become when one or both are faced with a new social situation and the need for immediate social contacts, the courting couple enter a brief engagement followed by marriage. Sometimes public engagement is omitted entirely and the first announcement of intention to marry comes with the marriage itself. The mere fact that marriage vows have been given does not nullify the necessity for the adjustment process to complete itself. It then continues into the marital state, complicating the adjustment to marriage. If the process is blocked, the husband and wife must go through the public legal procedure of divorce to withdraw from their responsibilities. Prior to marriage, failure of the two to adjust may terminate the relationship. Withdrawal at this point, however, is a private and individual act. Property settlements, alimony, possible custody of children, and the public exposure of quarrels are avoided.

Cultural Definitions of Eligibility for Marriage

Personal selection of the mate is part of the philosophy of American marriage. Nevertheless, selection is narrowed down to a relatively limited group within which the personal choice may be made with the approval of parents, friends, and community groups. Many of the restrictions are cultural in nature; some have already been discussed.

LEGAL RESTRICTIONS

Laws do not prescribe personal choices, but they proscribe marriages between certain groups or types of individuals.

Age of marriage is controlled by law. The most frequent minimum age for marriage with the parents' consent is 18 years for males and 16 for females; without consent of the parents, the most frequent minimum age is 21 for males and 18 for females. Table 13 gives the legal ages for marriage with and without parental consent for each state and, for comparison, the median age of first marriage in states where the information is available. The median tends to be several years later than the age for marriage without parental consent.

Socially interpreted, the legal minimum age for marriage is probably related more closely to the age at which schooling stops and earning begins than to any other factor. The minimum marital ages all tend to be below the age for voting or for inheritance of property. In terms of the processes leading to marriage, the minimum legal age approximates the period when steady dating becomes well established, with engagement following several years later and marriage about six years after initial dating. Only in a minority of cases does the young couple find the legal age a hindrance to marriage.

Mate selection is also subject to other legal regulations. The laws of all states prohibit marriage between those of close relationship—parent and child, sister and brother, aunt and nephew, uncle and niece, grandparent and grandchild; and marriage of first cousins is forbidden in

TABLE 13

LEGAL AGE OF MARRIAGE AND MEDIAN AGE OF FIRST MARRIAGE

| State | Legal Age of Marriage, July 1, 1965* | | | | Median Age of First Marriage*** | |
| | With consent of parents** | | Without consent of parents | | | |
	Males	Females	Males	Females	Males	Females
The Northeastern states						
Maine	16	16	21	18	22.5	19.7
New Hampshire	a	a	20	18	22.7	20.1
Vermont	18	16	21	18	22.6	19.9
Massachusetts	18	16	21	18		
Rhode Island	18	16	21	21	23.4	21.2
Connecticut	16	16	21	21	24.0	21.5
New York	16	16	21	18	23.4	20.7
New Jersey	18	16	21	18		
Pennsylvania	16	16	21	21	23.8	21.5
The North Central states						
Ohio	18	16	21	21		
Indiana	18	16	21	18		
Illinois	18	16	21	18		
Michigan	b	16	18	18	22.6	20.0
Wisconsin	18	16	21	18	23.0	20.5
Minnesota	18	16	21	18		
Iowa	18	16	21	18	22.1	19.7
Missouri	15	15	21	18		
North Dakota	18	15	21	18		
South Dakota	18	16	21	18	22.8	19.9
Nebraska	18	16	21	21	22.6	20.1
Kansas	18	16	21	18	22.0	19.5
The West						
Montana	18	16	21	21	22.7	19.6
Idaho	15	15	18	18	21.5	18.9
Wyoming	18	16	21	21	22.6	19.6
Colorado	16	16	21	18		
New Mexico	18	16	21	18		
Arizona	18	16	21	18		
Utah	16	14	21	18	22.2	19.5
Nevada	18	16	21	18		
Washington	17	17	21	18		
Oregon	18	15	21	18	22.0	19.5
California	18	16	21	18	22.6	19.9
Alaska	18	16	21	18	23.4	19.8
Hawaii	18	16	20	20		

TABLE 13 (*cont.*)

LEGAL AGE OF MARRIAGE AND MEDIAN AGE OF FIRST MARRIAGE

State	Legal Age of Marriage, July 1, 1965*				Median Age of First Marriage***	
	With consent of parents**		Without consent of parents			
	Males	Females	Males	Females	Males	Females
The South						
Delaware	18	16	21	18	22.8	20.5
Maryland	18	16	21	18	22.8	19.9
District of Columbia	18	16	21	18		
Virginia	18	16	21	21	22.8	20.7
West Virginia	18	16	21	21		
North Carolina	16	16	18	18		
South Carolina	16	14	18	18		
Georgia	18	16	19	19		
Florida	18	16	21	21	22.9	20.0
Kentucky	18	16	21	21		
Tennessee	16	16	21	21	22.1	19.6
Alabama	17	14	21	18	22.0	19.2
Mississippi	17	15	21	21	22.0	19.2
Arkansas	18	16	21	18		
Louisiana	18	16	21	21	22.2	19.5
Oklahoma	18	15	21	18		
Texas	16	14	21	18		

aBelow age of consent, parties need parental consent and permission of judge.

bNo parental consent provided for males.

*SOURCE: *The Book of the States, 1966-67* (Chicago: Council of State Governments, 1966), p. 385. The table of marriage laws was prepared by the Women's Bureau, U.S. Department of Labor.

**Some states make special provision for younger people to marry, for example, if the girl is pregnant.

***SOURCE: *Vital Statistics of the United States, 1959*, Sec. 2, "Marriage and Divorce Statistics" (Washington, D.C.: Government Printing Office, 1961), p. 2–21. The report covers only 29 states.

about two-thirds of the states. In addition to these blood relationships, some relationships based on marriage are also regarded in many states as a bar to marriage, the most common prohibition being that stepparent and stepchild may not marry. The marriages between blood relatives involve questions of inheritance as well as moral aversion to family endogamy. The marriage of stepparent and stepchild would not raise any question of heredity but arouses deep-seated aversions to incest, which are not limited to the strictly biological family. The insane and the feeble-minded in most states are forbidden to marry. In most states, too, premarital physical tests single out those with syphilis, who are not issued marriage licenses until the disease has been cured and a negative test is returned.

CULTURAL RESTRICTIONS

The chief nonlegal, cultural restrictions on the eligibility of young people for marriage to each other have been discussed in Chapter 10. Therefore, they will be mentioned only briefly.

Marriage within one's own race is the restriction most rigorously enforced by the mores. Persons of different races may marry, but so strong is the approval of marriage within the race and so severe the social penalties for out-marriage that few individuals feel the urge to marry into another race.

Religion sets the next limitation. The majority of people marry within their own religious faith. Although no law regulates marriage with reference to religion, the sanction of the church may be withheld from the one marrying into another religion, and especially so when the adherent of the other religion refuses to make concessions to the marriage pattern of the church. Thus the Catholic whose marriage to a non-Catholic has not been sanctified by the Catholic Church is regarded as not married but "living in sin." Traditionally, the Orthodox Jew who married outside his faith was officially declared to be dead.

A third limitation is the boundary of the ethnic culture. So long as families hold to the foreign culture of their youth or their ancestors, they circumscribe their children's social contacts by the ethnic culture, and the tendency is strong for marriages to occur within the ethnic group.

Less strong, but nevertheless a factor, is the inclusive nature of the social class. The tendency of people to marry others of the same occupational status and the same degree of education is essentially the tendency to marry within the social class to which the person belongs.

With reference to cultural characteristics, therefore, in the majority of marriages husband and wife have very similar cultural heritages, values, and associations. This natural sorting out of mates on a cultural basis is referred to as cultural homogamy (like-marriages), assortative mating, or cultural endogamy. The out-marriages that sometimes occur across cultural barriers are in the minority, generally are disapproved by both cultural groups, and frequently create problems of personal adjustment and family and community relationships.

Influence of Parents and Peer Groups in Mate Selection

The pressures exerted by institutions and public opinion for cultural endogamy are reinforced by the influence of parents and peer groups who favor culturally like-marriages.

PARENTAL INFLUENCE

Although we have spoken repeatedly of the independence of young people in choosing friends, establishing dating codes, and selecting a mate, nevertheless parents have not been entirely eliminated from the process; in fact, it may be that parents exert more influence in serious than in random or steady dating. A study of casual and serious dating showed that young people were not greatly concerned about their parents' approval of partners for casual dates, but 72 per cent wanted the courtship partner to meet the approval of their parents.[5]

At one time in the middle and upper classes, the parents had a definite role to play in the mate selection of their children and especially their daughters. The young man was not regarded as a suitor until he had asked the girl's father whether he could court his daughter with marriage as the objective or, after courting was under way, whether he could have her hand in marriage. The father was then in a position to approve the courtship or to send the young man away. Except in selected groups, this custom has died out.

Even though the parents may not directly try to influence the choice of a mate, general home influences prevail in many cases. For example, young people living at home tend more often than those living away from home to select mates of the same religious affiliation and of the same or adjacent socioeconomic status.[6] It may be that the influence is very indirect, since young people still living at home may have little opportunity to break out of the original family associations with people of like background, and limited opportunity to meet people of other religious or socioeconomic backgrounds.

[5]Robert O. Blood, "Uniformities and Diversities in Campus Dating Preferences," *Marriage and Family Living*, 18 (1956), 37–45.

[6]Robert H. Coombs, "Reinforcement of Values in the Parental Home as a Factor in Mate Selection," *Marriage and Family Living*, 24 (1962), 155–57.

Direct intervention by parents was found among 97 upper-middle-class, Protestant, white families living in an eastern metropolitan area.[7] At the time of the interviews with the parents, they had 195 married children, living away from home. Eighty-four per cent of the children had been directly influenced in mate selection. Parents testified that they had provided their children with a suitable social environment for "proper dating and courtship" within their social class. Parents also had persuaded or threatened to withdraw financial support in the case of children still dependent upon them. Only a few of the young people whose parents were opposed to their specific choice of a partner persisted in the engagement and eventually were married; 87 per cent complied with their parents' wishes.

Young people may openly rebel against their parents by elopement or a secret marriage. Others evade the issue by going away to college or moving to another city to work.

These devices remove the young person from the parent's direct influence. But in a more subtle way, the son or daughter is prevented from escaping the parent's influence. Attitudes ingrained since childhood cannot help but play a part in mate selection; the model of the parent's own marriage is always in the young person's mind as something to be imitated or avoided; and many of the personality needs of young adults stem from the parent-child relationship. The child whose needs are adequately met by one parent, whether father or mother, tends unconsciously to select a mate with some of the same qualities that the parent had, for in so doing he assures himself of continued satisfaction of his personality needs. When both parents have contributed to the child's needs, the mate may have traits found in both parents. This matching of mate to parents is not deliberate but is simply the natural result of an attempt to continue a satisfactory mode of life.[8]

INFLUENCE OF PEER GROUPS

Certain studies show the powerful influence of organized associations on mate selection. For example, the college sorority is presented in one study as an ascriptive group, that is, a group that selects its members

[7]Marvin B. Sussman, "Parental Participation in Mate Selection and Its Effect upon Family Continuity," *Social Forces*, 32 (1953–54), 76–81.

[8]Several studies throw some light on this question, but the data are not conclusive partly because few cases were studied and partly because resemblances are not clear-cut. Anselm Strauss, "The Influence of Parent-Images upon Marital Choice," *American Sociological Review*, 11 (October, 1946), 554–59; Anselm Strauss, "The Ideal and the Chosen Mate," *American Journal of Sociology*, 52 (November, 1946), 204–8.

on the basis of a certain type of family ascription (race, religion, social class).[9] The sorority therefore tends to be culturally homogeneous. This homogeneity is maintained in spite of the four-year turnover of membership by the control exerted over membership by alumnae, who are really surrogate parents. Through this control, parents protect their children from the "danger" inherent in large (especially state) heterogeneous universities that their children will break out of their ascribed status and mingle with and marry into other, less approved groups. The sorority dominates the life of its members, fills it with many activities, and so far as possible limits contacts with men to those of selected fraternities considered of suitable status for marriage. Dating and other mixed activities may be carried on between a certain sorority and fraternity, year after year, with strong disapproval by the peer group of deviation from this limitation. Both girls and men are assured of dates and limitation to partners who are socially suitable to parents and alumnae. Various rituals attend pinning and engagement that demonstrate approval of the peer groups and carry the couple along toward marriage.

Unorganized peer groups may also exert pressure for certain types of mate selection, but not to the extent that organized groups do.

Availability of Eligible Mates

In addition to cultural homogamy, various fortuitous factors over which the individual has little control also affect mate selection.

In our society mate selection takes place on the basis of personal contacts. It is not one of the prerogatives of parents to select mates unknown to their children, no matter how suitable these mates might seem to the parents. Nor are "go-betweens" used to find suitable mates. Marriage bureaus or "lonely heart" clubs are not in good repute, especially for young people. Among nonmobile groups, the selection is limited to a narrow geographical area. Small racial or ethnic colonies also contain a limited number of eligible people. Mobile groups sometimes increase their contacts with eligible partners; on the other hand, their mobility may seriously disturb the sex ratio.

The number of males per 100 females, called the sex ratio, may be a disturbing factor in mate selection. In 1960, for every 100 females in the United States there were 97.1 males; the sex ratio therefore was 97.1.[10]

[9]John Finley Scott, "The American College Sorority, Its Role in Class and Ethnic Endogamy," *American Sociological Review*, 30 (1965), 514–27.

[10]*Statistical Abstract of the United States, 1961* (Washington, D.C.: Government Printing Office, 1961), p. 26.

Since 1910 the sex ratio has been declining, owing in part to reduced immigration. The European immigration included large numbers of young men who helped to maintain an excess of males for many decades.

The overall sex ratio does not throw much light upon the marriage possibilities because the same ratio does not prevail for all age groups or in all communities. For some age groups and in some areas, the sex ratio is more favorable for marriage than in other groups or areas. In general, the situation is favorable for marriage for whichever sex is in the minority, other factors being equal. Women, being more passive than men in initiating proposals of marriage, are more dependent upon a favorable sex ratio than are men. When men are abundant, they compete for wives and marry many women who under other conditions might not have been selected for wives; with an abundance of women, men may be so selective that marginally attractive women remain unmarried.

The ages when marriages occur most frequently are the late teens and the twenties; therefore, sex ratios are especially important at these ages. For the age period 15–19 there is a slightly favorable situation for girls as there are 101 boys to every 100 girls. In the twenties, the men are favored since there are more women than men. For ages 20–24, the sex ratio is 95.3 and for ages 25–29, 96.3. However, girls usually marry men several years older than themselves. Ratios have therefore been computed between men in one five-year age period and women in the next younger period. With this staggering of age periods, girls in the 15–19 age period are very much disadvantaged, since the ratio of men aged 20–24 to these teenage girls is 80. When one considers that half of all first marriages involve women under the age of twenty, this lack of coordination in age seems serious. However, although most teenage girls marry men in their early twenties, 27 per cent marry boys in their teens, and a few teenage girls marry men who are much older than they are. The sex ratio between women aged 20–24 and men aged 25–29 is 96.5, a situation somewhat unfavorable to young women. Actually, most women in the early twenties marry men in the same five-year age range but a few years their senior. Others marry into the age range 25–29 and a few marry teenage boys.

The situation is further complicated by internal migration, which disturbs the natural sex ratio of different areas.[11] In the West, for ex-

[11]*United States Census of Population, 1960, United States Summary, General Population Characteristics* (Washington, D.C.: Government Printing Office, 1961), pp. XIII, 1–165.

ample, the sex ratio is 101. In the two newest states, it far exceeds this figure: Alaska has a sex ratio of 132 and Hawaii 115. Urban and rural sex ratios are in marked contrast: the urban ratio is 94 and the rural village and farm ratio 104. Marriage for women is favorable in the West and especially in Alaska and Hawaii, but unfavorable for men. Conversely, marriage is favorable for men in cities but unfavorable for women, and the reverse is true in rural areas.

For the total population of a community, the sex ratio may be well balanced, but very much unbalanced within racial or cultural groups. For example, Negro men have migrated in large numbers from some parts of the South, leaving a surplus of Negro girls with little prospect of marriage unless they follow the same lines of migration as the men. On the West Coast there are many unmarried male Chinese and Filipinos because of the abnormally high sex ratio; there simply are not enough women within their own or acceptable racial groups for all men to marry.

The sex ratio may be unbalanced for some one social class or educational level. In Yankee City, described by Warner, more upper-class young men than women moved from Yankee City to other cities, leaving stranded a number of upper-class women who were forbidden by their class mores to marry into a lower class: they therefore became lifelong spinsters.[12] College students who fail to make a selection while in college may later find themselves working in small towns where college graduates of the opposite sex are not available. The small-town woman schoolteacher may find herself in this position. Often, then, she marries someone of lower educational level, who on his part is willing to have a wife of higher educational level than himself. This combination is contrary to the usual matching of educational levels.

Sometimes the difficulty is not an unbalanced sex ratio in a limited group, but a total limitation in numbers that prevents a free choice. The marriage of Catholics with non-Catholics and Jews with non-Jews has been found to be higher in communities where the Catholic or the Jewish population is small. Some interracial marriages can be accounted for on the same basis, where a limited number of one race marry into a more numerous racial group.

In marriages that cross homogamous barriers, the pressure toward marriage outweighs the social disapproval. Some satisfactions of marriage are sacrificed in order to achieve other satisfactions.

[12]W. Lloyd Warner and Paul S. Lunt, *The Social Life of a Modern Community* (New Haven: Yale University Press, 1941).

Personal Choice of a Mate

Within the legal, cultural, and parental restrictions, young people make their mutual choice for marriage from the available eligible group. In the early stages of narrowing the field, they are probably motivated by the cultural concepts of their groups as to the ideal traits of a mate. In the later stages, personal preferences come to the fore.

CULTURAL CONCEPTS OF THE IDEAL MATE

Young people come into the mating period with cultural concepts of what the ideal mate should be like. Some of these concepts are a carry-over from earlier periods; some are in the process of developing from current situations. Whether or not they are actually suitable for the 1960's and 1970's, they nevertheless indicate expectations of what young people would like to find in a mate. Most of the studies in this area are of college students and therefore represent primarily middle-class expectations. They have been made in different types of institutions, in different regions, and with somewhat different methods.

Regardless of these differences in the studies, some marked similarities are found, suggesting the widespread and deep-rooted character of these cultural preconceptions of what a mate should be like.[13]

Students at the University of Wisconsin and Purdue University showed remarkable similarity in selecting from a long checklist the qua'ities they regarded as of most importance in a mate. Men and women also agreed on the most important traits but showed some variation on traits less frequently chosen as desirab'e. The eight traits most often checked by 628 University of Wisconsin students as indispensable were dependable character, emotional stability, pleasing disposition, mutual attraction or love, good health, desire for home and children, refinement and neatness, and ambition and industriousness. Purdue University students rated seven of these same traits as of most

---

[13]Ruth Shonle Cavan, "Dating in High School and College," in Cavan, ed., *Marriage and Family in the Modern World: A Book of Readings* (New York: Crowell, 1965); Harold T. Christensen, *Marriage Analysis* (New York: Ronald, 1950), p. 256, reporting responses of Purdue University students; Reuben Hill, "Campus Values in Mate Selection," *Journal of Home Economics*, 37 (1945), 554–58, for University of Wisconsin students; and Mirra Komarovsky, "What Do Young People Want in a Marriage Partner?" *Journal of Social Hygiene*, 32 (1946), 440–44, for students in a New York City college.

importance; they omitted ambition and industriousness and included consideration. Conventional sex standards or chastity rated lower than any of the above.

Certain traits that were rated lower than the eight most preferred reflect traditional roles. Women at both Wisconsin and Purdue gave desirable rating to "good financial prospect" and "ambition and industriousness." Woman, the homemaker, was sought by Purdue men, and the good cook and housekeeper by Wisconsin men.

Other traditional roles, as well as some changes in role, are reflected in the preferences of college men and women for mates whose status in age, education, and intelligence is the same as, less than, or more than their own. Only figures from the 1958 survey of opinions at "Alpha" college, a coeducational liberal arts college of some 400 students, will be given. This is a Middle West college enrolling primarily middle-class students, of whom about 70 per cent participated in the survey. Table 14 shows that, except in age, men prefer wives who have the same status as themselves. Women, however, tend to want husbands who are older, more intelligent, and with more education than themselves. Comparing this with earlier studies, there is a suggestion that men more than women are moving toward the desire for equality of husband and wife, whereas women tend to retain the earlier traditional attitude that the husband should have the higher status.

One can only speculate on what lies back of these choices. Are women

TABLE 14

PREFERENCE OF MEN AND WOMEN STUDENTS IN A MATE, WITH REFERENCE TO AGE, EDUCATION, AND INTELLIGENCE

PERCENTAGE DISTRIBUTION

What men wish in a wife	Less than self	Same as self	More than self	No reply	Total
Age of wife	53	30	5	12	100
Education	7	81	3	9	100
Intelligence	5	79	6	10	100
What women wish in a husband					
Age of husband	1	15	77	7	100
Education	0	29	64	7	100
Intelligence	0	42	54	4	100

SOURCE: Ruth Shonle Cavan, "Dating in High School and College," in Ruth Shonle Cavan, ed., *Marriage and the Family in the Modern World: A Book of Readings* (New York: Crowell, 1965).

simply more conservative than men? Has the older urge for equality, evident in the feminist movement, been spent? Do women feel insecure personally and economically and thus desire a more mature person for a husband and one able to earn a good living? Having been protected by their parents, more than boys are, do they wish to continue this state of dependence?

Or, one might ask, are men more realistic in their approach to national and international situations and the probability of war and their absence from their wives? Do they foresee the possibility that wives may have to become temporarily or permanently the heads of families? Are they more aware than women of the trend of women into employment with its demand for competence and independence? Do they perhaps feel insecure personally and financially and thus desire a wife who can be an equal partner? Or is there a possibility that they have been overprotected by their mothers, as some writers have claimed, and really are looking for a mother-substitute, but not to the extent of wishing to have a lower status than their wives?

Turning attention to current social situations, one might question the advisability of dependent wives in view of the following conditions: the increasing trend of married women into employment; separations of husband and wife because of military service, with or without war; the higher death rate of men; and the high divorce rate which places great demands upon the wife in terms of earning a living and in rearing children.

Generalizing from the studies cited, one may say that the college man desires a wife who has an attractive and dependable personality, who is healthy, well groomed, and affectionate, whose intelligence and education preferably are not greater than his own, who is several years younger, and who is a good homemaker. The college woman prefers a husband who is dependable and mature, in love with her, well groomed and mannered, whose intelligence and education preferably are greater than her own, who is older, and whose financial prospects are good and probably will be improved through his ambition and industriousness.

THEORIES OF PERSONAL CHOICE

The popular explanation of why two people out of the total number available and eligible as mates actually choose each other is that they fell in love. Psychologists and sociologists have not been content with this romantic explanation and have made various attempts to probe deeper into the personalities of the two who choose each other. The conscious or unconscious effect of the image of the parents that the man or woman carries over from childhood has already been mentioned. Spectacular cases in which the young person chooses a mate who exemplifies (or is the opposite) of a loved (or hated) parent are not hard to find. But it scarcely seems that this one strain of influence can be widened into a theory to explain all of mate selection.

Another theory asserts that marriages are homogamous, that is, people with like characteristics tend to marry each other. In social characteristics a strong case can be made for homogamy, since people tend to marry others of their own cultural, religious, and educational background. However, there are many exceptions.

A third theory has been constructed around the idea that people of opposite characteristics marry. From this general idea has come the theory of mate selection according to complementary needs.

THEORY OF COMPLEMENTARY NEEDS

According to the American philosophy of marriage, mutual love is the prime ingredient for a successful marriage. "Love" is a word that is loosely used, as Chapter 16 will show. The concept of love is introduced here in a preliminary manner since it is an important part of the theory of complementary needs.[14]

Winch, who has developed the theory of complementary needs, defines love as "the positive emotion experienced by one person (the person loving, or the lover) in an interpersonal relationship in which the second person (the person loved, or love-object) either (1) meets certain important needs of the first or (2) manifests or appears (to the first) to manifest personal attributes (e.g., beauty, skills, or status) highly prized by the first, or both."[15] The process of falling in love, therefore, might be defined as the process of finding a person who would give gratification to one's needs. Needs are not thought of as obvious or material but as psychological and even unconscious in nature. Winch adapted a list of needs developed by H. A. Murray, which are here given with abbreviated definitions.[16]

> Abasement, to invite blame or punishment
> Achievement, to strive to create something or to emulate others

[14]Robert F. Winch, *Mate-Selection: A Study of Complementary Needs* (New York: Harper, 1958); Thomas and Virginia Ktsanes, "The Theory of Complementary Needs in Mate-Selection," original article in Winch, Robert McGinnis, and Herbert R. Barringer, eds., *Selected Studies in Marriage and the Family* (New York: Holt, Rinehart and Winston, 1962), pp. 517–32.

[15]Winch, *op. cit.*, p. 88.

[16]*Ibid.*, p. 90, from H. A. Murray, *et al.*, *Explorations in Personality* (New York: Oxford University Press, 1938).

Approach, to seek interaction with others
Autonomy, to be independent of others
Deference, to admire or praise someone
Dominance, to influence or control another
Hostility, to fight or injure another
Nurturance, to sympathize with or help a person in need
Recognition, to arouse the admiration of others
Status aspiration, to desire a higher socio-economic status than
   one has (type of achievement)
Status striving, to work to alter one's status (type of achieve-
   ment)
Succorance, to be helped (opposite of nurturance)

To these twelve needs, Winch added three others: anxiety, emotional-
ity, and vicariousness.

To illustrate the theory of complementary needs: A person motivated by abasement would be drawn to a hostile person, who in turn
would be drawn to the abased person, each finding gratification in the
resulting relationship. Or a person with a strong desire for recognition
might love and be loved by a deferential person. Other pairs of complementary needs may be found; for example, nurturance and succorance
or status striving and status aspiration. The latter pairing of traits
might be found between a woman desirous of climbing the social status
ladder and a man willing and desirous of working hard for upward
mobility and wishing a wife who would support him in his efforts.
According to this type of pairing, the needs of the man and woman
would be complementary rather than alike ("opposites attract," instead of "like marries like"). Each, therefore, would find fulfillment of
his needs during a process in which he fulfilled the needs of the other.

Winch adds a number of qualifications to his formulation. The selection should normally take place within the cultural expectations of
who marries whom. Maturity is needed; the adolescent moved by the
glamor of a situation would scarcely select a mate on the basis of innate
needs. The person is not necessarily conscious of his needs, although
they nevertheless motivate him. All of a person's needs would not necessarily be met by his mate, although a certain number of important
ones would be, or the relationship would be too weak to endure. It is
necessary that each person have a rather wide field of eligible persons
of the opposite sex from which to choose the one who would give maximum gratification to his needs and whose needs he could also satisfy.
Each person, also, should be allowed free choice in the selection of a
mate, rather than being greatly influenced by his parents or having
them make the selection.

Winch and his associates tested their hypothesis by an intensive study of 25 couples. The statistical portion of the study gave some support to their hypothesis, although it did not demonstrate conclusively that mates selected each other solely on the basis of complementary needs. The study was sufficiently promising and ingenious that it called forth a generous amount of comment pro and con and some additional research. Some of the criticisms and suggestions for modification of the theory are given briefly.[17]

Studies that attempted to repeat Winch's research failed to give clear support to the theory, although they showed a slightly greater tendency toward unlike (complementary) needs than like needs between husband and wife or engaged couples. Apparently personality needs are too subtle for present methods to discover or measure them, or complementary needs are only one among many factors that determine mate selection. Like needs were found to be almost as influential as unlike ones; it may be that for some types of needs, likeness gives greater satisfaction than complementariness. Such an interpretation, for example, might mean that two ambitious, achieving persons would find greater satisfaction together than one achieving person and a deferential mate.

Other writers have commented on the fact that cultural expectations and the fitting together of cultural roles are also important. The upper-class girl is expected by her parents, and herself expects, to marry someone of the same social class. If the number of eligible upper-class young people is small, choices may be made more upon the basis of suitability than personal needs; if the roles are fulfilled, the marriage may be satisfactory to the couple. In fact, to some extent, needs are defined and their expression guided by the cultural dictates of different groups.

Attention has also been called to the fact that courtship and marriage are not static relationships but that interaction goes on at all times. Needs are slowly realized, brought into the open, and redefined. Each one may modify his own conception of needs in order to better help the mate realize his needs. Thus, as the sequence of dating, engagement, and eventually married life goes on, adjustments are made. Some needs are met within the marriage, some outside, and others are perhaps never met.

The culture demands that some needs should be met within marriage.

[17]Charles E. Bowerman and Barbara R. Day, "A Test of the Theory of Complementary Needs as Applied to Couples during Courtship," *American Sociological Review*, 21 (1956), 602–5; Alfred M. and Elizabeth B. Lee, *Marriage and the Family* (New York: Barnes and Noble, 1961), 158–60; James A. Schellenberg and Lawrence S. Bee, "A Re-Examination of the Theory of Complementary Needs in Mate Selection," *Marriage and Family Living*, 22 (1960), 227–32; George Simpson, *People in Families* (New York: Crowell, 1960), pp. 155–57.

Among these are sexual satisfaction and the production and rearing of children. Other needs are not necessarily confined to marriage; the ambitious husband may meet his needs at his occupation, the ambitious wife through community projects. The deferential husband may find a lowly niche in his occupation where he happily follows commands; the deferential wife may become a useful worker in her church; neither asks much from the other except a peaceful companionship.

Winch himself summarized the criticisms and studies undertaken by others to test the theory but came to no definite conclusions.[18]

The criticism of Winch's theory and the failure to establish it fully have not, however, disposed of the theory. Discussion and research continue. Winch was probing at an important side of mate selection. Cultural factors stake out the group within which eligible mates may be found. What determines the actual mutual selection of the one person for marriage? How much mutual satisfaction of needs is necessary to make the couple happy and to prevent conflict? How much mutuality should be evident during courtship; how much can be expected to develop during the marriage? Certainly a couple at war with each other in many areas would take more risk in marriage than a couple with at least some basic interlocking of needs. But a perfect meshing at the time of marriage is too much for any couple to expect.

Intimacies During Engagement

Discussion in the preceding chapter indicated that as the personal attachment in dating increased, sexual intimacies also tended to move toward heavy petting and intercourse. One might surmise that with engagement, intercourse would become the most widely approved mode of intimacy for the majority of men and women. According to Table 12, in the preceding chapter, this is the situation with men, 48 per cent of whom approve intercourse for engaged couples. Women, however, are more reluctant to move into intercourse; 60 per cent approve of heavy petting, but only 20 per cent of intercourse.

Christensen and Carpenter, who confined their query to intercourse, found that in their intermountain sample of students only 21 per cent of men and 7 per cent of women college students approved of inter-

[18]Robert F. Winch, "Another Look at the Theory of Complementary Needs in Mate-Selection," *Journal of Marriage and the Family*, 29 (1967), 756–62.

course during engagement.[19] In their midwestern sample, the attitude toward intercourse during engagement was more favorable, with 54 per cent of men students and 27 per cent of women students expressing approval. The differences found are probably primarily due to the backgrounds of the students in the various samples; for example, the intermountain students are primarily members of the Mormon church which maintains close control over its members.

As to actual sexual behavior during engagement, distinguished from the expressions of approval by college students given above, the study by Burgess and Wallin is one of the most informative so far produced.[20] Among their sample of 580 men and 604 women, primarily of middle-class origin, queried after marriage, 45 per cent had had intercourse with the spouse prior to marriage. This figure corresponds closely with the opinions of approval expressed by men in Table 12 and in the Christensen-Carpenter study for midwestern students. For women, the actual experience exceeds in frequency the opinions of approval expressed by women not yet engaged. It seems very probable that the women, abstractly disapproving of premarital sex relations, during engagement found themselves yielding to desire and to the importunities of their fiancés to engage in intercourse. They would be supported by the general philosophy that love justifies premarital intercourse. Intercourse with the last engagement partner before marriage does not tell the whole story, however, especially for the men. Half of the women and a third of the men had not had intercourse with anyone prior to marriage. Among those who had been sexually intimate with the fiancé(e), 28 per cent of the men and 10 per cent of the women had also had sex relations with some other person. For the women, it seems probable that this other experience may have been during some previous love affair or engagement, later broken. For the men, it probably represented a variety of situations—experiences during casual contacts for physical satisfactions only, contacts during random or steady dating, and in some instances previous engagements. Twenty-two per cent of the men and 2 per cent of the women had had sexual relations only with someone other than the fiancé (e). For the men at least, these experiences were not necessarily confined to the period before the engagement. Some men reported that they found the intimacies permitted

[19]Harold T. Christensen and George R. Carpenter, "Timing Patterns in the Development of Sexual Intimacy: An Attitudinal Report on Three Modern Western Societies," *Marriage and Family Living*, 24 (1962), 30–35.

[20]Ernest W. Burgess and Paul Wallin, *Engagement and Marriage* (Philadelphia: Lippincott, 1953), ch. 11.

by the fiancée frustrating in that they did not include intercourse. They therefore—sometimes with the knowledge and consent of the fiancée—occasionally visited a prostitute.

The total picture corroborates the general system of premarital sex relations already brought out in the preceding chapter. The woman regards sex relations as an expression of love. Some women prefer to keep this expression until after marriage; others feel that it is not wrong or at least is defensible during engagement. Some men during engagement continue to hold a double attitude toward sex: according to this view, intercourse is all right on a physical basis without a mutual tie of affection with women who hold the same view and who on the whole are not considered marriageable. It is also felt to be all right with a fiancée when there is mutual love. However, a large proportion of men join the women in abiding by the standard of complete abstinence until marriage. Other men, even when they have previously been more or less accustomed to sex satisfaction, wish to reserve the experience with their fiancées until after marriage.

The reactions of both abstainers and participants in sex relations among engaged people are also important. The most frequently stated reason for not having premarital intercourse, given in the Burgess-Wallin study, was the feeling on the part of one or both that such action was not right and that sex belonged to marriage.[21] No other single reason for refraining was given by more than a third of the number who stated that premarital indulgence was not right. The less frequent reasons, in declining order of frequency, were fear of pregnancy, possibility of weakening the relationship, fear of hurting parents' feelings, fear of social disapproval, or conditions that did not permit intercourse (about 7 per cent). Those who carried on intercourse tended to feel that the experience strengthened the relationship by deepening their love, giving increased understanding, and relieving physical tensions. Small numbers, however, feared social disapproval or pregnancy or had a sense of guilt.

When the abstainers and the participants in intercourse were compared as to scores on an engagement success scale, some difference was found between the two groups.[22] The average success scores of men stood as follows: never had intercourse with fiancée, 155.5; intercourse once or a few times, 146.0; often had intercourse, 147.4. The corresponding average scores for women were 154.3, 150.3, 147.4. A detailed chart shows that very high success scores tend to be linked with no intercourse, and extremely low scores with intercourse. However, as the averages show, the linkage is far from perfect.

[21] *Ibid.*, ch. 12.
[22] *Ibid.*

The Termination of Engagement

Ideally, the termination of an engagement is marriage. Actually, many engagements are broken. Only recently has the frequency of broken engagements been realized. Among 1,000 engaged couples who participated in the Burgess-Wallin study, 24 per cent of the men and 36 per cent of the women had broken one or more previous engagements, and 15 per cent later broke the engagement that existed when the study was started.[23] Broken engagements as well as the adjustment that follows are now an important part of the marital process.

On the basis of 131 cases of broken engagements, Burgess and Wallin found five causative factors.[24]

1. SLIGHT EMOTIONAL ATTACHMENT. Examples given are of young people not wholly or deeply in love, or who had fallen in love under special circumstances such as a summer vacation with limited eligible partners for dating, or the social whirl of a college campus. When deeper interest in someone else developed, the engagement was broken.

2. SEPARATION. The engagement did not survive long periods without personal contact, especially when the two were not able to communicate fully by correspondence.

3. PARENTAL OPPOSITION. Parents opposed a suitor or put pressure on son or daughter to enter into an engagement with someone of their choice. In either case, the engagement did not withstand the pressure.

4. CULTURAL DIVERGENCES. Often physical attraction or interest in the novelty of dating a person of different cultural background or standards led to engagement. When differences became more apparent, the engagement was broken. The obstacles most frequently found were differences in religion, nationality, region of the country, rural-urban background, and attitudes toward sex, race, interests, and ideals.

5. PERSONALITY PROBLEMS. These centered in incompatibilities and conflicts not arising from the factors previously listed. Examples were such personality problems as extreme dependency (on parents), fear of assuming the responsibilities of marriage, or (on the part of the girls) fear of the physical aspects of marriage. Incompat-

[23]*Ibid.,* p. 273.
[24]*Ibid.,* pp. 273–95.

ibility of temperament sometimes was the cause; for example, the engagement of two high-strung individuals or two moody ones. Unsatisfied personality needs or the demands of a career led to some broken engagements.

Using a small series of first-hand accounts of broken engagements, the author of this text was able to identify certain obstacles in the dating-engagement sequence that led to termination of the engagement. Three types were found. First, something may interfere with the progress of the dating-engagement sequence. The intrusive element may be the objection of parents, separation over a long period of time, illness of one partner, pressure from some institution, such as the church in an interreligious marriage, or some other factor not directly involved in the process itself. Second, the broken engagement may result from the inability of one or both of the partners to move from step to step through the sequence. The immature girl or boy may be able to enter the courtship phase but not accept the responsibilities of engagement; the philanderer may not be able to narrow his interests to one person as the conventional courtship demands. Third, although both may be able to follow through the entire sequence, they may not be well mated to each other and therefore find decreasing rather than increasing satisfaction in the sequence as it develops.

Sometimes more than one hazard appears in a courtship. For example, the immaturity of one partner (number two above) may be associated with interference of that partner's parents who try to direct the courtship (number one above). Or the person who has need for continued personal attention may not find this need met in the partner because of a long-continued separation (numbers three and one).

Although the final break may seem to come abruptly, usually it is the end of a disintegrating series of events. At some point the unifying effect of the dating-engagement sequence is counterbalanced by the disintegrating effect of the breaking-up process. Thereafter disintegration outweighs unification until the engagement is broken.

Because of the degree of personal involvement of one or both partners, personal disorganization often accompanies the broken engagement. Personality needs must be satisfied through other channels; emotional reactions, such as resentment, loneliness, jealousy, or hostility, must be dissipated; new social contacts must be established. Each person must become emotionally detached and individualized again.

The several aspects of broken engagements are illustrated through personal accounts.[25] The italicized statements in brackets call attention

[25]The writers were asked to put their accounts in the third person, even though, as in most cases, they referred to personal experiences.

to different phases of the dating-engagement and the disintegration sequences.

Curt, newly inducted into the army, first met Violet at an army camp service center dance where she and her mother were visiting her brother. Curt was invited to spend the week end at Violet's home in the city. Curt at this time was 19 and had just come from his home in a small Kansas town of 2,000 inhabitants; he had never before been away from home for any great length of time. Curt was soon spending as many week ends as possible with Violet. [*Violet—and her family—satisfy Curt's need for companionship and inclusion in a family.*]

Violet and Curt soon found themselves in love with each other. Violet was attracted as much if not more to the uniform than to Curt himself, although she did not realize this consciously. Curt found life in the city exciting. Violet, who was 17, was not only beautiful but an exciting girl to Curt, for she sang in a dance band. He readily adapted his week ends to Violet's manner of doing the town. Although Curt's parents had been opposed to dancing, drinking, smoking, and card-playing, and Curt previously had conformed to their expectations, now he found that he and Violet could live life to its fullest, so he thought, in a mad whirl of night clubs, drinking, love-making, and dancing. For both of them it was a wonderful romance. [*At this point, the sequence is still in the dating stage. Although the two are narrowing their interests to each other, the main emphasis is upon the excitement that each receives. Violet is flattered to have a man in uniform at her side, and Curt's ego is enhanced by the attention of a city girl who knows her way around in night life. The influence of Curt's parents is present but inhibited by Curt for the time being. Although no mention is made of Violet's parents, one may assume that they were not opposed to Violet's way of spending her week ends, and their unvoiced approval may have helped Curt to indulge in activities disapproved by his parents.*]

After three months of frequent week ends in the city, Violet and Curt mutually decided that they would become engaged. Curt's basic training was finished and it would soon be time for him to go overseas. [*The engagement is occurring while the couple are still in the dating stage and before identification and unity have occurred.*] The main reason that the couple were not married was that Curt knew the consternation the marriage would create in his family; he felt he might be better able to face the issue when he returned from the army. [*Indirect family influence is evident. Also, Curt is probably grasping for security in binding Violet to him before he goes into a new and dangerous experience.*]

Curt left for active military duty abroad two weeks after he became engaged. For Violet life continued in much the same manner as before, except that Curt was not with her to share the fast life that dance-band work afforded her. There was a frequent exchange of letters. However, it proved increasingly difficult for

Curt to write Violet because her letters were filled with trivial events, while he felt there was a greater job to be done. Curt was in the front lines for months at a time. He was wounded during his second year abroad and returned to the States, prematurely old and broken-spirited. [*The separation has given Curt new experiences and developed new needs—to take a responsible part in public affairs. He is still familiar with Violet's life, since she continued in the old round of activities; but she no longer shares his experiences or memories and cannot fill his new needs.*]

Upon his release from the army, Curt headed directly for Violet. When he met her he could scarcely believe his eyes for she was no longer a girl but a grown woman. In fact, she was an inch taller than Curt, which placed him at a disadvantage. It was difficult for them to find anything to talk about. After having seen death and destruction at its worst, Curt found Violet's trivial talk constantly irritating. He wondered why she couldn't come down to earth and see the more basic values of life rather than jabbering about the latest swing tune to be on the hit-parade. [*They no longer meet each other's needs, but are held together by the formality of engagement and the thought of marriage, which has become habitual over the months.*]

Curt wanted to get married but also he wanted to settle in a primarily rural section of the country. Violet could not think of giving up her present life and going off to live in the country with "a bunch of square farm characters." However, it was agreed that Violet would visit Curt's family in Kansas. Her visit was an unhappy experience for everyone. Their way of life was strictly nowhere as far as Violet was concerned, and the fact that she smoked and drank created ill-will toward her on the part of Curt's folks. [*The differences in values between Curt and Violet now become sharply defined, and it becomes more evident than before that, although each is ready for and wants marriage, they are not well mated with each other. The family influence becomes overt and is directed against Violet, whereas previously the influence had rested solely in Curt's early training and his foreboding of how his parents would react to Violet.*]

Curt discovered that during his absence, Violet had been going out with a sailor. Although Violet insisted the affair was purely platonic, Curt became suspicious. [*Violet has violated the convention of concentration of attention upon one person during an engagement. A long separation tends to re-establish a dating situation, the conventions of which conflict with the conventions of engagement: freedom to play the field as against pair dating only between the engaged couple, which is made impossible by long separations.*]

Soon after Violet returned home, she sent her ring to Curt and the engagement was at an end.

In summary, the factors involved fall under headings one and three. Factor one, intrusive elements, is apparent in the separation that forced an early engagement and prevented the romance from progressing to the identification and unity typical of an engagement, and in the influence of Curt's parents. Factor three is illustrated by the ability of Violet to meet the needs of a young, homesick rural boy lonely for affection and excited by the bright lights of the city, and by Curt's ability to meet the need of Violet, a young girl in a sophisticated environment of night clubs, for a personable escort. Later, after Curt's war experience, they are no longer well matched, and the sequence is blocked by their lack of responsiveness to each other's needs.

Although the engagement ended when Violet returned the ring, Curt and Violet still faced the problem of adjusting to nonengagement and conceiving of themselves as detached from each other. The account continues:

> For Violet the adjustment after the broken engagement was not difficult, for there had been no great emotional involvement. She resumed her vocal activities in the field of dance work, and in a few months became engaged to a dance musician whom she later married. [*Sharing a common field of interests, activities, and values, Violet and the musician probably meet each other's needs better than Violet and Curt could have done.*]
>
> Curt, in his search for something stable which might give purpose and meaning to his life, took up the study of agriculture. He did not date any of the home-town girls or girls at college for some months. He also spent much time in taverns, to his parent's dismay, trying to drown his sorrows. [*Curt's efforts at adjustment to the broken engagement and also to civilian life occurred simultaneously, and were of a type both to orient him toward a normal civilian and occupational life, and to induce personal demoralization.*]
>
> After some months, Curt began to date a girl in his home town who influenced him to stop his excessive drinking. A few months later, the two became engaged. [*In this girl, with the same background and system of values, who found good qualities in Curt, he is able to find appreciation and fulfillment of personal needs. His desire for his home town and the rural way of life perhaps indicate a need for security that he could not satisfy in a large city.*]

The case that follows illustrates all three factors in broken engagements.

> At 17, Bob was spending his summer vacation at home before returning to complete his senior year at prep school, where he had been sent because of family tensions. His mother, from her strong sense of devotion and love, had almost overwhelmed her son with direction and affection. Bob reacted by being stubborn, aggressive, and what his mother termed "wild."
>
> Bob met Laura at a party. Laura was 21 and a junior in college, but since Bob had always dated girls older than himself, they

found the difference in age no bar and began dating regularly. Laura was easygoing, sweet, and sincere. She always liked to help people and usually had gone with men who leaned on her for emotional help and understanding. [*At this point Bob and Laura meet each other's needs: Bob for a mother-substitute who reassures him but does not dominate as his own mother does; Laura for someone upon whom she can lavish devotion and help. We do not know the origin of this need of Laura's.*]

The two had many interests in common and got along well from the start; both were athletic, intelligent, and gregarious. Their families had similar educations and the same northern European cultural heritage. Both families were upper-middle class. [*These similarities helped them to build up mutual activities. They have essentially the same social-class and cultural values, which contribute to identification.*]

Bob and Laura corresponded throughout the next school year and attended social functions at each other's schools. By the time Laura was graduated from college and Bob from prep school in June, they were thinking of marriage. After a second summer of tennis, swimming, dancing, and making mutual friends, they became officially engaged. Although Bob's family thought he was too young for marriage, they approved the choice, as did Laura's family also. [*The family influence, especially on Bob's side, becomes a major factor in the engagement.*]

They planned to be married the following summer. Bob was looking forward to a good companionship with Laura and a life that was calmer and less filled with emotional tension than his had been. He felt also that his marriage would free him from his mother's control, since his mother was fond of Laura, who, for her part, understood Bob's immaturity and his desire to be a nonconformist and accepted him and had great belief in his future. [*Their needs are essentially the same as the previous summer—Bob for a gentler mother than his own and Laura for someone immature to help and mold.*]

During Bob's freshman year at college, he and Laura became officially engaged, with Bob's family buying the engagement ring. They planned to be married the following summer. But by the end of the school year, Bob began to fear the prospect of marriage. Laura was no longer as excellent a companion for him as she had been. While Bob was becoming more intellectually curious, Laura remained conservative and complacent. Perhaps the main cause of the difficulty was that Bob began to fear marriage itself, feared responsibility, feared failing, and all the more so because he felt himself falling out of love with Laura. [*Opposed factors are evident here. The pressure of Bob's family toward marriage and Laura's unquestioning acceptance of the marriage are opposed to Bob's increasing maturity and decreasing need for someone upon whom to lean. At the same time, he finds himself unready for marriage, fearing the responsibilities. Engagement brought him security, marriage threatens insecurity.*]

That summer Bob started dating other girls, although he was still engaged. [*Violation of engagement convention of dating only the partner is indicative of Bob's unreadiness for exclusive pair-relationship.*] Laura knew of his dating but accepted it and thought everything would iron itself out when they were married. [*Laura is the permissive parent.*] Bob became restless, never going to bed until five or six o'clock in the morning and having his sleep interrupted by nightmares. He didn't want to make any plans for the wedding and wanted to push it entirely out of his mind, as a child would. He postponed one tentative wedding date, and became angry at Laura's family who were unwilling to spend much money on the wedding and reception. [*Bob is still too immature and too much dominated by his mother to face the issue squarely and attempts childlike evasions, at the same time that his conflicts find an outlet in neurotic reactions.*]

Bob's mother bought Laura a wedding dress and fur coat and arranged for the two to take a honeymoon trip to South America. [*Heavy family pressure.*]

Bob's restlessness increased as the postponed wedding date approached. Finally his parents realized his intense unhappiness and helped him postpone the date again by saying he was too young to get married as he had three more years of college. Bob used this reason to break off the wedding plans. [*Bob's continued dependence on his parents makes it impossible for him to postpone the wedding without their approval.*] Laura and Bob discussed the whole situation and Laura came to the realization that Bob did not love her. Laura was very understanding. [*The forgiving parent.*] Laura and Bob broke their engagement entirely following a quarrel between their parents over the postponed wedding.

After a period of several months, Laura and Bob began to date again although not exclusively. Laura hoped to restore the old relationship, and Bob tried to fall in love with her again. He felt guilty about her unhappiness and thought that he could never fall in love with another girl until Laura was happily married. Whenever he started to go with another girl seriously, he feared she would break off their relationship, as he had done with Laura, as retribution for the pain he had caused Laura.

Factor one, intrusive elements, is found in Bob's college experience, which gives him added maturity and changes his personal needs. Factor two is clear in Bob's inability to carry the relationship beyond the steady-dating stage into a true courtship situation; in time he rebelled against steady dating. Factor three is evident for Laura, who was ready for marriage. Bob at first found security in Laura's love but later found her unable to meet his newly awakened and more mature needs. He found decreasing satisfaction in the relationship. Up to the time the account was written he had not fully freed himself from emotional guilt feelings.

Since one engagement may follow another, the attempt of young people to find partners with whom the dating-engagement sequence may reach a climax in marriage is repeated until couple after couple are well matched and the sequence can go to completion. A broken engagement is not a sign of a permanently broken heart or cause for lasting despair. Rather, it signifies the necessity for more careful selection of a partner.

Questions

1. If you are engaged or newly married, analyze your experience by the dating-engagement sequence. At what points did your experience differ from the process as outlined in the text? How do you account for the deviations?

2. Why is a fairly long period of courtship more closely associated with success or happiness in marriage than a short courtship?

3. What legal limitations are there to mate selection? Are these restrictions justified? Ought they be increased?

4. How might availability of eligible mates be increased? Discuss specific situations of nonavailability.

5. How does parental influence affect courtship and mate selection?

6. Read the Winch or Ktsanes references in the Bibliography on the theory of mate selection according to complementary needs. Make your own critical analysis.

7. In view of the widespread tolerance of sex relations during dating, why is it not more widely approved and experienced during engagement?

8. Discuss the points in the dating-engagement sequence where the process may break down.

9. Analyze a case of broken engagement according to the dating-engagement sequence.

Bibliography

BATES, A., "Parental Roles in Courtship," *Social Forces*, 20 (1942), 483–86.

BURCHINAL, LEE G., "The Premarital Dyad and Love Involvement," in Harold T. Christensen, ed., *Handbook of Marriage and the Family* (Chicago: Rand McNally, 1964), ch. 16.

BURGESS, ERNEST W., and PAUL WALLIN, *Engagement and Marriage* (Philadelphia: Lippincott, 1953).

CAVAN, RUTH SHONLE, ed., *Marriage and Family in the Modern World* (New York: Crowell, 1969), chs. 7, 11.

KERCKHOFF, A. C., and K. E. DAVIS, "Value Consensus and Need Complementarity in Mate Selection," *American Sociological Review*, 27 (1962), 295–303.

KIRKPATRICK, C., and T. CAPLOW, "Emotional Trends in the Courtship Experiences of College Students as Expressed by Graphs with Some Observations on Methodological Implications," *American Sociological Review*, 10 (1945), 619–26.

KTSANES, THOMAS and VIRGINIA, "The Theory of Complementary Needs in Mate Selection," in Robert F. Winch, Robert McGinnis, and Herbert R. Barringer, eds., *Selected Studies in Marriage and the Family* (New York: Holt, Rinehart, and Winston, 1962), pp. 517–32; reprinted in Ruth Shonle Cavan, ed., *Marriage and Family in the Modern World* (New York: Crowell, 1969).

SCOTT, JOHN FINLEY, "The American College Sorority, Its Role in Class and Ethnic Endogamy," *American Sociological Review*, 30 (1965), 514–27.

SUSSMAN, MARVIN B., "Parental Participation in Mate Selection and Its Effect upon Family Continuity," *Social Forces*, 32 (1953–54), 76–81.

WINCH, ROBERT F., "Another Look at the Theory of Complementary Needs in Mate-Selection," *Journal of Marriage and the Family*, 29 (1967), 756–62.

———, *Mate-Selection: A Study of Complementary Needs* (New York: Harper, 1958).

CHAPTER $I5$

Sexual Behavior

SEXUAL BEHAVIOR, both in acts and in the mind, is difficult to analyze because it stems from three origins rather than one: natural physiological processes common to all normal human beings; cultural and social norms that set up a web of definitions, restrictions, and approved areas of freedom of sex behavior; and psychological reactions of the individual as he works out the expression of his physiological sex drives. No one of the processes taken alone can be accepted as the fundamental one about which sexual behavior should center or which should control sexual behavior.

Physiological Processes

Although sex as a physiological process comes to maturity during the period immediately following puberty, a certain amount of restricted sexual expression is possible from infancy on and often occurs. Accidental or intentional stimulation of an infant's external sex organs produces pleasurable reactions in the child. Although such practices are not common, in a few primitive societies adults play with small children in this way,[1] and we find occasional records of sex stimulation and reaction of infants.[2] Surveys of sex experiences unveil a picture of wide-

[1]Clellan S. Ford and Frank A. Beach, *Patterns of Sexual Behavior* (New York: Harper, 1951), pp. 188–92.
[2]Alfred C. Kinsey, *et al.*, *Sexual Behavior in the Human Male* (Philadelphia: Saunders, 1948), p. 177.

spread masturbation in early as well as later childhood in the United States. In the Kinsey survey of sexual activities of males, boys as young as eight years were found to have masturbated; and by age 17, 90 per cent had masturbated at some time.[3] Girls were not exempt from this form of sexual expression. By age 10, 13 per cent had masturbated, according to the Kinsey survey, and by age 15, 28 per cent.[4] However, age by age, a much higher percentage of boys than of girls had had some experience with masturbation. This difference is in line with differences in later attitudes and experience with intercourse, as discussed in Chapter 13 and in this chapter.

It is not until after puberty, however, that sexual maturity is achieved by either boy or girl, when the pituitary glands, ovaries, and testes create and secrete the necessary hormones. The internal and external sex structures develop, as well as secondary sex characteristics, such as body hair, the beard of the boy, and the breasts of the girl. The sex glands begin to produce mature germ cells: ova (eggs) in the case of the female and sperm in the male. With the completion of this development during adolescence, full sexual intercourse with the probability of conception becomes possible. Internal physiological pressures and tensions tend to build up, especially in the male, creating discomfort until relieved. Although the sex drive is very powerful and at least in some persons very insistent, it is also very flexible. It is more flexible than the need for food, liquid, rest, or sleep, the denial of which after a certain period of time will result in death. Even lifelong denial of sex expression does not result in death; in fact, denial in time brings its own relief through certain safety valves provided by nature. Nevertheless, the natural and expected outcome of the sex drive is intercourse between two persons of opposite sex. Here again, however, we find a wide degree of latitude among different societies and among individuals in any one society as to the age when intercourse begins, how frequently it occurs once started, techniques of intercourse, and the exact pairing off of male with female. The physiological drive does not include a definite pattern of sexual behavior.

Social Norms

The flexible aspects of sex are controlled by socio-cultural norms in all human societies, primitive and civilized alike. Except in extreme cases, such as celibate religious groups, the norms strike some kind of balance

[3] *Ibid.*, p. 500.
[4] Alfred C. Kinsey, *et al.*, *Sexual Behavior in the Human Female* (Philadelphia: Saunders, 1953), p. 177.

between expression of sexual drives and the equally important need of each society to function smoothly and adequately in providing for all needs of its members. Sexual behavior, therefore, is nowhere allowed free and untrammeled expression in accordance with the impulses or even the considered judgment of individuals; it is integrated into the entire societal pattern of behavior. So important is it to maintain this integration that severe penalties are attached to violations of the sexual norms.

Norms That Preserve Family Life

Although societies differ in the details of their norms, certain restrictions of sexual behavior are common to all known societies. These regulations for the most part support the integrity of the family, which anthropologists, whose knowledge ranges round the world, regard as the most significant social unit. The common supporting regulations of sex are as follows:[5]

1.   Incest is universally forbidden, by even the most backward peoples. Moreover, the incest taboo extends beyond parents and children to include other, although not universally the same, relatives. Examples of incest sometimes cited for the Ptolemies of Egypt and the Incas of Peru do not pertain to the people as a whole but only to limited groups of high prestige where maintenance of status took precedence over other factors. The incest taboo is regarded as contributing to the integrity of the family by preventing sexual jealousy and rivalry, and to the cohesiveness of the community by binding families into a whole through intermarriage.

2.   All societies contain recognizable family groups consisting of a man, a woman, and children. These groups may form an independent family or be part of an extended or kinship family; nevertheless, this small-family unit is recognized. In some societies multiple husbands or wives may be acquired with social approval but usually are found in only a minority of families.

3.   Marriage between a man and woman is the legitimate way to found a family. Some ritual or definite form of behavior signifies the change of status from unmarried to married. It may be the simple giving of a gift and change of residence of some Eskimo

[5]George Peter Murdock, "A Comparative Anthropological Approach," in a symposium on "Sexual Behavior: How Shall We Define and Motivate What Is Acceptable," *Journal of Social Hygiene*, 36 (1950), 133–38; Margaret Mead, "The Sex Life of the Unmarried Adult in Primitive Society," in Ira S. Wile, ed., *Sex Life of the Unmarried Adult* (Garden City Publishing Co., 1940, reprinted from 1934), pp. 53–74; Ford and Beach, *op. cit.*, pp. 112–13.

groups or the elaborate church ritual of the upper-class American marriage, but it is recognized by the society where it occurs as the entrance upon family life with the assumption of new responsibilities and functions.

4. In general, societies disapprove of illegitimate birth. Even permissive societies give greater approval to legitimate births. With few exceptions it is generally conceded that the family is the primary agency for the physical care and the training or education of young children and that every child has the right to have socially recognized parents to assume his care. In primitive societies, as in ours, the pregnant girl usually marries or conceals the birth of the child, which is then adopted; in occasional societies she disposes of it by death immediately after birth.

5. Marriage is the most widely approved regular outlet for sexual expression for those of marriageable age. In a survey of 205 societies, chosen as a worldwide sample, Murdock found only five, or 2 per cent, that condoned adultery. A more detailed statement by Ford and Beach, based on 139 societies, classifies 39 per cent as approving of some type of extramarital sex relations; but only seven permitted complete freedom to the individual, corresponding to adultery. In the other societies the extramarital sex relations were strictly limited and served functions other than free sexual expression. One example is the wife-lending of the Chuckchee of Siberia, whereby a married man traveling to a distant community makes arrangements with some man in that community to share his wife, in exchange extending the same hospitality to his host when he visits his community. Another occasion of release from strict marital fidelity may be during some ceremony when men and women are expected to have sexual relations without regard to marital ties, perhaps as a magical means of insuring fertility of crops.

The societies that are marginal or that seem to have some highly individualistic patterns are few indeed, and no society exists that does not maintain strict sexual taboos and regulations that bring sexual activities within a framework of general societal organization and especially of adequate family functioning.

PREMARITAL SEX NORMS

The sweeping statement is often made by laymen that primitive people permit freedom of sex relations before marriage. Actually, primtiive societies come within the same range of premarital sex norms as civilized people, varying from very restrictive to very permissive, with the restrictive societies being in the minority. Ford and Beach classify primitive societies into three types.[6]

Restrictive societies not only hold virginity, especially for prepubescent girls, as of high value, but take positive measures to enforce the restriction of sexual relations.

Semirestrictive societies are those with formal restrictions that are not strictly enforced so long as violations remain more or less secretive.

Permissive societies permit sex play among children and young unmarried people as natural and normal; there are no moral implications. In some instances parents encourage it as contributory to successful marriage. The permissive attitude sometimes relates only to one sex or to certain age periods.

The early age of marriage of girls in many primitive societies actually reduces the length of time when sex play is allowed to a short period terminating in selection of a husband. The low number of pregnancies among unmarried girls reported from primitive societies tends to support the idea that sex relations are not unbridled. In other words, in permissive societies, sex takes its place as one phase of normal behavior to be integrated into activities of work, play, religion, and all other facets of life; it does not constitute a continuous orgy.

Civilized societies can also be placed in this threefold classification. Sweden, for instance, would fall into the semirestrictive class. The Swedish Population Commission, in its *Report on the Sexual Question*, places highest official approval on sex within marriage; realistically accepts the fact that in a situation where marriages are long delayed for economic reasons, premarital sex relations are practiced; does not condemn premarital intercourse when the couple are bound together by affection; but severely condemns promiscuity and prostitution.[7] Russia, after the revolution of 1917 and until 1944, was a permissive society. Sex relations and marriage were private affairs, illegitimacy carried no stigma, and divorce could be had upon application. Even so, certain limitations were set. The father was responsible for the support of all children whether or not they were born in wedlock. Also disapproval attached to promiscuity although not to semipermanent sexual unions. New laws passed in 1944 placed greater obligations on marriage and restrictions on divorce. Unmarried mothers, however, were given greater official recognition, with government allowances for each child. Russia thus moved toward the semirestrictive regulation of sex.

[6]Ford and Beach, *op. cit.*, pp. 180–92.
[7]Alva Myrdal, *Nation and Family* (New York: Harper, 1941), pp. 195–96.

The United States in the past was legally and religiously a restrictive society. An unofficial exception was made for unmarried young men, whose casual sexual exploits were condoned. That the United States has been moving toward a semirestrictive society is supported by data from several studies that show a marked increase in frequency of pre-marital intercourse in the United States for persons born after 1909 in comparison with the frequency for persons born prior to 1890. Terman, reporting on couples married at the time of the study, found that 86.4 per cent of husbands born after 1909 as compared with 49.4 per cent of those born before 1890 admitted premarital intercourse; 68.3 per cent of the younger wives but only 13.5 per cent of the older wives reported premarital intercourse.[8] Another study, reporting on very happily married couples, showed that 71.4 per cent of men born after 1909 as compared with 52.9 per cent of men born before 1890 had had premarital intercourse; among happily married women the correspond-ing percentages were 22.7 and 4.5.[9] Divorced men and women likewise showed an increase in premarital intercourse from the early period to the later one. The trend toward a semirestrictive pattern of sex behavior is further shown by the increase of intercourse with the future mate among the younger age group when compared with the older. This trend is indicative of acceptance of nonvirginity of the bride. Much of the earlier male premarital experience apparently was with prostitutes, whereas prospective wives were expected to be virgins.

The semirestrictive nature of American attitudes toward premarital sex experience is shown also by the widespread reluctance of police to arrest persons who engage in either premarital or extramarital inter-course. Prostitution, rape, or notoriously open nonmarital sex exploits may lead to arrest; when voluntary and noncommercial sexual activities are carried on with circumspection, arrests are rarely made even though the activities may be known. As one writer states, laws intended to con-trol or eliminate fornication (intercourse of the unmarried) or adultery (extramarital intercourse) are "in a state of suspended animation."[10]

[8]L. M. Terman, et al., Psychological Factors in Marital Happiness (New York: McGraw-Hill, 1938), p. 321.

[9]Harvey J. Locke, Predicting Adjustment in Marriage: A Comparison of a Divorced and a Happily Married Group (New York: Holt, 1951), pp. 136–37. Locke suggests that the incidence of premarital sex relations may actually be some-what higher, especially for women, as he discovered a tendency toward con-cealment of this information; he also believes that more older people may have indulged than reported the experience, but were inhibited about admitting it.

[10]Morris Ploscowe, Sex and the Law (New York: Prentice-Hall, 1951), p. 157; ch. 5 gives a detailed discussion of laws regarding premarital and extramarital sex relations and their nonenforcement.

Traditional attitudes, laws, and publicly stated mores condemn premarital sex relations; but actual behavior shows an increase in incidence over the years, with penalties not enforced or lightly applied, so long as public notoriety is avoided. The trend is toward semirestrictive control.

Definition of Sex in the United States

The increase in premarital intercourse and the accompanying leniency of attitude have their counterpart in the radical redefinition of sex that has been under way for at least 40 years. It may seem that this is an unduly long period for a change of attitude that is not yet generally accepted. It must be remembered, however, that in this country for many years sex had not only important social connotations but moral ones as well. Also, regardless of the deviations and violations that always existed, a fairly united front was presented by adults, leaders and laymen alike, on the meaning of sex and the relation of sex behavior to social welfare. Finally, even after a break had been made in the older definition and younger people became vocal in their efforts to find a new meaning, older people reared under the earlier, uniformly accepted conception protested and criticized. It is small wonder then that the attitudinal change has been slow and is still not firmly grounded or universally accepted. A brief review of the stages of change will give a perspective for understanding the present highly confused attitudes.

The Heritage of Attitudes

Puritanism identified sex with the baser qualities of human nature. Sufficiently realistic to recognize that sex must have some outlet for both physical and social reasons, the Puritan leaders sought to confine sex within the boundaries of family life, where its chief function was defined in terms of reproduction. Sex outside of marriage was sinful, and heavy penalties were applied not only to actual sexual misconduct but to such behavior as kissing in public.

Rules were sternly enforced both by the church, in its marked disapproval, and legally. Many of the older laws supporting the Puritan attitude have been repealed or are no longer enforced; but others remain, with great inconsistency in enforcement. Nevertheless, the Puritan attitude toward sex as sinful is still accepted in some religious groups and is widely influential in the attitude toward nonmarital sex behavior.

In the South contrasting attitudes developed as a reaction to the dominance of a two-class society widely separated in prestige—slave-owners backed by the wealth of plantations, and slaves. To women of his own social class the southern planter was extremely chivalrous, after as before marriage. Although the southern lady might flirt in a re-strained though provocative manner, any direct sexual approach before marriage was unthinkable to the gentleman. Sex after marriage was thought of as a function of the marital relationship and for the produc-tion of children to carry on the heritage of the family. At the same time, a more simple type of sex relation was possible and often obtained between the white planter and some comely slave girl. The planter, who already owned and provided for the girl, seems not to have regarded such a relationship as a violation of his code of conduct with women of his own class. Nor did he assume any special responsibility for any child that might result from the liaison, who psychologically as well as socially became identified with the Negro mother.

As the West was opened for settlement, the migrant carried with him his attitudes, southern or northern as the case might be. Much is made in popular literature and western motion pictures of the wild free life of the frontier, with bars and brothels as the most prominent institu-tions and debauchery occupying most of the time. Actually, to the extent that such a phase existed, it was a transitory one during the opening of areas that offered great and quick wealth and prior to the establishment of settled community life. The permanent settlement of the West was accomplished by families, and the economic and social development through cool-headed leaders. The wide-open town was pushed into the background and in time was represented only by small restricted areas in the larger cities. The familism of settlement was tinged, however, with greater individualism than had been true for many years in the more settled communities of the East. The necessity under frontier hardships for each member of the family to carry his share of the load tended to equalize the status of men and women, and at the same time to break down some of the refinements and niceties of sex relations and sex control. A dearth of churches and courts of law prevented the imposing of severe penalties for violations of the sexual code of the East. Sex became a more natural function, and people solved their sexual relationships on a practical basis, according as nearly as possible with the older code but much less restrictive in nature. Common-law marriages frequently occurred; or a young couple, with full approval of their families and neighbors, set up housekeeping and perhaps produced their first child before a legal marriage could be per-formed by the minister, whose circuit brought him to them only at widely spaced intervals of time. Unmarried men sent East for girls they had known as neighbors to come to the West and marry them there without the protective solicitude of parents. Matrimonial agencies sprang up to fill the need; the Caroline Fry Marriage Association and the Bloomer Marriage Association acted as go-betweens and arranged marriages. Occasionally a group of girls would be sent West by some enterprising agent, there to take their chances at finding a suitable husband among the young men eagerly awaiting the arrival of the group. In this freer life where young people made their own decisions, the old restrictions on sex tended to fade to a dim replica of the original stern Puritanical code. Nevertheless, sex was still related closely to marriage and children, and deviations from the code were regarded as violations rather than as individual rights, with, however, social condoning and willingness to forget and overlook the digression.[11]

Meanwhile, in the East another development started that was destined to spread rapidly westward—the Industrial Revolution and the growth of large cities. With this development came not only the crowding of many people with different cultural backgrounds and hence different conceptions of sex into close proximity to each other, but the freeing of women from economic dependence upon their fathers and husbands.

The feminists, who organized as early as 1848, in their battle for equality with men attacked the social order on many fronts: economic, educational, political, legal, and sexual. In all these areas they demanded the same rights, privileges, and opportunities as men. For many years the struggle for sexual equality did not approach sex directly, but was reflected indirectly in such things as the controversy over the growing tolerance for divorce; the reaction against marriage by some leading feminists as a lowering of their status as human beings; and the development of the birth-control movement to free women from excessive childbearing. The early feminist attitude toward sex, therefore, was in the nature of a protest against male control of the sexual situation before and after marriage. The feminists were not personally seeking greater freedom of sex expression. The sexual restrictions applied to women, however, were a symbol of their bondage and like the other symbols had to be abolished.

Finally, consideration must be given to a recurrence of strictness following the Civil War. Wars typically disturb human relationships and destroy many of the controls of settled community life. After the Civil War a reaction to this freedom, as well as to the freedom of the

[11]Arthur Charles Cole, *The Irrepressible Conflict, 1850–1865* (New York: Macmillan, 1934), p. 468.

preceding pioneer period, found expression in the activities of Anthony Comstock and others who became either genuinely concerned or panicky over the sexual freedom of the period. For example, prior to and immediately following the Civil War, divorce had been easier to obtain than at earlier periods and indeed in many states easier than at present. A number of states (at least seven) included in their divorce laws an "omnibus clause" that made it possible for the judge to grant a divorce not only for causes specified in the law but for any other cause that the judge might think justified a divorce. But in the five years following the close of the Civil War some of such clauses were repealed, and other states repealed it soon after.[12] In pre-Civil War decades great latitude appeared in the types of advertisements appearing in newspapers and in other material sent through the mail. Newspapers carried advertisements of abortionists, pills guaranteed to induce miscarriages, contraceptives, and thinly veiled notices of houses of prostitution.[13] Laws passed soon after the Civil War helped to eliminate such advertisements.

By the beginning of the twentieth century the heritage of sex definitions had become a tangle of conflicting attitudes and practices. Sex had the following definitions: a sin unless encompassed in marriage; an individual though secretive physical right outside of marriage; a privilege of men but not of women; a symbol of oppression; a means of producing children. The conflict became an active issue during and following World War I. Extravagant demands for freedom were placed in debate against demands for a return to more restrictive social norms and sterner measures of control; unlike the post-Civil War period when older social norms were reasserted, the post-World War I period fell to the newer trends.

THE DEBATE OF THE 1920'S

The tendency in the 1920's was to remove sex from its social context and regard it as a unique phase of life, a thing apart of great value in and of itself. The physical pleasure of sex to the individual was emphasized. This attitude contrasted with earlier approved concepts in which sex was a means to a social end, gaining its value through its

[12]James H. Barnett, *Divorce and the American Divorce Novel, 1858–1937: A Study in Literary Reflections of Social Influences* (Philadelphia: University of Pennsylvania, 1939), pp. 18–19.

[13]Carl Russell Fish, *The Rise of the Common Man, 1840–1850* (New York: Macmillan, 1927), pp. 152–55; Morris L. Ernst, "Changing Laws and Changing Attitudes," in Wile, *op. cit.*, pp. 212–32.

relationship to the family and reproduction. So far as sex existed apart from marriage it had been a thing of low value, debased, and unclean. The new definition gave it meaning wherever found, as an individual right and pleasure but not as a social value. Thus, the old concept that called for control and repression of sex began to yield to the new concept that opened the way for greater freedom.

In the 1920's repression of all types, and especially sex repression, was proclaimed dangerous to the personality because it caused emotional conflicts; psychoanalytic theories were cited in support of these declarations. Actually, much of the appeal to psychoanalytic theory was merely rationalization for the fearful breaking of the dam that had restricted the freedom of women on many fronts. For it was women, previously more restrained in their thinking and activities than men, who were especially active in tossing aside old social controls. This tendency was expressed in their hard-won right to vote, their reluctance to give up war jobs, their great desire for careers, their refusal to accept the long skirts and long hair that had been symbols of femininity, and their grasping after masculine prerogatives, such as smoking and freedom for premarital sex experiences. They represented the "new woman," free, independent, and self-reliant. They set the stage for a growing trend toward premarital sex relations between men and women of the same social class that has replaced the earlier pattern of men from one class associating sexually with women of a lower class, while those of their own class remained virgins until marriage.[14]

The 1920's did not give any new social evaluation to sex, and the physical evaluation was not universally accepted. The reaction of community leaders and other adults was one of shock and protest. Dire results were predicted for the individual, the family, and society in general as a result of the new individual and physical conception of sex, the matching of woman's behavior to man's, and the increase of premarital sex relations. The trend toward greater freedom also did not extend into the period beyond marriage, except for small radical groups which either sought to delay or altogether avoid marriage as too restrictive, or who visualized sex on two levels, one in the family for the production of children, another outside the family equally open to husband and wife for individual experimentation and pleasure. The chief change was a desire for freedom from old restraints, without too much thought of whether this freedom had any deeper implications, either for personality or for the family.

[14]For an excellent discussion by an anthropologist versed in psychology that presents the conflicts of the 1920's, see E. Sapir, "Observations on the Sex Problem in America," *American Journal of Psychiatry,* 8 (1928), 519–34. See also Goodwin Watson, *Youth After Conflict* (New York: Association Press, 1947).

The great debate of the 1920's made one positive contribution: it made sex a subject of open conversation among respectable people. Whereas previously sex had been almost exclusively the subject of smutty jokes in male groups and of secretive whispering among women, it then could be discussed openly and seriously in print and in mixed groups. This greater freedom of communication brought men's and women's points of view into juxtaposition and contributed to formulation of a jointly held point of view regarding the meaning of sex.

The fling of the 1920's was primarily one of youth. In time, greater maturity, marriage, children, and the depression of the 1930's had a sobering effect upon youth. But the experiments of the 1920's paved the way for a new attempt to define sex in social-psychological rather than physical or moralistic terms.

Diversity of Attitudes Toward Premarital Sex Behavior

By the 1960's the various trends of thought had crystallized into a number of positions, six of which have been defined by Rubin.[15]

1. Traditional repressive asceticism, the stand of the past, has already been discussed. Its rigid dichotomy into what is moral and what is immoral, and its enforcing by penalties imposed from outside the person as well as by personal standards, has steadily lost ground.

2. Enlightened asceticism is the term applied to a modification of the traditional point of view, whereby control over sexual expression is valued in developing self-discipline and avoiding self-indulgence in an important area of life.

    David Mace is cited by Rubin as a proponent of this point of view. Mace has called attention to the possible biological, psychological, and social implications for the couple and also for the institution of marriage and the family in general if free sexual unions became the universal pattern of behavior for all men and women. He has stated his own position as on the whole against premarital sex relations.[16]

[15]Isadore Rubin, "Transition in Sex Values—Implications for the Education of Adolescents," *Journal of Marriage and the Family*, 27 (1965), pp. 185–89; Albert Ellis and A. Babarbanel, eds., *Encyclopedia of Sexual Behavior* (New York: Hawthorn Books, 1961), pp. 247–57, 466–71.

[16]Walter R. Stokes and David M. Mace, "Premarital Sexual Behavior," *Marriage and Family Living*, 15 (1953), 234–39.

3. Rubin's third position is humanistic liberalism, which he feels is
    exemplified in the writings of Lester Kirkendall.[17] Kirkendall feels
    that premarital intercourse should be judged, not by rigid rules,
    but by the effect that it has on the personality. It is reprehensible
    if it creates distrust and suspicion; it may contribute to personality
    development if it creates personal integrity and self-respect for
    both partners to the relationship. He admits that it is very difficult
    for young people to determine, especially in advance, what the
    effect will be. His point of view would rule out all exploitative types
    of sex relationships.

    Another writer who falls into this general category is Ira Reiss,
    whose views have already been discussed in Chapter 13.

4. Humanistic radicalism goes beyond humanistic liberalism in that
    it advocates and urges complete freedom of sex relations for
    young people outside of marriage. Walter Stokes holds this posi-
    tion.[18] He calls attention to the following: sexual needs are part
    of the natural equipment of men and women, evident even in
    infancy; marriage counselors "have learned the unhappy relation-
    ship of childhood chastity demands to adult frigidity and impotence
    in marriage." Stokes states that because of "irrational prej-
    udice" many generations would be required to arrive at this state
    of freedom.

5. Fun morality is the viewpoint that sex is fun and as such contrib-
    utes to a healthy personality. This is a step beyond Stokes' position
    in its range of permissiveness and further divorces sex from mar-
    riage. Albert Ellis strongly urges this point of view.[19]

6. Sexual anarchy not only advocates sexual freedom but actively is
    opposed to chastity, virginity, and monogamy. A French jurist,
    René Guyon, supports this view, placing only the limitation that
    sexual expression should not be injurious to other people.[20]

As the six points of view are arranged by Rubin they range from
strict adherence to a formal moral code to complete abandonment of
personal or social controls or restraints. The moderate positions (Nos. 2

---

[17]Lester A. Kirkendall, *Premarital Intercourse and Interpersonal Relations* (New
York: Julian Press, 1961).

[18]Stokes and Mace, *op. cit.*, Kirkendall, Stokes, Reiss, and others have participated
in two symposia relative to the present discussion: "Sex Education of Adolescents,
An Exchange," *Marriage and Family Living*, 22 (1960), 317–32 and "Premarital Sexual Behavior: A Symposium," *Marriage and Family Living*, 24 (1962),
254–78.

[19]Albert Ellis, *If This Be Sexual Heresy* (New York: Lyle Stuart, 1963).

[20]René Guyon, *The Ethics of Sexual Acts* (New York: Alfred A. Knopf, 1934).

and 3) advocate flexible standards related to personal values and self-discipline. Interest in these positions seems to be on the increase, but the difficulty of establishing values to be sought and methods of instilling the needed self-discipline in young people prevents their adoption.

It should be noted that the concern of most of the writers cited is in premarital sex and its possible effects on young people as well as on marriage and the family. The status of possible children born from free unions is not discussed. Exploitation and obvious injury to the partner are ruled out.

OTHER CONFLICTS OF ATTITUDES

The situation is made more complex because of the lack of coordination among attitudes toward subjects closely related to premarital sex behavior. One such subject is premarital pregnancy. A girl or man may easily find adult approval by some individual or group for premarital intercourse, but if pregnancy occurs, as it does in many cases, they face the full brunt of disapproval of society in general. Although the heavy weight of public shame and ostracism of a few generations ago is not heaped upon the unmarried pregnant woman, the situation is a matter of personal shame and embarrassment to the woman and her parents.

Another related subject has to do with knowledge and availability of contraceptives. Young people may learn of their use from each other and may easily secure them. But there is no general move to acquaint young people with the effective use of contraceptives as part of a program of health or sex education. In fact, such a proposal almost certainly would arouse widespread protests. Nevertheless, such training is the logical correlate of current leniency toward premarital sex relations combined with disapproval of premarital pregnancy.

The attitudes of men toward the virginity of their brides are also muddled. Some are not opposed to lack of virginity, but others feel so strongly about the matter that they have tried during courtship to secure sex relations with a girl selected for marriage; if they succeed, they then drop all contact with the girl, reasoning that if the girl yielded to them, she might also yield to another.[21] It has been pointed out that girls equate intercourse with love; a girl might very well have thought that in yielding to a loved suitor she was making the final convincing guaranty of her love.

It would be logically possible to set up a coordinated system of sex

[21]Ira L. Reiss, "Sexual Codes in Teen-Age Culture," *Annals of the American Academy of Political and Social Science*, 338 (November, 1961), pp. 53–62.

behavior and marriage. One possible system would include early sex education and training in the technique of the more effective use of contraceptives, acceptance of premarital intercourse without feelings of fear, shame, or guilt, and adequate care for children of unmarried couples (when contraceptives failed) either by the mother, in children's homes, or through adoption. Another logical system would provide supervision of dating, training in the belief that sex should wait for marriage, education in the use of contraceptives near the time of marriage for those who wished to limit the number of children, and supportive help from parents and counselors in the early years of marriage to increase the stability of the family as an institution for rearing children. Under the first system, one might ask with David Mace: What would become of the institution of marriage and the family? At present, practices in the United States waver between these two systems.

A change in one part of a social system, such as marriage and the family, without corresponding changes in related parts usually places disadvantage on persons who seek an advantage from the change without awareness of the possible punitive results that will be set in motion in the older unchanged portions of the system. The young man, pursuing a policy of great freedom, nevertheless comes up against the realization that his bride may not be the virgin he desires. The girl, yielding to the young man for any one of a number of reasons, faces the fear and sometimes the actuality of an unwanted pregnancy.

The possibility of adult guidance has been further decreased by the disappearance of any personal supervision of informal social contacts between young people in dating or courting. The supervised school or college dance usually is followed by a prolonged period during which a couple or two visit a favorite eating or drinking place or park in a car. The conditions are favorable for necking, petting, and sometimes sexual relations. The control of premarital social and sexual relations has thus fallen into the hands of young people themselves, without adequate formulation of future marriage goals or skill in the methods of controlling potentially explosive situations.

The Extent of Premarital Sex Relations

The chapters on dating and engagement as well as the preceding sections of this chapter have indicated the confused and conflicting attitudes of young people and adults toward premarital sex relations.

What are the facts? Information will be limited to that uncovered by the Kinsey surveys of sexual behavior. Numerous small studies tend to corroborate the Kinsey findings.

PREMARITAL INTERCOURSE BY EDUCATIONAL LEVEL

Regardless of the age of informants at the time they were interviewed by the Kinsey investigators, they were asked about their sexual activities at different ages.[22] Their final educational level was also ascertained. On the basis of this information, the following facts appeared:

Among men who did not go beyond the eighth grade, 42 per cent had had intercourse by age 15; among those who had 9 to 12 grades of schooling, 45 per cent had had intercourse by age 15 and among those with more than 12 years of education, only 10 per cent. In other words, early teenage boys who were college-oriented followed a pattern of life that rarely included intercourse.

By age 20, premarital intercourse had become a regular part of life for 83 per cent of men with grade school education and for 75 per cent of those with high school education. Among college students at age 20, 44 per cent had had intercourse at some time. By age 25, the percentage in each category had increased, but the relative ranks by education were maintained. By this age, of course, most of the men would have married, leaving only a residue who for some reason had delayed marrying or who in some cases were unmarriageable.

Among women, all percentages are much lower than for men of corresponding age and education.[23] Among women with no more than eighth-grade education, 18 per cent had had intercourse by age 15; the percentage rose to 26 per cent by age 25. For the high school educated, the percentages were 5 for age 15 and 37 by age 25; for the college educated, 2 and 39 per cent respectively for the two ages. It is notable that adult women vary only slightly according to educational level, whereas men show a wide variation.

It is significant that for most of the categories only about a third as high a proportion of women as of men had intercourse. This situation can exist only because some women were promiscuous and ready to serve a number of men. Chapter 13 has already discussed the attitudes and relationships of young men to the pick-up, the prostitute, and, in contrast, to the girl of their own social class.

[22]Kinsey, et al., *Sexual Behavior in the Human Male*, p. 550.
[23]Kinsey, et al., *Sexual Behavior in the Human Female*, p. 333.

OTHER SOCIAL FACTORS

In general, a somewhat smaller percentage of people in rural areas than in cities had premarital intercourse. Fewer persons who were active in religious organizations, regardless of the religion, had premarital intercourse than those who were inactive.

TOTAL SEXUAL OUTPUT

Kinsey attempted to include all avenues of sexual expression in making an over-all statement of the amount of sexual activity. For example, for men he included masturbation, nocturnal emissions, petting to climax, homosexual activities, and contacts with animals. The amount of sexual expression through different methods varied with age, education, and various other social factors. The percentage of premarital intercourse in different groups reflects the type of expression rather than the force and prevalence of the sexual drive itself.

Premarital Intercourse and Pregnancy

As has been indicated, the increasing leniency of attitudes toward premarital intercourse does not go so far as to include approval of premarital pregnancy. Young people attempt to prevent premarital pregnancy by use of contraceptives, but often fail because they are inexpert in their use, cannot secure the most effective types, or use them sporadically.

The Kinsey data, based primarily on urban middle-class women, show that approximately a fifth of unmarried women who have intercourse become pregnant.[24] Premarital pregnancy creates a crisis, especially in the middle or upper class for the woman, her sexual partner, and her family. Ways of meeting the crisis vary from person to person and family to family.

Among the women queried by Kinsey's group, an analysis was made of the outcome of pregnancies that terminated while the women were still unmarried. Eighty-nine per cent of these premarital pregnancies were terminated by induced abortions, primarily for the express pur-

---

[24]Paul H. Gebhard, *et al.*, *Pregnancy, Birth, and Abortion* (New York: Harper, 1958), p. 39. This book was published after Kinsey's death, but is based on the data assembled during his lifetime.

pose of preventing the birth of the child.[25] Another 5 per cent of the pregnancies ended in spontaneous abortions. Only 6 per cent resulted in the birth of a child. This group constituted the illegitimate births, of which there are currently almost 300,000 per year.

Not all pregnancies in the Kinsey sample were terminated prior to marriage, by either abortion or birth. Of the total number of premarital pregnancies, 84 per cent were terminated prior to or without marriage, and 16 per cent were carried over into marriage. The chance that a child conceived before marriage will be born after marriage is about one to five. (Actually, in the Kinsey sample, some of the women were aborted after marriage, so that the chance of live birth after marriage was somewhat less than this.)

Each of the different ways in which the unmarried woman solves the problem of pregnancy has specific implications.

ABORTION

All states have laws making it a crime for anyone to induce an illegal abortion. What constitutes a legal abortion differs from state to state. Only two states by the middle of 1967 went beyond the longtime provision of legal abortion to save the life (or in a few cases preserve the health) of the mother. As stated in Chapter 2, in 1967 Colorado and North Carolina modified their laws to permit abortions whenever the pregnancy 1) results from incest or rape, 2) threatens grave damage to the woman's physical or mental health, or 3) is likely to result in the birth of a child with a severe mental or physical defect. The decision as to whether the woman's condition comes under one of these grounds is made by a panel of physicians. The laws do not give any special consideration to a premarital pregnancy (unless rape or incest is involved), nor do they make it possible for a woman, married or unmarried, to secure an abortion simply because she does not want to bear the child. Each individual case must be fitted into the provisions of the law. The situation therefore is only moderately different from that prior to 1967. Its seems probable, however, that as new laws are passed by additional states they will tend to include further justifications for abortion. In states with a high proportion of Catholics, however, the opposition will be strong and proposed new laws may be defeated time after time.

No one knows how many illegal abortions are performed each year; estimates run into the thousands—one as high as a million. Most illegal abortions are secured by married women, but it remains an avenue of

[25] *Ibid.*, pp. 54, 57.

escape for unmarried pregnant women. Since the act is illegal, everyone concerned is secretive about it. In a very few instances a case comes to public attention because the woman has been seriously injured or becomes infected through lack of sanitation on the part of the abortionist. Some cases that come to light are those in which the woman has tried to abort herself, with disastrous results of self-injury or infection. Only rarely can sufficient evidence be assembled to convict an abortionist.

One result of the present situation is that an illegal, not entirely safe, activity continues, morally condemned but tolerated as one way to escape the dilemma created by the combination of leniency toward premarital sex relations and condemnation of unmarried mothers.

BIRTH BEFORE MARRIAGE

Children who are born to unmarried mothers are known as illegitimate children, do not take their father's name, and cannot inherit from him. Although the father has some legal obligations to support the child, he rarely does so. Even when a case is brought to court, it is difficult to prove that a baby is the child of a specific man. Often the father leaves the community, or he has little money to be used for the child, or the mother prefers to avoid the publicity of a court hearing. Left with the responsibility for the child, the mother has a choice of ways to care for the child. She may keep it, assuming responsibility for its support and care, as is the tendency in certain lower-class groups. Middle-class women often try to conceal the fact that they have had an illegitimate child and place the child with an adoption agency or with some go-between who arranges for the child's adoption. The role of the unmarried mother is fully discussed in Chapter 19.

MARRIAGE AFTER CONCEPTION

Marriage between the pregnant mother and her sexual partner is not uncommon. Studies of a county in Utah and another in Indiana showed that a fifth of all first babies had been conceived before the marriage of their parents.[26] These marriages had extra hazards, as shown by the fact that a fifth of them ended in divorce, compared with half that pro-

[26]Harold T. Christensen, "Studies in Child Spacing: Premarital Pregnancy as Measured by the Spacing of the First Child from Marriage," *American Sociological Review*, 18 (1953), 53–59.

portion of other marriages with children.[27] These marriages are more fully discussed in Chapter 19.

Emotional Reactions to Premarital Sex Relations

It should be recognized that no widespread social disaster automatically results from premarital sex relations; in some measure they have been carried on for many generations by people who on the whole did not become personally maladjusted or fail in marital adjustment. However, a few studies and impressions from reading many case studies and life histories justify some suggestions as to the possible results of premarital sex behavior for individuals in whose social world it is disapproved.

1. The conditions under which premarital sex relations now occur engender anxiety. Fear of discovery and the possibility of arrest, with consequent family disapproval and loss of good name, create temporary fears and at times prolonged anxiety. For the girl there is the added fear of pregnancy unless careful precautions are observed. She also faces the future problem of whether her lack of virginity will interfere with marriage, or, if her relations are with her fiancé, whether he may fail to carry the relationship to the point of marriage.

2. If the act is in contradiction to earlier attitudes regarding chastity, mental conflict may develop with a sense of guilt and shame and a feeling that self-respect or the family's good name has been violated.

3. The act may be associated with deceit if the couple finds it necessary to use assumed names or to lie regarding marriage.

4. The physical conditions may contribute to the attitude that the relation is shameful. The back seat of a car, the side of a country road, or a motel room rented for an hour by the young man while the girl hides her face from the attendant gives an unsavory connotation to the event.

[27]Harold T. Christensen and H. W. Meissner, "Studies in Child Spacing: Premarital Pregnancy as a Factor in Divorce," *American Sociological Review*, 18 (1953), 641–44; Christensen and B. B. Rubenstein, "Premarital Pregnancy and Divorce: A Follow-Up Study by the Interview Method," *Marriage and Family Living*, 18 (1956), 114–23.

5.   The experience tends to be personally segmental and unintegrated into the total personality pattern. It may be contrary to ideas of honor, honesty, or morality instilled in childhood and therefore may be relegated to a sort of airtight compartment. It is brought into open consciousness, talked about, or planned for repetition, only under conditions unrelated to the usual round of life or with certain companions who will maintain the secrecy.

6.   Premarital sex relations tend to be socially segmental also. They cannot be discussed with family, close friends, the fiancé or fiancée, or later with husband or wife. When they occur between lovers they may later become a barrier and lead to the breakdown of the relationship. Only a rather sophisticated couple, somewhat withdrawn from the mores, are able long to defend their relationship. Even in lower-class groups, where sex is regarded as a natural function to be used and enjoyed, secrecy surrounds the activity.

Premarital Sex Relations and Social Stability

Premarital sex relations also have implications for the maintenance of society as a whole. They are often dismissed as a vagary of youth, as play, or as romance. Little consideration is given to the disintegrative effects of illicit pregnancies, care of illegitimate children, and the possible carry-over into marriage of promiscuous habits.

The group upon which youth depends for approval of premarital sex relations is the peer group of adolescents or youth, who form a small and to some extent exclusive social world of their own. When a group within the total society follows a pattern of conduct and sets up standards that run counter to the standards of the more inclusive society, social integration is threatened until either the behavior and standards of the minority group are brought into conformity with the standards or norms of the larger group, or the large-group norms are brought into conformity with the minority-group behavior. To the extent that the larger community simply reasserts its position without reasonable attempt at adjustment of one of the two types just suggested, it tends to force the smaller group into secretive behavior. The situation that we now have with many adolescents and youth running counter in both attitudes and behavior to the larger-group norms tends to be socially disintegrative. It would be more so, of course, if youth did not accept many of the other generally accepted sexual norms, such as monogamy, marriage as the ultimate goal, and legitimacy of birth.

Premarital Sex Relations and Adjustment in Engagement and Marriage

The relation of premarital intercourse to successful engagements has already been discussed in Chapter 14. The relationship, although slight, favors avoidance of intercourse prior to marriage.

Various attempts have been made to test the relationship of premarital intercourse with success in marriage. We know very little about this relationship because of the secrecy surrounding the experience. One study of marital adjustment shows a slightly higher frequency of good adjustment among couples who had not had premarital intercourse, a slightly lower frequency for those who had experienced intercourse only with the future spouse, and a still lower frequency of good adjustment for those who had been more casual in their relationship.[28] According to another study, a larger percentage of divorced than of happily married men reported premarital intercourse; few women, either divorced or happily married, reported premarital intercourse and the difference between the percentage for the two groups of women was not significant.[29] A third study found a positive though low relationship between abstinence from sex relations between fiancés and their later scores on tests of marital happiness, love, general marital satisfaction, and marriage permanence.[30]

From these three studies, we conclude that many couples who had had premarital intercourse were well adjusted in marriage, and that some who had been virgins at marriage did not make good adjustments. We are not sure of the exact process that takes place when premarital intercourse and poor adjustment are associated with each other. It is possible that attitudes developing from premarital intercourse may adversely affect marital adjustment. There is also another possibility: some personality traits that cause the unmarried person to turn to sex relations may also later cause marital maladjustment. For example, the girl who, against her better judgment, permits herself to be persuaded by the ardent youth to enter into sex relations may be generally lacking in independence and self-reliance; or the young man who enters into sexual exploits to prove his masculinity may continue to exhibit

[28]Terman, *op. cit.*, ch. 12.

[29]Locke, *op. cit.*, p. 133.

[30]Ernest W. Burgess and Paul Wallin, *Engagement and Marriage* (Philadelphia: Lippincott, 1953), pp. 367–71.

traits of immaturity. Indecisiveness and immaturity would interfere with good marital adjustment regardless of whether or not there had been premarital sex experience. In determining whether premarital sex relations hinder good marital adjustment, one should know other facts besides the mere incidence of such experience. For example, how frequently and under what conditions did the experience occur: was it an adolescent adventure in response to curiosity; an unpremeditated emotional episode; a regular pattern of visitation to prostitutes; or a part of casual or serious lovemaking between those of the same social class? In other words, what meaning did the experience have for the persons involved? Had the pattern of freedom and variety of contacts become habitual and therefore likely to be carried over into marriage, where limitation of intercourse to the spouse is part of the mores?

Marital and Extramarital Sex Relations

Unlike premarital intercourse, sex within the confines of marriage is not a segmental experience either psychologically or socially. It occurs with full public approval with a socially acceptable partner. Therefore, it is integrated into the personalities of the man and woman and receives the full support of community mores. As a part of the general pattern of married life, it is discussed in Chapter 17, "Marital Adjustment."

Extramarital sex relations, like premarital, are concealed and segmental. Since these are usually related to the adjustment of husband and wife, they are also discussed in Chapter 17.

Questions

1. In most societies, what is the function of social regulation of sex activities?
2. In the United States, what function or functions do sex regulations serve?
3. Attempt to prove or disprove the statement that the United States is moving toward a semirestrictive position with reference to premarital sex relations. In the future, is the United States likely to become a permissive society?
4. What conflicting attitudes on premarital sex are still current in the United States? How would you account for the confusion?
5. What are the arguments for and against increasing the legal

grounds for abortion? What will probably be the future trend of abortion laws?

6. What inconsistencies exist among attitudes toward premarital intercourse, premarital pregnancy, teaching unmarried young people the effective use of contraceptives, and the use of abortion? Suggest several different consistent policies that would eliminate the conflicts among these attitudes.

7. Which of the outcomes of premarital pregnancy now used by unmarried women seems to you best for the woman? For society?

8. What is the relation of premarital intercourse to good adjustment in marriage?

Bibliography

BELL, ROBERT R., *Premarital Sex in a Changing Society* (Englewood Cliffs, N.J.: Prentice-Hall, 1966).

CALDERONE, MARY STEICHEN, *Abortion in the United States* (New York: Paul B. Hoeber, 1958).

CAVAN, RUTH SHONLE, ed., *Marriage and Family in the Modern World, A Book of Readings* (New York: Crowell, 1969), ch. 9.

Commonweal, 86 (June 30, 1967). Contains four articles that discuss abortion from the Catholic point of view.

DUVALL, EVELYN MILLIS, *Why Wait till Marriage* (New York: Association Press, 1966).

EHRMANN, WINSTON, "Marital and Nonmarital Sexual Behavior," in Harold T. Christensen, ed., *Handbook of Marriage and the Family* (Chicago: Rand McNally, 1964).

ELLIS, ALBERT, *If This Be Sexual Heresy* (New York: Lyle Stuart, 1963).

FORD, CLELLAN S., and FRANK A. BEACH, *Patterns of Sexual Behavior* (New York: Harper, 1951).

GEBHARD, PAUL H., *et. al.*, *Pregnancy, Birth, and Abortion* (New York: Harper, 1958).

GROUP FOR THE ADVANCEMENT OF PSYCHIATRY, *Sex and the College Student* (New York: Atheneum, 1966).

KINSEY, ALFRED C., *et. al.*, *Sexual Behavior in the Human Female* (Philadelphia: Saunders, 1953).

_____, *Sexual Behavior in the Human Male* (Philadelphia: Saunders, 1948).

LOWE, DAVID, *Abortion and the Law* (New York: Simon and Schuster, 1966).

"Premarital Sexual Behavior: A Symposium," *Marriage and Family Living*, 24 (1962), 254–78.

REISS, IRA L., *Premarital Sexual Standards in America* (New York: Free Press, 1960).

_____, "Sexual Codes in Teen-Age Culture," *Annals of the American Academy of Political and Social Science*, 338 (November, 1961), 53–62.

_____, *The Social Context of Premarital Sexual Permissiveness* (New York: Holt, Rinehart and Winston, 1967).

RUBIN, ISADORE, "Transition in Sex Values—Implications for the Education of Adolescents," *Journal of Marriage and the Family*, 27 (1965), 185–89.

Sex Education of Adolescents: An Exchange, Marriage and Family Living, 22 (1960), 317–32.

16

Love and Marriage

IN OUR CULTURE, love is regarded as the primary motive for marriage. As a rule people do not consider marriage unless they are "in love" with each other. They do not say simply that they love each other; to be "in love" is not the same thing as to love. Love itself is a sentiment that may be lifelong; it is one of many attitudes that a person holds and that for many hours of the day—many days perhaps—may remain latent and still be expressed overtly when the proper stimulus appears. The person who is "in love" is dominated by his sentiment, which tends to obscure other attitudes and to be expressed overtly in words, facial expression, and bodily posture, whether or not the appropriate stimulus is present. On occasions when it cannot be openly expressed it suffuses mental life, and daydreams replace rational thought. The person deeply in love often dreams in sleep of the loved one. Love with this pervasive, trancelike quality is what is meant by being "in love." So closely linked in popular thinking are marriage and being in love that as soon as two young people feel the excitable reaction that they identify as love, they begin to think of marriage. Adolescents of 15 or 16, whose families have marked them for college and who therefore are far from a marriageable age, may nevertheless play with the thought of marriage. Their conversation swings from the fearful idea of an immediate elopement to the more serious prospect of an engagement of five or six years. Sometimes adolescents do marry at the peak of their in-loveness, and only later become aware that marriage is not the climax to being in love but is the beginning of a new way of everyday living.

Marriage for any other reason than being in love is popularly regarded as reprehensible. The institutional marriages officially uniting two families, which have a wider usage and older history than love-marriages, are scorned as distasteful and cold. The marriage of convenience, marriage of two old people, or marriage of a young woman and an older protective man are all open to criticism as not meeting the test of two people who are in love. "Love and love alone" is the popular conception of the proper basis for marriage.

The complexities of love, the confusion between being in love and loving, the tendency to mistake sexual attraction for love, and the place of love in marriage all merit discussion.

The Development of Love

DEFINITION OF LOVE

The verb "to love" is loosely used to indicate almost any pleasurable feeling, regardless of the object or stimulus that has aroused it. People often say they love a sunset, a certain kind of food, a new dress, a special type of dancing, an attractive person newly met, or the whole human race. These same people also love, but in a different way, their close friends, parents, siblings, children, and husband or wife. In this chapter the discussion of love is limited to the interpersonal bond that unites people.

Love may be defined as a pleasurable or joyous feeling aroused by some stimulus. The capacity for love is innate. Young babies coo, gurgle, and smile when they are fondled and cuddled. The child has the innate capacity to react in a certain way when pleased, and the fondling provides the stimulus for the pleasurable reaction.

ORIGIN OF LOVE

The baby's first reactions of pleasure are in response to physical satisfactions. The baby cries when he is hungry, wet, cold, or in pain. He smiles, coos, and cuddles when he is fed, dry, warm, fondled gently. His pleasure at first is in response to stimuli provided by his own physical sensations.

Soon, however, the child's feelings of pleasure are associated not only with his comfortable physical sensations but also with the person who induces those sensations. The child associates his mother or nurse with his physical pleasure, and, after many repetitions of the association, exhibits for the mother or nurse the same pleasurable reactions that were originally called for by his physical sensations alone. As other people come into the baby's social world he will come to love them also, if they provide pleasure. By a further linking of associations, the little child may show love responses to all women who resemble the mother.

Soon the child responds to other influences than physical care and comfort. If the person whom he loves as the giver of physical comforts (the mother usually) praises him, he comes to value that also. Even before the child can understand the words, he will respond to the caressing and approving tone of the mother. This response is reinforced when the mother catches up the baby and fondles him as she praises. Thus, early love grows out of physical comfort but is soon extended to those who praise and approve. It includes dependence upon the person who provides these satisfying experiences. Since the mother also loves the baby and is pleased by his smile and caresses, the relationship becomes mutual.[1]

LOVE OBJECTS

The baby's first responses of love are general and diffuse; they are not directed toward the person who arouses them. Soon, however, the loving adult seeks a personal response from the child, who is encouraged and urged to hug and kiss the mother, to pat the mother's cheek, and to become active in cuddling. Thus, the child learns the appropriate responses to the sensation of love—the ways in which he may express love. These responses, learned from the mother, are used throughout life to express love of many types and many degrees of intensity with many different people.

The child's responses to the mother are given as a sort of reward to the mother for her care and approval. The child's interest in love relationships is primarily directed inward toward his own satisfactions and gratification of his needs and drives. He feels the need to be loved before he feels the need to give love. This narcissistic or self-centered love is characteristic of the young child, reaching a climax at about age three to five.

During childhood, the child's love begins to turn outward, first to

---

[1]For a general discussion of love by a psychologist, see Percival M. Symonds, *The Dynamics of Human Adjustment* (New York: D. Appleton-Century, 1946), pp. 520–65.

members of the family, then to friends. The process is one of mutual satisfaction. The child finds that if he likes or loves another and expresses his preference, that person will respond with love reactions to him. Thus, the person whom the child hugs, kisses, smiles upon, approves of, will in turn hug, kiss, smile at, and approve of him. The child learns that giving love secures love in return.

Children vary in the degree to which they direct their love outward from themselves. In general, the child who is amply loved and thus made to feel wanted, secure, and worthwhile in his own family, will exhibit these attitudes in his relations with others. He has been worthy of being loved; he projects this feeling on those around him and unconsciously assumes that they too are worthy of being loved.

On the other hand, the child who has been denied parental love feels insecure and unworthy. In his later extrafamily contacts he will not only carry over his feelings of unworthiness but will project that attitude upon others and assume that they too are unworthy. Such a person has neither learned the techniques of expressing love toward others nor experienced the satisfaction to be secured from the love of others. He tends, therefore, to seek satisfactions within himself. Sometimes these satisfactions are on a physical level; sometimes in fantasy he imagines himself to be lovable and beloved, as he has witnessed these reactions in those around him.

The succession of new love objects that a child acquires tends to correspond to the social contacts that he has and his own maturing personality. Thus, it is almost inevitable that the first love objects of the child are the parents, and especially the mother who cares for him. Siblings and other members of the family or household follow. When the child's contacts expand beyond the family, friends of his own age are included within the circle of his love. Since children are encouraged in direct and subtle ways to play with those of their own sex, boys tend to form close ties with other boys, and girls with other girls. At adolescence, heterosexual social contacts are encouraged and love turns in this direction. After marriage and the birth of children, love is also directed toward children of either sex.

Nonsexual and Sexual Love

NONSEXUAL LOVE

Love and sex are sometimes erroneously assumed to be identical. One of the earliest expressions of pleasure (love) that the child exhibits comes from physical fondling. Certain portions of the body are especially associated by either nature or learning with pleasant physical sensations. They include the genital areas, breasts, and lips. Many other parts of the body also are responsive to stroking or gentle tickling. In our culture, the genital areas and breasts are associated with the idea of sex, and it is contrary to the mores to stimulate or permit the child to manipulate these portions of his own body. It is permissible to stimulate pleasurable sensations in the child through other types of tactile contacts, as by kissing, patting, and stroking almost any other part of the child's body. Most people do not associate this fondling of the child with sex stimulation, so long as they avoid the forbidden areas. The child himself knows nothing of sex as heterosexual intercourse, and even if he manipulates his own sex organs places the resulting sensations in the same category as other pleasant physical sensations.

Nonsexual physical contacts are common in infancy, tend to disappear during childhood, and to appear in a new setting during adolescence. In infancy, the contacts most often are between child and parents; in childhood, playmates are discouraged from ardent physical contacts and parents tend to decrease their fondling. Thus, there is a period of freedom from physical contacts but not of freedom from loving. During this period the child expands his love objects to include many outside the family. Expressions of love are symbolic; smiles, verbal expressions, secrets emphasizing an exclusive relationship, letters, poems, valentines, and gifts replace physical fondling. In adolescence physical contacts again appear, this time between boys and girls, but often without being related to any feeling of love.

Loving—even when expressed through physical fondling—therefore is not synonymous with sex. It occurs in relationships where sex is forbidden, and it neither carries sexual connotations nor arouses sexual desires on the part of participants. All elements of erotic interest between family members other than husband and wife are sternly repressed if they appear. Tenderness is the keynote of love between parents and children, and between brothers and sisters. It also characterizes friendships, and the associations in other primary groups, such as religious brotherhoods. In a more general expression, nonsexual love becomes altruism, or the desire to aid and protect others.

SEXUAL LOVE

Sex, in its simplest terms, is an instinctive biological drive, whose aim is to dissipate a physical tension. The motive of sex is selfish, the release of one's own tensions. The sexual object is merely a means to an end. At this level, sex is often spoken of as carnal, low, animalistic, and its expression usually is kept secretive. Because of the definition of sex as unworthy, some justification must be found for it. A social justification through the birth of children was formerly the highest motivation for sex, and strictly limited to marriage. Now, with a more personal definition of marriage, sex has found a new justification—as the expression of love. Although love and sex are now closely related and the deepest experiences of love and sex may occur between the same pair, they are not identical simply because they coincide.

Sexual love may be defined as intimate love between a man and woman who find sex a means of expression for their love. When two people love each other, they tend to identify themselves with each other. Part of this identification is on a psychological level; that is, they probe each other's thoughts and feelings and seek similarities and develop new attitudes in common. They like to do things together and especially to build up activities shared by themselves alone. When a man and woman love each other, shared sex experience becomes a symbol of their identification. Our culture requires privacy and secrecy for sex relations. It also approves only of sex relations between one pair over a period of time. Intercourse therefore becomes the ultimate in exclusive shared experiences and an almost ideal symbol of identification sought by those who love each other.

Although physical expressions of love have been at a minimum during childhood, the pattern of caressing and kissing lies in the memory and experience of each person. It is to be expected, therefore, that heterosexual love will use the old means of expression. The early tentative expression of liking or love between boy and girl is a duplication of the methods used in their families. With growing intimacy and the arousal of physical sexual feelings, these familial expressions seem inadequate, and new and more intimate techniques are sought to express their growing need to identify and to express love. New patterns are easily found, although rarely through the family. Motion pictures, certain illustrated magazines, pictures in advertisements, fiction, books on the art of love, popular songs, and the accounts of slightly older young people supply by example or description additional techniques. Eventually, the physical contacts that began as a duplication of early family expression will culminate in intercourse. Thus, the sex act may become an expression of love between man and woman, just as the stroking of the baby was an expression of love between mother and child.

Infatuation

As the child comes into adolescence, his rather diffuse love for family is overshadowed by a concentration of feeling directed toward a person of the opposite sex. At first this feeling is not worthy of the name of love, for it is a type that enhances the ego; only with maturity of personality does mature love also come to full flower. Nevertheless, these first brief stirrings of feeling for the opposite sex cannot be dismissed as unimportant. They are a step in the development of love, paralleling the early dating stage when ego-satisfaction outweighs other considerations.

Brief heady attractions between two people are called infatuations. They are especially typical of adolescents or older persons of immature personality. Infatuations build up rapidly, sometimes upon the basis of a single contact. They are like a balloon that is blown to maximum tension and then either explodes from its own inner tension or slowly loses air and shrivels.

Infatuation is in part a result of the situation in which the adolescent finds himself. After years of partial or complete separation from the other sex he suddenly finds himself urged to participate in mixed activities. He looks to the next older age group for a model for his new relationship and finds love. He feels that he too should be in love, and an artificially stimulated emotion is developed to fill the void. The infatuation may have its inception from a particularly romantic dance, moonlight boat ride, or other occasion that is out of keeping with everyday experiences. It is fed by what the adolescent has read or heard of romantic love. He runs through the overt pattern of love—the flattery, the tender words, the caress—and interprets his inner response to his own behavior as love.

The infatuation grows from a superficial attraction and tends to be unrelated to the total personality, although for a time it seems to absorb all the attention of the adolescent. It caters primarily to the boy's or girl's feeling of self-importance; at last he is experiencing this thing called love. He wishes to savor it to the full, and therefore other considerations and obligations are disregarded while he gives himself over to full appreciation of his new feelings.

When the infatuation begins with a particularly romantic situation, the infatuated person associates the thrill of the situation with the person who shared it. He builds up a fantasy-conception of the other's personality, based upon the few characteristics that stood out in the moments of romance. Sometimes the infatuation is still more remote from reality and may be completely one-sided; in fact, the object of the feeling may not know that he has been singled out for attention. With young adolescents or those without adequate heterosexual social contacts, the infatuation may be entirely in the realm of fantasy. The girl may become infatuated with a movie star, collecting photographs of him in romantic poses, seeing all the pictures in which he stars, sometimes repeatedly, and daydreaming about romantic situations in which she and the star figure.

We may perhaps say that adolescent infatuation results from the need of the boy or girl to experience a personal relationship with one of the opposite sex before the personality is ready for mature love. Among older persons other motives appear. Monotony or boredom may lead to a craving for adventure or thrill without responsibility or permanence. A person with a more fundamental love relationship that has become routinized may be susceptible to the momentary attraction of a spectacular personality. Sometimes lack of a satisfactory love object leads a person to seize upon a chance relationship with someone who attracts him, whipping it rapidly up to a froth that resembles but is not identical with lasting affection. Infatuation thrives also in a situation in which the person finds himself freed from the usual routines of his life or when he is detached from his usual friends or family. The short-lived romance of the summer vacation, the lake excursion, the ocean trip, or even the college year are typical of such situations. Infatuation, therefore, is an imitation of love, often mistaken by the young person but rarely by the older one for enduring love.

Sustaining an infatuation is difficult. When it is unreciprocated, it tends to fade and be replaced by other interests. When it is mutual, it continues for a longer time, but it is never permanent. In the mutual infatuation, each builds up an idealized conception of the other person. On dates each must live up to the imagined conception held by the other and each responds to that imagined personality. It is difficult to live in this unreal world or to find a succession of romantic situations that foster the imagined concepts. Consequently, the infatuation tends to break down rapidly. The person is forced in time to realize that the object of the infatuation does not meet the imagined conception; he has faults, loses his temper, is obstinate, has headaches or indigestion, is not always immaculately clothed, or able to maintain a scintillating conversation. The contrast with the imagined person is too great to be bridged, and the person may react violently against the object of the infatuation. He may despise, shun, hate him as ardently as he previously was attracted. These feelings often are really toward himself for his foolish overevaluation of the person, but are redirected toward the other person in order to save the infatuated one's feelings of pride and self-respect.

Even when there has not been extreme overidealization, the infatuation tends to break down with better acquaintance. It was formed on the basis of one segment of the personality, the meeting of one need— that for excitement, for example. But each person has many needs and the person who seemed so perfectly to meet one need under particularly propitious circumstances may not meet other needs as they arise. The good companion for an exciting round of dancing and dining may fail completely when the person needs sympathy or encouragement or a loyal working partner for some project.

When a relationship that began with infatuation continues, it usually changes in character. The fantasy-conception is replaced by one of more realistic nature inclusive of ordinary human faults. And the object of the infatuation is able to meet many (rather than one) needs of the person. The emotional level also changes and declines in intensity. The impossible is no longer expected of the object. Thus, the object of the infatuation may come to be classified as a friend rather than the romantic ideal or perfect person and may take his place among other friends, each of whom meets certain needs of the person and from no one of whom everything is expected.

Romantic Love

Romantic love is a highly personalized form of love in which love outweighs more practical considerations. One "falls into" romantic love and thereafter one is "in love." Because of the generally excitable quality of romantic love, it has often been confused with infatuation. It resembles infatuation in that it involves fantasy and idealization of the love object. It differs, however, in being more inclusive of the whole personality and more readily adjusted to the realities of marriage. Because of the confusion of romantic love and infatuation, romantic love has been repudiated by many as not having a genuine place in courtship and marriage. More recently, the concept of romantic love has been re-examined and found worthy to be considered one (but not the only) ingredient of happy and satisfying marriage.

Romance and romantic love have received bad names from their use in popular songs, fiction, and motion pictures. The fast-moving story that begins with a chance acquaintance on the beach or at a dance, moves rapidly into love-making, and ends with marriage after an interval of a few days really concerns infatuation more than romantic love. Attitudes of infatuation, not love of any kind, are expressed in such phrases as "soul mate," "the one and only," "I've waited for you all my life," "I can't live without you," and other statements that emphasize the egocentric reactions of the one in love. These presentations, entitled romance, are now part of the cultural heritage of all young people who attend movies, read popular magazines, or watch television. They encourage infatuations, misnamed as love.

HISTORICAL DEVELOPMENT

The historical connotations of romantic love also are somewhat different from its more recent meaning. Extolled in songs, poetry, and stories and described in social histories, early romantic love had a special meaning that grew out of restrictive social contacts.

Romantic or courtly love first appeared in Western civilization in the twelfth century, to define a relationship not previously provided for in social institutions. Institutional marriage did not provide for fulfillment of personal desires or for any contact of men and women outside of marriage. Through courtly love a young knight might dedicate himself to a married woman of high status, idealizing her and receiving recognition for his deeds of bravery. The relationship was impersonal and unrelated to sex, which was regarded as carnal, whereas courtly love was idealistic and spiritual. Much later, in Europe and again against the background of institutional marriages, romantic love was used as the justification for extramarital sexual alliances based on personal preferences. In many societies the correct marriage, arranged between two families, was supplemented by unofficial heterosexual relationships in which the couple paired off because of personal attraction. The women might be of the same social class as the men, married or unmarried, or of a lower class. In each case they provided for personal emotional needs, whereas marriage fulfilled social and family obligations.

Only more recently, and primarily in the United States, has initial entrance to marriage been through the gateway of romantic love. The combination of romantic love and marriage involves an attempt to coordinate love, sex and marriage into one unit of experience between one man and one woman. In the European social situations in which romantic love developed, marriage and sex relations were contained within an official relationship, whereas romantic love (and sometimes sex) with another partner remained outside of marriage on an individualistic basis. Marriage was the public and responsible relationship, romantic love the private and nonresponsible one. Marriage was permanent and stable, a means of conserving property and rearing children to continue the family name; romantic love lasted only so long as the personal preference for each other was fervid. Marriage and romantic love were, in fact, opposed to each other, serving different needs of people. The attempt to bring two such contradictory relationships into coincidence between two people involves tremendous difficulties.

If the traditional values of marriage are to be conserved, then something of romance must be sacrificed for stability and the needs of children. If romance rules, then partners may be changed time after time as one romantic episode gives way to another. Since our culture does not approve of such episodes outside of marriage, romance involves marriage and implies, at the end of the romance, divorce and remarriage. The epitome of romantic marriages is found among some of the much-publicized couples in Hollywood, where one marriage follows another in rapid succession, with the new romance highly developed before the previous marriage has been dissolved. With fewer changes of partners and less publicity, the same procedure marks many other marriages.

Romantic Love in the United States

Although romantic love has had a long history in Europe, its growth in the United States is not an attempt to reproduce a European pattern of culture. Rather, it developed out of special situations, an important one being the breakdown of family control as segments of families—and especially young people—migrated about the country, seeking land, work, and adventure. In the young world of the frontier, strength, ingenuity, and courage were highly valued; family connections were of less importance. People were judged more by personal traits than by family ties. Young people learned to think and act independently of their families. The combination of independence and high evaluation of personal traits placed selection of a mate on a personal basis and helped lay the foundation for the full development of romantic love.

The rise of the middle class was another factor; unhampered by upper-class ideals of continuity of family lines through arranged marriage, the middle class was free to follow individual preferences in courtship; at the same time, middle-class mores forbade the culmination of romantic love in sex relations outside of marriage. Individual

choice and romantic love might thrive, but they must find their fulfillment in marriage.

In the cities another influence pulled in the same direction. The
Industrial Revolution drew people, and especially women, away from
their narrow field of activities within the walls of the home and under
the supervision of parents. Women learned to be independent not only
economically but in their thinking about problems and in their attitude
toward themselves. They played a role unrelated to the family and
conceived of themselves not solely as members of the family but as
individuals. As individuals, they were entitled to free choice of mates,
and since they were able to support themselves they could take the
time to judge each suitor and reject those who seemed personally undesirable.

The variety of occupations that gradually opened to women called
forth different combinations of personality traits. Whereas the one role
previously open to women had tended to develop uniformity of personality, the new situation gave birth to distinctive personalities. Men
might choose now not between one good potential housewife and
another, but among the housewife type, the brisk businesswoman, the
cooperative social worker, the precise schoolteacher, and many other
types.

Labor-saving machinery in the city and on the farm and the movement of much labor from the home to the factory have provided a
previously unheard-of amount of leisure. Whereas courting at one time
had to be sandwiched in between long days of work in shop or fields,
with perhaps a little more leisure on Sunday (there was no two- or
three-day week end), now the evening may start at four in the afternoon
and the week end may last from Friday afternoon to Monday morning.
Time now encourages young people to spend many hours together.

To fill these vacant hours commercial recreation provides varied
activities, many calculated to increase the personal interest between the
sexes. Public dance halls, night clubs, and privately sponsored dances
make it possible for a young couple to dance every night in the week.
Often they go alone and do not meet anyone they know. They form a
small, although perhaps temporary, primary group, gaining privacy
from their status as strangers to all others. Attention is concentrated on
each other, and the soft lights, music, and embrace of the dance make
this attention romantic in nature. Thus, even a blind date may have
romantic elements. Motion pictures are another type of commercial
recreation that, by their content, stimulate romantic interests. By identification with the actor of the same sex, boy and girl thrill to the romance of the picture. Sitting shoulder to shoulder, hand in hand—or

actually embracing—the young couple in imagination feel themselves undergoing with each other the exciting love scenes of the picture.

With the great increase in independence of young people, and their freedom to leave home and support themselves elsewhere, has necessarily gone a decline in patriarchal authority. Familial control is much less intense than in early generations and more indirect. Social pressures emanate from the family, especially toward young people who still live at home, but direct commands or prohibitions rarely exist. Each young person is free to follow his romantic interests.

QUALITIES OF ROMANTIC LOVE

Romantic love in its pure form is the idealization of the emotion and sentiment of love itself. The person—or couple—enters a state in which the supreme motivating factor in his life is a feeling of devotion to another person and, of equal or greater importance, the personal satisfaction he receives from his devotion and the response to it. Although one person may fall in love with another who does not reciprocate, normally the process is mutual or it dies out. Thus, being in love is not something that occurs to one person, but involves two people and the interaction between them.

This interaction is exclusive to the two people. Whereas friends may wish to carry out their activities with congenial companions, the romantic couple seek privacy where a chain of stimulus and response may go on exclusively between them. Since privacy makes secrecy possible, the feeling of exclusiveness is further enhanced. The privacy and secrecy make identification easy, and the two build up a feeling of oneness and of separateness from the world. They create and exist in a little world of their own, furnished with their shared memories.

Sexual impulses are involved inasmuch as romantic love normally occurs only between a man and a woman. They are usually inhibited, however, so far as direct expression is concerned. Secondary contacts, as holding hands, nonpassionate kisses, and close dancing, give a certain degree of pleasant stimulation to each. Especially in the young and inexperienced lovers, these may not be identified as sexual in origin. Romantic love is thought to be pure and to verge on the spiritual; therefore, romantic lovers find it difficult to accept in the loved one—or in themselves—an interest in physical sexual pleasures.

Idealization of the loved one is a distinguishing feature of romantic love. Although all love relations involve a loss of objectivity, romantic love becomes in high degree divorced from reality. Each member of the relationship exhibits only a part of his personality, the part that responds to the expectations of the other. If the young man has whispered to the girl that she is beautiful, she will thereafter take special care in dressing and arranging her hair when she is to be with him, although at other times she is inclined to be careless about her personal grooming. If the girl has told the young man that he is thoughtful and considerate, he will go to extreme measures to think up and carry out special little pleasures for her, although in other relationships he may be inconsiderate or may impose upon others. When only a few special attributes of the personality are exposed, it is easy for the other person to build up an idealized conception of the lover. The imagined conception of the other's personality is based upon a few desirable phases of personality rather than upon the entire personality, good and bad. Because a few characteristics are unusually pleasing, it is assumed that the entire personality of the other is on the same plane.

The process of idealization is made easier, also, by the fact that romantic contacts take place under a rather standardized set of circumstances. The lovers withdraw to themselves. Therefore, neither sees the other in ordinary work or everyday contacts with others, where less ideal traits may appear. Nor do they see each other performing the ordinary tasks of the day or their reactions to these duties. Rather, romantic love develops in an atmosphere of dim lights, moonlight, romantic songs, soft music, love stories on the screen, dancing, and personal conversation. Here there are no frustrations, no competition, no external crises.

Romantic love places a low value on such conditions as wealth or social position or success in the real world. Concentration is on personal characteristics. Thus, the upper-class girl may have a romantic affair with a boy of the lower class if the boy has certain characteristics of strength or virility that appeal to her. Or the son of wealth and culture may fall romantically in love with a girl of limited background if she has beauty and grace. Practical considerations are disregarded. The upper-class boy or girl may risk or accept disinheritance and social ostracism rather than give up the loved one.

FUNCTIONS OF ROMANTIC LOVE

Although romantic love is of cultural origin, it serves certain psychological as well as social functions.

The long period between the beginning of adolescence and the acceptable social age for marriage has already been discussed. With the encouragement given to heterosexual social contacts, some device was bound to arise to channel the personal interests of young people for each other during this period. Infatuations, merging into more permanent romantic associations with more maturity, supply this need. Stimulating, thrilling, but not necessarily taken too seriously even by those involved, romance fills the dating period and becomes a halfway station to marriage; a way to sublimate gross sexual desires.

Psychologically, romantic love serves several purposes. It has some of the elements of a flight from reality—an escape from the prosaic working world, where one is appraised by his qualities and given status through competition, into a dream world where the idealized attitude of the partner gives one the illusion of perfection in himself. The activities and excitement of romance certainly are in contrast to the orderly and often monotonous activities of the day.

Love of any type gives security and a sense of being important to someone, of being cared for and protected. Romantic love makes this feeling possible on short notice. Also it removes the sense of loneliness that the detached young person may feel and provides not only incoming love but an object upon whom to expend love. It may contribute to the lover's own sense of importance; he may hold a mediocre position in business but be a great success as a romantic lover in the eyes of the girl who is his dating partner.

At times romantic love may become the justification for sexual relations. In fact, it is easily possible for young people to mistake sexual excitement for love, although one is physical in origin, the other attitudinal. In particular, the girl may make such an error, inasmuch as her early sexual reactions are more diffuse than the man's. Because of her training she is also more likely to need a strong rationalization to overcome her inhibitions. The man, responding to her demand for lovemaking, speaks the words of love and caresses her. If intercourse is the final result, that too is interpreted as love, although the pair may be only superficially attracted to each other.

OUTCOME OF ROMANTIC LOVE

Romantic love, with its exclusiveness, its extreme idealization, its disregard for practical considerations, is an unstable relationship in spite of its intensity. The spiraling process must eventually reach a limit; the couple must at some time bring their twosome into relationship with other people and groups; comparison of the idealized person with others follows; practical arrangements break into the situation. Although the pattern of romantic love is fairly clear, there is more variation in the outcome.

1. The affair may fall apart of its own weight. The very intensity of the relationship may be fatiguing. It is not easy for boy or girl always to meet the ideal conception of the other—always to be beautiful, well-dressed, sweet-tempered, sympathetic. Other interests intrude, and each may desire the companionship of other friends of both sexes. Practical demands of work, family duties, or studying for examinations may interfere with the concentration of time and activities upon each other. Sometimes the relationship can be brought down to a lower emotional level and maintained on a more realistic basis. But often the process simply brings disillusionment and disappointment, and the lovers fall out of love as they fell into love. The very short-lived romantic affairs verge into infatuations and leave only a momentary sadness when they end. Those of longer duration, which have aroused anticipations of continued love or have involved the prospect of marriage, may leave bitterness and deep disappointment when they are no longer tenable.

2. The romantic affair may always have been tempered by contact with reality. The young man may always have been able to admit to himself that the girl had a harsh laugh but considered this amply offset by her kindness and sympathy. Therefore, his idealization does not carry him completely away from reality but involves merely an underevaluation of her unpleasant qualities and an overevaluation of her good qualities. Romantic interludes of the two alone may have alternated with group contacts, a situation that has two results. The two do not center all their interest in each other and thus expose themselves to complete disappointment if the other fails to meet all needs. Also, each is able to observe the other in relation to other people in a variety of situations and thus make a more realistic evaluation of the other's personality than is possible under exclusive relationships.

    With the tempered romance, progression may take place into the combination of romantic and companionship interests that make permanent conjugal love possible. The relationship may then continue into marriage with a change of emphasis in the quality of the love relationship.

3. The highly keyed romantic love may continue into marriage without conversion to conjugal love, a situation that almost inevitably leads to conflict. The realities of married life are incompatible with the idealized conceptions of undiluted romantic love.

Love in Marriage

Romantic love has frequently been attacked as an unstable basis for marriage. It has been said that its overidealization breaks down under the impact of daily living, and that it is a fundamental cause of conflict and divorce. On the other hand, this point of view has been contested. It has been pointed out that with the loss of practical reasons for marrying and the high expectation of finding in marriage great happiness and relief from all frustrating experiences, love is perhaps the only bond strong enough to hold a couple together. If we assume the need for love on a personal basis, confining that love to marriage has strengthened marriage at a time when other marital functions are very weak.[2]

It has also been pointed out that too much emphasis has been placed on cultural similarities as the basis for a stable marriage. Individualism and a chance for personality growth are now also part of our ideal of marriage.[3] They require freedom of choice of mates and an appreciation of the spouse's needs and abilities on the part of each partner to the marriage. Romantic love provides for personal selection of the mate and evaluation of each other's needs and potentialities.

MATURE LOVE

The love that functions well in marriage is not the extreme type of romantic love. It is less demanding, less exclusive, and more tolerant. This love has been dubbed conjugal love by some writers.[4] It may also be called mature love.

Mature or conjugal love is compatible with the realities of marriage and later of family life inclusive of children. Thus, it is a type of love that makes it possible for the wife to accept her husband as still lovable when his chin is covered with a stubble of beard, when he is dirty and sweaty from a bout with the lawnmower or car, when he is cross because of some frustrating office experience, and when he is filled with anxiety over an unsettled business deal. It is also the type of love that

[2]The historical development of romantic love as well as an appraisal of its present function is given in Hugo G. Beigel, "Romantic Love," *American Sociological Review*, 16 (1951), 332–34.

[3]William L. Kolb, "Sociologically Established Family Norms and Democratic Values," *Social Forces*, 26 (1948), 451–56.

[4]Evelyn Millis Duvall and Rueben Hill, *When You Marry* (New York: D. C. Heath, 1945), pp. 170–71.

makes it possible for the husband to love his wife in spite of stringy hair, the nausea of pregnancy, the occasional poorly prepared meal, the sharp-tongued retort caused by anxiety or disappointment. And it is the type of love that holds husband and wife together and to their children when the baby cries throughout the evening or demands food or other care in the middle of the night; when parents must refuse enticing invitations in order to remain at home with young children; when the purchase of a new car must be delayed in order to straighten a youngster's teeth. These are the situations that romantic love has not prepared the young couple to manipulate successfully.

Romantic love remains in mature conjugal love but is strongly supplemented by other attitudes and types of interaction. There is still a strong element of idealization: each believes he has the best spouse in the world, or at least the best one for him; shortcomings are generously overlooked, and desirable traits are valued and praised.

The romantic ideal of exclusiveness remains so far as sexual love of another adult of the opposite sex is concerned, inclusive of physical contacts and sexual relations. But jealousy of contacts with those of one's own sex or of the married couple with other couples is eliminated. It must be recognized that this ideal is not always achieved in marriage. One or the other may supplement the marital relationship with an extramarital affair on either a physical or romantic basis; or one or the other or both may find they are no longer in love with the spouse, and a divorce follows.

Sexual impulses, present but inhibited before marriage, now find free expression. This situation in itself changes the quality of the love between the two, in that it removes a need to divert sexual interest into other channels or to seek expression in secondary ways or by subterfuge. The freedom to make love reduces the need for secret meetings or for love songs, dancing under soft lights, or presents of flowers. Such symbols of love tend to be attached only to special sentimental occasions, such as anniversaries, birthdays, or holidays, which formerly were the occasions for especially romantic episodes.

Replacing some of the romantic love and supplementing what remains is the growth of a new relationship that usually has its inception before marriage during the period of serious courtship and engagement. The new love is directed not toward the emotional responses and self-satisfactions of romantic love but toward the building of a mutual pattern of life, not limited to the present but extending into the indefinite future. Personality traits that are conducive to joint living gain in value, such as dependability, self-reliance, cooperativeness, sympathy, and unselfishness. The shift in emphasis is symbolized by the girl's willingness to forgo expensive dates in favor of a growing bank account and the man's interest in the girl's ability to make a home. Glamorous dates provided by the young man and beauty and grace on the part of the girl are no longer sufficient. The emotions of this new relationship are less highly keyed than those of romantic love. They are represented by such words as companionship, partnership, mutual helpfulness, sympathy, tenderness.

Mature love takes more account of reality, such as poverty or moderate income, the difficulties of adjusting differences in religious beliefs or social-class standing, differences or conflicts in moral standards, even such small items as differences in tastes for food, types of houses, hours for rising and going to bed. It is recognized that these and similar differences cannot be glossed over but will influence the daily interaction and mode of living of the couple.

Mature marital love provides many of the satisfactions that come from romantic love, but usually in a more permanent fashion. Security is part of the picture in that each feels both beloved and able to express his own love. The very fact of being loved and chosen for marriage increases the self-esteem of each, and therefore often self-reliance and ability. Protectiveness is mutual; there is always someone to lean upon for a short space of time.

In some ways mature conjugal love at its best is a correlation of several types of love: the narcissistic love of the child and the adolescent, in that each partner receives a glow of satisfaction from having been selected for love; nonsexual outgoing tender love that seeks to benefit the love object; sexual love; and romantic love.

Importance of Love in Present-Day Marriage

Love of some type is extremely important in present-day marriage. Many of the practical reasons for marriage have been removed by outside agencies that have taken over necessary functions formerly performed in the family. The personal attachment undoubtedly is the chief bond that holds husband and wife together. Not only have utilitarian functions disappeared, but the former stabilizing effects of supporting institutions, such as the church and primary community, have declined and new controls have been slow in developing. The one strong remaining bond is the personal relationship.

Questions

1. List as many popular uses as you can of the verb to love.
2. Discuss the relationship between the child's innate capacity to love and the social development of this capacity.
3. Are sex and love necessarily found together? Why does popular thought in America tend to associate them with each other?
4. Discuss the statement that infatuations are typical of adolescents or older persons of immature personality.
5. What is the difference between the present conception of romantic love in the United States and its historical connotation in Europe?
6. Why is romantic love not an adequate basis by itself for an enduring relationship?
7. How can romantic love be integrated into a stable marital relationship?

Bibliography

BIEGEL, H. G., "Romantic Love," *American Sociological Review*, 16 (1951), 326–34.

CAVAN, RUTH SHONLE, ed., *Marriage and Family in the Modern World* (New York: Crowell, 1969), ch. 8.

HORTON, DONALD, "The Dialogue of Courtship in Popular Songs," *American Journal of Sociology*, 62 (1957), 569–78.

MONTAGU, ASHLEY, ed., *Meaning of Love* (New York: Julian Press, 1953).

PRESCOTT, DANIEL A., "Role of Love in Human Development," *Journal of Home Economics*, 44 (1952), 173–76.

REIK, THEODOR A., *A Psychologist Looks at Love* (New York: Farrar and Rinehart, 1944).

ROUGEMONT, DENIS DE, *Love in the Western World* (New York: Harcourt, Brace, 1940).

SYMONDS, PERCIVAL M., *The Dynamics of Human Adjustment* (New York: D. Appleton-Century, 1946), pp. 520–65.

CHAPTER $I7$

Marital Adjustment

As THE dating-engagement sequence moves to its logical conclusion, couple after couple change their status from single to married. Women begin to make the transition in the late teens and push rapidly into marriage in the early twenties; by the late twenties the process is almost as complete as it will ever be. The process for men is similar, but begins in the twenties. The concentration of marriages in the early adult years has been typical of the United States for many years past, with a tendency for the median age of marriage to decline. For first marriages performed in 1966, the median age of grooms was 22.8 years and of brides 20.5 years.[1] One may fairly say that adjustment to marriage is the most important project of the girl in her late teens and early twenties and second only to vocational placement for the young man in early and mid-twenties.

This chapter deals with stages I through V of the family life cycle described in Chapter 11, that is, with the family of procreation. It focuses on husband-wife roles and interaction. The breakdown of this relationship is discussed in the following chapter. Parental roles are treated in a special chapter. To prevent repetition of material, the student should review Chapter 11 with special reference to stages I through V.

[1]*Statistical Abstract of the United States, 1967* (Washington, D.C.: Government Printing Office, 1967), p. 64.

The Nature of Marital Adjustment

Adjustment may be briefly defined as the process whereby people work out the satisfaction of their needs in all areas—physical, psychological, and social. Since deviation from cultural norms brings great disapproval, it is scarcely necessary to add that the process goes on within the range of freedom of personal behavior that is allowed by the social norms. Marital adjustment falls within this definition but has several special aspects because of the nature of marriage in our culture.

EXCLUSIVENESS OF MARITAL RELATIONSHIP

Marriage tends to be an exclusive association of two people. If the man and woman who marry have not already freed themselves from dependence upon their parents, they are expected to do it forthwith. Many jokes are made and cartoons drawn about the young wife who, after a spat, goes home to mother; or the young husband who still prefers his mother's cooking. It is popularly conceded that the young married couple have a right to an independent home where they are removed from close association with the parents of either. Needs previously satisfied through associations with those of greater maturity or younger or older siblings of the same or opposite sex are now to be satisfied through association with one of the opposite sex and approximately the same age. The couple are expected to finance their marriage, make their own decisions, consolidate their social life, and work out their interpersonal adjustment. In no other human relationship is so much expected from two young, relatively inexperienced people.

Marriage tends to be a pair relationship so far as friendships are concerned. The husband is not expected to meet his emotional or social needs through association with other women, nor the wife with other men. Each may continue to have friends of the same sex, but friends of the opposite sex must be shared with the spouse; they must be family friends rather than individual friends. Thus, most emotional and many social needs must be satisfied through one person, a limitation not imposed by the mores prior to engagement and marriage.

The husband has one outlet that many women do not have—his occupation. But occupational relationships are expected to be impersonal. They may satisfy needs for productive or creative activity and contribute to status and personal prestige; but wifely jealousy and public disapproval are quickly aroused if the husband becomes emotionally attached to any female fellow worker. The wife also has a special outlet, shared with the husband, but more especially her own, through her close relationship with her children. Her satisfactions here are affectional in nature and supplement her relationship with her husband, which is also affectional.

Even when there are children, the ideals of American marriage place allegiance between husband and wife on a higher level than parent-child attachments. It can truly be said that the deepest emotional satisfactions as well as social, financial, and household matters belong to the married couple as an exclusive pair.

Reciprocal Relationship

The exclusive nature of marriage gains significance when one realizes that husband and wife must be so nicely matched that each receives this maximum satisfaction for personal needs from the other. Not only does each receive satisfaction, but each must be able to give satisfaction to the other. People scorn the henpecked husband who gives but does not receive, and pity the browbeaten wife who serves her husband without affection or respect from him. Our present ideal of marriage is democratic and equalitarian: both husband and wife are entitled to a rich personal life; neither is expected to be resigned and self-sacrificing to the exclusion of compensating satisfactions from the other.

The democratic nature of the relationship also calls for mutual compromise and tolerance of any differences in attitudes or habits. Neither is expected to have a position of status or dominance so far superior to the other that one would make all the concessions to reach harmony and agreement and the other none.

Dynamic Quality of Marital Adjustment

Modes of interaction between husband and wife that yield mutual satisfaction tend to become habitual and predictable. Each learns to respect the deeply held convictions of the other; and each learns the little signs of restlessness and dissatisfaction that call for minor modifications of conduct. Each learns the personal happiness to be achieved by making the other happy and gaining the other's approval. Nevertheless, the relationship rarely becomes static. Both external changes that affect the marriage and personality changes require constant adjustment in the pattern of interaction.

The external changes may lie within the family itself, such as the birth of a child that necessitates a new marital relationship. Adjustment of the husband to a new job, or removal of the family to a new community of a different type from the old may have its counterpart in a new pattern of marital relationship. As the husband achieves new occupational responsibilities, much of his time and interests, previously wife-centered, may separate him from his wife. The wife must adjust to this situation. Migration from a rural to an urban environment, previously discussed, may involve reorganization of the husband-wife relationship and roles. The frequent separation of the young pair when the husband is called into military service creates its own peculiar problems of curtailed interaction.

Personalities also may change with the passage of time. The older dictum that the personality pattern is set by the time a child is four or five years of age is only partially true in a constantly changing social scene. New experiences destroy earlier personality formation, arouse new needs, and stimulate the mind to new interests and goals. Many couples who seemed well adjusted at one stage have found themselves at odds after one has fought in the front lines of a war, or attended college, or when both have attended college but different types. If marital adjustment is to survive personality changes, it must continue to be dynamic and to match change in one spouse with change in the other.

Personality changes are stimulated also by our present-day concept that marriage and family life should leave the door open for personality development not only of children but of husband and wife. Sometimes husband and wife are able to maintain their identity of interests and goals and to change in unison. But it also often happens that one becomes fixed at a certain stage of development while the other changes. Then the reciprocal quality of giving and receiving satisfaction for needs is threatened.

Marital adjustment, therefore, calls not only for coordination of personal qualities at the time of marriage but for a dynamic process of interaction to strengthen and maintain the relationship. Maintenance of coordination is not achieved by a laissez-faire attitude. Uncoordination is very likely to move into disintegration of the marriage unless deliberate effort is made to restore coordination when husband and wife begin to lose a sense of identification.

Personal Qualities Related to Good Marital Adjustment

Various measures of marital adjustment have been used in different studies: the estimation by husband or wife of his or her happiness; the estimate by others of the degree of happiness of a given marriage; agreements between husband and wife on matters pertaining to the marriage; and absence of conflict between the spouses. In general, the measures have to do with the subjective feelings of husband and wife about their marriage, or with more objective attempts to find the amount of agreement between husband and wife. Many studies have been made in the attempt to uncover the personal characteristics of men and women that contribute to good adjustment, however it is measured.

PERSONAL MATURITY

In Chapter 12, certain traits of the mature personality important for marital adjustment were discussed: integration of divergent attitudes and desires; narrowing of heterosexual interests to one person in conformity with our mores; self-reliance; and capacity for outgoing friendship. The same chapter also emphasized the necessity for the adolescent to free himself from childlike dependence upon his parents and to accept the adult masculine or feminine role. Failure of husband or wife to reach maturity before marriage places a heavy burden upon the spouse, who often must carry responsibilities for both that normally are equally shared. Examples of situations arising from immaturity are suggested here, garnered from case studies and observation:

The husband who secretly dates girls and the wife who flirts outrageously with men to reassure themselves—he of his virility, she of her youthfulness. Although married, they have not outgrown their adolescent dating attitudes.

The individual who seeks in the spouse a replica of a parent who has indulged and "spoiled" him and who expects the spouse to duplicate the parent's behavior.

Irresponsibility in spending.

The wife who expects her husband to leave his work for trivial reasons, such as to stay with her during a thunderstorm.

The husband who resents the attention his wife gives the new baby.

There is some evidence that girls are more likely than boys to come to adulthood with their attachment to their parents relatively unbroken.[2] The differential training of boys and girls encourages boys to become emancipated from their parents and permits them to have privacy in personal affairs, whereas girls are kept under the protective dominance of the parents. At marriage the girl finds it difficult to adjust

[2]Mirra Komarovsky, "Functional Analysis of Sex Roles," *American Sociological Review*, 15 (1950), pp. 508–16.

to the greater independence expected of a wife. In some instances she may adjust by assuming a dependent relationship to her husband, but the trend of the times is toward greater equality between husband and wife. The wife therefore suffers from the loss of her close attachment to her parents, and the husband resents the attachment, feeling that his wife's loyalty should be turned toward him.

When, as occasionally happens, the husband is the one who has been unable to detach himself from his parents, the tension is still more acute, since traditionally the husband has been independent whether or not his wife was, and a parent-dominated husband therefore runs counter to the social norms. An extreme attachment may lead to situations such as the following:

The mother disapproved of marriage for her sons and daughters, especially for the eldest son, who bought her many luxuries. When the second son married, he established his home near that of his parents. Each evening he visited his mother and often would lie on the bed and cry, saying he wanted to remain there and sleep in his old bed. The mother would comfort him and tell his wife to go on home, saying that her son would be all right in a few weeks. After a few months the son's wife left him, and he returned to his mother's home. Later she was reconciled with her husband, who succeeded in detaching himself to some extent from his mother. After ten years of marriage the son still drove twelve miles every other evening to see his mother. When the eldest son was in his thirties he married, against the wishes of his mother. The mother accompanied him and his wife on their honeymoon, during the course of which she made personal purchases amounting to some $150, which the son, as usual, paid. Upon their return home the mother wished to dictate the policies of her son's home, a procedure that his wife resented. As friction grew, the son sided with his mother. When the marriage was only two months old, the son was having lunch with his mother every day and spending several nights a week at his old home. Soon the son had agreed to help his mother buy a home. At this point the wife decided that her husband's attachment to his mother was so much greater than his attachment to her that harmony would never be possible; she therefore left her husband and secured a divorce.

PERSONALITY TRAITS

Most people are able to meet the ordinary stresses of life in a realistic manner, without undue fears and anxieties or retreat into fantasy. They approach life in a serene and optimistic mood and are friendly toward other people. Many people may be overly sensitive about some one or two aspects of their lives. A few have so many difficulties in accepting and adjusting to the usual strains of life that they are classified as neurotic. Their neurotic traits are symptoms of unresolved conflicts and unrelieved frustrations, which reveal themselves in exaggerated emotional reactions, fears, anxieties, compulsions, and symbolisms. Examples are the wife who dissolves into tears at the slightest opposition, who has unusual fears of pregnancy and childbirth, or who collects small china objects (symbols of babies) instead of having children; the husband who persistently refuses to allow his wife to work because he fears others will think he cannot support her; the parent who becomes unduly anxious and protective of adolescent children because of his own unresolved adolescent anxieties and guilt feelings, particularly with reference to sex; the husband's angry avoidance of household tasks because in his youth his mother forced him to do "girls' work"; the husband who periodically deserts his wife when some crisis arises; the wife who uses ill health or picks around at her food as a way of getting attention. It is impossible to list all the various ways in which neurotic attitudes show themselves.

Such neurotic reactions are related to happiness and adjustment in marriage. A careful study by Terman led him to conclude that unhappily married women were subject to wide emotional swings; they worried needlessly, lacked self-confidence, were overly sensitive, timid, and easily discouraged. They were unable to do painstaking work, and, finally, they were egotistic.[3] In compensation for some of these characteristics, they joined many societies or escaped through daydreams. They tended to be radical in social attitudes.

In contrast, happily married women were serene, optimistic, kindly, and cooperative. They were steady workers and sought conventional activities.

Unhappily married men were gloomy, ill at ease, and overly sensitive. They compensated by withdrawal or dominance of other people. Work habits were sporadic. They tended to hold radical attitudes.

Happily married men were even-tempered and stable, cooperative, and kindly in attitude toward their inferiors. Socially, they tended to be unself-conscious and were able to function in group relationships with initiative and responsibility. They tended to be conservative, cautious, and thrifty, and to uphold prevailing conventions.

Terman's study indicates that the mature, personally well-adjusted, conventional person tends to find happiness in marriage more often than the moody, insecure, unintegrated one. Terman tends to assume that these characteristics existed before marriage; it might also be

[3]L. M. Terman, *et al.*, *Psychological Factors in Marital Happiness* (New York: McGraw-Hill, 1938), chs. 6 and 7.

true, however, that the marriage relationship itself had produced or accentuated some of the reactions.

Another study, of 1,152 married individuals, corroborates some of Terman's findings. Low but positive correlations were found between self-estimates of marital happiness and the following traits: even-tempered, +.30; usually in good spirits, +.35; self-confident about own abilities, +.27. Conversely, negative correlations were found between marital happiness and the following reactions: often feel lonesome even when with others, —.31; often feel miserable, —.31; bothered by useless thoughts, —.30; and experience periods of loneliness, —.47.[4]

COMPATIBILITY

Although complete harmony is probably not to be expected in any human relationship, a high degree of harmony and compatibility is consistent with good marital adjustment. Compatibility is usually measured in studies of marriage by first locating areas of disagreement between husband and wife. The report of a recent Detroit study includes types of disagreements found among urban and suburban families.[5]

In response to an open-ended question about the chief matters of disagreement between themselves and their husbands, Detroit wives supplied an average of about two areas of disagreement, with a few naming three or four areas. Money was most frequently mentioned; a fourth of the wives gave money as the chief source of disagreement and another 18 per cent as a source of lesser disagreement. At every stage of the life cycle, money was an outstanding problem, except in the first few years of marriage before children were born; at this stage only 10 per cent of wives reported money disagreements, probably due to the double income when husband and wife were both employed.

Second in frequency as a source of disagreement were problems concerning children, primarily discipline. Sixteen per cent of wives regarded this as the chief source of disagreement and another 13 per cent

---

[4]E. W. Burgess and L. S. Cottrell, Jr., *Predicting Success or Failure in Marriage* (New York: Prentice-Hall, 1939), p. 56. The coefficients are tetrachoric coefficients of correlation; happiness was stated in five degrees running from very happy to very unhappy.

[5]Robert O. Blood, Jr., and Donald M. Wolfe, *Husbands and Wives: The Dynamics of Married Living* (Glencoe, Ill.: Free Press, 1960), ch. 9. The study was based on a systematic probability sample of families, with the wife being the only informant. Information was secured by structured and controlled interviews of an hour or more.

as a less important source. Disagreements over discipline reached a peak in the years when children were adolescents and then declined abruptly.

The third most frequent source of disagreement was recreation—either the type or the amount of time devoted to it. It was classified by 16 per cent of wives as the most important and by another 14 per cent as a more limited source of disagreement. Disagreements were especially numerous among the newlyweds.

Fourth in frequency were personality clashes, reported as the chief source of disagreement by 14 per cent of wives and as a secondary source by another 14 per cent. These disagreements also arose most frequently in the prechild period of marriage.

Of only minor importance as the cause of disagreements were in-law problems, roles of husband and wife, politics, religion, and sex. All these sources of disagreement were mentioned by a larger percentage of newly married wives than by those of longer marital experience.

Not all Detroit wives found disagreements in their marriage. Fifteen per cent said they and their husbands had none.

A rather free interpretation of this portion of the Detroit study leads to the conclusion that only a minority of married couples have no disagreements that seem of sufficient importance to report—or perhaps in some cases too serious to reveal. Some disagreements seem inherent in most American marriages.

An earlier study in the 1930's points up the relation of agreements to marital happiness. Burgess and Cottrell found high correlations between happiness and agreement on the following activities: handling finances, recreation, friends, dealing with in-laws, engaging in outside interests together, and leisure-time preferences.[6] In certain other areas, agreement was of less importance for happiness: agreement on caring for the baby and matters of conventionality were only moderately correlated with degree of happiness, and agreement on religious matters and table manners were of still less importance. All of these areas of interaction, however, had some correlation with happiness. When disagreements existed in more than one area, the chance of happiness was reduced. Many agreements made for happiness, many disagreements for unhappiness.

Incompatibility may also relate to more fundamental values in marriage. Children, now regarded as a matter of choice, constitute such a value. The meaning of sex to each partner and the desire of the wife for paid employment are other areas in which issues may exist that are

[6]Burgess and Cottrell, *op. cit.*, pp. 50–51, 53, 72.

difficult to adjust. When husband and wife disagree, each may feel justified in his position; nevertheless, tension and discontent may result.

In general, the failure to find congeniality does not indicate personal maladjustment of husband or wife so much as a failure of the two to dovetail their interests, values, and needs. It is conceivable that, unhappy together, the poorly matched pair might each find happiness if mated with someone who more nearly agreed with him and met his needs.

PERSISTENCE OF UNSUCCESSFUL MARRIAGES

Although the divorce rate is high, especially in the early years of marriage, not all unsatisfactory marriages end in divorce.

A study by LeMasters carried out intensive interviews with 36 couples (72 persons) whose marriages had been unsuccessful for at least 10 years but who had not separated or divorced.[7] It was true that the couples suffered from disillusionment with the romantic process and disenchantment with the marriage. Many of the individuals had acute symptoms of personal disorganization. Men most often exhibited alcoholism, occupational disorganization, and extramarital affairs; women, psychosomatic illness or neurotic-psychotic behavior. These symptoms were characteristic of less than half of the persons in the study.

LeMasters suggests several reasons why these couples remained together. Early in their marriage, the couple hoped to solve their problems. As children were born, parents remained together to give the children a home. In some cases, community position that might be damaged by a divorce or financial complications kept the marriage intact. In a few cases, hostility or the battle for dominance or "getting even" seemed to hold the couple together, as each struggled to keep the upper hand.

For many, personal disorganization was warded off by a number of devices. Women turned to their children or to community or church service for compensation. Men buried themselves in their jobs. Husband and wife might also develop different time patterns to reduce the number of hours spent together. LeMasters also calls attention to the fact that some persons were apparently better able to tolerate frustration than others. Some directed hostility away from the spouse.

[7] E. E. LeMasters, "Holy Deadlock: A Study of Unsuccessful Marriages," *Sociological Quarterly*, 21 (1959), pp. 86–91.

Sexual Adjustment

Sexual relations have been heralded by some writers as the keystone to marital happiness and are popularly thought to make or break the marriage. It is natural that such an attitude should arise, since sex is a special ingredient of marriage that differentiates it from other social relationships. We know that many young people are poorly informed on sexual matters and that fears and anxieties related to an unwanted pregnancy sometimes inhibit full sexual expression. Nevertheless, after the initial adjustment is made, sex becomes part of the total complex of interaction that constitutes married life. Lack of adjustment in other activities and interrelationships may be as fatal to the marriage as sexual maladjustment. It is true, however, that sexual adjustment is a very sensitive indicator of general adjustment, and dissatisfaction or conflict over sex relations may be symptomatic of other tensions. Good sexual adjustment requires as a background a sympathetic and cooperative relationship. Tension over handling of finances, quarrels about recreation or religion—in fact, conflict of any type—carries over into the more intimate relationships. Sexual adjustment, therefore, may be studied in its primary aspects in terms of biological drives and attitudes directed toward sex; and as a secondary reaction to adjustment in other areas.

PRIMARY SEXUAL ADJUSTMENT

Basically, intercourse rests upon normal organic structure and ability to function. In a limited number of cases sexual adjustment is prevented or made difficult because of some organic factor, such as structural malformation, disease, or temporary illness. These conditions are rare and if severe often prevent marriage.

The strength of the sexual drive differs among individuals, although it is not always clear whether the difference has a biological base or is related to attitudes toward sex. Whatever the origin, it is a factor in frequency of intercourse and in the sense of personal satisfaction secured. On the biological side, sexual drive among men decreases with age. Kinsey's report on marital intercourse of married males, covering 3,342 cases, shows a regular decrease in mean frequency of intercourse per week from 3.75 for married males aged 16 to 20, to 0.83 per week for ages 56–60.[8] The Kinsey study of women shows, as would be expected, a very similar decline of intercourse in marriage. Kinsey concluded from his data that the decline was related to the biological waning of the sexual drive in men and not to a similar change among women. He came to the conclusion that for both biological and social reasons men reached the peak of sexual desire early in life, whereas women were inhibited in youth but developed greater drive and experienced fewer inhibitions as they gained maturity and experience. These discrepancies in desire between husband and wife at a given age place sex relations in the category of activities where a specific effort is often needed to achieve mutual satisfaction.

Terman's study of happiness in marriage includes the relation of marital sex relations to happiness, as measured by a score based on a series of questions designed to reveal the degree of happiness.[9] For men aged 30 to 40 and their wives, low happiness scores were accompanied by infrequent intercourse whereas high happiness scores and high frequency of intercourse were found together. However, the association between happiness and frequency of intercourse was not complete. A minority of couples with low happiness scores had high frequency of intercourse. Terman's interpretation was that biological urges and habit were factors in frequency of intercourse that sometimes were more important than congeniality of husband and wife. He suggests also that in some cases frequent intercourse may continue regardless of unhappiness. The gratification of physical drives may come to be the one satisfying means of communion between husband and wife; or one mate, feeling that the marriage is becoming stale, may deliberately use sexual allure as a means of reviving interest. We may conclude, therefore, that in a general way frequency of intercourse is related to happiness, but that in some instances urgency of drives or persistence of habit overrides congeniality.

The above findings indicate that a more subtle approach to sexual adjustment than frequency of intercourse is needed. Terman throws some light on the relation of sexual satisfaction to happiness. By comparing frequency of intercourse with desire for intercourse, he discovered that happiness of both husband and wife was greatest among couples who both felt that their sexual needs were fully satisfied. When one received full satisfaction while the spouse was either undersatisfied or satiated, happiness was lower for both partners. When both

[8]Alfred C. Kinsey, et al., *Sexual Behavior in the Human Male* (Philadelphia: Saunders, 1948), p. 252; *Sexual Behavior in the Human Female* (Philadelphia: Saunders, 1953), ch. 9.
[9]*Op. cit.*, pp. 267–355.

were either undersatisfied or satiated, the happiness scores were still lower for both. Frequency of intercourse was less important than mutual satisfaction. Sexual relations thus appear as a mutual experience, related to happiness in the degree to which they give satisfaction to both husband and wife. Neither frequency nor individual satisfaction, but mutual satisfaction is of most importance to marital happiness. Thus, if either husband or wife has a strong sexual drive and the other a weak drive, complete happiness may be difficult to achieve.

Primary sexual adjustment is related to attitudes as well as to biological drives. It seems probable that attitudes toward sex are more favorable for adjustment at present than in the past. Although sex education is still meager and faulty, the trend is toward more complete information for both women and men and toward acceptance of intercourse for both as a natural and constructive experience. Nevertheless, for some couples, and especially wives, ignorance and inhibitive attitudes are a deterrent to easy adjustment.

FRIGIDITY

A topic of current discussion is frigidity, by which is meant the inability of the woman to have an orgasm or localized physical reaction to intercourse. Frigidity does not imply that she cannot have intercourse, but merely that she does not have an acute physical reaction. Many women have been happily married and have produced children without experiencing an orgasm. In extreme cases of frigidity the woman may wish to avoid intercourse itself, but as currently used the term does not apply to aversion to sex so much as to inability to respond fully. As women have learned more about sex, they have come to expect a full physical reaction equal to that of their husbands. Orgasm has become a symbol of full satisfaction; the wife who does not experience it feels deprived of her rights. Anxiety and intense effort to achieve it only add to the difficulty. The feeling of frustration may carry over to the husband. He may be accused openly or by implication of failing to bring his wife to a climax, and to the accusation he may respond by anger or a feeling of guilt. The many popular books on premarital training emphasize the importance of the husband in aiding his wife to full satisfaction. This great concern with frigidity and lack of orgasm, therefore, is not limited to the wife's feeling of deprivation, but may become a contentious subject leading to lack of satisfaction (and consequent diminution of happiness) for both husband and wife.

Total frigidity implies that the woman is never able to experience an orgasm.[10] Kinsey's study clearly shows that only 10 per cent of women married for 20 years or more had never reached orgasm. For the remainder, some combination of failure and success was typical of the sexual life of married women. Half of married women experienced orgasm during the first month of marriage (but not necessarily with every contact). By the end of the first year, 75 per cent were experiencing orgasm some of the time. Year by year the percentage who experienced orgasm at least some of the time increased, with the highest percentage coming when the women were between 31 and 40 years of age; after this age the percentage of contacts resulting in orgasm began to drop slowly.

From the above figures it is evident that very few women (10 per cent) are completely frigid. At the same time less than half of the nonfrigid women always or almost always experienced orgasm, the percentage increasing from 39 per cent during the first year of marriage to 47 per cent at the twentieth year. For any five-year period, from 11 to 17 per cent did not experience orgasm but had done so in the past. For most women, failure to respond is not a permanent condition.

Inability to have orgasm at any specific time may be related to fatigue or illness, anxieties and worries, conflict between husband and wife, or other temporary conditions. Continuous failure to respond may be related to physical factors but most often seems to be related to persistent personality problems, such as a deeply ingrained aversion to sexual contacts, subconscious fears or hates, or self-centered attitudes (narcissism). Frigidity often is symptomatic of other problems that must be solved in order to overcome the frigidity. The problems cited above are of a psychological nature. Vincent, on the basis of counseling clients who came with the complaint of frigidity, looked to the interaction between husband and wife for an explanation.[11] Frigidity was found to be symptomatic of the following interactional situations: misunderstandings and differences in attitudes between husband and wife of different social classes, which found their expression in sexual maladjustment; absence of physical love; overemphasis by the wife on techniques of love-making, when love is defined as synonymous with sex; lack of understanding between husband and wife; lack of self-respect on the part of the wife; and lack of the wife's understanding of the husband's reasons for sexual expression. Among these cases, frigidity was a symptom of a variety of difficulties in interaction between husband and wife.

[10]Kinsey, et al., *Sexual Behavior in the Human Female*, pp. 352–54, 371–91.
[11]Clark E. Vincent, "Social and Interpersonal Sources of Symptomatic Frigidity," *Marriage and Family Living*, 18 (1956), pp. 355–60.

Sexual Adjustment in Relation to Adjustment in Other Areas

Sexual adjustment tends to be affected by the degree of adjustment in other phases of the husband-wife relationship. Husbands and wives generally happy in their marriage are able to overlook some deficiencies of drive or attitude and to adjust satisfactorily in their sexual relationships. A pattern of satisfactory sexual relations that has been established during a period of general agreement and congeniality may, however, be destroyed if other tensions arise. Bitterness, anger, and disappointments affect this most intimate relationship. A mechanical carrying through of intercourse without active cooperation or evident enjoyment on the part of one will lessen or prevent satisfaction for the other. Sometimes the situation becomes still less personal, and sex is used as a technique of control. Either husband or wife can refuse to participate or can carry out the act in such a way that the other's satisfaction is lessened, or his ego feelings are attacked. The wife, for example, can use sex as a weapon: she can simulate orgasm to give her husband a feeling of achievement, or withhold any overt indication of pleasure in order to dominate or humiliate him.[12] In these situations, the crux of the problem is not in sex adjustment but in collateral interaction.

Extramarital Sex Relations

Marital infidelity is highly censured in American society. The monogamous ideal and the demand for legitimacy of children are both attacked by extramarital sex relations. The growing tolerance toward premarital intercourse does not extend to condoning of nonmarital sex relations by married people. All states recognize adultery as a cause for divorce and all but five provide criminal penalties for two persons living in adultery.

Nevertheless, Kinsey is able to report that from 27 to 37 per cent of married men studied by him at each five-year age period admitted having had extramarital intercourse at some time or other during their married lives.[13] Among married women, the percentage having extra-

---

[12]A. H. Maslow, "Self Esteem (Dominance-Feeling) and Sexuality in Women," *Journal of Social Psychology*, 16 (1942), 281.

[13]Kinsey, *et al., Sexual Behavior in the Human Male*, pp. 585ff.; *Sexual Behavior in the Human Female*, ch. 10.

marital sex relations increased from 7 per cent among married teen-agers (which includes approximately half of married women) to 26 per cent by age 40. Because of the stigma attached to extramarital sex behavior, Kinsey felt that the above percentages represented under-statements. Among men, lower-class men exceeded higher-class men in the proportion having extramarital sex relations; the differences were less marked among women.

Among both men and women, extramarital sex relations account for only a small proportion of sexual relations. The events are sporadic and infrequent, often incidental to special situations, as a trip away from home or a vacation. Long continued association with one partner is rare, although there is rarely complete promiscuity.

Interpretation of extramarital sex relations is much more difficult than a mere chronicling of incidence and frequency of experience. The secrecy that surrounds the experience is a tremendous obstacle to ade-quate study. Here and there, however, appear fragmentary explana-tions, usually based on cases that have come to the attention of mar-riage counselors or psychiatrists. They are offered here as suggestions rather than as conclusive diagnoses of the situation.

One explanation that has been advanced is that the biological drive is so strong and demands such variety of contact that a single partner is inadequate. The marital sex relationship may be satisfactory and mar-riage itself may be highly valued as the setting for security, children, and permanency, but limitation of all sexual activities to one person may be seriously frustrating.[14] Before marriage, it is freely recognized, interest centers first on one person, then on another; with marriage permanent fixation on one person is expected. But actually, it is con-tended, many people cannot adapt themselves to strict monogamy. They desire a variety of contacts. Divorce and remarriage is not the solution, for soon another change would be desired. Moreover, the person wants other values to be found in marriage. The solution, though it must be carried out furtively, is marriage plus extramarital sex relations.

An extremely simple biological explanation that attempts to account for differences in extramarital relations of men and women is offered by Kinsey,[15] who states that the male is easily aroused sexually by a variety of stimuli provided by conversations, pictures, advertisements,

[14]This point of view is advanced by C. C. Bowman, "Cultural Idealogy and Heterosexual Reality: A Preface to Sociological Research," *American Sociological Review*, 14 (1949), 627–29.

[15]Kinsey, *Sexual Behavior in the Human Male*, p. 589.

or memories. The average female, on the contrary, is rarely aroused except by actual tactile stimulations, such as love-making. The male in his ordinary round of life is therefore constantly aroused sexually, whereas the female usually is aroused only under special conditions of physical contact.

The sociologist is more inclined to look for explanations in the different social norms for men and women that permit men a limited area of freedom that is denied to women; or in social-class folkways and mores whereby sex is interpreted as a natural activity in the lower classes but as a moral issue in the higher classes; or, finally, in differences in ethnic culture that permit or restrain extramarital sex relations.

The psychologists and psychiatrists offer still other interpretations, related to personality problems of the individual or psychological maladjustment between husband and wife. One writer states that the emotionally immature man, among other types of infantile behavior, follows "patterns of compulsive sexual promiscuity (the so-called 'Don Juan Complex') in an effort to compensate for latent feelings of masculine inadequacy."[16] Maslow would take promiscuous sex relations out of the field of sex satisfactions altogether and interpret them as motivated by a desire for reassurance of continued attractiveness, the thrill of novelty, unconscious hostility for the spouse, and often the desire to conquer the opposite sex by "collecting scalps."[17] Such activities are especially likely to indicate insecure persons, who, while pursuing thrill and reassurance outside of marriage, enjoy a comfortable sexual relationship with the spouse.

Summing up psychological explanations, Seward states that extramarital sexual interests, whether they remain in fantasy or are carried out, should be regarded as symptoms rather than causes of marital maladjustment.[18] Some psychiatrists interested in marital adjustment urge that when extramarital relations of one spouse are discovered by the other, the discoverer should not immediately take offense or interpret the action as a personal affront; rather the entire marital relationship as well as the personality make-up of the digressing partner should be subjected to expert study.[19] The behavior, although it violates marital mores, may be symptomatic of situations that can be adjusted.

[16] Judd Marmor, "Psychological Trends in American Family Relationships," *Marriage and Family Living*, 13 (1951), 146.
[17] *Op. cit.*, p. 279.
[18] Georgene H. Seward, *Sex in the Social Order* (New York: McGraw-Hill, 1946), p. 204.
[19] John Levy and Ruth Munroe, *The Happy Family* (New York: Knopf, 1938).

Roles of Husband and Wife

The discussion thus far has centered on the interplay between husband and wife as individuals, but this interaction takes place in a larger context of social expectations of how husband and wife will function together. When these expectations or roles are clearly defined and coordinated in the society, each person learns as he matures what is expected of him in attitudes and behavior in his different group and institutional contacts. Expected roles have already been described in connection with social class. At present, however, roles are in a state of flux with alternate roles open to wives, especially in the middle class, where a state of uncoordination seems to exist. One role problem, therefore, centers in the choice of roles made by the wife and the way in which she coordinates them. A second problem concerns the coordination of the wife's roles with those of her husband.

ALTERNATIVE ROLES FOR WIVES

When women first began to work in offices and factories, their employment role usually did not conflict with the customary wifely roles of homemaker and mother. For the most part, only unmarried women worked, usually leaving their jobs when they married. Since those early days, many changes have occurred that increase rather than diminish the probability of role conflict. Employment of married women without children is now approved without question, but employment of mothers is a subject of controversy.

TRENDS OF EMPLOYMENT FOR WOMEN

In 1965, 37 per cent of all women, both single and married, aged 14 and over were employed.[20] In 1950, the percentage was 32; in 1940, 28; in 1930, 24; in 1920, 23; in 1900, 20; and in 1890, 18. Women now constitute 35 per cent of the entire labor force. They are a permanent and integral part of the labor force and could not be withdrawn without serious damage to production.

[20]*Statistical Abstract of the United States, 1967* (Washington, D.C.: Government Printing Office, 1967), p. 222; *1960 Handbook on Women Workers*, Women's Bureau No. 275 (Washington, D.C.: Government Printing Office, 1960), pp. 4–6.

The percentage of women who are employed is not the same for all ages or all types of marital status or all stages of the family life cycle. In some situations, the employment status is the dominant one; in others, it is subordinate to other roles. A generalized picture of the distribution of roles through the family life cycle follows:[21]

1. Before marriage, 75 per cent of women are employed.
2. Married, wife aged about 20–24, no children, 60 per cent employed.
3. Married, wife aged about 20–24, children under school age, 20 per cent employed; this percentage is increasing.
4. Wife aged about 30–45, children in school, 40 per cent employed.
5. Wife aged about 45–54, children independent, 40 per cent employed.
6. Wife approaching retirement, aged about 55–64, 25 per cent employed.
7. Retired, wife aged 65 and over, 7 per cent employed.

The above percentages are for women living with their husbands. Among widows and divorcees, the percentages of employed women are higher.

Some women are employed all through the course of married life. The wife's problem with roles is less the selection of which role to follow than the coordination of roles held simultaneously at different stages of the family life cycle. The day is past when "careers for women" were regarded as an alternative to marriage and motherhood. Now a young woman may prepare for the most exacting careers requiring many years of preparation without discarding the expectation of marriage. Most women do not have careers in the sense of a commitment to one type of occupation requiring the investment of time, money, and concentration of effort for preparation; rather, they enter work requiring routine preparation or training on the job. The semiprofessional, skilled, and semiskilled work that they do can be found in many communities; it may be abandoned and resumed; it can be fitted into full-time or part-time hours as the demands of homemaking and motherhood necessitate. If her husband moves from one locality to another, the wife resigns from her position and readily adapts her skills to the opportunities of the new location. She is not committed to either a career or homemaking, but is ready to combine and compromise.

[21]National Manpower Council, *Womanpower* (New York: Columbia University Press, 1957), pp. 10, 68–69; *1958 Handbook on Women Workers*, Women's Bureau Bulletin No. 266 (Washington, D.C.: Government Printing Office, 1958), p. 33; *1960 Handbook on Women Workers, op. cit.*, pp. 36, 40–45.

The Role of the Husband

The role of the husband has not been made the subject for research as has the role of the wife, nor are many articles written attempting to define his role. There is general acceptance that his familial function is to work as steadily as possible after appropriate preparation; to marry and give love, kindness, practical care, and material support to his family. He is condemned if he does not work or if he neglects, refuses to support, abuses, or deserts his wife and children. He may choose between one vocation and another; but he is not faced, as the woman is, with choice between fundamentally different and opposed roles. He may hold simultaneously a familial and a vocational role. The continuance of his roles rests, however, upon coordination with the role of his wife. The generally accepted masculine role, as outlined above, assumes that the wife will play the daily domestic role of homemaker and child-rearer. To the extent that this role is changed for the wife, the husband's role is disturbed and a new correlation of roles is demanded.

Coordination of Husband and Wife Roles

The importance of compatibility between the roles of husband and wife has been recognized for some time. A systematic analysis of the traditional and the new roles of women as they affect the relationships between husband and wife, made by Kirkpatrick some 30 years ago, is still of great value.[22] He says that three roles are open to the married woman, each of which carries its own privileges and obligations. If the obligations are not met by the wife and the privileges are not granted by husband and children, conflict and disorganization threaten.

The first role discussed is the wife-and-mother role, which entitles the woman to the privileges of economic security, including alimony in case of divorce, respect of the husband and children in her capacity as wife and mother, a certain amount of domestic authority, the loyalty of the husband, and the gratitude of the children. The obligations are bearing and rearing children, making a home including the actual tasks of housekeeping, economic subordination to the interests of the husband, financial dependence upon him, and a limited range of outside interests and activities. This centralization of interests and activities in the home marks the wife-and-mother role as the traditional one of the married woman.

[22]Clifford Kirkpatrick, "Ethical Inconsistencies in Marriage," *International Journal of Ethics*, 46 (1935–36), 444–60.

A second role is the companion role, which carries the privileges of sharing the pleasures of the husband, receiving a romantic emotional response, being admired, being allowed funds for dress and recreation, and having leisure for educational and social activities. The obligations are to maintain beauty, entertain the husband, make social contacts that are advantageous to him, and be an object of pride for him. This role has been called parasitic by less considerate writers, since the wife is more or less of an ornament in her husband's household, and a luxury inasmuch as she produces very little either in money or services.

The third role, that of the partner, implies that the wife works and is economically independent; she has equal authority with her husband in finances and performs only her fair share of domestic services; she has equal social and moral liberty with her husband. The role obligates her to contribute to the support of the home and children, in proportion to her income; to refuse alimony in case of divorce except for the support of children; to ask no special privileges and make no appeal to chivalry on the basis of being a woman.

In any one of the three situations, harmony would prevail if husband and wife agreed upon the role that each would play and if each then played the role consistently. Sometimes, however, roles are not well coordinated. The husband, let us say, has a preconception of what his role in the family should be; he comes into marriage with an expectation that he will have a certain status, perform certain functions, and receive certain responses from his wife. He may find that he is unable to meet these expectations; his role as he actually lives it out may be very different from his preconceived idea. A discrepancy that may amount only to slight irritation or may reach the proportions of a definite mental and emotional conflict then exists for him. His wife, likewise, may find herself unable to fulfill her expectations and play the role she had idealized beforehand as the one for her to play after marriage. She, too, may experience tension or inner conflict. Since one factor in the failure to reach role expectations usually is the failure of the spouse to play the supporting role, resentment and antagonism may be directed against the spouse.

In other situations, role conflict arises because external circumstances prevent the playing out of an anticipated role. Death or prolonged illness of the husband, his inability to find employment, or his induction into the armed services may create a situation in which it is impossible for the wife to play a wifely role; she may then be forced to assume a more aggressive wage-earning role, the headship of the family and position of authority. If, on the other hand, the wife has established a satisfactory career for herself, the serious illness of a child may force her to abandon it for the maternal role. The husband likewise may find himself confronted with external circumstances that prevent his playing his preferred role. The demands of his business may necessitate his absence from home for long periods of time or absorb so much time and energy that his family is neglected as less urgent. In each situation the person whose role is initially disturbed must adjust to a new role, and in response to this change the spouse must also adapt himself to a new role if coordination is to be maintained.

Even when the essential roles are agreed upon between husband and wife, one or the other may not be desirous of playing the chosen role consistently. Kirkpatrick points out that the wife may wish to claim the privileges of one role but not the obligations; for instance, if she works she may wish to retain the money for her own use instead of contributing proportionately to the family needs.[23] Or she may wish to play the wife-and-mother role but neglect the care of the children or evade household duties. On the other hand, the husband may expect his wife to accept the obligations of two roles, perhaps to work and at the same time carry full responsibility for household management, which the husband should share. Kirkpatrick concluded that women tend to seize the privileges of several roles, whereas their husbands emphasize the obligations of their wives' roles.

Decision-Making

Another approach to the relative importance of the roles of husband and wife and to the phases of family life in which they are most dominant is through what is sometimes called "the power structure" of the family. The relative "power" of husband and wife may be measured through a study of who makes decisions pertaining to family life. Formerly, the chief decision-maker undoubtedly was the father, with the mother customarily supporting his decisions and the children falling into line. When the status of women rose through increased legal rights and community activities, and especially when women began to contribute to the family income, the role of the husband and father as the chief decision-maker came into question. On the basis of their study of Detroit marriages, Blood and Wolfe came to the conclusion that the right to decide rests with the marriage partner who has the most resources to contribute in a given area.[24] At one time the husband brought into the family not only goods and income but also education, knowledge of the world, and skills in meeting community obligations.

[23] *Ibid.*
[24] Blood and Wolfe, *op. cit.*, ch. 2.

He was best able to make decisions. At present, the wife also has wide-spread knowledge through education; she also has skills; and she often contributes to income. She is also capable of making decisions.

As decision-making was realigned between husband and wife, two situations became apparent: (1) there are separate areas in which men and women dominate in making decisions, and there are still other areas in which they share the task; (2) no one pattern of decision-making is uniform for all families.

The husband is most clearly in authority on matters pertaining to his work. In the Detroit study, 90 per cent of men decided for themselves what job they would take; in the other 10 per cent, wives had some influence. A Florida study showed that in 98 per cent of the cases the husbands filled the role of chief income-provider, but were assisted by their wives in 38 per cent of the cases.[25] In the Detroit study, although 39 per cent of wives made decisions about their own jobs, 26 per cent of wives were controlled by the husband's decision, and in 32 per cent the husband was influential. The husband, then, is dominant in making decisions and assuming responsibilities about his own economic role, and is influential in decisions regarding his wife to a greater degree than she is with reference to his economic functions.

Decisions about expensive and relatively durable equipment, including a car, more often were vested in the husband than the wife, although in a minority of cases the wife had a share in decisions, according to the two studies. Shopping for daily needs fell more heavily upon the wife. In Detroit, decisions that were almost equally shared included vacations, housing, and medical matters.

From the Detroit and Florida studies, one may conclude that decisions and responsibilities regarding money for family use rest most heavily upon the husband, those concerning daily household expenses and children are primarily part of the wife's role, while other decisions are almost equally shared. However, in every area of decision-making some families do not follow the general pattern. Families are able to be flexible and perhaps assign decision-making to the one best qualified to act authoritatively. The Detroit study also showed that in only 1 per cent of families were all decisions made by one person. Even though husband or wife may dominate in certain areas, the total pattern is one of sharing. An overall view, however, showed that the dominance rating of the husband exceeded that of the wife. One may conclude

[25]Theodore B. Johannis, Jr., "Participation of Fathers, Mothers, and Teenage Sons and Daughters in Selected Family Economic Activity," *The Coordinator*, 6 (September, 1957), 15–16. The study is based on data from 1,027 high school sophomores from working-class families.

that the husband's role is slightly more authoritative than the wife's but that there is a strong trend toward equalitarianism in many areas.

HOUSEHOLD TASKS

Family roles are also shown by who performs daily tasks. According to the Detroit study, the traditional outdoor jobs of mowing the lawn, shoveling the sidewalks, and making repairs belonged to the husband.[26] The wife had her specialized functions: getting the husband's breakfast, straightening the living room when company was coming, doing the evening dishes, and similar work. The Florida study concentrated upon the care of children.[27] In every phase of child care, the mothers were more active than the fathers, but in every phase some fathers were active. Rearing children was definitely a shared activity, although each parent specialized in different areas. The father was relatively more active in teaching children ethics, facts, and skills, helping them choose a vocation, and in matters of discipline. The mother was relatively more active in the daily routines of getting children out of bed, fed, dressed, and so on.

COORDINATION ON A FAMILY BASIS

Authority and roles are not coordinated on a social basis; that is, there is no uniform pattern running throughout our society. Neither are the roles in conflict. Each family is privileged to work out its own assignment of roles. Perhaps the social expectation now is that husband and wife should be responsible for certain necessary tasks pertaining to the family, but should be free to devise their own methods of handling these responsibilities.

Prediction of Marital Adjustment

Adjustment has been discussed in terms of interaction between husband and wife as they work out a satisfactory companionship that meets the essential needs of each. Hazards to adjustment have been

[26]Blood and Wolfe, op. cit., ch. 3.

[27]Theodore B. Johannis, Jr., "Participation by Fathers, Mothers, and Teenage Sons and Daughters in Selected Child Care and Control Activity," *The Coordinator*, 6 (December, 1957), 31–32.

pointed out, some of which existed prior to marriage, others of which became apparent in the early years of marriage. With the discovery of factors that were either favorable or unfavorable to adjustment came the possibility of constructing marriage prediction scales. Like any other type of prediction, marital prediction scales forecast the future (type of future marital adjustment) from facts known in the present (prior to or in the early years of marriage).

A necessary element in prediction is a decision on what to use to indicate good adjustment—that is, what is being predicted? How can well-adjusted people be identified? Another necessity is an assemblage of premarital items known or thought to be related to the degree of marital adjustment.

Four mammoth research projects were carried out in the 1930's and 1940's and less extensive ones have followed in the effort to pinpoint predictive factors.

Ernest W. Burgess and Leonard Cottrell launched a study in the 1930's that yielded responses from 519 men and women.[28] They used as the criterion of marital adjustment a scale based on agreements between husband and wife, confidential relationship, feeling of satisfaction with the marriage, and presence or absence of neurotic traits. Through experimentation with a long questionnaire given to the same couples, Burgess and Cottrell identified 24 items for men and 20 for women, present prior to marriage, that distinguished poorly adjusted from well-adjusted couples.[29] These items were given weights that might be added into a total score. The questionnaire could then be given to unmarried persons and their scores compared with the scores of the married group; it would be assumed that their future marital adjustment would have the same degree of success as the adjustment of the married couples who made the same scores on the questionnaire. The questionnaire thus became a scale for prediction of marital adjustment as measured by the marital adjustment scale.[30]

The product moment correlation between the marital adjustment scale and the prediction scores was .51. Nevertheless the prediction scale could not be used successfully for individual prediction.

[28]Burgess and Cottrell, op. cit., pp. 64–65.

[29]Ibid., pp. 275–83. A revision of the prediction scale is given in Ernest W. Burgess and Harvey J. Locke, The Family (New York: American Book Co., 1950), pp. 760–71.

[30]It is important to note that prediction is made only in terms of the criterion of successful marriage that is used. The Burgess-Cottrell marital adjustment scale emphasizes agreements, congeniality, and evenly balanced personality. Their prediction scale therefore predicts attainment of this type of marriage relationship.

Table 15 shows the relationship between predictive and adjustment scores. Since the relationship is expressed in percentages the table serves as a table of probability. At the highest level of prediction scores, 80 per cent had very high adjustment scores; it might be assumed, therefore, that the chances were 80 out of 100 that persons who, prior to marriage, made prediction scores of 700–779 would make a very good marital adjustment. At the low end of the prediction scores, 75 per cent had very low adjustment scores; it might be assumed that persons making low scores before marriage could look forward to three chances out of four of making a poor marital adjustment. The middle range of scores, especially those between 380 and 539, have almost no predictive value.

Another prediction study that was carried out concurrently with the Burgess-Cottrell study was made by Terman.[31] Later, Burgess and Wallin studied the possibility of predicting from adjustment

TABLE 15

RELATION BETWEEN THE PREDICTION SCORES AND MARITAL ADJUSTMENT SCORES

Premarital prediction score	Marital adjustment score				No. of cases
	Very low	Low	High	Very high	
700–779	0.0%	10.0%	10.0%	80.0%	10
620–699	1.5	12.1	25.8	60.6	66
540–619	5.8	21.9	29.2	43.1	137
460–539	27.6	29.4	25.9	17.1	170
380–459	39.8	31.1	15.1	14.0	93
300–379	57.2	25.7	11.4	5.7	35
220–299	75.0	25.0	0.0	0.0	8
TOTAL					519

SOURCE: Ernest W. Burgess and Leonard S. Cottrell, Jr., *Predicting Success or Failure in Marriage* (Copyright 1939 by Prentice-Hall, Inc., New York), p. 284. Reprinted by permission of the authors and publisher.

during engagement to adjustment in marriage.[32] Locke attempted to predict good adjustment in marriage by comparing a group of divorced with a group of happily married people.[33] The last of these studies was published in 1953. None was sufficiently precise to make prediction

[31]Terman, *op. cit.*

[32]Ernest W. Burgess and Paul Wallin, *Engagement and Marriage* (Philadelphia: Lippincott, 1953).

[33]Harvey J. Locke, *Predicting Adjustment in Marriage: A Comparison of a Divorced and a Happily Married Group* (New York: Holt, 1951).

possible for an individual. All throw a great deal of light on background and personality items that are associated to some degree with successful marriage adjustment. One commentator on the whole field of prediction of successful marriage believes that the effort to predict has reached about as high a level of success as is possible with the techniques used in these early studies.[34] Limited studies continue, usually based to some extent on the early mammoth studies but less global in their approach and more sharply focused on specific types of marital adjustment or specific types of relationship between premarital variables and marital success. The objective is no longer limited to practical efforts to predict for individual marriages but is centered on wider theoretical aspects of marital processes.

Questions

1. How does the marital pair-relationship differ from other pair-relationships, such as parent-child, employer-employee, or friend-friend?

2. What can immature or neurotic persons do to increase their chances of happiness in marriage?

3. According to the Detroit study, what are the four chief sources of disagreement between husband and wife?

4. What are the most significant factors in good sexual adjustment in marriage?

5. Contrast the prevailing attitudes toward extramarital sex relations with the attitudes toward premarital sex relations. How would you account for the difference? If premarital sex relations gain more social approval, would you expect extramarital sex relations to increase in frequency and to gain in approval?

6. How can the married woman handle the conflicting roles that are open to her?

7. Why has the role of the husband changed from the traditional one to his current roles?

8. What are the possibilities and the limitations of prediction scales for marital adjustment?

[34]For a thorough discussion of prediction tests, see Charles E. Bowerman, "Prediction Studies," in Harold T. Christensen, ed., *Handbook of Marriage and the Family* (Chicago: Rand McNally, 1964), ch. 6.

Bibliography

BERNARD, JESSIE, "The Adjustment of Married Mates," in Harold T. Christensen, ed., *Handbook of Marriage and the Family* (Chicago: Rand McNally, 1964), ch. 17.

BLOOD, ROBERT O., and DONALD M. WOLFE, *Husbands and Wives: The Dynamics of Married Living* (New York: Free Press, 1960).

BOWERMAN, CHARLES E., "Prediction Studies," in Harold T. Christensen, ed., *Handbook of Marriage and the Family* (Chicago: Rand McNally, 1964).

BURGESS, E. W., and L. S. COTTRELL, JR., *Predicting Success or Failure in Marriage* (New York: Prentice-Hall, 1939).

_____, and PAUL WALLIN, *Engagement and Marriage* (Philadelphia: Lippincott, 1953).

CAVAN, RUTH SHONLE, ed., *Marriage and Family in the Modern World* (New York: Crowell, 1969), chs. 12, 13, 15.

CUBER, JOHN F., and PEGGY B. HARROFF, *The Significant Americans, A Study of Sexual Behavior among the Affluent* (New York: Appleton-Century, 1965).

HANSON, DONALD A., and REUBEN HILL, *"Families Under Stress,"* in Harold T. Christensen, ed., *Handbook of Marriage and the Family* (Chicago: Rand McNally, 1964), ch. 19.

KEPHART, WILLIAM M., "Legal and Procedural Aspects of Marriage and Divorce," in Harold T. Christensen, ed., *Handbook of Marriage and the Family* (Chicago: Rand McNally, 1964), ch. 23.

KINSEY, ALFRED C., et al., *Sexual Behavior in the Human Female* (Philadelphia: Saunders, 1953).

_____, *Sexual Behavior in the Human Male* (Philadelphia: Saunders, 1948).

LOCKE, HARVEY J., *Predicting Adjustment in Marriage: A Comparison of a Divorced and a Happily Married Group* (New York: Holt, 1951).

SPIEGEL, JOHN P., "The Resolution of Role Conflict within the Family," in Milton Greenblatt, Daniel J. Levinson, and Richard H. Williams, eds., *The Patient and the Mental Hospital* (Glencoe, Ill.: Free Press, 1957).

TERMAN, LEWIS M., et al., *Psychological Factors in Marital Happiness* (New York: McGraw-Hill, 1938).

"Women and Work," *Marriage and Family Living*, 23 (1961), entire issue.

CHAPTER $\boxed{18}$

Marital Disintegration and New Adjustment

WHEN HUSBAND and wife fail to find happiness in marriage or when some circumstance destroys their marital adjustment, a process of marital disintegration may replace the adjustment process. If disintegration runs its course, the marriage eventually will be terminated as a functional relationship. Although the psychological and social disunity is not necessarily followed by physical separation of husband and wife, separation often follows disintegration. When the separation is made final by a divorce, the marriage has ended as a contractual relationship and the couple are free to remarry.

Rates and Trends of Divorce

From 1944 through 1948, 400,000 or more divorces occurred each year, reaching a peak in 1946 with 610,000 divorces in one year. From 1949 to 1960 the number was slightly below 400,000 and since then slightly above.[1] Annulments are negligible, in 1963 numbering 12,701, which is equivalent to 3.0 per cent of divorces and annulments combined.

[1]*Divorce Statistics Analysis, United States—1963*, Public Health Service Publication No. 1000, Series 21, No. 13 (Washington, D.C.: Government Printing Office, 1967). For convenience the term divorces is used to refer to the combined figures for divorces and annulments.

Legal separations as distinct from divorces are not reported, and, of course there are no general figures for the informal separations that occur each year.

Divorce rates usually are stated in one of three ways: the number of divorces per 1,000 of the total population; the ratio of divorces granted in a given year to the number of marriages contracted in that year; and the number of divorces per 1,000 married females 15 years of age and over. 1) In 1963, divorces were equivalent to 2.3 per 1,000 of the total population of all ages.[2] Since each divorce involves two persons, twice 2.3 or 4.4 per 1,000 of the population were divorced in that year. 2) The number of divorces of 1963 equaled 26 per cent of the marriages of that year. This statement does not mean that the divorces were granted to the same couples who were married in 1963, as many of the couples had been married much longer. It does mean, however, that for every 3.8 marriages taking place that year, one marriage was dissolved. Nor is it valid to predict from these figures that 26 per cent of all marriages will end in divorce, since divorce rates differ with age of the population and would not be the same for all ages. 3) Divorces granted in 1963 affected 9.6 per 1,000 of married women aged 15 years and over (and a somewhat similar proportion of married men).

The above figures represent the record for one year. Among the population at any one time are not only the divorced of that year but also the divorced of many years previous. The remarriage rate for divorced people is high, however, so that the number living in a state of divorce at any one time is much lower, in 1966 amounting to 2.2 per cent of all males and 3.1 per cent of all females aged 14 and over.

The divorce rates in the United States have shown a long-term upward trend, with a temporary decline during the depression of the 1930's. The highest rates in the country's history came after the end of World War II, as Figure 23 shows. Since the war the rates have leveled off, with only minor variations from year to year. This rate is still higher than at any time prior to World War II.

The Disintegration Process

In spite of the frequency of divorce and the public tolerance (discussed in Chapter 2), it usually is a painful experience. Most people

[2]*Statistical Abstract of the United States, 1967* (Washington, D.C.: Government Printing Office, 1967), p. 33.

marry with great expectations of happiness and a successful life together; but divorce calls for a change of attitudes toward oneself, the
partner, and the marriage itself. Moreover, since the public image
of marriage is of a lifelong relationship, there are no ceremonies, rituals,
announcements, or ready-made modes of transition comparable to
those already in the culture to guide the couple into marriage. Aside
from the formalities of the legal proceedings, each divorcing couple
must work out their own adjustments. This flexibility may be to the
advantage of many couples and is in line with our policy of flexibility
in marital adjustment. For many people, however, the experience is
so unguided that it creates great insecurity and temporary personal
confusion.

Although husband and wife may not be completely happy, the marriage continues to function so long as each looks to the other for the

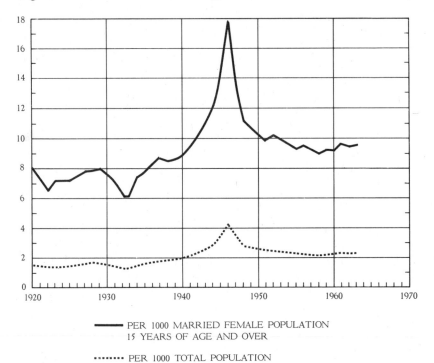

PER 1000 MARRIED FEMALE POPULATION
15 YEARS OF AGE AND OVER

•••••••• PER 1000 TOTAL POPULATION

FIGURE 23   *Divorce Rates: United States, 1920–63.*

SOURCE: *Divorce Statistics Analysis, United States, 1963,* Public Health Service Publication No. 1000, Series 21, No. 13 (Washington, D. C.: U. S. Department of Health,
Education, and Welfare, 1967), p. 5.

satisfaction of some fundamental needs and there is a workable degree of unity in daily patterns and future goals. In some marriages, however, estrangement enters, and husband and wife begin to deviate from the mutual-interaction process. They enter a process of disintegration that tends to be the reverse of the adjustment process. Identification is gradually lost, and roles become highly individuated and uncoordinated. The two partners no longer look to each other for satisfactions and happiness; they no longer consistently try to achieve better adjustment. As they turn away from each other, they begin to seek satisfactions outside the marriage. They may resort to other people—relatives, children, casual associates—for those functions usually performed in conjunction with the spouse. Or they may become personally disorganized or neurotic, seeking fulfillment of needs through fantasy, escape through illness or occasionally suicide, solution of fears through extreme anxieties, or bolstering of the ego through suspicion or braggadocio. They may evidence both the rejection of marriage and personality disorganization. One spouse may exhibit one set of reactions, the other a different pattern. Such estrangement, such denial of the marriage as a mutual relationship and a source of satisfactions, is the beginning of disintegration.

Since even in poorly adjusted marriages some progress usually has been made toward identification and unity, the reverse process typically creates emotional conflict in each individual. Some of the more obvious indications of this conflict are quarrels followed by reconciliation; temporary separations, sometimes made under the guise of visits to friends or relatives; or applications for divorce that are withdrawn and refiled. Gradually, however, the reconciliations become less frequent, the alienation deeper, the estrangement more open and complete.

Illustrations of the disintegration process are contained in the cases that follow. They are arranged according to the degree of identification that had been attained before the disintegration process began.[3]

Sometimes marriages occur with little or no sense of unity and identification between the pair, to be followed by early divorce. Forced marriages into which one or both enter unwillingly are often of this type. The first case describes a forced marriage following discovery that the girl was pregnant. Although the couple had been dating for some time, the relationship had not progressed to the courtship stage. The girl, but not the man, was emotionally involved; this one-sided relationship had not produced identification. It can scarcely be said, therefore, that a process of disintegration occurred. Nevertheless, the

[3]Unpublished cases.

girl at least had to adjust to the termination of her social relationship with the man which followed the divorce.

Jane, the middle child among five siblings, came from a lower-class family. Her father drank constantly so that the family was on relief most of the time. When Jane was 14 her father was accidentally killed. His death was a great shock to the family, as he had received their affection despite his shortcomings. Two of Jane's sisters were married, following pregnancy, a circumstance that did not disturb the family. At the age of 16 Jane fell in love with a Mexican boy several years her senior. He was from a large farm family and was upwardly mobile: intelligent, nicely dressed, a good dancer and athlete, and popular in school. Jane took the initiative and eventually succeeded in securing dates with Manuel. Soon after his graduation the two eloped and were married, as Jane was pregnant. It was agreed that Jane would remain in another town because of the gossip, while Manuel returned home. But Jane became homesick and returned, hoping for a reconciliation with Manuel. He refused to live with her and persuaded her to file suit for divorce.

In the following case, also, marital adjustment was not accomplished before the process of disintegration began. In this case divorce is very similar functionally to a broken engagement that occurs when a couple find themselves unable to identify with each other and unify their lives socially. Jim and Martha found that continued identification with their parents interfered with marital identification and unity. Their brief courtship also prevented development of premarital identification or the making of future plans with reference to parental relationships.

Jim and Martha grew up in a small mining community in the South, where they attended the same school and church and belonged to the same social groups. Martha's family was closely united, with all members of the family rallying around the protection and care of an invalid mother. Jim also belonged to a strongly unified family organized on a patriarchal basis with a strict but benevolent father. Jim and Martha began to date while in high school and by their senior year were in the courtship process. The relationship was broken, however, and each began to date others. A few months after graduation Martha moved with her parents to a distant city. Jim found work in his home town. His role in the family was abruptly changed when his father died suddenly, and at the age of 19 he became the head of the family charged with the support of his mother and a younger brother and sister.

Subsequently Jim and Martha began to correspond, and the following summer Martha returned to the small town to visit her relatives. She and Jim passed rapidly through a renewal of dating and courtship and were married within three months. Martha remained in the small town, with Jim and his family. Martha soon began to worry about her invalid mother in the distant city. She wanted her husband to move to the city, where she insisted he could earn enough to support them and also send money home to his mother. Jim suggested that Martha should visit her mother but then return to him. He felt that as head of the family he should decide where they would live. He also was just as reluctant to leave his mother as Martha was to be separated from her mother. There were many bitter arguments. Friends contributed conflicting advice. Finally Martha decided to return to her parents, a move that hurt Jim deeply.

Efforts at reconciliation followed, with Jim making a long visit to Martha but still refusing to move to the city. Martha suggested divorce as the solution, a proposal that Jim at first refused to consider. After an interval of time, however, he agreed and the couple were divorced.

In the case that follows husband and wife had widely different conceptions of marriage. Although the courtship lasted almost two years, they had not visualized the adjustment problems that would arise. In the face of objections from the wife's parents, the two were married without a planned wedding. The first two paragraphs of the case describe the differences in family backgrounds.

Mack had been reared in an orphanage and therefore lacked childhood experience in a normal family situation. He had attended only grade school, but work experience and reading had made him an interesting and competent person. In his twenties he married; he and his wife had two children, and were divorced. Four years after the divorce he met Edith. At this time his children were being cared for by relatives. He was a traveling man, accustomed to hotel life and touch-and-go contacts with groups that drank and spent money loosely; he ran up bills with little feeling of obligation about paying them promptly. He was not habituated to family life nor to a responsible father role. There are no available details about the first marriage and divorce.

Edith was reared in a family consisting of the parents and four children. They lived in a single house with a large yard. The family was well unified, sharing in work and recreation. There was no extravagance in spending; money was carefully used, and savings went into family projects. Edith had long earned her spending money. Unpaid bills and the use of money for drinking were unknown to the family pattern of living. Edith had had some college training as a librarian and was interested in education. She was 12 years younger than Mack.

[*Although the couple made an effort to coordinate their roles, they were not successful, and their roles continued to be highly individualized.*]

At the time of their marriage Edith did not fully appreciate the effect that different family experiences might have on their marriage. She expected to have children; she expected Mack to save his money and buy a home. Mack attempted to adjust to her ideas. He secured work in the city where Edith lived, and the two moved into an apartment; a year and a half later, at Edith's insistence, they moved into a house and took Mack's two children. Edith and the children liked each other, and their relationship was friendly and compatible. Mack, however, was not able to adjust to Edith's conception of marriage. He had never supported his children regularly and now found them an unwelcome financial burden. He did not like Edith's nondrinking friends. He could not confine himself to the neat pattern of family life idealized and expected by Edith.

[*These two were unable to reach agreement in many areas; they did not achieve full psychological identification nor develop common goals. They did not have a common social world, since neither liked the other's friends. With this unstable basis for marriage, disintegration came suddenly and completely, climaxing a growing realization that neither one was happy.*]

The crisis came about two years after the marriage when Mack announced that he had invited a large group of his friends to the house for a party the following evening. Edith protested that she could not prepare for them on such short notice. In the quarrel that followed, Mack struck Edith several times. The following day he did not bring his friends. Edith wanted to "make up," and Mack threatened to strike her again. She then told him she was leaving, and he drove her to her parents' home.

[*Edith turned to her parents for satisfaction of some of her needs —for sympathy and bolstering of her ego. The vacillation of attitude typical of many persons considering a divorce is also evident.*]

Edith immediately determined to get a divorce, but in the months that followed Mack made many efforts to see her and effect a reconciliation. He promised to meet her conditions for marriage. Edith refused to see him, fearing that she would then return to him and the unhappy situation. She had difficulty freeing herself from a feeling of responsibility toward him (when he was old, who would take care of him?) and toward his children. Her family and friends were sympathetic and finally she broke her identification sufficiently to file suit for divorce.

The following case shows the mounting tensions through a dozen years of marriage, although at the outset the marriage had many of the elements that are predictive of good adjustment. Husband and wife were increasingly unable to satisfy their personal needs in each other: sexual adjustment was poor, and the husband could not give his wife the social status that she craved. Nevertheless, a number of years passed before divorce was mentioned. The couple did not proceed quickly to divorce but attempted time after time to come to some adjustment. Gradually, however, they deviated further and further from a common life together and found less and less satisfaction in their marriage. Divorce came as the final step in a long process of disintegration.

Both husband and wife had grown up on farms in stable families without any record of divorce; both had some college education and had business positions, with the wife giving up her position at marriage and the husband continuing his education until he became a Certified Public Accountant. By the end of the second year the marriage was a failure, in the opinion of the couple; nevertheless, it continued because of family and social pressures.

Sexual adjustment was poor. The wife lacked knowledge, and the husband at the beginning of the marriage failed to understand her difficulties and made the situation worse.

Another basic difficulty was the feeling of social insecurity and inferiority on the part of the wife. Consequently she wished to live at a level beyond the income of an accountant. Money became a point of severe tension. Although the husband was advancing in his profession and felt that his income was as high as could be expected, his wife criticized and blamed him. A personal conflict situation developed. The wife implied that her husband was a failure; at the same time she seemed to feel inferior to him and found many opportunities in public to assert dominance over him, to his embarrassment. Her sharp tongue cut deeply; she seemed unable to relax and take life calmly.

In time the wife began to use the threat of divorce, which the husband wished to avoid, as a means of getting her own way. The husband more and more avoided conflicts by yielding to her wishes. Rather than solving the situation, this procedure caused more tensions in the wife.

After nine years of marriage a child was unexpectedly born to the couple. As they had earlier wanted a child but had given up hope of having one, the prospect of the baby and its presence gave a new point of adjustment. But the basic tensions were still present, and soon the wife was turning her resentment and desire to dominate upon the child. The husband tried to defend the child and conflicts became more frequent and tense than ever. The husband finally made the decision that a divorce was the only solution. The wife agreed, although she vacillated in her attitude when faced with the actuality of the situation. A separation of a year followed without reconciliation, after which the divorce was secured.

Premarital Conditions

Certain childhood relationships and early social contacts as well as length of engagement are related to marital adjustment. Locke's comparison of 200 happily married and 324 divorced couples living in the same community shows that the happily married more often than the divorced had happy childhoods with limited conflict with their parents, and their parents' marriages were more often happy and free from divorce.[4]

Selection of the mate for love, to have a home, on the basis of common interests, to satisfy sex desires, and to have children were more often associated with happiness than with divorce. Happily married women also more often than divorced women had an economic (security) motive. Approval of the choice of a mate by the parents also made for happiness. On the other hand, the divorced men, more often than the happy, married to escape loneliness, and divorced women to escape from their own families.

The divorced tended to know each other for shorter periods of time and to have shorter engagements, more conflict, and less affection during courtship than the happily married. Forced marriages because of premarital pregnancy were found in 41 cases among the divorced, but in only 3 cases among the happily married. The forced marriages usually took place after brief acquaintance and on the basis of casual contacts. It may be assumed that the premarital sex relations in these cases were on the physical level only and were not a part of developing affection during a courtship process.

PERSONALITY

It is not surprising to learn from Locke's study that divorced couples disagreed on more matters than the happily married.[5] More significant is the difference in attitude toward difficulties and disagreements between the two groups. In general, the happily married exhibited a more fundamental attachment to each other and greater security in their marriage. They were inclined to be tolerant, to overlook disagreements rather than make issues of them, and to regard conflicts as on the surface of an abiding relationship. The divorced had met difficulties with anger and personal criticism; they tended to separate temporarily when difficulties arose rather than to regard them as problems to be solved by mutual effort. Thus there was a basic difference in the conception of marriage held by the two groups.

[4]Harvey J. Locke, *Predicting Adjustment in Marriage: A Comparison of a Divorced and a Happily Married Group* (New York: Holt, 1951), chs. 5 and 6.
[5]*Ibid.*, pp. 81–84.

This difference in conception of marriage is shown in part by the reasons for marrying and the difference in length of engagement. It is also evident in the degree of individualism found in the divorced couples and the higher development of companionship and democracy among the happily married.[6] A free interpretation of Locke's findings would characterize the divorced as more ego-centered and rigid, the happily married as more out-going and adaptable.

Duration of Marriage and Children

DURATION OF MARRIAGE AT TIME OF DIVORCE

Some divorces occur before the first year of marriage has been completed, some after 40 years or more of marriage, and others at all periods in between. The median duration of first marriages that end in divorce is 7.7 years, and of remarriages 4.6 years.[7] The highest percentages of divorces, however, are clustered at the beginning of married life, as Table 16 shows. Almost a third of all divorces are granted in the first three years of marriage. Since a period of separation usually precedes the actual granting of the decree of divorce by the court, very little time has been allowed in these marriages for adjustment to take place. The percentage of divorces granted declines slowly through each added year of marriage, but never quite disappears.

CHILDREN

Among all divorced couples in 1963, 61.6 per cent had children under age 18 (Table 17). In 1963, 583,000 children lost one parent through divorce—assuming that the child remained with the other parent.[8] Since 1953 (when data first became available) the number of children per divorce has increased from 0.85 to 1.36 and the estimated total number from 330,000 to 583,000. When only divorced couples with children are considered, the number of children per couple rose from

[6]*Ibid.*, pp. 75–76, ch. 12.
[7]*Vital Statistics of the United States*, 1959, Vol. 1, Sec. 2, "Marriage and Divorce Statistics" (Washington, D.C.: Government Printing Office, 1961), pp. 2–30. Later reports do not separate divorces of first marriages from divorces of all marriages.
[8]*Divorce Statistics Analysis, United States—1963, op. cit.*, pp. 34–35.

TABLE 16

PERCENTAGE DISTRIBUTION OF DIVORCES AND ANNULMENTS
BY DURATION OF MARRIAGE: DIVORCE REGISTRATION AREAS,
TOTAL OF 22 REPORTING STATES, 1963

Duration of marriage in years	Per cent
Under 1 year	5.2
1 year	8.6
2 years	8.4
3 years	7.5
4 years	6.8
5 years	5.7
6 years	5.5
7 years	5.0
8 years	4.0
9 years	3.7
10–14 years, average per year	3.0
15–19 years, average per year	2.3
20–24 years, average per year	1.4
25–29 years, average per year	0.7
30 years and over*	

*Only 3 per cent of divorces are obtained after 29 years' duration of marriage.

SOURCE: *Vital Statistics of the United States, 1963*, Vol. III, "Marriage and Divorce" (Washington, D.C.: Government Printing Office, 1967), p. 2–8.

1.86 in 1953 to 2.16 in 1963. The total number of children under 18 of divorced parents runs into the millions.

While the presence of children may act as a deterrent to divorce, certainly it is not the deciding factor. In some cases, fundamental problems and attitudes may contribute to both the childlessness and the divorce. Also, some of the childlessness is accounted for by the large proportion of divorces in the early years of marriage. When the period of estrangement preceding the divorce is also taken into account, it is apparent that many couples have lived together as husband and wife only a short time.

Couples who work out an adjustment that survives the first few years of marriage generally have children. Later, if some disturbance occurs that makes the marriage intolerable, a divorce may be secured. For these later divorces, the rates for childless couples and couples with children show less and less variation with the duration of marriage.

Since the remarriage rate for divorced people is high, many different combinations of parents, stepparents, and children are possible. The adjustment of children to the divorce of their parents and to remarriage of parents is discussed in Chapter 19.

TABLE 17

PERCENT DISTRIBUTION OF DIVORCES AND ANNULMENTS,
BY NUMBER OF CHILDREN REPORTED ACCORDING TO
DURATION OF MARRIAGE: DIVORCE-REGISTRATION AREA, 1963
(BASED ON SAMPLE DATA)

Duration of marriage	All divorces and annul- ments	Number of children reported			
		None	1	2	3+
	PERCENTAGE DISTRIBUTION				
Under 1 year	100.0	84.8	11.2	1.7	2.3
1–2 years	100.0	57.5	34.6	6.3	1.5
3–4 years	100.0	38.5	35.5	20.5	5.5
5–9 years	100.0	28.7	22.0	25.9	23.5
10–14 years	100.0	24.4	15.9	23.2	36.5
15 years and over	100.0	34.5	19.2	19.5	26.8
TOTAL	100.0	38.4	23.9	18.7	19.0

SOURCE: *Divorce Statistics Analysis, United States—1963*, Public Health Service Publication No. 1000, Series 21, No. 13 (Washington, D. C.: Government Printing Office, 1967), pp. 34–35.

Social Situations and Divorce

From material presented in earlier chapters, we know that the pattern of family life varies from one social situation to another. We recognize differences between rural and urban families; lower-, middle-, and upper-class families; and families with different religious affiliations. Each social situation creates its distinctive hardships and tensions, and, to the extent that it represents cultural differences, has specific attitudes toward divorce. Therefore, from one social situation to another the proportion of family unadjustment, disintegration, and divorce may vary.

URBAN-RURAL DIFFERENCES

We usually assume that family disorganization and divorce are more often experienced by urban than rural families. Chapter 3 has shown that so far as the status of the population at any one period is concerned, the ratio of divorced women to married women is higher among urban than rural women. Current marital status does not indicate, however, the relative rates. People divorced in rural communities may move to cities and thereafter be included by the census in the urban population. Also, many divorced people remarry and thus return to the status of married.

Urban and rural communities must be compared according to the rate of divorces granted. Such comparisons usually use counties as the basic units, classified according to the largest city within each county. Rates are computed as number of divorces per 1,000 of the total population in each county.[9] The rural rates are probably understatements, since the rural total population includes a larger proportion of children than does the urban population. Actually, the results of the studies are inconclusive. Individual rural counties have higher rates than urban counties within the same state. When counties within a state are grouped according to the size of the largest city within each county, variations in rates are evident between the groups. In Iowa, for instance, counties without any towns as large as 2,500 population had the lowest divorce rates, 1.3 in 1947.[10] The rates increased regularly with urbanness of the counties to a rate of four in counties with one or more cities of 25,000. These figures support the thesis that the divorce rate is higher in urban than in rural communities. A Missouri study, however, shows a different pattern of rates.[11] For 1947, 33 rural counties with no city of 2,500 population had a divorce rate of 2.2 per 1,000 population; seven countries with cities of 10,000 or more had a rate of 7.5; St. Louis County (containing the city of St. Louis), however, had a rate of only 5.7. A similar county study for Illinois showed great irregularity of rates, with the lowest rate (1.8) in the most rural counties having no cities of 2,500 population, and the highest rate (4.5) in counties with cities of between 2,500 and 25,000.[12] Counties with larger cities had rates that fell between these extremes. Cook County, containing the city of Chicago, had a rate of only 2.8.

These results indicate the need for more exact studies of divorce

[9]The crudity of the method is a result of the type of information found in published reports.

[10]Kenneth L. Cannon, "Marriage and Divorce in Iowa, 1940–47," *Marriage and Family Living*, 9 (1947), 81–83, 98; since Cannon presented his data solely by graphs, the rates cited here are approximations only.

[11]"Missouri Marriage and Divorce Statistics, 1940–1947," *Journal of the Missouri Bar*, 4 (March, 1948), 38–39.

[12]Computed from population for 1950 and divorces for 1949. *1950 Census of Population, Preliminary Counts, Population of Illinois, by Counties: April 1, 1950*, Series PC-2, No. 40 (Washington, D.C.: Bureau of the Census, September 11, 1950); *Vital Statistics, Special Reports, Statistics on Divorces and Annulments, Specified States: 1949*, Vol. 36, No. 7 (Washington, D.C.: Federal Security Agency, August 3, 1951), pp. 111–12.

rates in urban and rural areas, which will take account of factors other than the size of population units. Suggested factors are ethnic and religious backgrounds, racial composition, educational and economic status, and mobility.

RELIGION

In the discussion of cross-cultural marriages in Chapter 10, it was shown that divorce rates tend to be lowest in Catholic-Catholic marriages, slightly higher in homogeneous Jewish or Protestant marriages, and still higher in varying degrees for different types of cross-religious marriages. For each type of marriage, however, the great majority of couples remain married at least during the early years of marriage.

SOCIAL CLASS

Although divorce has not been studied directly according to social-class divisions, certain data are suggestive. Descriptive material shows that aggressiveness is most common in lower-class families, and that crises occur with greater frequency.[13] The assumption that there is greater dissatisfaction is borne out by a study of 845 middle- and lower-class married people. Figure 24 shows the percentage distribution of husbands and wives in four social-class divisions according to good, fair, or poor marital adjustment. Good adjustment decreases and poor adjustment increases as social status declines. These data suggest that divorce rates also may vary according to social class.

The relation of frequency of divorce by social class has been approached indirectly by computing rates of divorce according to the occupational level of the men. Four studies of the 1940's and 1950's show that among urban occupations, divorce rates were lowest among professionals and proprietors, moderate among clerical and skilled workers, and highest among the semiskilled.[14] According to several studies, the unskilled have rates lower than the semiskilled, a fact that may be accounted for by the expense of divorce, religious affiliation, or lack of property that would necessitate a legal settlement.

[13]Chapters 5, 6, and 7.
[14]William J. Goode, *After Divorce* (Glencoe, Ill.: Free Press, 1956); William M. Kephart, "Occupational Level and Marital Disruption," *American Sociological Review*, 20 (1955), 456–65; Thomas P. Monahan, "Divorce by Occupational Level," *Marriage and Family Living*, 17 (1955), 322–24; H. Ashley Weeks, "Differential Divorce Rates by Occupation," *Social Forces*, 21 (1943), 34–37.

SOCIAL CLASS
AT MARRIAGE

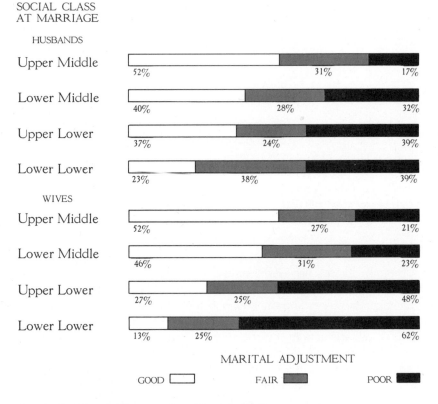

FIGURE 24   *Marital Adjustment According to Social Class.*

According to the Burgess-Cottrell scale of marital adjustment, higher percentages of middle-class than of lower-class people achieve good adjustment.

SOURCE: Julius Roth and Robert F. Peck, "Social Class and Social Mobility Factors Related to Marital Adjustment," *American Sociological Review*, 16 (1951), 479.

RACE

Statistical reports for divorces by race are incomplete. Nonwhites are not classified by race, although cultural differences among the races may result in differences in divorce rates. In three southern or border states (Tennesee, Virginia, Missouri) included in an official report, where most of the nonwhites are Negro, the divorce rates for whites and nonwhites varied only slightly.[15] In three northern states

[15]*Divorce Statistics Analysis, United States—1963, op. cit.*, pp. 16–17, 45.

(Rhode Island, Wisconsin, Iowa), the rates for nonwhites (primarily Negroes) were much higher than rates for whites. In Iowa, for example, the rate for Negroes was three times the rate for whites.

The above statements must be qualified to some extent.[16] They do not take account of informal separations, which are frequent among nonwhites in many states, often linked with common-law marriage. The regional differences may be accounted for in various ways: tensions in adjustment among migrating nonwhites, especially going from the rural south to the industrialized cities of the north, or personality differences among types of nonwhites who migrate.

DIFFICULTY OF ISOLATING SOCIAL FACTORS

No one of the social factors presented above shows an unequivocal correlation with divorce rates, although there is a tendency for rates to be lower in rural and large metropolitan than in medium urban areas; among couples affiliated with the same religious faith than in mixed marriages; in professional, managerial, and unskilled occupational groups than in middle-class groups or among the unemployed; and among whites than nonwhites. The effect of any one factor is decreased because a given couple may be subject to factors representing opposed pressures; for example, small town, mixed marriage, unskilled labor. Or the couple might be metropolitan, professional, and Catholic, thus representing three low-rate situations. More comprehensive studies are needed to uncover such interrelationships and also the way in which these general social factors are reflected in personal attitudes and patterns of marital interaction.

Adjustment to Divorce

Divorce is but a stage in marital disintegration and readjustment. The divorce marks the end of the marriage legally, defines obligations and relationships in a formal way, but leaves untouched the postdivorce adjustment of each individual. This adjustment covers a number of phases: resolving residual emotions and attitudes toward the marriage and the ex-spouse; readjusting one's conception of oneself; rearranging

[16]Jessie Bernard, *Marriage and Family among Negroes* (Englewood Cliffs, N.J.: Prentice-Hall, 1966), pp. 101–102.

personal habits, including finances and sexual satisfactions; and read-justing social life.[17]

Sometimes, when a long period of time intervenes between a defi-nite separation and the granting of a divorce, many of the above pro-cesses may take place prior to the divorce itself. Divorce in such cases may be secured not to terminate the marriage, which in reality was terminated at the time of the separation, but perhaps in order to settle property or to define legal relationships to children. Usually, however, the readjustment follows the divorce.

RESIDUAL EMOTIONS AND ATTITUDES

Although the attitude toward the ex-spouse may be neutral, often it is not. In Goode's interview study of over 400 urban divorced moth-ers, half of the women stated they felt indifferent toward their former husbands.[18] One out of ten expressed strong affection; one out of four wished the husband to be punished. Another one out of four admitted a willingness to remarry the husband under certain circumstances. The interviews indicated, however, that many of those expressing indifference really had considerable emotional content in their atti-tudes but were giving a conventional reply, since the divorced person is expected to be indifferent to the former mate.

The divorced person may still love the absent one. In other cases, the difficulties of personal and social adjustment may make the mar-riage in memory seem preferable to the later period. The marriage may be idealized; only the pleasurable aspects of periods of harmony may be remembered at such times.

The hostile and punitive attitude may have a realistic basis in mis-treatment. But it may also be a defensive reaction, to protect the person from admission of partial responsibility for the divorce and conse-quent feelings of guilt and failure.

The emotions felt, and their overt manifestations, do not fall into the same pattern in all cases. Goode states that repeated questions

[17]Not many studies have been made of adjustment to divorce. Willard Waller in *The Old Love for the New: Divorce and Readjustment* (New York: Liveright, 1930; Carbondale, Ill.: Southern Illinois University Press, 1967) analyzed 33 cases; such a limited number of cases obviously leads to illustrative types of adjustment rather than to a comprehensive analysis. Jessie Bernard includes divorced people in *Remarriage: A Study of Marriage* (New York: Dryden, 1956). A systematic study of 425 divorced women with children was made by Goode, *op. cit.*

[18]Goode, *op. cit.*, p. 201; also Goode, "Problems in Postdivorce Adjustment," *American Sociological Review*, 14 (1949), p. 400.

about sleep, forgetfulness, increased smoking or drinking, lessened efficiency or energy, lonesomeness, and so on, failed to reveal a definite pattern.[19] He believes that a more comprehensive study might uncover subpatterns of reactions, perhaps along social-class lines. He also believes that the emotional disturbance is not entirely due to the breakdown of the marriage itself, but that at least part is related to the conflict between the divorced person's inner problems of adjustment to a nonmarried state and the social expectation that he should be indifferent and show little affection for the divorced spouse.

These residual emotions impede adjustment to the divorced state and if not dissipated may hinder adjustment in a later marriage.

READJUSTING CONCEPTION OF SELF

An early reaction to divorce seems to be the tendency to place all the responsibility for it on the other person. Each spouse, whether he has demanded the divorce, acceded to the other's demand, or entered into a mutual agreement, feels the necessity to justify his action. This compulsion grows out of our attitude toward marriage and divorce. Regardless of the long-term upward trend in divorces, the social norm is still permanency of marriage. Any deviation must be explained and justified. When the couple belong to a religious group that strongly condemns divorce, personal defense is still more necessary because divorce is defined not merely as a violation of social customs but as the flaunting of a moral law. In addition to fear or dislike of social condemnation, the person often has a feeling of personal failure. The practice in our society of permitting young people to select their own mates and arrange for their own marriages places the responsibility for success or failure upon them personally. The young man who was elated over winning the most beautiful girl in his community and the girl who received a proposal from the most promising young man must now admit their errors in judgment. Also, marriage is regarded as a personal relationship in which each meets the needs of the other, as well as finding satisfaction for his own needs. Divorce signifies a failure, not only to find satisfaction, but to give satisfaction. The divorced person, therefore, often has his sense of personal adequacy, his self-assurance, his belief in himself shattered by the experience.

Marion divorced Harold after he had had several "affairs" with other women and finally wished to marry a woman with

19"Problems in Postdivorce Adjustment," p. 400.

whom he had secretly been living intermittently. Marion, who knew of his affairs, had previously offered to divorce him, but he had always assured her that the current affair was ended and that he did not want to be divorced. When the divorce was finally secured at Harold's request, Marion's first reaction was "numb frigidity like that of bereavement." As this feeling wore off she felt a keen sense of personal failure. She also felt disgraced as she was a devoted member of a church that condemned divorce; she felt that she had violated her moral standards. She found comfort in her friends and eventually began to date but asserted that she would never remarry. After five years' time, her feelings of failure and disgrace had changed very little. She learned to counteract a tendency to idealize her marriage by deliberately recalling its drawbacks. Some compensation for her feelings of failure resulted from her increased emotional serenity and the financial security of her job.[20]

Writing ten years after her divorce, a woman of 35 states:

At first, I was sure the divorce did not affect me, and I felt I would remarry and be happy, because I was sure I just made a bad decision and everything was wrong about our marriage. However, I now look backward and I can see that it has affected my attitude toward other men, my feeling of being able to decide to remarry. For many years I was sure that it was not my fault and that there was nothing wrong with me. I have just in the last few years started to analyze my own attitudes, opinions, expectations and behavior and realize they had a great deal to do with the marriage.[21]

Feelings of being "let down," unwanted, insecure, and a personal failure are mentioned by others who have described their reactions after a divorce.

Rearranging Personal Life

Marriage is both a personal relationship and a way of life. Even when a couple are in conflict and declare they no longer love each other, many joint patterns of behavior are continued. The wife may still manage the household and prepare the food that both eat; the husband may still pay the bills and depend upon his wife to attend to such personal needs as clean clothing and mending. Both may meet social obligations in the midst of estrangement. Sex relations, the most intimate part of marriage, often are discontinued early in the conflict period; but in other cases the couple continue sex relations through

[20]Unpublished record.
[21]Unpublished record.

habit, to meet mutual needs, or as part of the vacillation between harmony and conflict that often characterizes the marriage prior to a divorce. All these functions and relationships are disturbed and perhaps completely destroyed by separation and divorce; they also have many emotional connotations.

When there are children who remain with the mother, and she is able to retain the family home, the strain of her readjustment in daily habits is less severe than is the adjustment of the husband who leaves, or of the wife who finds it impossible or undesirable to maintain a house. Many women and some men retreat to their parents' home, where they may find solace in their parents' sympathy and may resume a filial relationship:

> Jim's mother and friends were very sympathetic. Through conversation they made him feel that maybe the divorce was the best thing after all. They reasoned that he was the man and his wife should live where he provided the place for them.[22]

Other women change their place and mode of living, seemingly seeking to destroy the old pattern of daily life.

> Janet, who never talked about her divorce even to intimate friends, used her share of the property settlement to buy a small house about five miles from her former home. She systematically sorted out all of her husband's possessions and left them in their old home, owned by her former husband. She burned all his letters to her and destroyed wedding mementos. She left all his photographs except one, and returned her wedding ring.[23]

Other men and women move away from the community and reconstruct life in a new social setting.

A financial adjustment usually is part of the divorce situation. Joint property is divided, sometimes with bitterness and a feeling of unfairness. Alimony may be allowed by the judge, although it is a less common practice than formerly for the wife to ask for or receive alimony. Alimony was a way of providing security for the divorced wife at a time when married women could not hold property and were completely dependent upon their husbands financially;[24] in an earlier period also they were less able to support themselves. At present there is less justification for alimony except in special cases, and alimony

[22]See the case of Jim and Martha, earlier in this chapter.
[23]Unpublished record.
[24]Robert W. Kelso, "The Changing Social Setting of Alimony Law," *Law and Contemporary Problems*, 6 (1939), 186–96.

thus becomes a psychological weapon or the focusing point for the conflict.[25] The man may resist, feeling resentful at the prospect of supporting an able-bodied woman to whom he is no longer married. He may object to the loss of purchasing power involved and especially so if he wishes to remarry. On the other hand, alimony relieves some men of a sense of guilt. They may feel that ample payment of alimony (and support of children) relieves them of all other responsibilities. The wife may use alimony as a punitive measure and insist upon financial payments as a way of maintaining power over her divorced husband. Other women, compelled to accept alimony because they have no means of self-support, may be humiliated by the situation. When the wife does not receive alimony, she becomes either dependent upon relatives or self-supporting. The middle-aged woman who has never been gainfully employed or who has lost her skills may either bitterly resent the necessity for self-support or find in it a new purpose and objective in her life.

Intimate and sexual relationships are difficult to adjust. The adult who has become accustomed to a close affectional and sexual union in marriage often finds single life irritating and frustrating. Regression to the family life in the parental family may partially solve the problem for some; concentration of affection on children for others. Dating and an overemphasis on social life is another solution tried by many, especially women. Men, more than women, may frankly cultivate sexual relations on a casual basis. Whirlwind love affairs, sometimes ending in marriage, are another effort at compensation. These affairs also have other meanings; they restore assurance to the divorced woman of her attractiveness and to the man of his masculine virility. They also offer public proof that the divorced person is indifferent, unhurt, and immune to the emotional ravages of the experience, although actually months or years may be required to repair the damage.

> Edith, whose marital history is given earlier in this chapter, began to date as soon as her divorce was granted. All her friends encouraged her to have a good time and introduced her to eligible men. Eight months after the divorce she became engaged, but broke the engagement after two weeks. She has continued to date many men, sometimes falling quickly in love with a man who in some way resembled the ex-husband, but later finding they were incompatible.

[25]Catherine Groves Peele, "Social and Psychological Effects of the Availability and the Granting of Alimony on the Spouses," *Law and Contemporary Problems*, 6 (1939), 283–92.

Readjustment of social life may be difficult.[26] Although there is greater leniency of attitude toward divorced persons than formerly, in some communities or toward members of some professions disapproval is still strong. Teachers and ministers are especially likely to be stigmatized if divorced. Sometimes the curiosity, sympathy, or facetiousness of friends is as trying as disapproval. Mutual friends of the couple are placed in a peculiar predicament: shall they "take sides," shall they retain both friendships but try to keep the two apart at social affairs by inviting first one and then the other, or shall they drop both? It seems probable that few divorced couples are really comfortable if invited to the same social function, although a high degree of sophistication may make it possible for the two to continue their old joint social contacts. If friends invite only one of the couple, the question arises of a partner. The divorced person himself may seek to withdraw from old joint associates, sometimes going to the extent of moving to another community. Others, however, rush into social life as an escape from loneliness and as proof that the divorce has not hurt them, that they are not failures, have not lost attractiveness, and so on.

Remarriage

Although the divorce experience may leave permanent scars or make lasting changes in attitude, it does not usually signify an end to married life for either partner.

REMARRIAGE OF THE DIVORCED

It is estimated that approximately two-thirds of divorced women and three-fourths of divorced men will eventually remarry.[27] While the interval of time between divorce and remarriage may vary from less than a year to more than 10 years, the median length of time is 2.7 years. Sixty-nine per cent of remarriages occur during the first three years after divorce.

Although remarriage seems to follow quickly after divorce, the differences between brides and grooms of first marriages and remarriages are marked. They are older: the median age of the bride at first marriage is 20.5 years, at remarriage 35.6 years; the median age of

[26]See the discussion of social life in Goode, *After Divorce*, ch. 17.
[27]Paul C. Glick, *American Families* (New York: Wiley, 1957), pp. 138–39.

the groom at first marriage is 23.0 years, at remarriage 40.2 years.[28] During this time, the husband has typically settled himself into his occupation and the wife has borne children. They have become estranged, divorced, adjusted to the status of being divorced; they have dated, courted, made a new selection of a mate, and married him. Some of these stages of course may overlap; for example, the selection of the new mate may precede the divorce.

Divorced people tend to choose for their second mates other divorced persons; this choice is true of 51 per cent of divorced brides and 52 per cent of divorced grooms.[29] Slightly more than a third of each sex selects a single person for the second spouse, and about 10 or 12 per cent a widowed person. Thus, over half of remarriages bring together people experienced with the techniques and roles of marriage, but with a new choice of partner necessitating the modification of old conceptions and roles to bring them into a new pattern of integration. The marriage of divorced persons with single persons bring together a person of experience and a novice. The adjustments called for here differ both from those of two divorced persons or two single persons.

FACTORS FOR AND AGAINST REMARRIAGE

In his study of divorced women, Goode emphasizes that the divorced woman has a poorly defined role in society.[30] The social expectation is that the adult woman will have a husband and usually children. The role of mother is rather well defined—she has certain obligations toward her children. The role of wife or wife-mother is also well defined. The role of the widow is perhaps the best structured; people sympathize with her and help her, and she is without the varying relationships found in marriage between wife and husband. The role of the divorced woman, especially when she has children, is ambiguous. Family and friends are not sure how they are expected to treat her. Someone other than the mother may have custody of the children, thus disturbing her normal maternal role. Some social disapproval clings to the role of divorcée. Normal social activities for adults are usually for couples, and the divorced person disrupts the pattern. The simplest way for the divorced person to regain status and integration into social institutions is to remarry. A new family is formed, with the roles of

[28]*Statistical Abstract of the United States, 1967* (Washington, D.C.: Government Printing Office, 1967), p. 64.

[29]*Vital Statistics of the United States,* 1959, Vol. 1, Sec. 2, "Marriage and Divorce Statistics" (Washington, D.C.: Government Printing Office, 1961), p. 2–9.

[30]*After Divorce,* ch. 15.

husband, wife, and parent reinstated. An approved status is regained. The couple fits into social life. Social pressure toward normal role fulfillment propels the divorced person toward remarriage.

Goode mentions other pressures toward remarriage. Friends find it awkward to fit divorced persons into social activities, and seek to find mates for them. Some married people regard a divorced person as a potential threat to their own marriage and urge remarriage. The divorced mother is told that she should remarry for the sake of her children. The need that the divorced person feels for sexual fulfillment is also a motive for marriage.

These pressures impinge unequally on people. Bernard mentions that some people do not wish to remarry.[31] She suggests that persons may have had an unhappy first marriage and do not wish to risk a repetition. A divorced woman may have an income that will stop with remarriage (as alimony does) or a satisfactory job that she does not want to leave. Children may deter her, since they may not react well to a new "father." Women who have not been well adjusted sexually in the first marriage may avoid a second one.

THE PROCESS OF REMARRIAGE

Remarriages take place by the same process as first marriages—through meeting eligible persons, dating, engagement, and marriage.[32] The young divorced woman, especially if she has no children, finds it easy to slip back into the young dating group. She is still youthful and her dating skills are intact; her experience in marriage may give her an attractive sophistication. The dating process tends to move quickly, and she is soon remarried. The older woman with children makes her appeal on a different basis. She no longer has the physical attraction of youth and is likely to be involved with homemaking and the needs of her children. In this role she makes her appeal, and the divorced man of her age who has been accustomed to a home or whose children are with their mother often finds this setting an attractive one.

Since the courtship process goes on through dating, it is not surprising that it is furthered by general social activities, membership in clubs, and beginning dating soon after the divorce—or even during the period of separation before the divorce. Indifference to the ex-husband is conducive to dating among women, according to Goode. Continued emotional involvement after separation or divorce prevents the woman from seeking dating contacts.

[31]Bernard, *op. cit.*, pp. 117–18.
[32]Goode, *After Divorce*, pp. 280–82.

The psychological process follows the same lines as in a first marriage, with certain modifications. Often, because the customary roles of husband and wife are already known, there is less romantic expectation and a more sober realization of mutual obligations. More important is the acceptance of oneself as a divorced person and acceptance of this same fact by the new mate.[33]

Legal Termination of Marriage

The discussion so far has emphasized psychological and social elements of marital disintegration. If the couple wish to make the dissolution of their marriage permanent and to relieve themselves of some of their obligations, they may secure a legal separation, a divorce, or—under certain circumstances—an annulment. Divorce is the most common method used.

Divorce is a legal decree that sets aside the contract of marriage. Although the decree may be granted by a judge after hearings lasting no more than a few minutes, divorce usually has other connotations to the couple than the mere termination of a legal contract. The very decision to make an irrevocable end to the marriage and thereby to risk the social disapproval that is often directed toward the divorced may create insecurity. The necessity on the part of the one filing the suit of accusing the partner of some form of misconduct in order to come within the framework of the law may offend the sensitive or the fairminded. Financial arrangements may be necessary but distasteful. Finally, the divorce precipitates the many phases of adjustment already described.

DIVORCE

Divorce relieves husband and wife of such privileges as sexual access or occupation of a common domicile and frees each for remarriage. However, certain obligations may be continued. By the terms of the individual divorce, the husband may be required to continue financial support of his wife through alimony. When there are minor children, one parent, usually the wife, receives custody of the children for

[33]Bernard, *op. cit.*, gives an elaborately detailed discussion of the many possible combinations of persons that may result from remarriage and the resulting problems arising from their interaction as a new family complex is formed.

whose care she is then responsible; the father usually is required to contribute to the support of the children.

The philosophy underlying divorce is that one party to the marriage has violated the marriage contract, whereas the other party is innocent. The innocent party, as plaintiff, may bring suit for divorce and must prove by evidence and witnesses that the spouse, who is the defendant, is guilty. The plaintiff must not admit in court any share of responsibility for the situation, and any agreement between husband and wife to end the marriage must be concealed. Now that divorce is recognized as the end result of a process of interaction and often is desired by both husband and wife, the court procedure is a farce. Nevertheless, until the laws are changed, the farce must be played out to the end. Each state has passed legislation listing with considerable detail the violations of the marriage contract for which a divorce will be granted. Few changes are made from year to year, but those that do occur usually add to the number and variety of causes. South Carolina, which until 1948 did not provide for any divorce, now allows divorce for adultery, desertion, physical cruelty, and drunkenness. New York state throughout its history until 1966 had only one legal ground for divorce—adultery. In 1966 four other causes were added: mental and physical cruelty, desertion, separation or absence of two years, and felony conviction or imprisonment.

Table 18 lists the causes and the number of states (including the District of Columbia) granting divorce for each cause. Divorce laws sometimes make fine distinctions between grounds for husband and wife; specify the length of time for desertion, habitual drinking, or insanity; and the length of time (if any) that must elapse before marriage to another person. Length of time that the person must reside in the state before filing suit for divorce is also specified, a period that ranges from six weeks in Idaho and Nevada to five years in Massachusetts. The most frequent period is one year, in 28 states. Only an inspection of the laws of each state can make all the distinctions clear.[34] This brief summary of laws is sufficient, however, to indicate the variety of grounds for divorce and the great specificity of misconduct that the plaintiff must prove. What actually happens, of course, is a fitting of the individual case into the legal requirements. A person may establish residence in a state requiring only a few weeks for the specific purpose of securing a divorce and then leave the state; an agreed-upon separation may be converted into desertion; or fraudulent

[34]Each issue of the *Book of the States,* published by the Council of State Governments, Chicago, carries a detailed table of the legal grounds of divorce for each state.

testimony may be given to prove adultery that never occurred (in New York prior to 1966).

Various reforms have been proposed. One is a federal divorce law, which would make the procedure uniform for all states and thus pre-

TABLE 18

LEGAL GROUNDS FOR DIVORCE, JULY 1, 1966

Cause	Number of states designating each ground for divorce
Adultery	51
Desertion, usually of one year's duration	48
Felony conviction or imprisonment	46
Mental and/or physical cruelty	45
Alcoholism	41
Impotency	32
Insanity, usually 3 to 5 years' duration	30
Nonsupport	30
Separation or absence, usually of 2 to 5 years' duration	26
Pregnancy at marriage	13
Drug addiction	12
Infamous crime	10
Bigamy	9
Fraudulent contract	7
Miscellaneous grounds, fewer than 4 states each	

SOURCE: Women's Bureau, U.S. Department of Labor.

vent people from establishing residence and securing a divorce in one state that could not be secured in the state of real residence. Another is the substitution of social-work procedures for the present legal ones, or their use as a supplementation to them.

ANNULMENT

An annulment is also a legally recognized type of separation that terminates marriage, but it differs from divorce in being justified by conditions existent before or at the time of marriage that invalidate the marriage itself, whereas divorce is granted for events that occur after the wedding. For example, a marriage may take place under conditions where the consent of one party is not clearly obtained: one of the pair may be feeble-minded or insane and not capable of realizing what he is doing; one may be intoxicated; one may be forced at gun point or through fear to enter into a marriage. Falsification of age by those under the legal age for marriage may be grounds for an annulment. Fraud may be involved when one person suffers from some condition that prevents full consummation of the marriage, as concealment of known sterility, of venereal disease, or pregnancy by another person. Annulments are also granted in cases of bigamy or failure to secure a divorce from a previous marriage.

Unlike divorce, which recognizes a legal marriage that is dissolved only from the date of the divorce, an annulment makes a marriage void and in effect declares that it never legally existed.[35] Annulment, therefore, does not provide for continuation or settlement of property rights acquired through marriage, for alimony, or for legitimacy or support of children. Since this situation often works a hardship on an innocent wife or child (who by an annulment becomes illegitimate), some states provide safeguards. New York, for example, permits alimony to be granted to the wife in an annulment suit and provides for the support of children. Other states include some of the usual causes for an annulment under causes for divorce and handle the dissolution of the marriage as a divorce, thus safeguarding the interests of the wife and children.

LEGAL SEPARATION

Although many people separate informally, the law in 25 states recognizes legal separations.[36] A legal separation is a partial divorce. Neither husband nor wife may demand the privilege of living with the other; at the same time neither is free to remarry.

VOLUNTARY NATURE OF MARRIAGE TERMINATION

If the marriage is legal in the first instance, termination comes only at the voluntary action of one or both partners. No condition makes a divorce mandatory. Divorce, therefore, is a legal procedure to be used at the discretion of one spouse to end the marriage. Although the legal provision is that the innocent or offended spouse shall bring the divorce suit, as a matter of custom the wife usually acts as plaintiff and brings the suit. This procedure saves her from the ignominy of being

[35]*The Legal Status of Women in the United States of America, United States Summary, as of January 1, 1953,* Women's Bureau Bulletin No. 157 (revised 1956), (Washington, D.C.: Government Printing Office, 1956), pp. 69–72.
[36]*Ibid.,* pp. 73, 77–80.

officially labeled as a failure in marriage and officially throws the blame on her husband. It also opens the way for her as the innocent parent to receive custody of her children and support from her husband, as the offending member of the marriage. Often the legal cause of divorce is only remotely or perhaps not at all related to the real factors in the marital maladjustment. The real reasons for maladjustment may be subtle ones involving frustrations, immaturity, or personal dissatisfactions not recognized by the law. Or the reason may be included in the divorce law but be of such a nature that the couple do not wish to reveal it. Hence the classification of causes of divorce based on court records does not help in an analysis of underlying causes of maladjustment; it simply reveals the legal grounds most often selected for the suit of divorce.

In one respect, therefore, divorce is a ritual of conformity to laws by which dissatisfied couples terminate a marriage that has already ended for one or both as a psychological and social relationship.

Need for Social Redefinition of Divorce

The traditional attitude toward divorce as a violation of sacred obligations or moral laws has hindered the development of procedures other than the strictly legal ones to carry husband and wife through the experience. Society has condemned and ignored; it has not sympathized and helped. There is no uniform collective attitude toward divorce or the divorced person. Some of the emotional disturbance attending a divorce is generated by this undefined situation and the conflict between the traditional opinion that marriage is inviolable and the actual fact that many people are breaking their marriages. In the course of time, social ideals for marriage and actual behavior will no doubt merge, or at least approach identity. But at present the divorced are running against the main current of opinion, or form a small independent stream of their own within the total social body.

In view of the high percentage of marriages that end in divorce, there is need to redefine divorce as a reasonable method of ending an unsatisfactory marriage rather than as a catastrophe because of personal failure and broken vows. Nevertheless, even with such a redefinition, which would relieve many personal conflicts, divorce would continue to be traumatic to husband, wife, and children through the breaking of personal ties and family disorganization. As a matter of social policy and personal happiness, care in mate selection and efforts at marital adjustment would still be paramount. But when, as often happens in a mobile urban society, the very basis of the marriage itself prevents adjustment, divorce should be considered as a solution. Goode, on the basis of his study of Detroit divorced women, suggests that marriage counselors (and others, it might be added) accept the fact that at present "many marriages are formed by incompatible individuals capable of happy marriages to others and the fact that a great proportion of marriages will end in divorce in any event."[37] He suggests, further, that in many cases the energy and effort of counselors to persuade a couple to continue their marriage in the face of insurmountable obstacles really condemn the couple to prolonged misery and maladjustment. It would be better, he believes, to advise such couples to divorce before the husband and wife become so emotionally dependent upon each other that the divorce will be a traumatic experience.

With a more accepting and less punitive attitude toward divorce, collective public opinion could exert a greater degree of control than at present when all divorces tend to be condemned or—the other extreme—divorce is regarded as a purely personal matter to be secured at the whim of husband or wife. New policies could be developed to help people determine the conditions under which divorce would be socially justified and at the same time personally beneficial. The way would then be opened for the formulation and natural growth of folkways and rituals to aid divorced people in their adjustment, just as, at present, we have accepted ways of helping people to adjust to severe illness or a death in the family.

Questions

1. What are the marks of marital disintegration? What is the logical end result?
2. How do the divorced and the nondivorced groups differ? Which differentiating features could be eliminated or controlled in the interest of greater marital stability?
3. At what period of marriage does the divorce rate reach its peak? Relate this period to the types of disagreement at different stages in the family life cycle (Chapter 11).
4. Are children a deterrent to divorce?

[37]William J. Goode, "Education for Divorce," *Marriage and Family Living*, 9 (1947), 36.

5. In what ways may religion affect the divorce rate?

6. What do you think is the most difficult aspect of adjustment to divorce?

7. How can you account for the high remarriage rate of people who have been divorced?

8. Compare the dating and courtship process for first marriages and for remarriages.

9. Discuss the philosophy and method involved in obtaining a legal decree of divorce. Are they in harmony with present-day attitudes toward divorce?

10. Suggest valid plans for (1) reducing the number of divorces and (2) bringing divorce procedures into line with present attitudes toward the function of marriage.

Bibliography

"Alimony," *Law and Contemporary Problems*, VI, 2 (1939), entire issue.

BERNARD, JESSIE, *Remarriage: A Study of Marriage* (New York: Dryden, 1956).

CAVAN, RUTH SHONLE, ed., *Marriage and Family in the Modern World: A Book of Readings*, (New York: Crowell, 1969), ch. 15, 16.

GLICK, PAUL C., *American Families* (New York: Wiley, 1957).

GOODE, WILLIAM J., *After Divorce* (Glencoe, Ill.: Free Press, 1956).

_____, "Education for Divorce," *Marriage and Family Living*, 9 (1947), 35–36.

_____, "Problems in Postdivorce Adjustment," *American Sociological Review*, 14 (1949), 394–401.

JACOBSON, PAUL H., and PAULINE F. JACOBSON, *American Marriage and Divorce*, (New York: Rinehart, 1959).

KEPHART, WILLIAM M., "Occupational Level and Marital Disruption," *American Sociological Review*, 20 (1955), 456–65.

LeMASTERS, E. E., "Holy Deadlock: A Study of Unsuccessful Marriages," *Midwest Sociologist*, 21 (July, 1959), 86–91.

LITWAK, EUGENE, "Three Ways in Which Law Acts as a Means of Social Control: Punishment, Therapy, and Education: Divorce Law a Case in Point," *Social Forces*, 24 (1956), 217–23.

"Migratory Divorce," *Law and Contemporary Problems*, II, 3 (1935), entire issue.

MONAHAN, THOMAS P., "Divorce by Occupational Level," *Marriage and Family Living*, 17 (1955), 322–24.

MUDD, EMILY H., *et al.*, *Marriage Counseling: A Casebook* (New York: Association Press, 1958).

PILPEL, HARRIET F., and THEODORA ZAVIN, *Your Marriage and the Law* (New York: Rinehart, 1952).

PLOSCOWE, MORRIS, *Sex and the Law* (New York: Prentice-Hall, 1951), chs. 2 and 3.

_____, *Truth about Divorce* (New York: Hawthorne Books, 1955).

WALLER, WILLARD, *The Old Love and the New: Divorce and Readjustment* (New York: Liveright, 1930; Carbondale, Ill.: Southern Illinois University Press, 1967).

CHAPTER $I9$

Parents of Children

MOST YOUNG people marry with the expectation of having children. The many polls made during the 1930's, 1940's, and 1950's as a rule show a low percentage of high school and college students and engaged couples as well as of married people who do not wish any children after marriage. The massive study of almost 2,000 engaged people of the late 1930's made by Burgess and Wallin showed that only 3.1 per cent of men and 2.5 per cent of women did not desire children.[1] A study of approximately 900 married Michigan women made in the 1950's included the question, "If you could choose, or if you could start over again, how many children would you want to have?" Only 3 per cent of women living in Detroit and 1 per cent of women living on farms said "none."[2] Among 239 male students at the University of Washington, only 1 per cent said they did not want any children in their future marriage.[3] From these studies we may conclude that marriage is not conceived of as the beginning of a couple relationship but as the first step toward a family relationship. However, many couples want to control both the number and spacing of births. More and more, the planned family is replacing the natural family as the ideal.

[1] Ernest W. Burgess and Paul Wallin, *Engagement and Marriage* (Philadelphia: Lippincott, 1953), p. 410.
[2] Robert O. Blood, Jr., and Donald M. Wolfe, *Husbands and Wives: The Dynamics of Married Living* (New York: Free Press, 1960), p. 118.
[3] Charles E. Bowerman, "Attitude Norms about Optimum Size of Family," *The Coordinator*, 4 (March, 1956), 8–12.

Number of Children

Desire for children does not mean that children will necessarily follow. Some men and women are incapable of having children because of sterility; marriage may be followed by widowhood or divorce before children are born, and unless there is a good second marriage the person normally remains childless regardless of desire for children; also family conflict, unforeseen poverty, adverse conditions, or illness may cause a couple to change their minds after marriage.

NUMBER OF CHILDREN WANTED

The widespread use of birth control methods makes it feasible for individuals and married couples to plan for a given number of children. Slightly over half of both men and women among the engaged couples of the 1930's wanted two children; approximately 30 per cent wanted three children.[4] Only 4 per cent of men and 3 per cent of women desired only one child; about 10 per cent desired four or more children. More recent studies show that the desired number of children has increased slightly. Detroit wives specified one child among 2 per cent of wives; two children among 23 per cent; three among 24 per cent; four among 36 per cent; and more than four among 12 per cent.[5] A third study of some 2,700 wives selected as a national scientific probability sample showed that 85 per cent of these women would prefer to have two to four children if they could relive their lives.[6] With a slightly less personal emphasis, these wives were also asked what they considered to be the ideal number of children: 94 per cent considered two to four children as ideal, with three or four being the most popular numbers. According to a Seattle study of 330 high school seniors, 5 per cent wanted no children or only one; 46 per cent wanted two; 30 per cent, three; and 17 per cent, four. Only 2 per cent wanted five or more.[7] Boys and girls were in agreement. The University of Washington students already referred to gave the following preferences: 38 per cent wanted two children; 36 per cent, three; and 18 per cent, four. At the extremes,

[4]Burgess and Wallin, *op. cit.*, p. 410.
[5]Blood and Wolfe, *op. cit.*, p. 118.
[6]Ronald Freedman, Pascal K. Whelpton, and Arthur A. Campbell, *Family Planning, Sterility, and Population Growth* (New York: McGraw-Hill, 1959), pp. 216–26.
[7]Bowerman, *op. cit.*

1 per cent wanted no children and 1 per cent, one child; 6 per cent wanted five or more children.

These statements indicate a widespread desire for children in moderate numbers. The birthrate may be used as an indication of changing conceptions of a desirable number of children.

THE BIRTHRATE

The birthrate shows both long-term and short-term trends. The long-term trend of the crude birthrate—the number of births per 1,000 population—has been downward. The Appendix shows that in the 1870's the birthrate was 37 per 1,000 population; with some variation during and after World War I, it declined to a low point of 16.7 in 1936, the heart of the depression. With increased prosperity, the birthrate rose slightly, fluctuated during World War II, and then rapidly rose to 25.8 in 1947. It then leveled off at about 24 per 1,000 population, where it remained until 1960. Since this date the rate has slowly declined to 18.5 in 1966. It is generally assumed that the primary cause of this decline is the use of the oral contraceptive pill. More exact figures take into account the proportion of the female population that is in the childbearing age, usually considered to be 14 to 45 years. The proportion of the population that is married and the age of marriage also affect the rate at any given time. Economic conditions and wars cause many of the short-term fluctuations.

Without regard to past causes or future trends, the family of the 1960's is receptive to two to four children, and this number seems to be widely accepted as the "standard" number of children that the average family should have. Freedman concluded that wives who wanted, expected, or had fewer than two children usually were subfecund, that is, they were not capable of bearing more children. Conversely, wives wanting, anticipating, or having more than five children often failed in their attempts to limit the number of children or belonged to religious groups that advocated large families.[8]

The discussion of social classes has already disclosed that the birthrate is higher in lower social classes than in higher ones, as shown by studies of social classes, income, occupational level, and education of the mother. Several explanations may be suggested for the differences. Lower-class families tend to accept children as a natural and normal consequence of marriage. Low-income families include a higher proportion of families of recent European origin, often affiliated with the

[8]Freedman, *et al., op. cit.,* pp. 103–15, 216–26.

Catholic Church; other groups, such as Puerto Ricans on the mainland and Mexican–Americans or newly arrived Mexicans, are also Catholic. Many of these same families come from rural backgrounds and, as with American rural families, tend to accept children as the natural result of marriage. It is true, also, that as educational level increases, the range of interests broadens and the desire for children often competes with other interests or with a desired standard of living. Another factor among low-income groups is the lack of accurate knowledge of reliable contraceptives and of money to purchase them.

The effect of religion is indicated by Table 19, which shows the highest average number of children per family to be among Roman Catholics, and the lowest among Jews.

TABLE 19

AVERAGE NUMBER OF CHILDREN PER WOMAN, AGED 45 AND OVER, WHO
HAD EVER BEEN MARRIED, BY RELIGIOUS AFFILIATION

Religion	Average number of children
Total population	2.8
Roman Catholic	3.1
Protestant	2.8
Jewish	2.2
Other, none, and not reported	2.7

SOURCE: *Statistical Abstract of the United States, 1961* (Washington, D.C.: Government Printing Office, 1961), p. 53.

Size of community as a factor was presented in Chapter 3. In general, the larger the city, the smaller the average number of children, with the great metropolitan centers having many fewer children than farm areas.

Control of Births

Discussions of birth control have three foci: attitudes toward limitation of births; methods of birth control; and spacing of births.

ATTITUDES TOWARD LIMITATION OF BIRTHS

In some societies and cultures it is a positive value for a woman to produce a large number of children and not to attempt by artificial means to limit the number. In some societies it is important for the wife to produce as many sons as she can. In our own rural past, children had an economic value. Many immigrant groups, rural in background, brought this same attitude toward large families with them. Moreover, efforts to avoid conception or to terminate the pregnancy often had negative religious sanctions and under certain conditions were illegal. Some of these attitudes and negative sanctions exist today in different parts of the United States.

According to the traditional attitudes of the Mormons, wives were expected to bear as many children as possible, for the status of the patriarch (husband or male Mormon ancestor) was enhanced by a large number of children, especially sons. They and their descendants were part of his family unit down the ages in eternity. Today, the Mormons still highly value large families.

The Catholic philosophy regards the essential purpose of sex functions as reproductive and, therefore, defines deliberate prevention of conception by artificial means as a sinful act. But self-denial in sex relations is not sinful; to prevent conception, this consists of avoiding intercourse during the period of the menstrual cycle when the woman is fertile. Conflicting statements have appeared regarding the purpose of such avoidance.[9] Many theologians regard observance of the infertile or "safe" period as indifferent from a moral standpoint. Opinions vary as to the reasons that justify avoiding intercourse during the fertile period. The consensus seems to be that conception should not be avoided for selfish purposes or for a general desire not to have children; avoidance is justified by such reasons as danger from pregnancy to the life or health of the mother, the likelihood of giving birth to a defective child, inability to provide the necessities of life to a child, or a serious housing crisis or similar social problem. According to the reason, limitation of intercourse to the safe period would be permanent or temporary.

Other organizations and individuals differ in their attitudes. A number of Protestant denominations have made formal statements in favor of family planning and voluntary childbearing.[10] The following denominations have been cited as making such statements, and undoubtedly others could be added: Augustana Evangelical Lutheran Church Synod (1954), Congregational Christian Churches, General

[9] Clement Simon Mihanovich, Brother Gerald J. Schnepp, and Rev. John L. Thomas, S.J., *Marriage and the Family* (Milwaukee, Wis.: Bruce Publishing Co., 1952), ch. 14; The Very Reverend Msgr. George A. Kelly, quoted by John Rock "We Can End the Battle Over Birth Control," *Good Housekeeping*, 153 (July, 1961), 44–45ff.

[10] "Religious Bodies Speak on Planned Parenthood," *Social Action*, 25 (December, 1958), 18–19.

Council (1931), Evangelical and Reformed Church, General Synod (1947), Methodist Church, Quadrennial Conference (1956), Protestant Episcopal Church, General Convention (1946), and United Lutheran Church, 20th Biennial Convention (1956). The statements indicate that planning for children should be regarded as a Christian responsibility in order to promote health, wholesome family life, and social well-being.

The chief spokesman for control of family size as a national policy is the Planned Parenthood Federation of America. An official of this organization has been quoted in Chapter 2 of this book as saying: "Planned parenthood is the utilization of medical knowledge for the procreation of the number of children any given couple want to have, born when the family is ready for them."[11] Although this statement implies that family planning depends upon the individual whim of the husband and wife, a rationale has developed to support the movement for family planning. Such reasons as the following are given: Every child will be a wanted child, and the emotional problems attached to the status of an unwanted child will be avoided; children can be spaced according to the health needs of the mother; births can be adjusted to economic status, housing facilities, and the career of the father; the likelihood of stillbirth is less when children are spaced two or three years apart than when the interval between births is less.[12] The Planned Parenthood Federation recognizes that not all couples have the number of children they desire; their program therefore includes dissemination of information on the possibilities of treatment for infertility.

In its early history, the Planned Parenthood Federation of America was called the American Birth Control League (1921).[13] Even before this date, Margaret Sanger had opened the first birth control clinic, in Brooklyn, and as a result was arrested for "maintaining a public nuisance." Margaret Sanger and her followers persisted in opening clinics, carrying on research, and propagandizing their philosophy of birth control, regardless of raids, arrests, and legislation opposing their work. Gradually, various organized groups and a segment of the public gave support to the movement. Margaret Sanger's original interest had arisen from her first-hand knowledge of the health hazards

---

[11]David Loth, "Planned Parenthood," *Annals of the American Academy of Political and Social Science*, 272 (November, 1950), 95–101.

[12]Publications of the Planned Parenthood Federation of America, Inc., 501 Madison Avenue, New York.

[13]*Birth Control, U.S.A.: Highlights of the Program*, pamphlet published by the Planned Parenthood Federation, undated.

of unspaced and unlimited births, gained through her services as a public health nurse in the East Side of New York City. The first objectives of the movement had been to alleviate the problems of the poor, through teaching women to use contraceptives. The later and present objectives do not emphasize merely limitation of the total number of children nor are they conceived as applicable only to the poor. A somewhat more positive approach is taken, to assist any and all, regardless of economic background, to plan for a certain number of children and to space them according to the wishes or needs of the parents. The objective of treatment for "involuntary sterility" was listed as one of the Federation's services for the first time in 1943. In forty years the movement has become national and international in scope, and has changed its emphasis from limiting the number of children born to poverty-stricken mothers to a positive program for helping couples have the number of children desired.

Although there is far from a uniform acceptance of the need for family planning, the various religious and secular groups have tended to move toward a common viewpoint—that there are family and social conditions under which it is beneficial to family and society to limit or space the births of children. It seems probable that the movement toward a common philosophy will continue, although perhaps not agreement on the optimum number of children that is socially desirable.

METHODS OF BIRTH CONTROL

The desire to prevent conception and to terminate unwanted conceptions before birth is evident in many primitive tribes and runs back into the remote history of present civilized nations.[14] The methods used were crude and often magical and therefore ineffective. Present methods are scientifically supported but are not always effective; nor are all types approved by different opinion-forming groups.

The rhythm method, which is widely accepted by Catholics and by others who wish to avoid chemical and mechanical devices, consists of refraining from intercourse during the few days each month when the woman is fertile and therefore likely to conceive. It is, however, an unreliable method, since many women are unable to determine with certainty each month when the fertile period is at hand.

Chemical measures that destroy the semen or mechanical devices

[14]Norman Himes, *Medical History of Contraception* (Baltimore: Williams and Wilkins, 1936).

that prevent the semen from having contact with the ovum have greater reliability than the rhythm method. Their use is sometimes regarded as an interference to the process of love-making that reaches its climax in intercourse or as a deterrent to full enjoyment. These contraceptives are banned by the Catholic Church as interfering artificially with the purpose of God.

The oral contraceptive pill gives almost complete control over conception if used regularly. Early fears of unfavorable side effects have been allayed, although such possible effects are still under study. Certain religious groups are opposed to it; other organized groups propagandize strongly for its use. Surveys and the mounting sales indicate widespread acceptance. The success of the pill has stimulated research into other methods, including experimentation with an injection that might be administered to a woman by a physician at fairly long intervals. Other possibilities include injections that might be given to the man, to suppress his sperm production. Another method is the use of the intra-uterine device (IUD), a small loop that can be inserted into the uterus by a physician and which prevents conception. Many women react negatively to the use of this device, sometimes because they do not like the idea of a foreign body remaining permanently in the uterus. It seems probable that other types of contraceptives will be developed in the near future.[15]

ABORTION

Abortion does not prevent conception but is a way of terminating pregnancy. Since induced (illegal) abortions are criminal acts and subject to severe penalties, they are performed with great secrecy, and no record of their occurrence is available. Evidence primarily on upper-middle- and upper-class women, published in 1958, indicated that one-fourth of pregnancies among young wives were terminated by an induced abortion.[16] This youthful period was followed by a period with a lower percentage of induced abortions. Subsequently, as couples sought to bring their childbearing to a close, induced abortions increased again.

The evidence on the use of contraceptives and abortions indicates the means by which American couples move toward their objective

[15]For two readable articles on the subject of birth control and specifically on the contraceptive pill, see Steven M. Spencer, "The Birth Control Revolution," *Saturday Evening Post* (January 15, 1966), 21–25, 64–70; [Survey on contraceptives] *McCall's Magazine*, 95, No. 2 (November, 1967), 96–97, 166–174.

[16]Paul H. Gebhard, *et al., Pregnancy, Birth, and Abortion* (New York: Harper, 1958), p. 119.

of two to four children. The sensitive periods of marriage come at the beginning when couples do not feel ready for babies, and at the approach of middle age, when they feel that their families are as large as they should be. When acceptable methods of contraceptives fail, some couples seek the aid of an abortionist.

SPACING OF CHILDREN

When nothing is done to prevent conception, the first child usually arrives approximately 13 months after marriage and subsequent children at intervals of 20 to 26 months.[17] Effective use of contraceptives may delay the birth of the first child for months or years. Newly married couples often have certain projects that they wish to accomplish before having the responsibility and expense of children. Such projects are especially likely to prevail among young people who have not completed their education, when the husband is not permanently established in his occupation, or when the couple wishes to reach a certain standard of living early in life.

Role Adjustment

With pregnancy and the birth of children, husband and wife adjust their roles in two ways: with reference to each other, and as parents of their children.

CHANGE IN HUSBAND-WIFE RELATIONSHIPS

With children, husband and wife have dual familial roles; to the husband role is added the father role, and to the wife role is added the mother role. The marital roles and the parental roles may be difficult to adjust; husband and wife whose roles were harmoniously coordinated before pregnancy may find their relationship seriously disturbed.

Often during the early period of marriage the role of the young wife resembles that of the "companion" as described in Chapter 17—the wife whose dominant activity is to look well and accompany her husband on pleasurable jaunts. With the birth of a baby the wife be-

---

[17]Regina Stix and Frank W. Notestein, *Controlled Fertility* (Baltimore: Williams and Wilkins, 1940); H. T. Christensen, "The Time-Interval between Marriage of Parents and the Birth of Their First Child in Utah County, Utah," *American Journal of Sociology*, 44 (1939), 518–25.

gins to shift to the mother role, which calls for a corresponding change in the role of the husband. The actual changes made may involve such things as the way evenings and weekends are spent, the wife being no longer free to accompany her husband to club, movie, or dance in the evening or to dash off at short notice on a week-end trip. Sometimes both husband and wife remain home and develop family activities; sometimes the husband spends certain evenings away from home with men friends, and on other evenings cares for the baby while his wife meets her women friends. Occasionally the husband attempts to substitute some woman friend for his wife as a companion in recreation; but this violates the middle-class mores and may lead to serious conflict between husband and wife.

When the wife has followed the partnership role, as developed by Kirkpatrick, children are fitted into the marital pattern with still greater difficulty.[18] The wife who has trained herself for a definite business or profession receives much of her feeling of worth and self-esteem from her success in following her chosen occupation. Accustomed to participating in the stimulating rush of vocational activity, where she pits her abilities against those of competitors or cooperators, she feels let down when her social world is restricted to the home and her activities and mental stimulation to the physical demands and limited capacities of a small child.

The husband in the partnership marriage must also make adjustments. For one thing, if his wife stops working, their joint income may be cut in half. The entire burden of support of the family is suddenly thrown upon him, at a time when medical care and the addition of a third member greatly increase expenses. If the standard of living has been based upon the joint income, it is often necessary to reduce it— to sell the car or move to a less expensive apartment. The husband may value his fatherhood more than material assets and regard the exchange of income for a baby as worth while. If he does not, he may resent the baby or the necessity of his wife's not working.

The husband may also find it difficult to adjust himself to the change in his wife's interests. Instead of talking about the problems and successes of her job she now relates the latest achievements of the baby. If she is trying to carry on her job after the birth of the baby, she may be harassed and overburdened with the two tasks and have little time or attention for him.

[18]Clifford Kirkpatrick, "Ethical Inconsistencies in Marriage," *International Journal of Ethics*, 46 (1935–36), 444–60.

SEXUAL ADJUSTMENT AFTER PREGNANCY

A study of 212 married couples at Michigan State College throws some light on the relation of the first pregnancy to sexual adjustment.[19] Sixty-three per cent of the pregnancies occurred before the end of the first year of marriage, 23 per cent in the second or third year, and 14 per cent later. Fifty-eight per cent of husbands and wives reported that the pregnancy had had no effect upon their sexual adjustment; for the most part these couples had a good adjustment prior to pregnancy. Seventeen per cent of the wives and 19 per cent of the husbands believed the pregnancy had improved adjustment; most of these people had had poor adjustment prior to pregnancy. Twenty-five per cent of the wives and 23 per cent of the husbands felt that the effect of pregnancy had been unfavorable; in these cases adjustment had been good before the pregnancy, but had decreased largely because of the fatigue of the wife from the care of the baby or because she felt less desire than at an earlier period. In approximately three-fourths of the cases, therefore, sexual adjustment either was not disturbed or was improved by the first pregnancy.

THE FIRST BABY

So acute were the problems of adjustment to the first baby observed by E. E. LeMasters that he interviewed 46 couples of middle-class status.[20] Thirty-eight of the couples reported that the birth of a child precipitated a crisis; that is, they were unprepared for the readjustment in roles called for by the addition of a baby to the marriage, changes in relative status positions, and reorientation of values. They experienced difficulty in accustoming themselves to meeting their needs through new channels or in new ways. Mothers reported such problems as the following: loss of sleep, physical exhaustion, dislike of excessive confinement to the home and loss of social contacts, lowered income in terms of needs, additional housework, worry over appearance, and decline in housekeeping standards. Many felt guilty because they were not "better mothers." Fathers suffered from many

[19] Judson T. Landis, Thomas Poffenberger, and Shirley Poffenberger, "The Effects of First Pregnancy upon the Sexual Adjustment of 212 Couples," *American Sociological Review*, 15 (1950), 766–72.

[20] E. E. LeMasters, "Parenthood as Crisis," *Marriage and Family Living*, 19 (1957), 352–55.

of the same adjustment problems and also mentioned the decline in
the sexual response of their wives, worry about a second pregnancy,
and, in general, "disenchantment" with the role of father. LeMasters'
conclusion was that people now tend to romanticize parenthood.
Courses in marriage preparation and the many popular books on marriage have tended to give a fairly realistic conception of marriage and
of the adjustments demanded, but have failed to prepare young people
for their future roles as parents.

A later study confirmed LeMasters' findings but added some qualifications. The crisis seems to be related to "(a) the state of the marriage
and family organization at the birth of the first child; (b) the couple's
preparation for marriage and parenthood; (c) the couple's marital
adjustment after the birth of the child; and (d) certain social background and situational variables such as the number of years married,
'planned parenthood,' and the age of the child," at the time of the
study. Recovery from the crisis seemed long-drawn-out for 40 per cent
of the couples experiencing a crisis; this group still experienced problems when, on the average, the child was a year old.[21]

A third study, using somewhat more precise techniques, did not
fully support the two earlier studies. It was made when the babies
were on the average 9.8 weeks old—younger than the average age in
the two previous studies. Except that fathers seemed concerned about
income, the parents generally were thrilled by their new parenthood.
With such diverse findings, the author of the third study suggests
additional studies with more careful selection of parents and more
precise methods.[22]

Changes in Roles of Parents: The Developmental Concept

The roles of parents gradually change in accordance with general
social changes that affect the family. One writer speaks of a century
of declining paternal authority.[23] The discussion in Chapter 17 of
the wife's role included the changing maternal role as women increasingly become permanent members of the labor force. New concepts of

[21]Everett D. Dyer, "Parenthood as Crisis: A Restudy," *Marriage and Family
Living*, 25 (1963), 196–201.

[22]Daniel F. Hobbs, Jr., "Parenthood as Crisis: A Third Study," *Journal of Marriage
and the Family*, 27 (1965), 367–72.

[23]J. M. Mogey, "A Century of Declining Paternal Authority," *Marriage and Family
Living*, 19 (1957), 234–39.

parenthood and new roles to fit the concepts are in the process of evolving.

One change has been from an authoritarian to a developmental conception of childrearing.[24] In general, parents do not conceive of themselves as authoritarian figures, issuing orders and demanding instant obedience. The role of disciplinarian is combined with the roles of teacher and counselor. The personality development of the child as a goal of childrearing has superseded the older goal of obedience without question. A current principle is that each child has a unique personality that he should be allowed to develop with some freedom. It is also conceded that under present conditions of mobility and complex urban conditions rules cannot be made that will fit all situations and last through a lifetime; therefore, children should be helped to become mature and well adjusted; they should be taught to examine the situations in which they find themselves and make rational decisions. Under the newer conceptions, the functions of parents are much more difficult to discharge than when parents assumed an authoritarian position and laid down rigid rules for their children to follow. The parents must understand both the world in which they live and at least the elements of child psychology; they must themselves be well organized personally.

PERMISSIVENESS

As the older pressure on the child to conform to the parents' rules and to an orderly regime lessened, a new concept of parent-child relationship developed—permissiveness. According to this concept, the child was given wide leeway in establishing his own schedule of activities; even the small infant was to find his own natural schedule for eating, sleeping, and waking. The older child was to be given as much freedom as possible both within and outside the home. For some people, permissiveness became a cult; in and of itself, freedom from restraint was good for the child. This extreme position overlooked the processes by which a child becomes socialized into his particular culture.[25] As parents and neighbors learned of the disruption to family and neighborhood life that attends extreme permissiveness in childrearing, controls

[24]Evelyn Millis Duvall, "Conceptions of Parenthood," *American Journal of Sociology*, 52 (1946), 193–203; Duvall, *Family Development* (Philadelphia: Lippincott, 1967), ch. 3; Rachel Ann Elder, "Traditional and Developmental Conceptions of Fatherhood," *Marriage and Family Living*, 11 (1949), 98–100, 106.

[25]See Chapter 12.

were again established over children, though without a full return to older forms of repressive measures.[26]

THE PERSON-CENTERED FAMILY

A new relationship of parents to children is implied in the phrase, person-centered family.[27] As authoritarianism of parents gave way to consideration for children, the family tended to become child-centered —a characteristic especially of the middle-class family. This concept yielded to another: that all members of the family were entitled to fulfillment of needs, that is, that the parent's generation need not. sacrifice their needs or curtail their own personality development in order to advance their children. This is not to imply neglect of the children nor the demand that children make great sacrifices for the parents. Rather, all members of the family should be considered and their needs and potentialities assessed. Children should contribute to the opportunities for parents to live a full life as well as vice versa.

A HYPOTHESIS CONCERNING ENTREPRENEURIAL AND BUREAUCRATIC FAMILIES

A study made in the Detroit area sought to relate emphases in child-rearing to the shift that is taking place in the economic world, from self-employment of the husband (the entrepreneur) to employment in a highly organized enterprise (the bureaucratic organization).[28] The entrepreneur acts as an individual and suffers or benefits from his own decisions and acts. It was part of the hypothesis of the study that when the father was an entrepreneur (or was employed in a loosely organized business), he would train his children to be self-reliant and self-controlled, to look to the future, and to be able to manipulate their environment. They would have to depend upon themselves as adults. The hypothesis also extended to childrearing in families in which the father was an employee of a large bureaucratic organization with a welfare orientation. The employee needed less independence,

[26]For a discussion of permissiveness and its consequences, see Robert O. Blood, Jr., "Consequences of Permissiveness for Parents of Young Children," *Marriage and Family Living*, 15 (1953), 209–12, and "A Situational Approach to the Study of Permissiveness in Child-Rearing," *American Sociological Review*, 18 (1953), 84–87.

[27]Ivan F. Nye and Lois W. Hoffman, *The Employed Mother in America* (Chicago: Rand McNally, 1963), ch. 1.

[28]Daniel R. Miller and Guy E. Swanson, *The Changing American Parent: A Study in the Detroit Area* (New York: Wiley, 1958).

since he was less often called upon to make crucial decisions, and an affable and cooperative personality, which would enable him to accommodate himself to membership in a large organization. He would therefore train his children to have these qualities. The authors of the study sought to find a connection between the father's economic life-organization and the details of childrearing in the home. The relationship was not clear-cut, but the study raises new questions regarding the relationship between parents and children, as well as needed changes in the goals of childrearing to fit the major changes in social life.

The Employed Mother

The employment of married women, including mothers, is now a generally accepted practice. Many employed mothers make concessions to the needs of their children, through part-time, temporary, or seasonal work.[29]

Regardless of concessions, many employed mothers suffer mental conflict regarding the care of their children. The feeling is strong that the mother is the best person to rear her children, especially in the preschool years, but whether she is or is not is sometimes a moot question. What is important in the choice of roles is not fact but feeling. The husband may feel that his wife should now remain at home, or he may be torn between his desire for her pay check and his fear that the children may be neglected. Grandparents, especially when the grandmother was not herself employed during her children's younger years, often are critical. Especially in upwardly mobile families, both husband and wife may fear loss of status if the wife works, particularly if her type of work does not carry some prestige. If a child becomes ill, the wife is torn between her obligation to her employer and to her child.

Against these oppositions to employment of the mother of young children, employed mothers erect strong rationalizations. Some say they become impatient with their children, whereas some elderly relative or paid housekeeper has more patience; or that it is better for a child to be in a nursery school with other children of his own age than at home alone or with older brothers and sisters. They point to the material advantages they can provide such as bicycles or better clothing, or cultural advantages such as dancing lessons or elaborate record

[29]*1965 Handbook on Women Workers*, Women's Bureau Bulletin No. 290 (Washington, D.C.: Government Printing Office, 1966), p. 44.

players. Some of these situations may provide an advantage to the child, but often they are cited by the wife to assuage her feeling of guilt over delegating the care of her child to someone else.

CARE OF CHILDREN

Neither public attitudes toward the mother's role nor public policy gives the mother much help in arranging care for young children. A study of child care arrangements that were made by fully employed mothers for children under the age of six showed that they placed a great variety of persons in charge of the children, as indicated in Table 20. The percentage of children cared for by the father suggests that either the father and mother worked on different shifts or the father was unemployed or unemployable. The great variety of types of care indicates that mothers individually make their own arrangements, in all probability according to individual ideas as to the adequacy of the type of care and the caretaker chosen.

Group (day-center) care was utilized for only 6 per cent of children. Few American communities have day-care centers or nursery schools; or they may have one or two for the children of mothers who must work from necessity. In general, the concept of group care for children is not part of the American culture. In various other countries, day nurseries are provided by public subsidies for the care of young children of employed mothers. The Scandinavian countries are outstanding in their provision of excellent small day nurseries where children still in the cradle as well as older preschool children may be left, with care provided also for the after-school hours of children in elementary school.

Research reports on the effect of the mother's employment on children are too numerous to summarize in detail.[30] Some conclude that the young child does not suffer from separation from the mother, provided that consistent care is given by a warm, friendly woman, or indeed in a group of such adults. If a child lives in a neighborhood where most mothers are employed, he accepts his mother's absence as normal and does not feel discriminated against. Among school children, clear-cut effects of employment of the mother on personality or academic achievement have not been found. Often other factors in the study that might affect adjustment or achievement, such as social class or ethnic culture, have not been controlled.

[30]Elizabeth Herzog, *Children of Working Mothers*, Publication No. 382–1960 of the Children's Bureau (Washington, D.C., 1960); Nye and Hoffman, *op. cit.*

TABLE 20

CHILD CARE ARRANGEMENTS OF WORKING MOTHERS' WITH CHILDREN UNDER
SIX YEARS OF AGE, FEBRUARY, 1965 (PER CENT DISTRIBUTION)

Type of arrangement	
Care in child's own home	47*
By father	15
By other relative	18
By nonrelative	15
Care in someone else's home	30
Other arrangements	23*
Group care (day care center, etc.)	6
Child looked after self	1
Mother looked after child while working	15
Mother worked only during child's school hours	1
Other arrangements	1
Number (in thousands)	3,778
Per cent	100

*Note: The subtotals add up to one more than the total for the first and third items.
This is as the figures stand in the source and is apparently due to rounding off of
numbers.

SOURCE: *1965 Handbook on Women Workers*, Women's Bureau Bulletin No. 290
(Washington, D.C.: Government Printing Office, 1966), p. 49.

Parenthood in the Divorced Family

When a married couple with children are divorced, the relationship
of parents to children changes drastically.

NUMBER OF CHILDREN OF DIVORCED PARENTS

Among the 64 million children under age 18 in 1960, an estimated
3.3 million were living with a parent who was currently separated or
divorced.[31] In addition, it was estimated that another 5 million children under 18 were living with a parent who had been divorced previously, but had remarried. In all, slightly over an eighth of all children
were not living with both of their own parents. Since divorces tend to
occur during the early years of marriage, many of the children were
young at the time of the divorce.

[31]Paul C. Glick, *American Families* (New York: Wiley, 1957), Table 96; Glick,
"Marriage Instability: Variations by Size of Place and Region," *Milbank Memorial Fund Quarterly*, XLI, 1 (January, 1963), 43–55. Estimates are based on
data from the Bureau of the Census and the National Office of Vital Statistics.

Loss of Parental Roles

When both parents are at home, they share in responsibilities for the children and tend to work out coordinated mother and father roles. With divorce, the coordination of roles is lost. Usually the children are placed in the custody of the "innocent party" by the trial judge. Since the wife usually brings the suit for divorce, she therefore is assumed to be the "innocent" party and obtains custody of the children. When the husband brings the suit and charges his wife with misconduct or a violation of the marriage contract, the children may be awarded to him. In occasional cases the children are awarded to a third party. Usually all the children in the family are kept together. The customary arrangement, however, is for the mother to have the custody of the children, with the father having certain privileges of visiting them or having them live with him periodically or visit him. One arrangement is for the children to live with the mother during the school year, spending vacations with the father. Usually the father is required by the court to pay a certain amount for the support of the children and sometimes alimony to his former wife. Therefore, in daily life during all or the greater part of the year, the children have daily association with their mother, whereas their contacts with the father become intermittent, although he continues to play one part of his traditional role—that of contributing to the support of the children. By this arrangement the child experiences discontinuity of family life, a situation that is both criticized and defended by social workers and judges. One judge lists the advantages as follows:[32]

1. The child retains contacts with both parents and has the love and advice of both; both are in a position to protect the child's future welfare.
2. The child has the opportunity to experience two homes; this arrangement is especially advantageous in states in which at a certain age the child may choose the parent with whom he will thereafter live.
3. The father is more willing to help his children if he knows them.

Others concerned with the welfare of children have stated the disadvantages as follows:

1. If the child is shifted about, he must adjust to two domestic situations and perhaps to two stepparents, if both real parents have

[32]Carl A. Weinman, "The Trial Judge Awards Custody in Children of Divorced Parents," *Law and Contemporary Problems*, 10 (1944), 726.

remarried; there is great risk of discontinuity of emotional and intellectual development.

2. The child becomes a means of communication between the divorced parents. Each may express his resentment toward the other through his treatment of the child, remarks about the other parent, and so on; the child not only carries the comments back and forth but is affected by them.[33]

3. The child may be used by one parent to punish the other. He may be urged to make exorbitant demands when he visits the other for toys, clothing, and the like; if the parent refuses the child may feel unloved by the parent.

4. As a result, the child may be torn in his loyalties between the parents: he may feel rejected by both; or he may detach himself from loyalty to either and play one off against the other. Although these situations may exist in the family with both parents present, they are more likely to arise in the divorced family.[34]

Even when the parent with whom the child is staying does not attempt to undermine the relationship to the other parent, the situation presents problems. Each child is in need of both a mother figure and a father figure to serve as models for emotional and social development. During the time when the mother has the children she must attempt to be both mother and father; when the children are with their father he must attempt the dual role. This duality is difficult at any time and especially so when it is played only at intervals and when the parent of the opposite sex has recently been playing both roles. For instance, the mother in her behavior toward the children, her comments, and her admiration of certain men may hold up one masculine role to the children, which is sadly shattered when they visit their father who presents an entirely different masculine type. If the mother has remarried, she has often chosen a second husband somewhat in contrast to the first; the children may then have serious conflicts in their attempts to accept both the stepfather and the father as part of their array of adult models. The reverse situation is true when the father attempts to be both father and mother, or when he presents to the children a stepmother who may be markedly different in personality from their own mother.

The mother often has a difficult time in that the support received from the father may not be sufficient for expenses or she may have

[33]Kingsley Davis, "Sociological and Statistical Analysis," *Law and Contemporary Problems*, 10 (1944), pp. 700, 708, for points 1 and 2.

[34]James S. Plant, "The Psychiatrist Views Children of Divorced Parents," *Law and Contemporary Problems*, 10 (1944), 815, for points 3 and 4.

refused alimony for herself. She then faces the necessity of working and providing substitute care for her children. If part of the original marital maladjustment was the mother's dislike of the domestic role, she may be happier and make a better adjustment to her children than before the divorce. But if the employment is disliked or constitutes a severe physical strain, resentment against her ex-husband may grow and be transmitted to the children.

The father may also face a financial problem, especially if he wishes to remarry and must support two households. He may become increasingly bitter against his first wife and perhaps against his children. Many fathers also suffer from their inability to maintain a close relationship with their children. Accounts by fathers give the hopeful attitude with which they at first agreed to the mother's having custody of the children. Each hoped and planned to play a father role in his week-end and vacation visits and to remain an influence in the development of his children. But he found that the children's lives soon became organized around their mother, school life, and friends; the father was an outsider. His children were ill at ease with him, reluctant to give up social plans at home for the legally allowed visits, and over longer visits became homesick for their mother and friends. The harder the father tried to please his children, the wider the rift became; moreover, the mother often resented the gifts or special events provided by the father. The children were momentarily impressed by the break in their routine and, the mother felt, unappreciative of the daily care that she provided. A father who tried to discipline his children found that they were rebellious and no longer accepted him as a person in authority. Even the most solicitous father found himself an outcast.

As is true of adjustment of marital roles in divorce, adjustment of parental roles is worked out on an individual basis with much variety. Society has not developed acceptable roles for the divorced parent.

The Stepparent

Although formally a man or woman becomes a stepparent with marriage to a spouse who has children from a previous marriage, functionally the role is developed through interaction between husband and wife and between parents and children.[35]

In the case of a first marriage on both sides, custom grants the couple

[35]Stepparent-stepchild relationships are discussed in the following: Jessie Bernard, *Remarriage: A Study of Marriage* (New York: Dryden, 1956), ch. 12; Edward Podolsky, "The Emotional Problems of the Stepchild," *Mental Hygiene*, 39 (January, 1955), 49–53; William Carlson Smith, *The Stepchild* (Chicago: University of Chicago Press, 1953).

an interlude of romance and privacy. The honeymoon and a home of
their own are part of the mores and support the idea that newly
married people are entitled to establish their married life without
interference from others. But these ideas are not shared by children.
If their father or mother, newly married, goes honeymooning, sends
the children to boarding school, or substitutes social affairs with the
new spouse for earlier family activities, the children interpret the
situation as neglect. They feel left out, unloved, rejected; they withdraw or rebel, as their temperament may dictate. The twice-married
husband or wife must continue to be a parent at the same time that
he or she is groom or bride. The new spouse must immediately be willing
and able to include the children in their pair relationship. Thus, the
relationship established between husband and wife affects the stepparent role.

The stepparent, however, cannot impose himself upon the child
without the child's consent. No matter how zealous and eager to perform his functions, he cannot do so unless he is accepted as a parent
by the child. Several conditions discussed below may cause the child
to reject, rather than accept, the stepparent.

The age of the child when the stepparent comes into the family
is a factor. Very young children who do not remember their own parent
tend to look upon the stepparent with the same confidence and love
that they would have felt toward the natural parent. Older children
have more difficulty, since they often must break the bond of loyalty
to the natural parent before accepting the stepparent.

If there has been a divorce and both parents are still living, the
child may find it impossible to accept the stepparent even as a friend,
provided he sees and remains attached to his own parent. The situation
becomes still more confusing when both divorced parents have remarried and the child finds four parents competing for his love and
loyalty. When halfsiblings and stepsiblings are added to the family,
the child may be still more uncertain of his relationship to the various
members of the family. The stepparent may easily differentiate between his own and his stepchildren, if he sees in the stepchild a rival
for the spouse's affection. The child may also reject the stepparent
who seems to steal the love of his own parent. The following description,
written by the daughter, shows the complete exclusion of the stepfather from the girl's life.

My parents were divorced when I was two and thereafter I
seldom saw my father. I never felt any love for him and had not
established any emotional ties to him. For eight years mother and
I lived alone. Then mother remarried. My stepfather seemed
always like a complete stranger to me and sort of an intruder
whom I disliked. As the years passed I became indifferent toward

him and never considered him really part of my family. Family to me was just mother. There were a lot of factors that helped prevent our becoming adjusted. My stepfather was a forty-year-old bachelor who had lived alone; it was hard for him to adjust to a family way of life. He had been brought up in a European family where the man was the complete authority in the home. He tried to establish some authority in our home but my reaction was negative. He resented my taking orders only from my mother, and I resented his trying to become head of the household, since I had always had to abide only by my mother's wishes. There is little that we can do as a family; my parents go out a lot to avoid the bickering between me and my stepfather.

Some of these situations no doubt underlie the statistics in Table 21, which are based on grade school and high school boys and girls from North Carolina and Ohio.[36] High scores and low scores on a scale of affectional orientation to parents form the basis for comparisons of parent-child relationships (medium scores are omitted from the report). A study of Table 21 leads to the following conclusions: high affectional relationship with the own mother declines and low affectional relationship increases when there is a stepfather instead of the own father. The presence of a stepfather therefore seems to disturb the child's relationship with his own mother; in some way he no longer feels as close to her. The same relationship does not hold for the child and father among children in grades 7 to 9. Children feel closer to the father when there is a stepmother than when the own mother is present, perhaps as compensation for the loss of the mother's love. When the affection for the own parent is compared with that for the stepparent of corresponding sex, the contrast is sharp. Affection for stepparents is extremely low compared with affection for own parents. This contrast holds for both boys and girls and younger and older children.

The same study shows that children adjust to stepparents in slightly better fashion when the broken family is the result of divorce rather than death, a situation especially marked for girls in relation to stepmothers. The suggestion is made that at the time of a divorce children are usually young and remarriage often takes place soon after the divorce. It is also suggested that if there has been tension preceding a divorce children may reject the parent and accept the stepparent, whereas in case of death the child may idealize the parent and not readily accept the stepparent. Other possible explanations are discussed, pointing to the need for study of social-psychological relationships.

[36]Charles E. Bowerman and Donald P. Irish, "Some Relationships of Stepchildren to Their Parents," *Marriage and Family Living*, 24 (1962), 113–21.

TABLE 21

AFFECTION FOR PARENTS AND STEPPARENTS, BY GRADE IN SCHOOL,
NORTH CAROLINA-OHIO SAMPLES, PERCENTAGE DISTRIBUTION

Parent pattern	Males		Females	
	Grades 7–9	10–12	Grades 7–9	10–12
Both own parents				
Mother: high	48.7	34.8	55.7	42.5
low	12.7	21.6	13.4	23.0
Father: high	47.5	31.6	32.2	22.6
low	18.3	30.9	29.3	41.7
Mother-stepfather				
Own mother: high	43.9	30.8	50.8	39.4
low	20.0	31.8	19.0	29.7
Stepfather: high	30.2	12.2	16.4	9.2
low	41.6	56.3	56.4	72.0
Father-stepmother				
Stepmother: high	22.5	15.9	22.0	18.9
low	45.1	59.4	54.2	66.0
Own father: high	58.3	29.4	41.7	24.1
low	18.1	29.4	31.7	42.6

Intermediate scores are omitted.
Numbers: own mother and father, 17, 738 students; mother and stepfather 1,112
and 1,115 respectively; father and stepmother, 254 and 252 respectively.

SOURCE: Charles E. Bowerman and Donald P. Irish, "Some Relationships of Stepchildren to Their Parents," *Marriage and Family Living*, 24 (1962), 113–21.

Unmarried Parents

The ratio of illicit births to all live births has steadily increased since
1938.[37] The estimated number of illicit births per 1,000 live births was
38.4 in 1938 and 49.6 in 1958. When illicit births are taken as a rate per
1,000 unmarried females, the rate rose by regular increments from 7.1
in 1940 to 14.1 in 1950, to 21.8 in 1960, and to 23.4 in 1965. The total
estimated number of children born to unmarried mothers in 1965 was
291,200; since each year adds a similar or larger number, the total
number of illegitimate children in the population is much greater than
this figure.

[37]*Vital Statistics of the United States, 1958*, Sec. 3, "Natality Statistics," Table 3-W,
p. 3–27; *Vital Statistics, Special Reports*, Vol. 47, No. 8, pp. 226–27; *Vital Statistics of the United States, 1965*, Vol. 1, "Natality," pp. 1–24, 1–25 (Washington,
D.C.: Government Printing Office, 1960, 1967); *Statistical Abstract of the United
States, 1967* (Washington, D.C.: Government Printing Office, 1967), p. 51.

CHARACTERISTICS OF UNMARRIED MOTHERS

Racially, the nonwhite (primarily Negro) population contributes a high proportion of the illicit births. Although nonwhites constitute only about 10 per cent of the total population, in 1965 they were responsible for 58 per cent of illicit births. In the same year, the ratio of illegitimate births to live births (number of illicit births per 1,000 live births) was 39.6 for whites and 263.2 for nonwhites.

The connotation of illicit births differs greatly among whites and among Negroes.[38] As a legacy from slavery, when legal marriages of

TABLE 22

AGE OF UNMARRIED MOTHERS, 1965

Age	Illegitimate live births per 1,000 unmarried women in specified age groups*	Percentage distribution of unmarried mothers by age**
10–14	0.7	2.1
15–19	16.7	42.2
20–24	38.8	31.1
25–29	50.4	12.6
30–34	37.1	6.7
35–39	17.1	4.0
40–44	4.4	1.3
TOTAL	23.4	100.0

*Vital Statistics of the United States, 1965, Vol. I, Natality Statistics (Washington, D.C.: Government Printing Office, 1967), pp. 1–24.

**Statistical Abstract of the United States, 1967 (Washington, D.C.: Government Printing Office, 1967), p. 51.

slaves were not demanded, has come an acceptance among lower-class Negroes of common-law marriages and transient unions. The unwed state of the mother is not morally condemned; she tends to keep her baby, and she and the baby are reabsorbed into the mother's parental family or maintain their own home.

Table 22 shows two relationships of illegitimate births to age of the mothers. Column 2 shows the number of illegitimate live births to every thousand unmarried women of specified age categories. Column 3 shows the percentage distribution of unmarried mothers. Thus,

[38]H. Hertz and S. W. Little, "Unmarried Negro Mothers in a Southern Urban Community; A Study of Attitudes toward Illegitimacy," Social Forces, 23 (1944), 73–79.

although 42.2 per cent of all unmarried mothers are 15 to 19 years old, the number of their children per 1,000 unmarried women is low, because of the large number of unmarried women in this age group. The reverse is true for age 25–29, which has a low percentage of the total number of unmarried mothers, but a high rate of illegitimate births per 1,000 unmarried women, because of the relatively few unmarried women in this age period.

Until recently most studies of unmarried mothers placed them in the lower economic level.[39] They were poorly educated and held jobs requiring few skills. But such a situation does not tell the whole story. Some girls hold jobs in bars, restaurants, dance halls, and hotels that cater to men who anticipate sexual relations. Granting these becomes part of the girl's job. Undoubtedly when pregnancies occur, abortions often follow; nevertheless, some illicit births come from this group of girls. Another segment of the total aggregate of unmarried mothers is composed of middle- and upper-class girls, a group that has rarely been studied. Most studies are based upon case records from welfare agencies or hospitals operated by such agencies. Middle- and upper-class girls are more likely to have private physicians and to make an effort to conceal the fact of their pregnancy and the birth of the baby. Their case records have not been readily accessible for study.

A study made in California that secured the cooperation of private physicians as well as public and welfare hospitals showed that unmarried motherhood is not limited to lower-class girls and women but extends into the middle class and upper class, as judged by educational and occupational levels of the mothers themselves and of their fathers.[40]

It seems probable that some middle- and upper-class girls have always been included among the unmarried mothers. However, the increased leniency toward premarital sex relations in the middle class may have resulted in an actual increase of unmarried parenthood among middle-class girls.

DISPOSITION OF CHILDREN

The experience of motherhood for many unmarried mothers is chiefly biological; that is, few of the white unmarried mothers become mothers

[39]D. F. Puttee and M. R. Colby, *The Illegitimate Child in Illinois* (Chicago: University of Chicago Press, 1937); A. M. Donahue, *Children of Illegitimate Birth Whose Mothers Have Kept Their Custody* (U. S. Department of Labor, Children's Bureau, 1928); Ruth Reed, *The Illegitimate Family in New York City* (New York: Columbia University Press, 1934).

[40]Vincent, *op. cit.*

socially, for few keep their children. Negro mothers tend to keep their children, however.

Unmarried mothers who come to the attention of social agencies are assisted in making realistic plans for the care of their babies. These more often than not include adoption, since the girls are rarely able to make any other plan that will assure a secure home for the baby where it will be able to develop normally. Several studies show that approximately two-thirds to three-fourths of illegitimate children are placed with social agencies for care and future adoption.[41]

The Sexual Partners

Earlier studies of illegitimacy pictured the sexual partner of the unmarried mother in the role of an exploiter—older, better educated, and more sophisticated than the woman. Vincent's study, made in the 1950's, erases this generalization.[42] He found that the man and woman were very similar in education and age. For example, among unmarried fathers who were college graduates, 70 per cent had caused a female college graduate to conceive, 17 per cent a woman who had attended college, 9 per cent a high school graduate, and only 4 per cent a woman with less education. At the other extreme, among men with less than 12 years of education, none had impregnated a female college graduate, only 2 per cent a woman who had attended college, 19 per cent a high school graduate, and 79 per cent a woman with less than 12 years of education. A comparison by age showed that 56 per cent of the sexual partners were not more than three years apart—a difference in age very similar to that found among married people.

When Vincent inquired about the relationship between the mother and her partner, he found that 55 per cent of the women regarded the relationship as a close friendship or love relationship, 25 per cent as a casual relationship, 3 per cent as rape, while 17 per cent did not answer. White women were much more likely than Negro women to specify love or friendship, while Negro women more often identified the relationship as casual.

The above facts suggest that the illegitimate births grew out of the steady and casual dating relationships now current, with their permissiveness toward premarital sex relations. However, premarital pregnancies do not necessarily result in births before marriage. Many pregnant

[41]Leontine R. Young, "Personality Patterns in Unmarried Mothers," *The Family* 26 (1945), 296–303; T. E. Sullenger and M. A. Nelson, *Problems of Illegitimacy in Nebraska* (Municipal University of Omaha, undated, multigraphed), p. 19.

[42]Vincent, *op. cit.*, ch. 4.

unmarried women find a solution in abortion; others marry the fathers of the unborn children. Only a small proportion actually bear children out of wedlock. Attention has therefore turned to the characteristics of the women and men who become unmarried parents.

MOTIVATIONS OF THE UNMARRIED MOTHER

Certain studies have interpreted premarital pregnancies in terms of the mother's unconscious psychological needs. According to this type of analysis, babies do not "just happen," but are a means by which the mother tries to solve problems, not by deliberate planning for a pregnancy, but by relationships that almost inevitably result in pregnancy. The girl often is not in love with or has little interest in continued contact with the child's father, but for inner reasons "needs" a baby. The situation seems to stem from the girl's home, although not from any one pattern of family relationships. Leontine Young's analysis of cases led her to the conclusion that "the great majority of unmarried mothers come from homes dominated by the mother."[43] Depending upon circumstances, the girl seems to desire either to present a baby to her mother or to show hostility and defiance toward her. The girl who has been dominated by her father may also attempt to solve psychological needs through pregnancy. She may seek revenge on a father who has emphasized the evils of sexual offenses; of she may vent on the father of her child the anger that she feels toward her own father. Numerous other psychological problems are discussed in Young's book.

Vincent's study included a comparison of young unmarried mothers with high school girls, matched for certain essential factors.[44] His studies failed to reveal the prevalence of dominance on the part of the mothers of unmarried mothers; the percentage of dominant mothers was if anything slightly greater among the high school girls. Vincent found several types of girls among the unwed mothers. One type was the friendly girl who dated widely and thus had many opportunities for sexual experience: when this girl had had little training in traditional mores at home or in church, the way was opened in some cases for intercourse and pregnancy. A second type was the immature, rather submissive girl who became absorbed in a peer group in adolescence apparently to compensate for lack of self-confidence. She thus tended to lose her identity with her mother and to follow incautiously peer patterns of conduct. A third type was composed of rather immature, impulsive girls, lacking in ambition and accomplishing little in school.

[43]Leontine R. Young, *Out of Wedlock* (New York: McGraw-Hill, 1954), chs. 3–7
[44]Vincent, *op. cit.*, chs. 5 and 6.

They were not fully accepted into peer groups and tended to use a feminine appeal to obtain love; they yielded readily to sexual demands and probably would continue to do so. Six other types are described by Vincent; he also notes that about a third of his cases did not fall into any type, thus suggesting the highly individualistic pattern of the factors entering into any one case.

It may be suggested that Young's study seems to be limited to unmarried mothers with definite psychological difficulties who were referred to a casework agency, whereas Vincent's covers a high percentage of all unmarried mothers who gave birth to a child in one county during a specified period of time. He therefore found a wide range of personality types and of external conditions that contributed in some way to pregnancy and birth.

THE UNMARRIED FATHER

Less is known about the unmarried father than the unmarried mother. The mother may refuse to reveal his name; she may not be sure who the father is, if she has been promiscuous; or the father may disappear and become "lost" even when his name is known. The chief reason for attempting to locate the father is to establish paternity and exact medical costs or support for the child, either through court proceedings or voluntarily. Many girls or their families, however, prefer to shoulder the financial burden rather than have the attendant publicity.

Premarital sex relations (and to some extent extramarital) are widespread among men and have been discussed in previous chapters. Why do some of these men not take precautions against making the woman pregnant, and why do a few seem to crave the birth of a child? This is a group that has led to a few special studies.

In analyzing the motivations and reactions of the unmarried father, Reider states that some men have unconscious needs to impregnate a woman, paralleling the unconscious needs found in some women.[45] Unsure of their virility, they need proof not through sexual intercourse alone but through procreation. Others, feeling themselves inferior, need proof of potency before they venture into marriage. Some express their hostility toward women by causing women to become pregnant. But for most men such neurotic tendencies are not dominant; they are engaged in sexual adventures, and the news of a pregnancy comes as a surprise and shock. Shame and guilt are common reactions.

Reider feels that most men are willing to accept some financial

[45]Norman Reider, "The Unmarried Father," *American Journal of Orthopsychiatry*, 18 (1948), 230–37; see also Young, *Out of Wedlock*, ch. 8.

responsibility, especially if pressure is put upon them during their first guilt reactions. A study of 241 cases in which the mother kept the custody of the child showed, however, that only one-third of the fathers contributed to the support of their children, either after court action, voluntarily, or by marrying the mother. Many of them settled all responsibility by a flat payment of $50 to $500.[46] It seems certain that a smaller percentage of fathers take responsibility when the child is adopted. Thus the fathers evade a fundamental aspect of the father role.

Men evade the responsibility for a number of reasons: The child is a by-product of sexual experience—usually of a casual nature—and the man really does not feel personally responsible. He may accept the custom of paying for illicit sexual adventures but not be ready to assume a larger payment or continuing support of a child. He also wishes to avoid publicity. He may believe that the child is not really his and rebel at the prospect of paying for another man's child. Others try to escape admission of paternity, because of shame, fear of being duped by the woman, or the feeling that they have been "suckers."[47]

The father therefore plays a parental role to an even lesser degree than the mother. At best, he has a slight financial relationship with his baby, without assuming the status of a father. He may not even be told by the mother that she is pregnant; he may deny the fact; he may admit the paternity but evade all responsibility except possible payments inadequate for the rearing of a child. Socially in relation to the child he does not function at all. Psychologically he probably has few paternal feelings.

MARRIAGE FOLLOWING PREMARITAL CONCEPTION

A halfway situation arises when the father and mother are married after pregnancy has progressed for some months.[48] We have discussed

[46]Donahue, op. cit., pp. 24–25.

[47]Maud Morlock, "Establishment of Paternity," Proceedings of the National Conference of Social Work (1940), 363–76; Margaret Marsh, "Common Attitudes toward the Unmarried Father," Proceedings of the National Conference of Social Work (1940), 377–87; Reider, op. cit.

[48]Harold T. Christensen, "Studies in Child Spacing: Premarital Pregnancy as Measured by the Spacing of the First Birth from Marriage," American Sociological Review, 18 (1953), 53–59; Christensen and H. W. Meissner, "Studies in Child Spacing: Premarital Pregnancy as a Factor in Divorce," American Sociological Review, 18 (1953), 641–44; Christensen and B. B. Rubenstein, "Premarital Pregnancy and Divorce: A Follow-up Study by the Interview Method," Marriage and Family Living, 18 (1956), 114–23.

the feelings of frustration and resentment that may accompany the unplanned-for and unwanted pregnancy after marriage. The pregnancy that occurs before marriage but where pressure is brought from some source (girl, her parents, social agencies) to effect a marriage may be much more frustrating, especially among middle-class people. Curtailment of high school or college education may force a complete change of life plans. The disapproval of parents usually is marked. Sometimes parents reject the couple completely, or they may exonerate their own child but refuse to have anything to do with the partner to the affair. At the present time when moral disapproval is less strong toward premarital sex relations than formerly, young friends of the couple may not condemn them for immorality but may ridicule them for having mismanaged their relationship or criticize them for failing to complete their education or establish a home before bringing a baby into the world. The lessened condemnation of premarital sex relations does not extend to the birth of a child before marriage. Young and old feel a strong sense of responsibility toward legitimacy of children.

Marriages to protect a pregnant woman or to "give the baby a name" have less chance of success than those based on mutual affection and congeniality. Even when the pregnancy occurs in the course of a courtship that might have led to marriage, the marriage has tensions because individual ambitions may have to be sacrificed and the couple must face the disapproval of family and friends. Often the marriage is hurriedly carried through in a period of panic and fear of discovery of the pregnancy by others, without planning for the future. When there is little affection between the couple and the marriage is one of the "shotgun" variety carried out under compulsion from parents or with threat of legal reprisals upon the man, the marriage has little chance of success.

The Adequate Parent

The adequate parent is one who is personally mature and well adjusted. His relationship to the child is both warm and responsible. He recognizes the child's need for love and dependence, and he receives recompense for providing these needs through the child's response and the satisfaction of helping the child to develop. He does not expect to satisfy all his emotional or status needs through the child, however, and so does not burden the child by demanding from him the love that should come from the spouse or the ego satisfactions that an occupation or other accomplishments should afford.

Sometimes the parent functions under conditions that impair the relationship to the child, such as the death of one parent, divorce, or stepparenthood. These conditions need not be completely destructive, however. They call for more effort on the part of the parent and ability to accept added responsibilities.

Questions

1. What is the number of children usually desired by parents? What does this show about the American idea of the "ideal family size"?
2. What are the probable reasons for the larger number of children in the lower-class than in the middle-class family?
3. What is birth control? What are the attitudes of different religious groups toward it?
4. What is the Planned Parenthood Federation of America? What were its objectives when it was first formed under the title of American Birth Control League? What are its objectives now?
5. What are the advantages of trying to control the number and spacing of children? The hazards?
6. What change in roles of husband and wife is occasioned by the birth of the first child?
7. What does LeMasters mean by "Parenthood as Crisis"?
8. Are parental roles and individualism in marriage in harmony or in opposition?
9. In view of present urban conditions, does the developmental or the traditional conception of parenthood give more promise for well-adjusted children?
10. What kind of child care is most advantageous for the child of an employed mother? Discuss both physical surroundings and quality of care.
11. What does the child lose by having an absentee father?
12. How can divorced parents best contribute to their children's personality development?
13. Why do stepparents and stepchildren find it difficult to assume normal parent-child roles?
14. Do you approve of present attitudes and policies for the treatment of unmarried parents and of illegitimate children? If not, what changes would you suggest?

Bibliography

LIMITATION AND SPACING OF CHILDREN

GUTTMACHER, ALAN F., *Babies by Choice or Chance* (New York: Doubleday, 1959).

LOTH, DAVID, "Planned Parenthood," *Annals of the American Academy of Political and Social Science*, 272 (November, 1950), 95–101.

RAINWATER, LEE, et. al., *And the Poor Get Children* (Chicago: Quadrangle Books, 1960).

———, *Family Design* (Chicago: Aldine, 1965).

PARENTHOOD

CAVAN, RUTH SHONLE, ed., *Marriage and Family in the Modern World* (New York: Crowell, 1969), chs. 10, 17, 18, 19.

DUVALL, EVELYN MILLIS, "Conceptions of Parenthood," *American Journal of Sociology*, 52 (1946), 193–203.

———, *Family Development* (Philadelphia: Lippincott, 1967), ch. 3.

DYER, EVERETT, "Parenthood as Crisis: A Restudy," *Marriage and Family Living*, 25 (1963), 196–201.

ENGLISH, O. SPURGEON, "The Psychological Role of the Father in the Family," *Social Casework*, 35 (1954), 323–29.

HALPERN, HOWARD, "Alienation from Parenthood in the Kibbutz and America," *Marriage and Family Living*, 24 (1962), 42–45.

HERZOG, ELIZABETH, *Children of Working Mothers*, Publication No. 382-1960 of the Children's Bureau (Washington, D. C.: 1960).

HOBBS, DANIEL F., JR., "Parenthood as Crisis: A Third Study," *Journal of Marriage and the Family*, 27 (1965), 367–72.

LEMASTERS, E. E., "Parenthood as Crisis," *Marriage and Family Living*, 19 (1957), 352–55.

MILLER, DANIEL R., and GUY E. SWANSON, *The Changing American Parent: A Study in the Detroit Area* (New York: Wiley, 1958).

MOGEY, J. M., "A Century of Declining Paternal Authority," *Marriage and Family Living*, 19 (1957), 234–39.

NYE, IVAN F., and LOIS W. HOFFMAN, *The Employed Mother in America* (Chicago: Rand McNally, 1963).

The Significance of the Father (New York: Family Service Association of America, 1959).

TASCH, RUTH J., "The Role of the Father in the Family," *Journal of Experimental Education*, 20 (June, 1952), 319–61.

DIVORCED PARENTS

"Children of Divorced Parents," *Law and Contemporary Problems*, X, 5 (1944), entire issue.

STEPPARENTS

BERNARD, JESSIE, *Remarriage: A Study of Marriage* (New York: Dryden, 1956), ch. 12.

BOWERMAN, CHARLES E., and DONALD P. IRISH, "Some Relationships of Stepchildren to Their Parents," *Marriage and Family Living*, 24 (1962), 113–21.

PODOLSKY, EDWARD, "The Emotional Problems of the Stepchild," *Mental Hygiene*, 39 (January, 1955), 49–53.

SMITH, WILLIAM C., *The Stepchild* (Chicago: University of Chicago Press, 1953).

UNMARRIED PARENTS

BERNARD, V. W., "Psychodynamics of Unmarried Motherhood in Early Adolescence," *Nervous Child*, 4 (1944–45), 26–45.

BLOCK, BABETTE, SYLVIA OSHLAG, FRANCES H. SCHERZ, and LEONTINE R. YOUNG, *Understanding the Psychology of the Unmarried Mother*, reprinted from *The Family* and *Journal of Social Casework*, 1945–1947 (Family Service Association of America, 122 East 22d Street, New York 10010).

DAVIS, K., "Illegitimacy and the Social Structure," *American Journal of Sociology*, 45 (1939), 215–33.

——, "The Forms of Illegitimacy," *Social Forces*, 18 (1939), 77–89.

FUTTERMAN, S., and J. B. LIVERMORE, "Putative Fathers," *Journal of Social Casework*, 28 (1947), 174–78.

HERZOG, ELIZABETH, "Unmarried Mothers: Some Questions to Be Answered and Some Answers to Be Questioned," *Child Welfare*, 41 (1962), 339–50.

REIDER, N., "The Unmarried Father," *American Journal of Orthopsychiatry*, 18 (1948), 230–37.

VINCENT, CLARK E., "Unmarried Fathers and the Mores: 'Sexual Exploiter' as an Ex Post Facto Label," *American Sociological Review*, 25 (1960), 40–46.

——, *Unmarried Mothers* (New York: Free Press, 1961).

YOUNG, LEONTINE R., *Out of Wedlock* (New York: McGraw-Hill, 1954).

20

The Later Years of Married Life

THE MIDDLE years of married life begin in the forties or early fifties when children reach adulthood, and through marriage pass from their family of orientation; simultaneously the middle-aged parents pass gradually, as child after child marries, from their period of procreation into the final family stage of gerontation. The period after children marry is typically a long one—some 25 to 30 years for the average couple, or equal to the total of all the preceding periods of the family life cycle. It breaks into two sub-periods: a post-parental period, lasting from approximately age 45 to age 65, when retirement typically calls for a change of roles; and a retirement period that brings not only unemployment and lowered income but widow- or widowerhood.

The Postparental Years

In many ways the postparental years are relatively uneventful when compared with the earlier periods of adjustment to marriage and of childrearing (see Chapter 11). Although the trend toward widowhood has begun, it is offset to some extent by the decrease in divorces. Marriage and family life have reached a fairly high degree of stability. Earlier tensions have eased: the children are reared; the complexity of interpersonal relationships has become simplified. Disagreements between husband and wife over older in-laws have all but ceased. Roles are stabilized and disagreements over personality differences are at a low point. Recreation and other activities are no longer a source of disagreements. While certain kinds of companionship have declined from earlier periods, organizational and friendship companionship are higher than at earlier periods. Rate of employment and consequently income are at their peak. The postparental couple is in a position to be independent and to give aid both to their married children and their old parents. In return they receive moderate amounts of aid and emotional gratification.

This generally favorable picture of the couple in middle age is marred by some evidence of general lessening of satisfaction with marriage, which some writers refer to as disenchantment with marriage. The measures used by Blood and Wolfe, satisfaction with love and marital satisfaction, begin their decline in the early years of marriage and do not show any sudden change at middle age.[1] In contrast, the percentage of couples without disagreements increases markedly.

A study by Pineo made use of an elaborate scale of marital satisfactions to measure disenchantment.[2] His longitudinal study of 400 couples over twenty years of married life showed a general decrease in marital satisfaction and adjustment, and a loss of intimacy as indicated by a feeling of loneliness and infrequency of confiding, kissing, and reciprocal settlement of disagreements. Decline of frequency of sexual intercourse was noted but was not linked with disenchantment, nor was a decrease in shared activities.

Pineo suggests an explanation for the process of disenchantment. A man and woman personally choose each other for marriage, the choice bringing together two people who are reasonably well adjusted to each other and to external circumstances at the time of marriage. But external changes reduce the "fit" between husband and wife and a gradual loss of satisfaction is the result.

It is significant that even when the loss of satisfaction was great, the 400 couples had remained married over the twenty-year period. It might be assumed that losses noted in the study were compensated for by gains in other areas of life, or that marriage even with dissatisfactions was preferable to returning to single status by way of divorce.

WITHDRAWAL OF YOUNG ADULT CHILDREN

Many parents, especially mothers, have a "lost" feeling when the last child leaves home. However, the withdrawal of children is rarely abrupt, partly because children leave the family one by one, as they

[1]Robert O. Blood and Donald M. Wolfe, *Husbands and Wives: The Dynamics of Married Living* (New York: Free Press, 1960), pp. 232, 265.
[2]Peter C. Pineo, "Disenchantment in the Later Years of Marriage," *Marriage and Family Living*, 23 (1961), 3–11.

reach maturity.[3] Also, children begin to "leave" the family long before they marry. With the little child's first inclusion in a play group, he is opposing a social group to the family..It is not until adolescence, however, that peer groups become strong competitors of the family and are a serious threat to family unity. The boy or girl begins to emancipate himself from the family when he finds his deepest satisfactions among his peers rather than with his parents. Sometime during adolescence the child begins to prefer attending the movies with his contemporaries instead of his parents, turns down the family picnic in favor of the peer-group bicycle hike, or protests vigorously over spending Christmas with out-of-town grandparents because it will mean the self-denial of a dance or tobogganing. The child is withdrawing from the family and entering autonomous social groups. The initiative for withdrawal usually comes from the child, who is supported in his emancipation by his peers and by a general philosophy that adolescents must make a heterosexual adjustment and free themselves from the family.[4] When adolescents enter college or begin to work and earn their own money, they withdraw further from the family group; even if they continue to live at home, they participate more and more in extrafamily groups. The final symbol of emancipation is the marriage of the son or daughter, since in our culture each newly married couple is expected to establish an independent family.

A corollary of social withdrawal is psychological independence. The dependent child who leaned heavily upon the parents for love and approval loses this need with increasing maturity. Identification with the parents is replaced by identification with the peer group or some members of it and finally identification with the spouse.

Each step that the child takes away from the social boundaries of the family, each advance in independence, necessitates an adjustment on the part of the parents. In part, the adjustment is social. The mother, who for many years kept her late afternoon hours free from engagements in order to be at home when children came from school, finds herself in an empty house when adolescent children lengthen the school day by athletic practice, extracurricular activities, or "dates" at the drugstore; when grown children have jobs that take them from home for the entire day or when they leave home for college, the leisure hours are greatly increased. The father is less affected than the mother,

[3]For an excellent discussion of anticipatory socialization for postparental life, see Irwin Deutscher, "Socialization for Postparental Life," in Arnold M. Rose, ed., *Human Behavior and Social Processes* (Boston: Houghton Mifflin, 1962), ch. 26.

[4]For a discussion of this situation from the point of view of the adolescent, see Chapter 12.

since he customarily spent less time with the children when they were young. But he also finds the house empty when adolescents rush from home early in the evening for football or basketball games or to study at a chum's home. As with any change in social groupings, the remnants of groups left after the withdrawal of some members must reorganize. The older patterns of interaction are impossible; new ones develop. The group thus reforms on the basis of those who remain; or new members are introduced into the membership to replace the old. In the case of the family, husband and wife may increase their own areas of interaction, building up couple activities as family activities die out. Also, they may increase nonfamily contacts through closer association with friends who are in a similar stage of the family cycle. The mother especially feels the need for increased social contacts. Observation suggests that many middle-aged women fulfill this need through increased community service; boards and committees of community agencies are heavily loaded with middle-aged women whose daytime hours are free. When women are reviewed by agency heads and boards for possible volunteer service, the presence or absence of children is an important factor; the woman whose children are adult or near-adult is the one invited to serve.

The movement of women into employment that began while children were still in school is maintained, with about 40 per cent of married women between ages 45 and 54 holding jobs.[5] The percentage then drops to 24 per cent for married women in later middle age, 55 to 64 years.

EMPLOYMENT OF MIDDLE-AGED WIVES

So long as children are at home, the interest of the employed mother is likely to be divided between her children and her job. With the departure of children, the life organization of the wife tends to focus more closely on her work. She may turn from part-time to full-time work; she may obtain specialized training for a more demanding type of work than she followed when children required her care or supervision. Some women who have not worked since their marriage enter employment for the first time. In terms of goals and interests, employment takes on a new meaning, and the woman's scale of values may shift. She may seek high status among fellow employees and with her employers to replace her lost status as a good mother. She may therefore

---

[5]*1960 Handbook on Women Workers*, Women's Bureau Bulletin No. 275 (Washington, D.C.: Government Printing Office, 1960), p. 36.

become more competitive. If she is successful, she may gain a high degree of ego-satisfaction that compensates for the loss of the earlier affectional relationship with her children.

The relationship between husband and wife changes with absorption in employment of the middle-aged woman. Whereas formerly they filled paternal-maternal roles or the wife served as companion to her husband, in middle age they assume partnership roles. Any role adjustment is difficult, not only for the person making the change, but also for others affected by interrole relationships. The wife cannot drastically change her role without her husband's making corresponding changes in his role. The wife, upon employment, cannot become a partner unless the husband adjusts and a new interactional pattern is established. These role and interrole changes often cause temporary tension and even conflict.

Various compensations may offset the strain of adjustment. Freed from responsibility for supervision and financial support of children, husband and wife have the opportunity to build up their companionship in lieu of intensive absorption in their respective jobs. They may use some of their income for pleasure trips, a new home, or cultural pursuits that were not possible earlier.

The early retirement of the wife from employment reemphasizes the privilege accorded her of making choices in roles. The spurt in employment of women at middle age suggests a fling at independence and an attempt to prove her ability to compete in a wider field than the home. Having gained these satisfactions she is ready to decrease the burdens that work places on her.

The Clinging Parent

In contrast to women who expand their activities in new directions with maturity of their children are those who cling to the mother role when no dependent children remain to be mothered. Fathers also sometimes resist giving up the role of protector and adult model to their children. Such parents continue to direct, supervise, and make decisions for adolescent and older sons and daughters. The role often becomes intensified and is overplayed as son or daughter ignores the parental directives or openly rebels. Parents who play an outmoded parental role underestimate the abilities of their children to look out for themselves and hence are riddled by fears and insecurities. They also see their only avenue for ego-satisfaction and status closing before them. Hence, the departure of a child for college or the marriage of son or daughter is treated as a bereavement, with parents grieving for the loss of the child's dependency as they might grieve over the physical death of the child. Sometimes this actual physical withdrawal of the child from the family and his acceptance of new adult roles in other groups is not sufficient to turn the parents' activities into other channels. There are parents who insist that a child attend college in the home town so that he may remain at home; or who move to a college town for the same reason. Other parents cling closely to the son or daughter who has married, the extreme cases being those who accompany the young married couple on their honeymoon, who insist that they share the parental home, or who attempt to plan the lives of the young couple. This attempted prolongation of the parental role has provoked many acrimonious in-law, and especially mother-in-law, jokes by which younger people unleash the hostility they cannot express overtly in personal relationships. In part, the jokes indicate immaturity on the part of the jokers, who are still struggling for independence from an older generation. In part, however, they spring from the failure of parents to find other roles to replace the parental one. When the young married couple live with the parents of one, as did an unusually large proportion of people after World War II, tensions easily arise over the conflict between attempted dominance by the parents and the desire of the young couple for autonomy. Very maternal women find great happiness in the situation since it not only permits them to continue the maternal role with their own adult children but to add to their brood the son-in-law or daughter-in-law and in time grandchildren. Such women not uncommonly use the term "children" inclusively to refer to the young parents and the grandchildren as though all were in the same category of immaturity and degree of dependency.[6]

Other middle-aged people, less enwrapped in parental roles, see in the maturity of their children a threat to their own youthfulness. Some try directly to evade the issue by insisting that sons or daughters in the early or middle twenties are not ready for marriage. Others identify themselves with their children and attempt to become members of their children's social circle. They may attach themselves to their adolescent children's groups, outdoing the young people in use of current slang, vigorous dancing, or vivid dressing. The mother may habitually refer to her husband and sons as "the boys," while her husband calls her and her daughters "the girls," implying contemporary status to middle-aged and adolescent. The mother may take pride in the fact that she is "accepted" by her daughter's friends as "one of them." With marriage of the son or daughter, the parents may continue this identification.

[6]For a full discussion of in-law relationships, see Evelyn Millis Duvall, *In-Laws: Pro and Con* (New York: Association Press, 1954).

The unoccupied mother may follow her daughter through all the rituals of an elaborate wedding with enthusiasm equal to the daughter's own; if the daughter wishes to curtail the social and ceremonial aspects of the wedding, the mother feels cheated. Finally, grandchildren are regarded less as members of a third generation than as children of the grandparents.

EMOTIONAL HINDRANCES

Emotional conflicts of earlier years that have not been solved may emerge into consciousness or become aggravated at middle age. Social insecurities or sexual tensions experienced by parents during their own adolescence, as well as guilt over early violation of sexual norms, may be reactivated. Submerged during the full and active years when children were young and safe in the family circle, these tensions now are projected upon the children who are assumed to have the same problems, feel the same inferiorities, make the same mistakes as the parents. Conversely, parents who have solved their earlier problems, who accept them as part of the progress toward maturity, are able to be more objective toward their children. They view their children as individual entities rather than revivals of their own adolescent personalities.

Husbands and wives who have failed to make a good marital adjustment and have turned to their children for the love and encouragement that normally comes from the spouse also face a difficult adjustment with independence of the children. Young children respond to the needs of their parents and find their own needs fulfilled in the close relationship. With maturity, however, they look elsewhere for emotional satisfactions, although the wrench to free themselves may be especially violent when the parent-child relationship has been extremely intimate. The widowed, divorced, or estranged mother who has found in her son a replacement for her husband may fight with every weapon at her command the introduction of a daughter-in-law into the family. The daughter-in-law is a rival for the son's affection and consideration, and according to our mores is entitled to a greater claim upon the man than his mother has. The father who is overly attached to his daughter may experience similar reactions toward his son-in-law.

CLIMACTERIC OF THE WIFE

Accidentally coincident in time with the departure of children are the biological changes of the climacteric, which create physical tensions and discomforts, and, of more importance to the family, psychological adjustments. Among women, the most noticeable outward change is the menopause or cessation of menstruation, which usually occurs during the forties. It is caused by changes in the sex glands and is accompanied by mild reactions, such as hot flushes (similar to severe blushing), languor, headaches, and digestive disturbances; it may also involve irritability, increased sensitivity to noise, emotional instability, and feelings of depression. These symptoms of slow glandular changes may extend over a period of five or six years.[7] Whether or not men also experience a climacteric in middle age is a matter of debate.[8]

The climacteric affects marriage and family life through its relation to reproduction, its effect on sex life, and its general interpretation as the end of youth.

With our present small families, most women have completed their reproductive period during their twenties or early thirties. The actual inability to conceive that comes with the menopause therefore is felt more as a symbol of loss of youthfulness and vitality than because it deprives the woman of additional children. Most women in their forties have long since produced all the children they desire and would be aghast at the prospect of a new baby. A few, feeling keenly the withdrawal of adolescent children, may long for dependent children, but as a rule they wish they could be young again and retrace the past rather than launch themselves into a new cycle of parenthood.[9] Never-

[7]Nathan W. Shock in Oscar J. Kaplan, ed., *Mental Disorders in Later Life* (Stanford, Calif.: Stanford University Press, 1945), pp. 44–45; A. A. Werner, "Sex Behavior and Problems of the Climacteric," in Morris Fishbein and E. W. Burgess, eds., *Successful Marriage* (New York: Doubleday, 1948), pp. 471–84.

[8]Shock says that cases of men with symptoms similar to those of women are rare and that the concept of a male climacteric is not generally accepted.—*loc. cit.* Another writer (Eugene Davidoff) in the same volume accepts the concept but states that difficulties of adjustment occur less frequently among men than women. Kaplan, *op. cit.*, pp. 187–88. Werner explicitly states that men experience a climacteric.—*op. cit.*, pp. 480–84.

[9]On the other hand, Helene Deutsch states that some women rush to produce one or two late children before the menopause shuts off the highly valued ability to reproduce. She attributes these births to a "thrust of activity" that results from the threatened blow to the ego given by the imminence of the climacteric. In other women the thrust of activity carries them into outside activities where they seek to create in some other field than the production of children. The urge toward late motherhood and the entrance into outside activities are analyzed by Deutsch as a defense mechanism against personal decline. They represent resistance to middle age.—Helene Deutsch, *Psychology of Women: A Psychoanalytic Interpretation*, Vol. II, *Motherhood* (New York: Grune and Stratton, 1945), pp. 457–59. The analysis in the preceding paragraphs of this chapter treats outside activities as compensations for maternal duties no longer possible, which, if successful, give status in a new area of activity. They are not directly related to the climacteric so much as to the withdrawal of children.

theless, many women face the forties with a distinct feeling that an era has come to an end in their personal lives. Although women do not gain status in our society through fertility beyond the production of two to four children, they gain it by youthful appearance and vigor. Changes in physical appearance and reduced capacity of the sense organs, energy, speed, and coordination come gradually over the years; there is no sudden decline at the climacteric. The mild physical symptoms of the menopause do, however, focus the woman's attention upon her body, and she often becomes fully aware for the first time that she no longer looks or acts as she did at the age of 20.

The woman's personal and family adjustments at the time of the menopause are important in determining her acceptance of it. Some of her reactions that verge on the neurotic are perhaps more closely related to her personal adjustment and relation to husband and children than to the physical changes. If her maturing children are withdrawing at this time, their rejection of her as a maternal figure may increase her anxieties and insecurities. If her husband is nearing the peak of his occupational striving, he may seem to neglect her. She may easily misinterpret these situations, viewing them not as growing out of external social relationships but as proof that her physical changes make her unattractive and unappealing. Clinical experience of psychiatrists and controlled studies emphasize that women with marked reactions to the menopause are those with previous neurotic symptoms or maladjustments, which become exaggerated at this time but are not created by the physical changes themselves.[10] This statement does not mean that the fears and insecurities are any the less real to the woman, but that their origins should be sought in personal adjustment and family relationships.

SEXUAL READJUSTMENT

When men and women come into middle and old age they encounter new social attitudes toward sex, of a disapproving and restrictive type. One writer attributes the restrictive attitude to "one ancient prejudice identifying sex with sin and another denying the right of sinning to elderly men and women."[11] It seems likely that the attitude derives also from the identification of sex with childbearing and the belief

---

[10]Franz Alexander, *Psychosomatic Medicine: Its Principles and Applications* (New York: Norton, 1950), 238–40; Norman Cameron in Kaplan, *op. cit.*, pp. 143–84; M. H. Greenhill, "A Psychosomatic Evaluation of the Psychiatric and Endocrinological Factors in the Menopause," *Southern Medical Journal* (Birmingham, Ala.), 39 (1946), 786–94.

[11]Cameron, *op. cit.*, p. 148.

that sex in older couples without the possibility of conception is licentious. Nowadays, of course, this attitude is not rational, for the use of contraceptives has divorced intercourse from conception for many families long before the menopause. In addition, there are erroneous folk beliefs of the absence of sexual capacity and desire in middle-aged and older persons. Although women are unable to bear children after the menopause, they do not lose their desire for sexual experiences. They are still able to participate in and derive satisfaction from sex relationships; in fact, being relieved of any fear of an undesired pregnancy, they may even enjoy the experience more freely than in earlier years.[12]

Whether or not men undergo physical changes in middle age similar to the climacteric in women, they usually lose neither the power to beget children nor the capacity for intercourse until some years later. There is, however, a decline in frequency of sexual activity and, one would infer, a decline in drive.[13] Complete loss of potency does not follow a uniform pattern for all men: a few men become impotent during middle age; on the other hand, some men are able to father children in extreme old age. By age 65, 25 per cent of Kinsey's sample of males were impotent; but at age 80, 25 per cent were still able to have intercourse. Thus, the occurrence of the male's impotency as measured by inability for intercourse may occur at any time over a long age range, in contrast to the concentration of the female climacteric within less than one decade of life. It must be remembered, however, that women may continue to have and enjoy intercourse after the menopause into extreme old age. There is therefore no sudden cessation of sexual activity at one age period for either men or women. Moreover, as men become impotent, their power declines gradually and without a sudden break; adjustment to nonsexual life may therefore be made gradually.

ADJUSTMENT OF MEN

The social and psychological adjustment of middle-aged men is usually regarded as less acute than that of their wives. Men have a dual set of satisfying relationships throughout marriage—family and vocation. Family and vocation are related to each other, in that family relationships may be an incentive to greater vocational effort or so disturbing that the man is unable to work at top capacity. Conversely,

[12]LeMon Clark, "Sex Life of the Middle Aged," *Marriage and Family Living*, 11 (1949), 58-60.

[13]Alfred C. Kinsey, *et al.*, *Sexual Behavior in the Human Male* (Philadelphia: Saunders, 1948), pp. 226-59, 567-68. See also this text, Chapter 11.

success or failure at work has repercussions upon family life, in terms of the standard of living and the respect in which the man is held by his wife and children. Nevertheless, the man usually has two outlets for personal satisfactions, whereas the woman more often has one. When children withdraw from the family, the father is less affected than the mother. Proud though he may be of his children, he is not so dependent upon them for status as is their mother. If his children are complete failures, he may feel his share in their failure less because he can turn to his work for success. Also, since he devotes less time than the mother to childrearing, he is less likely than she to attribute the shortcomings of children to personal failure as a good parent. (It should be noted that the woman who has consistently combined motherhood with a vocation may take a similar attitude toward her children, unless she shares the traditional attitude that the mother should devote her entire time to her children; then she may have an underlying feeling of insecurity and guilt even when her children meet every standard for success.) The middle-aged man's revaluation of himself is more likely to concern his vocational status than his status as a parent. Middle age is regarded as the "prime of life," the point when youthful drive is not yet noticeably diminished, experience is great, and the combination of the two carries the man to his peak of success. If he has reached success in middle life, he may relax later—even retire before old age—knowing that he has met social expectations. The man who has not found success easily, on the other hand, increases the pressure upon himself during middle age. He works under strain and tension and concentrates upon his business time and energy that previously had been divided between family and work. Many men during middle age are forced to realize that no matter how hard they try they cannot fulfill the American dream that "any boy can be President," or even that "home-town boy makes good." Younger men are promoted to positions above them. Only extreme lack of realism can prevent them from knowing that they have reached their maximum success and fallen short of what they once expected of themselves or what was expected of them by others. Their sense of failure and frustration may exhibit itself in irritability toward their wives, in irrational blame of their wives, or in depressions and withdrawal. Some men may turn to or increase extra-marital sexual affairs in the effort to prove to themselves that they are still young and virile.

SATISFACTORY READJUSTMENT

When husband and wife are in sympathetic communication with each other and understand that each has a problem of loss of status-giving activity, a feeling of uselessness, and especially for the wife a diminution of response-giving contacts, a closer relationship may develop. Each may turn to the other, as in the first years of marriage, as the chief source of personal satisfactions.

The description that follows is of a family that made a successful progress through the middle years.

The Martins are a family in the middle years. Their married son lives with his wife and little son some three hundred miles distant; their unmarried daughter is a secretary in a city a hundred miles away. During the period when they were rearing their children, the Martins lived in a comfortable six-room frame house in a middle-class neighborhood. Mrs. Martin, aided by her daughter, did all her housework, while Mr. Martin and his son made necessary repairs and usually redecorated their home, which they owned. As a moderately successful engineer, Mr. Martin was able to send his son to the state university and his daughter to the local junior college. The focus of family life was their home; here they entertained friends and relatives, listened to the radio, helped the children with their school work, and gave occasional parties for the son or daughter. The church provided their only organizational contact. Because of her close contacts with her children and her dearth of outside activities, Mrs. Martin found it difficult to relinquish her children. She wanted her son, who married immediately after his graduation, to postpone his marriage; and she tried in vain to persuade her daughter to find work in her home city so that she might remain at home. The father, however, maintained that both son and daughter must make their own decisions in these matters. Slowly, the Martins adjusted to the middle years. Persuaded by her daughter, who made frequent visits home, the mother began to patronize a beauty parlor and substituted gay hats and blouses for the more conservative ones she had previously worn; with the expense of childrearing ended, there was no longer the necessity for buying clothing that would outlast minor changes in style. She also joined the Woman's Club for the first time and faithfully attended their weekly meetings; her interest was thus aroused in many new fields and her conversation widened from domestic affairs to include current events and cultural subjects. In her middle years she thus seemed to become younger, both in appearance and outlook, than she had been during the time when she was absorbed in her children. The frame house now seemed too large for husband and wife, and too full of memories of their children; moreover, the neighborhood was changing and the new neighbors were not congenial. Mr. and Mrs. Martin therefore sold their home and bought a smaller house nearer the edge of the city. Unhampered by the care of children, Mrs. Martin occasionally accompanied her husband on business trips and from time to time visited her son or daughter.

Although the middle years brought greater freedom and a lessening of some responsibilities, they also brought the shadow of future problems. Mrs. Martin began to feel the twinges of arthritis. Moreover, for certain periods she assumed the care of her widowed mother, a woman in her eighties; this responsibility was shared with several sisters, for the mother preferred to make long visits with each daughter rather than to spend all her time in one place. Mr. Martin, still capable and in fact at the peak of his productive period, nevertheless began to feel his years. He declined a new and promising position in another city, for it seemed that the financial advantages of the new position would be a poor substitute for the security he felt in his current position, and that the cultural advantages of a larger city would not compensate for the strain of adjustment and the loss of old friends.[14]

Summing up the family situation of middle-aged people, we may regard it as a time of reappraisal and redirection for husband and wife. Physical changes, psychological independence of children, their withdrawal from the family as a social unit, and the vocational adjustments of the husband converge upon husband and wife during the forties or fifties. The impact of these forces upon husband and wife compels them to bring into consciousness previously half-denied facts of the mounting years and the maturity of children. Some men and women cannot face or accept these facts and look for some escape: identification with adolescents; clinging to the maternal or paternal role; neurotic reactions, especially on the part of the wife; seeking of extramarital sex relations, especially on the part of the husband. Other couples reorganize their lives, pulling their interpersonal relationships closer together, accepting a new status of equality with their mature children, and revising their roles to permit the wife to shift from a maternal to a partnership role with activities beyond the home.

Family Life of the Old

The changes that occur during middle age are primarily a reorientation of interests and activities of husband and wife. More far-reaching changes become evident by the late sixties. Table 23 shows the marital status of men and women in the decade 65–74 and for age 75 and over. The number of single people is low; these are the permanently unmarried. The number of widowers and widows increases greatly, and after age 75 this is the most common marital status for women. The divorced are a minute fraction of the total. Toward the end of life almost three-fourths of all women enter a postmarital status.

[14]Unpublished report.

CHRONIC ILLNESS

Death in old age may be preceded by a long period of chronic illness. The proportion of persons aged 65 and over with chronic illness (such as heart disease, cancer, diabetes, arthritis) is 77 per cent as compared with 38 per cent of people under age 65.[15]

TABLE 23

MARITAL STATUS OF MEN AND WOMEN,
AGED 65 AND OVER, 1966,
PERCENTAGE DISTRIBUTION

| | Men | | Women | |
Marital status	Aged 65–74	Aged 75 and over	Aged 65–74	Aged 75 and over
Single	7.4	7.4	7.6	6.9
Married	78.0	61.4	46.9	20.7
Widowed	11.2	29.8	43.3	71.0
Divorced	3.3	1.4	2.2	1.4
TOTAL	99.9	100.0	100.0	100.0

SOURCE: *Statistical Abstract of the United States, 1967* (Washington, D.C.: Government Printing Office, 1967), p. 33.

The illness of a child or young adult is likely to be acute and to have a definite beginning, short duration, and a definite end in recovery or death. Many of the illnesses of the old come slowly and insidiously, with ever-increasing handicaps. The illness becomes a part of the daily and yearly pattern of life, not only of the afflicted person, but of other members of the family who must adjust themselves to the presence and care of a chronic invalid. If there is a crisis it is at the point of some sudden change of condition, as the stroke that brings paralysis to the person who for years has suffered from high blood pressure; or the fall and broken hip that is suffered by an old person who has tottered up and down stairs with increasing difficulty; or the wandering from home and inability to recall the way back of the oldster with slowly failing memory. The crisis may bring home to the old person that he is old; it also brings a realization on the part of others that the old person is no longer capable of functioning independently.

The chronically ill person has needs not felt by the well. In addition to physical care, he also needs someone upon whom to lean for

[15]Staff report to the Special Committee on Aging, United States Senate (Washington, D.C.: Government Printing Office, 1961).

a sense of security and protection. His role changes from that of a self-reliant person to the childlike role of the invalid. Consequently the roles of others in the family change in adjustment to his new role and new needs. Since men tend to die at earlier ages than women, a common situation finds the elderly wife with an invalid husband from five to ten years older than herself. The man has the difficult problem of changing his conception of himself from self-sufficient to dependent and of accepting his wife in the dominant role. His functions shrink, his world contracts. In contrast, the role of the wife expands to encompass functions relinquished by her husband. She may not only be overburdened by the double duties but may have to learn many new skills and acquire knowledge formerly confined to the husband's role. If the husband's illness involves his mental capacities, she may find it advisable to be appointed his guardian and to take charge of all financial affairs. She may find this situation either a strain or a challenge as she struggles to understand a new field. At the same time that she is expanding her role she finds the fulfillment of many old needs denied her by her husband's illness, ranging all the way from his performance of heavy household tasks through recreation to satisfaction of affectional and perhaps sexual needs. When, perhaps after years of invalidism, the husband dies, the wife frequently feels a sense of great relief. One woman, happily married in her seventies, had nursed her husband through an illness of some four years' duration, during which he became progressively more and more helpless physically. She learned to manage all the household tasks, community contacts, and financial affairs. She gradually adjusted herself to the contraction of social activities and to the heartache of seeing her husband suffer. At his death she could not cry; she could not wish him to live longer. Having learned to handle all the practical problems alone, she continued to live in their large home, gradually expanding her social life to give additional satisfactions.

When the wife is invalid, the situation is to some extent reversed. The husband expands his functions to include those of housekeeper and nurse; the wife is compelled to see an inexpert male fumble with cooking, cleaning, and the serving of meals. Often, however, if the wife becomes a chronic invalid it is after the death of her husband and the adjustment is between the invalid and her adult children who then find themselves in the unaccustomed role of dominance over their parent, a reversal of their childhood years when they were dependent upon the mother for physical care and love. This parent-child adjustment often is more difficult than that between invalid and spouse.

THE POSTMARITAL FAMILY

The postmarital family consists of the widow or widower. When the husband dies first, the average length of widowhood is eleven years (Chapter 11). When the wife dies first, the widower lives about seven years before his own death. Since widowhood begins for many in middle age, a minority of men and women spend the last third or more of their lives alone, unless they remarry, a possibility that becomes more and more improbable the older the person becomes.

As has already been suggested, when widow- or widowerhood follows a long and trying illness on the part of the spouse, many adjustments have already been made to the postmarital role. When a reciprocal companionship has been maintained until the time of death, however, the change from marital to widowed status may create almost insurmountable hardships. Instead of the gradual adjustment possible with chronic illness, adjustment must be made abruptly to the absence of the deceased spouse. The companionship between a retired man and his wife may be closer than at earlier periods of their lives: their decrease in outside activities has increased their dependence upon each other, and often their social world has narrowed to the home and each other. When death removes one, the other feels that half of himself has suddenly been cut away. A younger person in similar circumstances tends to widen his activities, to seek new contacts and new interests, and, in time, to marry again. The old person often lacks the energy and flexibility for such broadening of activities and the assumption of new community roles. For many, life remains a stunted existence until death releases them also. One old woman whose companionship with her husband had been very close because of their childlessness, regarded her widowhood as a period of waiting until, in her firm belief, death would reunite them. "In the course of nature, the time will not be long until I go also," she said complacently.

Some old widows and widowers remarry, but the number of oldsters who do not remarry is very great. Since women outlive men, the sex ratio is very unbalanced in later years, and any program to encourage remarriage would fail because of the great excess of old women. The convention whereby women marry those of their own age or older inhibits many elderly widows from marrying men younger than themselves. Widowers are less handicapped, since they find an excess of women their own age and also may approach those younger than themselves. But a new marriage means the breaking up of old habits of life,

502 THE CYCLE OF FAMILY LIFE

adjusting to a new personality, and the comparison of the new spouse with the memory of the deceased. Moreover, public opinion tends to be opposed to the marriage of the old, for there is little understanding on the part of younger people of the affectional and social needs of the old. For these reasons, most widows and widowers tend to accept their half-lives, which may last over a long period of time.

EMPLOYMENT AND INCOME

Until age 65, approximately 90 per cent of all men in families are employed, for the most part full time.[16] For the age period of 65 and over, however, only 34 per cent are employed, 2 per cent are unemployed, and 64 per cent are not in the labor force, that is, are not looking for jobs. Not all men leave the labor force or employment on their sixty-fifth birthdays. However, age 65 is the most commonly

TABLE 24
FAMILY INCOMES OF MIDDLE-AGE AND OLD-AGE FAMILIES,
WITH AN EMPLOYED MALE MEMBER, 1961
(PERCENTAGE DISTRIBUTION)

Annual Family Income	Aged 45–64	Aged 65 and over
Less than $3,000	16	39
$3,000 to $4,999	21	26
$5,000 to $6,999	25	13
$7,000 and over	38	22
TOTAL	100	100

SOURCE: *Current Population Reports, Population Characteristics: December 29, 1961*, Series P-20, No. 112 (Washington, D.C.: Bureau of the Census, 1961), p. 16.

used age for compulsory retirement; it is also the age at which men become eligible for payments under Old Age and Survivors Insurance (usually called Social Security) and for various other benefits. Age 65 therefore is a turning point, and with each succeeding year additional men leave paid employment.

Table 24 shows the great contrast between the middle-age and old-age families. If the period of 65 years and over were divided into periods, the income would continue to decline, as many men are still employed during the five to ten years after age 65. For the unemployed group, 60 per cent represented families with less than $3,000 income.

[16]*Current Population Reports, Population Characteristics: December 29, 1961*, Series P-20, No. 112 (Washington, D.C., Bureau of the Census, 1961), p. 16.

Just as many wives find it necessary to change their roles and self-conceptions when the last child marries, men typically face the same necessity when they retire from work.[17] At the point of retirement the man usually conceives of himself as competent, reasonably successful at some level of work, useful to society, and able to care financially for his family. Family, friends, fellow-workers, and employers usually regard him in the same way. Retirement brings a number of changes, over and above increased leisure and lowered income.

The retired man is without means of carrying on his role, whether it was as day laborer, skilled mechanic, officer in a firm, or teacher, unless he can find a similar position open to men over retirement age. Some men are able to find such openings for a limited number of years, or they satisfy themselves with part-time work of some other kind. In any case, association with former co-workers has ended. In new work contacts and among nonwork associates, the retired man's status usually is lower than it was in his lifetime job. He rarely has the same prestige or receives the same respect, and is often regarded as old-fashioned, on the shelf, or aged because of his changed status, although there may be little or no change in his personality and capacities.

The retired man resists taking to himself the changed conception that others may have of him. He feels that he is the same person that he was before retirement, fully as capable and worthy of respect as during the preceding years. His internalized self-concept is of long standing and does not yield to external changes.

Perhaps because a large population segment of retired men is a recent phenomenon in the United States, society has not devised adequate substitute roles for work. The retired man tends to be adrift occupationally. Almost the only role provided for him is that of a "playboy." He may join leisure time clubs, many of which emphasize the age of members by such names as Golden Age Club, Borrowed Time Club, or Senior Citizens' Club. Here he may spend the time playing table games, shuffleboard, and the like, develop hobbies, and participate in picnics and parties. The playboy role at any age has never been a highly respected one in the United States, and many vigorous old people desire new opportunities to be productive. They do not want a generalized role as old people, who are set apart from other ages and from the mainstream of life. The result is often discontent and restlessness.

A possible outlet for the retired man is in his own home.   Husband

[17]This discussion is based on Ruth Shonle Cavan, "Self and Role in Adjustment During Old Age," in Arnold M. Rose, *op. cit.*, ch. 27.

and wife sometimes find a new companionship in sharing household tasks. But to many men, housework involves a lowering of status, and to many wives the inclusion of their husbands in household tasks disturbs their customary routines and presents a threat to their self-concept and role.

THE KINSHIP WEB

Chapter 11 showed the operation of the kinship web in three-generational families in the exchange of services. The oldest of the three received more aid than it gave in all areas: financial, housekeeping management, care in illness, and emotional gratification (help in child care of course was not appropriate to this generation). The oldest generation gave aid also but never to the same degree that it received aid.

Inter-kinship responsibilities show up strongly with reference to giving needed support of many types to the old. These forms of service do not imply the sharing of common living quarters, and often can be given when old parents and middle-aged children maintain independent homes.

LIVING ARRANGEMENTS

With retirement, lowered income, decline in physical vigor, and sometimes chronic illness and loss of the spouse, changes may be made in living arrangements. In accordance with the typical and approved type of American family, the husband-wife family is maintained until old age. Only small percentages of married men and women live otherwise.[18] The first break in living arrangements comes in late middle age, when the percentage of widows increases markedly over earlier years. For ages 65 to 74, only 42 per cent of women are living in a husband-wife relationship; 27 per cent live with relatives, either in their own home which they then head or in the relative's home; 25 per cent live alone, 3 per cent in other families, and 1.5 per cent in institutions. For ages 75 and over, only 20 per cent are living in a husband-wife relationship; some widows in this age period still maintain their own homes, but the percentage living with relatives has increased from 27 per cent to 44 per cent. Very few women even in very old age enter institutions—only 4 per cent.

[18]Information from census data for March, 1960, distributed at the Groves Conference on Marriage and the Family, 1962.

The living arrangement for men is somewhat different. When they become widowers, their solution less often is to combine household arrangements with a relative than to live alone. Few enter institutions.

With each change in living arrangements some changes have to be made in daily habits, roles, and self-conceptions, on the part of all who share the joint living quarters. The adjustments go far beyond new physical arrangements.

THE OLD PARENT IN THE FAMILY[19]

When the old parent comes to live with an adult child and his family, the enlarged family is faced with four types of adjustment.

1. When the elderly parent and his adult child have the same cultural beliefs, one basis for sound adjustment is at hand. Often, however, they adhere to different patterns, based upon different social experiences. The past 50 years have witnessed a marked growth of children away from their parents in cultural patterns. Examples are the migration of rural young people to cities and the assumption of urban attitudes and ways of living that may be wholly foreign to the rural parent who in later life may come to live with the urban son or daughter; the great increase in the number of young people completing high school or college as compared with the number of parents with similar education has created a wide difference between the generations in values and interests; the adult children and grandchildren of the foreign-born who surged into this country by the millions prior to 1915 follow an American pattern of culture that clashes with the remnants of foreign culture retained by the immigrant generation. These and other cultural conflicts often are dismissed by saying that "times have changed" and the parents should adjust. It cannot be overlooked, however, that more than conflicting cultural patterns are involved. The parents have woven into their personal standards and ideals the values of their culture and have invested these values with moral and religious significance. It is impossible for them to witness opposed behavior in their children or grandchildren without feelings of shock, fear, and anxiety. When the children have also invested their attitudes

[19]The following articles contributed to the discussion: Ruth Shonle Cavan, "Family Tensions between the Old and the Middle-Aged," *Marriage and Family Living,* 18 (1956), 323–27; Paul H. Glasser and Lois N. Glasser, "Role Reversal and Conflict between Aged Parents and Their Children," *Marriage and Family Living,* 24 (1962), 46–51; and E. E. LeMasters, "Social Class Mobility and Family Integration," *Marriage and Family Living,* 16 (1954), 226–32.

and behavior with moral significance an impasse exists. Only deep understanding of the relation between culture and ideals and great tolerance can bring harmony.

2. Often the old person must break his own social ties when he becomes a member of his child's family. Usually it is the old person who "breaks up" his home and moves into the household of a younger person. If the move is within one local community, he may be able to retain his friends, church membership, and social affiliations; he retains his social identity and the comfort of accustomed contacts. A move to another community may be almost disastrous. The social groups in which the old person normally is interested have elderly members who often form a closed group impenetrable by a new person. The burden of making new social contacts falls upon the newcomer at a time when self-assurance and desire for new experiences are overshadowed by the need for security and ready acceptance.

Few avenues are open to the old person to establish his status and his individuality in a new setting. In a community where he has lived for some years his status is established long before old age: he is known among friends and in his community as a steady worker, a church leader, a good parent, and so forth. He is an individual. As a member of his child's family in a new community he is all too likely to lose his individuality and be known only as Bob Brown's father or Judge Addison's aunt. He becomes a social nonentity. In his own mind, however, he thinks of himself in terms of his earlier status as acquired by birth, marriage, or occupation; he resents the lack of regard of the new community for him.

3. On the more personal side is the necessity to break old identifications and try to build new ones. Some of these identifications are with the status of the family in the old community—old Mrs. Smith is the daughter of a pioneer family; some are with material symbols that may relate to community status or to the intimacies of family life. The nonmaterial symbols are lost. Often the material symbols also must be left behind since the fully furnished household of son or daughter rarely has room for cherished pieces of furniture or an appropriate setting for the display of beloved photographs, handwork, or old china.

New identifications are hard for the old person to make. There are no memories attached to the new household, and on the personal side often there seems to be no place in the family circle for the old person. The husband and wife and their children have an integrated pattern of family interaction that forms a closed circle. When a new member is added through the birth of a child, the situation is very different. The baby seems to be an extension of the parents' personalities into the future; it offers many opportunities for parental pride, ambition, and feelings of accomplishment; it is small, loving, and appealing. The old person seems to demand as much or perhaps greater readjustment and sometimes physical care than a baby, but without compensating the caretaker in an equal amount.

4. Individual personalities also must be adjusted to each other. If it is assumed that husband, wife, and children have found mutually acceptable ways to fulfill each other's needs, the readjustment becomes one of helping the elderly parent find need-satisfactions and of finding in the old person satisfactions for some of their own needs. The general shifting necessarily brings both sacrifice and richness of experience. The child may have to yield some of his mother's attention to his grandparent but in return will receive added love from the grandparent. The husband may find his old mother demanding attention from him formerly given to his wife, but she may also assume some care of the children and thus release his wife for more free time with him. As with all periods of transition, the early period of readjustment may bring acute discomfort until a new network of interaction is woven.

These changes include adjustment of personal roles, with some possibilities of clashes. Although there are few studies on adjustment of roles in the three-generation family, personal accounts point to the adjustment between the old mother and her daughter or daughter-in-law as full of tension. The earlier role of the old mother as head of her home is in direct conflict with the corresponding role of the daughter or daughter-in-law as head of her home. The old mother may feel that her longer experience gives her precedence in making decisions and organizing the household; but the younger woman feels that her position as wife of the family head gives her the superior role. Another clash may occur between the old mother and her daughter-in-law for first place in her son's affections. The mother dwells on her long years of care of her son as a child and longs again to be first in his esteem. The young woman claims first place is due her as his wife. Only when such conflicts of roles have been adjusted so that each receives some satisfaction will the relationship become harmonious.

GRANDPARENTS

As with old parents, so also with grandparents—their status is not well defined. Much of what is written about grandparents is speculative or is based on a limited number of clinical cases. Few empirical studies have been made.

One study is based on 70 middle-class families, with children and one set of grandparents.[20] The grandparents were almost all middle-aged: grandfathers were primarily from mid-50's to late 60's, and grandmothers from early 50's to mid-60's. These grandparents were in the post-parental period rather than the old-age or retired period of family life and were still active in customary middle-age activities. Many were upwardly mobile, some were foreign-born, and Protestants and Jews predominated, only 17 per cent being Catholic. How much these various factors affected the findings is not shown. Most grandparents in the sample found their role pleasant and comfortable—59 per cent of grandmothers and 61 per cent of grandfathers. With the exception of a few cases with insufficient data, the remainder found the role difficult. For the grandmothers the greatest significance of the role was a sense of biological renewal (42 per cent)—of seeing oneself projected into the future or carrying on the family line. The second largest group (27 per cent) felt remote and little affected by the role; many of these women were still involved in employment or community affairs. The third most frequent effect on women was emotional self-fulfillment. The most frequently mentioned significance of the grandparent role on men was negative (29 per cent)—they felt remote from the role. Emotional fulfillment (27 per cent) and biological renewal (23 per cent) accounted for most other responses. The style in which the role of grandparent was fulfilled differed with age. Formality characterized the grandparents who were over 65 years old, while fun-seeking or the role of the "distant figure" were more frequent among grandparents under age 65.

Another suggested role of the older, retired grandfather, with time on his hands and a diminished range of interests, is that of an assistant to the mother of his grandchildren: caring for them when the mother is away, taking them to the park, and so on.[21] The suggestion has not been subjected to research.

Most of what has been written about grandparents has to do with the grandmother. One writer emphasizes that the grandchild fulfills an emotional need of the grandmother at a time when she feels that her period of usefulness is ended.[22] Since the child divides his love between his grandmother and his mother, the grandmother feels insecure and struggles for the child's devotion by indulging his whims and be-

[20]Bernice L. Neugarten and Karol K. Weinstein, "The Changing American Grandparent," *Journal of Marriage and the Family*, 26 (1964), 199–204.

[21]Cavan, *op. cit.*

[22]Hermann Vollmer, "The Grandmother: A Problem in Child-Rearing," *American Journal of Orthopsychiatry*, 7 (1937), 378–82.

littling his mother. Another writer, however, interprets the excessive love of a grandmother for her grandchildren as originating in guilt feelings caused by early neglect of her own children.[23] A third writer proclaims that "Grandmother made Johnny delinquent"[24] by arousing hostilities and aggressions in him. Still another report covers 15 cases in which the grandmothers tended to dominate their daughters, whom they lived with or near, and to usurp the mother role with their grand-children.[25] As a consequence, the daughters felt inadequate and the grandmother-daughter relationship became a major factor in the behavior problems of the children. These reports from the guidance clinic and the social worker's counseling room emphasize problem situations.

In a general statement that attempts to include all types of grand-mothers, Helene Deutsch says that "there are as many types of grand-mothers as there are individual types and characters of mothers."[26] She continues with a discussion of three types of good grandmothers. The first type of good grandmother is the woman who continues her motherhood through her grandchildren and thinks of the grandchildren simply as the youngest of her children. They give her a new opportunity to play the mother role and a new emotional satisfaction. The second type of grandmother has adjusted herself to the loss of the mother role when her children matured; through identification with her daughter or daughter-in-law, however, she experiences grandmotherhood as a "new edition" of her original role. In order to avoid a hateful compe-tition, she must be satisfied with a position of assistant mother and not attempt to impose her wishes or ideas of child training upon the child and his mother. The third type of good grandmother has made her peace with age and no longer reaches backward for her past motherhood or outward for identification with her daughter or daughter-in-law. She is tender and solicitous without seeking self-gratification in return. Consequently her grandchildren love her dearly. The only danger is that she may "spoil" her grandchildren by pampering them. Deutsch continues with a brief statement that there are also "wicked grand-mothers," who either do not want to be disturbed by their grand-children or whose envy for their daughters or daughters-in-law causes them to try to intrude between children and their parents.

[23]E. G. Fried and K. Stern, "The Situation of the Aged within the Family," *American Journal of Orthopsychiatry*, 18 (1948), 31–54.

[24]G. A. Strauss, "Grandmother Made Johnny Delinquent," *American Journal of Orthopsychiatry*, 13 (1943), 343–47.

[25]B. Borden, "The Role of Grandparents in Children's Behavior Problems," *Smith College Studies in Social Work*, 17 (1946), 115–16.

[26]*Op. cit.*, pp. 483–86.

The End of the Cycle

Family life is a series of alternating periods of adjustment and un-adjustment. To each change within the family and to the impact of external changes, the husband, wife, and children must adjust. When satisfactory adjustment has been reached, it tends to continue until another change calls for a new modification of attitude and behavior. A minority of families live in a continuous state of tension or disintegrate. Husbands and wives who obtain divorces as a way out of difficulties tend to remarry. Thus, the majority of the adult population is married until the transition in old age into widow- or widowerhood; even then the patterns of living established in the family are continued.

Adjustments in the 1960's differ from those of our earlier rural economy. Emphasis now is on interpersonal adjustments related to personal rather than utilitarian needs. Hardships that solidified the earlier rural family in its effort to survive now frequently disorganize families, each member of whom may seek an individual solution of problems. The qualities of a good husband or wife now place less stress on family background or property and more upon personal traits and compatibility than was true in the past. Recognition is also given to the importance of likenesses of social background.

Families that best survive strains and crises are both well integrated and adaptable. Held together by common bonds of affection and goals, they are nevertheless able to adjust roles and plans to changing conditions.

The need for adjusting continues into old age, the final adjustment being to death itself, which closes the family cycle.

Questions

1. Why is it necessary for the middle-aged couple to modify their roles?
2. What would you regard as good adjustment of middle-aged parents to their adolescent children? As poor adjustment?
3. Why do women seem to find adjustment to middle age more difficult than men?

4. What is the effect of employment of the middle-aged wife on her relationship to her husband?

5. How does the adjustment of the husband to middle age differ from that of his wife?

6. Report on a couple who have made a satisfactory adjustment to middle age. What seem to be the significant factors?

7. What changes in family organization follow the retirement of the husband?

8. What changes in marital roles are occasioned by chronic illness of husband or wife?

9. What roles are open to the husband after his retirement? Are they suitable for him?

10. What are the attitudes of married sons or daughters toward accepting an elderly parent into their household? Are these attitudes a logical sequence of our present conception of the function of marriage?

11. How can the elderly widow or widower best meet his psychological and social problems: by living alone; living with his children; or entering an institution? What are the advantages and disadvantages of each situation?

Bibliography

"Aging and Retirement," ed. by Ernest W. Burgess, *American Journal of Sociology*, 59 (January, 1954), entire issue.

ALBRECHT, RUTH, "The Parental Responsibilities of Grandparents," *Marriage and Family Living*, 16 (1954), 201–4.

_____, "Relationships of Older Parents with Their Children," *Marriage and Family Living*, 16 (1954), 32–35.

_____, "Relationships of Older People with Their Own Parents," *Marriage and Family Living*, 15 (1953), 296–98.

CAVAN, RUTH SHONLE, ed., *Marriage and Family in the Modern World* (New York: Crowell, 1969), chs. 13, 14, 15.

_____, E. W. BURGESS, R. J. HAVIGHURST, and HERBERT GOLDHAMER, *Personal Adjustment in Old Age* (Chicago: Science Research Associates, 1949).

CLARK, LE MON, "Sex Life of the Middle Aged," *Marriage and Family Living*, 11 (1949), 58–60.

CUMMING, ELAINE, LOIS R. DEAN, D. S. NEWELL, and ISABEL McCAFFREY, "Disengagement—A Tentative Theory of Aging," *Sociometry*, 23 (March, 1960), 23–35.

DUVALL, EVELYN MILLIS, *In-Laws: Pro and Con* (New York: Association Press, 1954).

GLASSER, PAUL H. and LOIS N., "Role Reversal and Conflict between Aged Parents and Their Children," *Marriage and Family Living*, 24 (1962), 46–51.

KAPLAN, OSCAR, ed., *Mental Disorders in Later Life* (Stanford, Calif.: Stanford University Press, 1945), chs. 7 and 8.

LEMASTERS, E. E., "Social Class Mobility and Family Integration," *Marriage and Family Living*, 16 (1954), 226–32.

NIMKOFF, M. F., "Changing Family Relationships of Older People in the United States during the Last Forty Years," *The Gerontologist*, 1 (June, 1961), 92–97.

ROSE, ARNOLD M., "Factors Associated with the Life Satisfaction of Middle-Class, Middle-Aged Persons," *Marriage and Family Living*, 17 (1955), 15–19.

———, ed., *Human Behavior and Social Processes* (Boston: Houghton Mifflin, 1962), chs. 26 and 27.

SHANAS, ETHEL, and GORDON F. STREIB, eds., *Social Structure and the Family* (Englewood Cliffs, N. J.: Prentice-Hall, 1965), chs. 4 and 6.

TIBBITTS, CLARK, ed., *Handbook of Social Gerontology* (Chicago: University of Chicago Press, 1960), ch. 13.

VEDDER, CLYDE B., ed., *Gerontology, A Book of Readings* (Springfield, Ill.: Charles C. Thomas, 1963), especially ch. 2.

———, ed., *Problems of the Middle-Aged* (Springfield, Ill.: Charles C. Thomas, 1965).

IV

Adjustment of Family and Society

CHAPTER $\boxed{21}$

Integration of Society and Family

THIS TEXT opened with a discussion of incompatibility and often conflicting values related to marriage and family life that create issues about which there are at present no uniform collective attitudes. These issues were analyzed as originating in two sets of social conditions: the transition from an agrarian to an urbanized culture; and the social mobility between social classes, subcultural groups (ethnic and religious), and races. This social analysis constituted Parts One and Two of this book. In Part Three, the orientation shifted to individual families and the interaction taking place within the family circle. The progress of family life was followed from the premarital activities of dating through marriage and into old age with its postmarital individual—the elderly widow or widower. In Part Three it was constantly necessary to refer to the social setting in which interaction took place. Now, at the end of the book, the task remains of examining trends toward greater integration of the family into the social organization, and of increased integration within the family.

Social Integration and Disintegration

In a strongly organized society, the various institutions tend to be well unified in two respects: they proclaim the same or mutually compatible social norms or values; and their functions dovetail together without undue overlapping and without leaving gaps in the services that people need.[1]

Integration as a static condition is easy to visualize in a stable and unchanging society. Over years of time the values become coordinated, and the various functions are distributed among the institutions. Moreover, functions and values are themselves integrated and support each other, and to a large extent are achieved by the institutions that subscribe to them. The coordinated values and functions are passed on from one generation to another and are constantly reinforced through legends, rituals, and ceremonies. When integration is viewed as a process through a period of time in a stable society, the institutions may be compared to so many regimented units, marching, halting, and wheeling in conformity with a master plan controlled by one system of values, with the movements of each unit synchronized with the movements of all other units.

In a changing society, however, the high degree of unity of values, the careful assignment of functions, and the synchronization of activities lack coordination. Some institutions retain much of the past; others revamp themselves to fit new conditions and, finding themselves out of step with more conservative institutions, tend to become separated from the main societal body and to lose sight of the total value system of society, although they may be well organized within themselves. In time, each institution may become a more or less autonomous unit within society, developing its own values and functions in relative independence from other institutions. Under these conditions societal integration is replaced by conflict and confusion between institutions. If this process—the development of independence by institutions—goes far enough, the society becomes generally disorganized. More often, however, a process of reorganization accompanies the process of disintegration. Although revised values may not be uniformly accepted throughout the society, a number of institutions will accept one set of social values or norms and bring their functions into conformity with each other. Thus, reorganization will offset the effects of confusion and conflict.

Unless the society again becomes stable, complete integration of values, functions, and pace of activities among institutions cannot be expected. As long as there is change of any sort (entrance of new cul-

---

[1]For discussions of integration, see Ronald Freedman, Amos H. Hawley, Werner S. Landecker, and Horace M. Miner, *Principles of Sociology* (New York: Holt, 1952), chs. 4, 5, and 13; Robin M. Williams, *American Society* (New York: Knopf, 1951, revised, 1960), chs. 11–14; Robert Cooley Angell, "The Moral Integration of American Cities," *American Journal of Sociology*, 57, Part 2 (July, 1951), especially pp. 115–22.

tural groups, social or technical inventions, depression, and wars), changes in values and functions must also be anticipated. One sociologist suggests that in a changing society stability of culture does not refer to a static condition but to "a dynamic process in which a delicately balanced system of values is maintained."[2]

In the light of this general statement about societal integration, let us look at the specific case of the family.

THE FAMILY IN THE INTEGRATION PROCESS

The family is one of the major social institutions. From a societal point of view the family is more than an intimate group whose members are seeking satisfaction of individual needs; traditionally, it is an institution ranking with such more formal organizations as the church, school, industry, or political system. It supports basic values related not only to personal needs but to society in general, some of which are maintenance of the population, indoctrination of children in societal culture, personality development of children, provision of a common family living unit, and maintenance of health. In the past, the family fulfilled these and other functions.

The issues presented in Chapter 2 are evidence of the inability of the family to maintain old values and functions under present urbanized conditions. The factory system alone destroyed the ideal of the family as a patriarchal organization with the father maintaining his headship through close personal contacts, sometimes on an hourly basis, with his wife and children. It destroyed, also, much of the ability of the father to support his family through all exigencies and crises, launch his children into productive activities, and save for the old-age needs of his wife and himself. The great improvement in medical practice that has prolonged life into old age has also changed family ideals and functions. As more and more people live into an old age for which they are unable to prepare themselves financially, they become an increasing—in some cases insuperable—burden upon the few children that now constitute the urban family; or they are threatened with a long dependency upon relief agencies. The separation of family members into diversified activities tends to break down the characteristics of the family as a primary group that typically exerts control over individual conduct and helps to establish integrated personalities. In like manner, other time-honored family values and functions were disturbed or destroyed by the development of modern urban institutions.

[2]Williams, *op. cit.*, p. 374.

The family seemed at odds with other institutions. Unaided, it could neither uphold societal values nor perform expected traditional functions. The process of societal disintegration with reference to the family tended to come to a climax after World War I. The increased employment of women and their break with the older restrictive moral codes, often viewed as a conflict between the sexes, in reality represented a movement toward conformity with the changed social conditions that had destroyed the older patriarchal family organization in which the husband and father had been able both to support and to give leadership to his family. In the 1930's the depression brought into sharp focus the inability of the family to continue as an independent economic unit and, in fact, the inability of the local community to care for the family in distress. At the same time the ease with which adolescents could escape from family supervision and control became apparent. During the depression great numbers of boys and some girls became transients, wandering aimlessly back and fourth across the country. Neither family, school, industry, nor law could control these wandering groups. In general, the urban family has found it difficult to cope with adolescents. Although school laws and labor laws tend to prolong the economic dependence of the child on the family, many adolescents have found ways to circumvent the law. The city child can falsify his age and secure work; he can evade the school attendance officer; he can, in the summer at least, sleep out in the "jungles" along railroad tracks or in vacant garages, houses, or stores. Automobiles, owned or stolen, carry him beyond the eyes of his family and the gossipy interest of neighbors. In many ways the urban conditions prevent the family from meeting social expectations based on the older rural situation.

Reintegration of Family and Society

In the United States reintegration of the family with other institutions has begun to take place. The process does not fall into a neat and precise system. Outmoded relationships exist alongside new and modern attempts at coordination, and great areas in need of coordination are still untouched. Governmental and various voluntary agencies overlap in their efforts. Some attempts at integration occur on the purely local level, others at the hands of state agencies, while the federal government and national organizations attempt to draw the entire picture together into some form of unity. Little has been done to redefine values. Many new services are in the nature of stopgaps for emergencies and not part of an overall plan. Certain aspects of the family have received intensive attention, others, equally significant, very little. Nevertheless, in this general and seemingly unguided stirring of interest and activity, certain organized movements and trends can be discerned.

Values and Norms

Two important movements have helped to crystallize new values. One of these, the feminist movement, has spent its force; another, the White House Conferences on children, has become a recurring phenomenon to re-evaluate children's needs and services at ten-year intervals.

The feminist movement, in its agitation for equality of women's status with men's, contributed to the transition from the patriarchal family to the present-day ideal of the partnership family in which husband and wife share equally in rights and responsibilities. Even the paternal family—which is still more characteristic than the partnership family—owes much to the feminist movement. The partnership and paternal families both give women high status, relative freedom in their choices of roles, and also increased responsibilities. These attributes of wives are now accepted as values of family life.

The feminist movement, after years of sporadic propaganda, was organized in 1848 at a Women's Rights Convention held in Seneca Falls, New York. In a "Declaration of Sentiments," it took its stand against disfranchisement of women, legal incapacity arising from marriage, unequal divorce laws, double standard of morals, occupational limitations, denial of educational opportunities, and subordination in church government.[3] The Nineteenth Amendment, which, in 1920, granted women the right to vote, is usually regarded as its major accomplishment. Other accomplishments of the movement for equality of women's opportunities with men have perhaps been more closely related to marriage and family life. One of these has been the trend of state laws toward giving married women separate property rights, the same right of inheriting property when there is no will that the husband would have if the wife died, the right to contract their services and receive their earnings, and the same rights and liabilities as litigants that their husbands have.[4] Control of property and earnings gives not only an

[3]Bernhard J. Stern, "Women, Position in Society: Historical," *Encyclopedia of the Social Sciences* (New York: Macmillan, 1937), Vol. 15, pp. 442–50.

[4]*The Legal Status of Women in the United States of America, United States Summary, as of January 1, 1953*, Women's Bureau Bulletin No. 157, revised 1956 (Washington, D.C.: Government Printing Office, 1956), pp. 9–59.

equal voice in family affairs but freedom for the married woman to carry out many of her personal interests and, in case of incompatibility or continued conflict, ability to support herself.

Over the years women have also gained entrance to colleges, universities, and many professional schools on an equal basis with men, although some specialized schools may limit the acceptance of women to a "quota." The exigencies of urban living and the effect of World War I accomplished another objective of the feminist movement— freedom for women to enter employment. Although it cannot be said that they have equal opportunities for all types of position, advancement, or earnings, nevertheless the way has been opened for women to use their own initiative regarding work. In many ways, therefore, the feminist movement helped to promote equality of men and women and to safeguard women as they moved from the home into the community. On the other hand, the feminist movement hindered marital adjustment in some respects. Since men had previously commanded political, educational, and economic opportunities, much of the struggle for equality was directed against men rather than against the institutions that excluded women. Many feminists became hostile in their attitudes toward men as persons, and bitter sex antagonism characterized the relationship between men and women. To the extent that this antagonism was carried over into marriage it tended to pit husband and wife against each other and to create opposition rather than cooperation.

Many of the objectives of the feminist movement have now been incorporated into the work of the Women's Bureau of the United States government. Organized in 1920 under the Department of Labor, the Women's Bureau acts as a clearing house for information on all matters that pertain to women workers. It collects, analyzes, and publishes information on employment, legislation concerning women, problems of special groups, such as older women or Negro women, and the civil and political status of women. Although it does not administer any laws, it supplies information and makes recommendations on proposed laws.[5] It might be called the watchdog of women's public rights.

The equality sought by the feminist movement, now incorporated in many laws and guarded by the Women's Bureau, has carried over into the family, where it is interpreted as a partnership between husband and wife. This partnership gives the wife many rights she did not have previously, but also gives her added responsibilities.

The second value-making movement is the series of White House Conferences on children. The effect of these has been to establish the

[5]The Women's Bureau, Its Purpose, Its Functions (Washington, D.C.: Women's Bureau), folder, undated.

child as a personality in his own right rather than as an adjunct of the family for its use or pleasure; at the same time, the family has been held to be the central agency in the child's development. The first White House Conference, on the Care of Dependent Children, convened in 1909 at the call of President Theodore Roosevelt. It emphasized the need of each child for home life as the most important force in his life. It was concluded that the child should not be deprived of his home except in cases of extreme unsuitability. An immediate outcome was the establishment by states of systems of Mother's Aid, whereby certain classes of mothers deprived of a husband's support could receive financial aid to enable them to maintain a home for their children. The movement for such aid culminated in the Aid to Dependent Children as part of the Social Security Act of 1935, whereby federal and state governments cooperate in granting aid for the maintenance of homes when the husband is dead or for certain reasons he is unable to support his family. Another result of the 1909 conference was the establishment of the Federal Children's Bureau in 1912 whose function is "to investigate and report upon all matters pertaining to the welfare of children and child life among all classes of our people." Specifically, the Children's Bureau has been concerned with infant mortality, the birthrate, orphanages, juvenile courts, desertion, dangerous occupations, accidents to and diseases of children, employment of children, juvenile delinquency, and legislation affecting children.

The repetitive nature of the White House Conference keeps the cause of children constantly before the public and points out new needs at ten-year intervals. The conference of 1919 was devoted to Child Welfare Standards. The conference of 1930 on Child Health and Protection was preceded by extensive research, which was reported at the time of the conference. The 1940 conference emphasized the position of children in a democracy, and that of 1950 stated that its purpose was "to consider how we can develop in children the mental, emotional, and spiritual qualities essential to individual happiness and to responsible citizenship, and what physical, economic, and social conditions are deemed necessary to this development."[6] In 1960, the conference took as its theme the promotion of opportunities for children and youth to realize their full potential for a creative life in freedom and dignity.

These successive conferences keep alive the importance of children, reaffirm the value of the home to the child, and give the home supportive aid through revitalized agencies and new services. Since the conferences are attended by professional and lay delegates from all parts

[6]Kathryn Close, "Everybody's Business—the Young of the Nation," *Survey*, 86 (1950), 535–40.

of the United States, the findings of the conferences tend to filter back into local communities and to give some uniformity to the formation of values as well as service to children.

In addition to these organized movements concerned with redefining marital and family values are the public statements of people who have given special attention to trends in family life and emerging valuations. Since each person speaks only for himself, we cannot be sure how far consensus of opinion on values would go among these specialists.

A number of the specialists cite stability as a desirable value of family life. By stability, however, they do not mean automatic continuity of marriage until it is terminated by the death of one spouse. Goode, after a careful consideration of various goals involving stability, happiness, and childrearing, concludes that the most widely accepted goal now is "family stability based on happiness."[7] Another sociologist carries the concept of stability further to include sufficient resiliency within the family to enable it to come back to normality in time of crisis and to maintain interrelationships that contribute to the emotional needs of the family members.[8] Stability is not conceived of as identical with continuity of the marriage; it is a special quality of marriage that enables individuals to achieve goals of their own while remaining married. It follows that when husband or wife no longer feels that the marriage contributes to his goals or happiness, divorce is the next step. Students of marriage now tend to take a middle ground on the subject of divorce: they do not condemn it; neither do they openly advocate it; rather, they recognize it as a logical conclusion to the conception of marriage whose highest value is the happiness or fulfillment of personal needs of husband and wife.[9] High valuation is thus not placed upon marriage permanence per se, but upon a marriage of sufficient value to husband and wife that they voluntarily continue the relationship.

Happiness and emotional needs are not narrowly conceived. More rounded statements speak of companionship, emotional security, personality development, and maximum expression of the personality. The

[7]William J. Goode, "Social Engineering and the Divorce Problem," *The Annals of the American Academy of Political and Social Science*, 272 (1950), 86–89. Volume 272 of *The Annals* is entitled *Toward Family Stability*.

[8]Ray H. Abrams, "The Concept of Family Stability," *Ibid.*, p. 7; Reuben Hill, "The American Family: Problem or Solution?" *American Journal of Sociology*, 53 (1947), 125–30.

[9]Emily H. Mudd, Abraham Stone, Maurice J. Karpf, and Janet Fowler Nelson, *Marriage Counseling: A Casebook* (New York: Association Press, 1958, pp. 26–27; Adolph S. Tomars, "Human Relations in a Changing Society," Ethical Frontiers Pamphlets (New York Society for Ethical Culture, 1949), pp. 28–30.

family in its ideal form is less concerned with housekeeping and more with homemaking, less with material needs and more with personality needs, than formerly.[10]

The equalitarian or partnership aspect of marriage has already been discussed as a value that was furthered by the feminist movement. Present-day writers on trends in family values almost unanimously identify an equalitarian relationship as of high value. It is widely spoken of as democracy in family life and as of value to children as well as parents.

Also unanimously accepted (and already discussed) is the tremendous value placed upon the personality development of children, with the family designated as the place where wholesome personalities are most readily nurtured.

Beyond these four values or goals for marriage and the family— fulfillment of personality needs, stability based upon such fulfillment, equalitarian relationships, and fine personality development of children —it is difficult to discover trends of sufficient strength to indicate consensus of opinion. It should be noted, also, that these values have not as yet been fully reached; they are in the nature of future goals toward which families and family agencies may work.

At the same time that these new values are emerging, the spokesmen for other groups reaffirm traditional values. Perhaps the most articulate group is the Catholic Church, whose values relating to marriage and the family are very different from those emerging from present urbanized society. Believing in unchanging, sacred values, the Church conceives of matrimony as instituted by God and subject to sacred laws. Family life, based on stable, monogamous marriage, is of high value. Divorce is forbidden. Sex receives sanction as the natural means provided for production of children, who are of extreme importance to the Church and to their parents, but is condemned as an end in itself; therefore, chemical and mechanical contraceptives, which interfere with the divine plan for children, are prohibited. Woman's basic function is to bear children and rear them in the Catholic faith. She therefore fulfills an important obligation and merits respect and reverence. Matched with the woman's role of mother and homemaker is the husband's role of provider and head of the family. Gainful employment for a woman is discouraged as being detrimental to her fundamental role for which nature and God designed her. Family life and children are of

---

[10]Hill, *op. cit.*; R. J. Havighurst, "The American Family, Essential and Accidental Functions," *Vital Speeches*, 14 (1948), 565–68; E. W. Burgess, "The Family and Sociological Research," *Social Forces*, 24 (1947), 1–6.

high value and financially should take precedence over costly pleasures or efforts to raise the standard of living.[11] Marriage and family life are thus closely linked with religious beliefs, and the Church sanctions, approves of, and supports marriages that conform to the values it upholds. These values in many ways resemble those commonly held a century ago. Whereas many non-Catholics have now come to regard marriage as a social institution and, consequently, as adaptable to changing social conditions, the Catholics, regarding marriage as in accordance with divine laws, view their family values as immutable. Nevertheless, in the United States, Catholics live under the same social conditions as non-Catholics. Will the Catholic Church be able to hold its adherents to the officially stated values or will the pressure of social conditions bring a deviation in behavior from the stated values?

TRANSFER OF FAMILY FUNCTIONS

Many family functions have been or are in the process of transfer to other institutions. This transfer often is regarded as indicative of the breakdown of the family. On the contrary, the transfer relieves the family of burdens that it cannot shoulder in an urban environment and thus releases it for more complete fulfillment of functions that are still retained. The transfer of functions has been going on for a long time, as the result of two factors. First, the growth of cities has made it impossible for families to perform many older functions. Physical protection, safe drinking water, disposal of sewage and garbage, and protection from contagious diseases must be handled on a community basis, for the safety of all. These services, having long since passed to community agencies, now are accepted as the normal duties of the community. Second, the highly specialized nature of some services has forced their conversion from family to organizational functions. Medical care, education, and recreation are examples; specialists trained in these and other fields bring their professional training to the service of many families. As people become accustomed to an outside service, they accept it, and the next generation rarely questions the loss of the function by the family. It is usually when functions are in the process of transfer that anxiety and suspicion as to the effect on the family arise. Even those who benefit by the transfer sometimes question the advisability of the change.

[11]For a complete discussion, see Edgar Schmiedeler, *Christian Marriage: An Analysis of and Commentary on the Marriage Encyclical* (The Catholic Conference on Family Life, 1312 Massachusetts Avenue, N.W., Washington, D.C., 1946); a brief summary is given in R. P. Odenwald, "Psychiatric and Religious Aspects of Marriage Problems," *Marriage and Family Living*, 14 (1952), 7–13.

The following functions were once handled by the family but are now the responsibility of other agencies.[12]

Regulation of marriage and family relationships by an outside institution (church or state) extends many generations into the past and is no longer questioned, although in some lines of the cultural ancestry families handled these matters themselves. Laws now regulate procedures for a legal marriage, rights and obligations of husband and wife, obligations between parents and children, inheritance, and dissolution of marriages.

Protection from physical disaster is handled by such special agencies as the military service and police and fire departments.

Education is the function of an elaborate system of public schools. Significantly, when public schools first spread across the country and pressure was put upon families to send their children regularly to school, many parents objected. They felt that the state had no right to deprive them of the work of their children or to make the decisions as to how much education their children should have. They regarded compulsory public education as a detriment to family life.

Health protection is shared by the family with a number of agencies. Public health agencies provide for control of contagion and conformity to sanitary standards; schools have added physical education programs, medical inspections, and healthful lunches to their programs; both public and private hospitals of many types are ready to care for the ill; doctors with many specialties are ready to assume responsibility for diagnosis and treatment.

Other functions have more recently been assumed by nonfamily institutions or are still subject to controversy.

Recreation has spread far beyond the family and is being claimed by special organizations. Community agencies such as park boards, settlement houses, some churches, and schools sponsor organized recreational programs. Commercial recreation has also had a phenomenal development through motion pictures, sports, public dance halls, and similar institutions that cater to large numbers of people.

Personality development, still regarded as one of the most highly valued functions of the family, has also become the task of a number of other agencies. Schools, churches, youth organizations, child-guidance clinics, and many social-work agencies are concerned with the personalities of children.

Economically, also, the family has not retained all its old functions.

[12]For a comprehensive statement of organizations handling functions once performed by the family as well as performing ameliorative services, see Muriel W. Brown, "Organizational Programs to Strengthen the Family," in Harold T. Christensen, ed., *Handbook of Marriage and the Family* (Chicago: Rand McNally, 1964), ch. 20.

Not long in the past the family was regarded as fully able to care for its own economic needs and to provide for dependents both old and young. Inasmuch as the transfer of economic functions away from the family is now in process, this area is full of controversy. Two movements have developed, toward compulsory savings, and toward the assumption by employers of financial responsibilities toward their employees, not only during periods when they are working, but also during periods of unemployment and after retirement. Old Age and Survivors Insurance (commonly called Social Security) is a system whereby employers and employees of certain classes of occupations pay specified amounts to the federal government, throughout the years of employment. The employee is forced to save something, and the employer to augment it. At age 65, regardless of whether or not the employee needs the money, he receives retirement payments. Provision is also made for payments to dependents both before and after the wage earner's death. Unemployment compensation also represents transfer of economic functions from the family to the employer. Employers pay to the federal government a certain percentage of their total payroll, from which unemployed persons are paid provided they are employable and unable to find work. Again, the question of need is not raised. Earlier provisions for payments in case of industrial accidents also place support upon the employer. In addition to these legal provisions for support from employers over and above payment for work performed, other types of financial payments are made by employers. Many industries have established pension plans to supplement the amounts received from Old Age and Survivors Insurance, thus assuming almost complete responsibility for support of their employees until death, regardless of how long they may live after retirement. This revolutionary movement whereby industry and business take over a responsibility traditionally the duty of the family has interesting implications, not all of which are clearly delineated. We do not know their full effect upon choice of an occupation, status of the husband, family thrift, or plans for retirement.

Many industries and business concerns are moving into other areas traditionally within the family circle. They provide recreational rooms and organized sports programs, assist young people in occupational choices by giving vocational aptitude tests, and help their employees solve personal or family problems through professional counseling.

Two areas in which there is agitation for other institutions to assume greater functions are medical care and housing.

At present medical care is provided for those who can afford the specialized and often expensive services of physicians and hospitals and for the impoverished who are completely unable to pay. The middle group with moderate incomes often finds itself handicapped. A movement for some form of federal health insurance supported by payroll taxes has been started. The high wages since the end of World War II have made the problem less acute than it was in the 1930's. In addition, many more programs have been established for hospital insurance, whereby people may make small payments individually or through their place of work in a group insurance plan that covers the basic cost of hospital care. Doctor's fees also are covered by some insurance plans.

The movement for federal public housing that began in 1933, with the construction of 21,800 units in 51 developments under the Public Works Administration, has become nationwide in scope. The projects are built and managed by a local housing authority but subsidized by the federal government; tenants are selected from applicants whose income does not exceed a prescribed amount, which varies with the number in the family. Later, if the income exceeds the maximum, the family is required to move, thus making way for another low-income family. Families in public housing projects are not "down-and-outers." They are primarily families with small children whose income is insufficient for them to buy or build a home and who are unable to find suitable housing for their children at rents they can afford to pay. Old people whose income is small also find a haven in public housing projects. Negroes, often discriminated against in the matter of housing, are eligible for federal housing units. The movement for public housing meets resistance from certain business interests that see a threat to their own profits or fear a general movement toward government ownership of business. Others regard it as a democratic procedure whereby the government is strengthening the family by making available comfortable and sanitary housing at feasible rents.

Both the formulation of new values and the absorption of earlier family functions by other institutions represent reintegration of the family and other institutions into a coordinated pattern of social organization. The reintegration is far from complete, but the lines of development that have been traced indicate the trend of change. As the transfer of some functions comes to be more universally accepted as a necessary adjustment to urbanism, families will be able to strengthen the performance of functions remaining to them.

Amelioration

Social incoordination often prevents individuals and families from meeting their needs adequately. Families often need special help in making adjustments and achieving or restoring integration among their members. One source of such help is the ameliorative agency, whose primary function is to step in with supportive aid or remedial training when a family is having difficulty with some phase of normal functioning. Its work is usually short term, a prime objective being to restore the family to independence. Ameliorative agencies should not be confused with the various institutions that have permanently assumed functions previously performed by families. These institutions provide services, open to all people of a certain classification, that are no longer regarded as the obligation of the family, whereas ameliorative agencies aid families themselves to improve or restore performance of functions still regarded as belonging to the family.[13] Thus amelioration preserves or increases the integration of the individual family, but does not materially increase social integration.

Ameliorative agencies are included in the loose classifications of social agencies and counseling services. Not all social agencies, however, are ameliorative: most agencies that work with youth are not, for they offer programs open to all boys and girls; some counseling services—for example, premarital counseling services open to anyone who wishes to come for educational purposes as well as those with acute problems—are not classified as ameliorative. Ameliorative services cover many areas of family life, often paralleling the normal services and sometimes being administered by the same institutions that provide other services to all families.

Laws not only set up the framework for the family, but also afford amelioration in certain cases of hardship. They make divorce available for the marriage that has become intolerable; they make it possible to compel the husband to meet his age-old obligation of support of wife and children; and they provide for care and treatment of unmanageable children.

Ameliorative laws often are administered through special courts established to aid the family in trouble. The juvenile court, first estab-

[13]In distinguishing between functions assumed by other institutions, which therefore represent a reintegration of family and society, and functions that are merely ameliorative, the following criterion was used. If the function serves all families of a large class, regardless of special hardship, it is regarded as a normal function of the institution that performs the service, and therefore reintegrative. If the function serves only families suffering a special handicap that prevents them from performing a function still regarded as belonging to the family, it is ameliorative. For example, Old Age and Survivors Insurance, financed by employer and employee and administered by the government, is now a normal function of industry and government to give support in old age—formerly purely an individual or family obligation. Old Age Assistance, however, is ameliorative only, since it is granted only to old people who can prove that they are in financial need; it is an ameliorative service of the federal and state governments offered old people in hardship.

lished in 1899, has jurisdiction over all juvenile offenders (except of the most serious type), rather than the criminal court. Acting on the theory that the child is a ward of the state, the juvenile court intervenes under special circumstances between parents and child, typically when the child is delinquent, dependent, or neglected. Although not all courts achieve the highest standards of treatment, the ideal is study of the child in all phases of his life, treatment of the difficulties, and a total future plan for him. The services of such a court are offered, not to all children, but to those who do not respond to the programs available to the masses of children, such as those of schools or recreational agencies. Juvenile courts have now been established by legislation in all states. Among other courts created by various states to aid the family that is unable to solve its own problems is the domestic relations court, originated in 1910 in Buffalo, with jurisdiction over all criminal activities relating to domestic affairs, including paternity cases. Nonsupport and desertion cases and sometimes divorce cases are handled in domestic relations courts. Family courts (first established in Hamilton County, Ohio, in which Cincinnati is located, in 1944) are another development; they tend to combine the functions of the domestic relations court and the juvenile court.

To aid the family in need of legal advice but without funds, Legal Aid Societies, financed by voluntary contributions, have been opened in many cities; Legal Aid Committees of local bar associations give a similar service.

Regardless of the general prosperity of the country, many families suffer poverty. Some types of poverty linked to the economic structure or to the aging of the human being are being brought under control by such previously discussed means as Old Age and Survivors Insurance, industrial pensions, and Unemployment Compensation. But there are still many families who cannot claim insurance or pensions as a result of normal employment during their employable years. People whose working days ended before these provisions went into effect, those who worked for occupations not included in the law, handicapped, chronically ill, and mothers of young children, all fall outside the normal provisions for support during unemployment. For these groups various types of ameliorative aid are available, but only for the person who can prove that he is destitute. As an example, Old Age Assistance, which was established under the Social Security Act, affords a minimum amount of support for old people. Though jointly financed by the federal government and the states, this aid is provided under a plan devised by each state; hence, the amounts differ from one state to another. Aid to Dependent Children, another provision of the Social

Security Act, makes it possible for mothers and children to remain together when the mother is a widow or the children for other specified reasons are deprived of their father's support. Again, financial need must be proved. The establishment of Aid to Dependent Children was an important step in giving the destitute family a bulwark against disintegration. In the colonial period, local authorities placed destitute children in almshouses; this system was followed by placement of children in individual homes as indentured servants, a plan that later developed into foster-home placement. Later the belief grew that the best place for the child is in his own home and that it was for the benefit of the child to aid the mother and make it possible for her to keep her children with her. Mother's Aid on a state basis began in 1911 and was succeeded in 1935 by the federal and state sponsored program of Aid to Dependent Children.

The educational system, in addition to schools for all normal children, increasingly has facilities for special classes of children—crippled, educable feeble-minded, hard of hearing and deaf, those with defective vision, and the blind. Some cities have special schools for problem children. In addition, states support residential schools of many types, for feeble-minded, deaf, and blind. Some states have residential schools for mentally disturbed children, and all have some provision for the training of delinquent boys and girls. These varied institutions relieve the family of heavy burdens in the special care and training of many types of children who are not able to benefit from the institutions provided for normal children.

When families cannot care for their own health problems, special agencies are ready to step in. Public hospitals, nursing homes, and infirmaries absorb both acutely ill and chronic invalids. Special hospitals care for the mentally afflicted. The family, struggling with its ill at home, may call upon the Visiting Nurses' Association.

Mental health has been of growing concern over the years, with concentration upon treatment in the early stages. There has been, therefore, a widespread growth of mental-health clinics, counseling centers, and child-guidance clinics to aid families unable to solve adjustment problems of their members.

Important as ameliorative agencies and services are to families undergoing hardship, they do not modify the underlying causes of the hardships and therefore cannot prevent a recurrence of the hardship or its appearance among other families. As the family becomes more and more integrated into urbanized society and other institutions assume functions that the family cannot handle, some of the hardships may disappear and the corresponding ameliorative services may not be needed. However, if our standards for health, education, recreation, and personality development continue to rise, conditions now thought of as normal may come to be defined as hardships, thus creating the demand for new ameliorative services.

Marriage and Family Education and Counseling

Another supportive movement is directed toward individuals, couples, or family units who are in need of assistance in marital or family adjustment. One phase of this movement is preparatory and is planned for young people prior to marriage; another phase of the service is focused upon poorly adjusted husbands and wives; and a third upon general family problems including children. In part, the movement is educational, planned to forestall trouble; in part, it is correctional, offering treatment to those already in difficulty. The same agency often offers both educational and remedial services.

EDUCATIONAL PROGRAMS

Family-life education at the secondary school level is designed to aid the student prior to or during his early courtship days to consider basic problems of adjustment and to direct his attention to some of the problems of the first years of marriage.[14] Therefore, the course is keyed to the students' present and future needs, with emphasis upon practical, everyday problems, such as dating, courtship, mate selection, premarital standards of conduct, desirable masculine and feminine roles and relationships, sex education, and parent-child relationships. Through reading, lectures by specialists, discussion, and personal counseling, the student is helped to understand his personal problems.

As is often true in new fields, the quality of aid given depends in large part upon the special preparation of the professional staff. Many teachers, especially the typical unmarried woman teacher, are hesitant about embarking upon a family-life course; the teacher needs not only to know the facts about courtship, sex, and marriage, but to have a healthful attitude toward these facts and to have solved any emotional problems of her own.

Community support is also necessary. In some communities, par-

[14]For a comprehensive discussion of family life education, consult Richard K. Kerckhoff, "Family Life Education in America," in Christensen, *op. cit.*, ch. 21.

ents, ministers, newspaper editors, and other adults have misunderstood the nature of family-life courses; school administrators therefore often carry on a general educational program in the community prior to establishing the course, drawing the Parent-Teacher Association, ministers, and others into a sponsoring group. Much community misunderstanding collects around the unit on sex education that is a part of most of the courses. This one unit may become so magnified in the public mind that other aspects of the course are forgotten; thus, in one community, after a period of community sponsorship, one parent induced a local newspaper to print a sensational story about the teaching of sex in the public schools. Only careful community work again established support of the course.

At the college level, courses on preparation for marriage have had enormous popularity since the first one was given for credit by Ernest R. Groves at Boston University in 1924. Soon transferring to the University of North Carolina, Groves further developed this type of course. The course has become a standard one in many colleges and universities. Individual counseling often accompanies the course and is regarded by some instructors as a necessary part of the program. The preparation-for-marriage course should not be confused with the systematic study of the family given in departments of sociology, which emphasizes social background of the family as well as interactional processes within the family. The preparation-for-marriage course usually has no prerequisites; it is a "service" course, open to all—or to all students of a certain class level—and designed to aid students in a wise selection of a mate and management of their own courtship and marital adjustment.

The movement for premarital courses has fanned out into the community with churches, Young Men's and Young Women's Christian Associations, community houses, and other agencies offering short popular courses for young men and women. Catholics have developed a special program of education for married life called Cana Conferences; either half days or entire days are devoted to the discussion of marriage and family problems under an expert leader. For these many courses, special outlines, pamphlets, and textbooks have been prepared, "translating" scientific findings into popular language.

It is difficult to know to what extent these many courses prevent marital unadjustment; it would seem logical to assume that as they reach more and more young people they will gradually establish new and less romantic standards of courtship and lead to a previewing before marriage of problems that may arise later. To the extent that they accomplish these ends, they should lead to better marital integration and greater happiness and stability of marriage.

A slightly different educational movement offers to parents study programs that center on problems of children. Parent-Teacher Associations, organized nationally through the National Congress of Parents and Teachers, sponsor mother-study groups. Many other organizations sponsor programs for parent education. Through these study groups parents are kept in touch with some of the newer findings in child psychology. Although there is a certain risk that what they learn is too fragmentary to be of much assistance to them and may simply create insecurity in their relationships with their children, if the leadership is good and the contact long continued this danger is reduced.

MARITAL COUNSELING

The first marriage counseling service is claimed by Drs. Abraham and Hannah Stone, who established such a service in New York City in 1929.[15] Fully developed counseling services are still few in number, among the best known being the American Institute of Family Relations in Los Angeles and the Marriage Council of Philadelphia. Counseling is carried on, however, in connection with many smaller agencies as well as by teachers and ministers. Attention is given to problems of both the unmarried and the married. The service is becoming professionalized with development of standards of training and national coordination through the American Association of Marriage Counselors.[16]

The field of marriage counseling is defined as primarily educational —to give young people and husbands and wives knowledge and insight into differences of viewpoints relating to areas of married life. People come to counselors seeking factual information, help in making decisions affecting their marriage, clarification of cultural conflicts between husband and wife, and understanding of personal differences. Sometimes they come with individual problems of maladjustment, neuroses, or even psychoses; these cases are not regarded as part of the legitimate clientele of the marriage counselor and are referred to a psychiatrist or mental-health clinic. The training advocated for the counselor is broad and primarily in the biological, sociological, and psychological

[15]Abraham Stone, "Marriage Counseling Today and Tomorrow," *Marriage and Family Living*, 12 (1950), 39.

[16]A full discussion of the field of counseling is given by Gerald R. Leslie, "The Field of Marriage Counseling," in Christensen, *op. cit.*, ch. 22.

fields, with special emphasis upon human relations and marriage and family fields. He needs to know when to refer his client to a specialist in some field as well as how to aid him to understand and manage his marital problems.

Family casework agencies also deal with marital problems, and at times seem to compete with marital counseling centers. Family casework originally was preoccupied with economic problems of the family. When the Social Security Act removed many financial problems from the private casework agencies through the creation of large-scale public relief (Old Age Assistance, Aid to Dependent Children, Unemployment Compensation, and so on), the private agencies had to redefine their function. They retained the family-adjustment side of their work and began to develop it, several substituting "family consultation," "family service," or some similar phrasing for "charity" in their names. They differ from the marital-counseling agency in that they usually handle all types of family problems, parent-child as well as marital, and of whatever origin except the purely financial. Many who come to them have serious personality problems and require some degree of therapeutic treatment on an individual basis. This treatment may be provided by the psychiatric caseworker who typically staffs the family agency, or it may be given by a psychiatrist. The family agency clearly overlaps the marital-counseling service in some areas, but it gives more extensive service and is also equipped to handle some types of personality maladjustment. Marital counseling is narrower and more highly specialized in its concentration upon marital adjustment of essentially normal people.

Counseling by teachers of family and marriage courses in high schools and colleges has already been mentioned. Ministers also are especially interested in the field of counseling. Based upon a background of ministerial help to people with personal problems, marriage counseling is a new specialization rather than entrance into a new field. Many seminaries now give some courses in counseling to aid the minister. It has been pointed out, however, that the minister is only secondarily a marital counselor and that his training usually has been much briefer than that of the professional counselor.[17] Many ministers limit their counseling to premarital conferences with couples who request the minister to perform their marriage ceremonies, whereas others are beginning to extend their services to poorly adjusted married couples as well. In addition to the usual counseling approach, ministers are peculiarly well equipped to draw attention to moral and religious ideals in relation to marriage.

[17]Sylvanus M. Duvall, "The Minister as Marriage Counselor, "*Marriage and Family Living*, 9 (1947), 63.

A few divorce courts operate a clinic to which the plaintiff is urged to go prior to a hearing. The marriage may be rehabilitated, although usually the estrangement is past repair by the time a suit for divorce is filed.

Counseling is both educational and remedial, aiding both couples in doubt about some information or line of action and those who have encountered some obstacle. Like courses of study, counseling is aimed at integration and stability of individual families.

Training of Leaders

Counselors find their training primarily in the graduate courses of universities. There is a great need, however, to train leaders who cannot attend the universities, and for coordinating and pointing up previous training in terms of marital and family problems. The summer workshop has become a popular and effective answer to this need. Stimulated by the National Council on Family Relations, workshops are now held in many sections of the country each summer. Teachers, ministers, social workers, and key community leaders meet for one to four weeks, to engage in concentrated discussion groups under the guidance of specialists. The participants then return to their home communities to use their new knowledge in their work or in stimulating new groups in study of the family. To prepare leaders for the Cana Conferences, Catholic University each summer holds a workshop for leaders.[18]

Research

Many movements toward better societal integration and ameliorative and educational services are based on trial-and-error attempts to stabilize or otherwise aid the family. Movements are not always coordinated, and sometimes much money and effort are expended upon relatively minor problems or upon the attempt to cure symptoms instead of finding the underlying causes. Gradually, research is providing information and analyzing marital and family processes. Sound programs make use of research findings and eagerly await new publications.

Popular though marital and family research is at present, it is a new field, offering many opportunities for different types of investigation.

[18]*Marriage and Family Living*, 13 (Winter, 1951), is a special workshop issue.

The present trends in research are indicative of the varied approaches now being made by widely different professional groups.

Demographic studies show long- and short-term trends in family life and offer basic data for isolating problems for further research. The United States Census, other official statistical reports, and attendant professional analyses provide information on number and types of families, their characteristics, and their dissolution, as well as trends in marriage and divorce rates, age of marriage, birth rates, and death rates. With the greatly increased interest in family research in recent years, official reports are becoming more detailed and are appearing with greater frequency than formerly.

Child psychology and child development have long been a special field of research for psychologists. Few sociologists have studied either children or adolescents, except juvenile delinquents. Since psychologists tend to emphasize individual development, an opportunity is present for sociological (or, better, interdisciplinary) research that would study the social roles of children and family interaction. Studies of adolescents would be especially helpful, with reference to masculine and feminine roles and the folkways and mores of dating.

With Kinsey's study of sexual behavior, biology has made a contribution to our knowledge of behavior related to marriage. The Kinsey reports set off a series of interdisciplinary conferences and stimulated a flood of books and articles that examined Kinsey's data critically and—of more significance—re-examined the lack of coordination between sexual moral standards and actual practice.

Since part of the present indirection of the family is due to the feeling that the traditional formulation of values and ideals cannot be made to fit current conditions, more research is needed in other areas. For example, divorce is in need of additional study.

Family life in other cultures than our own has long been a subject of interest to anthropologists. Earlier studies were limited to the more formal aspects of primitive families—kinship groupings, formal family organization, lines of descent, and the like. The writings of Margaret Mead introduced a new approach in which primitive people come to life as human beings with motivations, emotions, and patterns of personal interaction. The newer studies of other cultures make possible a re-examination of many of our concepts regarding the basic nature of human beings, processes of personality formation in the family, and forms of marital interaction.

Sociologists, also, have found the family a fertile field for research. The first studies, historical in nature, produced Goodsell's history of the European family and Calhoun's of the American colonial family. The development of the American Negro family has been thoroughly studied by Frazier. Rural and urban families have also been subjected to study. These studies analyze the family as a cultural product, changing in response to new social conditions.

Another trend of research has concentrated attention upon personal interaction within the family and especially between the courting couple and husband and wife. Mate selection and prediction of adjustment have received special attention. Since only a beginning has been made, research continues in these areas with frequent new publications.

Changing roles and adjustment of roles within the family constitute another field of interest. The increasing number of employed women is drawing attention to the question of roles. Research is badly needed in this area.

A strong beginning has been made in studying the reaction of families to social crises imposed from without, with economic depressions, war separations and reunions, and natural catastrophes as the fields for study. These great social crises afford a unique opportunity for study in an area where experiments cannot be set up or hardships deliberately imposed upon families.

Personal conflicts between husband and wife are only partially understood. The tendency to explain them in terms of overt tensions has given way to recognition that underlying psychological and sociological factors are also involved.

Many areas of research call for a multiple approach; it is encouraging, therefore, to know that specialists in biology, psychology, and the social sciences are converging upon the same marital and family problems.

As research findings accumulate, it may be anticipated that more rational efforts will gradually be made to readjust intrafamily relationships and to develop better coordination between the family and other institutions. The exact form of family that will emerge cannot be fully predicted, but present research indicates the need for a family that is flexible, with leeway for individual development; adjustable to external social conditions; keyed to mobility and social change; interdependent with other institutions; and ready to accept important though limited functions, such as meeting personal and sexual needs, giving emotional security, and rearing children for life in an industrialized, urban society.

Questions

1. How did the development of urban living threaten the integration of the family in the total society?

2. What new family values and norms are developing? What two movements have been important in their development?
3. The loss of family functions to other institutions often is regarded as a sign of family disintegration. Is it justifiable to regard the transfer of functions as a means of strengthening the family?
4. Distinguish between reintegrative transfer of functions and amelioration.
5. Why is amelioration necessary for the family?
6. Is it probable that education for marriage and family life will contribute to greater stability of marriage and more marital happiness? Support your answer.
7. Would it be advisable to require all applicants for a divorce to consult a marriage counselor or similar specialist in personal and social adjustment?

Bibliography

CHRISTENSEN, HAROLD T., ed., *Handbook of Marriage and the Family* (Chicago: Rand McNally, 1964), ch. 20, "Organizational Programs to Strengthen the Family"; ch. 21, "Family Life Education in America"; ch. 22, "The Field of Marriage Counseling."

Appendix

Marriage, Birth, and Divorce Rates in the United States

I. Number of marriages per 1,000 estimated midyear population *
II. Number of births per 1,000 population †
III. Divorces per 1,000 population ‡
IV. Divorces per 100 marriages occurring in the same year ‡
V. Divorces per 1,000 married women, 15 years of age and over ‡

Year	I	II	III	IV	V
1867	9.6		0.3	2.8	—
1868	9.0		0.3	3.0	—
1869	8.9		0.3	3.1	—
1870	8.8	(1871–75	0.3	3.1	—
1871	8.8	37.0)	0.3	3.2	—
1872	9.0		0.3	3.3	—
1873	9.0		0.3	3.4	—
1874	8.7		0.3	3.6	—
1875	9.1	(1876–80	0.3	3.4	—
1876	8.8	34.9)	0.3	3.6	—
1877	8.7		0.3	3.8	—
1878	8.8		0.3	3.8	—
1879	8.9		0.3	4.0	—
1880	9.0	(1881–85	0.4	4.3	—
1881	9.0	33.2)	0.4	4.5	—
1882	9.2		0.4	4.5	—
1883	9.3		0.4	4.6	—
1884	8.8		0.4	4.7	—
1885	8.9	(1886–90	0.4	4.6	—
1886	9.2	31.9)	0.4	4.8	—
1887	8.7		0.5	5.4	—
1888	8.8		0.5	5.3	—

Year	I	II	III	IV	V
1889	9.1		0.5	5.6	—
1890	9.0	(1891–95	0.5	5.8	—
1891	9.2	30.8)	0.6	6.0	—
1892	9.2		0.6	6.1	—
1893	9.0		0.6	6.2	—
1894	8.6		0.6	6.6	—
1895	8.9	(1896–1900	0.6	6.5	—
1896	9.0	29.8)	0.6	6.7	—
1897	8.9		0.6	6.9	—
1898	8.8		0.7	7.4	—
1899	9.0		0.7	7.6	—
1900	9.3	—	0.7	7.9	4.0
1901	9.6	—	0.8	8.2	—
1902	9.8	28.8	0.8	7.9	—
1903	10.0	—	0.8	7.9	—
1904	9.9	—	0.8	8.1	—
1905	10.0	—	0.8	8.0	—
1906	10.5	—	0.8	8.1	—
1907	10.8	27.7	0.9	8.2	—
1908	9.7	—	0.9	9.0	—
1909	9.9	—	0.9	8.8	—
1910	10.3	—	0.9	8.8	4.7
1911	10.2	—	1.0	9.3	—
1912	10.5	26.4	1.0	9.3	—
1913	10.5	—	0.9	8.9	—
1914	10.3	—	1.0	9.0	—
1915	10.0	25.1	1.0	10.3	—
1916	10.6	25.0	1.1	10.6	—
1917	11.1	24.7	1.2	10.7	—
1918	9.7	24.6	1.1	11.6	—
1919	11.0	22.3	1.3	12.3	—
1920	12.0	23.7	1.6	13.4	8.0
1921	10.7	24.2	1.5	13.7	—
1922	10.3	22.3	1.4	13.1	—
1923	11.0	22.2	1.5	13.4	—
1924	10.4	22.4	1.5	14.4	—
1925	10.3	21.5	1.5	14.8	—
1926	10.2	20.7	1.6	15.4	—
1927	10.1	20.6	1.6	16.3	—
1928	9.8	19.8	1.7	16.9	—
1929	10.1	18.9	1.7	16.7	—
1930	9.2	18.9	1.6	17.4	7.5
1931	8.6	18.0	1.5	17.7	7.1

Year	I	II	III	IV	V
1932	7.9	17.4	1.3	16.7	6.1
1933	8.7	16.6	1.3	15.0	6.1
1934	10.3	17.1	1.6	15.7	7.5
1935	10.4	16.8	1.7	16.4	7.8
1936	10.7	16.7	1.8	17.2	8.3
1937	11.3	17.1	1.9	17.2	8.7
1938	10.3	17.6	1.9	18.3	8.4
1939	10.7	17.3	1.9	17.9	8.5
1940	12.1	17.9	2.0	16.5	8.7
1941	12.7	18.9	2.2	17.3	9.4
1942	13.2	20.9	2.4	18.1	10.1
1943	11.8	21.5	2.6	22.8	11.0
1944	11.0	20.2	2.9	27.5	12.1
1945	12.2	19.6	3.5	30.8	14.5
1946	16.4	23.3	4.3	26.8	17.8
1947	13.9	25.8	3.4	24.2	13.7
1948	12.4	24.2	2.8	22.4	11.3
1949	10.6	24.0	2.7	25.1	10.8
1950	11.0	23.5	2.5	23.1	10.3
1951	10.4	—	2.5	23.9	9.9
1952	9.9	—	2.5	25.5	10.1
1953	9.2	—	2.5	25.2	9.9
1954	9.2	24.9	2.4	25.4	9.5
1955	9.3	24.6	2.3	24.6	9.3
1956	9.5	24.9	2.3	24.1	9.4
1957	8.9	25.0	2.2	25.1	9.2
1958	8.4	24.3	2.1	25.4	8.9
1959	8.5	24.1	2.2	26.4	9.3
1960	8.5	23.7	2.2	25.8	9.2
1961	8.5	23.3	2.3	26.7	9.6
1962	8.5	22.4	2.2	26.2	9.4
1963	8.8	21.7	2.3	25.9	9.6
1964	9.0	21.0	2.4	25.9	10.0
1965	9.2	19.4	2.5	26.9	—
1966	9.4	18.5	—	—	—

*Vital Statistics, Special Reports, Summary of Marriage and Divorce Statistics, United States, 1949, Vol. 36, No. 2 (Federal Security Agency, June 5, 1951), p. 24; Vital Statistics of the United States, 1959, Marriage and Divorce Statistics, Vol. I, Sec. 2 (U.S. Department of Health, Education, and Welfare, Public Health Service, National Office of Vital Statistics, 1961), pp. 2–17. Marriages refer only to those occurring in the United States. For 1959, Alaska is included; Vital Statistics of the United States, 1963, Marriage and Divorce, Vol. III, pp. 1–5; Statistical Abstracts of the United States, 1967 (Washington, D.C.: Government Printing Office, 1967), p. 63.

†Rates for 1871–1935 from A. J. Lotka, "Modern Trends in the Birth Rate," *Annals of the American Academy of Political and Social Science*, 188 (1936), 2–3; later rates from *Statistical Abstract of the United States, 1950*, p. 63; 1955, p. 59; 1961, p. 48; and 1967, p. 49.

‡*Vital Statistics, Special Reports, Summary of Marriage and Divorce Statistics, United States, 1949*, Vol. 36, No. 2 (Federal Security Agency, June 5, 1951), pp. 14, 24, 25; *Vital Statistics of the United States, 1959, Marriage and Divorce Statistics*, Vol. I, Sec. 2 (U.S. Department of Health, Education, and Welfare, Public Health Service, National Office of Vital Statistics, 1961), pp. 2–17. Divorces refer only to those occurring within the United States. Rates for 1959 include Alaska. *Vital Statistics of the United States, 1963, Marriage and Divorce*, Vol. III, pp. 2–5; *Statistical Abstract of the United States, 1967* (Washington, D.C.: Government Printing Office, 1967), p. 63.

Indexes

Index of Names

Index of Subjects